Lecture Notes in Computer Science   13720

More information about this series at https://link.springer.com/bookseries/558

Ilsun You · Taek-Young Youn (Eds.)

Information Security Applications

23rd International Conference, WISA 2022
Jeju Island, South Korea, August 24–26, 2022
Revised Selected Papers

 Springer

Editors
Ilsun You
Soonchunhyang University
Asan-Si, Korea (Republic of)

Taek-Young Youn 🅳
Dankook University
Yongin, Korea (Republic of)

ISSN 0302-9743   ISSN 1611-3349 (electronic)
Lecture Notes in Computer Science
ISBN 978-3-031-25658-5   ISBN 978-3-031-25659-2 (eBook)
https://doi.org/10.1007/978-3-031-25659-2

This Springer imprint is published by the registered company Springer Nature Switzerland AG
The registered company address is: Gewerbestrasse 11, 6330 Cham, Switzerland

Preface

This volume contains revised and selected papers which were submitted to and presented at the 23rd World Conference on Information Security Applications (WISA 2022) which was held at Jeju Island, Korea, during August 24–26, 2022. WISA 2022 provided an international forum for sharing original research results among specialists in various theories and practical applications.

We received 76 submissions, covering all areas of information security, and finally selected 30 papers to be presented at the conference. Among them, only 25 papers (32.9% of submitted papers) were selected for publication in this LNCS volume. We thank the authors for submitting meaningful papers to WISA 2022. We also thank the authors for their patience and cooperation during the back-and-forth process of comments and revisions requested by the editor and the reviewers. We were specially honored to have the two keynote talks by Willy Susilo (University of Wollongong), on "Cloud Computing Security," and Yi-Bing Lin (Miin Wu SOC Chair Professor) on "5G Private Network Security and Applications."

The conference was hosted by the Korea Institute of Information Security and Cryptography (KIISC) and sponsored by the Ministry of Science, ICT and Future Planning (MSIP) and National Intelligence Service (NIS), and co-sponsored by the Electronics & Telecommunications Research Institute (ETRI), the Korea Internet & Security Agency (KISA), the National Security Research Institute (NSR), and KONAI. The program chairs, Ilsun You (Kookmin University) and Taek-Young Youn, prepared a valuable program along with the Program Committee members listed here. The excellent arrangements for the conference venue were led by the WISA 2022 general chair, Okyeon Yi (Kookmin University), and organizing chairs, Jung Taek Seo (Gachon University) and Ki-Woong Park (Sejong University). Many people contributed to the success of WISA 2022. We would like to express our deepest appreciation to each of the WISA Program Committee and Organizing Committee members. Thanks to their invaluable support and sincere dedication, WISA 2022 was a success. Finally, we thank the Springer team for assistance with the LNCS proceedings.

September 2022   Ilsun You
                                                                                                          Taek-Young Youn

Preface

Organization

General Chair

Okyeon Yi   Kookmin University, South Korea

Program Committee Chairs

Ilsun You   Kookmin University, South Korea
Taek-Young Youn   Dankook University, South Korea

Organizing Committee Chairs

Jung Taek Seo   Gachon University, South Korea
Ki-Woong Park   Sejong University, South Korea

Poster Session Chairs

Hwanguk Kim   Sangmyung University, South Korea
Haehyun Cho   Soongsil University, South Korea

Program Committee

Pelin Angin   Middle East Technical University, Turkey
Joonsang Baek   University of Wollongong, Australia
Xiaofeng Chen   Xidian University, China
Jin-Hee Cho   Virginia Tech, USA
Dooho Choi   Korea University, South Korea
Swee-Huay Heng   Multimedia University, Malaysia
Hsu-Chun Hsiao   National Taiwan University, Taiwan
Jin Hong   University of Western Australia, Australia
Qiong Huang   South China Agricultural University, China
Eul Gyu Im   Hanyang University, South Korea
Yeongjin Jang   Oregon State University, USA
Hiroaki Kikuchi   Meiji University, Japan
Dongseong Kim   University of Queensland, Australia
Doowon Kim   University of Tennessee, Knoxville, USA
HeeSeok Kim   Korea University, South Korea
Hyunil Kim   DGIST, South Korea

Jong Kim	POSTECH, South Korea
Jongkil Kim	University of Wollongong, Australia
TaeGuen Kim	Soonchunhyang University, South Korea
Hyun Kwon	Korea Military Academy, South Korea
Yonghwi Kwon	University of Virginia, USA
Kyu Hyung Lee	University of Georgia, USA
Siqi Ma	University of New South Wales, Australia
David Mohaisen	University of Central Florida, USA
Masakatsu Nishigaki	Shizuoka University, Japan
Jason Nurse	University of Kent, UK
Younghee Park	San Jose State University, USA
Marcus Peinado	Microsoft, USA
Hyun Sook Rhee	Samsung Electronics, South Korea
Junghwan Rhee	University of Central Oklahoma, USA
Ulrich Rührmair	Ruhr University Bochum, Germany
Kouichi Sakurai	Kyushu University, Japan
Seog Chung Seo	Kookmin University, South Korea
Seung-Hyun Seo	Hanyang University, South Korea
Junji Shikata	Yokohama National University, Japan
Sang Uk Shin	Pukyong National University, South Korea
Seonghan Shin	AIST, Japan
Amril Syalim	University of Indonesia, Indonesia
Gang Tan	Pennsylvania State University, USA
Simon Woo	Sungkyunkwan University, South Korea
Toshihiro Yamauchi	Okayama University, Japan
Naoto Yanai	Osaka University, Japan
Meng Yu	Roosevelt University, USA

Organizing Committee

JongWook Baek	Gachon University, South Korea
Namkyun Baik Busan	University of Foreign Studies, South Korea
Jungsoo Park	Soongsil University, South Korea
Hangbae Chang	Chung-Ang University, South Korea
Byeongcheol Choi	ETRI, South Korea
Daeseon Choi	Soongsil University, South Korea
Hyojin Cho	Soongsil University, South Korea
KwangHee Choi	KISA, South Korea
Won Seok Choi	Hansung University, South Korea
Dongguk Han	Kookmin University, South Korea
Jaecheol Ha	Hoseo University, South Korea
Manpyo Hong	Ajou University, South Korea
Seokhie Hong	Korea University, South Korea

Souhwan Jung	Soongsil University, South Korea
Yousung Kang	ETRI, South Korea
ChangHoon Kim	Daegu University, South Korea
Geonwoo Kim	ETRI, South Korea
Howon Kim	Pusan National University, South Korea
Hwanguk Kim	Sangmyung University, South Korea
Jin Cheol Kim	KEPCO-KDN, South Korea
Jongsung Kim	Kookmin University, South Korea
Sungmin Kim	Sungshin Women's University, South Korea
Tae-Sung Kim	Chungbuk National University, South Korea
Kibom Kim	NSR, South Korea
WonHo Kim	NSR, South Korea
Woo-Nyon Kim	NSR, South Korea
Hun Yeong	Kwon Korea University, South Korea
Jin Kwak	Ajou University, South Korea
Daesung Moon	ETRI, South Korea
Changhoon Lee	Seoul National University of Science and Technology, South Korea
Dong Hoon Lee	Korea University, South Korea
Imyeong Lee	Soonchunhyang University, South Korea
Jong-Hyouk Lee	Sejong University, South Korea
Kyungho Lee	Korea University, South Korea
Manhee Lee	Hannam University, South Korea
SeokJoon Lee	Gachon University, South Korea
Sungjae Lee	KISA, South Korea
Donghwan Oh	KISA, South Korea
Heekuck Oh	Hanyang University, South Korea
Hyung-Geun Oh	NSR, South Korea
Jin Young Oh	KISA, South Korea
Yunheung Paek	Seoul National University, South Korea
Kyung-Hyune Rhee	Pukyong National University, South Korea
HwaJung Seo	Hansung University, South Korea
Kyungho Son	Kangwon National University, South Korea
Jungsuk Song	Korea Institute of Science & Technology Information, South Korea
Jaecheol Ryou	Chungnam National University, South Korea
Yoojae Won	Chungnam National University, South Korea

Contents

Security Management

Cryptography

Collision-Resistant and Pseudorandom Hash Function Using Tweakable Block Cipher

Shoichi Hirose[(✉)] [ID]

University of Fukui, Fukui, Japan
hrs_shch@u-fukui.ac.jp

Abstract. This paper presents a method to construct a keyed Merkle-Damgård hash function satisfying collision resistance and the pseudorandom function property using a tweakable block cipher in the TWEAKEY framework. Its compression function adopts double-block construction to achieve sufficient level of collision resistance. Not only does the padding of the proposed keyed hash function not employ Merkle-Damgård strengthening, but it is also not injective. Due to the novel feature, the proposed keyed hash function achieves the minimum number of calls to its compression function for any message input. The proposed keyed hash function is shown to be optimally collision-resistant in the ideal cipher model. It is also shown to be a secure pseudorandom function if the underlying tweakable block cipher in the TWEAKEY framework is a secure tweakable pseudorandom permutation in two tweakey strategies.

Keywords: Hash function · Collision resistance · Pseudorandom function · Tweakable block cipher

1 Introduction

Background. Cryptographic hash functions are an important primitive in cryptography. They are classified into two classes: Unkeyed hash functions and keyed hash functions. The characteristic security requirement of an unkeyed hash function is collision resistance, which is the intractability of finding a pair of distinct inputs mapped to the same output. On the other hand, a keyed hash function is required to be a pseudorandom function (PRF) [10], which is indistinguishable from a uniform random function.

If a keyed hash function is a PRF satisfying collision resistance, then one can use it for computationally hiding and computationally binding string commitment. In addition, it has recently been shown that one can use it to achieve interesting cryptographic schemes such as compactly committing authenticated encryption with associated data (ccAEAD) [8,11] and hash-based post-quantum EPID signatures [6]. In this paper, a keyed hash function satisfying collision resistance and the PRF property is called a collision-resistant and pseudorandom hash function.

© Springer Nature Switzerland AG 2023
I. You and T.-Y. Youn (Eds.): WISA 2022, LNCS 13720, pp. 3–15, 2023.
https://doi.org/10.1007/978-3-031-25659-2_1

HMAC [1] is a standardized keyed hash function in FIPS PUB 198-1 [9]. It is a collision-resistant and pseudorandom hash function. However, it is not so efficient for short message inputs.

Contribution. We present a method to construct a collision-resistant and pseudorandom hash function using a tweakable block cipher (TBC) in the TWEAKEY framework [19]. It is a kind of Merkle-Damgård iterated hash function [7,20]. Its compression function adopts the double-block (DBL) construction [12] using a TBC to achieve sufficient level of collision resistance. Its domain extension extends KMDP$^+$ [13] to achieve a PRF using the DBL compression function.

The proposed construction does not use the Merkle-Damgård strengthening for padding. Due to the feature, it achieves the minimum number of calls to its compression function for any message input under the assumption that the message input is fed only into the message-block input of its compression function.

The proposed construction is shown to be optimally collision-resistant in the ideal cipher model. It is also shown to be a secure PRF if the underlying TBC in the TWEAKEY framework is a secure tweakable pseudorandom permutation (PRP) in two tweakey strategies. In one tweakey strategy, the underlying TBC is required to be a secure tweakable PRP against related-key attacks. However, the related-key attacks are not so powerful in that the key-deriving functions are chosen by the designers.

Related Work. There have been proposals of keyed hash functions satisfying the PRF property and collision resistance: HMAC [1], EMD [4], Keyed-MDP [15], and KMDP$^+$ [13]. All the constructions mentioned above except KMDP$^+$ use the Merkle-Damgård strengthening for their padding. Thus, in terms of the number of calls to the underlying compression function, our proposed construction is more efficient than these constructions though they are competitive to ours.

The Merkle-Damgård hash function keyed via the initial value with prefix-free padding is shown to be a secure PRF if its compression function is a secure PRF [2]. Our proof on the PRF property is based on this proof.

Iwata and Kurosawa designed a CBC-MAC function called CMAC [21], which achieves the minimum number of calls to its block cipher [17,18]. Though it is shown to be a secure PRF if its block cipher is a secure PRP, it is not aimed at collision resistance.

Organization. Notations and definitions are given in Sect. 2. The proposed construction is presented in Sect. 3. It is shown to satisfy collision resistance in the ideal cipher model in Sect. 4. It is shown to be a secure PRF if the underlying tweakable block cipher in the TWEAKEY framework is a secure tweakable PRP in two tweakey strategies in Sect. 5.

2   Preliminaries

Let $\Sigma := \{0, 1\}$. Let $(\Sigma^n)^* := \bigcup_{i \geq 0} \Sigma^{ni}$ and $(\Sigma^n)^+ := \bigcup_{i \geq 1} \Sigma^{ni}$. Let $\varepsilon \in \Sigma^0$ be the empty sequence.

The length of a sequence $x \in \Sigma^*$ is denoted by $|x|$. The least significant bit of x is denoted by $\mathsf{lsb}(x)$. For sequences $y_i, y_{i+1}, \ldots, y_{i+j} \in \Sigma^*$, their concatenation is denoted by $y_i \| y_{i+1} \| \cdots \| y_{i+j}$ or $y_{[i, i+j]}$.

For sequences $x, y \in \Sigma^*$, $x \oplus y$ represents bit-wise XOR of x and y. If $|x| > |y|$, then $x \oplus y := x \oplus (0^{|x|-|y|} \| y)$.

Let $s \leftarrow S$ represent that s is an element chosen uniformly at random from a set S.

For integers a, b, and d, let $a \equiv_d b$ represent $a \equiv b \pmod{d}$.

2.1 Cryptographic Hash Function

A cryptographic hash function is a function mapping an input of arbitrary length to an output of fixed length. It is often called simply a hash function. The characteristic security requirement of a hash function is collision resistance.

Let H^P be a hash function using a primitive P. In this paper, P is assumed to be an ideal TBC. Namely, P is chosen uniformly at random from the set of all TBCs with the same domain and range.

Let **A** be an adversary trying to find a colliding pair of inputs for H^P, which are a pair of distinct inputs mapped to the same output. **A** can make encryption and decryption queries to its oracle P. The advantage of **A** against H^P for collision resistance is given by

$$\mathrm{Adv}_{H^P}^{\mathrm{col}}(\mathbf{A}) := \Pr[(X, X') \leftarrow \mathbf{A}^P : H^P(X) = H^P(X') \wedge X \neq X'].$$

It is assumed that **A** makes all the queries to P necessary to compute both $H^P(X)$ and $H^P(X')$.

2.2 Pseudorandom Function

Let $f : \mathcal{K} \times \mathcal{X} \to \mathcal{Y}$ be a keyed function with its key space $\mathcal{K}$. A security requirement of f is indistinguishability from a uniform random function. The goal of an adversary **A** against f is to distinguish between $f_K(\cdot) := f(K, \cdot)$ and a random oracle $\rho : \mathcal{X} \to \mathcal{Y}$, where $K \leftarrow \mathcal{K}$. **A** has either f_K or ρ as an oracle and outputs 0 or 1. The advantage of **A** against f as a PRF is defined as

$$\mathrm{Adv}_f^{\mathrm{prf}}(\mathbf{A}) := \left| \Pr\left[\mathbf{A}^{f_K} = 1\right] - \Pr\left[\mathbf{A}^{\rho} = 1\right] \right|.$$

f is called a secure PRF if no efficient adversary **A** has any significant advantage. The advantage can be extended to adversaries with multiple oracles:

$$\mathrm{Adv}_f^{p\text{-}\mathrm{prf}}(\mathbf{A}) := \left| \Pr[\mathbf{A}^{f_{K_1}, f_{K_2}, \ldots, f_{K_p}} = 1] - \Pr[\mathbf{A}^{\rho_1, \rho_2, \ldots, \rho_p} = 1] \right|,$$

where $(K_1, \ldots, K_p) \leftarrow \mathcal{K}^p$ and $\rho_1, \ldots, \rho_p$ are independent random oracles.

2.3   Tweakable Block Cipher in TWEAKEY Framework

A TBC in the TWEAKEY framework is a function $\tilde{e} : \Sigma^\nu \times \Sigma^n \to \Sigma^n$ with its tweakey space Σ^ν such that, for every $Y \in \Sigma^\nu$, $\tilde{e}(Y, \cdot)$ is a permutation. We assume that $\tilde{e} : \Sigma^\nu \times \Sigma^n \to \Sigma^n$ is a family of TBCs with their key space and tweak space Σ^κ and Σ^τ, respectively, satisfying $\Sigma^\nu = \Sigma^\kappa \times \Sigma^\tau$.

Let $\mathcal{P}_{\tau,n}$ be the set of all tweakable permutations over Σ^n with their tweak space Σ^τ. Namely, for every $\varpi \in \mathcal{P}_{\tau,n}$ and every $T \in \Sigma^\tau$, $\varpi(T, \cdot)$ is a permutation over Σ^n.

A security requirement of a TBC $e : \Sigma^\kappa \times \Sigma^\tau \times \Sigma^n \to \Sigma^n$ is indistinguishability from a tweakable uniform random permutation. The advantage of an adversary $\mathbf{A}$ against e as a tweakable PRP (TPRP) is defined as

$$\mathrm{Adv}_e^{\mathrm{tprp}}(\mathbf{A}) := \left| \Pr[\mathbf{A}^{e_K} = 1] - \Pr[\mathbf{A}^{\varpi} = 1] \right|,$$

where $K \leftarrow \Sigma^\kappa$ and $\varpi \leftarrow \mathcal{P}_{\tau,n}$. $\mathbf{A}$ is allowed to make queries in $\Sigma^\tau \times \Sigma^n$ adaptively to its oracle e_K or ϖ and outputs 0 or 1.

The following lemma is a kind of PRP/PRF switching lemma [5,16] for a TBC.

Lemma 1. *For any adversary $\mathbf{A}$ against a TBC $e : \Sigma^\kappa \times \Sigma^\tau \times \Sigma^n \to \Sigma^n$ taking at most t time and making at most q queries to its oracle, there exists an adversary $\mathbf{X}$ against e such that*

$$\mathrm{Adv}_e^{\mathrm{prf}}(\mathbf{A}) \le \mathrm{Adv}_e^{\mathrm{tprp}}(\mathbf{X}) + q^2/2^{n+1}$$

and $\mathbf{X}$ takes at most t time and makes at most q queries.

2.4   PRF and TPRP Under Related-Key Attack

Let $f : \mathcal{K} \times \mathcal{X} \to \mathcal{Y}$. Let Φ be a set of functions from $\mathcal{K}$ to $\mathcal{K}$. Let $\mathbf{A}$ be an adversary against f making a related-key attack restricted to Φ (Φ-RKA) [3]: $\mathbf{A}$ is given $g[K] : \Phi \times \mathcal{X} \to \mathcal{Y}$ such that $g[K](\varphi, X) := g(\varphi(K), X)$ as an oracle, where g is either f or a random oracle $\rho : \mathcal{K} \times \mathcal{X} \to \mathcal{Y}$ and $K \leftarrow \mathcal{K}$. φ is called a key-deriving function. The advantage of $\mathbf{A}$ against f as a PRF under a Φ-RKA is defined as

$$\mathrm{Adv}_{f,\Phi}^{\mathrm{prf\text{-}rka}}(\mathbf{A}) := \left| \Pr[\mathbf{A}^{f[K]} = 1] - \Pr[\mathbf{A}^{\rho[K]} = 1] \right|.$$

f is called a secure PRF under Φ-RKAs if no efficient adversary $\mathbf{A}$ has any significant advantage. The advantage of $\mathbf{A}$ with p oracles is defined as

$$\mathrm{Adv}_{f,\Phi}^{p\text{-}\mathrm{prf\text{-}rka}}(\mathbf{A}) := \left| \Pr[\mathbf{A}^{f[K_1],\ldots,f[K_p]} = 1] - \Pr[\mathbf{A}^{\rho_1[K_1],\ldots,\rho_p[K_p]} = 1] \right|,$$

where $(K_1, \ldots, K_p) \leftarrow \mathcal{K}^p$ and $\rho_1, \ldots, \rho_p$ are independent random oracles.

For a TBC e, $\mathrm{Adv}_{e,\Phi}^{\mathrm{tprp\text{-}rka}}(\mathbf{A})$ and $\mathrm{Adv}_{e,\Phi}^{p\text{-}\mathrm{tprp\text{-}rka}}(\mathbf{X})$ are defined similarly.

The following lemma is a kind of PRP/PRF switching lemma against adversaries making related-key attacks [14] for a TBC e.

Lemma 2. *Let* **A** *be any adversary with p oracles against e taking at most t time and making at most q_i queries to its i-th oracle for $1 \leq i \leq p$. Let $q := q_1 + \cdots + q_p$. Then, there exists an adversary* **X** *against e such that*

$$\mathrm{Adv}_{e,\varPhi}^{p\text{-prf-rka}}(\mathbf{A}) \leq p \cdot \mathrm{Adv}_{e,\varPhi}^{\text{tprp-rka}}(\mathbf{X}) + q^2/2^{n+1}$$

and **X** *takes at most $t + O(qT_e)$ time and makes at most $\max\{q_1, q_2, \ldots, q_p\}$ queries, where T_e represents the time required to compute e.*

3   Proposed Construction

Let $E : \varSigma^\nu \times \varSigma^n \to \varSigma^n$ be a TBC in the TWEAKEY framework such that $\nu \geq 2n$. The proposed construction $\mathsf{C}^E : \varSigma^n \times \varSigma^* \to \varSigma^{2n}$ is described in Algorithm 1. It is also depicted in Fig. 1. For the PRF property, C^E is viewed as a keyed function with its key space $\varSigma^n$. C^E incorporates constants $IV \in \varSigma^n$ and $c_{00}, c_{01}, c_{10}, c_{11}, \delta \in \varSigma^n \setminus \{0^n\}$. δ is a constant such that $\mathsf{lsb}(\delta) = 1$. $c_{00}, c_{01}, c_{10}, c_{11}$ are distinct from each other. $\mathsf{cf}^E : \varSigma^{2n} \times \varSigma^{\nu-n} \to \varSigma^{2n}$ is a compression function such that

$$\mathsf{cf}^E(V_{i-1}, M_i) := E(V_{i-1}\|M_{i,0}, M_{i,1})\|E(V_{i-1}\|M_{i,0}, M_{i,1} \oplus \delta),$$

where $M_i = M_{i,0}\|M_{i,1}$ and $|M_{i,1}| = n$. If $\nu = 2n$, then $M_{i,0} = \varepsilon$. $\mathsf{pad} : \varSigma^* \to (\varSigma^{\nu-n})^+$ is a padding function such that

$$\mathsf{pad}(M) := \begin{cases} M & \text{if } |M| > 0 \text{ and } |M| \equiv_{\nu-n} 0 \\ M\|10^a & \text{otherwise,} \end{cases}$$

where a is the non-negative integer such that $|\mathsf{pad}(M)|$ is the smallest multiple of $\nu - n$. Notice that $\mathsf{pad}(\varepsilon) = 10^{\nu-n-1}$.

Remark 1. Let sw be a permutation over $\varSigma^n \times \varSigma^n$ such that $(x_0, x_1) \mapsto (x_1, x_0)$. Then, for any $(V_{i-1}, M_i) \in \varSigma^{2n} \times \varSigma^{\nu-n}$, $\mathsf{cf}^E(V_{i-1}, M_i \oplus \delta) = \mathsf{sw}(\mathsf{cf}^E(V_{i-1}, M_i))$. For the PRF property, C^E is designed so that the *reflectiveness* of cf^E does not appear at the last call to cf^E. Notice that $\mathsf{lsb}(M_m) \neq \mathsf{lsb}(M_m \oplus \delta)$.

Algorithm 1: The proposed construction $\mathsf{C}^E : \Sigma^n \times \Sigma^* \to \Sigma^{2n}$

---

input : (K, M)
output: $\mathsf{C}^E(K, M)$
$M_1 \| M_2 \| \cdots \| M_m \leftarrow \mathsf{pad}(M);$ /* $|M_i| = \nu - n$ for $1 \le i \le m$ */
$V_0 \leftarrow K \| IV;$
for $i = 1$ **to** $m - 1$ **do** $V_i \leftarrow \mathsf{cf}^E(V_{i-1}, M_i);$
if $|M| > 0 \wedge |M| \equiv_{\nu-n} 0 \wedge \mathsf{lsb}(M_m) = 0$ **then** $c \leftarrow c_{00};$
if $|M| > 0 \wedge |M| \equiv_{\nu-n} 0 \wedge \mathsf{lsb}(M_m) = 1$ **then** $c \leftarrow c_{01};$
if $(|M| = 0 \vee |M| \not\equiv_{\nu-n} 0) \wedge \mathsf{lsb}(M_m) = 0$ **then** $c \leftarrow c_{10};$
if $(|M| = 0 \vee |M| \not\equiv_{\nu-n} 0) \wedge \mathsf{lsb}(M_m) = 1$ **then** $c \leftarrow c_{11};$
$V_m \leftarrow \mathsf{cf}^E(V_{i-1} \oplus c, M_i);$
return $V_m;$

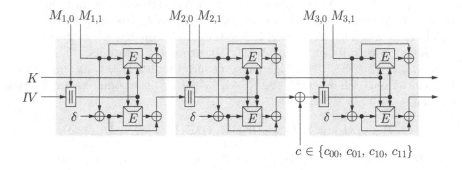

Fig. 1. The proposed construction

4   Collision Resistance

Any adversary needs $\Omega(2^n)$ queries to find a colliding pair of inputs for C^E under the assumption that E is an ideal cipher:

Theorem 1. *For any adversary* **A** *making at most q queries,*

$$\mathrm{Adv}^{\mathrm{col}}_{\mathsf{C}^E}(\mathbf{A}) \le 7q/(2^n - 2q) + 5q(q-1)/(2^n - 2q)^2.$$

Proof. Suppose that **A** finds a colliding pair of inputs, (K, M) and (K', M') for C^E. Then, $\mathsf{C}^E(K, M) = \mathsf{C}^E(K', M')$ and $(K, M) \neq (K', M')$. Without loss of generality, suppose that $|M| \le |M'|$. Let $\mathsf{pad}(M) = M_1 \| M_2 \| \cdots \| M_m$ and $\mathsf{pad}(M') = M'_1 \| M'_2 \| \cdots \| M'_{m'}$.

(i) Suppose that $m = m' = 1$. If $K \neq K'$, then **A** finds a colliding pair for cf^E. Otherwise, $M \neq M'$.
   - If $|M| = |M'| = \nu - n$, then **A** finds a colliding pair for cf^E since $\mathsf{pad}(M) \neq \mathsf{pad}(M')$.
   - If $|M| < \nu - n$ and $|M'| < \nu - n$, then **A** finds a colliding pair for cf^E since $\mathsf{pad}(M) \neq \mathsf{pad}(M')$.

– If $|M| < \nu - n$ and $|M'| = \nu - n$, then

$$\mathsf{cf}^E(K\|(IV \oplus c), M_1) = \mathsf{cf}^E(K\|(IV \oplus c'), M_1'),$$

where $c \in \{c_{10}, c_{11}\}$ and $c' \in \{c_{00}, c_{01}\}$. Thus, **A** finds a colliding pair for cf^E since $\{c_{10}, c_{11}\} \cap \{c_{00}, c_{01}\} = \emptyset$.

(ii) Suppose that $m = 1$ and $m' \geq 2$. Then,

$$\mathsf{cf}^E(K\|(IV \oplus c), M_1) = \mathsf{cf}^E(V_{m'-1}' \oplus c', M_{m'}'),$$

where

$$c \in \begin{cases} \{c_{00}, c_{01}\} & \text{if } |M| = \nu - n, \\ \{c_{10}, c_{11}\} & \text{if } |M| < \nu - n, \end{cases} \qquad c' \in \begin{cases} \{c_{00}, c_{01}\} & \text{if } |M'| \equiv_{\nu-n} 0, \\ \{c_{10}, c_{11}\} & \text{if } |M'| \not\equiv_{\nu-n} 0. \end{cases}$$

If $(K\|(IV \oplus c), M_1) \neq (V_{m'-1}' \oplus c', M_{m'}')$, then **A** finds a colliding pair for cf^E. Otherwise, $M_1 = M_{m'}'$ and the least significant n bits of $V_{m'-1}'$ equals $IV \oplus c \oplus c'$. Thus, **A** finds an input for cf^E such that the least significant n bits of the corresponding output equals

– IV if $|M| = \nu - n$ and $|M'| \equiv_{\nu-n} 0$,
– IV if $|M| < \nu - n$ and $|M'| \not\equiv_{\nu-n} 0$, and
– $IV \oplus c_{00} \oplus c_{10}$ or $IV \oplus c_{01} \oplus c_{11}$ otherwise.

(iii) Suppose that $m \geq 2$ and $m' \geq 2$. Then,

$$\mathsf{cf}^E(V_{m-1} \oplus c, M_m) = \mathsf{cf}^E(V_{m'-1}' \oplus c', M_{m'}')$$

where

$$c \in \begin{cases} \{c_{00}, c_{01}\} & \text{if } |M| \equiv_{\nu-n} 0, \\ \{c_{10}, c_{11}\} & \text{if } |M| \not\equiv_{\nu-n} 0, \end{cases} \qquad c' \in \begin{cases} \{c_{00}, c_{01}\} & \text{if } |M'| \equiv_{\nu-n} 0, \\ \{c_{10}, c_{11}\} & \text{if } |M'| \not\equiv_{\nu-n} 0. \end{cases}$$

If $(V_{m-1} \oplus c, M_m) \neq (V_{m'-1}' \oplus c', M_{m'}')$, then **A** finds a colliding pair for cf^E. Otherwise, $V_{m-1} \oplus V_{m'-1}' = 0^n\|(c \oplus c')$ and $M_m = M_{m'}'$.

– If $|M| \equiv_{\nu-n} 0$ and $|M'| \not\equiv_{\nu-n} 0$, or $|M| \not\equiv_{\nu-n} 0$ and $|M'| \equiv_{\nu-n} 0$, then **A** finds a colliding pair for cf^E wrt $0^n\|(c_{00} \oplus c_{10})$ or $0^n\|(c_{01} \oplus c_{11})$, that is, a pair of inputs (V_{m-2}, M_{m-1}) and $(V_{m'-2}', M_{m'-1}')$ such that $\mathsf{cf}^E(V_{m-2}, M_{m-1}) \oplus \mathsf{cf}^E(V_{m'-2}', M_{m'-1}')$ equals $0^n\|(c_{00} \oplus c_{10})$ or $0^n\|(c_{01} \oplus c_{11})$.
– Suppose that $|M| \equiv_{\nu-n} 0$ and $|M'| \equiv_{\nu-n} 0$. Then, since $M_m = M_{m'}'$, $c = c'$ and $V_{m-1} = V_{m'-1}'$. If $m = m'$, then **A** finds a colliding pair for cf^E since $(K, M) \neq (K', M')$. If $m < m'$, then **A** finds a colliding pair for cf^E or an input for cf^E such that the least significant n bits of the corresponding output equals IV.
– Suppose that $|M| \not\equiv_{\nu-n} 0$ and $|M'| \not\equiv_{\nu-n} 0$. This case is similar to the case above. Thus, **A** finds a colliding pair for cf^E or an input for cf^E such that the least significant n bits of the corresponding output equals IV.

Thus, a colliding pair for C^E implies for cf^E

1. a colliding pair,
2. a colliding pair wrt $0^n\|(c_{00} \oplus c_{10})$ or $0^n\|(c_{01} \oplus c_{11})$, or
3. an input mapped to an output whose least significant n bits equals IV, $IV \oplus c_{00} \oplus c_{10}$ or $IV \oplus c_{01} \oplus c_{11}$.

Let us consider an adversary $\tilde{\mathbf{A}}$ running $\mathbf{A}$. For each query $\mathbf{A}$, $\tilde{\mathbf{A}}$ makes at most 2 queries. Thus, $\tilde{\mathbf{A}}$ makes at most $2q$ queries in total.

For a query of $\mathbf{A}$, if $\tilde{\mathbf{A}}$ already knows the corresponding answer, then $\tilde{\mathbf{A}}$ simply returns it to $\mathbf{A}$. Suppose that $\tilde{\mathbf{A}}$ does not know the answer. If the query of $\mathbf{A}$ is an encryption query (TK, PT), then $\tilde{\mathbf{A}}$ asks (TK, PT) and $(TK, PT \oplus \delta)$ to E and receives replies CT and CT', respectively. Then, $\tilde{\mathbf{A}}$ returns CT to $\mathbf{A}$. If the query of $\mathbf{A}$ is a decryption query (TK, CT), then $\tilde{\mathbf{A}}$ asks (TK, CT) to E^{-1}, receives a reply PT and returns it to $\mathbf{A}$. Then, $\tilde{\mathbf{A}}$ asks $(TK, PT \oplus \delta)$ to E and receives a reply CT'. In both of the cases, $\tilde{\mathbf{A}}$ gets (TK, PT, CT) and $(TK, PT \oplus \delta, CT')$. Notice that $\mathsf{cf}^E(TK_{\mathrm{v}}, TK_{\mathrm{m}}\|PT) = (CT \oplus PT)\|(CT' \oplus PT \oplus \delta)$ and $\mathsf{cf}^E(TK_{\mathrm{v}}, TK_{\mathrm{m}}\|(PT \oplus \delta)) = (CT' \oplus PT \oplus \delta)\|(CT \oplus PT)$, where $TK = TK_{\mathrm{v}}\|TK_{\mathrm{m}}$ and $|TK_{\mathrm{v}}| = 2n$. Also notice that, if $CT \oplus CT' = \delta$, then $\mathsf{cf}^E(TK_{\mathrm{v}}, TK_{\mathrm{m}}\|PT) = \mathsf{cf}^E(TK_{\mathrm{v}}, TK_{\mathrm{m}}\|(PT \oplus \delta))$.

Let (TK_j, PT_j, CT_j) and $(TK_j, PT_j \oplus \delta, CT'_j)$ be the tuples obtained by $\tilde{\mathbf{A}}$ for the j-th query of $\mathbf{A}$. Let $U_j := CT_j \oplus PT_j$ and $U'_j := CT'_j \oplus PT_j \oplus \delta$. Then, for an execution of $\tilde{\mathbf{A}}$, the j-th query of $\mathbf{A}$ induces 1 or 2 above for cf^E if $U_j = U'_j$ or there exists some $j' < j$ such that

- $U_j\|U'_j \in \{U_{j'}\|U'_{j'}, U_{j'}\|(U'_{j'} \oplus c_{00} \oplus c_{10}), U_{j'}\|(U'_{j'} \oplus c_{01} \oplus c_{11})\}$,
- $U_j\|U'_j \in \{U'_{j'}\|U'_{j'}, U'_{j'}\|(U'_{j'} \oplus c_{00} \oplus c_{10}), U'_{j'}\|(U'_{j'} \oplus c_{01} \oplus c_{11})\}$,
- $U'_j\|U_j \in \{U_{j'}\|U'_{j'}, U_{j'}\|(U'_{j'} \oplus c_{00} \oplus c_{10}), U_{j'}\|(U'_{j'} \oplus c_{01} \oplus c_{11})\}$, or
- $U'_j\|U_j \in \{U'_{j'}\|U'_{j'}, U'_{j'}\|(U'_{j'} \oplus c_{00} \oplus c_{10}), U'_{j'}\|(U'_{j'} \oplus c_{01} \oplus c_{11})\}$.

Thus, the probability that the j-th query of $\mathbf{A}$ induces 1 or 2 above for cf^E is at most $10(j-1)/(2^n - 2q)^2 + 1/(2^n - 2q)$. The probability that it induces 3 above for cf^E is at most $6/(2^n - 2q)$. Since $\mathbf{A}$ makes at most q queries,

$$\sum_{j=1}^{q}(10(j-1)/(2^n - 2q)^2 + 7/(2^n - 2q)) \le 7q/(2^n - 2q) + 5q(q-1)/(2^n - 2q)^2.$$

It is also an upper bound on $\mathrm{Adv}^{\mathrm{col}}_{\mathsf{C}^E}(\mathbf{A})$. $\square$

5 Pseudorandom-Function Property

The proposed construction C^E treats the TBC $E : \Sigma^\nu \times \Sigma^n \to \Sigma^n$ in the TWEAKEY framework in two tweakey strategies: $\Sigma^\nu := \Sigma^n \times \Sigma^{\nu-n}$ in one strategy and $\Sigma^\nu := \Sigma^{2n} \times \Sigma^{\nu-2n}$ in the other strategy. We denote E in the former and the latter tweakey strategies by $\dot{E}$ and $\ddot{E}$, respectively.

For $\ddot{E}$, we consider related-key attacks with related-key-deriving functions $\Phi := \{\mathrm{id}, \mathrm{sw}, \mathrm{x}_{c_{00}}, \mathrm{x}_{c_{01}}, \mathrm{x}_{c_{10}}, \mathrm{x}_{c_{11}}, \mathrm{sw} \circ \mathrm{x}_{c_{00}}, \mathrm{sw} \circ \mathrm{x}_{c_{01}}, \mathrm{sw} \circ \mathrm{x}_{c_{10}}, \mathrm{sw} \circ \mathrm{x}_{c_{11}}\}$, where

- id is the identity permutation over Σ^{2n},
- sw is a permutation over $\Sigma^n \times \Sigma^n$ such that $(x_0, x_1) \mapsto (x_1, x_0)$, and
- for $c \in \Sigma^n$, x_c is a permutation over Σ^{2n} such that $x \mapsto x \oplus c$.

C^E is a secure PRF if $\dot{E}$ is a secure TPRP and $\ddot{E}$ is a secure TPRP under Φ-related-key attacks:

Theorem 2. *For any adversary* $\mathbf{A}$ *against* C^E *taking at most t time and making at most q queries each of which has at most ℓ blocks after padding, there exist adversaries* $\dot{\mathbf{A}}$ *against* $\dot{E}$ *and* $\ddot{\mathbf{A}}$ *against* $\ddot{E}$ *such that*

$$\mathrm{Adv}_{\mathsf{C}^E}^{\mathrm{prf}}(\mathbf{A}) \le \mathrm{Adv}_{\dot{E}}^{\mathrm{tprp}}(\dot{\mathbf{A}}) + (\ell - 1)q \, \mathrm{Adv}_{\ddot{E},\Phi}^{\mathrm{tprp\text{-}rka}}(\ddot{\mathbf{A}}) + \ell q^2 / 2^{n+1} + (\ell - 1)q/2^n.$$

Both $\dot{\mathbf{A}}$ *and* $\ddot{\mathbf{A}}$ *take at most about* $t + O(\ell q \, T_E)$ *time and make at most $2q$ queries, where T_E is time required to compute E.*

Proof. Let $\mathsf{I}^c : \Sigma^{2n} \times (\Sigma^{\nu-n})^+ \to \Sigma^{2n}$ be a keyed function specified in Algorithm 2. For an integer $k \ge 0$ and functions $\zeta : \Sigma^* \to \Sigma^{2n}$ and $\eta : (\Sigma^{\nu-n})^* \to \Sigma^{2n}$, let $\mathsf{Hy}[k]^{\zeta,\eta} : \Sigma^* \to \Sigma^{2n}$ be a function specified as follows: For $M \in \Sigma^*$ such that $\mathbf{pad}(M) = M_1 \| M_2 \| \cdots \| M_m$ and $|M_i| = \nu - n$ for $1 \le i \le m$,

$$\mathsf{Hy}[k]^{\zeta,\eta}(M) := \begin{cases} \zeta(M) & \text{if } m \le k, \\ \mathsf{I}^c(\eta(M_{[1,k]}), M_{[k+1,m]}) & \text{if } m > k, \end{cases}$$

and

$$c \leftarrow \begin{cases} c_{00} & \text{if } |M| > 0 \wedge |M| \equiv_{\nu-n} 0 \wedge \mathsf{lsb}(M_m) = 0, \\ c_{01} & \text{if } |M| > 0 \wedge |M| \equiv_{\nu-n} 0 \wedge \mathsf{lsb}(M_m) = 1, \\ c_{10} & \text{if } (|M| = 0 \vee |M| \not\equiv_{\nu-n} 0) \wedge \mathsf{lsb}(M_m) = 0, \\ c_{11} & \text{if } (|M| = 0 \vee |M| \not\equiv_{\nu-n} 0) \wedge \mathsf{lsb}(M_m) = 1. \end{cases} \qquad (1)$$

Notice that $M_{[1,0]} = \varepsilon$.

Suppose that ζ is a random oracle and η is a random function such that

- $\eta(\varepsilon) \leftarrow \Sigma^n \times \{IV\}$, and
- for every $k \ge 1$ and $M_{[1,k]}$ such that $\mathsf{lsb}(M_k) = 0$, $\eta(M_{[1,k]}) \leftarrow \Sigma^{2n}$ and $\eta(M_{[1,k]} \oplus \delta) \leftarrow \mathsf{sw}(\eta(M_{[1,k]}))$.

Then,

$$\mathsf{Hy}[0]^{\zeta,\eta}(M) = \mathsf{I}^c(\eta(\varepsilon), M_{[1,m]})$$

and c is chosen as specified by Formula (1). Thus, $\mathsf{Hy}[0]^{\zeta,\eta}$ is equivalent to C^E. $\mathsf{Hy}[\ell]^{\zeta,\eta}$ works as a random oracle for any $M \in \Sigma^*$ such that $\mathbf{pad}(M)$ consists of at most ℓ blocks. Since every query made by $\mathbf{A}$ is assumed to consist of at most ℓ blocks after padding,

$$\mathrm{Adv}_{\mathsf{C}^E}^{\mathrm{prf}}(\mathbf{A}) = \left| \Pr[\mathbf{A}^{\mathsf{Hy}[0]^{\zeta,\eta}} = 1] - \Pr[\mathbf{A}^{\mathsf{Hy}[\ell]^{\zeta,\eta}} = 1] \right|.$$

Let $\Delta_k := \left| \Pr[\mathbf{A}^{\mathsf{Hy}[k]^{\zeta,\eta}} = 1] - \Pr[\mathbf{A}^{\mathsf{Hy}[k+1]^{\zeta,\eta}} = 1] \right|$. Then,

$$\mathrm{Adv}_{\mathsf{C}^E}^{\mathrm{prf}}(\mathbf{A}) \le \Delta_0 + \Delta_1 + \cdots + \Delta_{\ell-1}. \qquad (2)$$

For Δ_0, let $\mathbf{D}_0$ be an adversary against $\dot{E}$. $\mathbf{D}_0$ runs $\mathbf{A}$ and produces the same output as $\mathbf{A}$. It also simulates the oracle of $\mathbf{A}$ using its oracle. Let $\dot{F} : \Sigma^{\nu-n} \times \Sigma^n \to \Sigma^n$ be the oracle of $\mathbf{D}_0$, which is either $\dot{E}_K$ or $\dot{\rho}$, where $K \leftarrow \Sigma^n$ and $\dot{\rho}$ is a random oracle. For each query M of $\mathbf{A}$ such that $\mathrm{pad}(M) = M_1 \| \cdots \| M_m$, $\mathbf{D}_0$ acts as follows: For $1 \le i \le m$, $M_i := M_{i,0} \| M_{i,1}$, where $|M_{i,0}| = \nu - 2n$ and $|M_{i,1}| = n$.

- If $m = 1$, then $\mathbf{D}_0$ asks $((IV \oplus c) \| M_{1,0}, M_{1,1})$ and $((IV \oplus c) \| M_{1,0}, M_{1,1} \oplus \delta)$ to $\dot{F}$ and returns $\mathrm{cf}^{\dot{F}}(K \| (IV \oplus c), M_1)$ to $\mathbf{A}$.
- If $m \ge 2$, then $\mathbf{D}_0$ asks $(IV \| M_{1,0}, M_{1,1})$ and $(IV \| M_{1,0}, M_{1,1} \oplus \delta)$ to $\dot{F}$ and returns $\mathsf{l}^c(\mathrm{cf}^{\dot{F}}(K \| IV, M_1), M_{[2,m]})$ to $\mathbf{A}$.

In both of the cases above, c is chosen as specified by Formula (1). $\mathbf{D}_0$ implements $\mathsf{Hy}[0]^{\zeta,\eta}$ as the oracle of $\mathbf{A}$ if its oracle is $\dot{E}_K$. It implements $\mathsf{Hy}[1]^{\zeta,\eta}$ if its oracle is $\dot{\rho}$ since $\dot{\rho}((IV \oplus c_{00}) \| M_{1,0}, M_{1,1})$, $\dot{\rho}((IV \oplus c_{01}) \| M_{1,0}, M_{1,1})$, $\dot{\rho}((IV \oplus c_{10}) \| M_{1,0}, M_{1,1})$, $\dot{\rho}((IV \oplus c_{11}) \| M_{1,0}, M_{1,1})$ and $\dot{\rho}(IV \| M_{1,0}, M_{1,1})$ are independent from each other. Thus,

$$\Delta_0 = \left| \Pr[\mathbf{D}_0^{\dot{E}_K} = 1] - \Pr[\mathbf{D}_0^{\dot{\rho}} = 1] \right| = \mathrm{Adv}_{\dot{E}}^{\mathrm{prf}}(\mathbf{D}_0). \tag{3}$$

$\mathbf{D}_0$ takes at most about $t + O(\ell q T_E)$ time and makes at most $2q$ queries.

Suppose that $1 \le k \le \ell - 1$. For Δ_k, let $\mathbf{D}_k$ be an adversary making a Φ-related-key attack on $\ddot{E}$. $\mathbf{D}_k$ runs $\mathbf{A}$ and produces the same output as $\mathbf{A}$. It also simulates the oracle of $\mathbf{A}$ using its oracle. $\mathbf{D}_k$ has q oracles $\ddot{F}_i[K_i] : \Sigma^{\nu-2n} \times \Sigma^n \to \Sigma^n$ for $1 \le i \le q$. They are either $\ddot{E}[K_1], \ldots, \ddot{E}[K_q]$ or $\ddot{\rho}_1[K_1], \ldots, \ddot{\rho}_q[K_q]$, where $K_i \leftarrow \Sigma^{2n}$ and $\ddot{\rho}_i$ is a random oracle for $1 \le i \le q$. For the j-th query M of $\mathbf{A}$, let $\mathrm{pad}(M) = M_1 \| \cdots \| M_m$, where $M_i := M_{i,0} \| M_{i,1}$, $|M_{i,0}| = \nu - 2n$ and $|M_{i,1}| = n$ for $1 \le i \le m$. Suppose that $m \le k$. Then, $\mathbf{D}_k$ simulates ζ and returns $\zeta(M)$ to $\mathbf{A}$. Suppose that $m > k$. Let $\mathcal{J}$ be a set of integers j' such that $j' < j$ and the j'-th query M' of $\mathbf{A}$ satisfies $m' > k$ and $M'_{[1,k]} = M_{[1,k]} \vee M'_{[1,k]} = M_{[1,k-1]} \| M_{k,0} \| (M_{k,1} \oplus \delta)$, where $\mathrm{pad}(M') = M'_1 \| \cdots \| M'_{m'}$. Let $j^* \leftarrow j$ if $\mathcal{J} = \emptyset$ and $j^* \leftarrow \min \mathcal{J}$ otherwise. Let M^* be the j^*-th query of $\mathbf{A}$. Then, for the j-th query M of $\mathbf{A}$, $\mathbf{D}_k$ acts as follows:

- Suppose that $m = k + 1$. Then,
  - $\mathbf{D}_k$ asks $(\mathsf{x}_c, M_{k+1,0}, M_{k+1,1})$ and $(\mathsf{x}_c, M_{k+1,0}, M_{k+1,1} \oplus \delta)$ to $\ddot{F}_{j^*}[K_{j^*}]$ and returns $\mathrm{cf}^{\ddot{F}_{j^*}}(K_{j^*} \oplus c, M_{k+1})$ to $\mathbf{A}$ if $j^* = j$ or $j^* < j \wedge M^*_{[1,k]} = M_{[1,k]}$, and
  - $\mathbf{D}_k$ asks $(\mathsf{sw} \circ \mathsf{x}_c, M_{k+1,0}, M_{k+1,1})$ and $(\mathsf{sw} \circ \mathsf{x}_c, M_{k+1,0}, M_{k+1,1} \oplus \delta)$ to $\ddot{F}_{j^*}[K_{j^*}]$ and returns $\mathrm{cf}^{\ddot{F}_{j^*}}(\mathsf{sw}(K_{j^*}) \oplus c, M_{k+1})$ to $\mathbf{A}$ otherwise.

  In both of the cases above, c is chosen as specified by Formula (1).
- Suppose that $m \ge k + 2$. Then,
  - $\mathbf{D}_k$ asks $(\mathsf{id}, M_{k+1,0}, M_{k+1,1})$ and $(\mathsf{id}, M_{k+1,0}, M_{k+1,1} \oplus \delta)$ to $\ddot{F}_{j^*}[K_{j^*}]$ and returns $\mathsf{l}^c(\mathrm{cf}^{\ddot{F}_{j^*}}(K_{j^*}, M_{k+1}), M_{[k+2,m]})$ to $\mathbf{A}$ if $j^* = j$ or $j^* < j \wedge M^*_{[1,k]} = M_{[1,k]}$, and

- $\mathbf{D}_k$ asks $(\mathsf{sw}, M_{k+1,0}, M_{k+1,1})$ and $(\mathsf{sw}, M_{k+1,0}, M_{k+1,1} \oplus \delta)$ to $\ddot{F}_{j^*}[K_{j^*}]$ and returns $\mathsf{l}^c(\mathsf{cf}^{\ddot{F}_{j^*}}(\mathsf{sw}(K_{j^*}), M_{k+1}), M_{[k+2,m]})$ to $\mathbf{A}$ otherwise.

In both of the cases above, c is chosen as specified by Formula (1).

In the process above, for the j-th query M, if $M_{[1,k]}$ is new, that is, $\mathcal{J} = \emptyset$, then $\mathbf{D}_k$ uses the new oracle $\ddot{F}_j[K_j]$ to compute the answer to the query. It implies that new K_j, which is chosen uniformly at random, is assigned to new $M_{[1,k]}$. Suppose that the oracles of $\mathbf{D}_k$ are $\ddot{E}[K_1], \ldots, \ddot{E}[K_q]$. Then, $\mathbf{D}_k$ implements $\mathsf{Hy}[k]^{\varsigma, \eta}$ as the oracle of $\mathbf{A}$. On the other hand, suppose that the oracles of $\mathbf{D}_k$ are $\ddot{\rho}_1[K_1], \ldots, \ddot{\rho}_q[K_q]$. Then, $\mathbf{D}_k$ implements $\mathsf{Hy}[k+1]^{\varsigma, \eta}$ if $K_i \neq \mathsf{sw}(K_i)$ for every i sich that $1 \leq i \leq q$. Thus,

$$\Delta_k = \mathrm{Adv}_{\ddot{E}, \Phi}^{q\text{-prf-rka}}(\mathbf{D}_k) + \left| \Pr[\mathbf{D}_k^{\ddot{\rho}[K_1], \ldots, \ddot{\rho}[K_q]} = 1] - \Pr[\mathbf{A}^{\mathsf{Hy}[k+1]^{\varsigma, \eta}} = 1] \right|$$

$$\leq \mathrm{Adv}_{\ddot{E}, \Phi}^{q\text{-prf-rka}}(\mathbf{D}_k) + q/2^n. \tag{4}$$

$\mathbf{D}_k$ takes at most about $t + O(\ell q T_E)$ time and makes at most $2q$ queries.

From Inequality (2), Equalities (3) and (4), and Lemmas 1 and 2, there exist adversaries $\dot{\mathbf{A}}$ and $\ddot{\mathbf{A}}$ such that

$$\mathrm{Adv}_{CE}^{\mathrm{prf}}(\mathbf{A}) \leq \mathrm{Adv}_{\dot{E}}^{\mathrm{tprp}}(\dot{\mathbf{A}}) + (\ell - 1)q \cdot \mathrm{Adv}_{\ddot{E}, \Phi}^{\mathrm{tprp\text{-}rka}}(\ddot{\mathbf{A}}) + \ell q^2/2^{n+1} + (\ell - 1)q/2^n.$$

Both $\dot{\mathbf{A}}$ and $\ddot{\mathbf{A}}$ take at most about $t + O(\ell q T_E)$ time and make at most $2q$ queries.   □

Algorithm 2: $\mathsf{l}^c : \Sigma^{2n} \times (\Sigma^{\nu-n})^+ \rightarrow \Sigma^{2n}$

---

input : $(W, X_1 \| X_2 \cdots \| X_x)$
output: $\mathsf{l}^c(W, X_1 \| X_2 \cdots \| X_x)$
$V_0 \leftarrow W;$ /* $|X_i| = \nu - n$ for $1 \leq i \leq x$ */
for $i = 1$ **to** $x - 1$ **do** $V_i \leftarrow \mathsf{cf}^E(V_{i-1}, X_i)$ $V_x \leftarrow \mathsf{cf}^E((V_{x-1} \oplus c, X_x);$
return $V_x;$

Acknowledgements. This work was supported by JSPS KAKENHI Grant Number JP21K11885.

References

1. Bellare, M., Canetti, R., Krawczyk, H.: Keying hash functions for message authentication. In: Koblitz, N. (ed.) CRYPTO 1996. LNCS, vol. 1109, pp. 1–15. Springer, Heidelberg (1996). https://doi.org/10.1007/3-540-68697-5_1
2. Bellare, M., Canetti, R., Krawczyk, H.: Pseudorandom functions revisited: the cascade construction and its concrete security. In: Proceedings of the 37th IEEE Symposium on Foundations of Computer Science, pp. 514–523 (1996)

14   S. Hirose

3. Bellare, M., Kohno, T.: A theoretical treatment of related-key attacks: RKA-PRPs, RKA-PRFs, and applications. In: Biham, E. (ed.) EUROCRYPT 2003. LNCS, vol. 2656, pp. 491–506. Springer, Heidelberg (2003). https://doi.org/10.1007/3-540-39200-9_31
4. Bellare, M., Ristenpart, T.: Multi-property-preserving hash domain extension and the EMD transform. In: Lai, X., Chen, K. (eds.) ASIACRYPT 2006. LNCS, vol. 4284, pp. 299–314. Springer, Heidelberg (2006). https://doi.org/10.1007/11935230_20
5. Bellare, M., Rogaway, P.: Code-based game-playing proofs and the security of triple encryption. Cryptology ePrint Archive, Report 2004/331 (2006). http://eprint.iacr.org/
6. Boneh, D., Eskandarian, S., Fisch, B.: Post-quantum EPID signatures from symmetric primitives. In: Matsui, M. (ed.) CT-RSA 2019. LNCS, vol. 11405, pp. 251–271. Springer, Cham (2019). https://doi.org/10.1007/978-3-030-12612-4_13
7. Damgård, I.B.: A design principle for hash functions. In: Brassard, G. (ed.) CRYPTO 1989. LNCS, vol. 435, pp. 416–427. Springer, New York (1990). https://doi.org/10.1007/0-387-34805-0_39
8. Dodis, Y., Grubbs, P., Ristenpart, T., Woodage, J.: Fast message franking: from invisible salamanders to encryptment. In: Shacham, H., Boldyreva, A. (eds.) CRYPTO 2018. LNCS, vol. 10991, pp. 155–186. Springer, Cham (2018). https://doi.org/10.1007/978-3-319-96884-1_6
9. FIPS PUB 198-1: The keyed-hash message authentication code (HMAC) (2008)
10. Goldreich, O., Goldwasser, S., Micali, S.: How to construct random functions. J. ACM **33**(4), 792–807 (1986). https://doi.org/10.1145/6490.6503
11. Grubbs, P., Lu, J., Ristenpart, T.: Message franking via committing authenticated encryption. In: Katz, J., Shacham, H. (eds.) CRYPTO 2017. LNCS, vol. 10403, pp. 66–97. Springer, Cham (2017). https://doi.org/10.1007/978-3-319-63697-9_3
12. Hirose, S.: Some plausible constructions of double-block-length hash functions. In: Robshaw, M. (ed.) FSE 2006. LNCS, vol. 4047, pp. 210–225. Springer, Heidelberg (2006). https://doi.org/10.1007/11799313_14
13. Hirose, S.: Collision-resistant and pseudorandom function based on Merkle-Damgård hash function. In: Park, J.H., Seo, S. (eds.) ICISC 2021. LNCS, vol. 13218, pp. 325–338. Springer, Cham (2021). https://doi.org/10.1007/978-3-031-08896-4_17
14. Hirose, S., Ideguchi, K., Kuwakado, H., Owada, T., Preneel, B., Yoshida, H.: An AES based 256-bit hash function for lightweight applications: Lesamnta-LW. IEICE Trans. Fundam. **E95-A**(1), 89–99 (2012)
15. Hirose, S., Park, J.H., Yun, A.: A simple variant of the Merkle-Damgård scheme with a permutation. In: Kurosawa, K. (ed.) ASIACRYPT 2007. LNCS, vol. 4833, pp. 113–129. Springer, Heidelberg (2007). https://doi.org/10.1007/978-3-540-76900-2_7
16. Impagliazzo, R., Rudich, S.: Limits on the provable consequences of one-way permutations. In: Goldwasser, S. (ed.) CRYPTO 1988. LNCS, vol. 403, pp. 8–26. Springer, New York (1990). https://doi.org/10.1007/0-387-34799-2_2
17. Iwata, T., Kurosawa, K.: OMAC: One-key CBC MAC. Cryptology ePrint Archive, Report 2002/180 (2002). https://ia.cr/2002/180
18. Iwata, T., Kurosawa, K.: OMAC: one-key CBC MAC. In: Johansson, T. (ed.) FSE 2003. LNCS, vol. 2887, pp. 129–153. Springer, Heidelberg (2003). https://doi.org/10.1007/978-3-540-39887-5_11

19. Jean, J., Nikolić, I., Peyrin, T.: Tweaks and keys for block ciphers: the TWEAKEY framework. In: Sarkar, P., Iwata, T. (eds.) ASIACRYPT 2014. LNCS, vol. 8874, pp. 274–288. Springer, Heidelberg (2014). https://doi.org/10.1007/978-3-662-45608-8_15
20. Merkle, R.C.: One way hash functions and DES. In: Brassard, G. (ed.) CRYPTO 1989. LNCS, vol. 435, pp. 428–446. Springer, New York (1990). https://doi.org/10.1007/0-387-34805-0_40
21. NIST Special Publication 800-38B: Recommendation for block cipher modes of operation: The CMAC mode for authentication (2005)

Provably Secure Password-Authenticated Key Exchange Based on SIDH

Theo Fanuela Prabowo$^{(\boxtimes)}$ and Chik How Tan

Temasek Laboratories, National University of Singapore, Singapore, Singapore
{tsltfp,tsltch}@nus.edu.sg

Abstract. Password-authenticated key exchange (PAKE) schemes are cryptographic schemes for securely establishing a shared session key between a client and a server communicating over an insecure channel by using a low-entropy password. In this paper, we propose a PAKE based on SIDH, where the password is used to derive a torsion points obfuscator independent of ephemeral keys. We analyze its security and prove that it is secure in the Bellare-Pointcheval-Rogaway (BPR) model, assuming the hardness of the supersingular isogeny computational Diffie-Hellman (SI-CDH) problem.

Keywords: SIDH · Isogeny · Password authenticated key exchange

1 Introduction

Post-quantum cryptosystems refer to cryptographic schemes which are secure not only against threats from classical computers, but also against adversaries with access to quantum computers. Such schemes are important as the discovery of Shor's algorithm [15] has highlighted that some problems and cryptographic schemes which were previously believed to be secure can be solved quite efficiently using a quantum computer. As progress in building quantum computers has been significant in the last few years, the field of post-quantum cryptography has also been studied more extensively. As a result, many post-quantum cryptosystems have been proposed and analyzed. These schemes are based on various problems, such as lattices problems, solving multivariate quadratic equations, etc.

Isogeny-based cryptography is a branch of post-quantum cryptography which is based on finding isogenies (certain kind of maps) between elliptic curves. It was first proposed by Couveignes in [6] and gained a renewed interest ever since the proposal of SIDH (supersingular isogeny Diffie-Hellman) in [9], which is an isogeny-based post-quantum key exchange protocol. Similar to the classical Diffie-Hellman key exchange, SIDH does not provide security against active adversary (e.g. impersonation attack). To overcome this, one may use authenticated key exchange (AKE) or password-authenticated key exchange (PAKE) schemes.

Both AKE and PAKE schemes aim to securely establish a common shared key between two parties communicating over an insecure channel. The difference

© Springer Nature Switzerland AG 2023
I. You and T.-Y. Youn (Eds.): WISA 2022, LNCS 13720, pp. 16–28, 2023.
https://doi.org/10.1007/978-3-031-25659-2_2

between these schemes is that for AKE, all parties (clients and servers) have a pre-established long-term secret key - public key pair. Hence, a public key infrastructure (PKI) is needed for AKE schemes. On the other hand, PAKE scheme does not require a PKI. Rather, for PAKE, each client/user has a low-entropy password, which is also securely stored by the server. Due to having less requirement, PAKE schemes are more widely used than AKE schemes in practical applications.

The first PAKE scheme was proposed by Bellovin and Merritt in [2]. Since then, many other PAKE schemes have been proposed, such as EKE [3], J-PAKE [12], PAK [4], etc. They are mostly based on the hardness of computing discrete logarithm or the classical Diffie-Hellman problem, and thus not post-quantum secure. More recently, a few post-quantum alternatives have also been proposed.

Prior to this work, there are few proposed isogeny-based PAKE schemes [17,18]. The PAKE proposed in [18] adapts the EKE scheme [3] to the SIDH setting. However, it is later shown to be insecure in [1]. In fact, [1] also shows that most PAKE based on the classical Diffie-Hellman will be insecure when adapted to the SIDH setting. The PAKE proposed in [17] is secure as there is currently no known attack on it. However, it does not have a formal security proof. Another attempt to construct isogeny-based provably secure PAKE-like scheme is the work of Qi and Chen [14]. However, the scheme proposed in [14] is not exactly a PAKE as the servers are required to have secret key - public key pairs (while the clients only need a low-entropy password). In this paper, we propose another PAKE scheme based on SIDH. Furthermore, we also analyze its security and prove that it is secure in the BPR model, which is the standard security model used to prove security of PAKE schemes.

The rest of this paper is organized as follows. In Sect. 2, we briefly review the SIDH key exchange, as well as some isogeny-based hard problems. In Sect. 3, we present our proposed PAKE scheme. We then analyze its security and give a formal security proof in the BPR model in Sect. 4. Finally, the paper is concluded in Sect. 5.

2   Preliminaries

2.1   SIDH

In this section, we review the SIDH key exchange protocol, which was introduced in [9]. For background on elliptic curves and isogenies, please refer to [8,10,16].

Let p be a prime of the form $\ell_1^{e_1} \ell_2^{e_2} f \pm 1$, where ℓ_1, ℓ_2 are distinct small primes. Let $E : y^2 = x^3 + 6x^2 + x^1$ be a supersingular elliptic curve defined over $\mathbb{F}_{p^2}$.

---

[1] Note that in the original SIDH [9] and SIKE [13] proposal, the starting curve was proposed to be $y^2 = x^3 + x$. However, it was later realised to have some security issues as the number of 2 and 3-isogenous curves (up to isomorphism) to this curve are less than ideal. As such, in the second round submission to the NIST call for PQC standardization, the starting curve for SIKE is revised to be $y^2 = x^3 + 6x^2 + x$. The reader is referred to [13, Section 1.3.2] for more details.

Suppose $\{P_1, Q_1\}$ and $\{P_2, Q_2\}$ are bases for the torsion subgroups $E[\ell_1^{e_1}]$ and $E[\ell_2^{e_2}]$ respectively.

The key exchange between two parties, Alice and Bob, is as follows. Alice chooses a secret $a \in \mathbb{Z}_{\ell_1^{e_1}}$. She then computes the isogeny whose kernel is given by $\langle P_1 + [a]Q_1 \rangle$, say $\phi_A : E \rightarrow E_A = E/\langle P_1 + [a]Q_1 \rangle$. She sends $(E_A, \phi_A(P_2), \phi_A(Q_2))$ to Bob. Similarly, Bob chooses a secret $b \in \mathbb{Z}_{\ell_2^{e_2}}$ and computes an isogeny $\phi_B : E \rightarrow E_B = E/\langle P_2 + [b]Q_2 \rangle$ with kernel given by $\langle P_2 + [b]Q_2 \rangle$. Then sends $(E_B, \phi_B(P_1), \phi_B(Q_1))$ to Alice. Alice then computes an isogeny $\tau_A : E_B \rightarrow E_{AB}$ with kernel given by $\langle \phi_B(P_1) + [a]\phi_B(Q_1) \rangle$. The shared key is the j-invariant of the codomain curve E_{AB}. Bob gets the shared key in a similar fashion, i.e. he computes an isogeny $\tau_B : E_A \rightarrow E_{BA}$ with kernel given by $\langle \phi_A(P_2) + [b]\phi_A(Q_2) \rangle$. The shared key is $j(E_{BA})$. The SIDH key exchange described above can be visualised using the following diagram.

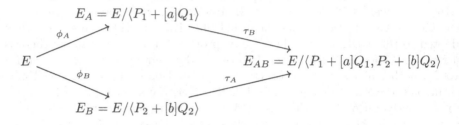

2.2 Standard Isogeny-Based Hard Problems

The security of SIDH is based on the following standard hard problems.

Definition 1 (SI-CDH Problem). *Let* param $:= (p, \ell_1, \ell_2, e_1, e_2, E, P_1, Q_1, P_2, Q_2)$ *be the public parameters for SIDH. Suppose* $\phi_A : E \rightarrow E_A$ *and* $\phi_B : E \rightarrow E_B$ *are isogenies with kernel given by* $\langle P_1 + [a]Q_1 \rangle$ *and* $\langle P_2 + [b]Q_2 \rangle$ *respectively (for some* $a \leftarrow \mathbb{Z}_{\ell_1^{e_1}}$ *and* $b \leftarrow \mathbb{Z}_{\ell_2^{e_2}}$). *The SI-CDH (supersingular isogeny computational Diffie-Hellman) problem is: given* param *and* $E_A, \phi_A(P_2), \phi_A(Q_2), E_B, \phi_B(P_1), \phi_B(Q_1)$, *compute* $j(E_{AB})$, *where* $E_{AB} = E_A/\langle \phi_A(P_2) + [b]\phi_A(Q_2) \rangle \cong E_B/\langle \phi_B(P_1) + [a]\phi_B(Q_1) \rangle \cong E/\langle P_1 + [a]Q_1, P_2 + [b]Q_2 \rangle$.

For any probabilistic polynomial time (ppt) algorithm $\mathcal{A}$, *the advantage of solving SI-CDH is defined to be*

$$\text{Adv}_{\mathcal{A}}^{\text{SI-CDH}} = \Pr[\mathcal{A}(\text{param}, E_A, \phi_A(P_2), \phi_A(Q_2), E_B, \phi_B(P_1), \phi_B(Q_1)) = j(E_{AB})].$$

The SI-CDH assumption assumes that for any ppt algorithm $\mathcal{A}$, *the advantage of solving SI-CDH problem is negligible.*

Definition 2 (SI-DDH Problem). *Let* param $:= (p, \ell_1, \ell_2, e_1, e_2, E, P_1, Q_1,$
$P_2, Q_2)$ *be the public parameters for SIDH. Suppose* $\phi_A : E \to E_A$ *and* $\phi_B : E \to$
E_B *are isogenies with kernel given by* $\langle P_1 + [a]Q_1 \rangle$ *and* $\langle P_2 + [b]Q_2 \rangle$ *respectively*
(for some $a \leftarrow \mathbb{Z}_{\ell_1^{e_1}}$ *and* $b \leftarrow \mathbb{Z}_{\ell_2^{e_2}}$ *). Set* $j_1 \in \mathbb{F}_{p^2}$ *to be random and* $j_0 := j(E_{AB})$,
where $E_{AB} = E_A/\langle \phi_A(P_2) + [b]\phi_A(Q_2) \rangle \cong E_B/\langle \phi_B(P_1) + [a]\phi_B(Q_1) \rangle \cong E/\langle P_1 +$
$[a]Q_1, P_2 + [b]Q_2 \rangle$.

The SI-DDH (supersingular isogeny decisional Diffie-Hellman) problem is:
given param, $E_A, \phi_A(P_2), \phi_A(Q_2), E_B, \phi_B(P_1), \phi_B(Q_1)$, *and* j_b, *where* $b \leftarrow \{0, 1\}$
is randomly sampled bit, determine b.

Other related isogeny hard problems can be found in [11, 19].

3   The Proposed PAKE

3.1   Description of the Proposed PAKE

In this section, we describe our proposed password authenticated key exchange
whose security is based on the hardness of the SI-CDH problem (see Definition 1).
Let p be a prime of the form $p = \ell_1^{e_1} \ell_2^{e_2} f \pm 1$, for some small distinct primes
ℓ_1, ℓ_2. Let $E : y^2 = x^3 + 6x^2 + x$ be a supersingular elliptic curve defined over $\mathbb{F}_{p^2}$.
Fix bases $\{P_1, Q_1\}$ and $\{P_2, Q_2\}$ for $E[\ell_1^{e_1}]$ and $E[\ell_2^{e_2}]$ respectively. For a given
security parameter λ, let $\mathcal{H}_1 : \{0, 1\}^* \to \{i \in [0, \min\{\ell_1^{e_1}, \ell_2^{e_2}\}] : \gcd(i, \ell_1) =$
$1, \gcd(i, \ell_2) = 1\}$ and $\mathcal{H}_2 : \{0, 1\}^* \to \{0, 1\}^{2\lambda}$ be hash functions. Our proposed
PAKE is depicted in the following diagram (Table 1). Client A and a server B
shares a common low entropy password pw_A and would like to establish a shared
session key K.

In the proposed PAKE, the client and the server generate ephemeral secret
keys $a \in \mathbb{Z}_{\ell_1^{e_1}}$ and $b \in \mathbb{Z}_{\ell_2^{e_2}}$ respectively. The shared key K is computed as $K =$
$\mathcal{H}_2(j(E_{AB})$, exchanged messages$)$, where $E_{AB} \cong E/\langle P_1 + [a]Q_1, P_2 + [b]Q_2 \rangle$. In
order to allow the server to compute $E_{AB} = E_A/\langle \phi_A(P_2) + [b]\phi_A(Q_2) \rangle$, the client
sends E_A as well as some images of $\phi_A : E \to E_A$. Instead of sending $\phi_A(P_2)$
and $\phi_A(Q_2)$ as in the usual SIDH key exchange, the client sends "obfuscated
images" $P_A := [h^{-1}]\phi_A(P_2)$ and $Q_A := [h]\phi_A(Q_2)$ to the server, where the
obfuscator $h = \mathcal{H}_1(\mathsf{pw}_A, \dots)$ is dependent on the client's password pw_A. This
allows the server to compute E_{AB} as $E_{AB} = E_A/\langle [h]P_A + [bh^{-1}]Q_A \rangle$ as long as
the server knows the password pw_A. Similarly, the server sends E_B as well as
the obfuscated images $P_B := [h^{-1}]\phi_B(P_1)$ and $Q_B := [h]\phi_B(Q_1)$ to the client,
enabling the client to compute $E_{BA} = E_B/\langle [h]P_B + [ah^{-1}]Q_B \rangle$. If the passwords
used by the client and the server are different, the resulting key derived by the
client and the server will also be different, and so they fail to establish a shared
key. This provides authenticity and prevents impersonation attack.

In Table 1, the server B needs to check whether $e(P_A, Q_A) = e(P_2, Q_2)^{\ell_1^{e_1}}$
while the client A is required to check whether $e(P_B, Q_B) = e(P_1, Q_1)^{\ell_2^{e_2}}$. We
shall remark that these two equalities should hold if the scheme is followed
properly. We start by proving the following lemma.

Table 1. The proposed PAKE

Client A		Server B
$a \leftarrow \mathbb{Z}_{\ell_1^{e_1}}$		
$h = \mathcal{H}_1(\mathrm{pw}_A, E, P_1, Q_1, P_2, Q_2)$		
$h' = h^{-1} \bmod \ell_1^{e_1}, \quad h'' = h^{-1} \bmod \ell_2^{e_2}$		
$\phi_A : E \rightarrow E_A = E/\langle P_1 + [a]Q_1 \rangle$		
$P_A = [h'']\phi_A(P_2), \; Q_A = [h]\phi_A(Q_2)$	$\xrightarrow{(E_A, P_A, Q_A)}$	check $e(P_A, Q_A) \overset{?}{=} e(P_2, Q_2)^{\ell_1^{e_1}}$
		if not, then terminate
		$b \leftarrow \mathbb{Z}_{\ell_2^{e_2}}$
		$h = \mathcal{H}_1(\mathrm{pw}_A, E, P_1, Q_1, P_2, Q_2)$
		$h' = h^{-1} \bmod \ell_1^{e_1}, \quad h'' = h^{-1} \bmod \ell_2^{e_2}$
		$\phi_B : E \rightarrow E_B = E/\langle P_2 + [b]Q_2 \rangle$
	$\xleftarrow{(E_B, P_B, Q_B)}$	$P_B = [h']\phi_B(P_1), \; Q_B = [h]\phi_B(Q_1)$
check $e(P_B, Q_B) \overset{?}{=} e(P_1, Q_1)^{\ell_2^{e_2}}$		
if not, then terminate		
$E_{BA} = E_B/\langle [h]P_B + [ah']Q_B \rangle$		$E_{AB} = E_A/\langle [h]P_A + [bh'']Q_A \rangle$
$K = \mathcal{H}_2(j(E_{BA}), E_A, P_A, Q_A, E_B, P_B, Q_B)$		$K = \mathcal{H}_2(j(E_{AB}), E_A, P_A, Q_A, E_B, P_B, Q_B)$

Lemma 1. *Let N be an integer coprime to p and $\phi : E_1 \rightarrow E_2$ be an isogeny between elliptic curves over $\mathbb{F}_{p^2}$. If $P, Q \in E_1[N]$. Then $e(\phi(P), \phi(Q)) = e(P, Q)^{\deg(\phi)}$.*

Proof. Note that $\phi(Q) \in E_2[N]$. Let $\widehat{\phi} : E_2 \rightarrow E_1$ be the dual of ϕ. Then

$$e(\phi(P), \phi(Q)) = e(P, \widehat{\phi}(\phi(Q))) \quad \text{(by [16, III, Proposition 8.2])}$$
$$= e(P, [\deg(\phi)]Q) = e(P, Q)^{\deg \phi}.$$

Remark 1. *We note that* $e(P_A, Q_A) = e([h'']\phi_A(P_2), [h]\phi_A(Q_2)) = e(\phi_A(P_2), \phi_A(Q_2))^{h''h} = e(\phi_A(P_2), \phi_A(Q_2))$. *Moreover, by Lemma 1,* $e(\phi_A(P_2), \phi_A(Q_2)) = e(P_2, Q_2)^{\ell_1^{e_1}}$ *as* $\deg(\phi_A) = \ell_1^{e_1}$. *Thus,* $e(P_A, Q_A) = e(P_2, Q_2)^{\ell_1^{e_1}}$.
Similarly, we have $e(P_B, Q_B) = e(P_1, Q_1)^{\ell_2^{e_2}}$.

3.2 Comparison with Relevant Works

The proposed PAKE is similar to the PAKE proposed by Taraskin et al. [17] as both schemes use the (hash of the) password to obfuscate the torsion points in the ephemeral SIDH public key. In [17], the password is hashed into a matrix Ψ, which is an element of the group
$$Y_2(\ell_i, e_i) := \left\{ \begin{pmatrix} a & b \\ c & d \end{pmatrix} \in \mathbb{Z}_{\ell_i^{e_i}}^{2 \times 2} : ad - bc \equiv 1 \bmod \ell_i^{e_i}, \; c \equiv 0 \bmod \ell_i \right\} \text{ for } i = 1, 2;$$
the torsion points $\phi(P), \phi(Q)$ are then obfuscated via matrix multiplication $\Psi \cdot (\phi(P), \phi(Q))^T$. In our PAKE, the password is hashed into a number $h \leq \min\{\ell_1^{e_1}, \ell_2^{e_2}\}$ which is relatively prime to ℓ_1 and ℓ_2. The torsion points $\phi(P), \phi(Q)$ are then obfuscated to $([h^{-1}]\phi(P), [h]\phi(Q))$. Note that this can also be thought of as obfuscation via matrix multiplication $\Psi_h \cdot (\phi(P), \phi(Q))^T$, where
$$\Psi_h := \begin{pmatrix} h^{-1} & 0 \\ 0 & h \end{pmatrix} \in Y_2(\ell_i, e_i).$$

The difference between our PAKE and that in [17] is that in our scheme, the torsion points obfuscator h is independent of the ephemeral public key generated by the client/server, while in [17], the torsion points obfuscator Ψ is dependent on the isomorphism class of the curve (E_A or E_B) in the ephemeral public key generated by the client/server. For this reason, a session of [17] uses two obfuscators $\Psi_A \in Y(\ell_1, e_1)$ (dependent on the ephemeral public key E_A generated by the client) and $\Psi_B \in Y(\ell_2, e_2)$ (dependent on the ephemeral public key E_B generated by the server). This causes difficulty for giving security proof of [17].

Another related scheme is the scheme proposed by Qi and Chen in [14]. This scheme is also some kind of authenticated key establishment scheme using client's password. It is proven secure in the BPR model. However, the scheme is not exactly a PAKE scheme as the servers are required to have a secret key - public key pair. Thus, this scheme requires public key infrastructure or a trusted central authority to certify the servers' public key. As the scheme is obtained by combining ideas from password-based authentication method and key encapsulation mechanism, the authors of [14] call it a PBKEM scheme. We also note that for the PBKEM scheme proposed in [14], each party needs to perform 4 isogeny computations to establish a shared session key, while for our PAKE scheme, each party only needs to perform 2 isogeny computations.

4   Security Analysis of the Proposed PAKE

4.1   Informal Security Analysis

In this section, we provide some informal security analysis of the PAKE scheme proposed in Sect. 3.

Security Against Offline Dictionary Attack. In offline dictionary attack, given the messages sent by the client and the server in a particular session, the adversary aims to find the client's password, possibly by checking through all possible passwords in the password dictionary.

The messages sent by the client and the server in a session are $(E_A, P_A = [h'']\phi_A(P_2), Q_A = [h]\phi_A(Q_2))$ and $(E_B, P_B = [h']\phi_B(P_1), Q_B = [h]\phi_B(Q_1))$, where $h' = h^{-1} \bmod \ell_1^{e_1}$ and $h'' = h^{-1} \bmod \ell_2^{e_2}$.

The adversary may guess the client's password, say the guess is pw$'$. He then computes $\overline{h} = \mathcal{H}_1(\text{pw}', E, P_1, Q_1, P_2, Q_2)$ as well as $\overline{h'} = \overline{h}^{-1} \bmod \ell_1^{e_1}$ and $\overline{h''} = \overline{h}^{-1} \bmod \ell_2^{e_2}$. The adversary computes the Weil pairing $e([\overline{h}]P_A, [\overline{h''}]Q_A)$ and $e([\overline{h}]P_B, [\overline{h'}]Q_B)$ in order to get some information on whether his guess is correct.

However,

$$
\begin{aligned}
e([\overline{h}]P_A, [\overline{h''}]Q_A) &= e([\overline{h}][h'']\phi_A(P_2), [\overline{h''}][h]\phi_A(Q_2)) \\
&= e(\phi_A(P_2), \phi_A(Q_2))^{\overline{h}h''\overline{h''}h} \\
&= e(\phi_A(P_2), \phi_A(Q_2))^{(\overline{h}\overline{h''})(hh'')} \\
&= e(\phi_A(P_2), \phi_A(Q_2)),
\end{aligned}
$$

where the last equality follows from the fact that $(\overline{h}h'')(hh'') \equiv 1 \cdot 1 \equiv 1 \bmod \ell_2^{e_2}$. Similarly, $e([\overline{h}]P_B, [\overline{h'}]Q_B) = e(\phi_B(P_1), \phi_B(Q_1))$.

Therefore, the Weil pairing computation $e([\overline{h}]P_A, [\overline{h''}]Q_A)$ (resp. $e(\overline{h}P_B, \overline{h'}Q_B)$) always gives the same result $e(\phi_A(P_2), \phi_A(Q_2))$ (resp. $e(\phi_B(P_1), \phi_B(Q_1))$) regardless of the password guessed by the adversary. Hence, the adversary cannot check whether his guess is correct or not through Weil pairing computations.

Forward Security. We now show that the proposed PAKE is forward secure, i.e. even if the adversary knows the client's password, as well as the messages exchanged in a past session, the adversary is unable to recover the shared session key established in that session.

Given pw_A and $E_A, P_A, Q_A, E_B, P_B, Q_B, c$, as well as the public parameters. The adversary is able to compute $h = \mathcal{H}_1(\mathsf{pw}_A, E, P_1, Q_1, P_2, Q_2)$. But in order to compute $E_{BA} = E_B/\langle[h]P_B + [ah']Q_B\rangle$, the adversary must know the value of a. However, computing a (or equivalently ϕ_A) given $E, E_A, \phi_A(P_2), \phi_A(Q_2)$ is assumed to be difficult.

Similarly, in order to compute $E_{AB} = E_A/\langle[h]P_A + [bh'']Q_B\rangle$, the adversary must know the value of b. However, computing b (or equivalently ϕ_B) given $E, E_B, \phi_B(P_1), \phi_B(Q_1)$ is assumed to be difficult.

Therefore, the adversary cannot compute the session key $K = \mathcal{H}_2(j(E_{BA}), E_A, P_A, Q_A, E_B, P_B, Q_B)$ even if he knows the password pw_A as well as $E_A, P_A, Q_A, E_B, P_B, Q_B, c$. So, the proposed PAKE is forward secure.

Security Against Impersonation Attack. Suppose an adversary pretends to be client A and would like to maliciously established a shared session key with the server posing as client A (without knowing client A's password pw_A).

The adversary can generate a valid $a \in \mathbb{Z}_{\ell_1^{e_1}}$ and the corresponding $\phi_A : E \to E_A = E/\langle P_1 + [a]Q_1\rangle$ as this does not require the password pw_A. However he cannot compute $h = \mathcal{H}_1(\mathsf{pw}_A, E, P_1, Q_1, P_2, Q_2)$. At best, he could try to make a guess pw' for the password and compute $\overline{h} = \mathcal{H}_1(\mathsf{pw}', E, P_1, Q_1, P_2, Q_2)$. He then computes the corresponding $\overline{h'} = h^{-1} \bmod \ell_1^{e_1}$, $\overline{h''} = h^{-1} \bmod \ell_2^{e_2}$, as well as the points $\overline{P_A} = \phi_A([\overline{h''}]P_2)$ and $\overline{Q_A} = \phi_A([\overline{h}]Q_2)$. He proceeds to send $(E_A, \overline{P_A}, \overline{Q_A})$.

In response, the adversary will get a valid (E_B, P_B, Q_B) from the server. Thereafter, the adversary can compute $E_{BA} = E_B/\langle[\overline{h}]P_B + [a\overline{h'}]Q_B\rangle$ to finally get $\overline{K} = \mathcal{H}_2(j(E_{BA}), E_A, \overline{P_A}, \overline{Q_A}, E_B, P_B, Q_B)$. We note that

$$\begin{aligned}
E_{BA} &= E_B/\langle[\overline{h}]P_B + [a\overline{h'}]Q_B\rangle \\
&= E_B/\langle[\overline{h}h']\phi_B(P_1) + [a\overline{h'}h]\phi_B(Q_1)\rangle \\
&= E_B/\langle\phi_B(P_1) + [a(\overline{h'}h)^2]\phi_B(Q_1)\rangle \\
&= E_B/\langle\phi_B(P_1 + [a(\overline{h'}h)^2]Q_1)\rangle \\
&= E/\langle P_1 + [a(\overline{h'}h)^2]Q_1, P_2 + [b]Q_2\rangle.
\end{aligned}$$

On the other hand, the server will compute $E_{AB} = E_A/\langle[h]\overline{P_A} + [bh'']\overline{Q_A}\rangle$ and $K = \mathcal{H}_2(j(E_{AB}), E_A, \overline{P_A}, \overline{Q_A}, E_B, P_B, Q_B)$. Note that

$$
\begin{aligned}
E_{AB} &= E_A/\langle[h\overline{h''}]\phi_A(P_2) + [bh''\overline{h}]\phi_A(Q_2)\rangle \\
&= E_A/\langle\phi_A(P_2) + [b(h''\overline{h})^2]\phi_A(Q_2)\rangle \\
&= E_A/\langle\phi_A(P_2 + [b(h''\overline{h})^2]Q_2)\rangle \\
&= E/\langle P_1 + [a]Q_1, P_2 + [b(h''\overline{h})^2]Q_2\rangle.
\end{aligned}
$$

Observe that $\langle P_1 + [a(\overline{h'}h)^2]Q_1, P_2 + [b]Q_2\rangle \neq \langle P_1 + [a]Q_1, P_2 + [b(h''\overline{h})^2]Q_2\rangle$ unless $\overline{h} \equiv h \bmod \ell_1^{e_1}$ and $\overline{h} \equiv h \bmod \ell_2^{e_2}$, which (with high probability) happens only if $pw' = pw_A$. In other words, the shared key computed by the adversary and the server will be different (with high probability) unless the adversary guesses client A's password correctly.

To sum up, without knowing the password, the adversary fails to establish the same shared session key with the server. Hence, the proposed PAKE is secure against impersonation attack.

4.2 Security in the BPR Model

In this section, we will give a formal security proof for the proposed PAKE. We start by describing the security model used to formally analyse the security of PAKE schemes, namely the BPR model proposed by Bellare, Pointcheval, and Rogaway in [5]. It has some resemblance to the Canetti-Krawczyk (CK) model [7] for security of AKE schemes.

In the BPR model, we consider multiple parties. Each party P is either client ($P \in \mathcal{C}$) or server ($P \in \mathcal{S}$). In this model, protocols are initiated by clients and responded by servers. Each client $A \in \mathcal{C}$ has a password pw_A; and each server has a collection of client's passwords $\{pw_A\}_{A \in \mathcal{C}}$.

Each client engages in a number of sessions with servers. The instance of party $P \in \mathcal{C} \cup \mathcal{S}$ running its n-th session is denoted by Ω_P^n. An instance Ω_P^n *accepts* when it completes its computation of session key; and it *terminates* when it will not send any more message. We note that termination may occur without acceptance (e.g. in the case of malformed incoming messages).

In the BPR model, each client $A \in \mathcal{C}$ generates a password pw_A and each server $B \in \mathcal{S}$ receives and stores all client passwords. This password-generation process happens out-of-view of the adversary.

After the above initialization phase, the adversary in the BPR model controls all communication between parties, and may modify or replace any message between any parties. This is formalised by giving adversary access to the following oracles.

- Send(P, n, M): Sends message M to the instance Ω_P^n (the n-th session of party P), in response to which Ω_P^n performs the specified steps of the protocol.
- Execute(A, m, B, n): If $A \in \mathcal{C}$, $B \in \mathcal{S}$, and neither Ω_A^m nor Ω_B^n has been used, then a fresh protocol interaction between Ω_A^m and Ω_B^n is executed (conducted

in a correct and undisrupted way). The transcript of the execution is then provided to the adversary.

- Corrupt(P): The adversary is given the password possessed by party P. If $P \in \mathcal{C}$, the adversary is given pw_P. If $P \in \mathcal{S}$, the adversary is given all the clients' passwords stored by P.
- Reveal(P, n): The adversary is given the resulting session key of Ω_P^n (the n-th session of party P) if it exists.

After interacting with the users through the above queries, the adversary chooses the n-th session of party P and make a test query Test(P, n). The test query must be made on a *fresh* session. To properly define what it means for Ω_P^n to be fresh, we first define *partnered session*.

Definition 3 (Partnered Session). *A pair of sessions Ω_A^m and Ω_B^n are called partnered if all of the following are true:*

- *either $A \in \mathcal{C}$ and $B \in \mathcal{S}$; or $A \in \mathcal{S}$ and $B \in \mathcal{C}$.*
- *Ω_A^m and Ω_B^n have both accepted (i.e. they have both computed their session key).*
- *Ω_A^m's peer is B and Ω_B^n's peer is A.*
- *Ω_A^m and Ω_B^n have the same message transcript and session key.*
- *No other oracle Ω_P^i accepts with the same message transcript.*

Definition 4 (Fresh Session). *An instance Ω_P^n is called fresh if none of the following is true:*

- *Reveal(P, n) has been issued.*
- *Reveal(Q, m) has been issued, where Ω_Q^m is the partner of Ω_P^n.*
- *Corrupt(R) was issued for some $R \in \mathcal{C} \cup \mathcal{S}$ and Send(P, n, M) was issued for some message M.*

Once Test(P, n) query has been made on a fresh session, a random bit $b \leftarrow \{0, 1\}$ is sampled. If $b = 0$, then the adversary is given the session key computed in Ω_P^n. If $b = 1$, then the adversary is given a random string of the same length. The adversary is to guess the bit b. The adversary wins if he can guess the bit b with noticeable advantage. The adversary can still continue to perform Send, Execute, Corrupt, Reveal queries even after the Test query has been made. The only restriction is that these queries cannot be made on the Test session and its partner session.

Letting p to be the probability that the adversary $\mathcal{A}$ determines the bit b correctly, we set $\mathrm{Adv}(\mathcal{A}) := |p - \frac{1}{2}|$. Let q_s be the number of Send queries and N be the size of the password dictionary (i.e. the number of all possible passwords). As the adversary can always perform an online dictionary attack, i.e. by guessing the password and use Send query to check whether the guess is correct, a PAKE scheme is considered to be secure if $\mathrm{Adv}(\mathcal{A}) \leq \frac{q_s}{N} + \varepsilon$, where ε is negligible.

Theorem 1. *The proposed PAKE is secure in the BPR model.*

Proof. We shall prove the result via a sequence of game G_i for $i \in \{0, 1, 2\}$, where G_0 is the standard BPR security game. For $0 \le i \le 2$, we denote by p_i the probability that the adversary wins in Game G_i (i.e. the probability that the adversary guesses the bit b in the Test session correctly). Let q_s, q_e, q_h denote the number of Send queries, Execute queries, and hash queries respectively. Let N be the size of the password dictionary and n be the total number of clients.

Game G_0: This is the standard BPR security game, where the adversary can control all communication by making various queries (Send, Execute, Corrupt, Reveal and Test query). In the Test session, a bit $b \leftarrow \{0, 1\}$ is randomly sampled. Then the adversary is given a value, which is either the session key computed in the Test session or a random value (depending on the bit b). The adversary wins if he can guess the bit b correctly. We have

$$\mathrm{Adv}(\mathcal{A}) = |p_0 - \frac{1}{2}|.$$

Game G_1: This game is the same as G_0 except that the random oracles $\mathcal{H}_1, \mathcal{H}_2$ are simulated as usual by maintaining hash lists L_1, L_2 such that for any query u to these random oracles, returns v if there is already an item (u, v) in the corresponding list L_i (for $i = 1, 2$), otherwise returns a randomly chosen v and stores (u, v) in the corresponding list L_i. Also, the oracle instances are simulated for all $\mathcal{A}$'s oracle queries by doing exactly as the real instance would do. It is thus clear that G_0 and G_1 are indistinguishable from the view of the adversary. Therefore,

$$p_1 = p_0.$$

Game G_2: This game is the same as G_1 except that the game is aborted if there is a collision in the ephemeral values generated in different sessions; or if there is a collision in the output of the hash queries. We then have

$$|p_2 - p_1| \le \frac{q_h^2}{2^{\lambda+1}} + \frac{(q_s + q_e)^2}{2 \min\{\ell_1^{e_1}, \ell_2^{e_2}\}}.$$

We now estimate the probability that the adversary wins Game G_2. We divide into two cases.

Case 1: the Test session Ω_P^m has a partnered session $\Omega_{P'}^n$. Then, for any given SI-CDH instance $(E_U, P_U, Q_U, E_V, P_V, Q_V)$, one can construct an algorithm $\mathcal{B}$ to solve the given SI-CDH instance (i.e. compute $j(E_{UV})$ if $\mathcal{A}$ wins in the security experiment. The algorithm $\mathcal{B}$ works as follows. It first randomly chooses the m_0-th session of $A_0 \in \mathcal{C}$ (i.e. $\Omega_{A_0}^{m_0}$) as its guess for the client instance of the Test session. Suppose $\Omega_{B_0}^{n_0}$ is the partner session of $\Omega_{A_0}^{m_0}$. When $\Omega_{A_0}^{m_0}$ is activated, $\mathcal{B}$ sets and outputs $(E_A, P_A, Q_A) = (E_U, \lfloor h'' \rfloor P_U, \lfloor h \rfloor Q_U)$, where (E_U, P_U, Q_U) is from the given SI-CDH instance and $h = \mathcal{H}_1(\mathsf{pw}_A, E, P_1, Q_1, P_2, Q_2)$. Thereafter, when $\Omega_{B_0}^{n_0}$ is activated, $\mathcal{B}$ sets and outputs $(E_B, P_B, Q_B) = (E_V, \lfloor h' \rfloor P_V, \lfloor h \rfloor Q_V)$, where (E_V, P_V, Q_V) is from the given SI-CDH instance. For all other sessions, $\mathcal{B}$ executes them according to the protocol specification. We note that $\mathcal{B}$ is able to response appropriately to any of the adversary's oracle queries except on $\Omega_{A_0}^{m_0}, \Omega_{B_0}^{n_0}$ (which are the parties in the Test session). Therefore, the only way for

$\mathcal{A}$ to get an advantage in winning G_2 is if he has made an $\mathcal{H}_2$-query of the form $(j(E_{UV}), E_U, [h'']P_U, [h]Q_U, E_V, [h']P_V, [h]Q_V)$. In this case, $\mathcal{B}$ obtains $j(E_{UV})$, which is a solution to the given SI-CDH instance. We note that the probability that the Test session is indeed on $\Omega_{A_0}^{m_0}$ as guessed by $\mathcal{B}$ is at least $\frac{1}{n \cdot (q_s + q_e)}$. On the other hand, the probability that $\mathcal{B}$ picks $j(E_{UV})$ out of the possibly many hash queries of the form $\mathcal{H}_2(*, E_U, [h'']P_U, [h]Q_U, E_V, [h']P_V, [h]Q_V)$ is at least $\frac{1}{q_h}$. Thus, the probability that $\mathcal{B}$ successfully solves the given SI-CDH instance is at least $\frac{|p_{2,1} - 1/2|}{n \cdot (q_s + q_e) \cdot q_h}$, where $|p_{2,1} - 1/2|$ denote the advantage of the adversary to win Game G_2 in this case. Hence,

$$|p_{2,1} - \frac{1}{2}| \leq n(q_s + q_e)q_h \mathrm{Adv}_{\mathcal{B}}^{\mathrm{SI-CDH}}.$$

Case 2: the Test session has no partnered session, i.e. the adversary impersonates one of the party in the Test session via a Send-query. But the session key computed by the client and server in the Test session would be different if the wrong client's password is used (as explained in the last subsection of Sect. 4.1). Thus, the adversary may only succeed if he guesses and uses the correct password when impersonating a party of the Test session. So, the advantage of the adversary to win G_2 in this case is

$$|p_{2,2} - \frac{1}{2}| \leq \frac{q_s}{N}.$$

It follows that $|p_2 - \frac{1}{2}| \leq n(q_s + q_e)q_h \mathrm{Adv}_{\mathcal{B}}^{\mathrm{SI-CDH}} + \frac{q_s}{N}$. Hence,

$$\mathrm{Adv}(\mathcal{A}) = |p_0 - \frac{1}{2}| \leq |p_0 - p_1| + |p_1 - p_2| + |p_2 - \frac{1}{2}|$$
$$\leq \frac{q_h^2}{2^{\lambda+1}} + \frac{(q_s + q_e)^2}{2 \min\{\ell_1^{e_1}, \ell_2^{e_2}\}} + n(q_s + q_e)q_h \mathrm{Adv}_{\mathcal{B}}^{\mathrm{SI-CDH}} + \frac{q_s}{N}.$$

5   Conclusion

Password-authenticated key exchange (PAKE) schemes are cryptographic schemes for securely establishing a shared session key between a client and a server communicating over an insecure channel by using a low-entropy password. Some isogeny-based PAKE schemes have been proposed prior to this work. However, they are either insecure [18] or does not have a security proof [17]. In this paper, we constructed an SIDH-based PAKE scheme. In the proposed scheme, the low-entropy password is used to derive an obfuscator h that is independent of the ephemeral keys generated by the users. The same obfuscator is used to obfuscate the torsion points generated by the client and the server. We analyzed the security of the proposed PAKE scheme and showed that it is secure in the BPR model, assuming the hardness of the SI-CDH problem.

References

1. Azarderakhsh, R., Jao, D., Koziel, B., LeGrow, J.T., Soukharev, V., Taraskin, O.: How not to create an isogeny-based PAKE. In: Conti, M., Zhou, J., Casalicchio, E., Spognardi, A. (eds.) ACNS 2020. LNCS, vol. 12146, pp. 169–186. Springer, Cham (2020). https://doi.org/10.1007/978-3-030-57808-4_9
2. Bellovin, S.M., Merritt, M.: Encrypted key exchange: password-based protocols secure against dictionary attacks. In: IEEE Computer Society Symposium on Research in Security and Privacy, S&P 1992, pp. 72–84. IEEE (1992)
3. Bellovin, S.M., Merritt, M.: Augmented encrypted key exchange: a password-based protocol secure against dictionary attacks and password file compromise. In: ACM Conference on Computer and Communications Security, CCS 1993, pp. 244–250. ACM (1993)
4. Boyko, V., MacKenzie, P., Patel, S.: Provably secure password-authenticated key exchange using Diffie-Hellman. In: Preneel, B. (ed.) EUROCRYPT 2000. LNCS, vol. 1807, pp. 156–171. Springer, Heidelberg (2000). https://doi.org/10.1007/3-540-45539-6_12
5. Bellare, M., Pointcheval, D., Rogaway, P.: Authenticated key exchange secure against dictionary attacks. In: Preneel, B. (ed.) EUROCRYPT 2000. LNCS, vol. 1807, pp. 139–155. Springer, Heidelberg (2000). https://doi.org/10.1007/3-540-45539-6_11
6. Couveignes, J.-M.: Hard homogeneous spaces. IACR Cryptology ePrint Archive 2006/291 (1997). https://eprint.iacr.org/2006/291.pdf
7. Canetti, R., Krawczyk, H.: Analysis of key-exchange protocols and their use for building secure channels. In: Pfitzmann, B. (ed.) EUROCRYPT 2001. LNCS, vol. 2045, pp. 453–474. Springer, Heidelberg (2001). https://doi.org/10.1007/3-540-44987-6_28
8. De Feo, L.: Mathematics of isogeny based cryptography. CoRR, abs/1711.04062 (2017). https://arxiv.org/pdf/1711.04062.pdf
9. De Feo, L., Jao, D., Plût, J.: Towards quantum-resistant cryptosystems from supersingular elliptic curve isogenies. J. Math. Cryptol. **8**(3), 209–247 (2014)
10. Galbraith, S.D.: Mathematics of Public Key Cryptography. Cambridge University Press, Cambridge (2012)
11. Galbraith, S.D., Vercauteren, F.: Computational problems in supersingular elliptic curve isogenies. Quantum Inf. Process. **17**(10), 1–22 (2018). https://doi.org/10.1007/s11128-018-2023-6
12. Hao, F., Ryan, P.: J-PAKE: authenticated key exchange without PKI. In: Gavrilova, M.L., Tan, C.J.K., Moreno, E.D. (eds.) Transactions on Computational Science XI. LNCS, vol. 6480, pp. 192–206. Springer, Heidelberg (2010). https://doi.org/10.1007/978-3-642-17697-5_10
13. Jao, D., et al.: SIKE: supersingular isogeny key encapsulation (2017). https://sike.org
14. Qi, M., Chen, J.: Authentication and key establishment protocol from supersingular isogeny for mobile environments. J. Supercomput. **78**(5), 6371–6385 (2021). https://doi.org/10.1007/s11227-021-04121-8
15. Shor, P.W.: Polynomial-time algorithms for prime factorization and discrete logarithms on a quantum computer. SIAM J. Comput. **26**(5), 1484–1509 (1997)
16. Silverman, J.: The Arithmetic of Elliptic Curves. Graduate Texts in Mathematics, Springer, New York (2009)

17. Taraskin, O., Soukharev, V., Jao, D., LeGrow, J.T.: Towards isogeny-based password-authenticated key establishment. J. Math. Cryptol. **15**(1), 18–30 (2021). https://doi.org/10.1515/jmc-2020-0071
18. Terada, S., Yoneyama, K.: Password-based authenticated key exchange from standard isogeny assumptions. In: Steinfeld, R., Yuen, T.H. (eds.) ProvSec 2019. LNCS, vol. 11821, pp. 41–56. Springer, Cham (2019). https://doi.org/10.1007/978-3-030-31919-9_3
19. Urbanik, D., Jao, D.: SoK: the problem landscape of SIDH. In: Proceedings of the 5th ACM on ASIA Public-Key Cryptography Workshop, APKC 2018, pp. 53–60. ACM, New York (2018). https://doi.org/10.1145/3197507.3197516

Group Signatures with Designated Traceability over Openers' Attributes in Bilinear Groups

Hiroaki Anada[1]([✉]), Masayuki Fukumitsu[2], and Shingo Hasegawa[3]

[1] Aomori University, Aomori 030-0943, Japan
anada@aomori-u.ac.jp
[2] University of Nagasaki, Nagayo 851-2195, Japan
fukumitsu@sun.ac.jp
[3] Tohoku University, Sendai 980-8576, Japan
shingo.hasegawa.b7@tohoku.ac.jp

Abstract. Anonymity and traceability are two properties that are seemingly difficult to be compatible. "Group signatures with designated traceability" that was introduced at CANDAR 2021 is a group signature scheme in which a signer is capable of designating openers by specifying an opening access structure. In this paper, we give an instantiation of the scheme in the algebraic setting of bilinear groups.

Keywords: Group signature · Openers · Attributes · Bilinear groups

1 Introduction

Anonymity is a privacy property that is having more and more importance. Personal data should be protected against growing of big data analysis with machine learning. On the other hand, traceability is a managerial property that is needed in case that a trouble or doubtful matter happens. These two security properties are seemingly difficult to be compatible, but cryptographers tried to resolve the problem in the area of anonymous digital signature schemes. That is, message-dependent opening [14], accountable tracing [11] and especially accountable ring signatures [15], and bifurcated anonymous signatures [12]. The notion of group signatures with designated traceability [4], GSdT, was recently introduced approach. In its scheme, a signer is able to designate openers who can open a group signature and identify its signer, where the designation is by specifying an access structure over openers' attributes. This feature is claimed to be an ability with which users who generate anonymous tokens actively control traceability against authorities. A generic construction of GSdT was shown in the previous work [4], but it was unknown whether such cryptographic primitive can be instantiated with reasonable performance. In this paper, we give an instantiation of GSdT

This work was supported by The Telecommunication Advancement Foundation (TAF), and JSPS KAKENHI Grant Number JP19K20272.

I. You and T.-Y. Youn (Eds.): WISA 2022, LNCS 13720, pp. 29–43, 2023.
https://doi.org/10.1007/978-3-031-25659-2_3

in the setting of bilinear groups. We employ "Type III pairing" [8], which is well-investigated for implementation.

The generic construction of GSdT given in [4] follows the generic construction of "partially dynamic group signatures" [5]. That is, a group-signer first generates a (normal) signature on a message, encrypts the signature and his/her identity-data with certification data using opener's public-key, and appends a proof that the ciphertext is certainly generated under the public keys and the message by a registered user, in zero-knowledge. In [4], a ciphertext-policy attribute-based encryption is adapted for the encryption. This is why a group-signer can specify an access structure over openers' attributes, and has the above ability. Hence the generic construction consists of three building blocks; an EUF-CMA secure digital signature scheme Sig, an adaptive IND-CPA secure payload-hiding ciphertext-policy attribute-based encryption scheme ABE, and a non-interactive zero-knowledge proof system Π.

1.1   Our Contribution

There can be a few strategies to instantiate GSdT in the setting of discrete logarithm. One of the strategies is via the Fiat-Shamir transformation [7]. However, if we choose the strategy, then the verification equations of a group signature include the relation between the input and output of the employed hash function. This feature causes an obstcle because, in the setting of discrete logarithm, an efficient hash function is not known (to the best of the authors' knowledge). Another strategy is via the "structure-preserving signatures (SPS)" ([1] etc.). A better feature of the strategy is that SPS fits the Groth-Sahai NIZK [6,9], which work as a proof of a signature. The remaining problem of the latter strategy is that most of the existing ABE schemes utilize bilinear groups and a message is encrypted by multiplying a blinding factor in the *target group*. If we try to satisfy the constraint, then the algorithm Sig has to generate a signature in the target group. However, SPS schemes generate a signature in the source groups by-design, and hence those ABE schemes cannot be employed.

In this paper, our choice is to employ a pairing-free ABE scheme proposed by Herranz [10] so that a group-signer can encrypt all the elements, which are user's identity, its public key, their certification data and a signature, in each of the source groups. Thanks to the choice we can employ SPS and the Groth-Sahai NIZK. A remark is that the pairing-free ABE scheme [10] has an "irregular" limitation to compensate for pairing-freeness; that is, the maximum number of users that is the maximum number of openers has to be fixed when the scheme is setup.

Thus, our approach to instantiate the generic construction of GSdT [4] is to select the following three building blocks; Sig is "compact structure-preserving signatures with almost tight security" [2], ABE is "pairing-free CP-ABE with limited number of users" [10], and Π is "one-time simulation-sound Groth-Sahai NIZK" [9,13]. These selection enables us to satisfy all the security properties in the generic construction [4]; correctness, anonymity, traceability and non-frameability based on the SXDH assumption on the Type-III biliner groups [2].

2   Preliminaries

λ denotes the security parameter. $\mathcal{BG}(\cdot)$ denotes an algorithm that generates bilinear groups. $\mathcal{BG}$ takes as input 1^λ and returns $(p, e, \hat{\mathbb{G}}, \check{\mathbb{G}}, \mathbb{G}_T, \hat{G}, \check{G})$. Here p is a prime of bit-length λ, $\hat{\mathbb{G}}$, $\check{\mathbb{G}}$ and $\mathbb{G}_T$ denote cyclic groups of order p, $\hat{G}$ and $\check{G}$ denote generators of $\hat{\mathbb{G}}$ and $\check{\mathbb{G}}$. $e : \hat{\mathbb{G}} \times \check{\mathbb{G}} \to \mathbb{G}_T$ denotes a bilinear map, which satisfies the following conditions (1) and (2): (1) $e(\hat{G}, \check{G})$ is a generator of $\mathbb{G}_T$. (2) There exists no homomorphism of $\hat{\mathbb{G}}$ to $\check{\mathbb{G}}$ that is computable within poyonomial-time in λ, and vice versa. Such a map e is called a Type-III pairing [8]. We denote hereafter elements of $\hat{\mathbb{G}}$ with "hat" $\hat{}$ and elements of $\check{\mathbb{G}}$ with "check" $\check{}$.

2.1   Syntax of GSdT

A group Signature scheme with designated traceability over Openers' Attributes, which is denoted by GSdT, consists of nine probabilistic polynomial-time (PPT) algorithms (GKG, OKG, UKG, Join, Iss, GSign, GVrfy, Open, Judge).

- GKG($1^\lambda, \kappa$) $\to$ (gpk, ik, omk). This PPT algorithm is executed by the group manager of the scheme. GKG takes as input the security parameter λ and an index κ that determines the data of the attribute universe. In this paper, κ also contains the upper bound L of the number of openers. GKG returns a group public key gpk, an issuing key ik that is used to issue a certificate for a user and an opening master secret key omk.
- OKG(gpk, omk, j, X) $\to$ $\boldsymbol{ok}[\mathsf{j}]$. This PPT algorithm is executed by the group manager of the scheme. OKG takes as input gpk, omk, j that identifies an opener and X that is a set of opener's attributes. Note that X is also called a set of key attributes. OKG returns an opening key $\boldsymbol{ok}[\mathsf{j}]$. Note that $\boldsymbol{ok}[\mathsf{j}]$ contains the data of X.
- UKG(1^λ) $\to$ (upk, usk). This PPT algorithm is executed by a user in the scheme before he/she joins the group[1]. UKG takes as input 1^λ. Then UKG returns a user public key upk and a user secret key usk.
- Join and Iss. These interactive PPT algorithms are executed by a user and the issuer of the scheme, respectively. Join takes as input gpk, i, upk_i and usk_i. Join generates a pair of a public key and a secret key $(pk_\mathsf{i}, sk_\mathsf{i})$. Join signs pk_i to generate a signature $sig_\mathsf{i})$ by using usk_i. Join sends $(pk_\mathsf{i}, sig_\mathsf{i})$ to Iss.
  Iss receives them and takes as input gpk, ik, i and upk_i. Iss generates a certificate $cert_\mathsf{i}$. Iss sends $cert_\mathsf{i}$ to Join.
  Join receives it and sets $\boldsymbol{gsk}[\mathsf{i}] := (\mathsf{i}, pk_\mathsf{i}, sk_\mathsf{i}, cert_\mathsf{i})$. It is a group-signing key of the user. On the other hand, Iss sets $\boldsymbol{reg}[\mathsf{i}] := (pk_\mathsf{i}, sig_\mathsf{i})$ and writes it in the registration table $\boldsymbol{reg}$ of the group.
- GSign($gpk, \boldsymbol{gsk}[\mathsf{i}], Y, m$) $\to$ (Y, σ_0). This PPT algorithm is executed by a user of the scheme. GSign takes as input gpk, $\boldsymbol{gsk}[\mathsf{i}]$, an access structure Y and a

---

[1]   This is because a user should sign his/her second public key generated by him/herself when it joins the group. On the other hand, its first public key should be maintained based on an authentic system such as a public-key infrastructure.

message m. GSign returns a group signature (Y, σ_0). Hereafter (Y, σ_0) is often denoted by σ. Also, when m is an element of the source groups of the bilinear groups, m is denoted by $\hat{M}$ or $\check{M}$.

- GVrfy($gpk, m, (Y, \sigma_0)$) $\rightarrow$ 1/0. This deterministic polynomial-time algorithm is executed by any verifier (of a group signature) in the scheme. user of the scheme. GVrfy takes as input gpk, m and σ. GVrfy returns a boolean 0 or 1.
- Open($gpk, \boldsymbol{ok}[j], \boldsymbol{reg}, m, (Y, \sigma_0)$) $\rightarrow$ (i, τ). This PPT algorithm is executed by openers of the scheme. Open takes as input gpk, $\boldsymbol{ok}[j]$, $\boldsymbol{reg}$, m and σ. Open returns a user ID string i($\in \mathbb{N}$) and a proof τ of legitimate opening.
- Judge($gpk, i, \boldsymbol{upk}[i], m, (Y, \sigma_0), \tau$) $\rightarrow$ d. This deterministic polynomial-time algorithm is executed by any judge (of an opening of a group signature) in the scheme. Judge takes as input gpk, i, $\boldsymbol{upk}[i]$, m, σ and τ. Judge returns a boolean 0 or 1.

2.2 Security Definitions of GSdT

Based on the previous work [4,5] we need the following oracles for the security definitions of our GSdT: AddOO is "add-opener" oracle. AddUO is "add-user" oracle. StoUO is "send to user" oracle. StoIO is "send to issuer" oracle. USKO is "user secret key" oracle. GSignO is "group-signing" oracle. CrptOO is "corrupt-opener" oracle. CrptUO is "corrupt user" oracle. OpenO is "opening signature" oracle. RRegO is "read registration table" oracle. WRegO is "write registration table" oracle. ChaO$_b$ is "challenge for b" oracle. HU is the set of honest users. CU is the set of corrupted users. OP is the set of openers. MS is the set of "queried message and replied signature" pairs. CO is the set of corrupted oracles. We note that AddOO and CrptOO are added in the definition of [4] compared with the definition of "partially dynamic group signature scheme" [5]. Using these oracles, the following experimental algorithms **Expr** are defined. (For the details, see [4]). Correctness. If for any unbounded algorithm **A** the advantage $\mathbf{Adv}^{\mathrm{corr}}_{\mathrm{GSdT}, \mathbf{A}}(\lambda) = 0$, then GSdT is said to have correctness.

$\mathsf{Expr}^{\mathrm{corr}}_{\mathrm{GSdT}, \mathbf{A}}(1^{\lambda}, \kappa)$

   $(gpk, ik, omk) \leftarrow \mathsf{GKG}(1^{\lambda}, \kappa), \mathrm{CU} \leftarrow \emptyset, \mathrm{HU} \leftarrow \emptyset, \mathrm{OP} \leftarrow \emptyset$

   $(i, m, Y) \leftarrow \mathbf{A}(gpk : \mathsf{AddOO}(\cdot, \cdot), \mathsf{AddUO}(\cdot), \mathsf{RRegO}(\cdot))$

   If i $\notin$ HU then return 0; If $\boldsymbol{gsk}[i] = \varepsilon$ then return 0

   $\sigma \leftarrow \mathsf{GSign}(gpk, \boldsymbol{gsk}[i], Y, m)$

   If $\mathsf{GVrfy}(gpk, m, \sigma) = 0$ return 1

   $\mathrm{OS}_Y \leftarrow \{j \in \mathrm{OP} \mid \mathcal{R}^{\kappa}(X, Y) = 1 \text{ for } (X, ok_0) \leftarrow \boldsymbol{ok}[j]\}$

   For j $\in \mathrm{OS}_Y$ do

     $(i', \tau) \leftarrow \mathsf{Open}(gpk, \boldsymbol{ok}[j], \boldsymbol{reg}, m, \sigma)$

     If i $\neq$ i' or $\mathsf{Judge}(gpk, i, \boldsymbol{upk}[i], m, \sigma, \tau) = 0$ then return 1

   Return 0;

$\mathbf{Adv}^{\mathrm{corr}}_{\mathrm{GSdT}, \mathbf{A}}(\lambda) \overset{\mathrm{def}}{=} \Pr[\mathsf{Expr}^{\mathrm{corr}}_{\mathrm{GSdT}, \mathbf{A}}(1^{\lambda}, \kappa) = 1].$

Anonymity. If for any PPT algorithm $\mathbf{A}$ the advantage $\mathbf{Adv}_{\mathsf{GSdT},\mathbf{A}}^{\mathrm{anon}}(\lambda)$ is negligible in λ, then GSdT is said to have anonymity.

$\mathsf{Expr}_{\mathsf{GSdT},\mathbf{A}}^{\mathrm{anon}\text{-}b}(1^\lambda, \kappa)$ // $b \in \{0, 1\}$

$\quad (gpk, ik, omk) \leftarrow \mathsf{GKG}(1^\lambda, \kappa)$

$\quad \mathrm{CU} \leftarrow \emptyset, \mathrm{HU} \leftarrow \emptyset, \mathrm{MS} \leftarrow \emptyset, \mathrm{CO} \leftarrow \emptyset, \mathrm{OP} \leftarrow \emptyset$

$\quad d \leftarrow \mathbf{A}(gpk, ik : \mathsf{ChaO}_b(\cdot, \cdot, \cdot, \cdot), \mathsf{AddOO}(\cdot, \cdot),$

$\qquad \mathsf{OpenO}(\cdot, \cdot, \cdot), \mathsf{StoUO}(\cdot, \cdot), \mathsf{WRegO}(\cdot, \cdot), \mathsf{USKO}(\cdot),$

$\qquad \mathsf{CrptOO}(\cdot), \mathsf{CrptUO}(\cdot, \cdot))$

$\quad$ Return d;

$\mathbf{Adv}_{\mathsf{GSdT},\mathbf{A}}^{\mathrm{anon}}(\lambda) \overset{\mathrm{def}}{=}$

$|\Pr[\mathsf{Expr}_{\mathsf{GSdT},\mathbf{A}}^{\mathrm{anon}\text{-}0}(1^\lambda, \kappa) = 1]| - |\Pr[\mathsf{Expr}_{\mathsf{GSdT},\mathbf{A}}^{\mathrm{anon}\text{-}1}(1^\lambda, \kappa) = 1]|.$

Traceability. If for any PPT algorithm $\mathbf{A}$ the advantage $\mathbf{Adv}_{\mathsf{GSdT},\mathbf{A}}^{\mathrm{trace}}(\lambda)$ is negligible in λ, then GSdT is said to have traceability.

$\mathsf{Expr}_{\mathsf{GSdT},\mathbf{A}}^{\mathrm{trace}}(1^\lambda, \kappa)$

$\quad (gpk, ik, omk) \leftarrow \mathsf{GKG}(1^\lambda, \kappa), \;\; \mathrm{CU} \leftarrow \emptyset, \mathrm{HU} \leftarrow \emptyset, \mathrm{OP} \leftarrow \emptyset$

$\quad (m, (Y, \sigma_0)) \leftarrow \mathbf{A}(gpk, omk : \mathsf{StoIO}(\cdot, \cdot), \mathsf{AddUO}(\cdot), \mathsf{RRegO}(\cdot), \mathsf{USKO}(\cdot), \mathsf{CrptUO}(\cdot, \cdot))$

$\quad$ If $\mathsf{GVrfy}(gpk, m, (Y, \sigma_0)) = 0$ then return 0

$\quad$ Find X s.t. $\mathcal{R}^\kappa(X, Y) = 1$; $\;\; ok \leftarrow \mathsf{OKG}(gpk, omk, 0, X)$

$\quad (i, \tau) \leftarrow \mathsf{Open}(gpk, ok, \boldsymbol{reg}, m, (Y, \sigma_0))$

$\quad$ If $i = 0$ or $\mathsf{Judge}(gpk, i, \boldsymbol{upk}[i], m, (Y, \sigma_0), \tau) = 0$ then return 1 else return 0;

$\mathbf{Adv}_{\mathsf{GSdT},\mathbf{A}}^{\mathrm{trace}}(\lambda) \overset{\mathrm{def}}{=} \Pr[\mathsf{Expr}_{\mathsf{GSdT},\mathbf{A}}^{\mathrm{trace}}(1^\lambda, \kappa) = 1].$

Non-frameability. If for any PPT algorithm $\mathbf{A}$ the advantage $\mathbf{Adv}_{\mathsf{GSdT},\mathbf{A}}^{\mathrm{trace}}(\lambda)$ is negligible in λ, then GSdT is said to have non-frameability.

$\mathsf{Expr}_{\mathsf{GSdT},\mathbf{A}}^{\mathrm{nf}}(1^\lambda, \kappa)$

$\quad (gpk, ik, omk) \leftarrow \mathsf{GKG}(1^\lambda, \kappa), \;\; \mathrm{CU} \leftarrow \emptyset, \mathrm{HU} \leftarrow \emptyset, \mathrm{OP} \leftarrow \emptyset$

$\quad (m, (Y, \sigma_0), i, \tau) \leftarrow \mathbf{A}(gpk, ik, omk : \mathsf{StoUO}(\cdot, \cdot),$

$\qquad \mathsf{WRegO}(\cdot, \cdot), \mathsf{GSignO}(\cdot, \cdot, \cdot, \cdot), \mathsf{USKO}(\cdot), \mathsf{CrptUO}(\cdot, \cdot))$

$\quad$ If the following are all true then return 1 else return 0 :

$\qquad$ - $i \in \mathrm{HU} \wedge \boldsymbol{gsk}[i] \neq \varepsilon$

$\qquad$ - $\mathsf{Judge}(gpk, i, \boldsymbol{upk}[i], m, (Y, \sigma_0), \tau) = 1$

$\qquad$ - A did not query $\mathsf{USKO}(i) \vee \mathsf{GSignO}(i, m)$;

$\mathbf{Adv}_{\mathsf{GSdT},\mathbf{A}}^{\mathrm{nf}}(\lambda) \overset{\mathrm{def}}{=} \Pr[\mathsf{Expr}_{\mathsf{GSdT},\mathbf{A}}^{\mathrm{nf}}(1^\lambda, \kappa) = 1].$

3   Our Instantiation

In this section, we give an instantiation of the generic construction of GSdT in [4]. In our instantiation, we build-in as Sig the structure-preserving signature scheme of Abe et al. [2], as ABE the "pairing-free" CP-ABE of Herranz [10], and as Π the Groth-Sahai NIZK [6] with modification by Libert-Yung [13] for one-time simulation-soundness. Hereafter, let $pp := (p, e, \hat{\mathbb{G}}, \check{\mathbb{G}}, \mathbb{G}_T, \hat{G}, \check{G}) \leftarrow \mathcal{BG}(1^\lambda)$ denote the public parameters, but pp is not written as input though it is always input to the algorithms below. Before giving our instantiation, we briefly recall the generic construction of GSdT in [4].

3.1   Generic Constriction of GSdT in [4]

Their generic construction GSdT = (GKG, OKG, UKG, Join, Iss, GSign, GVrfy, Open, Judge) is intuitively given by replacing an IND-CCA secure public key encryption part of "partially dynamic group signatures" [5] with an adaptive IND-CPA secure payload-hiding CP-ABE. The building blocks are therefore an EUF-CMA secure Sig, an adaptive IND-CPA secure payload-hiding CP-ABE ABE, and two simulation-sound NIZKs $\Pi = (\Pi_a, \Pi_b)$.

A group signature σ of a message m issued by the generic construction consists of a ciphertext C and a proof π_a. C is an ABE-ciphertext of signer's identity data and a (normal) signature, which can be decrypted by an opener who has an attribute X satisfying an access structure Y. On the other hand, π_a is a proof with Π_a that the signer who belongs to the group indeed signs m and that C is the encryption of the signer's identity data and a signature. The proof π_a instead of just a signature of m guarantees anonymity, while adding the ciphertext C as a part of a group signature ensures traceability.

Let us briefly recall the formal construction. GKG generates gpk, ik and omk. gpk consists of two common reference strings $\mathbf{crs}_a$ and $\mathbf{crs}_b$ of Π_a and Π_b, a public key pk_a of ABE, and a public key pk_s of Sig. ik is the secret key sk_s of pk_s in the similar manner to [5]. omk generated by GKG is the master secret key msk_a of pk_a. OKG takes as input gpk, an opener master key omk, opener's id string j, and an attribute set X. Then OKG on input (omk, j, X) generates a secret key $ok[j]$ by running the key generation algorithm of ABE. UKG, Join and Iss are the same as those of [5]. Namely, UKG generates a key pair of Sig that are used to sign user's public key pk_i of Sig which will be registered, while during the group-joining protocol between Join and Iss, the issuer generates a signature $cert_i$ of user's id string i and user's public key pk_i as a certificate for the registration to the group. The resulting secret key $gsk[i]$ of the user i is $(i, pk_i, sk_i, cert_i)$, where sk_i is the secret key corresponding to pk_i.

GSign takes as input a group public key gpk, a secret key $gsk[i] = (i, pk_i, sk_i, cert_i)$ of an user i, an access structure Y, and a message m. GSign issues a signature s of m by running the signing algorithm of Sig on input (sk_i, m), GSign generates a ciphertext C of $\langle i, pk_i, cert_i, s \rangle$ by running the encryption algorithm of ABE on input $(pk_a, Y, \langle i, pk_i, cert_i, s \rangle)$. Then GSign generates by using Π_a a proof π_a that proves that the signature s and the ciphertext C are correctly computed. Finally GSign returns $\sigma = (C, \pi_a)$ as a group signature. GVrfy merely checks whether or not π_a is indeed correct.

As the same idea as [5], Open decrypts C to $\langle i, pk_i, sk_i, cert_i \rangle$ by using the decryption algorithm of ABE on input $(pk_a, ok[j], C)$ with opener's key $ok[j]$. Then Open generates by using Π_b a proof π_b that proves that C is decrypted correctly. Finally Open returns an opening information containing the opened id i and the proof π_b. Since $ok[j]$ is the secret key of ABE for the attribute set X, Open can correctly decrypt C if the attribute set X satisfies the access structure Y embedded into C. Judge, by checking π_b, can verify that Open executes the opening process honestly. (For more detail, see [4].)

3.2 Key Generation and User Joining

We describe here our algorithm GKG that generates a group public key gpk, an issuing key ik and an opening master secret key omk. As for our interactive algorithms of user-joining Join and certificate-issuing Iss, we note a remark.

Group-Key Generation

- GKG$(1^\lambda, \kappa) \rightarrow (gpk, ik, omk)$. GKG takes as input the security parameter λ and an index κ that determines the attribute universe $\{1, \ldots, N\}$ and the upper bound L of the number of openers. It first generates a common reference string (CRS) of binding mode for the proof system $\Pi = (\Pi_a, \Pi_b)$ as Diffie-Hellman tuples, as follows. That is, for $i = a, b$ GKG generates $\chi_i, \xi_i, \chi_i', \xi_i' \in_R \mathbb{Z}_p$, $\hat{Q}_i := \hat{G}^{\chi_i}, \hat{U}_i := \hat{G}^{\xi_i}, \hat{V}_i := \hat{G}^{\chi_i \xi_i}, \check{Q}_i := \check{G}^{\chi_i'}, \check{U}_i := \check{G}^{\xi_i'}, \check{V}_i := \check{G}^{\chi_i' \xi_i'}$. Then,

$$\hat{crs}_a := \begin{bmatrix} \hat{G} & \hat{Q}_a \\ \hat{U}_a & \hat{V}_a \end{bmatrix}, \check{crs}_a :=, \begin{bmatrix} \check{G} & \check{Q}_a \\ \check{U}_a & \check{V}_{a,} \end{bmatrix}, \hat{crs}_b := \begin{bmatrix} \hat{G} & \hat{Q}_b \\ \hat{U}_b & \hat{V}_b \end{bmatrix}, \check{crs}_b :=, \begin{bmatrix} \check{G} & \check{Q}_b \\ \check{U}_b & \check{V}_{b.} \end{bmatrix}. \tag{1}$$

Then GKG generates a public key of ABE and a master secret key as follows, where $M := L + 2N$ [10].

For $at = 1, \ldots, N$: for $j = 1, \ldots, M$:

$$y_{at,j} \in_R \mathbb{Z}_p, \ y_{at,j}' \in_R \mathbb{Z}_p, \ \hat{Y}_{at,j} := \hat{G}^{y_{at,j}}, \ \check{Y}_{at,j} := \check{G}^{y_{at,j}'}$$

$$pk_a := ((\hat{Y}_{at,j})_{1 \leq at \leq N}^{1 \leq k \leq M}, (\check{Y}_{at,j})_{1 \leq at \leq N}^{1 \leq k \leq M}), \ msk_a := ((y_{at,j})_{1 \leq at \leq N}^{1 \leq k \leq M}, (y_{at,j}')_{1 \leq at \leq N}^{1 \leq k \leq M}). \tag{2}$$

Then, GKG generates CRS of binding mode for $\Pi_{s,0}$ and $\Pi_{s,1}$ of the Groth-Sahai NIZK [6] as follows, which is needed when the issuer execute Sig to generate a signature as a certificate for user's identity.

$$\hat{crs}_{s,0} := \begin{bmatrix} \hat{G} & \hat{Q}_{s,0} \\ \hat{U}_{s,0} & \hat{V}_{s,0} \end{bmatrix}, \hat{crs}_{s,1} :=, \begin{bmatrix} \hat{G} & \hat{Q}_{s,1} \\ \hat{U}_{s,1} & \hat{V}_{s,1} \end{bmatrix}, \check{crs}_{s,1} :=, \begin{bmatrix} \check{G} & \check{Q}_{s,1} \\ \check{U}_{s,1} & \check{V}_{s,1} \end{bmatrix}. \tag{3}$$

Then, GKG generates exponent values as follows.

$$x_0 \in_R \mathbb{Z}_p, \; x_1 = x_2 := 0. \tag{4}$$

Then, GKG generates the secret keys of the ElGamal encryption as follows.

$$y_0, y_1, y_2 \in_R \mathbb{Z}_p, \; \check{Y}_0 := \check{G}^{y_0}, \check{Y}_1 := \check{G}^{y_1}, \check{Y}_2 := \check{G}^{y_2}. \tag{5}$$

Then, GKG generates commitments as follows.

$$[\hat{x_0}]_0 := \mathsf{Com}(\hat{\mathbf{crs}}_{\mathsf{s},0}, x_0; r_{x_{00}}), \; [\hat{x_1}]_0 := \mathsf{Com}(\hat{\mathbf{crs}}_{\mathsf{s},0}, x_1; r_{x_{10}}),$$
$$[\hat{y_0}]_0 := \mathsf{Com}(\hat{\mathbf{crs}}_{\mathsf{s},0}, y_0; r_{y_{00}}), [\check{x_2}]_1 := \mathsf{Com}(\check{\mathbf{crs}}_{\mathsf{s},1}, x_2; r_{x_{21}}),$$
$$[\check{y_0}]_1 := \mathsf{Com}(\check{\mathbf{crs}}_{\mathsf{s},1}, y_0; r_{y_{01}}), [\hat{y_1}]_1 := \mathsf{Com}(\hat{\mathbf{crs}}_{\mathsf{s},1}, y_1; r_{y_{11}}),$$
$$[\check{y_2}]_1 := \mathsf{Com}(\check{\mathbf{crs}}_{\mathsf{s},1}, y_2; r_{y_{21}}), \tag{6}$$

where $[\hat{x_g}]_i$ and $[\check{x_h}]_j$ are computed as follows.

$$[\hat{x_g}]_i := \mathsf{Com}(\hat{\mathbf{crs}}_{\mathsf{s},i}, x_g; r_{x_{gi}}) = (\hat{U}_{\mathsf{s},i}^{x_g} \hat{G}^{r_{x_{gi}}}, (\hat{V}_{\mathsf{s},i}\hat{G})^{x_g} \hat{Q}_{\mathsf{s},i}^{r_{x_{gi}}}),$$
$$[\check{x_h}]_j := \mathsf{Com}(\check{\mathbf{crs}}_{\mathsf{s},j}, x_h; r_{x_{hj}}) = (\check{U}_{\mathsf{s},j}^{x_h} \check{G}^{r_{x_{hj}}}, (\check{V}_{\mathsf{s},j}\check{G})^{x_h} \check{Q}_{\mathsf{s},j}^{r_{x_{hj}}}).$$

Then, GKG generates key pairs as follows, where n_1 and n_2 are the numbers of messages in the source groups $\hat{G}$ and $\check{G}$, respectively, in one execution of Sig.

$$\omega \in_R \mathbb{Z}_p, \; \check{G}_r := \check{G}^{\omega}, \text{For } i = 1, \ldots, n_1 + 1 : \; \gamma_i \in_R \mathbb{Z}_p, \check{G}_i := \check{G}_r^{\gamma_i}, \tag{7}$$

$$\mu \in_R \mathbb{Z}_p, \; \hat{G}_r := \hat{G}^{\mu}, \text{For } j = 1, \ldots, n_2 : \; \psi_j \in_R \mathbb{Z}_p, \hat{G}_j := \hat{G}_r^{\psi_j}. \tag{8}$$

In total,

$$pk_{\mathsf{s}} := (\hat{G}, \check{G}, \hat{\mathbf{crs}}_{\mathsf{s},0}, \hat{\mathbf{crs}}_{\mathsf{s},1}, \check{\mathbf{crs}}_{\mathsf{s},1}, \check{Y}_0, \check{Y}_1, \check{Y}_2,$$
$$[\hat{x_0}]_0, [\hat{x_1}]_0, [\hat{y_0}]_0, [\check{x_2}]_1, [\check{y_0}]_1, [\hat{y_1}]_1, [\check{y_2}]_1,$$
$$\check{G}_r, \check{G}_1, \ldots, \check{G}_{n_1}, \hat{G}_r, \hat{G}_1, \ldots, \hat{G}_{n_2}), \tag{9}$$
$$sk_{\mathsf{s}} := (x_0, y_0, y_1, y_2,$$
$$r_{x_{00}}, r_{x_{10}}, r_{x_{21}}, r_{y_{00}}, r_{y_{01}}, r_{y_{11}}, r_{y_{21}},$$
$$\omega, \gamma_1, \ldots, \gamma_{n_1+1}, \mu, \psi_1, \ldots, \psi_{n_2}). \tag{10}$$

As a result, GKG returns the following values.

$$\mathsf{Return}\big(gpk := (1^{\lambda}, (\hat{\mathbf{crs}}_a, \check{\mathbf{crs}}_a, \hat{\mathbf{crs}}_b, \check{\mathbf{crs}}_b), pk_{\mathsf{a}}, pk_{\mathsf{s}}), omk := msk_{\mathsf{a}}, \; ik := sk_{\mathsf{s}}\big).$$

Opening-Key Generation

- OKG(gpk, omk, j, X) $\rightarrow \boldsymbol{ok}[\mathsf{j}]$. OKG takes as input gpk, omk, j and X, where j and X are an id string of an opener and an attribute subset. Then, OKG samples $\boldsymbol{a} = (a_1, \ldots, a_M) \in_R (\mathbb{Z}_p)^M$, where equations $\boldsymbol{a} \cdot (x_{\mathsf{at},1}, \ldots, x_{\mathsf{at},M}) = 1$ holds for $\mathsf{at} \in X$ (see [10]). As a result, OKG returns $\boldsymbol{ok}[\mathsf{j}] := sk_X^{\mathsf{j}} = (\mathsf{j}, X, \boldsymbol{a})$.

User-Key Generation

- $\mathsf{UKG}(1^\lambda) \to (upk, usk)$. UKG takes as input λ. In an analogous way in Sect. 3.2, UKG generates user's public key and secret key as follows.

$$upk := (\hat{G}, \check{G}, \hat{\mathbf{crs}}_{u,0}, \hat{\mathbf{crs}}_{u,1}, \check{\mathbf{crs}}_{u,1}, \check{Y}_0, \check{Y}_1, \check{Y}_2, [\hat{x_0}]_0, [\hat{x_1}]_0, [\check{y_0}]_0, [\check{x_2}]_1, [\check{y_0}]_1, [\hat{y_1}]_1, [\check{y_2}]_1,$$
$$\check{G}_r, \check{G}_1, \dots, \check{G}_{n_1}, \hat{G}_r, \hat{G}_1, \dots, \hat{G}_{n_2}), \tag{11}$$

$$usk := (x_0, y_0, y_1, y_2, r_{x00}, r_{x10}, r_{x21}, r_{y00}, r_{y01}, r_{y11}, r_{y21},$$
$$\omega, \gamma_1, \dots, \gamma_{n_1+1}, \mu, \psi_1, \dots, \psi_{n_2}). \tag{12}$$

Note here that subscripts $_u$ are omitted except for CRS. As a result, UKG returns (upk, usk).

User-Joining and Certificate-Issuing The user-joining and certificate-issuing algorithms, Join and Iss respectively, are interactive. Roughly, these algorithms consist of the signing and verification algorithms of the structure-preserving signatures (SPS). The details in our instantiation are the same as in [2] combined with the generic construction of GSdT [4].

3.3 Generating and Verifying a Group Signature

We describe here our algorithm GSign that generates a group signature σ. Then we describe our algorithm GVrfy that verifies a message-signature pair. (For the equations in Fig. 1 and Fig. 2, please consult Sect. 4.3 and 4.4 of [2]. For the algorithms P_a and V_a, please consult [6] and [13] for more details.)

Generating a Group Signature

- $\mathsf{GSign}(gpk, \boldsymbol{gsk}[\mathsf{i}], Y, \hat{M}) \to \sigma = (C, \pi_a)$. GSign takes as input gpk, $\boldsymbol{gsk}[\mathsf{i}]$, Y and $\hat{M}$. First, GSign generates a signature s on $\hat{M}$ by using the structure-preserving signature Sig [2]:

$$s = (\check{A}, \hat{Z}, \hat{R}, \check{E}_{z_0}, \check{E}_{z_1}, \check{E}_s, \hat{E}_{z_2}, \hat{E}_t, [\hat{z_0}]_0, [\hat{z_0}]_1, [\check{z_1}]_1, [\check{z_2}]_1,$$
$$\rho_{0,0}, \rho_{0,1}, \rho_{1,0}, \rho_{1,1}, \rho_{1,2}, \rho_{1,3}). \tag{13}$$

Second, GSign encrypts user's identity, its public key, their certification data and the signature, $\langle \mathsf{i}, pk_{\mathsf{i}}, cert_{\mathsf{i}}, s \rangle$ by using the pairing-free encryption ABE [10]. We note here that all the entries of this plaintext are elements of $\hat{G}$ or $\check{G}$ by the structure of Sig. Owing the feature, all the entries can be encrypted within each group, $\hat{G}$ or $\check{G}$, by using ABE. The procedure below is the case that Y is a t-out-of-n threshold access structure, for simplicity. In general, Y can be any monotone access structure [3,10]. Let us denote an element of $\hat{G}$ or $\check{G}$ by $\hat{X}$ or $\check{X}$, respectively. Then the encryption of $\hat{X}$ with ABE is $\hat{C}_{\hat{X}} := (\hat{C}_{\hat{X},0}, (\hat{C}_{\hat{X},\mathsf{at},j})_{1 \leq \mathsf{at} \leq n}^{1 \leq j \leq M})$, where

$$r_{\hat{X}} \in_R \mathbb{Z}_p, \ \hat{C}_{\hat{X},0} := \hat{X}\hat{G}^{r_{\hat{X}}}, \text{for } \mathsf{at} = 1, \dots, n: \text{ for } j = 1, \dots, M:$$

$$\text{find a deg. } t-1 \text{ random poly. } f_{\hat{X},\mathsf{at}}(x) \in \mathbb{Z}_p[x]$$
$$\text{s.t. } f_{\hat{X},\mathsf{at}}(0) = 0, \ \hat{C}_{\hat{X},\mathsf{at},j} := \hat{Y}_{\mathsf{at},j}^{r_{\hat{X}}} \hat{G}^{f_{\hat{X},\mathsf{at}}(j)}. \tag{14}$$

The encryption $\check{C}_{\check{X}}$ of $\check{X}$ with ABE is described by replacing $\hat{X}$ with $\check{X}$. In total, the ciphertext C is the following form.

$$C = (Y, C_0), C_0 = ((\hat{C}_{\hat{X}})_{\hat{X}}, (\check{C}_{\check{X}})_{\check{X}}),$$

$$\text{where } \hat{X} \text{ and } \check{X} \text{ run the entries of } \langle i, pk_i, cert_i, \sigma \rangle. \quad (15)$$

Third, GSign generates a proof π_a of the statement $(pk_a, pk_s, \hat{M}, C)$ by using the simulation-sound non-interactive zero-knowledge proof Π_a [13] with CRS $(\hat{\text{crs}}_a, \check{\text{crs}}_a)$ and the witness $(i, pk_i, cert_i, s, (r)_C)$. That is, GSign executes the prove-algorithm as $P_a(1^\lambda, (pk_a, pk_s, \hat{M}, C), (i, pk_i, cert_i, s, (r)_C, (\hat{\text{crs}}_a, \check{\text{crs}}_a))$, where $(r)_C$ denotes all the randomness sampled in generating the ciphertext C. We describe here the pairing-product equations in Fig. 1 and Fig. 2, which are used to generate π_a. Note in Fig. 1 and Fig. 2 that $\widehat{X} = \hat{C}_{\hat{X},0}/\hat{G}^{r\hat{x}}$ and $\overline{\check{X}} = \check{C}_{\check{X},0}/\check{G}^{r\check{x}}$ mean the corresponding entries of a plaintext of the ciphertext C with ABE. (We omit the details of the entries of π_a in this paper.)

Finally, GSign returns a group signature $\sigma = (C, \pi_a)$.

Verifying a Group Signature

- GVrfy$(gpk, (\hat{M}, \sigma)) \to 0/1$. GVrfy takes as input gpk and $(\hat{M}, \sigma)$. GVrfy parses σ as (C, π_a). Then GVrfy executes the verification algorithm as $V_a(1^\lambda, (pk_a, pk_s, \hat{M}, C), \pi_a, (\hat{\text{crs}}_a, \check{\text{crs}}_a))$. GVrfy returns the boolean 0 or 1 returned by V_a.

3.4   Opening and Judging

We describe here our algorithm Open that opens a group signature σ to return an identity with a proof of legitimate opening. Then we describe our algorithm Judge that judges the opening result. (For the algorithms V_a, P_b and V_b, please consult [6] and [13] for more details.)

Opening a Group Signature

- Open$(gpk, ok[j], reg, \hat{M}, \sigma) \to (i, \tau)$. Open takes as input gpk, $ok[j]$, reg, $\hat{M}$ and σ. First, Open parses $ok[j](= sk_X^j)$ as (j, X, a) and σ as (C, π_a). When the opener's attributes X satisfies the access structure Y, that is, when t or more attributes of the key attributes X is in Y (a threshold access structure), Open obtains a decryption result M by executing the decryption algorithm Dec of ABE with input (pk_a, sk_X^j, C). Then Open parses M as $\langle i, pk, cert, s \rangle$. Then Open refers the i-th row of the registration table reg, and sets $(pk_i, sig_i) := (\varepsilon, \varepsilon)$ if the i-th row is ε, or reads out (pk_i, sig_i) otherwise.

Second, Open generates a proof π_b of the statement $(pk_a, C, i, pk, cert, s)$ (legitimate opening) by using the non-interactive zero-knowledge proof Π_b [6] with CRS $(\hat{\text{crs}}_b, \check{\text{crs}}_b)$ and the witness $(sk_X^j, (r)_C)$. That is, Open executes the prove-algorithm 'a' as $P_b(1^\lambda, (pk_a, C, i, pk, cert, s), (sk_X^j, (r)_C), (\hat{\text{crs}}_b, \check{\text{crs}}_b))$. (We omit the details of the entries of π_b in this paper.)

Third, Open executes the verification algorithm 'a' as $\mathsf{V}_a(1^\lambda,$ $(pk_a, pk_s, \hat{M}, C), \pi_a, (\hat{\mathbf{crs}}_a, \check{\mathbf{crs}}_a))$. If the result is 0 or $pk \neq pk_\mathsf{i}$ or $\boldsymbol{reg}[\mathsf{i}] = \varepsilon$, then Open sets $(\mathsf{i}, \tau) := (0, \varepsilon)$. Otherwise, it sets $\tau := (pk_\mathsf{i}, sig_\mathsf{i}, \mathsf{i}, pk, cert, s, \pi_b)$. Finally, Open returns the opening result (i, τ).

Judging an Opened Result

- Judge$(gpk, \mathsf{i}, \boldsymbol{upk}[\mathsf{i}], m, \sigma, \tau) \to 0/1$. Judge takes as input gpk, i, $\boldsymbol{upk}[\mathsf{i}]$, m, σ and τ. First, Judge parses σ as (C, π_a). If $(\mathsf{i}, \tau) = (0, \varepsilon)$, then Judge executes the verification algorithm 'a' as $\mathsf{V}_a(1^\lambda, (pk_a, pk_s, \hat{M}, C), \pi_a, (\hat{\mathbf{crs}}_a, \check{\mathbf{crs}}_a))$, and returns the boolean 0 or 1 returned by V_a.

Second, Judge parses τ as $(\overline{pk}, \overline{sig}, \mathsf{i}', pk, cert, s, \pi_b)$. Judge executes the verification algorithm 'b' as $\mathsf{V}_b(1^\lambda, (C, \mathsf{i}', pk, cert, \sigma), \pi_b, (\hat{\mathbf{crs}}_b, \check{\mathbf{crs}}_b))$. If it returns 0, then Judge also returns 0. Otherwise, if the following three conditions all hold, then Judge returns 1, and otherwise, 0.

$$\mathsf{i} = \mathsf{i}', \ \mathsf{Vrfy}(\boldsymbol{upk}[\mathsf{i}], \overline{pk}, \overline{sig}) = 1, \ \overline{pk} = pk. \tag{16}$$

$$e(\overline{\check{B}}, \check{G}) = e(\hat{G}, \overline{\check{Z}})e(\hat{G}_r, \overline{\check{R}})\prod_j e(\hat{G}_j, \overline{\check{X}}_j), \tag{17}$$

$$e(\hat{G}, \overline{\check{A}}) = e(\overline{\hat{Z}}, \check{G})e(\overline{\hat{R}}, \check{G}_r)\prod_i e(\overline{\hat{X}}_i, \check{G}_i), \tag{18}$$

where $\hat{X}_i$ and $\check{X}_j$ run the entries of $(\langle \mathsf{i}, pk_\mathsf{i} \rangle, cert_\mathsf{i})$

$$e(\overline{\hat{C}_{z_0,1}}, \check{G})e(\overline{\hat{C}_{x_0,1}}, \check{G}^{-1})e(\overline{\hat{C}_{x_1,1}}, \overline{A^{-1}}) = e(\hat{G}, \check{\pi}_{0,0}),$$

$$e(\overline{\hat{C}_{z_0,2}}, \check{G})e(\overline{\hat{C}_{x_0,2}}, \check{G}^{-1})e(\overline{\hat{C}_{x_1,2}}, \overline{A^{-1}}) = e(\hat{Q}_0, \check{\pi}_{0,0}),$$

$$e(\overline{\hat{C}_{z_0,1}\hat{C}_{z_1,1}^{-1}}, \overline{\check{D}_{x_2,1}})e(\overline{\hat{C}_{z_0,1}\hat{C}_{z_1,1}^{-1}}, \overline{\check{D}_{z_2,1}^{-1}}) = e(\hat{G}, \check{\pi}_{1,0,1})e(\hat{\theta}_{1,0,1}, \check{G}),$$

$$e(\overline{\hat{C}_{z_0,2}\hat{C}_{z_1,2}^{-1}}, \overline{\check{D}_{x_2,1}})e(\overline{\hat{C}_{z_0,2}\hat{C}_{z_1,1}^{-1}}, \overline{\check{D}_{z_2,1}^{-1}}) = e(\hat{Q}_1, \check{\pi}_{1,0,1})e(\hat{\theta}_{1,0,2}, \check{G}),$$

$$e(\overline{\hat{C}_{z_0,1}\hat{C}_{z_1,1}^{-1}}, \overline{\check{D}_{x_2,2}})e(\overline{\hat{C}_{z_0,1}\hat{C}_{z_1,1}^{-1}}, \overline{\check{D}_{z_2,2}^{-1}}) = e(\hat{G}, \check{\pi}_{1,0,2})e(\hat{\theta}_{1,0,1}, \check{Q}_1),$$

$$e(\overline{\hat{C}_{z_0,2}\hat{C}_{z_1,2}^{-1}}, \overline{\check{D}_{x_2,2}})e(\overline{\hat{C}_{z_0,2}\hat{C}_{z_1,1}^{-1}}, \overline{\check{D}_{z_2,2}^{-1}}) = e(\hat{Q}_1, \check{\pi}_{1,0,2})e(\hat{\theta}_{1,0,2}, \check{Q}_1), \tag{19}$$

For $\hat{X}_i$ running the $\hat{\mathbb{G}}$-entries of $(\langle \mathsf{i}, pk_\mathsf{i} \rangle, cert_\mathsf{i})$:

$$\text{for } \mathbf{at} = 1, \ldots, n : \text{ for } j = 1, \ldots, M : \hat{C}_{\hat{X}, \mathbf{at}, j} = \hat{Y}_{\mathbf{at}, j}^{r\hat{x}} \hat{G}^{f\hat{x}, \mathbf{at}(j)}, \tag{20}$$

For $\check{X}_j$ running the $\check{\mathbb{G}}$-entries of $(\langle \mathsf{i}, pk_\mathsf{i} \rangle, cert_\mathsf{i})$:

$$\text{for } \mathbf{at} = 1, \ldots, n : \text{ for } j = 1, \ldots, M : \check{C}_{\check{X}, \mathbf{at}, j} = \check{Y}_{\mathbf{at}, j}^{r\check{x}} \check{G}^{f\check{x}, \mathbf{at}(j)}. \tag{21}$$

Fig. 1. Equations that should be satisfied by the ABE encryption of a message $\langle \mathsf{i}, pk_\mathsf{i} \rangle$ and a signature $cert_\mathsf{i}$. Here $\overline{\hat{X}} = \hat{C}_{\hat{X},0}/\hat{G}^{r\hat{x}}$, $\overline{\check{X}} = \check{C}_{\check{X},0}/\check{G}^{r\check{x}}$.

$$e(\hat{G}, \overline{\check{A}}) = e(\overline{\check{Z}}, \check{G})e(\overline{\hat{R}}, \check{G}_r)e(\hat{M}, \check{G}_1),$$

$$e(\overline{\hat{C}_{z_0,1}}, \check{G})e(\overline{\hat{C}_{x_0,1}}, \check{G}^{-1})e(\overline{\hat{C}_{x_1,1}}, \overline{\check{A}^{-1}}) = e(\hat{G}, \check{\pi}_{0,0}),$$

$$e(\overline{\hat{C}_{z_0,2}}, \check{G})e(\overline{\hat{C}_{x_0,2}}, \check{G}^{-1})e(\overline{\hat{C}_{x_1,2}}, \overline{\check{A}^{-1}}) = e(\hat{Q}_0, \check{\pi}_{0,0}),$$

$$e(\overline{\hat{C}_{z_0,1}\hat{C}_{z_1,1}^{-1}}, \check{D}_{x_2,1})e(\overline{\hat{C}_{z_0,1}\hat{C}_{z_1,1}^{-1}}, \check{D}_{z_2,1}^{-1}) = e(\hat{G}, \check{\pi}_{1,0,1})e(\hat{\theta}_{1,0,1}, \check{G}),$$

$$e(\overline{\hat{C}_{z_0,2}\hat{C}_{z_1,2}^{-1}}, \check{D}_{x_2,1})e(\overline{\hat{C}_{z_0,2}\hat{C}_{z_1,1}^{-1}}, \check{D}_{z_2,1}^{-1}) = e(\hat{Q}_1, \check{\pi}_{1,0,1})e(\hat{\theta}_{1,0,2}, \check{G}),$$

$$e(\overline{\hat{C}_{z_0,1}\hat{C}_{z_1,1}^{-1}}, \check{D}_{x_2,2})e(\overline{\hat{C}_{z_0,1}\hat{C}_{z_1,1}^{-1}}, \check{D}_{z_2,2}^{-1}) = e(\hat{G}, \check{\pi}_{1,0,2})e(\hat{\theta}_{1,0,1}, \check{Q}_1),$$

$$e(\overline{\hat{C}_{z_0,2}\hat{C}_{z_1,2}^{-1}}, \check{D}_{x_2,2})e(\overline{\hat{C}_{z_0,2}\hat{C}_{z_1,1}^{-1}}, \check{D}_{z_2,2}^{-1}) = e(\hat{Q}_1, \check{\pi}_{1,0,2})e(\hat{\theta}_{1,0,2}, \check{Q}_1), \quad (22)$$

For $\hat{X}_i$ running the $\hat{\mathbb{G}}$-entries of σ :

$$\text{for at} = 1, \ldots, n : \text{for } j = 1, \ldots, M : \hat{C}_{\hat{X}, \text{at}, j} = \hat{Y}_{\text{at}, j}^{r\check{x}} \hat{G}^{f\check{x}, \text{at}(j)}, \quad (23)$$

For $\check{X}_j$ running the $\check{\mathbb{G}}$-entries of σ :

$$\text{for at} = 1, \ldots, n : \text{for } j = 1, \ldots, M : \check{C}_{\check{X}, \text{at}, j} = \check{Y}_{\text{at}, j}^{r\check{x}} \check{G}^{f\check{x}, \text{at}(j)}. \quad (24)$$

Fig. 2. Equations that should be satisfied by a message $\hat{M}$ and ABE encryption of a signature σ. Here $\overline{\hat{X}} = \hat{C}_{\hat{X},0}/\hat{G}^{r\check{x}}, \overline{\check{X}} = \check{C}_{\check{X},0}/\check{G}^{r\check{x}}$.

4 Properties

In this section, we analyse security and performance of our instantiation of GSdT theoretically.

4.1 Security

We first note that our security properties of our GSdT is under the SXDH assumption on the Type-III biliner groups [2,8]. The assumption implies that the DDH assumption holds for both $\hat{\mathbb{G}}$ and $\check{\mathbb{G}}$ [2,8]. The security properties are stated by the following four theorems.

Theorem 1 (Correctness). *For any unbounded algorithm* **A**, $\mathbf{Adv}_{GSdT,\mathbf{A}}^{corr}(\lambda) = 0$.

Proof (sketch). The correctness of Sig and ABE and the completeness of $\Pi = (\Pi_a, \Pi_b)$ yield the correctness of GSdT due to the correctness of the generic construction (Theorem 1 in [4]). □

Theorem 2 (Anonymity). *If the SXDH assumption holds, then for any* PPT *algorithm* **A**, $\mathbf{Adv}_{GSdT,\mathbf{A}}^{anon}(\lambda)$ *is negligible in* λ.

Proof (sketch). If the SXDH assumption holds, then the DDH assumption holds for both $\hat{\mathbb{G}}$ and $\check{\mathbb{G}}$. Therefore, ABE (CP-ABE [10]) is adaptive IND-CPA secure(, that is, payload-hiding). Besides, if the SXDH assumption holds, then Π_a [13] is simulation-sound and computational zero-knowledge. Also, if the SXDH assumption holds, then Π_b [6] is computational zero-knowledge. These yield the anonymity of GSdT due to the anonymity of the generic construction (Theorem 2 in [4]). □

Theorem 3 (Traceability). *If the SXDH assumption holds, then for any* PPT *algorithm* **A**, $\mathbf{Adv}_{GSdT,\mathbf{A}}^{trace}(\lambda)$ *is negligible in* λ.

Proof (sketch). If the SXDH assumption holds, then Sig [2] is EUF-CMA secure. Besides, if the SXDH assumption holds, then Π_a [13] is sound. Also, if the SXDH assumption holds, then Π_b [6] is sound. These yield the traceability of GSdT due to the traceability of the generic construction (Theorem 3 in [4]). □

Theorem 4 (Non-frameability). *If the SXDH assumption holds, then for any* PPT *algorithm* **A**, $\mathbf{Adv}_{GSdT,\mathbf{A}}^{nf}(\lambda)$ *is negligible in* λ.

Proof (sketch). If the SXDH assumption holds, then Sig [2] is EUF-CMA secure. Besides, if the SXDH assumption holds, then Π_a [13] is sound. Also, if the SXDH assumption holds, then Π_b [6] is sound. These yield the non-frameability of GSdT due to the non-frameability of the generic construction (Theorem 4 in [4]). □

4.2 Asymptotic Performance

We analyse the performance related to a group member because it would be critical in most of real scenarios. The analysis is by asymptotic evaluation of data lengths and computational amounts. Table 1 shows the performance. The left subtable shows the bit lengths of a group-signing key sk_i and a group signature σ. On the other hand, The right subtable shows the computational amount of the algorithms of generating and verifying a group signature, GSign and GVrfy, respectively. Here n is related to a t-out-of-n access structure over openers' attributes, L is the maximum number of openers and N is the size of the attribute universe.

We can see that, except the bit-length of sk_i, the asymptotic behaviors are linear to $L + 2N$. This is because of the (not good) feature of the pairing-free ABE.

Table 1. Performance analysis: Data length and computational amount

data	bit length		algorithm	amount
$\boldsymbol{gsk}[\mathrm{i}]$	$O(\lambda)$		GSign	$O(\lambda n(L+2N))$
σ	$O(\lambda n(L+2N))$		GVrfy	$O(\lambda n(L+2N))$

5   Conclusion

In this paper, we gave an instantiation of GSdT in the algebraic setting of bilinear groups. In future work, we give details of the algorithms and estimation of the performance in terms of the number of group elements and the number of group-multiplication and pairing-computation.

Acknowledgements. The authors would like to express sincere thanks to the anonymous reviewers for their technical comments.

References

1. Abe, M., Fuchsbauer, G., Groth, J., Haralambiev, K., Ohkubo, M.: Structure-preserving signatures and commitments to group elements. In: Rabin, T. (ed.) CRYPTO 2010. LNCS, vol. 6223, pp. 209–236. Springer, Heidelberg (2010). https://doi.org/10.1007/978-3-642-14623-7_12
2. Abe, M., Hofheinz, D., Nishimaki, R., Ohkubo, M., Pan, J.: Compact structure-preserving signatures with almost tight security. In: Katz, J., Shacham, H. (eds.) CRYPTO 2017. LNCS, vol. 10402, pp. 548–580. Springer, Cham (2017). https://doi.org/10.1007/978-3-319-63715-0_19
3. Anada, H., Arita, S., Sakurai, K.: Proof of knowledge on monotone predicates and its application to attribute-based identifications and signatures. IACR Cryptology ePrint Archive 2016, 483 (2016). http://eprint.iacr.org/2016/483
4. Anada, H., Fukumitsu, M., Hasegawa, S.: Group signatures with designated traceability. In: Proceedings of the Ninth International Symposium on Computing and Networking, CANDAR 2021, Matsue, Japan, 23–26 November 2021 (2021)
5. Bellare, M., Shi, H., Zhang, C.: Foundations of group signatures: the case of dynamic groups. In: Menezes, A. (ed.) CT-RSA 2005. LNCS, vol. 3376, pp. 136–153. Springer, Heidelberg (2005). https://doi.org/10.1007/978-3-540-30574-3_11
6. Escala, A., Groth, J.: Fine-tuning Groth-Sahai proofs. In: Krawczyk, H. (ed.) PKC 2014. LNCS, vol. 8383, pp. 630–649. Springer, Heidelberg (2014). https://doi.org/10.1007/978-3-642-54631-0_36
7. Fiat, A., Shamir, A.: How to prove yourself: practical solutions to identification and signature problems. In: Odlyzko, A.M. (ed.) CRYPTO 1986. LNCS, vol. 263, pp. 186–194. Springer, Heidelberg (1987). https://doi.org/10.1007/3-540-47721-7_12
8. Galbraith, S.D., Paterson, K.G., Smart, N.P.: Pairings for cryptographers. Discret. Appl. Math. **156**(16), 3113–3121 (2008). https://doi.org/10.1016/j.dam.2007.12.010
9. Groth, J., Sahai, A.: Efficient non-interactive proof systems for bilinear groups. In: Smart, N. (ed.) EUROCRYPT 2008. LNCS, vol. 4965, pp. 415–432. Springer, Heidelberg (2008). https://doi.org/10.1007/978-3-540-78967-3_24. http://dl.acm.org/citation.cfm?id=1788414.1788438
10. Herranz, J.: Attribute-based versions of Schnorr and ElGamal. Appl. Algebra Eng. Commun. Comput. **27**(1), 17–57 (2015). https://doi.org/10.1007/s00200-015-0270-7
11. Kohlweiss, M., Miers, I.: Accountable metadata-hiding escrow: a group signature case study. Proc. Priv. Enhancing Technol. **2015**(2), 206–221 (2015). https://doi.org/10.1515/popets-2015-0012

12. Libert, B., Nguyen, K., Peters, T., Yung, M.: Bifurcated signatures: folding the accountability vs. anonymity dilemma into a single private signing scheme. In: Canteaut, A., Standaert, F.-X. (eds.) EUROCRYPT 2021. LNCS, vol. 12698, pp. 521–552. Springer, Cham (2021). https://doi.org/10.1007/978-3-030-77883-5_18
13. Libert, B., Yung, M.: Non-interactive CCA-secure threshold cryptosystems with adaptive security: new framework and constructions. In: Cramer, R. (ed.) TCC 2012. LNCS, vol. 7194, pp. 75–93. Springer, Heidelberg (2012). https://doi.org/10.1007/978-3-642-28914-9_5
14. Sakai, Y., Emura, K., Hanaoka, G., Kawai, Y., Matsuda, T., Omote, K.: Group signatures with message-dependent opening. In: Abdalla, M., Lange, T. (eds.) Pairing 2012. LNCS, vol. 7708, pp. 270–294. Springer, Heidelberg (2013). https://doi.org/10.1007/978-3-642-36334-4_18
15. Xu, S., Yung, M.: Accountable ring signatures: a smart card approach. In: Quisquater, J.-J., Paradinas, P., Deswarte, Y., El Kalam, A.A. (eds.) CARDIS 2004. IIFIP, vol. 153, pp. 271–286. Springer, Boston, MA (2004). https://doi.org/10.1007/1-4020-8147-2_18

Grover on SPARKLE

Yujin Yang, Kyungbae Jang, Hyunji Kim, Gyeongju Song,
and Hwajeong Seo$^{(\boxtimes)}$

IT Department, Hansung University, Seoul, South Korea
hwajeong84@gmail.com

Abstract. Quantum computers that take advantage of quantum
mechanics efficiently model and solve certain hard problems. In particular, quantum computers are considered a major threat to cryptography in
the near future. In this current situation, analysis of quantum computer
attacks on ciphers is a major way to evaluate the security of ciphers. Several studies of quantum circuits for block ciphers have been presented.
However, quantum implementations for Authenticated Encryption with
Associated Data (AEAD) are not actively studied.

In this paper, we present a quantum implementation for authenticated ciphers of SPARKLE, a finalist candidate of the National Institute of Standards and Technology (NIST) Lightweight Cryptography
(LWC) project. We apply various techniques for optimization by considering trade-off between qubits and gates/depth in quantum computers.
Based on proposed quantum circuit, we estimate the cost of applying key
search using Grover's algorithm, which degrades the security of symmetric key ciphers. Afterward, we further explore the expected level of post-
quantum security for SPARKLE on the basis of post-quantum security
requirements of NIST.

Keywords: Quantum computer · Grover algorithm · Lightweight
block cipher · SPARKLE · Authenticated Encryption with Associated
Data

1 Introduction

Quantum computers utilizing quantum mechanics can efficiently model the certain hard problems and solve them in polynomial-time [1]. As these quantum
computers develop, the safety of ciphers based on these hard problems is threatened. It is well known that the Shor algorithm can solve the factorization and discrete logarithm problems of Rivest-Shamir-Adleman (RSA) and Elliptic Curve

This work was partly supported by Institute for Information & communications Technology Promotion (IITP) grant funded by the Korea government (MSIT) (No.2018-
0-00264, Research on Blockchain Security Technology for IoT Services, 50%) and this
work was partly supported by Institute for Information & communications Technology Planning & Evaluation (IITP) grant funded by the Korea government (MSIT)
(<Q|Crypton>, No. 2019-0-00033, Study on Quantum Security Evaluation of Cryp-
tography based on Computational Quantum Complexity, 50%).

© Springer Nature Switzerland AG 2023
I. You and T.-Y. Youn (Eds.): WISA 2022, LNCS 13720, pp. 44–59, 2023.
https://doi.org/10.1007/978-3-031-25659-2_4

Cryptography (ECC) [2], which are public key cryptosystems, in polynomial-time [3,4]. In response to the serious security threat to the public key cryptography system, NIST is working on a post-quantum cryptography project to standardize a new cryptographic system that can replace RSA and ECC algorithms.

Grover's Algorithm is well known for reducing the security level of the symmetric key cryptography since it can reduce the complexity of searching for a secret key by as much as square root. Although less of a threat than the Shor algorithm, the Grover algorithm makes it impossible to assert the full security of ciphers.

Accordingly, studies are being conducted to implement ciphers as quantum circuits and to analyze threats to the Grover algorithm. Starting with the most famous symmetric key cipher (i.e. AES) [5–8], the field of research has expanded to lightweight ciphers [9–13] in recent years. However, the only quantum implementation for AEAD is the quantum implementation for KNOT by Baksi et al. [14].

In this paper, we present a quantum implementation of AEAD among the authenticated cipher family of SPARKLE [15], the final candidate of the NIST LWC project. We apply various techniques, such as parallelization and compact reversible operations, to our quantum circuit in order to optimize the quantum circuit by considering the trade-off between qubits and gates/depth. Based on our optimized quantum circuit, we estimate the cost of applying key search by using Grover's algorithm. Finally, we evaluate the post-quantum security level of SPARKLE based on the post-quantum security requirements of the NIST. The source code of the proposed method is provided as open-source[1].

1.1 Our Contribution and Organization

Our contributions are as follows:

1. We report the first quantum implementation of all parameters of SCHWAEMM, which is AEAD of lightweight block cipher SPARKLE.
2. We optimize the quantum circuit of SCHWAEMM by reducing the number of qubits using inverse operations and fake padding. By implementing quantum additions in parallel, the depth of the quantum circuit is reduced, significantly.
3. We estimate the quantum resources for applying Grover's algorithm on SCHWAEMM and evaluate the post-quantum security based on the proposed quantum circuit.

The organization of this paper is as follows. Section 2 presents the background of SPARKLE, quantum implementation, and the Grover search algorithm. In Sect. 3, the proposed quantum implementation is presented. In Sect. 4, we evaluate the proposed quantum circuit for SCHWAEMM. Section 5 estimates Grover key search cost for the proposed SCHWAEMM quantum circuit. Further, the NIST post-quantum security level for SCHAEMM is evaluated based on the estimated cost. Finally, Sect. 6 concludes the paper.

---

[1] https://github.com/YangYu34/SPARKLE_SCHWAEMM.git.

2   Background

2.1   SPARKLE

SPARKLE is a lightweight cipher designed based on the sponge structure, which is the final candidate for NIST lightweight cipher standardization. SPARKLE consists of ESCH that belongs to hash function family, and SCHWAEMM that belongs to authenticated cipher family.

SPARKLE Permutation. SPARKLE permutation, a cryptographic permutation, consists of ARX-box (Addition, Rotation, and XOR) Alzette and linear diffusion layer which has a linear layer of Feistel structure. This permutation is key because it is used in all steps of SCHWAEMM except for Padding Data.

The process of SCHWAEMM consists of 5 steps and is given as:

Padding Data. This process pads associated data A and message M according to the given block sizes (e.g. 128, 192, and 256). The padding function $Pad_r(M)$ used when $|M| < r$ performs $M||00000001||0^i$ operation ($i = (-|M| - 1) \ mod \ r$). It can reduce collision resistance by using domain extensions.

State Initialization. This process initializes the internal state S. Since S is used throughout the encryption phase, initializing S is important. The sequentially connected value of key K and nonce N becomes S. According to the predetermined size, the left value of S is defined as S_L and the right value of S is defined as S_R. Only state initialization is completed when S is put into the SPARKLE function and then SPARKLE permutation is performed. At this time, it should be noted that the number of SPARKLE permutation rounds varies depending on which operation is performed, depending on the parameter. The number of SPARKLE permutation rounds depends on the parameter.

Processing of Associated Data. This process puts S and associated data A that has padded as inputs into feedback function ρ_1, which is calculated on Eq. (1) In order to prevent trivial collision, if A is the last block, XOR operation is performed with the predefined constant $const_A$ to S_R. After that, S is renewed by performing XOR operation and SPARKLE permutation.

$$\rho_1 : (S, D) \mapsto (S_2||(S_2 \oplus S_1)) \oplus D \qquad (1)$$

Encrypting. This process is to encrypt the messages M. First of all, S is updated by performing SPARKLE permutation in the same way as in the previous step. At this time, $const_M$, which is predefined together with $const_A$, is used as a constant which is XORed to S_R. After that, S and M are puts to ρ_2 function that is $\rho_2 : (S, M) \mapsto S \oplus M$ in order to encrypt messages. S is put in $trunc_t$ function that returns the t leftmost bits of the input data in order to delete the padded data. As a result, ciphertext C is generated with the same size as M.

Finalization. This process generates the final return value which consists of ciphertext C, and an authentication tag T. T is the result of XOR operation between S_R and key K. The final return value is the concatenation of C and T.

Figure 1 shows the process of SCHWAEMM-128/128. In the case of 128, 192, and 256 parameters, the overall structure is the same. Only the size of instances is different. On the other hand, in 256/128, the $W_{c,r}$ process is added to the same structure. $W_{c,r}$, which performs rate-whitening, is ORed with S_R corresponding to the inner part with the outer part.

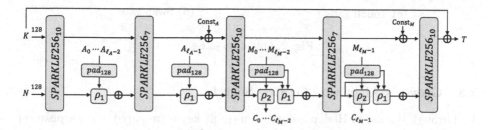

Fig. 1. Process of SCHWAEMM128-128.

2.2 Quantum Gates

Quantum gates are the fundamental building blocks of quantum computing. In this section, we describe the quantum gates needed to implement cryptographic operations of ciphers. Quantum gates that are essential and quite frequently used in implementing quantum circuits of ciphers are shown in Fig. 2.

The X gate shown in Fig. 2(a), also known as the NOT gate, is equivalent to the classical bit flip and is the simplest reversible logic gate. The NOT gate returns 1-output for 1-input and inverts the received qubit.

The CNOT gate shown in Fig. 2(b) stands for a controlled-not gate and returns a 1-qubit output for a 2-qubit input. If the control qubit is $|1\rangle$, the target qubit is negated. In other words, the target qubit is determined by the control qubit. The CNOT gate is able to generate entangled (i.e. non-separable) states contrary to the single-qubit gates.

The Toffoli gate shown in Fig. 2(c) stands for a controlled-controlled-not gate. It returns 1-output for 3-inputs. The target qubit is flipped if the two control qubits are $|1\rangle$.

The Swap Gate shown in Fig. 2(d) returns a 2-qubit output by exchanging values for a 2-qubit input.

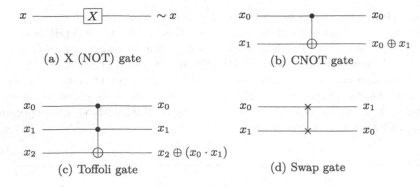

Fig. 2. Quantum gates.

2.3 Grover's Algorithm for Key Search

1. Through the use of Hadamard gates, n-qubit key is prepared in superposition $|\psi\rangle$. It has the same amplitude at all state of the qubits then:

$$|\psi\rangle = H^{\otimes n} |0\rangle^{\otimes n} = \left(\frac{|0\rangle + |1\rangle}{\sqrt{2}}\right) = \frac{1}{2^{n/2}} \sum_{x=0}^{2^n - 1} |x\rangle \qquad (2)$$

2. The cipher implemented as a quantum circuit is placed in oracle. In oracle $f(x)$, the plaintext is encrypted using the key of superposition state. Consequently, ciphertexts in regard to all of the key values are generated. By comparing to the known ciphertext, the sign of the solution key is changed to a negative number. The sign is changed to negative by the condition $(f(x) = 1)$, and this condition applies to all states.

$$f(x) = \begin{cases} 1 \text{ if } Enc(key) = c \\ 0 \text{ if } Enc(key) \neq c \end{cases} \qquad (3)$$

$$U_f(|\psi\rangle |-\rangle) = \frac{1}{2^{n/2}} \sum_{x=0}^{2^n - 1} (-1)^{f(x)} |x\rangle |-\rangle \qquad (4)$$

3. Finally, the diffusion operator serves to amplify the amplitude of the negative sign state. The diffusion operator requires no special skills to implement because it is usually generic.

3 Quantum Implementation of SPARKLE

3.1 SPARKLE Permutation

ARX-Box Alzette. Addition, XOR, and Rotation operations in quantum are essential in the ARX-box Alzette implementation. The XOR operation is simply implemented using the CNOT gate. Rotation operation can be implemented using Swap gates, but we implement logical swap that only changes the index of qubits. Thus, no quantum resources are used for rotation operations in our quantum implementation.

In classical computers, addition operations do not have that high overhead compared to XOR and AND operations. In contrast, in quantum computers, the overhead for implementing quantum addition is relatively high. Quantum addition is implemented as a combination of several Toffoli, CNOT, and X gates. More quantum resources are required than for XOR (i.e. CNOT) and AND (i.e. Toffoli) operations. Accordingly, several quantum adders for optimizing addition on a quantum computer have been presented [16–19].

We adopt an improved quantum adder with a ripple-carry approach [19] (i.e. CDKM adder). This quantum adder is efficiently implemented when $n \geq 4$. Since there are only additions with $n = 32$ in our work, we can implement an improved quantum adder, effectively. This quantum adder is further improved for modular additions where the carry value does not need to be computed. As a result, an optimal quantum adder that requires only one ancilla qubit is used in the ARX-box Alzette quantum circuit. For n-qubit quantum addition, $(2n - 3)$ Toffoli gates, $(5n - 7)$ CNOT gates, and $(2n - 6)$ X gates are used, with a depth of $(2n + 3)$. Details of the quantum adder implementation can be found in our source code and [19].

In Alzette, *AddConstant*, which XORs the constant c to 32-qubit x, is implemented with only X gates, not CNOT gates. Since the constant c is a known value, we perform X gates on 32-qubit x according to the position where the bit of c is 1. For example, if the condition is $c = 3$, it performs X gates on $x[0]$ and $x[1]$ qubits of 32-qubit x. This saves qubits and CNOT gates by using only X gates. A quantum implementation of the ARX-box Alzette is described in Algorithm 1.

Algorithm 1. Quantum implementation of Alzette.

Input: 32-qubit x and y, Constant c, Adder carry ac
Output: x, y
  1: $x \leftarrow ADD((y \ggg 31), x, ac)$
  2: $y \leftarrow \text{CNOT32}((x \ggg 24), y)$
  3: $x \leftarrow AddConstant(x, c)$
  4: $x \leftarrow ADD((y \ggg 17), x, ac)$
  5: $y \leftarrow \text{CNOT32}((x \ggg 17), y)$
  6: $x \leftarrow AddConstant(x, c)$
  7: $x \leftarrow ADD(y, x, ac)$
  8: $y \leftarrow \text{CNOT32}((x \ggg 31), y)$
  9: $x \leftarrow AddConstant(x, c)$
 10: $x \leftarrow ADD((y \ggg 24), x, ac)$
 11: $y \leftarrow \text{CNOT32}((x \ggg 16), y)$
 12: $x \leftarrow AddConstant(x, c)$
 13: **return** x, y

Linear Diffusion Layer. In the Feistel round phase of linear diffusion layer denoted by $\mathcal{L}_{n_b}$, $t_x \leftarrow (t_x \oplus (t_x \ll 16) \lll 16)$, it should be performed. However, implementing this formula as-is will result in unnecessary gate usage.

To prevent this, 16 CNOT gates are not used by XORing t_{xL}, which is the left 16 qubits of t_x, to t_{xR}. Next, the 16-qubit rotation process can be implemented using the SWAP gate since the left and right values are simply swapped. However, the left and right of t_x are used interchangeably in order to reduce the resources. In other words, the following XOR operation is divided into 16-qubit and performed using t_{xL} as the right value of t_x and t_{xR} as the left value of t_x. For example, if $y_0 \oplus t_x$ is implemented as a circuit, the operation is performed in this way: $y_{0R} \oplus t_{xL}$, $y_{0L} \oplus t_{xR}$.

Compute() and Uncompute() are meta functions provided by ProjectQ, which, if Compute() designs to perform certain function, Uncompute() reverses the actions performed in Compute(). Instead of allocating qubits to t_x and t_y, recycling x_0, y_0 by utilizing Compute() and Uncompute() saves two qubits.

$\mathcal{L}_4$, $\mathcal{L}_6$, and $\mathcal{L}_8$ are used for SPARKLE256, SPARKLE384, and SPARKLE512, respectively. Details of the implementation is found in Algorithms 2. Since the quantum circuit design of $\mathcal{L}_b(\mathcal{L}_4, \mathcal{L}_6,$ and $\mathcal{L}_8)$ differs only in the number of variables and the overall structure is the same, only the quantum circuit of $\mathcal{L}_4$ is shown in Algorithm 2.

SPARKLE Permutation. The SPAKRLE permutation quantum circuit is implemented by combining the previously introduced ARX-box Alzette and the linear diffusion layer. The quantum circuit implementation for SPARKLE256$_r$ is described and the same applies to other parameters. Within a round of SPARKLE256$_r$, Alzette runs 4 times, and we execute them in parallel. The quantum adder we adopted requires one carry qubit ac for addition. Since the carry qubit is initialized to 0 after addition, it can be used in all Alzette boxes. However, this imposes a sequential structure of the circuit, which significantly increases the depth. To solve this, we allocate four carry qubits $(ac_{0\sim3})$ to operate four Alzettes, simultaneously. Without a doubt, it would be more efficient to reduce the depth by a quarter instead of using only three more qubits. Algorithm 3 describes a quantum implementation of SPARKLE256$_r$.

Algorithm 2. Quantum implementation of $\mathcal{L}_4$.

Input: 128-qubit $x_{0\sim3}$, and $y_{0\sim3}$
Output: x, y

1: // Feistel round
2: **Transform** x_0:   ▷ Compute()
3:     $x_0 \leftarrow \text{CNOT32}(x_1, x_0)$
4:     $x_{0L} \leftarrow \text{CNOT16}(x_{0R}, x_{0L})$
5: $y_{2R} \leftarrow \text{CNOT16}(x_{0L}, y_{2R})$
6: $y_{2L} \leftarrow \text{CNOT16}(x_{0R}, y_{2L})$
7: $y_2 \leftarrow \text{CNOT32}(y_0, y_2)$
8: $y_{3R} \leftarrow \text{CNOT16}(x_{0L}, y_{3R})$
9: $y_{3L} \leftarrow \text{CNOT16}(x_{0R}, y_{3L})$
10: $y_3 \leftarrow \text{CNOT32}(y_1, y_3)$
11: Reverse(**transform** x_0)   ▷ Uncompute()

12: **Transform** y_0:   ▷ Compute()
13:     $y_0 \leftarrow \text{CNOT32}(y_1, y_0)$
14:     $y_{0L} \leftarrow \text{CNOT16}(y_{0R}, y_{0L})$
15: $x_{2R} \leftarrow \text{CNOT16}(y_{0L}, x_{2R})$
16: $x_{2L} \leftarrow \text{CNOT16}(y_{0R}, x_{2L})$
17: $x_2 \leftarrow \text{CNOT32}(x_0, x_2)$
18: $x_{3R} \leftarrow \text{CNOT16}(y_{0L}, x_{3R})$
19: $x_{3L} \leftarrow \text{CNOT16}(y_{0R}, x_{3L})$
20: $x_3 \leftarrow \text{CNOT32}(x_1, x_3)$
21: Reverse(**transform** y_0)   ▷ Uncompute()

22: // Branch permutation
23: $(x_0, x_2) \leftarrow \text{SWAP32}(x_0, x_2)$
24: $(x_1, x_3) \leftarrow \text{SWAP32}(x_1, x_3)$
25: $(y_0, y_2) \leftarrow \text{SWAP32}(y_0, y_2)$
26: $(y_1, y_3) \leftarrow \text{SWAP32}(y_1, y_3)$
27: $(x_0, x_1) \leftarrow \text{SWAP32}(x_0, x_1)$
28: $(y_0, y_1) \leftarrow \text{SWAP32}(y_0, y_1)$
29: **return** x, y

3.2 SCHWAEMM

In this section, the quantum circuit implementation of SCHWAEMM-128/128 is described in detail and can be extended with other parameters. We also describe our quantum implementation by assuming that the input associated data A and the message M have a length of 32 bits.

Padding Data. The padded data of Associated data A and Message M are used only when performing XOR operations with internal state S in the ρ_1 function. That is, A and M do not need to maintain the padding state because they are used as volatile in the encryption stage. Since only meaningful data (mostly the

---

Algorithm 3. Quantum implementation of $SPAKRLE256_r$.

Input: 128-qubit $x_{0\sim3}$, and $y_{0\sim3}$, Adder carry $ac_{0\sim3}$, Constant $c_{0\sim7}$
Output: x, y
1: **for** $i = 0$ to r **do**
2:     $y_0 \leftarrow AddConstant(y_0, c_{(i\%8)})$
3:     $y_1 \leftarrow AddConstant(y_1, i)$

4:     // Parallel Azlettes
5:     $(x_0, y_0) \leftarrow Alzette(x_0, y_0, c_0, ac_0)$
6:     $(x_1, y_1) \leftarrow Alzette(x_1, y_0, c_1, ac_1)$
7:     $(x_2, y_2) \leftarrow Alzette(x_2, y_0, c_2, ac_2)$
8:     $(x_3, y_3) \leftarrow Alzette(x_3, y_0, c_3, ac_3)$

9:     // Linear Diffusion Layer
10:     $(x_{0\sim3}, y_{0\sim3}) \leftarrow \mathcal{L}_4(x_{0\sim3}, y_{0\sim3})$
11: **end for**
12: **return** x, y

---

non-padded part) is used when performing the actual operation, we can get the value we want by only operating on the non-padded part and the data worth operating on. We call this technique *fake padding*. The implementation of fake padding is easily extended according to the lengths of input A and M. Also, the implementation details are described assuming that A and M lengths are 32-bit.

We do not allocate padding qubits to A and M in order to compute only useful data in ρ_1. This saves 32-qubit and reduces the number of 64 CNOT gates. Because it reduces the number of 64 CNOT gates, which are more expensive than X gate, and 32 qubits, although the X gate is increased by 1, therefore it is a reasonable trade-off.

State Initialization. Key K and nonce N are initialized differently depending on parameters, and most parameters except 256/128 have the characteristic as $|K| = |N|$. S is allocated as many qubits as $|N| + |K|$x because of $S = N||K$. N and K is put into S in sequence using CNOT gates when initializing S. There are no additional qubits because it is simply an operation of putting N and K into S. After that, if SPARKLE permutation is performed for n_s of rounds suitable for each parameter, the state initialization operation is completed.

Processing of Associated Data. As mentioned in the padding data phase, non-padded A is used when calculating $\rho_1(S_L, A)$. In the same way as the existing operation, A is XORed to S_L using CNOT gates. In the data padding step, a padding function Pad_r is performed that appends with the single 1 and 0s mentioned in Sect. 2.1 to A to fill the r-bit block. Because XORing 0s is no change even, there is no need to implement these with quantum gates, but single 1 must be XORed. Further, the CNOT gate can be replaced with an X gate because XOR operation of the single 1 has the same value as using the NOT operation.

When A is XORed to S_L, X gate is used for a single XOR operation on S_L. As a result, we efficiently implement it using only a single X gate instead of 32 CNOT gates.

AddConstant, which XORing the constant $const_A$, is implemented with only X gates as in Alzette. The quantum circuit of processing of associated data is described in Algorithm 4.

Algorithm 4. Quantum implementation of processing of associated data.

Input: State S, Associated data A, Constant of A $const_A$
Output: S
1: $S_R \leftarrow AddConstant(const_A, S_R)$

2: // $\rho_1(S_L, A)$
3: $S_L \leftarrow \text{SWAP64}(S_{L1}, S_{L2})$
4: $S_{L1} \leftarrow \text{CNOT64}(S_{L2}, S_{L1})$
5: $S_L \leftarrow \text{CNOT32}(A, S_L)$
6: $S_L \leftarrow \text{X}(S_L)$
7: $S_L \leftarrow \text{CNOT128}(S_R, S_L)$

8: // SPRAKLE Permutation
9: $S \leftarrow \text{SPARKLE256}_{10}(S)$
10: **return** S

Encrypting and Finalization. In encrypting, the result of XORing M and S_L is the ciphertext C (i.e. $trunc_t(\rho_2(S_L, M))$). Since S_L and M are later used in finalization, in-place computation (i.e. $S_L = S_L \oplus M$ or $M = M \oplus S_L$) is not possible. It has to be implemented as $C = S_L \oplus M$. This is not an overhead in classical computers, but in quantum computers we have to allocate new 32 qubits for C. This is inevitable, so we reduce the use of CNOT gates by using X gates to copy the value of M to the newly allocated ciphertext C. Then, we compute ciphertext C by XORing S_L to C using CNOT gates.

In finalization, AddConstant, which XORs the constant $const_M$ of encryption, is also implemented using only X gates as before. Operations of ρ_1 and SPARKLE permutation have the same mechanism as the previous step, except for using M instead of A. Authentication tag T is generated by XORing key K to S_R. In this case, in-place computation (i.e. $S_R = S_R \oplus K$) is possible. Rather than creating a T, K is XORed to S_R and S_R is used instead of T. Consequently, no additional qubits are allocated, and less quantum resources are used. Finally, the ciphertext C is appended with the authentication tag T and returned. Details of the quantum circuit implementation are shown in Algorithm 5.

Figure 3 shows a diagram of the quantum circuit for the SCHWAEMM128-128/128.

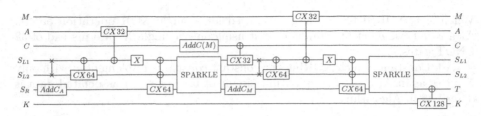

Fig. 3. The quantum circuit of SCHWAEMM128-128 (A and M are 32-qubit).

4 Performance

In this section, we evaluate the performance of proposed SCHWAEMM quantum circuits by estimating the quantum resources. Large-scale quantum computers in which proposed quantum circuits can operate have not yet been developed. Thus, we implement and simulate quantum circuits using ProjectQ, a quantum programming tool on a classical computer.

ProjectQ's internal library, `ClassicalSimulator`, is limited to simple quantum gates (e.g. X, CNOT, and Toffoli), enabling simulation using numer-

---

Algorithm 5. Quantum implementation of encrypting and finalization.

Input: State S, Message M, Constant of M $const_M$, Key K, Ciphertext C
Output: $C\|S_R$

1: **Encrypting:**
2:   $//C \leftarrow trunc_t(\rho_2(S_L, M)))$
3:   $C \leftarrow$ Allocate new qubits of length $|M|$
4:   $AddConstant(M(\text{classical}), C)$
5:   $C \leftarrow \text{CNOT32}(S_L, C)$

6: **Finalization:**
7:   $S_R \leftarrow AddConstant(const_M, S_R)$

8:   $// \rho_1(S_L, M)$
9:   $S_L \leftarrow \text{SWAP64}(S_{L1}, S_{L2})$
10:   $S_{L1} \leftarrow \text{CNOT64}(S_{L2}, S_{L1})$
11:   $S_L \leftarrow \text{CNOT32}(M, S_L)$
12:   $S_L \leftarrow \text{X}(S_L)$
13:   $S_L \leftarrow \text{CNOT128}(S_R, S_L)$

14:   $//\text{SPARKLE Permutation}$
15:   $S \leftarrow \text{SPARKLE256}_{10}(S)$

16:   $//S_R \oplus K$
17:   $S_R \leftarrow \text{CNOT128}(K, S_R)$
18: **return** $C\|S_R$

Table 1. Quantum resources required for SCHWAEMM quantum circuits.

Cipher	#CNOT	#X	#Toffoli	Toffoli depth	#qubits	Depth
SCHWAEMM-128/128	102,976	35,951	29,280	2,440	612	8,598
SCHWAEMM-256/128	170,872	59,873	48,312	2,684	870	9,591
SCHWAEMM-192/192	170,808	59,873	48,312	2,684	870	9,591
SCHWAEMM-256/256	249,056	87,062	70,272	2,928	1,128	10,605

ous qubits. This feature allows ClassicalSimulator to verify implementations by classically computing the output for a specific input to the implemented SCHWAEMM quantum circuit. Another internal library, ResourceCounter, is used for estimation of detailed quantum resources. Unlike ClassicalSimulator, ResourceCounter does not run quantum circuits and counts only quantum gates and circuit depth. There is no limit to quantum gates.

In order to proceed with the standardized evaluation in all parameters, the encryption is based on the case where Associated Data A and Message M are 32-bit. Table 1 shows the quantum resources required to implement SCHWAEMM quantum circuits at the NCT (NOT (X), CNOT, Toffoli) level.

The actual implementation of the Toffoli gate consists of a combination of Clifford gates and T gates. There are several options for decomposing the Toffoli gate [20–22]. In this work, we decompose into 7 T gates + 8 Clifford gates following the method of [20] (which is frequently adopted in quantum-related studies). Simply, one Toffoli gate has 7 T gates, 8 Clifford gates, a T-depth of 4, and a full depth of 8. Table 2 shows detailed quantum resources required for SCHWAEMM quantum circuits at the Clifford + T level.

Table 2. Quantum resources required for SCHWAEMM quantum circuits in detail.

Cipher	#CNOT	#1qCliff	#T	T-depth	#qubits	Full depth
SCHWAEMM-128/128	278,656	94,511	204,960	9,760	612	59,687
SCHWAEMM-256/128	460,744	156,497	338,184	10,736	870	65,783
SCHWAEMM-192/192	460,680	156,497	338,184	10,736	870	65,783
SCHWAEMM-256/256	670,688	227,606	491,904	11,712	1,128	71,906

5 Cost Estimation for Grover Key Search

Grover's algorithm (Sect. 2.3) consists of an oracle that finds a solution and a diffusion operator that amplifies the amplitude of the solution. The diffusion operator requires no special technique to implement, and its overhead is negligible. Thus, in most cases [5,7,13,14], the cost of Grover's algorithm is estimated with only the quantum resources required for oracle. Quantum resources for oracle are determined by the efficiency of the quantum circuit implemented. Following this, we also estimate the cost for the oracle only.

In oracle, our proposed SCHWAEMM quantum circuit works twice as illustrated in Fig. 4. In the intermediate process, there is a process to verify that the ciphertext matches the known ciphertext, but for simplicity of comparison, this is excluded from the count. Since the quantum circuit operates sequentially, the cost for oracle is calculated as (Table 2 × 2) excluding the number of qubits. As can be seen, the performance of Grover key search depends on the efficiency of the implemented quantum circuit. Table 3 shows the quantum resources required for Grover's oracle on SCHWAEMM.

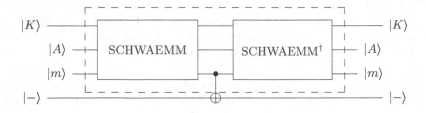

Fig. 4. Grover's oracle on SCHWAEMM.

Table 3. Quantum resources required for Grover's oracle on SCHWAEMM.

Cipher	#CNOT	#1qCliff	#T	T-depth	#qubits	Full depth
SCHWAEMM-128/128	557,312	189,022	409,920	19,520	613	119,374
SCHWAEMM-256/128	921,488	312,994	676,368	21,472	871	131,566
SCHWAEMM-192/192	921,360	312,994	676,368	21,472	871	131,566
SCHWAEMM-256/256	1,341,376	455,212	983,808	23,424	1,129	143,812

Grover key search recovers with high probability after sufficiently increasing the amplitude of the solution key through numerous iterations of the oracle and diffusion operator. When recovering an n-bit key (i.e., 2^n search space), the Grover algorithm is well known to iterate $\sqrt{2^n}$ times. However, after Grover's algorithm was presented, the authors of [23] suggested that $\lfloor \frac{\pi}{4} \cdot \sqrt{2^n} \rfloor$ iterations are optimal through a detailed analysis of Grover's iterations. Following this, Grover key search cost is calculated as (Table 3 · $\lfloor \frac{\pi}{4} \cdot \sqrt{2^n} \rfloor$) excluding the number of qubits. Table 4 shows the quantum resources required for Grover's key search on SCHWAEMM. Additionally, Table 4 shows the Grover attack cost specified by NIST according to the key size.

According to the NIST security requirements [24], the Grover attack cost is 2^{170}, 2^{233}, and 2^{298} in the order of AES-128, AES-192, and AES-256, and the security level gradually increases starting from Level 1. The attack cost for AES estimated by NIST (calculated as Total gates × Total depth) follows Grassl et al.'s quantum circuit implementation for AES [5]. NIST's post-quantum security requirements specify that ciphers should be comparable to or higher than the Grover attack cost for AES in order to claim security from quantum computers. If the Grover attack cost for SCHWAEMM is evaluated based on NIST's post-quantum security requirements, it is exposed to attack at a lower cost than AES with the same key size. Since an attack is possible with fewer quantum resources, an appropriate security level cannot be achieved.

However, it should be pointed out that the AES attack cost estimated by NIST is the result of 2016, and implementations for optimizing quantum circuits for AES have recently been proposed [6–8,25]. Among them, Jaques et al. significantly reduced the attack costs for AES-128, 192, and 256 to 2^{157}, 2^{221}, and 2^{285} [7]. NIST noted that the estimated cost in post-quantum security requirements should be conservatively evaluated if the results of significantly reducing the quantum attack cost are presented. Thus, compared with the attack cost for AES estimated in [7], SCHWAEMM achieves an appropriate security level according to the key size.

Table 4. Quantum resources required for Grover's key search on SCHWAEMM.

Cipher	Total gates	Total depth	Cost	NIST security
SCHWAEMM-128/128	$1.732 \cdot 2^{83}$	$1.431 \cdot 2^{80}$	$1.239 \cdot 2^{164}$	2^{170}
SCHWAEMM-256/128	$1.431 \cdot 2^{84}$	$1.577 \cdot 2^{80}$	$1.128 \cdot 2^{165}$	2^{170}
SCHWAEMM-192/192	$1.431 \cdot 2^{116}$	$1.577 \cdot 2^{112}$	$1.128 \cdot 2^{229}$	2^{233}
SCHWAEMM-256/256	$1.041 \cdot 2^{149}$	$1.723 \cdot 2^{144}$	$1.795 \cdot 2^{293}$	2^{298}

6 Conclusion

We present quantum circuit implementations of the AEAD instances SCHWAEMM of the lightweight cipher SPARKLE in this work. This is the first implementation of SCHWAEMM as a quantum circuit. Our implementation has been optimized by applying various techniques to minimize the cost. In this implementation, we focus a bit more on reducing qubit complexity than on depth complexity. We estimate the cost of our quantum circuit needed to run the Grover's algorithm and evaluated the security level of SCHWAEMM against the post-quantum security requirements criteria of NIST. Future work is to analyze the cost of Grover's attack for other final candidate algorithms of the NIST LWC project and evaluate the post-quantum security strength.

References

1. Abrams, D.S., Lloyd, S.: Nonlinear quantum mechanics implies polynomial-time solution for NP-complete and #P problems. Phys. Rev. Lett. **81**(18), 3992 (1998)
2. Tsai, K.-L., Leu, F.-Y., Wu, T.-H., Chiou, S.S., Liu, Y.-W., Liu, H.-Y.: A secure ECC-based electronic medical record system. J. Internet Serv. Inf. Secur. (JISIS) **4**, 47–57 (2014)
3. Shor, P.W.: Polynomial-time algorithms for prime factorization and discrete logarithms on a quantum computer. SIAM Rev. **41**(2), 303–332 (1999)
4. Singh, K., Rangan, C.P., Banerjee, A.: Lattice based efficient threshold public key encryption scheme. J. Wirel. Mob. Netw. Ubiquit. Comput. Dependable Appl. (JoWUA) **4**, 93–107 (2013)
5. Grassl, M., Langenberg, B., Roetteler, M., Steinwandt, R.: Applying Grover's algorithm to AES: quantum resource estimates. In: Takagi, T. (ed.) PQCrypto 2016. LNCS, vol. 9606, pp. 29–43. Springer, Cham (2016). https://doi.org/10.1007/978-3-319-29360-8_3
6. Langenberg, B., Pham, H., Steinwandt, R.: Reducing the cost of implementing the advanced encryption standard as a quantum circuit. IEEE Trans. Quantum Eng. **1**, 1–12 (2020)
7. Jaques, S., Naehrig, M., Roetteler, M., Virdia, F.: Implementing Grover oracles for quantum key search on AES and LowMC. In: Canteaut, A., Ishai, Y. (eds.) EUROCRYPT 2020. LNCS, vol. 12106, pp. 280–310. Springer, Cham (2020). https://doi.org/10.1007/978-3-030-45724-2_10
8. Zou, J., Wei, Z., Sun, S., Liu, X., Wu, W.: Quantum circuit implementations of AES with fewer qubits. In: Moriai, S., Wang, H. (eds.) ASIACRYPT 2020. LNCS, vol. 12492, pp. 697–726. Springer, Cham (2020). https://doi.org/10.1007/978-3-030-64834-3_24
9. Jang, K., Choi, S., Kwon, H., Kim, H., Park, J., Seo, H.: Grover on Korean block ciphers. Appl. Sci. **10**(18), 6407 (2020)
10. Jang, K., Song, G., Kim, H., Kwon, H., Kim, H., Seo, H.: Efficient implementation of PRESENT and GIFT on quantum computers. Appl. Sci. **11**(11), 4776 (2021)
11. Jang, K., Choi, S., Kwon, H., Seo, H.: Grover on speck: quantum resource estimates. Cryptology ePrint Archive (2020)
12. Jang, K., et al.: Grover on PIPO. Electronics **10**(10), 1194 (2021)
13. Bijwe, S., Chauhan, A.K., Sanadhya, S.K.: Quantum search for lightweight block ciphers: GIFT, SKINNY, SATURNIN. Cryptology ePrint Archive (2020)
14. Baksi, A., Jang, K., Song, G., Seo, H., Xiang, Z.: Quantum implementation and resource estimates for rectangle and knot. Quantum Inf. Process. **20**(12), 1–24 (2021). https://doi.org/10.1007/s11128-021-03307-6
15. Beierle, C., et al.: Schwaemm and Esch: lightweight authenticated encryption and hashing using the sparkle permutation family. NIST Round, vol. 2 (2019)
16. Draper, T.G., Kutin, S.A., Rains, E.M., Svore, K.M.: A logarithmic-depth quantum carry-lookahead adder. arXiv preprint quant-ph/0406142 (2004)
17. Takahashi, Y., Tani, S., Kunihiro, N.: Quantum addition circuits and unbounded fan-out. arXiv preprint arXiv:0910.2530 (2009)
18. Draper, T.G.: Addition on a quantum computer. arXiv preprint quant-ph/0008033 (2000)
19. Cuccaro, S.A., Draper, T.G., Kutin, S.A., Moulton, D.P.: A new quantum ripple-carry addition circuit. arXiv preprint quant-ph/0410184 (2004)

20. Amy, M., Maslov, D., Mosca, M., Roetteler, M., Roetteler, M.: A meet-in-the-middle algorithm for fast synthesis of depth-optimal quantum circuits. IEEE Trans. Comput. Aided Des. Integr. Circuits Syst. **32**, 818–830 (2013)
21. Fedorov, A., Steffen, L., Baur, M., da Silva, M.P., Wallraff, A.: Implementation of a Toffoli gate with superconducting circuits. Nature **481**(7380), 170–172 (2012)
22. Ralph, T., Resch, K., Gilchrist, A.: Efficient Toffoli gates using qudits. Phys. Rev. A **75**(2), 022313 (2007)
23. Boyer, M., Brassard, G., Høyer, P., Tapp, A.: Tight bounds on quantum searching. Fortschr. Phys. **46**, 493–505 (1998)
24. NIST. Submission requirements and evaluation criteria for the post-quantum cryptography standardization process (2016). https://csrc.nist.gov/CSRC/media/Projects/Post-Quantum-Cryptography/documents/call-for-proposals-final-dec-2016.pdf
25. Almazrooie, M., Samsudin, A., Abdullah, R., Mutter, K.N.: Quantum reversible circuit of AES-128. Quantum Inf. Process. **17**, 1–30 (2018)

Network Security

Quality-of-Service Degradation in Distributed Instrumentation Systems Through Poisoning of 5G Beamforming Algorithms

Borja Bordel[2,3,5]($\boxtimes$) , Ramón Alcarria[2,3,5] , Joaquin Chung[2,3] ,
Rajkumar Kettimuthu[2,3] , Tomás Robles[1] , and Iván Armuelles[4]

[1] Universidad Politécnica de Madrid, Madrid, Spain
tomas.robles@upm.es
[2] Argonne National Laboratory, Lemont, IL, USA
{bbordelsanchez,ralcarriagarrido,chungmiranda}@anl.gov,
kettimut@mcs.anl.gov
[3] Consortium for Advanced Science and Engineering, The University of Chicago, Chicago, USA
[4] Universidad de Panamá, Panamá, Panamá
ivan.armuelles@up.ac.pa
[5] Universidad Politécnica de Madrid, Madrid, Spain

Abstract. Instrumentation systems are essential in many critical applications such as air defense and natural disaster prediction and control. In these systems, the Quality-of-Service, measurement capacity, resilience, and efficiency are higher than in traditional monolithic instruments, thus ultra-reliable low latency, broadband, and massive communications are required to communicate all those machines. In such scenario, 5G communication technologies are seen as a promising solution. To achieve that, 5G networks provide a new radio interface in which hundreds of antennas are used to serve around tens of users in each frequency slot. This approach is only feasible if all those antennas are controlled by a hybrid transmission and reception chain, where radio beams are conformed. However, this approach opens the door to innovative cyber-physical attacks. For instance, digital and analog beamforming algorithms may be poisoned to spread the energy in the free space, deny the 5G communication services, and use that as a vector to attack and degrade the instrumentation systems. In this paper, we describe a new method for poisoning 5G beamforming algorithms based on passive radio-obstacles. Our mathematical framework allows an attacker to manage an obstacle made of unit cells of absorbent materials and varactors, so it can mix and reflect MIMO radio signals in such a way beamforming algorithms get confused and spread all the energy into free space. To validate the proposed approach, a simulation scenario was built, where different beamforming algorithms were considered. Results show the proposed attack is successful with all kinds of hybrid and analog beamforming algorithms, so more than 90% of the available power is spread in the free space and Quality-of-Service of instrumentation systems is degraded around 77%.

Keywords: 5G networks · Beamforming poisoning · Instrumentation systems · Cybersecurity · Quality-of-Service · Cyber-physical attack

© Springer Nature Switzerland AG 2023
I. You and T.-Y. Youn (Eds.): WISA 2022, LNCS 13720, pp. 63–76, 2023.
https://doi.org/10.1007/978-3-031-25659-2_5

1 Introduction

Instrumentation systems are essential in many critical applications [1]. For instance, air defense infrastructures, volcanic or tsunami activity monitoring solutions, and hurricane prediction and control centers need every day more precise and faster measurements. To achieve that precision, exogenous effects caused by thermic noise, the ionosphere, the Earth's magnetic field, or perturbations in the Earth's mantle must be removed [2]. Typically, the most efficient approaches to remove noise are based on several concurrent measurements taken at very distant points (from some meters to thousands of kilometers) [3]. Then, all those geographically sparse measurements are mixed and the final result is calculated through an algorithm for error reduction (such as mean square error) [4]. This scheme, however, requires all instruments to be calibrated in the same way [5], to be synchronized [6] and, if those measurements are the input for a control system, to be able to operate in real time [7] (thus communication and computational delays must be extremely small).

The answer to this emerging need is distributed instrumentation systems, where specialized probes, instruments, and computing nodes are deployed in different locations and collaborate to produce the final measurements [8]. In distributed instrumentation systems, the Quality-of-Service (QoS), measurement capacity, resilience, and efficiency are higher than in traditional monolithic instruments, thus ultra-reliable low latency, broadband and massive communications are required to communicate all those machines [9].

In recent demonstrations, distributed instrumentation systems have been employed, for example, to capture a picture of the Sagittarius A* black hole [10]. However, in those use cases, measurements are collected for a long period of time and transmitted and processed offline. Nevertheless, other applications such as hurricane prediction and control centers present real-time QoS requirements that wireless communication technologies cannot easily match. On the one hand, wired solutions (such as optical fibers) could meet the expected QoS, but the required deployment cost is enormous. Wireless access networks are easy to deploy, but they cannot guarantee reliable operation of critical infrastructures. In this scenario, 5G mobile (wireless) communication technologies are the most suitable answer [5], as they are envisioned to provide ultra-reliable, low latency (URLLC), enhanced broadband (eMBBC), and massive machine-type communications (mMTC) services.

To achieve the required levels of QoS, the radio interface of 5G networks is designed to employ new spectrum frequencies (millimetric waves and beyond) [11]. However, these waves have a short range and massive MIMO (Multiple-Input Multiple-Output) must be employed to address the of challenge providing sufficient capacity and coverage [12]. The MIMO systems can concentrate the transmission power in the area where the users (instrumentation devices) are, and receptors can compose signals from different directions in a constructive interference. Thus, hundreds of antennas are needed to serve tens of users in each frequency slot. However, this approach is only feasible if all these antennas are controlled by a hybrid transmission and reception chain, where radio beams are conformed, so all the antennas direct their power in the direction the users are.

The MIMO approach, nevertheless, opens the door to innovative cyber-physical attacks [13]. For instance, digital and analog beamforming algorithms may be poisoned to spread the energy into the free space, denying the 5G communication services [15], and using that as a vector to attack and degrade the instrumentation systems and, finally, the critical applications. Some approaches to poison beamforming algorithms based on active components and the transmission of radio signals have been reported [14]. However, the required equipment is costly and complicated to manage (it needs, for example, a power supply). This fact may cause these new cyber-physical risks to get underestimated, but other cheaper and equally effective attacks are feasible.

In this paper, we describe a new method for poisoning 5G beamforming algorithms based on passive radio-obstacles. We propose a mathematical framework that allows an attacker to manage an obstacle made of unit cells of absorbent materials and varactors, so it can mix and reflect MIMO radio signals in such a way beamforming algorithms get confused and sparse all the energy into the free space. The obstacle is described by its geometry and firmware, so it can be easily manufactured. In order to validate the proposed approach, a simulation scenario was built, where different 5G beamforming algorithms were considered.

The rest of the paper is organized as follows: Sect. 2 describes the state-of-the-art on techniques for poisoning 5G beamforming algorithms; Sect. 3 describes the proposed attack including the geometry calculation framework of the obstacle; Sect. 4 presents an experimental validation; and Sect. 5 concludes the paper.

2 Techniques for Poisoning 5G Beamforming Algorithms

Related work about techniques for poisoning 5G beamforming algorithms are based on active components, transmitting signals that create destructive interferences. In order to calculate the signal vector that generates those interferences, machine learning algorithms have been described [14, 16]. Other approaches propose mathematical frameworks to calculate the required additive noise to reduce the Signal-Noise Ratio (SNR) and deny the 5G communication services [17]. Other approaches take advantage of multi-carrier schemes to mix all frequencies and degrade the final Quality-of-Service [18]. However, the implementation and success of active mechanisms that require complex and costly equipment is usually much less probable than simpler approaches. Although critical infrastructures may suffer all kinds of attacks, in this paper we focus on passive approaches that are simpler, cheaper and thus, more probable (making the risk higher). In general, studies about passive approaches to poisoning 5G beamforming algorithms are very sparse. Most common articles are focused on protecting the mobile networks against electromagnetic attacks and cyberwarfare scenarios [19]. However, these active attacks are not the main threat for distributed instrumentation systems.

Only a few passive mechanisms for poisoning beamforming algorithms have been reported. They can be classified in two groups: metasurfaces and reconfigurable intelligent surfaces. Metasurfaces [20], typically, are obstacles with a special geometry, so they reflect and scatter radio signals, but they are useless if beamforming algorithms change the beam, or the geometry of the scenario changes. Therefore, this approach is not flexible enough to represent a relevant risk for most distributed instrumentation systems. On the other hand, reconfigurable intelligent surfaces [21] are two-dimensional obstacles that replicates the structure of a MIMO antenna, with several cells making up the global geometry. Each cell, when excited, changes its structure and response, so it can reflect or absorb radio signals differently according to the users' needs. This approach is very powerful, as the reconfigurable surface may be programmed to cancel any change for improvement applied by the beamforming algorithms. In this paper we are employing this approach.

3 A Reconfigurable Surface for Poisoning 5G Beamforming Algorithms

There are two basic approaches to poison 5G beamforming algorithms and deny next generation mobile communication services: (1) absorbing all power from the base station, so the MIMO antenna moves the beam looking for users in other area; and (2) generating several reflected power signals, so the MIMO antenna opens the beam and power gets scattered into the free space. Depending on the specific beamforming algorithm to get poisoned, these two basic approaches are implemented in different ways. The following subsections introduce a general model for the obstacle we are using to poison the beamforming algorithms (Sect. 3.1), the beamforming algorithms under study and the proposed poisoning schemes (Sect. 3.2), and the physical implementation of the proposed obstacle according to the characteristics of 5G radio channels (Sect. 3.3).

3.1 Reconfigurable Surface Modeling

To poison beamforming algorithms, we propose a regular rectangular array, with N rows and M elements (unit cells) in every row (see Fig. 1). Every cell in this obstacle, together with the transmission and return channels, define a Linear Time Independent (LTI) system. In this context, every cell may apply the following changes to radio signals (independently or all together): reflection, absorption, or change the signal polarity.

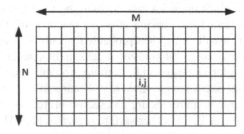

Fig. 1. Basic geometry for the obstacle (square array)

For every unit cell or element $e_{i,j}$ in the passive array, we can define an impulse response $h_{i,j}$. Thus, the malicious output signal $y_{i,j}$ received in the base station and aimed to poisoning the beamforming algorithm may be calculated from the input signal x initially generated by the radio station Eq. (1) using the convolution operation.

$$y_{i,j} = x(t) * h_{i,j}(t) = \int_{-\infty}^{\infty} x(u) * h_{i,j}(t-u)du \qquad (1)$$

With this notation, the carrier frequency is embedded into signals, and it is not explicit. However, in 5G networks, different frequency bands are employed. Then, it may be useful to include this parameter in an explicit manner. Using the complex baseband notation, every signal may be separated in two terms: the information signal (baseband) $x_{i,j}^{base}(t)$ and the carrier frequency f_c, Eq. (2).

$$x(t) = x^{base}(t)e^{-j2\pi f_c t} \tag{2}$$

The impulse response $h_{i,j}(t)$ is composed of three effects in cascade: the impulse response of the transmission channel $\alpha_{i,j}(t)$, the impulse response exclusively caused by the obstacle $\theta_{i,j}(t)$, and the impulse response for the return channel $\beta_{i,j}(t)$. These effects are combined using the convolution, Eq. (3).

$$h_{i,j}(t) = \alpha_{i,j}(t) * \theta_{i,j}(t) * \beta_{i,j}(t) \tag{3}$$

Then, the poisoning radio signal $y(t)$ finally received by the base station is the addition of all radio signals, reflected or absorbed by each one of the cell units $y_{i,j}(t)$. Moreover, we must consider the possibility of the base station to receive a radio signal through a direct channel (i.e., not affected by the poisoning surface). This "clear signal" $y_d(t)$ is also added to the final poisoning radio signal, Eq. (4). The same reasoning may be done to deduct the global impulse response for the entire obstacle $h(t)$, Eq. (5).

$$y(t) = y_d(t) + \sum_{i=1}^{N}\sum_{j=1}^{M} y_{i,j}(t) \tag{4}$$

$$h(t) = h_d(t) + \sum_{i=1}^{N}\sum_{j=1}^{M} N(t)$$

$$= h_d(t) + \sum_{i=1}^{N}\sum_{j=1}^{M} \left[\alpha_{i,j}(t) * \theta_{i,j}(t) * \beta_{i,j}(t)\right] \tag{5}$$

Besides, we must consider the additive noise $w(t)$, that is actually added to any communication system. In this case we consider Gaussian Noise. If we assume now the information radio signals have a bandwidth of B Hertz, then 5G reception chains in the base station will apply a low-pass filter with this passband. In the time domain, this filter is a *sinc* signal $p(t)$, Eq. (6). So, the final signal actually being injected into the beamforming algorithm is the filtered one $z(t)$, Eq. (7).

$$p(t) = \sqrt{B}sinc(B \cdot t) = \sqrt{B} \cdot \frac{sin(B \cdot t)}{B \cdot t} \tag{6}$$

$$z(t) = p(t) * \left[y(t) + w(t)\right] \tag{7}$$

Therefore, the effective impulse response $h_{eff}(t)$ is the convolution of the filter transfer function and the reconfigurable surface response, Eq. (8).

$$h_{eff}(t) = h(t) * p(t) \tag{8}$$

Now, as the transmission channel, the obstacle and the return channel are LTI systems, their impulse response may be modeled as the composition of a delay and an attenuation, Eq. (9). The attenuation is caused by power absorbed by materials and the medium, and it is represented by a reflection coefficient, ρ_α, ρ_β and ρ_θ. In general, reflection coefficients are calculated in terms of power, but radio signal are referred in terms of voltage. Thus, a square root is needed. Delays τ_α, τ_β and τ_θ are modeled as a delta function, Eq. (10). Although coefficients and delays caused by transmission and returns channels cannot be controlled by our poisoning obstacle, reflection coefficient ρ_θ and delay τ_θ may be manipulated by reconfiguring the surface.

$$y_{i,j}(t) = \sqrt{\rho_{i,j}} x_{i,j}\left(t - \tau_{i,j}\right) \tag{9}$$

$$h_d(t) = \sqrt{\rho_d} \cdot e^{-j2\pi f_c t} \cdot \delta(t - \tau_d)$$

$$\alpha_{i,j}(t) = \sqrt{\rho_\alpha^{i,j}} \cdot e^{-j2\pi f_c t} \cdot \delta\left(t - \tau_\alpha^{i,j}\right)$$

$$\theta_{i,j}(t) = \sqrt{\rho_\theta^{i,j}} \cdot e^{-j2\pi f_c t} \cdot \delta\left(t - \tau_\theta^{i,j}\right)$$

$$\beta_{i,j}(t) = \sqrt{\rho_\beta^{i,j}} \cdot e^{-j2\pi f_c t} \cdot \delta\left(t - \tau_\beta^{i,j}\right) \tag{10}$$

Then, the poisoning radio signal may be obtained putting together all previous elements, Eq. (11). Where the joint amplitude loss $\sqrt{\rho_\alpha^{i,j} \cdot \rho_\theta^{i,j} \cdot \rho_\beta^{i,j}}$ and joint delay $\tau_\alpha^{i,j} + \tau_\theta^{i,j} + \tau_\beta^{i,j}$ are tunable. However, not all amplitude values are possible to generate, as the Cauchy-Schwarz inequality defines a maximum value for this magnitude, Eq. (12).

$$z(t) = p(t) * \left[\left(\sqrt{\rho_d} \cdot e^{-j2\pi f_c \tau_d}\right) \cdot x(t)\right]$$
$$+ p(t) * \left(\left[\sum_{i=1}^{N}\sum_{j=1}^{M} \sqrt{\rho_\alpha^{i,j} \cdot \rho_\theta^{i,j} \cdot \rho_\beta^{i,j}} \cdot e^{-j2\pi f_c\left(\tau_\alpha^{i,j}+\tau_\theta^{i,j}+\tau_\beta^{i,j}\right)}\right] \cdot x(t)\right) \tag{11}$$
$$+ w(t) * p(t)$$

$$\left| \sqrt{\rho_d} \cdot e^{-j2\pi f_c \tau_d} + \sum_{i=1}^{N}\sum_{j=1}^{M} \sqrt{\rho_\alpha^{i,j} \cdot \rho_\theta^{i,j} \cdot \rho_\beta^{i,j}} \cdot e^{-j2\pi f_c\left(\tau_\alpha^{i,j}+\tau_\theta^{i,j}+\tau_\beta^{i,j}\right)} \right|^2$$
$$\leq \left| \sqrt{\rho_d} + \sum_{i=1}^{N}\sum_{j=1}^{M} \sqrt{\rho_\alpha^{i,j} \cdot \rho_\theta^{i,j} \cdot \rho_\beta^{i,j}} \right|^2 \tag{12}$$

$$\vec{u} = u_1\vec{u_x} + u_2\vec{u_y} + u_3\vec{u_z} \tag{13}$$

$$\tau_\theta^{i,j} = \begin{pmatrix} cos(\varphi) \cdot cos(\varepsilon) \\ cos(\varepsilon) \cdot sin(\varphi) \\ sin(\varepsilon) \end{pmatrix} \cdot \left(u_1 \; u_2 \; u_3\right) \tag{14}$$

Tunable delays may be generated by controlling the reflection angles in every unit cell in the surface. If we consider φ the Azimuth angle of the reflected signal and ε the elevation angle of the reflected radio wave, then the delay depends on the incidence vector $\vec{u}$, Eq. (13) and the carrier wavelength λ, Eq. (14).

3.2 Considered Beamforming Algorithms and Proposed Poisoning Algorithm

In 5G networks, three basic beamforming algorithms are considered [22]: digital techniques, analog techniques, and hybrid technologies. In digital schemes, beams are conformed according to information explicitly transmitted by the user devices. These algorithms can only be poisoned through active techniques such as false information injection or electromagnetic attacks. In this paper we are not addressing these techniques. Furthermore, these beamforming algorithms are not common in future 5G networks, as they are slow and costly for user devices and the base station.

In analog solutions, beams are conformed according to the result of an amplitude comparison procedure based on very directive antennas. Two antennas with overlapped Gaussian radiation diagrams, Eq. (15), receive the same radio signal. Being ϑ the zenith angle, G_o an amplitude parameter, ϑ_G the inclination of the radiation diagram and σ the 3dB beam width of the radiation diagram, and using an envelope receptor and a logarithmic amplifier, we can obtain two analog electric signals proportional to the input zenith angle of the radio signal, Eq. (16). Combining both signals, Eq. (17), and solving the underlying mathematical problem, it is possible to obtain an input for 5G beamforming algorithms to modify and optimize the beams in MIMO antennas.

$$
\begin{aligned}
G_1 &= G_o \cdot exp\left\{ -\frac{2,776}{\vartheta_G^2}(\vartheta - \sigma)^2 \right\} \\
G_2 &= G_o \cdot exp\left\{ -\frac{2,776}{\vartheta_G^2}(\vartheta + \sigma)^2 \right\}
\end{aligned}
\tag{15}
$$

$$
\begin{aligned}
logA_1 &= log\left(G_o \cdot exp\left\{ -\frac{2,776}{\vartheta_G^2}(\vartheta - \sigma)^2 \right\} \right) \\
logA_2 &= log\left(G_o \cdot exp\left\{ -\frac{2,776}{\vartheta_G^2}(\vartheta + \sigma)^2 \right\} \right)
\end{aligned}
\tag{16}
$$

$$
log\left(\frac{A_1}{A_2}\right) = -\frac{2,776}{\vartheta_G^2}\left[(\vartheta - \sigma)^2 - (\vartheta + \sigma)^2\right]
\tag{17}
$$

Against this beamforming algorithm, we propose a poisoning algorithm based on the introduction of two simultaneous radio signals in the amplitude comparison system. One of these signals is the original direct signal. The other one is the poisoning signal. In this approach, all unit cells in the reconfigurable surface generate the same radio signal. The objective is to make the beamforming algorithm detect users in the maximum zenith angle ($\vartheta = \mp\frac{\pi}{2}rad$), where there is only free space. To do that, the reconfigurable surface must introduce a $\tau_\theta^{i,j} = \frac{\pi}{2}$ delay. This delay may be achieved through the proper elevation and Azimuth angles in the reflected radio signal.

Hybrid techniques are the third and last kind of beamforming algorithms in 5G. These technologies are in fact the most promising and developed, although they are not practical nowadays as one transmission chain is needed per individual element in the MIMO antenna. In this approach, radio signals are sampled to feed a digital optimization algorithm in a microcontroller. Several sampling techniques have been analyzed. Even the very simple one-bit Analog-to-Digital conversion (ADC) has received great attention lately. In our paper we are considering a general sampling method, Eq. (18), based on pulse amplitude modulation with a sampling period of T_s seconds, as our proposal is valid for all techniques meeting the Nyquist criterion.

$$z[k] = z(k \cdot T_s) = \sum_m z[m] \cdot p\left(\frac{k - m}{B}\right) \quad being \quad k, m \in \mathbb{N} \tag{18}$$

In general, the optimization algorithm in 5G hybrid beamforming techniques may apply two different approaches: the capacity maximization or the received signal strength (RSS) maximization. Considering ϕ the Azimuth angle and ϑ the zenith angle of the beams, d_h the horizontal distance between elements in the MIMO antenna, d_v the horizontal distance between elements in the MIMO antenna, N_{MIMO} the number of horizontal elements in the MIMO antenna, M_{MIMO} the number of vertical elements in the MIMO antenna, and (finally) $H(i, j)$ a matrix describing the incident electromagnetic power over the surface of the MIMO antenna, it is possible to calculate a matrix A_{eff}, Eq. (19), usually named as preferred matrix index (PMI), representing the users distribution around the antenna. The RSS maximization algorithm looks for the optimal Azimuth and zenith angles, so the norm of this PMI is maximum, Eq. (20). The capacity maximization approach looks for the optimal angles, so the binary logarithm of the PMI's norm is maximum, Eq. (21).

$$A_{eff} = \left(e^{-j\frac{2\pi}{\lambda}d_h\sin(\vartheta)} \ldots e^{-j\frac{2\pi}{\lambda}d_hN_{MIMO}\sin(\vartheta)}\right) \cdot H$$
$$\cdot \begin{pmatrix} e^{-j\frac{2\pi}{\lambda}d_v\sin(\phi)} \\ \ldots \\ e^{-j\frac{2\pi}{\lambda}d_vM_{MIMO}\sin(\phi)} \end{pmatrix} \tag{19}$$

$$\max_{\phi,\vartheta}\left(\left|A_{eff}\right|^2\right) \tag{20}$$

$$\max_{\phi,\vartheta}\left\{\log_2\left(\left|A_{eff}\right|^2\right)\right\} \tag{21}$$

In order to poison these hybrid beamforming algorithms, we can only manipulate the incident power distribution of the antenna, $H(i, j)$. We have identified two basic poisoning strategies. In the first one, a homogenous power distribution is created over the surface of the MIMO antenna. Thus, beamforming algorithms will increase the beams' width and power will spread across a large area. In the second one, radio signals will be cancelled in the central area of the MIMO antenna and will be enhanced in the borders. Thus, beams will take extreme Azimuth and zenith angles, scattering the power into the free space. In both cases, the poisoning signal may be directly calculated from expressions, Eqs. (11), (14) and (18).

3.3 Physical Implementation and 5G Radio Channel Characteristics

Power reflection and absorption in every radio system is caused by the different impedance between two media. In the transmission and return channels, this change in the impedance is caused by the difference between the MIMO antenna surface (in the base station) and the air's impedance. Therefore, it cannot be controlled by the poisoning obstacle and algorithm. Hereinafter we are naming Z_o the air impedance. Z_o is a complex number with magnitude and phase, that are different depending on the carrier frequency, the power to be transmitted and the air's environmental conditions (e.g., temperature, humidity, and orography). On the other hand, reflection coefficients $\rho_\theta^{i,j}$ and delays $\tau_\theta^{i,j}$ are caused by the difference in impedance between the surface of the reconfigurable obstacles' unit cell in the i-th, j-th position and the air. Power reflection may be easily calculated using the Fresnel's equations, Eq. (22). From this expression, some other analytical expression can be deducted, Eq. (14). Being, $Z_{i,j}$ the impedance of the obstacles' unit cell in the i-th, j-th position.

$$\mu_{i,j} = \frac{Z_{i,j}(V_{i,j}) - Z_0}{Z_{i,j}(V_{i,j}) + Z_0} \tag{22}$$

In general, the obstacle's impedance is also different depending on the carrier frequency, the incident power and other environmental conditions. However, in order to allow the poisoning obstacle to be reconfigurable, each unit cell must be manufactured with an array of varactors. Varactors have the property to change their impedance according to the applied voltage $V_{i,j}$. This voltage can be small, and no strong current is needed. In general, for a given general conditions (such as the employed frequency band), variations in impedance caused by small changes in carrier frequencies or environmental factors (e.g., temperature or humidity) are negligible compared to changes caused by varactors. Thus, low-cost microcontrollers may manage a reconfigurable surface, applying to each varactor the required voltage to get the expected impedance and, finally, the needed poisoning radio signal.

Although, currently, some MIMO technologies are using the 3.5 GHz band to generate spatial multiplexing, in this approach no beamforming is applied. Several beams are configured in a static and immutable way. However, future 5G networks and their New Radio (NR) interface are envisioned to use the 28 GHz frequency band to apply MIMO beamforming. In this band, there is an extra power loss between 20 dB and 25 dB, compared to traditional frequency bands in mobile networks. Besides, at this frequency the attenuation caused by rain and atmospheric absorption is not the main cause of signal degradation. If the poisoning obstacle or the final users are indoor, a moderate power loss between 30 dB and 40 dB, caused by exterior materials in building (e.g., brick or glass) must be applied. Indoor materials such as drywalls introduce a power loss between 4 dB and 7 dB.

In 5G NR, a standard bandwidth of 400 MHz is employed, although numerology (i.e., the number of carriers introduced in every frequency band) and as a result, the effective bandwidth, are flexible. Also, the subcarrier spacing (SCS) and symbol duration are flexible. In distributed instrumentation systems, URLLC and eMBBC require large bandwidths, short symbol durations, and large SCS. On the contrary, mMTC usually need larger symbols and larger SCS. However, as current distributed instrumentation systems tend to be geographically sparse, mMTC may be ignored.

4   Experimental Validation: Simulation and Results

In order to evaluate the performance of the proposed poisoning strategy, we present a preliminary experiment employing simulated instruments. The objective of this experiment is to analyze whether the poisoning obstacle and algorithm could force the MIMO antennas in the base station to scatter their power into free space, and how this would affect the QoS of distributed instrumentation systems.

Our simulation scenario is composed of one 5G base station operating at 28 GHz frequency band and a variable number of instrumentation devices (between three and 20). Devices could turn on and off randomly to represent real operation patterns. Radio channel characteristics were defined according to Sect. 3.3. A medium size square service area of 12 hectares was simulated. Base station was placed in the central point, while instruments where randomly distributed. No relevant buildings are considered in the area. This scenario is adequate for distributed instrumentation systems in national parks, military bases, or other isolated critical infrastructures such as nuclear power stations or astronomy observatories. The poisoning obstacle was modeled according to Sect. 3 descriptions, and all three poisoning strategies for the two kinds of 5G beamforming algorithms under study were analyzed.

Three parameters were monitored: latency, bitrate, and power concentration. QoS was controlled through the effective communication latency and bitrate. On the other hand, power scattering was controlled by analyzing the amount (percentage) of power from the base station that is influencing the surface of the geographical are under study (power concentration). Every simulation scenario represented 24 h of network operations. Besides, in order to remove any exogenous effect, all simulations were repeated twelve times and final results were obtained as the average value of all runs. To perform these studies, we employed a simulation scenario described and executed using MATLAB 2017a software. All simulations were performed using a Linux architecture (Linux 16.04 LTS) with the following hardware characteristics: Dell R540 Rack 2U, 96 GB RAM, two processors Intel Xeon Silver 4114 2.2 G, HD 2TB SATA 7,2 K rpm.

Figure 2, Fig. 3 and Fig. 4 show our experimental results. As can be seen in Fig. 2, power concentration quickly decreases and after five hours of operation only ~10% of power influences the surface of the area under study. Similar behavior can be seen in latency (Fig. 3) and bitrate (Fig. 4), with a reduction of up to 77% in the original QoS. The only exception is produced by hybrid beamforming poisoning when the attack consists of scattering the transmission power around the whole area. In this case power concentration does not reduce, but QoS is affected in a similar way as with the other algorithms.

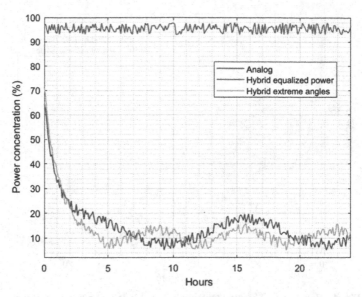

Fig. 2. Experimental results: Evolution of the power concentration

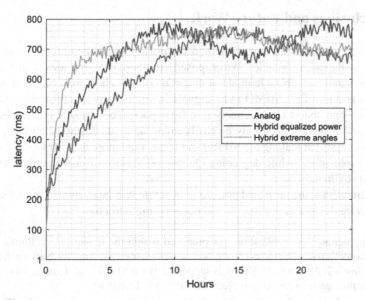

Fig. 3. Experimental results: QoS evolution (latency) as a function of time

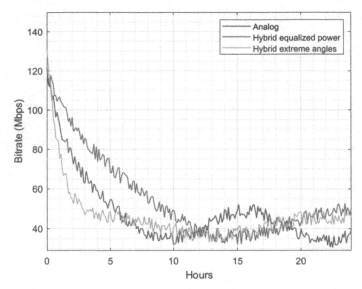

Fig. 4. Experimental results: QoS evolution (bitrate) as a function of time

5   Conclusions and Future Work

In this paper, we described a new method for poisoning 5G beamforming algorithms based on passive radio-obstacles. We proposed a mathematical framework that allows an attacker to manage an obstacle made of unit cells of absorbent materials and varactors, so it can mix and reflect MIMO radio signals in such a way beamforming algorithms get confused and sparse all the energy into free space. The obstacle is described by its geometry and firmware, so it may be easily manufactured. Results show the proposed attack is successful at making the MIMO antenna spread more than 90% of the available power into free space, while degrading Quality-of-Service of instrumentation systems to 77% approximately.

In future works, the proposed poisoning obstacle will be evaluated in real scenarios with hardware devices and a specific 5G network infrastructure.

Acknowledgments. This publication was produced within the framework of Ramón Alcarria and Borja Bordel's research projects on the occasion of their stay at Argonne National Laboratory (José Castillejo's 2021 grant). This work is supported by the Ministry of Science, Innovation and Universities through the COGNOS project (PID2019-105484RB-I00).

References

1. Nidhin, T.S., Bhattacharyya, A., Behera, R.P., Jayanthi, T., Velusamy, K.: Understanding radiation effects in SRAM-based field programmable gate arrays for implementing instrumentation and control systems of nuclear power plants. Nucl. Eng. Technol. **49**(8), 1589–1599 (2017)

2. Bordel, B., Alcarria, R., Robles, T., Sánchez-Picot, Á.: Stochastic and information theory techniques to reduce large datasets and detect cyberattacks in ambient intelligence environments. IEEE Access **6**, 34896–34910 (2018)
3. Yan, Z., Zhang, X.: Assessment of the performance of GPS/Galileo PPP-RTK convergence using ionospheric corrections from networks with different scales. Earth Planets Space **74**(1), 1–19 (2022). https://doi.org/10.1186/s40623-022-01602-9
4. Bordel, B., Alcarria, R., Robles, T.: Prediction-correction techniques to support sensor interoperability in industry 4.0 systems. Sensors **21**(21), 7301 (2021)
5. Bordel, B., Alcarria, R., Chung, J., Kettimuthu, R., Robles, T.: Evaluation and modeling of microprocessors' numerical precision impact on 5G enhanced mobile broadband communications. In: Rocha, Á., Ferrás, C., López-López, P.C., Guarda, T. (eds.) Information Technology and Systems. ICITS 2021. Advances in Intelligent Systems and Computing, vol. 1330, pp. 267–279. Springer, Cham (2021). https://doi.org/10.1007/978-3-030-68285-9_26
6. Bordel, B., Orúe, A.B., Alcarria, R., Sánchez-De-Rivera, D.: An intra-slice security solution for emerging 5G networks based on pseudo-random number generators. IEEE Access **6**, 16149–16164 (2018)
7. Bordel, B., Alcarria, R., Sanchez de Rivera, D., Martín, D., Robles, T.: Fast self-configuration in service-oriented smart environments for real-time applications. J. Ambient Intell. Smart Environ. **10**(2), 143–167 (2018)
8. Rao, N.S., et al.: Software-defined network solutions for science scenarios: performance testing framework and measurements. In: Proceedings of the 19th International Conference on Distributed Computing and Networking, pp. 1–10, January 2018
9. Bordel, B., Alcarria, R., Robles, T., Iglesias, M.S.: Data authentication and anonymization in IoT scenarios and future 5G networks using chaotic digital watermarking. IEEE Access **9**, 22378–22398 (2021)
10. Akiyama, K., et al.: First Sagittarius a* event horizon telescope results. I. The shadow of the supermassive black hole in the center of the Milky Way. Astrophys. J. Lett. **930**(2), L12 (2022)
11. Sanchez, B.B., Sánchez-Picot, Á., De Rivera, D.S.: Using 5G technologies in the internet of things handovers, problems and challenges. In: 2015 9th International Conference on Innovative Mobile and Internet Services in Ubiquitous Computing, pp. 364–369. IEEE, July 2015
12. Chataut, R., Akl, R.: Massive MIMO systems for 5G and beyond networks—overview, recent trends, challenges, and future research direction. Sensors **20**(10), 2753 (2020)
13. Bordel, B., Alcarria, R., Robles, T.: Denial of chain: evaluation and prediction of a novel cyberattack in blockchain-supported systems. Futur. Gener. Comput. Syst. **116**, 426–439 (2021)
14. Catak, E., Catak, F.O., Moldsvor, A.: Adversarial machine learning security problems for 6G: mmWave beam prediction use-case. In: 2021 IEEE International Black Sea Conference on Communications and Networking (BlackSeaCom), pp. 1–6. IEEE, May 2021
15. Bordel, B., Alcarria, R., Robles, T., Sanchez-de-Rivera, D.: Service management in virtualization-based architectures for 5G systems with network slicing. Integr. Comput. Aided Eng. **27**(1), 77–99 (2020)
16. Sheth, K., Patel, K., Shah, H., Tanwar, S., Gupta, R., Kumar, N.: A taxonomy of AI techniques for 6G communication networks. Comput. Commun. **161**, 279–303 (2020)
17. Mukherjee, A., Swindlehurst, A.L.: Poisoned feedback: the impact of malicious users in closed-loop multiuser MIMO systems. In: 2010 IEEE International Conference on Acoustics, Speech and Signal Processing, pp. 2558–2561. IEEE, March 2010
18. Ozpoyraz, B., Dogukan, A.T., Gevez, Y., Altun, U., Basar, E.: Deep learning-aided 6G wireless networks: a comprehensive survey of revolutionary PHY architectures (2022)

19. Kuzlu, M., Catak, F.O., Cali, U., Catak, E., Guler, O.: The adversarial security mitigations of mmWave beamforming prediction models using defensive distillation and adversarial retraining (2022). arXiv preprint arXiv:2202.08185
20. Biswas, S.R., Khaliji, K., Low, T.: Graphene plasmonic metasurface for beam forming and gas sensing. In: 2019 IEEE Research and Applications of Photonics in Defense Conference (RAPID), pp. 1–3. IEEE, August 2019
21. Di Renzo, M., Danufane, F.H., Tretyakov, S.: Communication models for reconfigurable intelligent surfaces: from surface electromagnetics to wireless networks optimization (2021)
22. Ahmed, I., et al.: A survey on hybrid beamforming techniques in 5G: architecture and system model perspectives. IEEE Commun. Surv. Tutor. **20**(4), 3060–3097 (2018)

An Effective Approach for Stepping-Stone Intrusion Detection Using Packet Crossover

Lixin Wang(✉), Jianhua Yang, and Austin Lee

Columbus State University, Columbus, GA 31907, USA
{wang_lixin,yang_jianhua,lee_austin}@columbusstate.edu

Abstract. An effective approach for stepping-stone intrusion detection (SSID) is to estimate the length of a connection chain, which is referred to as the network-based detection approach. In this paper, we propose an effective network-based approach for SSID using packet crossover. Existing network-based approaches for SSID are either not effective, or not efficient as they require a large number of TCP packets to be captured and processed. Some other existing network-based approaches for SSID do not work effectively when the fluctuation of the packets' RTTs is large and requires the length of a connection chain to be pre-determined, and thus these existing detection methods have very limited performance. Our proposed algorithm for SSID using packet crossover can effectively determine the length of a downstream connection chain without any pre-assumption about the length of a connection chain as well as not requiring a large number of TCP packets being captured and processed, and thus our proposed SSID algorithm is more efficient. Since the number of packet crossovers can be easily calculated, our proposed detection method is easy to use and implement. The effectiveness, correctness and efficiency of our proposed algorithm for SSID are verified through well-designed network experiments.

1 Introduction

Intruders usually launch attacks on remote target systems through compromised hosts, aiming to reduce the chance of being detected [1–6, 10, 12–18]. These compromised hosts used by intruders are called stepping-stones. With stepping-stone intrusion (**SSI**), an attacker uses a chain of stepping-stones on the Internet as relay hosts and remotely login these hosts by employing SSH, rlogin, or telnet. An intruder operates at a local host and sends attacking packets that are relayed via stepping-stones until they arrive at a remote target host.

Typically, in an SSI, an intruder sets up a connection chain as shown in Fig. 1 in which the attacker utilizes SSH to remotely login to the stepping-stones and then launch an attack. In Fig. 1, Host 0 is assumed to be the attacker's host that is used to login to stepping-stone hosts Host 1, Host 2,…, Host i − 1, Host i, Host i + 1,…, and Host N − 1. Host N represents the remote target system that is under attack. In order to perform SSI detection, any stepping-stone host (other than the attacker's host and the target system) can serve as a sensor machine where a detection program such as TCPdump is installed and used to capture packets. In this figure, Host i is assumed to be a detection sensor

© Springer Nature Switzerland AG 2023
I. You and T.-Y. Youn (Eds.): WISA 2022, LNCS 13720, pp. 77–88, 2023.
https://doi.org/10.1007/978-3-031-25659-2_6

machine with a detection program running. The connection from Host $i - 1$ to Host i is referred to as an incoming connection to Host i, and the connection from Host i to Host $i + 1$ is referred to as an outgoing connection from Host i. In terms of the sensor Host i, the part of the connection chain from the attacker's Host 0 to the sensor Host i is called a upstream connection chain, and the part of the connection chain from the sensor Host i to the target system Host N is called a downstream connection chain. If there is at least one relayed pair between all the incoming connections and all the outgoing connections, then it is most likely that Host i is used as a stepping-stone and the session is manipulated by hackers. The purpose of SSI detection (**SSID**) is to determine whether the detecting sensor Host i is used as a stepping-stone host by a hacker.

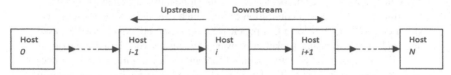

Fig. 1. A sample of connection chain.

If we compare all the outgoing connections with all the incoming connections of the same host and then see if there exists a relayed pair, this process may give us some idea whether there is a possible intrusion or not. This type of detection approach is called host-based SSID [2, 4, 5, 12–18]. With this approach we only focus on a single host (the sensor) detection. This type of methods usually generate high false-positive errors because legitimate applications such as web servers often employ stepping-stones to access remote servers. Also, this type of SSID is not effective when intruders use time-jittering and/or chaff permutation to manipulate the sessions established.

Another type of approaches for SSID is to estimate the length of a connection chain, which is referred to as the network-based detection approaches [1, 7, 9, 11]. That is, this type of methods try to estimate the number of connections from the intruder's host to the remote target host (as shown in Fig. 1). This number is referred to as the length of the connection chain. If there exist three or more connections in a connection chain from the user's host to the remote server, it means that the user attempts to gain access to a remote server host via three or more relay hosts. Clearly, the more hosts used in an interactive session to gain access to a remote server, the slower the network communication. It is well-known that most legitimate applications never use three or more hosts as stepping-stones to access a remote server. If any user tries to access a remote server through three or more stepping-stones hosts, it is highly suspicious that it is a malicious intrusion.

Next, we present a literature review focusing on network-based approaches for SSID. The first network-based approach for SSID is the work [11] by Yung in 2002. Its basic idea is to calculate the length of a connection chain length by computing a Send packet's RTT and matching it with an ACK packet sent from the next adjacent host in the connection chain. The false positive error produced by the detection method proposed in [11] is decreased a little bit. However, Yung's method for SSID generates high false negative errors. The reason for this is that the connection chain setup in [11] had some issues, and there is no way to capture the actual Echo packet for each Send packet. Instead, it used the ACK packets to match the corresponding Send packets. The 2nd work using network-based approach for SSID is the work [7] by Yang et al. that proposed the step-function detection approach to calculate the length of a connection chain in a local area network (LAN). One of the major improvements of the detection method proposed in [7] over the one proposed in [11] is that [7] used a totally different way to set up a connection chain so that an Echo packet can be captured for each corresponding Send packet. The step-function method for SSID reduced both the false positive error and the false negative error, compared with the detection method proposed in [11]. That is, the key idea of the step-function approach in [7] is to obtain the RTTs by matching a Send packet with its corresponding Echo packet. However, the SSID method developed in [7] only worked effectively when the data communications are limited within a LAN. In the context of Internet, instead, Yang et al. proposed a conservative and greedy packet matching algorithm for SSID [8]. However, this conservative algorithm can only match very few packets and thus the SSID approach is very ineffective.

The clustering and partitioning data mining algorithm for SSID by Yang et al. [9] is a well-known network-based approach. The authors of [9] proposed an algorithm for SSID by using a clustering and partitioning data mining method to calculate the RTTs of Send packets. The previously network-based approaches match Send and Echo packets by only comparing one Echo packet with a Send packet at a time. The work [9] checked all the possible packets for packet matching and made the matching process more accurate. In [9], the packets' RTTs are calculated using the maximum-minimum distance clustering algorithm (MMD). The number of connections in the chain is determined according to the number of clusters generated by the MMD data mining algorithm. The results obtained from [9] indicated that this approach can more accurately estimate the length of a connection chain than all of the prior SSID algorithms. However, the clustering and partitioning approach developed in [9] requires that a huge number of packets captured and processed, and thus this detection algorithm is not efficient.

The work [1] addressed the issue existing in [9] and developed an SSID algorithm by mining network traffic using the k-Means clustering algorithm. The SSID algorithm proposed in [1] does not require a large number of packets to be captured and processed, and thus it is more efficient than MMD clustering and partitioning approach proposed in [9]. However, with the k-Means clustering algorithm, k represents the number of clusters and must be pre-determined. This makes the performance of the SSID method proposed in [1] very limited. Also, the detection method with the k-Means clustering does not work effectively when there are large fluctuations of the packets' RTTs. The authors of [19] assumed that the number of packet crossovers is approximately proportional to the length of a given connection chain, then used this assumption to determine whether a connection chain is long or not with all the TCP packets captured at the victim host, assuming it is the sensor host. However, [19] did not verify whether this assumption is true or not. Neither technical proofs nor network experiments were provided to verify the assumption used in [19].

In this paper, we propose an effective network-based approach for SSID using packet crossover. We first verify using well-designed network experiments a claim: the length of a downstream connection chain from the sensor to the target strictly increases with the packet crossover ratio, which is the ratio of the number of packet crossovers over the total number of Send and Echo packets. Then we use the above claim to develop an innovative SSID algorithm that can effectively determine the length of a downstream connection chain without any pre-assumption about the length of a connection chain as well as not requiring a large number of TCP packets being captured and processed. Also, our proposed SSID algorithm is efficient and easy to use and implement as the packet crossover ratio is easy to compute.

The remaining of this paper is organized as follows. In Sect. 2, preliminary knowledge needed for proposing the SSID algorithm are given. In Sect. 3, we estimate the length of a downstream connection chain using packet crossover. Network experiments and performance analysis for our proposed detection algorithm are presented in Sect. 4. Finally, we conclude this paper and give some future research directions in Sect. 5.

2 Preliminaries

In this section, we introduce some basic concepts in computer networks that are required to design our detection algorithm for SSI, and the rationale of using crossover packets to estimate the length of a connection chain.

2.1 Definitions of Send/Echo Packets

Let us use Fig. 1 to define Send and Echo packets. We assume Host i is a detection sensor. In the *incoming connection* of Host i, a Send packet is defined as a TCP packet received at Host i and sent from Host $i - 1$, with the flag bit TCP.Flag.PSH set; an Echo packet is defined as a TCP packet received at Host $i - 1$ and sent from Host i, with the TCP.Flag.PSH flag bit set. In the *outgoing connection* from Host i, a Send packet is defined as a TCP packet received at Host $i + 1$ and sent from Host i, with the TCP.Flag.PSH flag bit set; an Echo packet is defined as a TCP packet received at Host i and sent from Host $i + 1$, with the TCP.Flag.PSH flag bit set.

We use an example to explain which Send packet and Echo packet are a matched pair. When a user types a command on a command line in a Linux system, such as "ls", it might be sent to the server in one or two packets. Suppose that the command "ls" is sent to the remote server in two separate Send packets: "l" and "s". When "l" is typed on the user's command line, the packet will be sent to the server side. Once this Send packet is echoed, an Echo packet sent back to the user's host, letter "l" will be shown on the terminal of the user's host. Such Send and Echo packets are called a matched pair. For the other letter "s", a matched pair can be similarly obtained: a Send "s" and an Echo "s". Using the timestamps of a matched pair of Send and Echo packets, their packet RTT can be easily computed. The length of the connection of an interactive TCP session is represented by the RTT of a matched packet pair. The RTT computed from the matched pair of the Send and Echo packets of "l" is different from the RTT computed from the matched pair of the Send and Echo packets of "s", these two numbers are very close to each other because these two RTTs stand for the length of the same connection in different time periods. A Send packet could be echoed by one or Echo packets. Also, an Echo packet could echo one or more Send packets.

2.2 Packet Crossover

Packet crossover is a phenomenon in which a new Send (request) packet meets an Echo (reply) packet of a previous Send packet along the connection chain between a client host and a server host. For example, in Fig. 2 below, we have a connection chain starting from the client (Host 1), to Host 2, then to Host 3, and finally to the server (Host 4), where Host 2 and Host 3 are the stepping-stone hosts in this chain. The Send packets S1, S2 and S3 (marked red in the figure) are sent from the client host to the server, and their Echo packets are respectively, E1, E2, and E3 (marked green in the figure). From the standpoint of the client host, the sequence of these six packets is S1, S2, E1, S3, E2, and E3. Therefore, there are two occurrences of packet crossovers in this scenario.

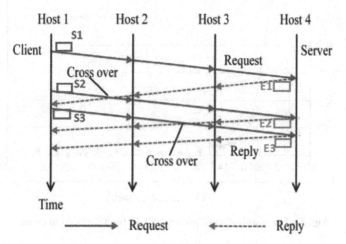

Fig. 2. A sample of packet crossover in a connection chain of four hosts.

2.3 The Distribution of Packets' RTTs in a Connection Chain

A packet RTT of a TCP connection is the sum of four time-delays including processing delay, queuing delay, transmission delay, and propagation delay of the underlying connection. For a connection chain-based SSI detection, the length of a connection chain is estimated by using the packet RTTs. The RTTs obtained from matched Send and Echo pairs can be used to represent the network traffic. Yang et al. [7] showed that the length of a connection chain is equal to the number of clusters that are produced by using the RTTs obtained from the connection chain.

V. Paxson and S. Floyd [14] found the fact that packet RTTs obtained from a connection chain obey Poisson distribution. This can be used to match TCP packets and further estimate the number of connections in an extended connection chain. Figure 3 shows a typical experiment from which packet RTTs obey Poisson distribution, where the Y-axis represents the probability of the occurrence of each RTT, and the X-axis represents the values of the RTTs with unit of microsecond. The values of the RTTs shown in Fig. 3

were from the packets collected from a connection chain composed of four connections. With this experiment, most values of the RTTs are close to the mean $\mu = 138,500$ (ms) of all the RTTs, with at least 95% of the RTT values in the range between 137,000 (ms) and 141,000 (ms) (refer to Fig. 3 below).

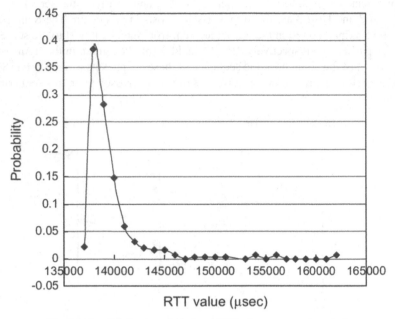

Fig. 3. The distribution of packets' RTTs for a connection chain

Assume that a random variable X follows the Poisson distribution, and its mean and standard deviation are represented by μ and σ, respectively. Then we have

$$|X - \mu| \leq 2\sigma.$$

Based on this inequality, most values of the random variable X must be around its mean value μ. The difference between X and its mean μ is upper bounded by 2σ. According to our above discussion, the packet RTTs obtained from a connection chain follow Poisson distribution. In other words, most values of the packet RTTs obtained from a connection chain of fixed length must be around its mean within a circle with radius 2σ. Therefore, the RTTs corresponding to a connection chain with fixed length belong to the same cluster with the mean μ being the cluster center. Thus, if a detection algorithm can be developed to obtain the number of such data clusters, then we could easily obtain the matched packets and estimate the length of the connection chain.

It is well-known that many legitimate applications such as Web servers usually use other servers as stepping-stones to access a remote application server. But for most such legitimate applications, they never use three or more hosts as stepping-stones to access a remote server. It is easy to see that the more hosts used to access a remote server, the slower the network traffic. If there are no intention to hide malicious activities, it is unnecessary to access a remote server via three or more stepping-stones as it could make the performance of the remote accessing not acceptable. Therefore, it is reasonable to assume that if a host uses three or more stepping-stones to access a remote server, that host is highly suspicious a malicious intruder. This assumption is popularly used in almost all network-based approaches for SSI detection in the literature.

2.4 The Rationale to Detect SSI Based on the Length of a Connection Chain

Using one host as a stepping-stone is very common in legal applications. For example, one such a popular application is a web application. Accessing a web server via a browser may result in accessing a database server through the web server because most web forms need data from its database which normally resides in another separate remote server. In this scenario, from the browser to the web server, then to the database server, the web server obviously plays a role of a stepping-stone host.

However, it is well-known that it is quite rare to use more than three hosts as stepping-stones for legitimate applications. Clearly, the more hosts to pass through to access a remote target system, the slower the network traffic is. If there were no malicious behaviors to hide, it is neither wise nor necessary to access a target indirectly via more than three hosts as the process would produce a great amount of network traffic, resulting in inefficiency of the accessing process. Therefore, it is reasonable to assume that it is highly suspicious to hide malicious activities if three or more stepping-stone hosts are used to access a remote server. Thus, to detect stepping-stone intrusion, we can estimate the number of stepping-stone hosts used in a connection chain. That is, this detection method is to estimate the length of a connection chain. The longer a connection chain is, the more suspicious the session is.

To the best of our knowledge, it is currently still a long-standing open problem to estimate the length of the upstream connection from the attacker host to the sensor, even though some researchers made several attempts to propose methods toward solving this problem. However, none of these methods for upstream detection is considered as an effective one. In this paper, we also focus on estimating the length of a downstream connection from the sensor to the target host. Since the length of an upstream connection is at least one, if a downstream connection has two or more hosts used as stepping-stones, then there are definitely three or more stepping-stone hosts used to access a remote server, and thus it is highly suspicious that there is an intrusion in such a case.

3   Estimate the Length of a Downstream Connection Chain Using Packet Crossover

In this section, we present an effective method to estimate the length of a downstream connection chain using packet crossover. From our discussion in Sect. 2, it is most likely that there is a malicious intrusion if the length of a downstream connection is at least two as the length of the upstream connection is at least one.

We claim that the length of a downstream connection chain from the sensor to the target host strictly increases with the ratio of packet crossover for a given connection chain. Intuitively, this claim is certainly true. Let us use the above Fig. 2 as an example to explain the claim. The more stepping-stone hosts between the client (Host 1) and the server (Host 4), the longer for the Echo packet E1 to arrive at Host 1 from Host 4. As a consequence, the chance will be higher for the Send packet S2 to cross over with the Echo packet E1. The same is true for the crossover between S3 and E2.

Before we present our algorithm for SSID, let us design an algorithm to compute the packet crossover ratio using the raw PCAP files captured from a connection chain of a fixed length. The captured raw PCAP files need to be preprocessed so that for a connection of fixed length, the packet timestamp, packet type (either Send or Echo based on the definitions given in Sect. 2), and the index of Send or Echo packets. The index of the first Send packet is one. The same is true for the first Echo packet. At the end of this preprocessing, every raw PCAP file is converted into a corresponding TXT file that contains three columns: packet timestamp, packet type, and index of Send or Echo packets. Such a TXT file is used as the input file of the following algorithm to compute the ratio of packet crossover.

Algorithm 1 (Compute Packet Crossover Ratio)

Input: a TXT file containing packet timestamp, packet type (Send or Echo), and index of Send or Echo
Output: Packet Crossover Ratio

```
sendIndex, echoIndex, crossoverCount = 0
while more packets in data capture file:
        if currentPacket is Acknowledgement:
                discard packet
                break

        else if currentPacket is Echo:
                if echoIndex less than sendIndex:
                        crossoverCount+=(sendIndex–echoIndex)
                echoIndex += 1

        else if (currentPacket is Send):
                sendIndex += 1
PacketCrossoverRatio = crossoverCount / (2 * echoIndex)
Print PacketCrossoverRatio
```

In order to make our results more accurate, we can repeat our network experiment N times and capture N datasets for a connection chain of fixed length, and then to calculate the average packet crossover ratio over the N captured datasets. The connection chain length can be one, two, three, four, five or six. For example, for a connection chain of length one, we capture N datasets from it and then calculate the average packet crossover ratio over the N captured datasets according to the above Algorithm 1. We then perform the same tasks for the connection chains of length two, three, four, five or six, respectively.

Next, we use the obtained packet crossover ratios and the above claim to design an effective algorithm to detect SSI. We first define an intrusion threshold value of the average packet crossover ratio. The *intrusion threshold ratio* is the average packet crossover ratio we obtained from the downstream connection chain of length two. Since the length of the upstream chain is at least one, it is most likely that there is an intrusion if the length of the downstream chain is at least two. Therefore, while monitoring the network traffic and capturing packets, if an obtained packet crossover ratio is greater than the intrusion threshold ratio, it is for sure that the length of the whole connection chain will be at least three, which indicates an intrusion.

If an obtained packet crossover ratio is less than the intrusion threshold ratio, we can conclude that the length of the downstream connection is less than two, according to the above claim. However, since we do not know the upper bound of the upstream connection length, we are unable to tell whether there is an intrusion or no intrusion in such a case.

4   Network Experiments and Performance Analysis

In this section, we verify the claim we made in Sect. 3 through a well-designed network experiment. That is, we will verify that the length of a downstream connection chain (from the sensor to the target) strictly increases with the ratio of packet crossover for a given connection chain.

To set up our experimental environment, we used two local hosts and six geographically dispersed Amazon Web Services; all hosts in the experiment ran Ubuntu operating system. We created a long connection chain by using Secure Shell (SSH) to sequentially connect to each host in the connection chain from the attacker host (see Fig. 4). In other words, a single terminal appearing on the local attacker host was used to create the entire connection chain by using sequential remote access. From our local PC in Georgia, USA running Ubuntu with IP address 168.27.2.101, we remotely accessed Host 2 (the second local host and our first stepping-stone), located in Georgia, USA with IP address 168.27.2.103. We then extended the connection chain by using Host 2 as a stepping-stone to remotely access Host 3, located in Virginia, USA with public IP address 54.175.200.189. We then extended the connection chain again by using Host 3 as a stepping-stone to remotely access Host 4, located in London, England with public IP address 35.178.87.47. We then extended the connection chain by using Host 4 as a stepping-stone to remotely access Host 5, located in Virginia, USA with public IP address 3.87.217.13. We then extended the connection chain by using Host 5 as a stepping-stone to remotely access Host 6, located in Tokyo, Japan with public IP address 54.65.202.87. We then extended the connection chain by using Host 6 as a stepping-stone to remotely access Host 7 (our last stepping-stone), located in Paris, France with public IP address 15.188.87.227. We then extended the connection chain for the final time by using Host 7 as a stepping-stone to remotely access Host 8 (the Victim host), located in Virginia, USA with public IP address 54.86.84.197; this final connection completed the 7-connection chain. To capture network traffic, we used another local host uninvolved in the connection chain to remotely access the hosts Host 2 through Host 7, each using SSH on an independent terminal. The tool TCPdump is used to capture the data for the downstream connection chain on each of these sensor hosts. For example, at Host 2 we captured the traffic from the connection between Host 2 and Host 3; at Host 3 we captured the traffic from the connection between Host 3 and Host 4).

Once the TCPdump program ready to capture network traffic at each sensor host, we entered standard Linux commands for about three minutes into the long-chain terminal

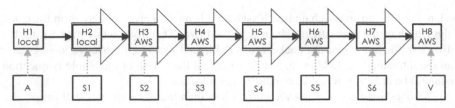

Fig. 4. A connection chain of seven connections with Hosts 2 through 7 serving as sensors used to capture traffic from the downstream chain. Red arrows indicate the connection used for packet capture. For example, when H2 serves as the sensor, then we capture the network traffic between H2 and H3.

(E.g., ls, cd, mkdir, etc.) at the attacker host (Host 1) and captured all packets from the indicated connection. We captured ten data sets in total, with each data set comprising one file at each of the six sensor hosts in the connection chain. After capturing the data at each sensor, we ran our Packet Crossover Ratio algorithm to calculate the packet crossover ratio.

Our claim is that the length of a downstream connection chain strictly increases with the ratio of packet crossover for a given connection chain. Our experimental results support this claim: the length of a downstream connection chain increases stably with the packet crossover ratios (0.0375 corresponding to the number of connections equal to 1 and 1.0820 corresponding to the number of connections equal to 1 6 (refer to Table 1 below). The intrusion threshold 0.52245 is the average packet crossover ratio derived from a downstream chain of two connections. We consider any downstream connection with a packet crossover ratio above this intrusion threshold to be malicious with high probability, as the length of an upstream chain is at least one.

Table 1. The length of a downstream chain strictly increases with packet crossover ratio. "DS" stands for data set. AVG-Ratio is the average packet crossover ration over the ten data sets collected from a connection chain of the specified length.

# of Conn	DS-1	DS-2	DS-3	DS-4	DS-5	DS-6	DS-7	DS-8	DS-9	DS-10	AVG-Ratio
1	0.0094	0.046	0.0362	0.1308	0.0147	0.0287	0.0303	0.0316	0.0074	0.0399	0.0375
2	0.4686	0.5331	0.4528	0.7945	0.4647	0.457	0.5106	0.4407	0.513	0.5895	0.52245
3	0.6948	0.7721	0.7453	1.1571	0.7206	0.6577	0.753	0.6818	0.7498	0.8567	0.77889
4	0.7823	0.9393	0.9169	1.3617	0.9456	0.776	0.9076	0.7648	0.868	1.073	0.93352
5	0.8688	1.0607	1.0266	1.5346	1.0603	0.8638	1.0621	0.8577	0.987	1.2176	1.05392
6	0.9129	1.0864	1.0549	1.5605	1.0882	0.8889	1.0864	0.876	1.0205	1.2452	1.08199

Figure 5 below clearly shows the positive relationship between the number of connections in a chain and the packet crossover ratios.

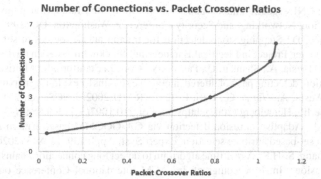

Fig. 5. This figure illustrates how the number of connections strictly increases with the packet crossover ratio.

5 Conclusion

In this paper, we developed an effective network-based method for SSID by estimating the length of a downstream connection chain using packet crossover. Previously known network-based SSID approaches are either not effective, or not efficient since a large number of TCP packets must be captured and processed, or with very limited performance as the length of a connection chain must be pre-determined. Since the number of packet crossovers can be easily computed, our proposed algorithm for SSID in this paper can be easily implemented to effectively determine the length of a downstream connection chain without any pre-assumption about the length of a connection chain. Our proposed detection algorithm does not require a large number of TCP packets captured and processed, and thus it is efficient. Well-designed network experiments were conducted to verify that the length of a downstream connection chain strictly increases with the packet crossover ratio.

As for future research directions, one may use the idea of packet crossover ratio to estimate the length of a whole connection chain, including both the downstream and upstream connections.

Acknowledgment. This work of Drs. Lixin Wang and Jianhua Yang is supported by the National Security Agency NCAE-C Research Grant (H98230-20-1-0293) with Columbus State University, Georgia, USA.

References

1. Wang, L., Yang, J., Xu, X., Wan, P.-J.: Mining network traffic with the k-means clustering algorithm for stepping-stone intrusion detection. Wirel. Commun. Mob. Comput. **2021** (2021). Article ID 6632671
2. Blum, A., Song, D., Venkataraman, S.: Detection of interactive stepping stones: algorithms and confidence bounds. In: Jonsson, E., Valdes, A., Almgren, M. (eds.) RAID 2004. LNCS, vol. 3224, pp. 258–277. Springer, Heidelberg (2004). https://doi.org/10.1007/978-3-540-30143-1_14

3. Bishop, M.: UNIX security: threats and solutions. In: Invited Talk Given at the 1995 System Administration, Networking, and Security Conference, Washington, DC (1995)
4. Bhattacherjee, D.: Stepping-stone detection for tracing attack sources in software-defined networks. Degree Project in Electrical Engineering, Stockholm, Sweden (2016)
5. Donoho, D., Flesia, A., Shankar, U., Paxson, V., Coit, J., Staniford, S.: Multiscale stepping-stone detection: detecting pairs of jittered interactive streams by exploiting maximum tolerable delay. In: Wespi, A., Vigna, G., Deri, L. (eds.) RAID 2002. LNCS, vol. 2516, pp. 17–35. Springer, Berlin, Heidelberg (2002). https://doi.org/10.1007/3-540-36084-0_2
6. Liu, J., et al.: Adaptive intrusion detection via GA-GOGMM-based pattern learning with fuzzy rough set-based attribute selection. Expert Syst. Appl. **139**, 112845 (2020)
7. Yang, J., Huang, S.-H.S.: A real-time algorithm to detect long connection chains of interactive terminal sessions. In: Proceedings of 3rd ACM International Conference on Information Security (Infosecu 2004), Shanghai, China, pp. 198–203 (2004)
8. Yang, J., Huang, S.-H. S.: Matching TCP packets and its application to the detection of long connection chains. In: Proceedings of 19th IEEE International Conference on Advanced Information Networking and Applications (AINA 2005), Taipei, Taiwan, China, pp. 1005–1010 (2005)
9. Yang, J., Huang, S.S.-H.: Mining TCP/IP packets to detect stepping-stone intrusion. J. Comput. Secur. **26**, 479–484 (2007)
10. Yang, J., Wang, L., Lesh, A., Lockerbie, B.: Manipulating network traffic to evade stepping-stone intrusion detection. Internet Things **3**, 34–45 (2018)
11. Yung, K.H.: Detecting long connecting chains of interactive terminal sessions. In: Wespi, A., Vigna, G., Deri, L. (eds.) RAID 2002. LNCS, vol. 2516, pp. 1–16. Springer, Heidelberg (2002). https://doi.org/10.1007/3-540-36084-0_1
12. Phaal, P., Panchen, S., McKee, N.: InMon corporation's sFlow: a method for monitoring traffic in switched and routed networks. RFC 3176, IETF (2001)
13. Staniford-Chen, S., Heberlein, L.T.: Holding intruders accountable on the internet. In: Proceedings of the IEEE Symposium on Security and Privacy, Oakland, CA, pp. 39–49 (1995)
14. Paxson, V., Floyd, S.: Wide-area traffic: the failure of poisson modeling. IEEE/ACM Trans. Netw. **3**(3), 226–244 (1995)
15. Wang, L., Yang, J.: A research survey in stepping-stone intrusion detection. EURASIP J. Wirel. Commun. Netw. **2018**(1), 1–15 (2018). https://doi.org/10.1186/s13638-018-1303-2
16. Wang, X., Reeves, D.: Robust correlation of encrypted attack traffic through stepping-stones by flow watermarking. IEEE Trans. Dependable Secure Comput. **8**(3), 434–449 (2011)
17. Chen, Y., Wang, S.: A novel network flow watermark embedding model for efficient detection of stepping-stone intrusion based on entropy. In: Proceedings of the International Conference on e-Learning, e-Business, Enterprise Information Systems, and e-Government (EEE), WorldComp 2016 (2016)
18. Zhang, Y., Paxson, V.: Detecting stepping-stones. In: Proceedings of the 9th USENIX Security Symposium, Denver, CO, pp. 67–81 (2000)
19. Huang, S.-H.S., Zhang, H., Phay, M.: Detecting stepping-stone intruders by identifying crossover packets in SSH connections. In: 2016 IEEE 30th International Conference on Advanced Information Networking and Applications (AINA). IEEE (2016)

Software-Defined Network Based Secure Internet-Enabled Video Surveillance System

Mathew Del Castillo[1], Harvey Hermosa[1], Philip Virgil Astillo[1], Gaurav Choudhary[2], and Nicola Dragoni[2(✉)]

[1] Department of Computer Engineering, University of San Carlos, Cebu, Philippines
{18100735,18100379,pvbastillo}@usc.edu.ph
[2] DTU Compute, Technical University of Denmark (DTU), 2800 Lyngby, Denmark
{gauch,ndra}@dtu.dk

Abstract. The Internet-of-Things is driving significant change to the video surveillance network system, allowing access to video data anywhere and at any time. Despite the tremendous benefits, the system is faced with an insider threat, causing service interruption. Current management strategies for this system are inflexible and lack security incident mitigation. This paper offers a cost-effective, flexible, and security-oriented management system based on the software-defined network technology for the video surveillance network using commercial-off-the-shelf components. A management interface was developed for the formulation of network-enforced flow rules and the visualization of network performance. The system was tested with scenarios, such that the stations within the network were exposed to high and low network demand applications. The bandwidth visualization showed an distinguishable outcomes When the surveillance network system was overwhelmed with ping flooding attack by insiders. Enforcing the appropriate for rules successfully mitigates such Denial-of-Service attack, originating within the network infrastructure. The network bandwidth immediately return to their normal state after the malicious device was logically removed.

Keywords: Software-defined network · IoT · Video surveillance system · Monitoring system

1 Introduction

The Internet of Things (IoT) is an interconnection of physical objects that consists of sensors, software, and other technologies - all of which collect and share data of their target environment. Accordingly, these devices are also connected to the Internet, establishing a connection with dispersed nodes [11]. The increasing value of IoT fuelled more and more physical security providers to migrate their video surveillance infrastructures in the IoT ecosystem [10,14,17]. Networked cameras in the IoT ecosystem can lead to automating processes that uses visual

© Springer Nature Switzerland AG 2023
I. You and T.-Y. Youn (Eds.): WISA 2022, LNCS 13720, pp. 89–101, 2023.
https://doi.org/10.1007/978-3-031-25659-2_7

information. Unfortunately, the migration opened cybersecurity challenges. In particular, Internet Protocol (IP) network cameras have become one of the targets for hackers [3]. Meanwhile, many surveillance system providers offer expensive and complex security, management, and privacy systems [16,20]. The high cost could be one of the reasons why small-scale enterprise put cybersecurity subscriptions as their least priority. The implications of such allows the possibility of a study to be done on a more simpler and budget friendly while keeping flexibility, security and maintainability.

The integration of an IoT-enabled surveillance system with Software-Defined Networking (SDN) architecture can support in defending against several cybersecurity threats. The SDN technology permits an administrator to have full control over the network with the use of various rules governing the traffic flow [2,6]. Inexpensive commercial-off-the-shelf microcomputer, like Raspberry-pi, can be configured to operate as an SDN-enabled switch. Hence, small-scale business can then setup their own surveillance network IP camera with low cost. Accordingly, business owners view live streaming video remotely and monitor network-related performance. In turn, this work offers low-cost secure video surveillance infrastructure with network management and monitoring system. This provides owner high degree of control over their setup to ensure continuous operation.

1.1   Problem Background

The Denial-of-Service (DoS) and data leakages are one of the many critical threats in a networking system that involves an IP Camera Monitoring System. Despite the numerous advantages of combining the IP with IoT in a monitoring system, it is nevertheless vulnerable to a number of cyber security concerns [9,20,22]. One of the common causes is a malicious insider, typically a malevolent individual affiliated with the organization and has privileged access to the organization's assets. In addition, employee's cybersecurity ignorance are often leveraged by many hackers as their point of entry to their workstation and to the network infrastructure. Unfortunately, on-board mitigation solutions are designed to address external threats and are often not sensitive enough to detect an internal threat [4,12]. Thus, the availability of real-time data can be harmed by DoS or distributed DoS (DDoS) attacks restricting the availability of video footage. Cyberattacks also aim on compromising the confidentiality and integrity of node data. As a result, attackers will successfully execute this harmful espionage and malign companies and businesses, resulting in its image being tarnished in the society and global markets [7,9,20,22].

The various security issues faced by the traditional networking scheme make it necessary to address these problems. One of these issues is the availability of real-time conditions in the field, which is essential as a monitoring system needs to transmit the data without any interruptions efficiently. Numerous studies have emphasized the importance of ensuring surveillance IP cameras, which are also vulnerable to a significant danger to users' security and privacy. These works reveal that IP cameras, like other WiFi-connected devices, are subject to hacking, blocking, and eavesdropping, disrupting their operations and data transfer in real-time [1]. This work offers an inexpensive solution in maintaining and monitoring the video surveillance network system through the Software-Defined Networking technology.

1.2 Contribution of the Paper

The attainment of this work is focalized on the development of a secure Internet-enable video surveillance system under a new networking paradigm, called Software-Defined Network.

The main contributions of this work are as follows:

- Built the physical setup of the SDN based video surveillance network system. This includes provision of internet connection to all hosts (e.g., IP camera, computer station).
- Developed a simple Graphical User Interface (GUI) for the SDN management interface which is used to define the flow-rules and received by the SDN-switch upon command by the administrator.
- Evaluated the security and effectiveness of the system against an insider Denial-of-Service attack.

1.3 Significance of the Study

This research would create an effective and alternative solution to the security issues faced by the traditional networking scheme of surveillance system. The proposed solution could ease in monitoring the security and quickly react to security incidents. The prototype monitoring system developed in this work could open more research avenues in the future.

Lastly, the research will therefore be beneficial to the following:

- Small-scale businesses in both urban and rural areas that are interested in a secure and effective Video Surveillance monitoring system.
- Entrepreneurs that are interested in investing into a new software networking scheme for a monitoring system that uses the Internet Protocol Camera.
- Concerning establishing an SDN testbed, it could serve as a starting point for future research in the department, e.g., building dynamic security management systems in conjunction with other technologies like Network Function Virtualization (NFV) as applied to any target use cases.

2 Related Literature Review

2.1 Application of an IoT-Based System

The IoT concept in this research is introduced in an information system of video surveillance to support the information and security measures of the environment. To further understand and incorporate different principles of this system, it is essential to base the foundation of this research on previous examples of

IoT video surveillance systems. Mainly, video surveillance systems that deliver video with the function to be continuously observed by administrators or other personnel [19]. The simultaneously collected and processed video data can provide comprehensive insights rather than isolated incidents to the person with authority. This would strengthen physical security and security-related operations across a wide range of domains and sectors by enabling a quicker and more appropriate response to any incident. Through these concepts, the researcher will be able to adapt and merge some concepts together to produce a completely unique principle of applying an IoT-based System [19].

2.2   Security and Prevention Features

Recent research has concentrated on network traffic monitoring and surveillance camera examination. Some of these studies look into probable attacks, while others look into network traffic behaviour. [1,15,20]. Implementation of the IoT-based system is not limited only to monitoring but extends to security and prevention of data loss. This can be done through the utilization of Raspberry Pi with the networking architecture of SDN. To further explore the small print of the implementation, the descriptive terms of the following are: "The Raspberry Pi may be a low cost, credit-card sized computer that plugs into a computer monitor or TV and uses a regular keyboard and mouse. It is a capable device that allows people of all ages to explore computing and to find out the way to program in languages like Scratch and Python [21]" and for the networking system: "SDN could be a specification approach that permits the network to be intelligently and centrally controlled, or 'programmed,' using software applications. This helps the users to manage the whole network consistently and holistically, irrespective of the underlying network technology [5]".

3   Secure Internet-Enabled Video Surveillance System

Figure 1 shows the operational workflow of the working system. It starts by configuring the network-related information of each device, such as the IP address and ports that will be utilized in transmitting the operational data. This information assists in creating the flow rules through the SDN application. A flow rule refers to a list of packet flows allowed or denied in the network. By default, all packet flows are allowed within the network. Accordingly, packet-dropping control is achieved by adding a corresponding flow rule with the "DENY" action. Once the network infrastructure is established, it will proceed with the monitoring application.

3.1   Environment Setup

The overall system is set up with a hierarchical network. The lower layer is introduced with a Raspberry Pi (RPi), which is configured with the Open vSwitch open-source tool to operate as an SDN switch. A set of SDN hosts, at most 4

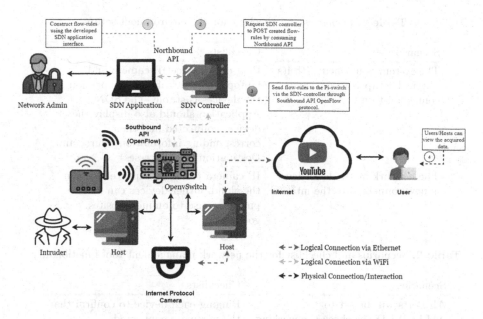

Fig. 1. SDN-based secure internet-enabled video surveillance system architecture

devices (1 IP camera, at least 1 and at most 3 other devices), will be connected via ethernet cables. Four USB ports of RPi are attached with a USB to ethernet port converter, while its onboard ethernet port will be utilized as the connection to the Internet, providing all hosts access to Internet services. Accordingly, the IP camera is configured to transfer video captures to a local server within SDN, serving as the video streaming server. The service leverages the Open Broadcaster Server (OBS) application, which is configured to transfer video capture to live streaming services.

Meanwhile, the upper layer consists of at least one computer or laptop, serving as a control and monitoring unit (CMU) of administrators over the SDN network (lower layer). A wireless router will be utilized to connect the CMU and the RPi switch wirelessly. In turn, the CMU will not be restricted to a single station, i.e., the station is installed with the necessary applications or tools and its user is given privileged access. Additionally, CMU will not be tied to a fixed location, allowing administrators to control and monitor anywhere within proximity. Table 1 summarizes scenarios and checklists to verify the network environment is successfully set up partially.

3.2   Network Management Tool

In this work, a Graphical User Interface (GUI) was developed that will serves as the network management tool, providing the necessary functions for the administrator. Accordingly, the tool is composed of three modules namely, *Connection*

Table 1. Scenarios and checklist for the environment setup

Scenarios	Checklists
The system is finished with its physical setup with devices connected to it	Ping each device(IP camera and laptops) to check if each connection to the devices is stable. The SDN Application should also display the devices connected and their corresponding information(Source and Destination IP Addresses)
The network at the lower level is now connected to the internet	IP camera transfers capture video to the cloud. Other devices can receive ping response to online websites, e.g., google.com

Table 2. Scenarios and checklist for the network management tool functionality

Scenarios	Checklists
All Ports will be set to "ALLOWED" to check the working condition of the Network Management Tool	Pinging each device to confirm that the ports are connected
All Ports will also be set to "BLOCKED" to check if the Networking Management Tool can control the connected devices	Ping each device to confirm its connection is blocked
The Network Administrator is able to view the connected devices through the SDN Application	The GUI should display the information(Source and Destination IP addresses) of each connected device in the connection list
The Network Administrator is able to give permission on each connected device	The GUI should allow the network administrator to send flow rules that will allow or block each connected device
The Network Administrator is able to view the Network Bandwidth of each connected device of each port	The GUI should display the Network Throughput of each port

List tab, *Flow List* tab, *Graphical Network Bandwidth* visualization, as shown in Fig. 2.

The *Connection List* tab simply automatically list down in a table the network information of all the hosts devices that includes Device Number, MAC address, IP Address, and physical port connection. Meanwhile, the *Flow List* module consist of Add and Edit operations, allowing administrators to manage and enforce flow rules. In this tab, the flow rules are listed with the necessary information such as Source IP, Destination IP, Network Protocol, and Action (DENY or ALLOW). Furthermore, the *Graphical Network Bandwidth* visualization displays in close to real-time the network performance. This graph can provide information as to how much data is being transferred and received by the devices at a given timeframe. In this current state, the graphical presentation will also serve as a visual reference of the administrator in determining whether a security incident occurs. Note that automatic intrusion detection within the network is yet out of the scope in the system. Moreover, other features such as switch display selection, displaying the assigned flow list, connected devices information, and network activity of selected switch are also included. This feature is only included to prepare the tool for future works. In verifying whether the tool is working according to the specifications, different scenarios and checklists were identified, as listed in Table 2.

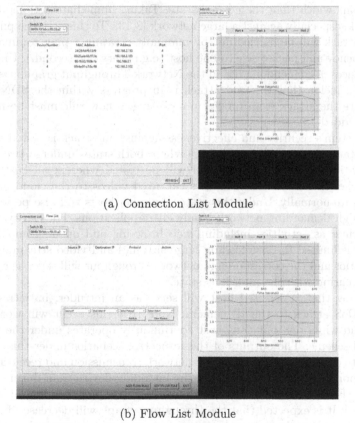

(a) Connection List Module

(b) Flow List Module

Fig. 2. Network management interface

3.3   DDOS Attack and Mitigation

The verification of the system's security measures is evaluated through a Ping Flood attack, which is used as a test case for the network performance under two network load states, e.g., heavy and light network load. Normally, ping requests are used to test the connectivity of two computers by measuring the round-trip time from when an ICMP echo request is sent to and when an ICMP echo reply is received [13, 18]. However, this request can also be exploited as an attack to overwhelm target devices with unusable data packets, disrupting the normal network behavior of the target devices. Executing a ping flood is dependent on attackers knowing the IP address of their target. A targeted local disclosed ping flood targets a single device on a local network. An attacker needs to have physical access to the computer in order to discover its IP address. A successful attack would result in the target computer being taken down. In case of ping flood incidents, the attacking computer and the target device consume more network bandwidth than the normal state. Taking immediate actions mitigates DoS attack, especially against a large network [8, 13]. To this end, the ping flooding DoS attack will be carried out by manually creating a ping command with high frequency and packet size to one host (e.g., every one second,). Under such circumstances, a tremendous rise in the Network Throughput graph is expected, building suspicion that the said attack is in progress within the SDN system. To mitigate the attack from further progressing, a flow rule must be manually edited or added.

The system's security and effectiveness against an attack is tested with two network states (normal and malicious) where both states undergo two network load activities. Primarily, the system will be tested wherein all hosts behave normally, i.e. the IP camera transfers captured videos to the cloud and other hosts operate normally. Under this state, the other hosts will also perform both low and high demanding network bandwidth applications. For clarity, we refer to the former as activities including web browsing and opening emails, while the latter is limited to downloading large size files and video streaming. These test scenarios and the corresponding network throughput will serve as a baseline when comparing with the malicious state.

Following that, a selected host will serve as an intruder, initiating a ping flooding DoS attack to the IP camera. Note that this event will work in the background while the malicious host continuously operates under the two network load scheme. The outputs of the respective scenarios under this state are expected to display a relatively higher network transmission and reception bandwidth in ports of the IP Camera and the intruding device than during the normal state. Finally, the flow rule that will block the ping flooding attack shall be enforced. It is expected that the throughput graph will decrease, if not zero. Table 3 summarizes the test scenarios and corresponding expected results.

Table 3. Scenarios and expected results for security testing

Scenarios	Checklists
Normal state with low demanding network bandwidth applications	The devices should display low activity across the graph in the Network Management Tool
	Video data transferred to the cloud is complete or uncut
Normal state with high demanding network bandwidth applications	The devices should display relatively higher activity across the graph in the Network Management Tool
	Video data transferred to the cloud is complete or uncut
Intrusion incident with low demanding network bandwidth application	The devices should first display low activity and eventually rise or show high spikes across the Network Throughput graph. Particularly, the Network Throughput graph of ports of IP Camera and the intruding device shows relatively higher value or spikes
	Video data transferred to cloud is broken
Intrusion incident with high demanding network bandwidth application	The device should first display relatively higher throughput and eventually rise or show high spikes across the Network Throughput graph. Particularly, the Network Throughput graph of ports for IP Camera and the intruding device shows relatively higher value or spike
	Video data transferred to the cloud is broken
Enforce the flow rule to mitigate the attack	The devices shall eventually decrease its throughput, if not closeto zero
	Video data transferred to the cloud eventually shows no broken data

4   Results and Discussion

Figure 3 shows a relatively low network bandwidth output when the SDN hosts PC and IP camera were exposed to low network-demanding applications. On the one hand, Figs. 3a and 3b presents the correlation of the transmitted and received data to and from the host PC and the IP camera at the normal network state. The spikes shown in 3a is caused by the loading and running of a number of preset websites, while the fluctuations shown in Fig. 3b is caused by the communication between the IP camera and the local server. On the other hand, Figs. 3c and 3d respectively presents both the transmission and reception bandwidth of the host

PC and IP camera, in which the former initiate ping flooding attack to the latter. Note that the host PC is conducting the attack at the background while browser is simultaneously loading and running preset websites. The occurrence of flooding attack shows a matching spikes and sharp increase on the transmission and reception data rate. Furthermore, when the appropriate flow rule that blocks ICMP requests from host PC was enforce, the attack was mitigated, which can be translated from decrease of network bandwidth of the host PC.

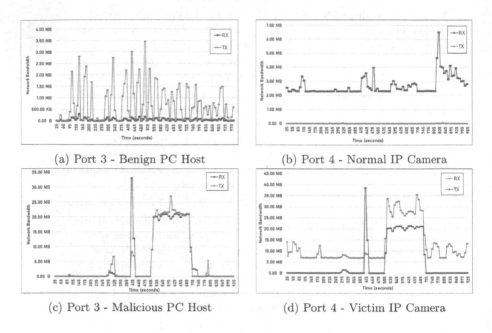

(a) Port 3 - Benign PC Host   (b) Port 4 - Normal IP Camera

(c) Port 3 - Malicious PC Host   (d) Port 4 - Victim IP Camera

Fig. 3. Network bandwidth visualization under low network demand applications

Meanwhile, Fig. 4 shows a higher network bandwidth output when hosts were exposed to higher network-demanding applications. In this case, the spikes shown in Fig. 4a are caused by the buffering and streaming of videos from YouTube. Further, the network bandwidth tremendously increased, as shown in Figs. 4c and 4d, when security incident occurred. However, it was also mitigated by enforcing an ICMP request blocking flow rule. In turn, the transmission and reception bandwidth of the two host devices decrease instantaneously.

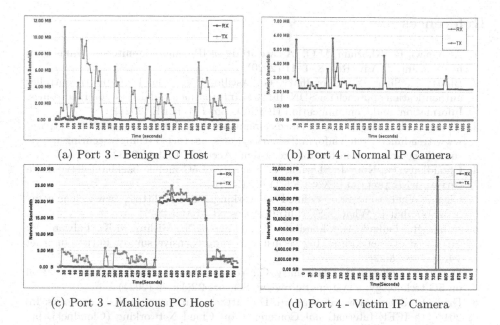

(a) Port 3 - Benign PC Host   (b) Port 4 - Normal IP Camera

(c) Port 3 - Malicious PC Host   (d) Port 4 - Victim IP Camera

Fig. 4. Network bandwidth visualization under high network demand applications

5 Conclusion and Future Works

In this paper, a working and stable physical setup of an SDN based video surveillance network system is presented with provisions of internet connection to all its hosts. Using this system, the researchers were able to successfully develop a simple Graphical User Interface(GUI) for the management interface and test the system using the test case scenarios. Based on the tests, the system was able to monitor in real-time and prevent a simulated insider Denial-of-Service attack.

With the conclusion of this study, it was determined that there is still a greater potential to improve and develop the functionalities of this system. Therefore, the following suggestions were conceptualized for improvement and enhancement of the research study:

- An automated warning and prevention system which will automatically notify the administrator, detect the source of the intrusion and neutralize a simulated or actual intrusion event on the system.
- A user interface guide, tips and tutorial for new users or administrators on the usage of the GUI which will allow accessibility and ease of access.

Acknowledgements. This work has been supported by project TRANSACT funded under H2020-EU.2.1.1. - INDUSTRIAL LEADERSHIP - Leadership in enabling and industrial technologies - Information and Communication Technologies (grant agreement ID: 101007260).

References

1. Alshalawi, R., Khozium, M.O.: A case study of IP camera monitoring traffic veri-fication. Int. J. Adv. Res. **8**, 1–11 (2020)
2. Bhatt, C., Sihag, V., Choudhary, G., Astillo, P.V., You, I.: A multi-controller authentication approach for SDN. In: 2021 International Conference on Electronics, Information, and Communication (ICEIC), pp. 1–4. IEEE (2021)
3. Cheng, J.: Securing IP surveillance cameras in the IoT ecosystem (2018). https://www.trendmicro.com/vinfo/mx/security/news/internet-of-things/securing-ip-surveillance-cameras-in-the-iot-ecosystem. Accessed 16 July 2022
4. Choudhary, G., Kim, J., Sharma, V.: Security of 5G-mobile backhaul networks: a survey. arXiv preprint arXiv:1906.11427 (2019)
5. Ciena: What is software-defined networking (SDN)? https://www.ciena.com/insights/what-is/What-Is-SDN.html. Accessed 14 Mar 2021
6. Dangi, R., Jadhav, A., Choudhary, G., Dragoni, N., Mishra, M.K., Lalwani, P.: ML-based 5G network slicing security: a comprehensive survey. Future Internet **14**(4), 116 (2022)
7. Dangi, R., Lalwani, P., Choudhary, G., You, I., Pau, G.: Study and investigation on 5G technology: a systematic review. Sensors **22**(1), 26 (2021)
8. Dridi, L., Zhani, M.F.: SDN-guard: DoS attacks mitigation in SDN networks. In: 2016 5th IEEE International Conference on Cloud Networking (Cloudnet), pp. 212–217. IEEE (2016)
9. GeeksforGeeks: Difference between software defined network and traditional net-work (2020). https://www.geeksforgeeks.org/difference-between-software-defined-network-and-traditional-network/. Accessed 23 Apr 2021
10. Gulve, S.P., Khoje, S.A., Pardeshi, P.: Implementation of IoT-based smart video surveillance system. In: Behera, H.S., Mohapatra, D.P. (eds.) Computational Intel-ligence in Data Mining. AISC, vol. 556, pp. 771–780. Springer, Singapore (2017). https://doi.org/10.1007/978-981-10-3874-7_73
11. IBM: What is the internet of things, and how does it work? (2020). https://www.ibm.com/blogs/internet-of-things/what-is-the-iot/. Accessed 23 Apr 2021
12. Imperva: What is an insider threat: Malicious insider attack examples: Imperva. https://www.imperva.com/learn/application-security/insider-threats/. Accessed 10 June 2021
13. Imperva: What is a ping flood: ICMP flood: DDoS attack glossary: Imperva (2020). https://www.imperva.com/learn/ddos/ping-icmp-flood/. Accessed 26 Apr 2021
14. Jyothi, S.N., Vardhan, K.V.: Design and implementation of real time security surveillance system using IoT. In: 2016 International Conference on Communi-cation and Electronics Systems (ICCES), pp. 1–5. IEEE (2016)
15. Kenny, S.: What are the cybersecurity issues in video surveillance? https://www.axis.com/blog/secure-insights/what-are-the-cybersecurity-issues-in-video-surveillance/. Accessed 02 June 2021
16. Kim, H., Kim, J., Ko, Y.B.: Developing a cost-effective openflow testbed for small-scale software defined networking. In: 16th International Conference on Advanced Communication Technology, pp. 758–761. IEEE (2014)
17. Lin, T., Kang, J.M., Bannazadeh, H., Leon-Garcia, A.: Enabling SDN applica-tions on software-defined infrastructure. In: 2014 IEEE Network Operations and Management Symposium (NOMS), pp. 1–7. IEEE (2014)
18. McKeown, N., et al.: OpenFlow: enabling innovation in campus networks. ACM SIGCOMM Comput. Commun. Rev. **38**(2), 69–74 (2008)

19. Penfold, A.: IoT is reshaping the future of video surveillance (2022). https://www.azena.com/insights/iot-reshaping-future-surveillance. Accessed 10 June 2021
20. Rametta, C., Baldoni, G., Lombardo, A., Micalizzi, S., Vassallo, A.: S6: a smart, social and SDN-based surveillance system for smart-cities. Proc. Comput. Sci. **110**, 361–368 (2017)
21. RaspberryPi: What is a raspberry pi? https://www.raspberrypi.org/help/what-%20is-a-raspberry-pi/. Accessed 14 Mar 2021
22. Rice, D.: Cyber security and IP cameras: Everyone's concern. https://www.sdmmag.com/articles/94748-cyber-security-ip-cameras-everyones-concern. Accessed 02 June 2021

TLS Goes Low Cost: When TLS Meets Edge

Intae Kim[1]([✉]) [iD], Willy Susilo[1] [iD], Joonsang Baek[1] [iD], Jongkil Kim[2] [iD], and Yang-Wai Chow[1] [iD]

[1] School of Computing and Information Technology, Institute of Cybersecurity and Cryptology, University of Wollongong, Wollongong, NSW 2522, Australia
{intaekim,wsusilo,baek,caseyc}@uow.edu.au
[2] Department of Cyber Security, Ewha Womans University, Seoul 03760, Republic of Korea
Jongkil@ewha.ac.kr

Abstract. Recently, we have witnessed an upward trend in adopting the Transport Layer Security version 1.3 (TLS 1.3) to numerous applications (Google Cloud [25], Microsoft software products [20], CloudFlare [27]). Although TLS 1.3 provides higher efficiency than the previous versions of TLS, its handshake protocol still requires the server to send its certificate to the client which consumes a significant amount of network bandwidth. Moreover, the client becomes idle while it is waiting for the certificate to arrive. This latency is one of the causes of the TLS handshake delay. Adequate adoption of edge computing can increase the efficiency of traditional server client architectures. In this paper, we envision a new paradigm to adopt edge computing into TLS to improve the efficiency of session establishment. Our new architecture will motivate researchers to consider the edge in improving the TLS protocol in the future. TLS-EC (TLS with Edge Computing) protocol improves the TLS 1.3 handshake efficiency by reducing server-side certificate transmission overhead and network latency between server and client through edge computing. We also present the implementation of TLS-EC, which shows a reduction in both the handshake time and the bandwidth consumption between the server and the client during the TLS handshake. In particular, our experiments indicate that bandwidth consumption can be reduced by 33% and 49%, respectively, for ECDSA and RSA-based certificates with 128-bit security level compared to TLS 1.3 full handshake.

Keywords: Edge computing · TLS 1.3 · Latency utilization · Bandwidth reduction · Handshake time reduction

1 Introduction

Edge computing is an emerging technology to provide outsourced computing resources such as data storage and processing power to its users by moving computations and data storage to the edge of a network, located close to the users on behalf of the cloud servers. Therefore, most of the communication which

I. You and T.-Y. Youn (Eds.): WISA 2022, LNCS 13720, pp. 102–113, 2023.
https://doi.org/10.1007/978-3-031-25659-2_8

impacts on service quality for users is made only at the boundary of the network. Thanks to the geographical closeness of the edge nodes, the delay in accessing outsourced resources from the users is reduced significantly. Moreover, the overall network traffic overhead is reduced since data are less likely to travel between users and cloud servers than between users and edge nodes. Consequently, the introduction of edge computing can increase the efficiency of traditional server-client architectures.

TLS 1.3 [22] is the most recent version of Transport Layer Security (TLS) protocol. A growing number of websites, including Google and Facebook, now support TLS 1.3 [16]. One of the most distinguished properties of TLS 1.3 is the fast handshake process. Due to the physical distance between the client and the server, the round trips of handshake messages are the dominant factor causing a delay in establishing a connection between them.

In this paper, we present a new paradigm to introduce edge computing to TLS 1.3. We show that edge computing can take part in the TLS 1.3 protocol to further improve the efficiency of its handshake (the basic full TLS handshake) protocol. In today's networking environment where ultra low delay is required for a better service quality, establishing a secure session (e.g., TLS handshake) even using TLS 1.3 is considered as a significant bottleneck. With this in mind, our goal in this work is to optimize certificate delivery using the edge to cut down the time and network traffic overhead for authenticating the server, while ensuring the same level of security as TLS 1.3. Since certificate messages take a large portion of the entire handshake traffic, they often result in long latency in TLS. Besides, transmitting the certificates imposes large overhead on the server which needs to repeatedly distribute them to numerous clients. Our idea is to separate the handshake in order to process the certificate delivery, in parallel, and assign the edge node as a proxy role that sends certificates to clients on behalf of the server. This is to take advantage of the fact that as the edge node is located very close to the client, a quick response from it is possible. We emphasize that by using existing edges, there is no need to introduce some special edges only to act as a proxy. Our proposed protocol can be viewed as a mode that utilizes the edge added to the TLS 1.3 protocol. This protocol is used instead of the TLS 1.3 full handshake protocol only when the user can get the server's certificate from the edge.

For the case of no edges or using functions and protocols (e.g., 0-RTT [22], certificate revocation [7], OCSP [23], pinning [14], transparency [18], and so on) that are not directly related to the certificate, TLS 1.3 protocol will be used. We observe that, since the certificate and the server information are public, there is no security problem for the edge node to store and disseminate the server's certificates.[1] This approach will make it possible for the client to perform parts

---

[1] Our TLS-EC protocol may not be used if Encrypted Server Name Indication [21] and Encrypted ClientHello are employed to prevent leaking private information about the connection. However, these two works are under discussion, and how they will actually work has yet to be determined. Therefore, we are not going to discuss this issue in this paper. Our work in this paper can serve as a stepping stone to construct a protocol that improves the efficiency of TLS 1.3 by applying edge computing to the standardization when these two works are standardized in the future.

of the TLS handshake processes before receiving a server's response. This way, session negotiation can be completed using less network bandwidth in less time.

2   Related Works

The existing study on TLS 1.3 mainly have focused on analyzing the security and efficiency of TLS 1.3 in various environments. The works appeared in [3,8, 9,11] provided formal security analyses of the draft version of TLS 1.3 before its standardization was completed [22]. In particular, the security analysis based on the automatic cryptographic protocol verifiers was conducted using the symbolic model or the computational model. Note that the symbolic model is mainly verified using ProVerif [5] or Tamarin [12], and the computational model employs CryptoVerif [4].

Moreover, even after its standard was established, it is also used to find the problems occurring when TLS 1.3 is applied to various special environments. The following studies were conducted to supplement the problems that were not covered in TLS 1.3. [6] analyzed the security of key exchange and cryptographic protocols, proposed a breakdown resilience problem, and suggested a solution to the problem. [13] explained the cause of the TLS 1.3 vulnerability, demonstrated an attack on OpenSSL's TLS implementation, and suggested an appropriate method to prevent it.

There have been some approaches to deal with efficiency in TLS. [29] presented an energy-efficient cryptographic acceleration system for HTTPS using OpenSSL. This system increases the efficiency of the TLS protocol by providing energy-efficient encryption through HW/SW co-design. [15] reduced handshake time by allowing sessions to be shared between applications. [19] presented a new protocol. It reduces the handshake time by providing implicit mutual authentication without a certificate by sending a ciphertext using identity-based cryptography (IBC) with ClientHello message. However, this approach introduces additional negotiation of cryptographic system parameters for IBC, which the client and server need to perform.

Some research has been directed to take advantages of edge computing to achieve efficiency improvements in various systems. [10] used edge nodes to increase the efficiency of VANET's message authentication process. [26] improved the efficiency of content delivery networks by using edge computing as a proxy for a domain server. [17] improved the scheme's efficiency by reducing the computing operation that each user has to pay for decryption by employing edge computing. However, to our knowledge, there has been no research focusing on improving the efficiency of TLS 1.3 based on the edge computing paradigm.

3   TLS-EC (TLS with Edge Computing) Protocol

In this section, we describe the details of our protocol, which we call "TLS-EC (TLS with Edge Computing)". TLS-EC utilizes edge nodes to improve the efficiency of the TLS 1.3 handshake protocol while retaining the same security level of the original TLS 1.3 handshake protocol.

3.1   Our Approach

After sending the ClientHello message in TLS 1.3, the client becomes idle until it receives a ServerHello message from the server. Only after the client has received all these messages, it can proceed to the next step of the handshake process.

We argue that leaving the client idle at the beginning of the handshake process reduces the efficiency of the TLS 1.3 handshake as a whole. To improve this, we propose to employ the edge computing environment to introduce some parallelism into the client's sequential executions of the TLS 1.3 handshake protocol. Our idea is to separate the process of transmitting and verifying the server's certificate from the TLS 1.3 handshake protocol and have the edge transfer the server's certificate to the client on behalf of the server.

The rationale for the separation is as follows. Among the messages generated by the server in TLS 1.3, the Certificate message is encrypted with the newly generated session key during the handshake for security, but the certificate itself does not change for long. Besides, the content of the Certificate message depends only on the certificate data and is essentially independent of the server's other messages. On the other hand, the CertificateVerify message is a signature created by hashing the handshake messages using the certificate's private key for the server authentication purpose. That is, the purposes of the CertificateVerify message are 1) to verify that the server owns the private key corresponding to the certificate by allowing the client to verify the signature in the CertificateVerify message using the server's (long-term) public key from the certificate message, and 2) to guarantee integrity for the handshake process up to this point. Thus, since the server's public key and the Certificate Authority (CA)'s signature on it in the Certificate message are independent of anything else, Certificate can be sent to the client *in advance* from the edge, instead of the server. This way, the client can verify the server's certificate while it is waiting to receive messages from the server. Moreover, the server does not need to send the Certificate message directly to the client.

The advantages of our approach are summarized as follows.

- Our approach helps the client and the server reduce the time required to complete a handshake as the client does not have to be idle after it transmits the ClientHello message to the server.
- Since the client does not need to obtain the server's certificate directly from the server, the server can save a little computing power and a significant amount of certificate transmission overhead required to compute the message and transmit the Certificate message from the server to the client. (Note that the size of the Certificate message is the largest among TLS 1.3 handshake messages.) This brings enormous benefits to the server.
- Ours has very little impact on composition and presentation of other handshake messages, so it inherits all the security features provided by TLS 1.3.

3.2   TLS-EC Protocol

Now, we provide the details of the proposed TLS-EC protocol. Before discussing the TLS-EC protocol, we list the main assumptions of the protocol for ease of understanding.

- The TLS-EC protocol only replaces the TLS 1.3 full handshake protocol in which the server sends a certificate.
- The server is authenticated using a certificate created with a valid root certificate from a trusted certification authority.
- The edge is a local router and has all certificates (including intermediate certificates) of servers requested by the client.
- The edge is closer to the client than the server. So client-edge latency is much lower than client-server latency.
- The edge has enough performance to simultaneously handle the TLS-EC protocol to all users who used the edge.
- The client has information about which server the edge can present the certificate of.
- The client has all valid root certificates from the trusted certificate authorities and can use the root certificates to verify the server's certificate.
- All cryptographic primitives used in the protocol are secure.

TLS-EC Handshake Protocol. In TLS-EC, the client requests connections to both the server and the edge. The handshake between the client and the server is similar to that in the original TLS 1.3. The client also performs a handshake with the edge. Ideally, the communication between the client and the edge should be completed before the client receives the ServerHello message from the server. The details of the TLS-EC handshake are illustrated in Fig. 1.

First, the TLS-EC Handshake protocol starts by generating two ClientHelloEC messages, which will be sent to the server and the edge, respectively. The ClientHelloEC messages for the TLS-EC protocol have the **edge** extension compared to the TLS 1.3 protocol. Nevertheless, the other parts remain the same. The client sends these messages to the server and the edge at the same time. Naturally, the ClientHelloEC message arrives first at the edge because it is closer to the client.

When the edge receives the ClientHelloEC message, it identifies the server by using the **server_name** extension in the message and finds the server's certificate. If there is no matched certificate (in its storage), the edge returns an error message to the client. On the other hand, if the edge has the server's certificate, the edge generates EdgeResponse, Certificate, and Finished messages.

The EdgeResponse message has the same format as the ServerHello message in the Client-Server communication. That is, the EdgeResponse message is just a ServerHello message sent by the edge, but we use different names to easily distinguish between them. Certificates and Finished messages are identical to those sent by the server except that they are encrypted using the **edge_handshake_traffic_key**. After this step, the edge will no longer be involved.

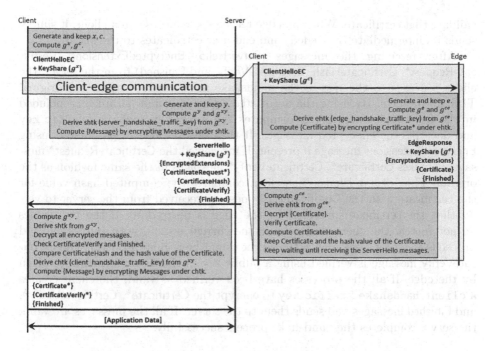

Fig. 1. TLS-EC handshake protocol

If the client does not receive a certificate from the edge (in the case where the edge does not have the server's certificate) or the received certificate is invalid, it informs the situation to the edge, discontinues the current session with the server, and proceeds to a new session with the server using the regular TLS 1.3. If the client receives a valid certificate, it computes the hash value for the certificate and waits for the ServerHello message. Note that it is highly likely that the client receives the certificate before the ServerHello message comes because the client-to-server latency is much longer than the client-to-edge latency due to the fact that the edge is located closer to the client.

The server receiving the ClientHelloEC message proceeds to the handshake in the same as the original TLS 1.3 with the following exceptions: The server sends the (pre-computed) hash value for the certificate, CertificateHash message, instead of the Certificate message. The CertificateVerify message now contains a signature on all the messages and CertificateHash message. By doing this, the client can verify that the edge has sent the latest certificate.

In the whole TLS-EC protocol, there is no part where the edge can be involved in generating the server_handshake_traffic_key used to encrypt messages coming after the ServerHello message from the server. Note that the edge does not need to be concerned about the server's response to the ClientHelloEC message sent by the client to the server. The edge receives a certificate from the server in advance and also receives the intermediate certificates needed to validate that certificate. When an edge receives a request from a client, it simply sends its intermediate (if needed) and end-user certificates to the client.

After receiving the messages (ServerHello, EncryptedExtensions, CertificateRequest*, CertificateHash, CertificateVerify, and Finished) from the server, the client proceeds to the rest of the handshake in the same way as the original TLS 1.3 protocol. By using the negotiated cipher suit and parameters included in the ServerHello message, it computes the server_handshake_traffic_key and decrypts the encrypted messages. It then sets the rest of parameters using EncryptedExtensions message if present. If it received the CertificateRequest* message, it makes Certificate*, CertificateVerify* messages in the same fashion as the original TLS 1.3 handshake. The client compares the computed hash value for the certificate with the CertificateHash message received from the server to verify that the certificate provided by the edge is up-to-date. If the two values do not match, the client discontinues the current session with the server, and proceeds to a new session with the server using the regular TLS 1.3. The CertificateVerify message is verified using a public key in the server's certificate given by the edge. If all the processes have been verified as valid, the client creates a client_handshake_traffic_key to encrypt the Certificate*, CertificateVerify*, and Finished messages and sends them to the server. If all the messages are valid, the server completes the handshake process successfully.

4   Security Evaluation

In this section, we evaluate the security of TLS-EC by symbolic verification using ProVerif [5]. ProVerif is one of the most popular formal cryptographic protocol verifiers and provides a formal specification language to construct a verification model of the protocol along with an automatic execution environment.

We show that TLS-EC achieves the same level of security as the TLS 1.3 protocol by verifying the security of Client-Edge Communication and Client-Server Communication. There are a total of 5 secret keys generated by TLS-EC: edge_handshake_traffic_key, server_handshake_traffic_key, client_handshake_traffic_key, server_application_traffic_key, and client_application_traffic_key. We should consider whether these keys do not leak out. To formally verify this, we define the following queries to see whether an attacker can access the keys created during this process:

- attacker (edge_handshake_traffic_key)
- attacker (server_handshake_traffic_key)
- attacker (client_handshake_traffic_key)
- attacker (server_application_traffic_key)
- attacker (client_application_traffic_key)

where the "attacker (KEY)" means a query that attackers try to make KEY. The secret key used in the Client-Edge communication is edge_handshake_traffic_key shared between the client and the edge. In the Client-Server communication, four secret keys are established as a result of the communication process. Two handshake keys, server_handshake_traffic_key and client_handshake_traffic_key, are established to deliver handshake message securely. The other two keys, server_application_traffic_key and client_application_traffic_key, are set for the secure application data transmission. These keys are only shared between these two parties (e.g., client and edge or client and server) and does not leak to any others. Additionally, to verify whether the Client-Edge Communication and Client-Server Communication protocols are working properly, we define the four events: MatchingChannel-BindingE, MatchingChannelBinding, MatchingHTKeyE, and MatchingAEKey.

The MatchingChannelBindingE and MatchingChannelBinding events occur when the endpoints of each connection in the channel between the client and the edge and between the client and the server are properly matched, respectively. Similarly, the MatchingHTKeyE and MatchingAEKey events occur when the keys used in each connection in the channel between the client and the edge and between the client and the server are properly matched, respectively.

As a result of performing formal verification of all queries and events mentioned above, we are able to verify that the Client-Edge and Client-Server communications are working correctly and that an attacker (an entity that does not join each communication) cannot access any secret keys.

Although the Client-Edge and the Client-Server communications proceed at the same time and to the same client, the security parameters established in each communication are created independently. Therefore, the verification result of the Client-Server communication means that the edge can be considered as one of the attackers who want to get the key because it does not participate in the Client-Server communication protocol. The result of the four queries which simulate Client-Server communication shows their keys do not leak out to any outsider include the edge. Therefore, it is verified that the Client-Server communication is secure against the attackers including the untrusted edge. In addition, we are also able to confirm that the both communications are working properly as all channels and keys in the communications are properly matched.

5 Performance Evaluation

In this section, we present performance evaluation results of TLS-EC and compare them with TLS 1.3 in terms of the handshake time and the network bandwidth. Here, we define the handshake time is the time from when the client sends the ClientHelloEC message to the server until it sends the Finished message. And we also define the network bandwidth is the size of data transmitted by the server to the client. It is for measuring the change in data that the server must transmit. We exclude the amount of data the server receives as it is comparable for both TLS 1.3 and TLS-EC. For the size of data transmitted and received by client, refer to Sect. 5.1.

Implementation Setting. We implemented TLS-EC using Boringssl [2]. In our implementation, the client was deployed on a Raspberry Pi 3 Model B+ with Ubuntu Mate Linux OS. The server is deployed on the n1-standard-1 machine of Google Cloud Platform with Ubuntu-1804-Bionic installed. The edge was deployed on a desktop computer with Intel i7-8700 CPU, 16GB DDR4, and Ubuntu on Windows 10.

Network Settings. The client is connected to the edge with a wireless network. The edge and the server are connected through a wired network over the Internet. We assume that the client communicates with the server only through the edge as the edge acts as a router to the client, which also provides certificates for TLS-EC protocol.

For our analysis, we chose two types of certificates with 128-bit security level that are recommended by NIST [1]. We named the certificates based on the signature algorithm they use: ECDSA 256 is the ECDSA based certificate generated using the 256-bit elliptic curve (secp256r1) public key and sha256ECDSA signature algorithm. RSA 3072 is the RSA based certificate generated using 3072 bits of RSA public key. In addition, it is using sha256RSA signature algorithm. The ECDSA based algorithm has the advantage of guaranteeing the same level of security with a shorter key than the RSA based algorithm, but has the disadvantage of requiring higher computational overhead [28]. In our experiment, it is assumed that the depth of the certificate chains is 2, and the root certificate is already imported to the client. Therefore, it only needs to verify the server's certificate during TLS-EC handshake.

For each certificate used to authenticate a server in TLS 1.3 and TLS-EC, we measured the bandwidth and handshake time of the client's 1,000 connections with the server and took the average taken by excluding 5% from the top and bottom tails of them.

We compared the network bandwidth consumption and handshake time of TLS-EC with that of TLS 1.3 in regards to the use of the RSA and ECDSA based certificates.

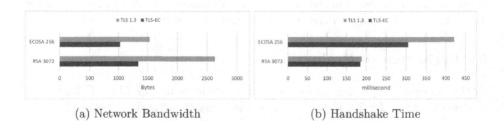

(a) Network Bandwidth   (b) Handshake Time

Fig. 2. Results with 128-bit security level certificates

In terms of network bandwidth consumption, when using TLS-EC, ECDSA 256 and RSA 3072 consume approximately 33% and 49% less bandwidth, respectively. Therefore, regardless of what type of certificate is used, TLS-EC turns out to provide higher bandwidth efficiency. This result is summarized in Fig. 2a.

In terms of handshake time, TLS-EC is about 19% faster when RSA 3072 is used, and about 47% faster when ECDSA 256 is used, compared with TLS

1.3. Even if the difference between TLS 1.3 and TLS-EC with ECDSA 256 is greater than those with RSA 3072, due to the underlying algorithmic performance, handshake with RSA 3072 is completed earlier than that with ECDSA 256. This result is summarized in Fig. 2b.

To conclude, compared with TLS 1.3, TLS-EC can achieve high efficiency in terms of both network bandwidth and handshake time.

5.1   Discussion

We envision that our TLS-EC can be more and more beneficial as we demand higher levels of security in the future. In particular, in the environment used post-quantum, secure algorithms may require a longer signature with more computational overhead [24]. TLS-EC can be future-proof in that it will provide efficiency for TLS in such the environment too.

Overhead on the Internal Network. For the convenience of exposition, we define the network by separating it into two parts, internal (local) network and external network. The internal network is a network between the client and the edge. The external network is a network between the edge and the cloud server and includes all networks except the internal networks.

Although TLS-EC shows better overall performance than TLS 1.3 in terms of external network bandwidth and handshake time, slight inefficiencies are caused by the communication between the client and the edge in the internal network. This is because the client additionally sends the ClientHelloEC message to the edge, and receives EdgeResponse and Finished messages from the edge. We measured that this additional communication at the internal network incurs about 1 KB more data exchange compared with the TLS 1.3 handshake protocol.

However, we argue that the additional data transfer will not have a significant impact on the external network and the internal network: There are not many clients on the internal network and one client will not run a handshake with many servers in a short time. Even if it happens, the congestion will happen only in the internal network where the client connected, which does not affect the other internal networks and external network.

6   Conclusion

In this paper, we proposed TLS-EC, a new TLS protocol that improves the efficiency of TLS 1.3 through the edge computing paradigm. TLS-EC achieves shorter latency than TLS 1.3 because the client can complete computationally intensive tasks while waiting for the server's initial response. Moreover, traffic incurred by TLS handshake between the edge and the server is reduced significantly as most certificate messages are exchanged only between the client and the edge, which are almost directly connected to each other. Furthermore, TLS-EC reduces workloads imposed on the server as the server no longer needs to transmit its certificate to every client. We showed that TLS-EC guarantees the same level of security as TLS 1.3 even with an untrusted edge by formal verification using ProVerif. We also thoroughly implemented TLS-EC using the Boringssl library. Our performance analysis showed that TLS-EC is indeed more efficient than TLS 1.3 in terms of both bandwidth consumption and handshake time. Thus, TLS-EC can be adopted easily for real-world applications. We anticipate that security and practicality of TLS-EC will broaden the horizon of edge computing for secure applications.

References

1. Barker, E.: Nist special publication 800-57 part 1, revision 5. NIST, Technical report (2020). https://doi.org/10.6028/NIST.SP.800-57pt1r5, https://csrc.nist.gov/publications/detail/sp/800-57-part-1/rev-5/final
2. Benjamin, D.: Boringssl (2016). https://boringssl.googlesource.com/boringssl/
3. Bhargavan, K., Blanchet, B., Kobeissi, N.: Verified models and reference implementations for the TLS 1.3 standard candidate. In: 2017 IEEE Symposium on Security and Privacy (SP), pp. 483–502. IEEE (2017). https://doi.org/10.1109/SP.2017.26
4. Blanchet, B.: Composition theorems for CryptoVerif and application to TLS 1.3. In: 2018 IEEE 31st Computer Security Foundations Symposium (CSF), pp. 16–30. IEEE (2018). https://doi.org/10.1109/CSF.2018.00009
5. Blanchet, B., Smyth, B., Cheval, V., Sylvestre, M.: ProVerif 2.00: automatic cryptographic protocol verifier, user manual and tutorial (2018), originally appeared as Bruno Blanchet and Ben Smyth (2011) ProVerif 1.85: Automatic Cryptographic Protocol Verifier, User Manual and Tutorial
6. Brendel, J., Fischlin, M., Günther, F.: Breakdown resilience of key exchange protocols: NewHope, TLS 1.3, and hybrids. In: Sako, K., Schneider, S., Ryan, P.Y.A. (eds.) ESORICS 2019. LNCS, vol. 11736, pp. 521–541. Springer, Cham (2019). https://doi.org/10.1007/978-3-030-29962-0_25
7. Cooper, D., Santesson, S., Farrell, S., Boeyen, S., Housley, R., Polk, W.: RFC 5280: internet x. 509 public key infrastructure certificate and certificate revocation list (CRL) profile. Internet Engineering Task Force (IETF) (2008)
8. Cremers, C., Horvat, M., Hoyland, J., Scott, S., van der Merwe, T.: A comprehensive symbolic analysis of TLS 1.3. In: Proceedings of the 2017 ACM SIGSAC Conference on Computer and Communications Security, pp. 1773–1788 (2017). https://doi.org/10.1145/3133956.3134063
9. Cremers, C., Horvat, M., Scott, S., van der Merwe, T.: Automated analysis and verification of TLS 1.3: 0-RTT, resumption and delayed authentication. In: 2016 IEEE Symposium on Security and Privacy (SP), pp. 470–485. IEEE (2016). https://doi.org/10.1109/SP.2016.35
10. Cui, J., Wei, L., Zhang, J., Xu, Y., Zhong, H.: An efficient message-authentication scheme based on edge computing for vehicular ad hoc networks. IEEE Trans. Intell. Transp. Syst. **20**(5), 1621–1632 (2018). https://doi.org/10.1109/TITS.2018.2827460
11. Dowling, B., Fischlin, M., Günther, F., Stebila, D.: A cryptographic analysis of the TLS 1.3 handshake protocol candidates. In: Proceedings of the 22nd ACM SIGSAC conference on computer and communications security, pp. 1197–1210 (2015). https://doi.org/10.1145/2810103.2813653
12. Dreier, J., Hirschi, L., Radomirovic, S., Sasse, R.: Automated unbounded verification of stateful cryptographic protocols with exclusive or. In: 2018 IEEE 31st Computer Security Foundations Symposium (CSF), pp. 359–373. IEEE (2018). https://doi.org/10.1109/CSF.2018.00033

13. Drucker, N., Gueron, S.: Selfie: reflections on TLS 1.3 with PSK. J. Cryptol. **34**(3), 1–18 (2021). https://doi.org/10.1007/s00145-021-09387-y
14. Evans, C., Palmer, C., Sleevi, R.: RFC 7469: public key pinning extension for http. Internet Engineering Task Force (IETF) (2015)
15. Hiller, J., Henze, M., Zimmermann, T., Hohlfeld, O., Wehrle, K.: The case for session sharing: relieving clients from TLS handshake overheads. In: 2019 IEEE 44th LCN Symposium on Emerging Topics in Networking (LCN Symposium), pp. 83–91. IEEE (2019). https://doi.org/10.1109/LCNSymposium47956.2019.9000667
16. Holz, R., et al.: Tracking the deployment of TLS 1.3 on the web: a story of experimentation and centralization. ACM SIGCOMM Comput. Commun. Rev. **50**(3), 3–15 (2020). https://doi.org/10.1145/3411740.3411742
17. Kim, J., Camtepe, S., Susilo, W., Nepal, S., Baek, J.: Identity-based broadcast encryption with outsourced partial decryption for hybrid security models in edge computing. In: Proceedings of the 2019 ACM Asia Conference on Computer and Communications Security, pp. 55–66 (2019). https://doi.org/10.1145/3321705.3329825
18. Laurie, B., Langley, A., Kasper, E.: RFC 6962: certificate transparency. Internet Engineering Task Force (IETF) (2013)
19. Li, P., Su, J., Wang, X.: iTLS: lightweight transport-layer security protocol for IoT with minimal latency and perfect forward secrecy. IEEE Internet Things J. **7**(8), 6828–6841 (2020). https://doi.org/10.1109/JIOT.2020.2988126
20. Mackie, K.: Microsoft updates its TLS 1.3 support plans in windows, office 365 and.net (2020). https://redmondmag.com/articles/2020/08/20/microsoft-tls-1-3-support-plans.aspx
21. Rescorla, E., Oku, K., Sullivan, N., Wood, C.A.: Encrypted server name indication for TLS 1.3. IETF draft (2019). https://tools.ietf.org/html/draft-ietf-tls-esni-02. Accessed 14 Dec 2018
22. Rescorla, E., et al.: RFC 8446: the transport layer security (TLS) protocol version 1.3. Internet Engineering Task Force (IETF) (2018)
23. Santessona, S., Myers, M., Ankney, R., Malpani, A., Galperin, S., Adams, C.: RFC 6960: X. 509 internet public key infrastructure online certificate status protocol-OCSP. Internet Engineering Task Force (IETF) (2013)
24. Sikeridis, D., Kampanakis, P., Devetsikiotis, M.: Post-quantum authentication in TLS 1.3: a performance study. In: Network and Distributed Systems Security (NDSS) Symposium (2020). https://doi.org/10.14722/ndss.2020.24203
25. Silverlock, M., Redner, G.: Bringing modern transport security to google cloud with TLS 1.3 (2020). https://cloud.google.com/blog/products/networking/tls-1-3-is-now-on-by-default-for-google-cloud-services
26. Stebila, D., Sullivan, N.: An analysis of TLS handshake proxying. In: 2015 IEEE Trustcom/BigDataSE/ISPA, vol. 1, pp. 279–286. IEEE (2015). https://doi.org/10.1109/Trustcom.2015.385
27. Sullivan, N.: Introducing TLS 1.3 (2016). https://blog.cloudflare.com/introducing-tls-1-3
28. Toradmalle, D., Singh, R., Shastri, H., Naik, N., Panchidi, V.: Prominence of ECDSA over RSA digital signature algorithm. In: 2018 2nd International Conference on I-SMAC (IoT in Social, Mobile, Analytics and Cloud)(I-SMAC) I-SMAC (IoT in Social, Mobile, Analytics and Cloud)(I-SMAC), pp. 253–257. IEEE (2018). https://doi.org/10.1109/I-SMAC.2018.8653689
29. Xiao, C., Zhang, L., Liu, W., Bergmann, N., Xie, Y.: Energy-efficient crypto acceleration with HW/SW co-design for HTTPS. Futur. Gener. Comput. Syst. **96**, 336–347 (2019). https://doi.org/10.1016/j.future.2019.02.023

5G-AKA, Revisited

SeongHan Shin[✉]

National Institute of Advanced Industrial Science and Technology (AIST),
2-3-26, Aomi, Koto-ku, Tokyo 135-0064, Japan
seonghan.shin@aist.go.jp

Abstract. The 5G primary Authentication and Key Agreement (5G-AKA) protocol has received much attention in the literature. However, most of the 5G-AKA and relevant AKA protocols do not guarantee forward secrecy. In this paper, we propose a secure AKA (for short, AKA⋆) protocol that provides UE (User Equipment) anonymity and forward secrecy for 5G and beyond networks. Also, we formally prove the security of the AKA⋆ protocol in the random oracle model under the CDH (Computational Diffie-Hellman) problem. Moreover, we discuss several aspects of the AKA⋆ protocol, and compare the AKA⋆ and relevant protocols (EAP-AKA, EAP-AKA', EAP-AKA' FS, 5G-AKA and 5G-AKA') in terms of efficiency, forward secrecy, UE anonymity and UE unlinkability.

Keywords: 5G security · 5G-AKA · UE anonymity · Forward secrecy

1 Introduction

Currently, the fifth generation (5G) mobile network and telecommunication standard [1,2] has been developed to meet the needs of enhanced mobile broadband, massive machine-type communications, and ultra-reliable and low-latency communications. Among several building blocks in this standard [1], the 5G primary Authentication and Key Agreement (5G-AKA) protocol [5], designed and mandated by 3GPP (3rd Generation Partnership Project) consortium, is of utmost importance for 5G security. The 5G-AKA protocol is a new version of the AKA variants used for 3G and 4G networks. In the 5G-AKA protocol, a UE (User Equipment) and an HN (Home Network) can authenticate each other and establish key materials (i.e., anchor keys) for protecting subsequent 5G communications. A distinctive feature of the 5G-AKA protocol is that it provides enhanced mobile users' privacy where a SUPI (Subscriber Permanent Identifier) of UE is sent to HN in the form of ciphertext by using ECIES (Elliptic Curve Integrated Encryption Scheme) KEM (Key Encapsulation Mechanism) [27,37–39] with HN's public key.

There are many works on the 5G-AKA protocol in the literature. In [7], D. Basin et al. provided a comprehensive formal model of the 5G-AKA protocol and evaluated the model with respect to the 5G security goals using the security protocol verification tool Tamarin [4,32,36]. Then, they found that some critical security goals for the 5G-AKE protocol are not met. In [11], R. Borgaonkar et al. showed a new privacy attack on subscriber privacy against all the AKA variants (including 5G-AKA) by exploiting a

© Springer Nature Switzerland AG 2023
I. You and T.-Y. Youn (Eds.): WISA 2022, LNCS 13720, pp. 114–127, 2023.
https://doi.org/10.1007/978-3-031-25659-2_9

logical vulnerability in the protection mechanism of SQN (Sequence Number). Also, A. Koutsos [28] showed that all the known privacy attacks (except the IMSI (International Mobile Subscriber Identity)-catcher attack) are possible in the 5G-AKA protocol, and then proposed a modified 5G-AKA protocol that satisfies the unlinkability property and is proven in the Bana-Comon logic model [6]. After describing that the 5G-AKA protocol is still vulnerable to a series of active linkability attacks, Y. Wang et al. [42] proposed a privacy-preserving 5G-AKA (called, 5G-AKA') that is secure against active linkability attacks by encrypting a random challenge of HN with an ECIES-KEM key and is compatible with the SIM cards and SNs (Serving Networks). By using Tamarin [4,32,36], they also proved that the 5G-AKA' protocol achieves privacy, authentication, and secrecy. Very recently, IETF EMU WG initiated work on an EAP-AKA' FS protocol [14] that provides the EAP-AKA' protocol [26] with forward secrecy. Basically, the EAP-AKA' FS protocol is a simple combination of the EAP-AKA' [26] and Diffie-Hellman key exchange [13] protocols.

1.1 Motivation and Our Contributions

Affected by Snowden's disclosures of pervasive surveillance [21–23,31,35], TLS 1.3 [25] is designed to provide forward secrecy where a client and a server first execute the Diffie-Hellman key exchange protocol [13], and all the subsequent messages are encrypted with a Diffie-Hellman key in the handshake protocol. This prevents an attacker who obtained long-term secrets from decrypting any past communications. However, most of the 5G-AKA and relevant AKA protocols do not guarantee forward secrecy.

In this paper, we propose a secure AKA (for short, AKA*) protocol that provides UE anonymity and forward secrecy for 5G and beyond networks [3]. This protocol keeps up with the 5G-AKA protocol structure where the first message is for sending a SUCI (Subscriber Concealed Identifier), and the second and third exchanged messages are a challenge/response type of authentication. The main idea of the AKA* protocol is 1) to send a randomized identifier for UE anonymity and 2) to employ the DCR signature scheme in Sect. 2.3 for a challenge/response type of authentication and forward secrecy. Also, we formally prove the security of the AKA* protocol in the random oracle model [10] under the CDH (Computational Diffie-Hellman) problem. Moreover, we discuss several aspects of the AKA* protocol, and compare the AKA* and relevant protocols (EAP-AKA [17], EAP-AKA' [26], EAP-AKA' FS [14], 5G-AKA [5] and 5G-AKA' [42]) in terms of efficiency, forward secrecy, UE anonymity and UE unlinkability.

2 Preliminaries

2.1 Notation

Let $k \in \mathbb{N}$ be the security parameter. Let $\{0,1\}^*$ be the set of finite binary strings and $\{0,1\}^k$ be the set of binary strings of length k. Let $A\|B$ be the concatenation of A and B. If U is a set, then $u \xleftarrow{\$} U$ indicates the process of selecting u at random and uniformly over U. If U is a function (whatever it is), then $u = U$ indicates the process of assigning the result to u. Let N be the identity of HN.

Also, let $\lambda \in \mathbb{N}$ be the security parameter. Let $\mathcal{G}$ be the group generation algorithm that takes as input 1^λ and outputs a group description $(\mathbb{G}, q, g)$ where $\mathbb{G}$ is a finite cyclic group of prime order q with g as a generator and its operation is denoted multiplicatively. In the aftermath, all the subsequent arithmetic operations are performed in modulo p unless otherwise stated where p is a prime, $s \ (\geq 2)$ is a positive integer and $p = sq + 1$. Also, $H_1, H_2 : \{0,1\}^* \to \mathbb{Z}_q^*$ and $H_3, H_4, H_5 : \{0,1\}^* \to \{0,1\}^k$ are descriptions of cryptographic hash functions (e.g., SHA-3 [34]).

2.2 Computational Assumption

Here, we define the CDH (Computational Diffie-Hellman) problem.

Definition 1 (CDH Problem). *Let $\mathcal{G}$ be the group generation algorithm described above. A (t, ε)-CDH$_\mathbb{G}$ adversary is a probabilistic polynomial time (PPT) machine $\mathcal{B}$, running in time t, such that its success probability $\mathsf{Succ}_\mathbb{G}^{cdh}(\mathcal{B})$, given random elements g^α and g^β to output $g^{\alpha\beta}$, is greater than ε. We denote by $\mathsf{Succ}_\mathbb{G}^{cdh}(t)$ the maximal success probability over every adversaries, running within time t. The CDH problem states that $\mathsf{Succ}_\mathbb{G}^{cdh}(t) \leq \varepsilon$ for any t/ε not too large.*

2.3 Exponential Challenge-Response Signature Schemes

In this subsection, we describe the Exponential Challenge-Response (XCR) and Dual XCR (DCR) signature schemes [29] where a valid signature is not only message-specific but also challenge-specific.

XCR Signature Scheme. A signer $\hat{A}$ has a private key $a \xleftarrow{\$} \mathbb{Z}_q^*$ and a public key $A \equiv g^a$. A verifier (or challenger) $\hat{B}$ provides a message m together with a challenge Y where $\hat{B}$ chooses a random element $y \xleftarrow{\$} \mathbb{Z}_q^*$ and computes $Y \equiv g^y$. A signature of $\hat{A}$ on message m using challenge Y is defined as a pair $(X, Y^{x+H_1(X,m)\cdot a})$ where $\hat{A}$ chooses a random element $x \xleftarrow{\$} \mathbb{Z}_q^*$ and computes $X \equiv g^x$. The verifier $\hat{B}$ accepts a signature pair (X, σ) as valid (for message m and with respect to challenge $Y \equiv g^y$) if and only if both $X \neq 0$ and $(X \cdot A^{H_1(X,m)})^y = \sigma$ hold. Hereafter, we denote by $XSIG_{\hat{A}}(X, m, Y) \overset{\text{def}}{=} Y^{x+H_1(X,m)\cdot a}$ the second element of an XCR signature pair. In [29], the XCR signature scheme is proven to be EUF-CMA secure (see below) in the random oracle model [10] under the CDH problem of Definition 1.

Definition 2 (Security of XCR). *An XCR signature scheme XCR is said to be secure against existential forgery on adaptively chosen message attacks (EUF-CMA secure) if, for any probabilistic polynomial time adversary $\mathcal{F}$, there exists a negligible function $\varepsilon(\cdot)$ in the security parameter λ such that $\Pr[\mathsf{Exp}_{XCR}^{euf\text{-}cma}(\mathcal{F}) = 1] \leq \varepsilon(\cdot)$ in the experiment $\mathsf{Exp}_{XCR}^{euf\text{-}cma}(\mathcal{F})$ defined as below:*

1. $\mathcal{G}(1^\lambda)$ outputs $(\mathbb{G}, q, g)$.
2. Adversary $\mathcal{F}$ is given two random values A, Y_0 where $A, Y_0 \in \mathbb{G}$.

3. *During this experiment, $\mathcal{F}$ has access to a signing oracle O_{Sign} (representing a signer $\hat{A}$ with the private key a and public key A) which takes as input a challenge Y and a message m, and returns a signature pair $(X, XSIG_{\hat{A}}(X, m, Y))$ where O_{Sign} chooses a random element $x \xleftarrow{\$} \mathbb{Z}_q^*$ and computes $X \equiv g^x$ afresh with each query. $\mathcal{F}$ is allowed a polynomial number of queries to O_{Sign} where the queries (Y, m) are chosen adaptively by $\mathcal{F}$.*
4. *Adversary $\mathcal{F}$ outputs a triple (X_0, m_0, σ).*

The output of the experiment is defined to be 1 if the following two conditions hold: (a) The pair (X_0, σ) is a valid XCR signature of $\hat{A}$ on message m_0 with respect to challenge Y_0 (i.e., $X_0 \neq 0$ and $\sigma = XSIG_{\hat{A}}(X_0, m_0, Y_0)$); and (b) The pair (X_0, m_0) did not appear in any of the responses of O_{Sign} to $\mathcal{F}$'s queries. Otherwise, the output of the experiment is 0. We denote by $\mathsf{Adv}_{XCR}^{\text{euf-cma}}(\mathcal{F}) = \Pr[\mathsf{Exp}_{XCR}^{\text{euf-cma}}(\mathcal{F}) = 1]$ the adversary's advantage in attacking the XCR signature scheme XCR.

DCR Signature Scheme. In the DCR signature scheme, any two parties $\hat{A}$ and $\hat{B}$ can interact with each other with the dual role of challenger and signer, and each produces a signature that no third party can forge. A party $\hat{A}$ (resp., $\hat{B}$) has a private key $a \xleftarrow{\$} \mathbb{Z}_q^*$ (resp., $b \xleftarrow{\$} \mathbb{Z}_q^*$) and a public key $A \equiv g^a$ (resp., $B \equiv g^b$). Let m_1, m_2 be two messages. A DCR signature of $\hat{A}$ and $\hat{B}$ on messages m_1, m_2 is defined as a triple of values: X, Y and $DSIG_{\hat{A}, \hat{B}}(m_1, m_2, X, Y) \stackrel{\text{def}}{=} g^{(x+d \cdot a)(y+e \cdot b)}$ where $X \equiv g^x$ and $Y \equiv g^y$ are challenges chosen by $\hat{A}$ and $\hat{B}$, respectively, and $d = H_1(X, m_1)$ and $e = H_2(Y, m_2)$. A fundamental property of the DCR signature is that, after exchanging the values X and Y (with x and y randomly chosen by $\hat{A}$ and $\hat{B}$, respectively), both $\hat{A}$ and $\hat{B}$ can compute and verify the same signature $DSIG_{\hat{A}, \hat{B}}(m_1, m_2, X, Y)$ as follows:

$$DSIG_{\hat{A}, \hat{B}}(m_1, m_2, X, Y) = g^{(x+d \cdot a)(y+e \cdot b)} = (Y \cdot B^e)^{x+d \cdot a} = (X \cdot A^d)^{y+e \cdot b}. \quad (1)$$

Intuitively, a DCR signature is an XCR signature of $\hat{A}$ on message m_1 under challenge $Y \cdot B^e$ and, at the same time, an XCR signature of $\hat{B}$ on message m_2 under challenge $X \cdot A^d$. In [29], the DCR signature scheme (i.e., the DCR signature of $\hat{A}$ with respect to B) is proven to be EUF-CMA secure in the random oracle model [10] under the CDH problem of Definition 1.[1] For the security of DCR, Definition 2 should be modified with the followings: (1) In step 3, the queries to O_{Sign} are of the form (Y, m, m_2) and the signature by O_{Sign} is the pair $(X, XSIG_{\hat{A}}(X, m, Y \cdot B^e))$ where $e = H_2(Y, m_2)$; and (2) In step 4, $\mathcal{F}$ outputs a quadruple (X_0, m_0, m_2, σ) where m_2 is an arbitrary message chosen by $\mathcal{F}$. Accordingly, the output of the experiment is defined to be 1 if (a) $X_0 \neq 0$ and $\sigma = XSIG_{\hat{A}}(X_0, m_0, Y_0 \cdot B^e)$; and (b) The pair (X_0, m_0) did not appear in any of the responses of O_{Sign} to $\mathcal{F}$'s queries. We denote by $\mathsf{Adv}_{DCR}^{\text{euf-cma}}(\mathcal{F}) = \Pr[\mathsf{Exp}_{DCR}^{\text{euf-cma}}(\mathcal{F}) = 1]$ the adversary's advantage in attacking the DCR signature scheme DCR.

---

[1] Actually, the proof in [29] shows that it is EUF-CMA secure even if adversary $\mathcal{F}$ is given the private key b of $\hat{B}$ (but not the private key of $\hat{A}$). For more details, please refer to [29].

```
Public parameters: G, q, g, H₁, H₂, H₃, H₄, H₅

UE (SUPI)                                                    HN (N)
Initialization

U ←$ {0,1}ᵏ
a ←$ Z*_q, A ≡ gᵃ          (U, A, SUPI)
                        ──────────────────→
                            (N, B)            b ←$ Z*_q, B ≡ gᵇ
                        ←──────────────────
Store (SUPI, U, (a, A ≡ gᵃ), N, B)          Store (N, (b, B ≡ gᵇ), U, A, SUPI)
```

Fig. 1. **Initialization** phase where A and B are raw public keys of UE and HN, respectively

3   A Secure AKA Protocol for 5G and Beyond Networks

In this section, we propose a secure AKA (for short, AKA*) protocol that provides UE anonymity and forward secrecy for 5G and beyond networks [3]. This protocol keeps up with the 5G-AKA protocol structure where the first message from UE to HN is for sending a SUCI or GUTI (Globally Unique Temporary Identity) of UE, and the second and third exchanged messages are a challenge/response type of authentication between UE and HN. The main idea of the AKA* protocol is 1) to send a randomized temporary identifier (to be computed with a DCR signature) for UE anonymity and 2) to employ the DCR signature scheme in Sect. 2.3 for a challenge/response type of authentication and forward secrecy. In the AKA* protocol, we do not assume PKI (Public Key Infrastructure), meaning that raw public keys of UE and HN do not need to be checked (e.g., via CRL (Certificate Revocation List) [18] or OCSP (Online Certificate Status Protocol) [20]). The AKA* protocol consists of **Initialization** and **Authentication and Key Agreement** phases.

3.1   Initialization

First, UE randomly chooses his/her temporary identifier U from $\{0,1\}^k$. Also, UE chooses a private key $a \xleftarrow{\$} \mathbb{Z}_q^\star$ and computes a public key $A \equiv g^a$. Then, UE sends (U, A) to HN along with SUPI. After receiving (U, A, SUPI) from UE, HN chooses its private key $b \xleftarrow{\$} \mathbb{Z}_q^\star$ and computes a public key $B \equiv g^b$, and then sends (N, B) to UE where N is HN's identifier. Finally, UE stores $(\text{SUPI}, U, (a, A \equiv g^a), N, B)$ secretly and HN holds $(N, (b, B \equiv g^b), U, A, \text{SUPI})$ secretly. Note that A and B are raw public keys of UE and HN, respectively. This initialization phase (see Fig. 1) should be done once and securely between UE and HN.

3.2   Authentication and Key Agreement

In this phase, UE and HN execute the AKA* protocol, whenever needed, over insecure networks in order to share an authenticated session key to be used for protecting sub-

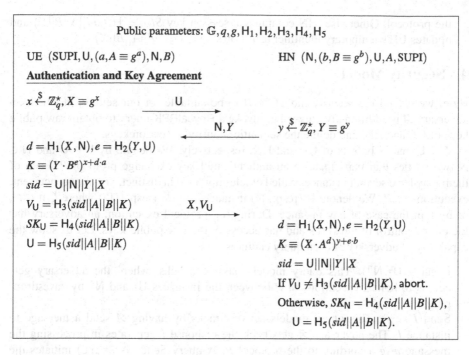

Fig. 2. A secure AKA (for short, AKA*) protocol for 5G and beyond networks where A and B are raw public keys of UE and HN, respectively

sequent communications. This phase of the AKA* protocol has four steps as below (see also Fig. 2).

Step 1. The UE chooses a random element $x \overset{\$}{\leftarrow} \mathbb{Z}_q^{\star}$ and computes a Diffie-Hellman public value $X \equiv g^x$. Then, UE sends his/her temporary identifier U to HN.

Step 2. The HN chooses a random element $y \overset{\$}{\leftarrow} \mathbb{Z}_q^{\star}$ and computes a Diffie-Hellman public value $Y \equiv g^y$. After receiving a message U from UE, HN sends back its identifier N and Diffie-Hellman public value Y to UE.

Step 3. After receiving a message (N, Y) from HN, UE computes $d = H_1(X, N)$ and $e = H_2(Y, U)$. Using his/her private key a, UE computes a DCR signature $K \equiv (Y \cdot B^e)^{x+d \cdot a}$ (i.e., an XCR signature $XSIG_{UE}(X, N, Y \cdot B^e)$ on message N under challenge $Y \cdot B^e$). With a session identifier $sid = U||N||Y||X$, UE computes his/her authenticator $V_U = H_3(sid||A||B||K)$, and then sends (X, V_U) to HN. Also, UE computes a session key $SK_U = H_4(sid||A||B||K)$ and updates his/her temporary identifier as follows: $U = H_5(sid||A||B||K)$.

Step 4. After receiving a message (X, V_U) from UE, HN computes $d = H_1(X, N)$ and $e = H_2(Y, U)$. Using its private key b, HN computes a DCR signature $K \equiv (X \cdot A^d)^{y+e \cdot b}$ (i.e., an XCR signature $XSIG_{HN}(Y, U, X \cdot A^d)$ on message U under challenge $X \cdot A^d$). Then, HN checks whether the authenticator V_U is valid or not. If $V_U \neq H_3(sid||A||B||K)$ where a session identifier $sid = U||N||Y||X$, HN aborts the protocol. Otherwise, HN computes a session key $SK_N = H_4(sid||A||B||K)$ and updates UE's temporary identifier as follows: $U = H_5(sid||A||B||K)$.

4   Security Model

Here, we extend the security model [8,9] to be suitable for our setting, in which an adversary $\mathcal{A}$ is additionally allowed to invoke a RevealRPK-query to obtain raw public keys of UE and HN, and define the semantic security of session keys.

Let **U** and **N** be sets of UE and HN, respectively. We denote by $U \in \mathbf{U}$ and $N \in \mathbf{N}$ two parties that participate in an authenticated key exchange protocol P. Each of them may have several instances called oracles involved in distinct, possibly concurrent, executions of P. We denote U (resp., N) instances by U^ζ (resp., N^η) where $\zeta, \eta \in \mathbb{N}$, or by I in the case of any instance. During the protocol execution, an adversary has the entire control of networks and has access to the raw public keys. Let us show the capability of adversary $\mathcal{A}$ each query captures:

- Execute(U^ζ, N^η): This query models passive attacks, where the adversary gets access to honest executions of P between the instances U^ζ and N^η by eavesdropping.
- Send(I, msg): This query models active attacks by having $\mathcal{A}$ send a message to instance I. The adversary $\mathcal{A}$ gets back the response I generates in processing the message msg according to the protocol P. A query Send(U^ζ, Start) initiates the protocol, and thus the adversary receives the first flow message.
- Reveal(I): This query handles misuse of the session key (e.g., use in a weak symmetric-key encryption) by any instance I. The query is only available to $\mathcal{A}$, if the instance actually holds a session key, and the latter is released to $\mathcal{A}$.
- RevealRPK(U/N): This query allows the adversary to obtain the raw public keys of UE and HN.
- Test(I): This oracle is used to see whether or not the adversary can obtain some information on the session key by giving a hint on the key. The Test-query can be asked at most once by the adversary $\mathcal{A}$ and is only available to $\mathcal{A}$ if the instance I is fresh[2]. This query is answered as follows: One flips a (private) coin $b \in \{0, 1\}$ and forwards the corresponding session key SK (Reveal(I) would output) if $b = 1$, or a random value with the same size except the session key if $b = 0$.

The adversary $\mathcal{A}$ is provided with random coin tosses, some oracles and then is allowed to invoke any number of queries as described above, in any order. The aim of the adversary is to break the privacy of the session key (a.k.a., semantic security) in the context of executing P.

Definition 3 (AKE Security).   *The AKE security is defined by the game* **Game**$^{\mathrm{ake}}(\mathcal{A}, P)$, *in which the ultimate goal of the adversary is to guess the bit b involved in the Test-query by outputting this guess b'. We denote the AKE advantage, by* $\mathrm{Adv}_P^{\mathrm{ake}}(\mathcal{A}) = 2\Pr[b = b'] - 1$, *as the probability that $\mathcal{A}$ can correctly guess the value of b. The protocol P is said to be (t, ε)-AKE-secure if $\mathcal{A}$'s advantage is smaller than ε for any adversary $\mathcal{A}$ running time t.*

---

[2] We say that an instance I is fresh unless the Reveal(I)-query is asked by an adversary $\mathcal{A}$.

5 Security Proof of AKA*

In this section, we show that the AKA* protocol of Fig. 2 is provably secure in the random oracle model [10] under the CDH problem of Definition 1.

Theorem 1. *Let P be the AKA* protocol of Fig. 2. For any adversary $\mathcal{A}$ within a polynomial time t, with less than q_{se} active interactions with the parties (Send-queries) and q_{ex} passive eavesdroppings (Execute-queries), $\mathsf{Adv}_P^{ake}(\mathcal{A}) \leq \varepsilon$, with ε upper-bounded by*

$$\frac{(q_{ex}+q_{se})^2}{q} + \frac{4q_{se}}{2^k} + 12n^2 \cdot q_{se} \times \mathsf{Adv}_{DCR}^{euf-cma}(\mathcal{F}), \tag{2}$$

where n is the cardinalities of **U** *and* **N***, and k is the output length of* H_j*, for* $j = 3,4,5$.

Proof. In this proof, we define a sequence of games starting at the real protocol $\mathbf{G}_0$ and ending up at $\mathbf{G}_4$ where we bound the probability of each event by using Shoup's difference lemma [40]. For clarity, we denote by Event_i an event Event considered in **Game** $\mathbf{G}_i$.

Game $\mathbf{G}_0$: This is the real protocol in the random oracle model. We are interested in the following event: S_0 which occurs if the adversary correctly guesses the bit b involved in the Test-query

$$\mathsf{Adv}_P^{ake}(\mathcal{A}) = 2\Pr[\mathsf{S}_0] - 1. \tag{3}$$

Game $\mathbf{G}_1$: In this game, we simulate the hash oracles (H_j, but as well additional hash functions, for $j = 1,2,3,4,5$ which will appear in the game $\mathbf{G}_3$) by maintaining hash lists Λ_{H} and $\Lambda_{\mathsf{H}'}$ (see below). We also simulate all the instances, as the real parties would do, for the Send-queries and for the Execute, Reveal, RevealRPK and Test-queries. From this simulation, we can easily see that the game is perfectly indistinguishable from the real attack.

- For a hash-query $\mathsf{H}_j(\mathsf{q})$ (resp., $\mathsf{H}_j'(\mathsf{q})$), such that a record $(j,\mathsf{q},\mathsf{r})$ appears in Λ_{H} (resp., $\Lambda_{\mathsf{H}'}$), the answer is r. Otherwise, one chooses a random element $\mathsf{r} \xleftarrow{\$} \mathbb{Z}_q^*$, for $j = 1,2$, or $\mathsf{r} \xleftarrow{\$} \{0,1\}^k$, for $j = 3,4,5$, answers with it, and adds the record $(j,\mathsf{q},\mathsf{r})$ to Λ_{H} (resp., $\Lambda_{\mathsf{H}'}$).

Game $\mathbf{G}_2$: For an easier analysis in the following, we cancel games in which some collisions (Coll_2) are unlikely to happen:
- Collisions on the partial transcripts $(\mathsf{U},(\mathsf{N},Y),(X,V_{\mathsf{U}}))$: Any adversary tries to find out one pair (Y,X), coinciding with the challenge transcript, and then obtain the corresponding session key using the Reveal-query. However, at least one party involves with the transcripts, and thus one of Y and X is truly uniformly distributed.

The probability is bounded by the birthday paradox:

$$\Pr[\mathsf{Coll}_2] \leq \frac{(q_{ex}+q_{se})^2}{2q}. \tag{4}$$

Game G_3: In order to make the authenticator, session key and temporary identifier unpredictable to any adversary, we compute them using the private oracles H'_j (instead of H_j) so that the values are completely independent from the random oracles. We reach this aim by modifying the simulation as follows: (1) In **Step 3**, we compute the authenticator $V_U = H'_3(U||N||Y||X||A||B)$, session key $SK_U = H'_4(U||N||Y||X||A||B)$ and temporary identifier $U = H'_5(U||N||Y||X||A||B)$; and (2) In **Step 4**, we compute the authenticator $V_N = H'_3(U||N||Y||X||A||B)$, session key $SK_N = H'_4(U||N||Y||X||A||B)$ and temporary identifier $U = H'_5(U||N||Y||X||A||B)$, and abort the protocol if $V_U \neq V_N$. Accordingly, we do no longer need to compute the DCR signature K in **Step 3** and **Step 4**.

The games G_3 and G_2 are indistinguishable unless some specific hash queries are asked, denoted by event $\mathsf{AskH}_3 = \mathsf{AskH}3_3 \vee \mathsf{AskH}4w3_3 \vee \mathsf{AskH}5w34_3$:

- $\mathsf{AskH}3_3$: $H_3(U||N||Y||X||A||B||K)$ has been queried by $\mathcal{A}$ to H_3 for some execution transcripts $(U, (N, Y), (X, V_U))$;
- $\mathsf{AskH}4w3_3$: $H_4(U||N||Y||X||A||B||K)$ has been queried by $\mathcal{A}$ to H_4 for some execution transcripts $(U, (N, Y), (X, V_U))$, but event $\mathsf{AskH}3_3$ did not happen.
- $\mathsf{AskH}5w34_3$: $H_5(U||N||Y||X||A||B||K)$ has been queried by $\mathcal{A}$ to H_5 for some execution transcripts $(U, (N, Y), (X, V_U))$, but both events $\mathsf{AskH}3_3$ and $\mathsf{AskH}4w3_3$ did not happen.

The authenticator and temporary identifier are computed with random oracles that are private to the simulator, then one can remark that it cannot be guessed by the adversary, better than at random for each attempt, unless the same partial transcript $(U, (N, Y), (X, V_U))$ appeared in another session with a real instance (U^ζ or N^η). But such a case has already been excluded in game G_2. A similar remark holds on the session key:

$$\Pr[S_3] \leq \frac{2q_{se}}{2^k} + \frac{1}{2}. \tag{5}$$

Game G_4: In this game, we evaluate the probability of event AskH. Let $\mathsf{ForgeDCR}_4$ be an event that adversary $\mathcal{A}$ asks a hash-query $H_j(U||N||Y||X||A||B||K)$, for $j = 3, 4, 5$, where K is a valid DCR signature. Since $\mathsf{AskH}_4 = \mathsf{AskH}3_4 \vee \mathsf{AskH}4w3_4 \vee \mathsf{AskH}5w34_4$, the probability of event AskH_4 is bounded by

$$\Pr[\mathsf{AskH}_4] \leq 3\Pr[\mathsf{ForgeDCR}_4]. \tag{6}$$

For the above right term, we construct an adversary $\mathcal{F}$ who breaks the EUF-CMA security of the DCR signature scheme DCR by using an adversary $\mathcal{A}$ who breaks the semantic security of the AKA* protocol.

Let n be the cardinalities of $\mathbf{U}$ and $\mathbf{N}$, and we assume that $U \in \mathbf{U}$ and $N \in \mathbf{N}$ are the target parties. We first set a random value $A \in \mathbb{G}$, given to adversary $\mathcal{F}$, as UE's public key. For a $\mathsf{Send}(U^\zeta, (N, Y))$-query, adversary $\mathcal{F}$ gets a signature pair $(X, XSIG_{UE}(X, N, Y \cdot B^e))$ by asking a query (Y, N, U) to the signing oracle O_{Sign}, and then replies with (X, V_U) where $V_U = H_3(U||N||Y||X||A||B||XSIG_{UE}(X, N, Y \cdot B^e))$. Also, we introduce a random value $Y_0 \in \mathbb{G}$, given to adversary $\mathcal{F}$, in the simulation of HN as follows: For a $\mathsf{Send}(N^\eta, U)$-query, adversary $\mathcal{F}$ sets $Y = Y_0$ by guessing that it is the test instance for the target parties, and then replies with (N, Y). If adversary $\mathcal{A}$ correctly guesses the bit b involved in the Test-query, adversary $\mathcal{F}$ outputs a forged signature pair from that challenge transcript $(\mathsf{U}, (\mathsf{N}, Y_0), (X_0, V_\mathsf{U}))$ as follows: $(X_0, \mathsf{N}, \mathsf{U}, XSIG_\mathsf{UE}(X_0, \mathsf{N}, Y_0 \cdot B^e))$. So, the probability of event ForgeDCR$_4$ is bounded by

$$\Pr[\mathsf{ForgeDCR}_4] \leq 2n^2 \cdot q_{\mathsf{se}} \times \mathsf{Adv}_{DCR}^{\mathsf{euf\text{-}cma}}(\mathcal{F}) . \tag{7}$$

Combining inequalities (4), (5), (6) and (7), one gets

$$\Pr[S_0] \leq \frac{(q_{\mathsf{ex}} + q_{\mathsf{se}})^2}{2q} + \frac{2q_{\mathsf{se}}}{2^k} + \frac{1}{2} + 6n^2 \cdot q_{\mathsf{se}} \times \mathsf{Adv}_{DCR}^{\mathsf{euf\text{-}cma}}(\mathcal{F}). \tag{8}$$

Finally, one can get the result as desired by noting that $\mathsf{Adv}_P^{\mathsf{ake}}(\mathcal{A}) = 2\Pr[S_0] - 1$.

6 Discussions

In this section, we discuss several aspects of the AKA* protocol with respect to security properties, efficiency, and implementation perspective. Also, we compare the AKA* protocol with relevant protocols (EAP-AKA [17], EAP-AKA' [26], EAP-AKA' FS [14], 5G-AKA [5] and 5G-AKA' [42]) in terms of efficiency, forward secrecy, UE anonymity and UE unlinkability.

6.1 UE Anonymity

In the AKA* protocol, UE temporary identifier U is updated with the DCR signature K that is shared between UE and HN. This identifier is similarly functioning as GUTI [5] because they are both temporary identifiers renewed every time and can be used in at most one session. However, UE temporary identifier U differs from GUTI in the sense that GUTI should be reissued by HN independently from the 5G-AKA protocol. Also, this kind of identifier can be a countermeasure to DoS (Denial-of-Service) attacks consuming heavy modular exponentiation computations on the HN side.

6.2 Forward Secrecy

The AKA* protocol guarantees forward secrecy since the ephemeral Diffie-Hellman key exchange [13] is inherent in the construction of the DCR signature scheme [29]. So, the AKA* protocol is much more efficient than the EAP-AKA' FS protocol [14] which is a simple combination of the EAP-AKA' [26] and Diffie-Hellman key exchange [13] protocols.

6.3 Explicit Mutual Authentication

Explicit mutual authentication of the AKA* protocol can be achieved by adding the fourth message flow from HN to UE as follows: At the end of **Step 4**, HN computes its authenticator $V_\mathsf{N} = \mathsf{H}_6(sid||A||B||K)$, where $H_6 : \{0,1\}^* \rightarrow \{0,1\}^k$, and sends V_N to UE who checks the validity of V_N.

6.4   UE Unlinkability

In the AKA* protocol, UE unlinkability is tightly related to the synchronization of UE temporary identifier U. If an attacker blocks the third message flow from UE to HN, the temporary identifier U on the UE side is inconsistent with the U on the HN side. A straightforward solution might be to make UE keep a pair of identifiers (U_{t-1}, U_t) where U_{t-1} (resp., U_t) is the temporary identifier of the last (resp., current) session. In this case, the above attacker can easily break UE unlinkability because UE uses the identifier U_{t-1} in the current session for synchronization. Though the AKA* protocol itself does not provide UE unlinkability in a stronger security notion as above, it can be solved by adding one round of message exchanges (i.e., the fourth message flow from HN to UE, and the fifth message flow from UE to HN) in order to confirm that both parties have actually updated the UE temporary identifier U.

6.5   Efficiency

Let $\mathsf{Exp}_\mathbb{G}$ and $\mathsf{MExp(m)}_\mathbb{G}$ be a modular exponentiation g^x in $\mathbb{G}$ and an m-fold multi-exponentiation $g_1^{x_1} \cdots g_m^{x_m}$ in $\mathbb{G}$, respectively. The computation cost of $\mathsf{MExp(m)}_\mathbb{G}$ is 1 exponentiation plus 2^m multiplications, which for small $m = 2$ or $m = 3$ is essentially the same as 1 exponentiation [33,41]. Since the DCR signature K needs $1\mathsf{MExp(2)}_\mathbb{G}$, the computation costs (i.e., $1\mathsf{Exp}_\mathbb{G} + 1\mathsf{MExp(2)}_\mathbb{G}$ on each side) of the AKA* protocol are almost same as those of the Diffie-Hellman key exchange protocol [13]. If pre-computation (i.e., computing X and Y in advance) is allowed, the computation costs of each side are reduced to $1\mathsf{MExp(2)}_\mathbb{G}$. Compared to the Diffie-Hellman key exchange [13], the AKA* protocol requires one hash size of communication costs and one message flow additionally.

6.6   Implementation Perspective

In order to avoid subgroup order checks of the received Diffie-Hellman public values X and Y in the AKA* protocol, we can use a "secure" prime $p = sq + 1$ [16,19,30] such that q is a sufficiently large prime divisor of $(p-1)/2$, and every factors of $(p-1)/2$ are also primes comparable to q in size. Also, the AKA* protocol can be directly implemented over elliptic curve groups because neither FDH (Full-Domain Hash) [15] nor IC (Ideal Cipher) [12] is used in its construction.

6.7   Comparison

Here, we compare the AKA* protocol of Sect. 3 with relevant protocols (EAP-AKA [17], EAP-AKA' [26], EAP-AKA' FS [14], 5G-AKA [5] and 5G-AKA' [42]) in terms of efficiency, forward secrecy (FS), UE anonymity and UE unlinkability. For a fair comparison, the following assumptions are applied: (1) We do not consider roaming scenario (i.e., SN); (2) The computation and communication costs of ECIES-KEM/DEM [27,37–39] (used in 5G-AKA [5] and 5G-AKA' [42]) and ECDHE [24] (used in EAP-AKA' FS [14]) are counted in the group description $(\mathbb{G}, q, g)$; and (3) $1\mathsf{Exp}_\mathbb{G} \approx 1\mathsf{MExp(2)}_\mathbb{G}$ due to [33,41].

Table 1. Comparison of the AKA* and relevant protocols where R is a (128-bit) random challenge $RAND$, SE is AES-128 in ECB mode, and $|l|$ indicates a bit-length of l

Protocols	Computation costs of		Communication costs	FS	UE anonymity /unlinkability
	UE	HN			
EAP-AKA [17], EAP-AKA' [26]			$\|U\|+\|N\|$ $+\|R\|+7\|H\|$	No	No /No
EAP-AKA' FS [14]	$2\mathrm{Exp}_G$	$2\mathrm{Exp}_G$	$\|U\|+\|N\|+2\|p\|$ $+\|R\|+8\|H\|$	Yes	No /No
5G-AKA [5]	$2\mathrm{Exp}_G$	$1\mathrm{Exp}_G$	$\|N\|+\|p\|+\|SE\|$ $+\|R\|+4\|H\|$	No	Yes /No
5G-AKA' [42]	$2\mathrm{Exp}_G$	$1\mathrm{Exp}_G$	$\|N\|+\|p\|$ $+2\|SE\|+4\|H\|$	No	Yes /Yes
AKA* (Sect. 3)	$1\mathrm{Exp}_G+$ $1\mathrm{MExp}(2)_G$	$1\mathrm{Exp}_G+$ $1\mathrm{MExp}(2)_G$	$\|U\|+\|N\|$ $+2\|p\|+\|H\|$	Yes	Yes /Yes

We summarize a comparative result in Table 1. It is clear that only the AKA* and EAP-AKA' FS [14] protocols provide forward secrecy. However, the AKA* protocol is much more efficient than EAP-AKA' FS [14] with respect to communication costs. In addition, the AKA* protocol guarantees UE anonymity and UE unlinkability, while the EAP-AKA' FS protocol [14] does not.

Acknowledgements. We sincerely appreciate the anonymous reviewers' constructive and valuable comments on this paper.

References

1. 3GPP. https://www.3gpp.org/
2. 5G. https://www.etsi.org/technologies/mobile/5g
3. 5G & Beyond. https://www.nist.gov/programs-projects/5g-beyond
4. Tamarin prover. https://github.com/tamarin-prover
5. 3GPP TS 33.501: Security architecture and procedures for 5G system (Release 17), September 2022. https://portal.3gpp.org/desktopmodules/Specifications/SpecificationDetails.aspx?specificationId=3169
6. Bana, G., C.-Lundh, H.: A computationally complete symbolic attacker for equivalence properties. In: CCS 2014, pp. 609–620. ACM (2014)
7. Basin, D., Dreier, J., Hirschi, L., Radomirovic, S., Sasse, R., Stettler, V.: A formal analysis of 5G authentication. In: CCS 2018, pp. 1383–1396. ACM (2018)
8. Bellare, M., Pointcheval, D., Rogaway, P.: Authenticated key exchange secure against dictionary attacks. In: Preneel, B. (ed.) EUROCRYPT 2000. LNCS, vol. 1807, pp. 139–155. Springer, Heidelberg (2000). https://doi.org/10.1007/3 540 45539 6_11
9. Bellare, M., Rogaway, P.: Entity authentication and key distribution. In: Stinson, D.R. (ed.) CRYPTO 1993. LNCS, vol. 773, pp. 232–249. Springer, Heidelberg (1994). https://doi.org/10.1007/3-540-48329-2_21
10. Bellare, M., Rogaway, P.: Random oracles are practical: a paradigm for designing efficient protocols. In: CCS 1993, pp. 62–73. ACM (1993)
11. Borgaonkar, R., Hirschi, L., Park, S., Shaik, A.: New privacy threat on 3G, 4G, and upcoming 5G AKA protocols. Proc. Priv. Enhanc. Technol. (PoPETs) **2019**(3), 108–127 (2019)

12. Coron, J.-S., Patarin, J., Seurin, Y.: The random oracle model and the ideal cipher model are equivalent. In: Wagner, D. (ed.) CRYPTO 2008. LNCS, vol. 5157, pp. 1–20. Springer, Heidelberg (2008). https://doi.org/10.1007/978-3-540-85174-5_1
13. Diffie, W., Hellman, M.: New directions in cryptography. IEEE Trans. Inf. Theory **22**(6), 644–654 (1976)
14. IETF Internet-Draft: Forward Secrecy for the Extensible Authentication Protocol Method for Authentication and Key Agreement (EAP-AKA' FS) (2022). https://datatracker.ietf.org/doc/html/draft-ietf-emu-aka-pfs-07
15. IETF Internet-Draft: Hashing to Elliptic Curves (2022). https://www.ietf.org/archive/id/draft-irtf-cfrg-hash-to-curve-16.html
16. IETF RFC 2785: Methods for Avoiding the "Small-Subgroup" Attacks on the Diffie-Hellman Key Agreement Method for S/MIME (2000). https://www.rfc-editor.org/rfc/rfc2785.html
17. IETF RFC 4187: Extensible Authentication Protocol Method for 3rd Generation Authentication and Key Agreement (EAP-AKA) (2006). https://www.rfc-editor.org/rfc/rfc4187.html
18. IETF RFC 5280: Internet X.509 Public Key Infrastructure Certificate and Certificate Revocation List (CRL) Profile (2008). https://www.rfc-editor.org/rfc/rfc5280.html
19. IETF RFC 6628: Efficient Augmented Password-Only Authentication and Key Exchange for IKEv2 (2012). https://www.rfc-editor.org/rfc/rfc6628.html
20. IETF RFC 6960: X.509 Internet Public Key Infrastructure Online Certificate Status Protocol - OCSP (2013). https://www.rfc-editor.org/rfc/rfc6960.html
21. IETF RFC 7258: Pervasive Monitoring Is an Attack (2014). https://www.rfc-editor.org/rfc/rfc7258.html
22. IETF RFC 7435: Opportunistic Security: Some Protection Most of the Time (2014). https://www.rfc-editor.org/rfc/rfc7435.html
23. IETF RFC 7624: Confidentiality in the Face of Pervasive Surveillance: A Threat Model and Problem Statement (2015). https://www.rfc-editor.org/rfc/rfc7624.html
24. IETF RFC 7748: Elliptic Curves for Security (2016). https://www.rfc-editor.org/rfc/rfc7748.html
25. IETF RFC 8446: The Transport Layer Security (TLS) Protocol Version 1.3 (2018). https://www.rfc-editor.org/rfc/rfc8446.html
26. IETF RFC 9048: Improved Extensible Authentication Protocol Method for 3GPP Mobile Network Authentication and Key Agreement (EAP-AKA') (2021). https://www.rfc-editor.org/rfc/rfc9048.html
27. ISO/IEC 18033-2:2006: Information technology —Security techniques—Encryption algorithms—Part 2: Asymmetric ciphers (2006). https://www.iso.org/standard/37971.html
28. Koutsos, A.: The 5G-AKA authentication protocol privacy. In: EuroS&P 2019, pp. 464–479. IEEE (2019)
29. Krawczyk, H.: HMQV: a high-performance secure Diffie-Hellman protocol. In: Shoup, V. (ed.) CRYPTO 2005. LNCS, vol. 3621, pp. 546–566. Springer, Heidelberg (2005). https://doi.org/10.1007/11535218_33
30. Lim, C.H., Lee, P.J.: A key recovery attack on discrete log-based schemes using a prime order subgroup. In: Kaliski, B.S. (ed.) CRYPTO 1997. LNCS, vol. 1294, pp. 249–263. Springer, Heidelberg (1997). https://doi.org/10.1007/BFb0052240
31. Lyon, D.: Surveillance After Snowden. Wiley, Hoboken (2015)
32. Meier, S., Schmidt, B., Cremers, C., Basin, D.: The TAMARIN prover for the symbolic analysis of security protocols. In: Sharygina, N., Veith, H. (eds.) CAV 2013. LNCS, vol. 8044, pp. 696–701. Springer, Heidelberg (2013). https://doi.org/10.1007/978-3-642-39799-8_48
33. Menezes, A.J., van Oorschot, P.C., Vanstone, S.A.: Handbook of Applied Cryptography, pp. 617–618. CRC Press (1996)

34. NIST FIPS PUB 202: SHA-3 Standard: Permutation-Based Hash and Extendable-Output Functions (2015). https://nvlpubs.nist.gov/nistpubs/FIPS/NIST.FIPS.202.pdf
35. Rogers, M., Eden, G.: The snowden disclosures, technical standards, and the making of surveillance infrastructures. Int. J. Commun. **11**, 802–823 (2017)
36. Schmidt, B., Meier, S., Cremers, C., Basin, D.: Automated analysis of Diffie-Hellman protocols and advanced security properties. In: Computer Security Foundations Symposium (CSF) 2012, pp. 78–94. IEEE (2012)
37. SECG SEC 1: Elliptic Curve Cryptography (2009). https://www.secg.org/sec1-v2.pdf
38. SECG SEC 2: Recommended Elliptic Curve Domain Parameters (2010). https://www.secg.org/sec2-v2.pdf
39. Shoup, V.: A Proposal for an ISO Standard for Public Key Encryption (version 2.1) (2001). https://www.shoup.net/papers/iso-2_1.pdf
40. Shoup, V.: OAEP reconsidered. J. Cryptol. **15**(4), 223–249 (2002)
41. Straus, E.G.: Addition chains of vectors. Amer. Math. Monthly **71**(7), 806–808 (1964)
42. Wang, Y., Zhang, Z., Xie, Y.: Privacy-preserving and standard-compatible AKA protocol for 5G. In: USENIX Security Symposium 2021, pp. 3595–3612. USENIX Association (2021)

Privacy Enhancing Technique

Membership Privacy for Asynchronous Group Messaging

Keita Emura[1]($\boxtimes$)(iD), Kaisei Kajita[2], Ryo Nojima[1], Kazuto Ogawa[1], and Go Ohtake[2]

[1] National Institute of Information and Communications Technology, Tokyo, Japan
k-emura@nict.go.jp
[2] Japan Broadcasting Corporation, Tokyo, Japan

Abstract. The Signal protocol is a secure messaging protocol providing end-to-end encrypted asynchronous communication. In this paper, we focus on a method capable of hiding membership information from the viewpoint of non group members in a secure group messaging (SGM) protocol, which we call "membership privacy". Although Chase et al. (ACM CCS 2020) have considered the same notion, their proposal is an extension of Signal so called "Pairwise Signal" where a group message is repeatedly sent over individual Signal channels. Thus, for the number of group users n, their protocol is not scalable where each user is required $O(n)$ computational and communication costs for updating keys. In this work, we extend the Cohn-Gordon et al. SGM protocol (ACM CCS 2018), which we call the Asynchronous Ratcheting Trees (ART) protocol, to add membership privacy. The ART protocol is scalable where each user is required $O(\log n)$ computational and communication costs for updating keys. We employ a key-private and robust public-key encryption (Abdalla et al., TCC2010/JoC2018) for hiding membership-related values in the setup phase. Furthermore, we concentrate on the fact that a group common key provides anonymity. This fact is used to encrypt membership information in the key update phase. Our extension does not affect the forward secrecy and post-compromise security of the original ART protocol. Our modification achieves asymptotically the same efficiency of the ART protocol in the setup phase. Any additional cost for key update does not depend on the number of group members (specifically, one encryption and decryption of a symmetric-key encryption scheme and one execution of a key-derivation function for each key update are employed). Therefore, the proposed protocol can add membership privacy to the ART protocol with a quite small overhead.

1 Introduction

Background. Researches on secure messaging have been much popular. Besides end-to-end encryption, secure messaging protocols provide *asynchronicity* where a sender is not required to aware whether a receiver is online or not, *forward*

© Springer Nature Switzerland AG 2023
I. You and T.-Y. Youn (Eds.): WISA 2022, LNCS 13720, pp. 131–142, 2023.
https://doi.org/10.1007/978-3-031-25659-2_10

secrecy (FS) where even if state information (i.e., long-term secret keys or any values used in subsequent operations) is leaked, previously derived session keys are still hidden, and *post-compromise security* (PCS) where if an intermediate stage completes with no corruption by an adversary after all of secrets are compromised, then subsequent stages are still secure. Basically, a key update procedure is crucial for providing FS and PCS. In addition to two-party messaging, secure group messaging (SGM) protocols also have been proposed [3,4,10].

On Membership Privacy in SGM. As an SGM scenario, let us assume that a user participates in an online symposium (with many sessions) several times; for example, when the symposium consists of many courses held at different days. Then, due to asynchronicity, the organizer can set up the online system, even if the participants are offline. Also, due to FS and PCS, the past and future contents are not disclosed, even if the present secret information is disclosed. This is important for a pay-per-view service. Let us consider a privacy if the symposium is held in offline. In this case, a participant is aware of who participates in the symposium (here, we simply consider that he/she can see other participants in the venue), whereas it would be better to hide the participants in the symposium from the nonparticipants, unless the organizer intentionally discloses the membership information, and all participants agree with it. Moreover, if one knows that a particular person speaks more than the others, then this person might be identified. Thus, it would be better to hide the speakers (according to the anonymity in the usual sense). Therefore, in SGM related to multiple participants, where membership privacy (containing anonymity), is very important. Chase et al. [7] have considered the same notion. Because the SGM protocol is an extension of the Signal protocol where each group member needs to run the (one-to-one) Signal protocol for all other group members, respectively, their protocol is not scalable (i.e., it requires $O(n)$ computational and communication costs in the key update phase). So, to the best of our knowledge, no such a SGM protocol (with scalability) has been proposed so far.

We remark that anonymity is not enough to provide membership privacy. For example, Backes et al. [5] proposed a group signature scheme providing membership privacy though conventional group signatures basically provide anonymity. We remark that Chen et al. [8] have considered to add anonymity to the ART protocol that hides the user who sent a message. However, they did not consider hiding membership information. As a result, membership information can be disclosed in their protocol. It is noted that they introduced a trusted third party (TTP) to hide the position information, which is necessary for key updating (See Sect. 2). However, it is highly undesirable to introduce a TTP in the end-to-end encryption context.

Our Contribution. In this paper, we extend the Cohn-Gordon et al. SGM protocol [10], which we call the Asynchronous Ratcheting Trees (ART) protocol, to add membership privacy, which hides the participants and also the participant who sends a message. To achieve this, we basically do not modify the original key update procedure for directly employing FS and PCS of the ART protocol. Moreover, the ART protocol requires $O(n)$ (resp. $O(\log n)$) computational and communication costs in the setup phase for the initiator (resp. for each user), and requires $O(\log n)$ computational and communication costs in the key update phase, where n is the number of users belonging to the SGM protocol. We consider to keep this efficiency as much as possible even membership privacy is additionally provided.

We employ key-private and robust public-key encryption [1,2] for hiding membership-related values in the setup phase. Our modification achieves asymptotically the same efficiency of the ART protocol in the setup phase. Furthermore, we concentrate on the fact that a group common key provides anonymity. This fact is used to encrypt membership information in the key update phase. It is noted that the ART protocol also introduces a group common key called a "stage key" to add a message authentication code (MAC). The aim is to authenticate updated public keys (See Sect. 2). We also introduce a similar common key to encrypt membership information in the key update phase. By employing the common MAC key-generation procedure of the ART protocol, the additional key update cost does not depend on the number of group members. Specifically, one encryption and decryption of a symmetric-key encryption scheme and one execution of a key-derivation function for each key update are employed. In this way, membership privacy can be added to the ART protocol with a quite small overhead.

Martiny et al. [13] analyzed the sealed sender functionality, where an encrypted message contains sender information, and showed that it can be broken by identifying the sender. They assumed that most messages receive a quick response, i.e., when a user device receives a message, the device will automatically send back a delivery receipt to the sender. In our work, such a deanonymization attack due to quick responses and due to communication-related value such as IP address are out of the scope, and it is not considered.

Assuming an Initiator. Cohn-Gordon et al. [10] introduced an initiator who setups a group and generates initial secret keys of group members. We remark that the initiator does not know secret keys of group members after key updating. Thus we assume that the initiator is trusted in the setup phase (as in the ART protocol). In the above mentioned online symposium, the organizer can be an initiator, and we do not consider initiator anonymity since the organizer is obviously a member.

2   Cohn-Gordon et al. SGM Protocol (ART)

In this section, the Cohn-Gordon et al. SGM protocol [10], called Asynchronous Ratcheting Trees (ART), is described. Let $\mathbb{G}$ be a group with prime order p, and $H : \mathbb{G} \to \mathbb{Z}_p$ be a hash function.[1] Furthermore, a key-derivation function (KDF), which is used to derive a stage key, is modeled as a random oracle.[2]

---

[1] In [10], H is defined as a mapping from a group element to a $\mathbb{Z}_p$ element that uses the corresponding DH key as the secret key of the parent node. For simplicity, we define H as a hash function.

[2] Cohn-Gordon et al. employed HKDF with SHA256 for key derivation.

Basically, the ART protocol described in [10] is a tree Diffie–Hellman (DH) key agreement. Each user is assigned to a leaf node, and a secret key of a parent node is defined as the DH key of the children nodes. More specifically, let a secret key of a node be $K_1 \in \mathbb{Z}_p$, and a secret key of the sibling node be $K_2 \in \mathbb{Z}_p$. Then, each public key is defined as g^{K_1} and g^{K_2}, respectively. From the DH key $g^{K_1 K_2}$, the secret key and the public key of the parent node are defined as $H(g^{K_1 K_2})$ and $g^{H(g^{K_1 K_2})}$.

Setup Phase. Next, we explain how to asynchronously setup these node secret keys K. The basic concept is to employ a strong one-round authenticated key exchange protocol. The initiator runs the protocol "locally" using his/her own secret keys and a public key of a group member. Let us assume that each user publishes a key pair $(\mathsf{IK}, \mathsf{EK})$ in a PKI. Here, IK stands for "identity key", and EK stands for "ephemeral prekey". The corresponding secret keys are denoted as ik and ek, respectively. Intuitively (which is not entirely correct), $(\mathsf{IK}, \mathsf{ik})$ is a key pair of a signature scheme used for authentication, $(\mathsf{EK}, \mathsf{ek})$ is a key pair of a key exchange protocol, and EK is defined as $\mathsf{EK} = g^{\mathsf{ek}}$. For a strong one-round authenticated key exchange protocol, it is required that

$$\mathsf{KeyExchange}(\mathsf{ik}_I, \mathsf{IK}_R, \mathsf{ek}_I, \mathsf{EK}_R) = \mathsf{KeyExchange}(\mathsf{ik}_R, \mathsf{IK}_I, \mathsf{ek}_R, \mathsf{EK}_I)$$

holds. That is, a key generated by the secret key of an initiator $(\mathsf{ik}_I, \mathsf{ek}_I)$ and a public key of a receiver $(\mathsf{IK}_R, \mathsf{EK}_R)$ is equal to a key generated by a secret key of the receiver $(\mathsf{ik}_R, \mathsf{ek}_R)$ and the secret key of the initiator $(\mathsf{IK}_I, \mathsf{EK}_I)$. Cohn-Gordon et al. stated that although any key exchange protocol satisfying the above requirement can be employed, they assumed X3DH [12] as the underlying key exchange protocol. Due to the one-round key exchange, the initiator (and a group member) can locally run the key exchange protocol if the public key of the partner is obtained. Thus, they can asynchronously (i.e., regardless of the partner being online or offline) exchange a key.

The setup phase run by an initiator is described as follows. Let n be the group size, and the initiator is also a member of the group. For simplicity, the initiator is regarded as the user 1, and $(\mathsf{IK}_1, \mathsf{EK}_1)$ is the initiator's public key managed by the PKI.

[Initiator]:

1. Randomly choose a setup key $\mathsf{suk} \in \mathbb{Z}_p$, and compute $\mathsf{SUK} = g^{\mathsf{suk}}$.
2. Obtain other members' key pairs $n - 1$ $\{(\mathsf{IK}_i, \mathsf{EK}_i)\}_{i=2}^{n}$ from PKI.
3. Randomly choose $K_1 \in \mathbb{Z}_p$.
4. For $(\mathsf{IK}_i, \mathsf{EK}_i)$ $(i = 2, 3, \ldots, n)$, locally run the underlying strong one round authenticated key exchange protocol $K_i \leftarrow \mathsf{KeyExchange}(\mathsf{ik}_1, \mathsf{IK}_i, \mathsf{suk}, \mathsf{EK}_i)$. Here, the initiator indicates ik_1 and suk as secret keys.
5. Compute all public keys associated to nodes to the tree $T = (g^{K_1}, \ldots, g^{K_{2n-2}})$. Here, the root node is excluded. Moreover, delete all secret keys (except K_1) $(K_2, \ldots, K_{2n-2})$.
6. Generate a signature σ on $(\{(\mathsf{IK}_i, \mathsf{EK}_i)\}_{i \in [1,n]}, \mathsf{SUK}, T)$ using ik_1.
7. Broadcast $(\{(\mathsf{IK}_i, \mathsf{EK}_i)\}_{i \in [1,n]}, \mathsf{SUK}, T)$ and σ.

Each user $i \in [2, n]$ receives $(\{(\mathsf{IK}_i, \mathsf{EK}_i)\}_{i\in[1,n]}, \mathsf{SUK}, T)$ and σ, and runs the following procedure.

[User i ($i \in [2, n]$)]:

1. Check the validity of σ using the verification key IK_1.
2. If σ is valid, then run $K_i \leftarrow \mathsf{KeyExchange}(\mathsf{ik}_i, \mathsf{IK}_1, \mathsf{ek}_i, \mathsf{SUK})$.
3. Compute the tree key tk using K_i and public keys T
4. Derive the stage key $\mathsf{stgk} \leftarrow \mathsf{KDF}(0, \mathsf{tk}, \{\mathsf{IK}_i\}_{i\in[1,n]}, T)$.

Key Update Phase. Next, we explain how the secret and public keys are updated. When a user updates his/her own secret key K, he/she randomly selects $K' \in \mathbb{Z}_p$ and computes public keys on the path (i.e., from the leaf node associated with the user to the root node). All group members can derive the tree key using their own secret key and updated public keys. However, they need to know which public keys are updated. Thus, the position information, which indicates which leaf node is assigned to the user, is additionally required. Furthermore, these public keys are required to be generated by a group member. Thus, the user computes a MAC for the position information and public keys on the path, and broadcasts the MAC, his/her position information, and the public keys. Here, the MAC key is the current stage key stgk. After receiving the MAC, any group member can check the validity of the MAC since these group members also have a stgk. If the MAC is valid, the group members derive the new tree key and the new stage key. Specifically, each user $i \in [1, n]$ runs the procedure described below. Let the current secret key be K_i and the position information be j.

[User i ($i \in [1, n]$)]:

1. Randomly choose $K_i' \in \mathbb{Z}_p$.
2. Compute public keys on the path (i.e., from the leaf node associated with the user i to the root node). Here, the public key of the root node is excluded because the secret key of the root node is regarded as the tree key. Let T' be a set of updated public keys.
3. Compute a MAC on $j||T'$ using stgk, and broadcast the MAC and $j||T'$.
4. Remove stgk and derive the new stage key using the new tree key.

Each user $k \in [1, n]\backslash\{i\}$ receives the MAC and $j||T'$, and runs the following procedure.

[User k ($k \in [1, n]\backslash\{i\}$)]:

1. Check the validity of the MAC using stgk.
2. If the MAC is valid, then remove stgk and derive the new stage key using the new tree key.

Security: Here, we briefly explain that the ART protocol provides FS and PCS. FS requires that even if long-term secret keys $(\mathsf{ik}, \mathsf{ek})$ and random values selected in latter stages are revealed after a user computes a tree key tk, tk still remains secret from nongroup members. Intuitively, the ART protocol provides FS due to the randomness of the updated key K'. That is, K' is independently selected by the previous key K. Thus, knowledge of K' does not affect that of K. We emphasize that K needs to be erased in the key update phase mentioned above, and K is not included in the state information. Here, implicitly assume that a user, whose state information is disclosed, has updated his/her own key at least once. If no key update is run, the leaf key K is computed by the long-term secret keys (and public keys of the initiator). Thus, the tree key can be derived. Moreover, implicitly assume that state information disclosure occurs after at least two key updates. If only one key update is run, the previous tree key can be computed by the long-term secret keys (and public keys of the initiator), and FS does not hold. In summary, when $n \geq 3$, the ART protocol provides FS if all group members run the key update at least once.

PCS requires that even if all secret values are disclosed, a tree key tk shared in an after stage still remains secret from nongroup members if one no-disclosure stage exists. Since a stateless protocol does not provide PCS [9], a stage key stgk$'$ is derived by the current tree key tk$'$ and the previous stage key stgk, where stgk$' \leftarrow$ KDF(stgk, tk$'$, $\{\mathsf{IK}_i\}_{i \in [1,n]}, T'$). Let us assume that an adversary obtains a user's secret values at a particular stage, and another user runs the key update in the next stage without the adversary being involved. Then, the adversary can compute the current tree key from the secret values obtained in the previous stage and the current public keys broadcasted by the user. Therefore, the user, whose secret key has been disclosed, is required to run the key update (i.e., the user randomly selects K') without the adversary being involved. In this way, the adversary cannot compute the current tree key since he/she does not know K'. At the same time, the adversary cannot derive the current stage key stgk$'$ since the current tree key is required. However, the adversary knows the previous stage key stgk, and thus, the adversary can send a message with a MAC computed by stgk. Thus, implicitly, the user is required to run the key update and send the updated public keys and his/her position information with a MAC computed by stgk before the adversary sends a message. In summary, the ART protocol provides PCS after a user, whose secret key has been disclosed, runs the key update once without the adversary being involved.

3 Proposed Protocol

In this section, the proposed SGM protocol, which provides membership privacy by extending the ART protocol, is presented. For simplicity, we assume that a key is updated when a message is sent. Thus, hiding the user who sends a message is the same as hiding the user who updates a key. We assume that a particular user has the role of initiator, and the user always participates in groups (although any user can be an initiator for each group in the ART protocol). Moreover, no membership privacy for the initiator is considered. If a path size, i.e., the number of nodes from a leaf to the root is not the same for all users, the size detracts anonymity. Therefore, we employ a complete binary tree structure (although any binary tree structure can be employed in the ART protocol).

High-Level Description. We extract which part of the ART protocol leaks membership privacy, and briefly explain how to provide membership privacy.

1. In the setup phase, a set of public kyes of group members $\{(\mathsf{IK}_i, \mathsf{EK}_i)\}_{i \in [1,n]}$ is contained to a message $(\{(\mathsf{IK}_i, \mathsf{EK}_i)\}_{i \in [1,n]}, \mathsf{SUK}, T)$ sent from the initiator. We do not consider to hide $(\mathsf{IK}_1, \mathsf{EK}_1)$ because these keys are for the initiator.
   - For hiding $\{(\mathsf{IK}_i, \mathsf{EK}_i)\}_{i \in [2,n]}$, we employ key private and robust public key encryption [1,2]. Briefly, for different two key pairs $(\mathsf{PK}, \mathsf{DK}) \leftarrow \mathsf{KeyGen}(1^k)$ and $(\mathsf{PK}', \mathsf{DK}') \leftarrow \mathsf{KeyGen}(1^k)$, and for a ciphertext $C \leftarrow \mathsf{Ecn}(\mathsf{PK}, M)$ of a message M under PK, it is key private when no information of PK is revealed from C, and it is robust if $\perp \leftarrow \mathsf{Dec}(C, \mathsf{DK}')$. Moreover, it is weak robust when C is generated by the Ecn algorithm.[3] This essentially employs a generic construction of anonymous broadcast encryption proposed by Libert et al. [11].
   - In addition to $(\mathsf{IK}, \mathsf{EK})$, we assume that a public key PK of a key private and robust public key encryption scheme is also managed by PKI. In the setup phase, the initiator chooses a secret key k for a symmetric encryption scheme, encrypts $\{(\mathsf{IK}_i, \mathsf{EK}_i)\}_{i \in [2,n]}$ using k, and encrypts k and position information of a user i using PK_i. Each user can obtain $\{(\mathsf{IK}_i, \mathsf{EK}_i)\}_{i \in [2,n]}$ and own position information only if the user i is a member.
   - Since the ART protocol requires $O(n)$ computation and communication costs for the initiator, additionally employing key private and robust public key encryption in the setup phase does not affect asymptotic complexity of the original protocol. However, if we directly employ key private and robust public key encryption, the efficiency of each user in the setup phase is worsened from $O(\log n)$ to $O(n)$ due to the decryption procedure. That is, if each user does not know which ciphertext can be decrypted owing to key privacy, then $n/2$-times decryptions are required on average. Thus, we additionally employ a tag-based hint system [11] that provides efficient decryption. Employing the hint system achieves asymptotically the same efficiency of the ART protocol in the setup phase. Briefly, a hint system consists of $(\mathsf{KeyGen}_h, \mathsf{Hint}, \mathsf{Invert})$: the key generation algorithm KeyGen_h takes a security parameter as input, and outputs a key pair $(\mathsf{PK}^h, \mathsf{DK}^h)$. The hint generation algorithm Hint takes a tag t, a public key PK^h, and a random coin r, and outputs a pair (U, H). The inversion algorithm Invert takes DK^h, t, and U as input, and outputs either a hint H or $\perp$. Here, U only depends on r and not on PK^h, and the same r and U are commonly used for all users. Moreover, two security notions hold where, Anonymity: hints generated under two distinct public keys are indistinguishable, and Strong robustness: for two distinct secret keys

---

[3] Such a public key encryption scheme can be constructed easily. For example, for a key private public key encryption scheme, e.g., the ElGamal encryption, a random R is contained to a public key and for encryption of M, encrypt $M\|R$. The decryption algorithm decrypts a ciphertext, obtains $M\|R'$, and outputs M if $R' = R$ and $\perp$, otherwise.

$DK_0^h \neq DK_1^h$ and a common (t, U), the same hint is not generated, i.e., $\mathsf{Invert}(DK_0^h, t, U) \neq \mathsf{Invert}(DK_1^h, t, U)$ holds.

2. In the key update phase, a user who updates the key declares position information. This information distinguishes users that detracts anonymity.

   - It is required that only the group members obtain the position information. We concentrate on the authentication in the key update phase of the ART protocol, which employs a common stage key as a MAC key. Such a common key provides anonymity. Therefore, each user, who updates the key, encrypts his/her position information using a common encryption key.

   - For PCS, this common encryption key needs to be updated. For this purpose, hash chains are employed as in the ART protocol. Let mack be a MAC key, which was originally described as stgk, and let enck be an encryption key. In the setup phase, mack is derived from 0 and the first tree key, whereas enck is derived from 1 and the first tree key. Both are derived from the current tree key and the previous mack and enck, respectively. This structure enables PCS. As in the authentication in the ART protocol, only the group members can derive enck and obtain the position information of the user who updates the key. Moreover, by employing a common encryption key, anonymity is not detracted.

   - Any additional cost for key update does not depend on the number of group members (specifically, one encryption and decryption of a symmetric key encryption scheme and one execution of a key-derivation function for each key update are employed). In this way, membership privacy can be added to the ART protocol with a quite small overhead.

3. When a stage key is derived, a set of public keys of group members $\{IK_i\}_{i \in [1,n]}$ is contained to the input of KDF.

   - Due to the $\{IK_i\}_{i \in [1,n]}$ encryption in the setup phase, only the group members know which identity key is included. Thus, one may think that each user locally stores $\{IK_i\}_{i \in [1,n]}$ and then uses it to derive the stage key. However, if an adversary obtains state information, $\{IK_i\}_{i \in [1,n]}$ is also disclosed. Thus, we discuss why $\{IK_i\}_{i \in [1,n]}$ is required to derive the stage key. Cohn-Gordon et al. stated that KDF takes $\{IK_i\}_{i \in [1,n]}$ as input to satisfy partnering. Intuitively, partnering means that different session and nongroup members cannot derive the same stage key. Since KDF is modeled as a random oracle, if the output is the same, then the input is also the same. Moreover, the probability that a set of public keys T and the current tree key tk are the same as those of another session is negligible due to the randomness of K. Thus, in the proposed protocol, $\{IK_i\}_{i \in [1,n]}$ is removed from the KDF input.

We give our proposed protocol as follows.

Setup Phase. We give the setup phase as follows. In addition to (IK, EK) managed by PKI, we introduce a key pair (PK, DK) of a key private and robust public key encryption, and a key pair (PK^h, DK^h) of a hint system.

[Initiator]:

1. Randomly choose a setup key $\mathsf{suk} \in \mathbb{Z}_p$, and compute $\mathsf{SUK} = g^{\mathsf{suk}}$.
2. Obtain other members' key pairs $n - 1$ $\{(\mathsf{IK}_i, \mathsf{EK}_i, \mathsf{PK}_i, \mathsf{PK}_i^h)\}_{i=2}^n$ from PKI.
3. Randomly choose $K_1 \in \mathbb{Z}_p$.
4. For $(\mathsf{IK}_i, \mathsf{EK}_i)$ $(i = 2, 3, \dots, n)$, locally run the underlying strong one round authenticated key exchange protocol $K_i \leftarrow \mathsf{KeyExchange}(\mathsf{ik}_1, \mathsf{IK}_i, \mathsf{suk}, \mathsf{EK}_i)$. Here, the initiator indicates ik_1 and suk as secret keys.
5. Compute all public keys associated with nodes in the tree $T = (g^{K_1}, \dots, g^{K_{2n-2}})$. Here, the root node is excluded. Furthermore, delete all secret keys (except K_1) $(K_2, \dots, K_{2n-2})$.
6. Randomly choose a secret key k of a symmetric encryption scheme. Encrypt $\{(\mathsf{IK}_i, \mathsf{EK}_i)\}_{i \in [2,n]}$ using k, and let C_{pk} be the ciphertext.
7. Encrypt $\mathsf{IK}_1 \| j \| k$ using PK_j $(j = 2, 3, \dots, n)$ where IK_1 is regarded as a label and j is position information. Let CT_j be the ciphertext.[4]
8. Choose r and run $(U, H_j) \leftarrow \mathsf{Hint}(\mathsf{IK}_1, \mathsf{PK}_j^h, r)$ for $(j = 2, 3, \dots, n)$. Remark that the same r is used and thus U is a common value for all users.
9. Generate a signature σ on $((\mathsf{IK}_1, \mathsf{EK}_1), \mathsf{C}_{\mathsf{pk}}, U, \{(H_j, \mathsf{CT}_j)\}_{j \in [2,n]}, \mathsf{SUK}, T)$ using ik_1.
10. Broadcast $((\mathsf{IK}_1, \mathsf{EK}_1), \mathsf{C}_{\mathsf{pk}}, U, \{(H_j, \mathsf{CT}_j)\}_{j \in [2,n]}, \mathsf{SUK}, T)$ and σ.

Each user $i \in [2, n]$ receives $((\mathsf{IK}_1, \mathsf{EK}_1), \mathsf{C}_{\mathsf{pk}}, U, \{(H_j, \mathsf{CT}_j)\}_{j \in [2,n]}, \mathsf{SUK}, T)$ and σ, and runs the following procedure.

[User i ($i \in [2, n]$)]:

1. Check the validity of σ using the verification key IK_1. If σ is not valid, then abort.
2. If σ is valid, run $H \leftarrow \mathsf{Invert}(\mathsf{DK}_i^h, \mathsf{IK}_1, U)$. If $H \neq H_j$ for all $j = 2, 3, \dots, n$, then abort. Let j be the smallest index such that $H = H_j$. Let $\mathsf{IK} \| j \| k$ be the decryption result of CT_j. If $\mathsf{IK} \| j \| k = \bot$, then abort. If $\mathsf{IK} \neq \mathsf{IK}_1$, then abort. Otherwise, decrypt C_{pk} using k and obtain $\{(\mathsf{IK}_i, \mathsf{EK}_i)\}_{i \in [2,n]}$.
3. Run $K_i \leftarrow \mathsf{KeyExchange}(\mathsf{ik}_i, \mathsf{IK}_1, \mathsf{ek}_i, \mathsf{SUK})$.
4. Compute the tree key tk using K_i and public keys T
5. Derive the two stage key $\mathsf{mack} \leftarrow \mathsf{KDF}(0, \mathsf{tk}, T)$ and $\mathsf{enck} \leftarrow \mathsf{KDF}(1, \mathsf{tk}, T)$.

Key Update Phase. In the key update phase, as in the ART protocol, a user randomly selects $K' \in \mathbb{Z}_p$ and computes a set of updated public keys. Since the user has enck and mack, the user encrypts his/her position information using enck (here, any IND-CPA symmetric encryption scheme can be employed) and computes a MAC on the ciphertext and the set of updated public keys using mack. The user broadcasts the MAC, the ciphertext, and the set of updated public keys, locally derives a new tk' and new stage keys enck' and mack', and removes previous tk, enck, and mack. When group members receive the MAC, the ciphertext, and the set of updated public keys, they derive a new tk' and new

---

[4] Here, the position j of the user i and the index of the ciphertext do not have to be the same. Here, for the sake of simplicity, we use the same j for both indexes.

stage keys enck′ and mack′ and remove the previous tk, enck, and mack if the MAC is valid under mack. Specifically, each user $i \in [1, n]$ runs the procedure described below. Let the current secret key be K_i, and the position information be j.

[User i ($i \in [1, n]$)]:

1. Randomly choose $K_i' \in \mathbb{Z}_p$.
2. Compute public keys on the path (i.e., from the leaf node associated by the user i to the root node). Here, the public key of the root node is excluded because the secret key of the root node is regarded as the tree key. Let T' be a set of updated public keys.
3. Encrypt j using enck. Let C be the ciphertext.
4. Compute a MAC on C$||T'$ using mack, and broadcast the MAC and C$||T'$.
5. Remove enck and mack, and derive the new stage keys using the new tree key.

Each user $k \in [1, n] \backslash \{i\}$ receives the MAC and C$||T'$, and runs the following procedure.

[User k ($k \in [1, n] \backslash \{i\}$)]:

1. Check the validity of the MAC using mack.
2. If the MAC is valid, then decrypt C and obtain position information j.
3. Remove enck and mack, and derive the new stage keys using the new tree key.

Security: First, we discuss whether or not the proposed modification affects the security of the ART protocol. A stage key for authentication mack is derived by a hash chain, as in the ART protocol. In the proposed protocol, a stage key for encryption enck is also derived from a different hash chain. These stage keys are derived from the previous stage keys (initialized to 0 for mack and 1 for enck, respectively) and the current tree key. Thus, even if they are disclosed, their impact is the same as that of the ART protocol. Moreover, enck is not used for authentication. Thus, its disclosure does not affect the PCS of the ART protocol. Finally, the technique for updating a key is exactly the same as that of the ART protocol. Therefore, the proposed modification does not affect the FS and PCS in the ART protocol.

Next, we demonstrate that the proposed protocol provides membership privacy. In the setup phase, a set of public keys of group members $\{(\mathsf{IK}_i, \mathsf{EK}_i)\}_{i \in [2, n]}$ is encrypted. Thus, the ciphertext reveals no information on these keys. Moreover, due to the key privacy of the underlying public-key encryption scheme, the ciphertext does not disclose any information, which is used by PK_i for encryption. In addition, due to the anonymity of the hint system, the hint does not disclose any information, which is used by PK_i. In addition, due to the robustness of the underlying public-key encryption scheme and the hint system, a legitimate group member can decrypt a ciphertext, and the proposed modification does not affect the protocol execution. During the key update phase, a user who updates his/her own key, encrypts his/her position information using a common key (a stage key enck for encryption). Thus, the ciphertext does not disclose any information about the user who updates a key. We remark that the updated public keys are randomized due to the randomness of the leaf key. Thus, information about the user who updates a key is not disclosed by the updated public keys. If the length of a user path is different from that of other users, the anonymity is not provided because anyone can distinguish whether two users who update the keys are the same or not. Therefore, a complete binary tree structure is assumed in the proposed protocol. If the number of group members is not a power of 2, dummy users are added (i.e., in the setup phase, the initiator selects a leaf secret key K_d for a dummy user d). Alternatively, it might be enough to encrypt T' by enck. However, usually encryption does not hide the plaintext size. In this case, padding is required.

Membership Privacy for Group Members. Our main goal is to provide membership privacy from the viewpoint of non group members. In addition, it would be better to discuss membership privacy for group members which may be useful in some cases where group members also do not know who the other group members are (except the initiator). For example, in the online symposium scenario, the organizer setups the protocol as the initiator, and group members are participants of the symposium. Then, it may be not always necessary to know who the other participants are. (BTW, Chase et al. [7] do not consider this case). In the proposed protocol, the initiator sends a ciphertext of $\{(\mathsf{IK}_i, \mathsf{EK}_i)\}_{i \in [2,n]}$ to group members, and they know who the other members are from $\{(\mathsf{IK}_i, \mathsf{EK}_i)\}_{i \in [2,n]}$. Since we have removed $\{\mathsf{IK}_i\}_{i \in [1,n]}$ from the input of KDF, and members can generate a key via a strong one round authenticated key exchange protocol if they know $(\mathsf{IK}_1, \mathsf{EK}_1)$, our protocol works well even if $\{(\mathsf{IK}_i, \mathsf{EK}_i)\}_{i \in [2,n]}$ is not sent to group members. Concretely, the initiator encrypts $\mathsf{IK}_1 \| j$ using PK_j ($j = 2, 3, \ldots, n$), and let CT_j be the ciphertext, and generates a signature σ on $((\mathsf{IK}_1, \mathsf{EK}_1), \{\mathsf{CT}_j\}_{j \in [2,n]}, \mathsf{SUK}, T)$ using ik_1. We remark that anonymity does not hold since a user who updates a key sends position information which can be used for distinguishing whether two key updates are run by the same user or not. That is, the modified protocol provides "pseudonymity" for group members where each user is linkable via key update, and still provides membership privacy from the viewpoint of non group members.

4   Conclusion

In this paper, we propose an SGM protocol capable of providing membership privacy. The proposed protocol is an extension of the ART protocol with a quite small overhead that maintains the FS and PCS capabilities and scalability of the ART protocol. Alwen et al. [4] proposed a formal security model for SGM, but no initiator was specified, unlike the ART protocol and our protocol. Giving an extension of the Alwan et al. security model to provide membership privacy is left as a future work.

The ART protocol, which is our main target, has been updated and currently is known as the Messaging Layer Security (MLS) protocol. The Internet Engineering Task Force (IETF) has created a working group, and has discussed the MLS protocol. Currently (September 8, 2022), Draft 16 is the newest version [6]. As the main difference, in MLS, or rather TreeKEM, a user who updates a key encrypts secret values assigned to nodes using public keys of other users. That is, the user needs to know other group members explicitly. This seems there is no way to provide membership privacy for group members. However, providing membership privacy from the viewpoint of non group members may be possible. Further discussion is left as a future work.

References

1. Abdalla, M., Bellare, M., Neven, G.: Robust encryption. In: Micciancio, D. (ed.) TCC 2010. LNCS, vol. 5978, pp. 480–497. Springer, Heidelberg (2010). https://doi.org/10.1007/978-3-642-11799-2_28
2. Abdalla, M., Bellare, M., Neven, G.: Robust encryption. J. Cryptol. **31**(2), 307–350 (2018)
3. Alwen, J., Coretti, S., Dodis, Y., Tselekounis, Y.: Security analysis and improvements for the IETF MLS standard for group messaging. In: Micciancio, D., Ristenpart, T. (eds.) CRYPTO 2020. LNCS, vol. 12170, pp. 248–277. Springer, Cham (2020). https://doi.org/10.1007/978-3-030-56784-2_9
4. Alwen, J., Coretti, S., Dodis, Y., Tselekounis, Y.: Modular design of secure group messaging protocols and the security of MLS. In: ACM CCS, pp. 1463–1483 (2021)
5. Backes, M., Hanzlik, L., Schneider-Bensch, J.: Membership privacy for fully dynamic group signatures. In: ACM CCS, pp. 2181–2198 (2019)
6. Barnes, R., Beurdouche, B., Robert, R., Millican, J., Omara, E., Cohn-Gordon, K.: The messaging layer security (MLS) protocol. Internet-Draft draft-ietf-MLS-protocol-16, Internet Engineering Task Force (2022). https://datatracker.ietf.org/doc/draft-ietf-mls-protocol/16/. Work in Progress
7. Chase, M., Perrin, T., Zaverucha, G.: The signal private group system and anonymous credentials supporting efficient verifiable encryption. In: ACM CCS, pp. 1445–1459 (2020)
8. Chen, K., Chen, J.: Anonymous end to end encryption group messaging protocol based on asynchronous ratchet tree. In: ICICS, pp. 588–605 (2020)
9. Cohn-Gordon, K., Cremers, C., Garratt, L.: On post-compromise security. In: IEEE CSF, pp. 164–178 (2016)
10. Cohn-Gordon, K., Cremers, C., Garratt, L., Millican, J., Milner, K.: On ends-to-ends encryption: asynchronous group messaging with strong security guarantees. In: ACM CCS, pp. 1802–1819 (2018)
11. Libert, B., Paterson, K.G., Quaglia, E.A.: Anonymous broadcast encryption: adaptive security and efficient constructions in the standard model. In: Fischlin, M., Buchmann, J., Manulis, M. (eds.) PKC 2012. LNCS, vol. 7293, pp. 206–224. Springer, Heidelberg (2012). https://doi.org/10.1007/978-3-642-30057-8_13
12. Marlinspike, M.: The X3DH key agreement protocol, revision 1, 04 November 2016. https://signal.org/docs/specifications/x3dh/
13. Martiny, I., Kaptchuk, G., Aviv, A.J., Roche, D.S., Wustrow, E.: Improving signal's sealed sender. In: NDSS (2021)

On Membership Inference Attacks to Generative Language Models Across Language Domains

Myung Gyo Oh[ID], Leo Hyun Park[ID], Jaeuk Kim[ID], Jaewoo Park[ID],
and Taekyoung Kwon[✉][ID]

Graduate School of Information, Yonsei University, Seoul 03722, South Korea
{myunggyo.oh,dofi,freak0wk,jaewoo1218,taekyoung}@yonsei.ac.kr
http://seclab.yonsei.ac.kr/

Abstract. The confidentiality threat against training data has become a significant security problem in neural language models. Recent studies have shown that memorized training data can be extracted by injecting well-chosen prompts into generative language models. While these attacks have achieved remarkable success in the English-based Transformer architecture, it is unclear whether they are still effective in other language domains. This paper studies the effectiveness of attacks against Korean models and the potential for attack improvements that might be beneficial for future defense studies.

The contribution of this study is two-fold. First, we perform a membership inference attack against the state-of-the-art Korea-based GPT model. We found approximate training data with 20% to 90% precision in the top 100 samples and confirmed that the proposed attack technique for naive GPT is valid across the language domains. Second, in this process, we observed that the redundancy of the selected sentences could hardly be detected with the existing attack method. Since the information appearing in a few documents is more likely to be meaningful, it is desirable to increase the uniqueness of the sentences to improve the effectiveness of the attack. Thus, we propose a deduplication strategy to replace the traditional word-level similarity metric with the BPE token level. As a result, we show 6% to 22% of the underestimated samples among the selected samples.

Keywords: Generative language model · Korean-based GPT · Membership inference · Training data extraction attack · Confidentiality

1 Introduction

Deep learning (DL)-based neural language models (neural LMs) are rapidly advancing in their respective subfields of natural language processing (NLP), such as neural machine translation (NMT) [3,35], question answering (QA)

© Springer Nature Switzerland AG 2023
I. You and T.-Y. Youn (Eds.): WISA 2022, LNCS 13720, pp. 143–155, 2023.
https://doi.org/10.1007/978-3-031-25659-2_11

[10,29], and text summarization [39,40]. Along with these advances, recent studies have shown that LMs can leak memorized training data by well-chosen prompts [7,8,15,18,23,24,31,33,34,38]. In particular, generative LMs (*e.g.*, GPT family) are a prime target for membership inference (MI) attacks because they can automatically yield samples from being inferred. Carlini *et al.* [8] identified 604 actual training data by selecting 1,800 unique candidates in GPT-2 [26]. Furthermore, their follow-up study confirmed that the memorization capacity of LMs had a log-linear relationship with the model size [7]. Considering the current circumstance that GPT-based architectures are widely adopted as core engines in real applications [9,20], the MI attacks against LMs are a substantial threat.

While these attacks have achieved remarkable success in the English-based Transformer architecture, it is unclear whether they are still effective in other language domains. For example, many languages have grammatical characteristics different from English: no (or flexible) spacing, case-insensitive characters, and relatively free word order in a sentence. On the contrary, Carlini *et al.*'s work assumed case-sensitivity and rigorous spacing by targeting the English model. To the best of our knowledge, there is no case of studying an MI attack with this language difference.

In this paper, we study the MI attacks on Korean-based generative LMs. As we mentioned above, Korean has very different characteristics compared to English. For example, a spacing is more complicated and a character is case-insensitive. Moreover, the word order is more flexible so that its minor change may not affect the meaning of a sentence. Starting from the prior elegant work of Carlini *et al.* [8], we sample 100,000 texts from the LM (Sect. 3.2). We score the texts using four metrics based on each loss of samples and select the top-100 potential members (Sect. 3.3). Finally, we compute the approximated precision through the manual search (Sect. 3.4). The main difference between ours and Carlini *et al.*'s work [8] is the subsequent verification of the inference results.

Given their interesting assumption—formalized as being k-eidetic memorization—that the less mentioned information in the documents is unintentional and potentially harmful, increasing the uniqueness of selected top-k samples is necessary. Following the assumption, we more strictly perform deduplication (Sect. 3.4) based on the similarity between each prediction. We verify the effectiveness of our method by checking the number of *underestimated* samples where the newly calculated similarity exceeds a threshold so that judged to be a duplicate, unlike the previous result.

Our two-fold contribution based on the experimental results is as follows:

- We verify that the existing MI attack is effective against the state-of-the-art (SOTA) Korean-based GPT model (Sect. 4.3). Our finding that well-defined MI attacks may not depend on the language domain motivates future research toward multilingual (or universal) MI attacks.
- We refine the existing deduplicating strategy to improve the uniqueness of selection in the MI process (Sect. 4.4). A practical attack requires dedupli-

cation because the knowledge appearing in a few documents is likely to be meaningful information.

We publish the experimental code to reproduce the main empirical results: https://github.com/seclab-yonsei/mia-ko-lm.

2 Background of Language Modeling

Training Objective. The LM f explores the weight $\hat{\theta}$ that maximizes the appearance probability for each element in a given training corpus $\mathcal{D} = \{x^i\}_{i=1}^{N}$ in the pre-training process. The probability that each sentence $x_{1:n} = [x_1, \ldots, x_n]$ appears from f can be expressed as Eq. 1 by the chain rule.

$$\Pr(x_{1:n}; \theta) = \Pr(x_1, \ldots, x_n; \theta) = \prod_{j=1}^{n} \Pr(x_j \mid x_{<j}; \theta) \tag{1}$$

LM f takes a step of gradient descent to minimize negative log-likelihood:

$$\mathcal{L}(\theta) = -\sum_{i=1}^{N} \log \Pr(x_{1:n}^i; \theta) = -\sum_{i=1}^{N} \sum_{j=1}^{n} \log \Pr(x_j^i \mid x_{<j}^i; \theta) \tag{2}$$

$$\theta \leftarrow \theta - \alpha \nabla_\theta \mathcal{L}(\theta) \tag{3}$$

where α is the step size of the gradient.

Inference. The LM f auto-regressively predicts the next word from the given words iteratively during the inference phase:

$$\hat{x}_t = \arg\max_{x_t \in \mathcal{X}} \log \Pr(x_t \mid x_{<t}; \theta) \tag{4}$$

where $\mathcal{X}$ is the set of all tokens that the LM can explore.

GPT Family. The Transformer structure proposed by Vaswani *et al.* [35] in 2017 overwhelms existing recurrent neural network-based models in performance of NMT, leading to rapid development in NLP. Since then, the GPT family using only the decoder block of Transformer has shown exceptionally superior performance in natural language generation (NLG) [4,6,9,26,27,36].

3 Methodology

In this section, we describe an approach to attack the Korean model. We first define the attacker's capabilities and objectives (Sect. 3.1). Afterward, we explain the method to generate texts following the threat model (Sect. 3.2), determine the member/non-member of the sampled data through MI (Sect. 3.3), and verify the GT of the selected data (Sect. 3.4). In this process, we introduce the modified Carlini *et al.*'s deduplication to suit the characteristics of the Korean language.

3.1   Threat Model

Adversary's Capabilities. Assume that the attacker has a black-box attack environment that can access the input/output of the pre-trained LM f. The attacker does not have access to the weights inside the f, training data distribution, architecture knowledge, and output of the hidden layer. Nevertheless, for a chosen prompt $p = [p_1, \ldots, p_n]$, the attacker can compute the output $s = f(p; \theta) = [p \parallel s_1, \ldots, s_m]$ of the LM. The attacker can control the hyperparameters for generating the output s, $e.g.$, adjusting the resulting's min/max length and considering various sampling strategies [16,27].

Adversary's Objectives. Given an input x and access to the pre-trained LM f, an attacker infers whether $\hat{x} \in \mathcal{D}_{\text{train}}$ for $\hat{x} \in \mathcal{D}_{\text{infer}}$ [17]. We assume an attacker conducting an untargeted attack that acquires data without aiming or deriving for specific data. The attacker maximizes the MI precision by selecting the set of top-k samples $\mathcal{A}$ among numerous samples obtained from f:

$$\hat{\mathcal{A}} = \arg\max_{\substack{\mathcal{A} \subset \mathcal{D}_{\text{infer}} \\ |\mathcal{A}|=k}} \sum_{\hat{x} \in \mathcal{A}} \mathbb{1}\left(\exists x \in \mathcal{D}_{\text{train}} : \texttt{match}(x, \hat{x}) \geq m\right) \tag{5}$$

where `match` is a substring matching function that determines memorization, and m is a threshold that controls the lower bound of matching characters (Sect. 3.4).

3.2   Text Generation

For MI, we first approximate the population by generating a sufficiently large number of samples. When selecting the next word, we auto-regressively sample the words with the top-40 probabilities. The output statement is 256 tokens, excluding the input prompt. For random sampling, we use a special token [EOS] (end of the sentence) as a prompt to inform the end of the sentence.

3.3   Membership Inference

The MI process is performed on the generated sample to select data with a high probability of being in the training data. MI attack on machine learning (ML) starts with the assumption that the data used for training is overfitting (or memorized) more than the data not used for training ($i.e.$, test dataset) [32]; the data already learned once will have relatively high confidence. We use four out of six evaluation metrics proposed by Carlini et $al.$ [8] (Table 1) to capture the confidence difference. We select potential member sentences with the top-k duplicates removed by scoring the samples on the four metrics. The other two metrics, which we did not use, measure the loss ratio of two different sized (XL versus medium or small) models for a single sentence.

Table 1. A brief introduction to the four evaluation indicators we used. PPL and `Window` metrics score better with lower values, `zlib` and `Lowercase` metrics with higher values.

Shortcut	Abstractive evaluation method	Lower best	Higher best
PPL	log (Perplexity)	✓	–
zlib	(zlib Entropy) /PPL	–	✓
Lowercase	log (Lowercase Perplexity) /PPL	–	✓
Window	log (min {Perplexity of Sliding Windows})	✓	–

Perplexity. We calculate the perplexity (PPL) of the output sentences from the LM as the geometric mean of the sentence probabilities over the length. Intuitively, the PPL is the number of confusing words for every time step. The lower the value, the more confident the LM is about the sentence, and the higher the value, the more confused the LM is.

Comparing with Zlib Entropy. LM sometimes yields an unexpected output; it produces an incoherent gibberish output or degenerates repetition [16]. Although the PPL effectively filters out unfamiliar phrases that do not fit the syntax, it sometimes gives a very high score to unexpectedly repeated output sentences (*e.g.*, "[1] [2] [3] ..." or "----- ..."). Carlini *et al.* attempted filtering by calculating the entropy of a sentence based on the zlib [14] compression algorithm to alleviate this phenomenon. The lower the PPL and the higher the zlib of the sentence at the same time, the closer it is to a probable member.

Comparing with Lowercase Texts. In the case of English text containing sufficient uppercase characters, such as newspaper article titles and product names, converting the sentences to lowercase may dramatically raise the PPL. We select the `Lowercase` as one of the metrics since even the Korean text can include various English characters.

Calculating Minimum Perplexity by Sliding Window. There is a possibility that the inference result is not wholly similar to the actual member and is included only in some segmentation. Carlini *et al.* calculated the lowest PPL among 50 tokens by sliding the sentence. Since the stride is unclear, we set it to 16, considering the time cost.

3.4 Verification

We verify whether the selected top-k samples by MI are members or not. The dataset used for training is not publicly available, and the property (distribution) in which the data was collected is also unspecified. Since the GT is unidentified, we collected approximated reference documents by manually searching each sample with the Google search engine as a suboptimal approach.

Table 2. An example of a non-duplicated sentence with high similarity by intrinsic evaluation. We use `difflib` [1] to highlight common areas. In the existing method [8], the similarity with the reference was underestimated to 0.443. However, our method raises the similarity to 0.549 and judges it as a duplicate.

Reference (Top-31)
◆ 우리가 잘 몰랐던 24가지 ◆ 1,미국의 수도 워싱턴D.C 에 고층건물이 없는 이유 워싱턴D.C 에는 고층 건물이 없습니다. 그 이유는 국회의사당(높이 94m) 보다 더높은 건물을 지을 수 없도록 건축법이 제정돼 있기 때문입니다. 2. 미국 국회의사당에는 의자가 국회의원 수보다 적게 배치가 돼 있다. 회의에 늦게 참석하는 의원은 뒤에 선채로 회의에 참여해야 되고 물론 명패도 없으니 화난다고 명패를 내던질 수도 없거니와 만일 기물을 내던졌다간 법의 준엄한 법의 심판을 받게됩니다. 우리 나라 국회에도 적용했으면.... 3. 피카소의 그림이 루브르 박물관에 있을까? 루브르 (The Louvre) 박물관에 전시되는 작품은 그 작가가 죽은지 60년이 지나야 전시될 수 있습니다. 단 한사람의 예외가 있었는데 그것은 프랑스의 화가 조오지 브라크 (George Braque1882~1963) 입니다. 4. 매미의 일생 하룻밤 을 살기 위해서 매미는 17년 동안 땅속에서 번데기로 살다가 17년이 지난후 화려한 잠을 깨면 비로서 성숙된 매미로 변신되어

Non-Duplicated Hypothesis (Top-75; Similarity: 0.443 → 0.549)
우리가 잘 몰랐던 事實 이곳 미국 칼리포니아에 거주하는 폴 임(Paul Lim) 박사의 저서 ('우리가 모르고 있는 모든 것이 이 책 속에 있었다.')를 참고 했으며 사진들은 별도로 자료를 수집하여 편집하였습니다 美國의 首都 워싱턴 D.C 에 高層建物이 없는 理由 워싱턴D.C 에는 고층 건물이 없습니다. 그 이유는 국회의사당(높이 94m) 보다 더 높은 건물을 지을수 없도록 건축법이 제정돼 있기 때문입니다. 워싱턴 D.C 의 미국 국회의사당 <參考> 미국 국회 의사당에는 의자가 국회의원수 보다 적게 배치가 돼 있습니다. 회의에 늦게 참석하는 의원은 뒤에 선채로 회의에 참여해야되고 물론 명패도 없으니 화난다고 명패를 내던질 수도 없거니와 만일 기물을 내던졌다간 법의 준엄한 법의 심판을 받게 됩니다. 피카소의 그림이 루브르 博物館에 있을까? 루브르 (The Louvre) 박물관에 전시되는 작품은 그 작가가 죽은 지 60년이 지나야 전시 될 수 있습니다. 단 한사람의 예외가 있었는데 그것은

Candidate Deduplication. In order to maximize the amount of information in the unique output sentences, we deduplicate two sentences when the similarity between them exceeds a certain threshold. Two duplicated sentences are the same or similar. We deleted the identical sentences except one for efficient indexing. If they are not the same but similar to some degree, we perform deduplicating by the similarity function based on trigram multiset. We obtained a family of sets `tri` by binding three adjacent tokens (*i.e.*, trigram). We describe two deduplication method, including our new strategy with BPE tokenization, as follows:

- **Word Level** tokenization is a traditional way of splitting each token by whitespace and punctuation [8]. Simple to use and understand, but it might not be a suitable method for tokenizing Korean text with complicated spacing.
- **Byte Pair Encoding** (BPE) [13] tokenization is one of NLP's most popular subword segmentation algorithms [30]. Prior knowledge of vocabulary mapping is required when pre-training the target LM, but generally, we can expect to divide the text into more precise units than word-level division. This modification was motivated by insufficient previous deduplicating, in which some similar texts were included in top-k (Table 2).

We calculate the similarity between tokenized sentences (*i.e.*, predictions) and deduplicate them based on that. For some sentence s is similar with t if and only if $\frac{|\text{tri}(s) \cap \text{tri}(t)|}{|\text{tri}(s)|} \geq \alpha$ for the threshold $\alpha = 0.5$.

Substring Matching. The raw document text (called *reference*) collected by the searching trivially includes the inference result (called *hypothesis*). Given reference $r = [r^1, \ldots, r^p]$ and hypothesis $h = [h^1, \ldots, h^q]$ where $p > q$ and each element means a character, h is memorized if $r^{i..i+m} = h^{j..j+m}$ for some indexes i and j. We set threshold $m = 50$.

4 Evaluation

4.1 Environments

We performed text generation and MI attacks on a single machine environment with two NVIDIA Quadro RTX 6000 (24 GB) GPUs. We omit other components since they do not significantly affect the reproduction of experimental results.

4.2 Target System

We experiment with the Korean-based SOTA generative LM, KoGPT6B-ryan1.5b-float16 (KoGPT) [21]. The pre-trained KoGPT is open for research in HuggingFace [37], and since the number of parameters is large enough, we considered it is effective MI would be possible [7]. In addition, the corporation to which the team belongs has a search engine that can collect high-quality source data. The high quality of the training data leads to more complete outputs and contributes to the consistency (*i.e.*, reproducibility) of the experiment results.

4.3 Effectiveness of Membership Inference Across Language Domains

Table 3 shows the quantitative results of MI. We identified 89 and 90 actual members out of 100 potential members for the metric PPL and zlib, respectively. We searched only 20 samples with the Lowercase metric, 33 fewer than the prior result. We detected 52 samples with Window, 19 more than before; yet, it did not show performance improvement as much as PPL or zlib metric.

Although we detected more redundant samples than in the previous work, it is *premature* to conclude that the KoGPT model is vulnerable. Since our target system is 4.0× larger than that of Carlini *et al.* (Sect. 4.2), the memorization capacity may differ. Carlini *et al.* used the GPT-2 (XL) [8] with 1542M parameters, and we used KoGPT [21] with 6167M parameters. Memorization definition is also a significant factor influencing precision. Carlini *et al.* reported a potentially membered sample to OpenAI and received only "member/non-member" results; *i.e.*, they overlooked a precise threshold of memorization. On the other hand, we considered a case in which 50 tokens of BPE tokenized texts were duplicated (Sect. 3.4).

Table 4 provides examples of top-1 sentences for each metric. PPL and zlib entropy metrics showed the same output. Lowercase metric contained many

Table 3. Quantitative results of MI using four metrics. Each result means the number of samples found with the corresponding metric out of 100. The leading cause of finding more members than prior work in `PPL`, `zlib`, and `Window` metrics is the increase in the number of parameters in LM. On the other hand, the `Lowercase` metric shows poor performance due to differences in language domains; attempt to use the characteristics of English words from Korean-based LM.

Target system	Tokenization	Metrics			
		PPL	zlib	Lowercase	Window
GPT-2 (XL)	Word-level	9	59	**53**	33
KoGPT	Word-level	89	90	20	52
KoGPT	BPE	**91**	**91**	18	**59**

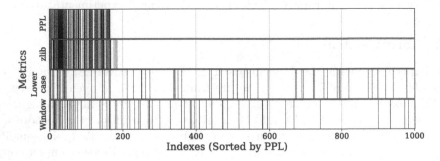

Fig. 1. Selection points of each metric for the top-1000 samples in ascending order of `PPL`. `PPL` and `zlib` metrics tend to focus on common samples. On the other hand, `Lowercase` and `Window` metrics look at different aspects of the generated sample.

English uppercase characters and had a low `PPL` at the same time. `Window` metric includes trivial (*i.e.*, repeated and boring) segments in the middle of the sentence.

The selection of the four metrics is not focused on specific outputs but instead on looking at different parts. As shown in Fig. 1, the top-k `PPL` and `zlib` samples often overlap. Nonetheless, `Lowercase` and `Window` indicated an even distribution of the index regardless of the `PPL`. Evaluating different aspects of the generated text is crucial as it enriches the distribution of selected samples.

4.4   Improving Uniqueness of Inferred Samples

As we mentioned above (Sect. 3.4), we modified the existing word-level sentence similarity with the BPE token level to improve the uniqueness of inference results. The BPE token-level method found 6 to 22 more duplicated samples from each metric (Table 5), showing that the previous method underestimated the similarity of such samples. We believe that the significantly larger number of underestimations found in the `Window` metric is not meaningful. Multiple prompts with the same `PPL` may appear if the metric looks at only a partial window (almost 20%) instead of all tokens.

Table 4. The output sentence with the highest score for each metric. We masked the personal information included in the output with ██. The part obscured by the character "*" is presumed to be de-identified before pre-training.

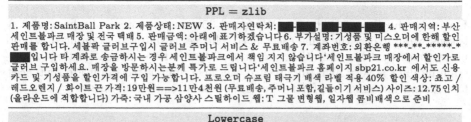

PPL = zlib
1. 제품명: SaintBall Park 2. 제품상태: NEW 3. 판매자연락처: ██-██, ██-██-██ 4. 판매지역: 부산 세인트볼파크 매장 및 전국 택배 5. 판매금액: 아래에 표기하겠습니다 6. 부가설명: 기성품 및 미스오더에 한해 할인 판매를 합니다. 세블팍 글러브구입시 글러브 주머니 서비스 & 무료배송 7. 계좌번호: 외환은행 ***-**-*****-* ██입니다 타 계좌로 송금하시는 경우 세인트볼파크에서 책임 지지 않습니다 '세인트볼파크 매장에서 할인가로 글러브 구입하세요. 매장을 방문하시는분께 특가로 드립니다 '세인트볼파크 홈페이지 sbp21.co.kr 에서도 신용 카드 및 기성품을 할인가격에 구입 가능합니다. 프로오더 슈프림 태극기 배색 라벨 적용 40% 할인 색상: 쵸고 / 레드오렌지 / 화이트 끈 가격: 19만원===>11만4천원 (무료배송, 주머니 포함,길들이기 서비스) 사이즈: 12.75인치 (올라운드에 적합합니다) 가죽: 국내 가공 삼양사 스틸하이드 웹: T 그물 변형웹, 일자웹 콤비배색으로 준비

Lowercase
1. 제품명: SaintBall Park 2. 제품상태: NEW 3. 판매자연락처: ██-██, ██-██-██ 4. 판매지역: 부산 세인트볼파크 매장 및 전국 택배 5. 판매금액: 아래에 표기하겠습니다 6. 부가설명: 기성품 및 미스오더에 한해 할인 판매를 합니다. 세블팍 글러브구입시 글러브 주머니 서비스 & 무료배송 7. 계좌번호: 외환은행 ***-**-*****-* ██입니다 타 계좌로 송금하시는 경우 세인트볼파크에서 책임 지지 않습니다 '세인트볼파크 매장에서 할인가로 글러브 구입하세요. 매장을 방문하시는분께 특가로 드립니다 '세인트볼파크 홈페이지 sbp21.co.kr 에서도 신용 카드 및 기성품 20% 할인가격에 구입 가능합니다. 미즈노 MVP GXF55 FIRST BASE MITT 가격: 14만원 (무료배송) 색상: 블랙/탄 바로 길들여집니다.. 부드럽습니다 미즈노 GXC 56 CATCHER'S MITT 가격: 14만원 (무료배송) 색상: 블랙 미국 글러브 치고는 하드합니다 미즈노 GPM1251 BASEBALL GLOVE 12", 12.

Window
이번에 새로 산 거는요....^^; (새로 산거고 다른거고..) 아참.. 제 이름은.. ██ ██ 이구요.. 나이는.. ██살 이예요..^^ (나이를 너무 일찍 밝혔나요..^^?) 이 애들은.. 저희학교 5대 킹카예요..^^ (제 친구들이 너무 착해요..♡) ----------------------------------- 처음 쓰는 글이라 좀 엉성한데요.. 읽어 주셔서 넘 감사해요.. 다음번에는 더 좋은 주제와 내용으로 찾아 올께요.. 그럼 안녕히.~~~ ♡ ----------------------------------- ——※※[雪花] 일본소녀 이토유리코 그녀가 한국에 떳다?!※※ 카페:http://cafe.daum.net/██[水流花流水香]에서 퍼왔습니다. 불펌금 지!! -----------------------------------

Table 5. The number of underestimated cases. The word-level similarity method is being top-k, but our method is not.

Eval. item	Metrics			
	PPL	zlib	Lowercase	Window
# of Underrated	6	6	7	**22**

Since only 100 samples were selected, we must be careful not to interpret the experimental results prematurely. Nevertheless, discovering potentially underestimated members of about 6% per metric is encouraging. This result suggests that our method can increase about 6%p more information entropy in the limited top-k sample selection environment.

5 Discussion

Inference Sample Properties. Since we experimented with an untargeted attack, we did not consider any properties of the inferences. A targeted attack that maximizes the risk of privacy leakage of training data resulting from MI outcomes is a promising future research area. Researchers can extend the experiment to investigate policy issues that may arise from the output, regardless of member/non-member results [5]. A simple example is an issue of copyright and intellectual property (IP) infringement driven by leakage of the memorized training data.

Entirely the Same Outputs. We found 35 curious sentences[1] whose all 256 tokens were utterly the same (Sect. 3.4). The *verbatim* outputs induced two or more times by LM imply that the possibility of the sentence existing in the training data is very high. In advance, we have obliterated duplicate sentences for efficient indexing, but further research is still required in future.

Possible Mitigations. Differential privacy (DP) is one of the most well-known techniques to guarantee the strong privacy of training data [11,12]. Despite the proven privacy concept [2,17,25], there is a tradeoff between DP and the utility of the ML model. Alternatively, some recent studies attempt to enhance performance while reducing memorization for specific data by deduplicating training data [19,22]. Lee *et al.* reduced memorized training data's emission amounts by a factor of ten using deduplication of training data [22].

6   Related Work

Extracting Training Data from Large Language Models. Carlini *et al.* proposed a MI attack pipeline targeting a generative LM [8]. They deduplicated sentences by calculating a word-level trigram-multiset based on whitespaces and punctuations in a sentence. In contrast, we considered that the deduplicating strategy is an overly rough assumption for determining the similarity of sentences and improved it by the BPE token-level similarity (Sect. 3.4).

Quantifying Memorization Across Neural Language Models. Carlini *et al.* performed extensive experiments on GPT-J [36] and GPT-Neo [4] for quantitative analysis of factors that increase the memorization capability of LM. As a result, they identified three attributes that significantly influence memorization; bigger models, repeated strings, and more extended context. They confirmed that the LM could accurately reproduce the target sentence with a chosen length-k prompt. Afterward, they expanded the study to the T5 [28] masked LM (MLM) as a replication experiment. We conducted experiments only on models trained by the next word prediction (NWP) strategy (Sect. 4.2), not MLM. We did not study memorization according to the selection of input prompts; this is due to the characteristics of the target system for which training data is not publicly available. We plan to expand the experiment to public LMs trained on publicly available datasets in the future.

---

[1] Two, three, and five identical sentences appear 6, 1, and 4 times, respectively.

Deduplicating Training Data Makes Language Models Better. Lee *et al.* showed that duplication of training data for LM reduces the diversity of outputs and increases the likelihood of exposing the members [22]. They generated 100,000 samples, each with a maximum length of 512 BPE tokens. They defined that the LM remembers tokens if each output has exactly 50 token substrings in the training data. As a result, they showed that LM memorized more than 1% of the generated tokens. We maintain their memorization definition while reducing the token length limit from "less than 512" to "exactly 256". This process prevents the experimental results (precision) from being exaggerated.

7   Conclusion

This paper studied the effectiveness and improvements of the existing MI attack for the SOTA Korean-based GPT model. We confirmed that the existing attack strategies are still sufficient for data extraction of the Korea-based LM. In addition, PPL and zlib metrics yield up to 80%p higher than the prior results. We established that the existing deduplicating procedure during this attack process is not rigorous enough. We identified 6 to 22 more duplicated samples than the existing method by replacing the word-level trigram similarity with the BPE token-level one. Since the knowledge that appears in fewer documents is more likely to be meaningful, increasing the uniqueness of the selected samples increases the effectiveness and diversity of the attack.

We plan to gradually expand the experiment on LM memorization, one of the possible mitigations. Future studies will help understand the fundamental cause of confidentiality leaks for LM. We believe that our study on confidentiality infringement serves as an opportunity to raise the awareness of all researchers, developers, and administrators about security issues.

Acknowledgments. We thank the reviewers for their insightful feedback. This work was supported by the National Research Foundation of Korea (NRF) grant funded by the Korea government (MSIT) (No. NRF-2019R1A2C1088802).

References

1. difflib – helpers for computing deltas. https://docs.python.org/3/library/difflib.html, Accessed 01 May 2022
2. Abadi, M., et al.: Deep learning with differential privacy. In: Proceedings of the 2016 ACM SIGSAC Conference on Computer and Communications Security, pp. 308–318 (2016)
3. Bahdanau, D., Cho, K., Bengio, Y.: Neural machine translation by jointly learning to align and translate. arXiv preprint arXiv:1409.0473 (2014)
4. Black, S., Gao, L., Wang, P., Leahy, C., Biderman, S.: Gpt-neo: Large scale autoregressive language modeling with mesh-tensorflow. If you use this software, please cite it using these metadata 58 (2021)
5. Brown, H., Lee, K., Mireshghallah, F., Shokri, R., Tramèr, F.: What does it mean for a language model to preserve privacy? arXiv preprint arXiv:2202.05520 (2022)

6. Brown, T., et al.: Language models are few-shot learners. Adv. Neural Inf. Process. Syst. **33**, 1877–1901 (2020)
7. Carlini, N., Ippolito, D., Jagielski, M., Lee, K., Tramer, F., Zhang, C.: Quantifying memorization across neural language models. arXiv preprint arXiv:2202.07646 (2022)
8. Carlini, N., et al.: Extracting training data from large language models. In: 30th USENIX Security Symposium (USENIX Security 2021), pp. 2633–2650 (2021)
9. Chen, M., et al.: Evaluating large language models trained on code. arXiv preprint arXiv:2107.03374 (2021)
10. Devlin, J., Chang, M.W., Lee, K., Toutanova, K.: Bert: pre-training of deep bidirectional transformers for language understanding. arXiv preprint arXiv:1810.04805 (2018)
11. Dwork, C.: Differential privacy: a survey of results. In: Agrawal, M., Du, D., Duan, Z., Li, A. (eds.) TAMC 2008. LNCS, vol. 4978, pp. 1–19. Springer, Heidelberg (2008). https://doi.org/10.1007/978-3-540-79228-4_1
12. Dwork, C., McSherry, F., Nissim, K., Smith, A.: Calibrating noise to sensitivity in private data analysis. In: Halevi, S., Rabin, T. (eds.) TCC 2006. LNCS, vol. 3876, pp. 265–284. Springer, Heidelberg (2006). https://doi.org/10.1007/11681878_14
13. Gage, P.: A new algorithm for data compression. C Users J. **12**(2), 23–38 (1994)
14. Gailly, J.l., Adler, M.: Zlib compression library (2004)
15. Hayes, J., Melis, L., Danezis, G., De Cristofaro, E.: Logan: membership inference attacks against generative models. In: Proceedings on Privacy Enhancing Technologies (PoPETs), De Gruyter, vol. 2019, pp. 133–152 (2019)
16. Holtzman, A., Buys, J., Du, L., Forbes, M., Choi, Y.: The curious case of neural text degeneration. arXiv preprint arXiv:1904.09751 (2019)
17. Hu, H., Salcic, Z., Sun, L., Dobbie, G., Yu, P.S., Zhang, X.: Membership inference attacks on machine learning: a survey. ACM Comput. Surv. (CSUR) **54**, 1–37 (2021)
18. Jagannatha, A., Rawat, B.P.S., Yu, H.: Membership inference attack susceptibility of clinical language models. arXiv preprint arXiv:2104.08305 (2021)
19. Kandpal, N., Wallace, E., Raffel, C.: Deduplicating training data mitigates privacy risks in language models. arXiv preprint arXiv:2202.06539 (2022)
20. Kim, B., et al.: What changes can large-scale language models bring? intensive study on hyperclova: billions-scale Korean generative pretrained transformers. arXiv preprint arXiv:2109.04650 (2021)
21. Kim, I., Han, G., Ham, J., Baek, W.: Kogpt: Kakaobrain Korean (hangul) generative pre-trained transformer. https://github.com/kakaobrain/kogpt (2021)
22. Lee, K., et al.: Deduplicating training data makes language models better. arXiv preprint arXiv:2107.06499 (2021)
23. Lehman, E., Jain, S., Pichotta, K., Goldberg, Y., Wallace, B.C.: Does bert pre-trained on clinical notes reveal sensitive data? arXiv preprint arXiv:2104.07762 (2021)
24. Mireshghallah, F., Goyal, K., Uniyal, A., Berg-Kirkpatrick, T., Shokri, R.: Quantifying privacy risks of masked language models using membership inference attacks. arXiv preprint arXiv:2203.03929 (2022)
25. Nasr, M., Songi, S., Thakurta, A., Papemoti, N., Carlin, N.: Adversary instantiation: lower bounds for differentially private machine learning. In: 2021 IEEE Symposium on Security and Privacy (SP), pp. 866–882. IEEE (2021)
26. Radford, A., Narasimhan, K., Salimans, T., Sutskever, I.: Improving language understanding by generative pre-training (2018)

27. Radford, A., Wu, J., Child, R., Luan, D., Amodei, D., Sutskever, I., et al.: Language models are unsupervised multitask learners. OpenAI Blog **1**(8), 9 (2019)
28. Raffel, C., et al.: Exploring the limits of transfer learning with a unified text-to-text transformer. arXiv preprint arXiv:1910.10683 (2019)
29. Roller, S., et al.: Recipes for building an open-domain chatbot. arXiv preprint arXiv:2004.13637 (2020)
30. Sennrich, R., Haddow, B., Birch, A.: Neural machine translation of rare words with subword units. arXiv preprint arXiv:1508.07909 (2015)
31. Shejwalkar, V., Inan, H.A., Houmansadr, A., Sim, R.: Membership inference attacks against nlp classification models. In: NeurIPS 2021 Workshop Privacy in Machine Learning (2021)
32. Shokri, R., Stronati, M., Song, C., Shmatikov, V.: Membership inference attacks against machine learning models. In: 2017 IEEE Symposium on Security and Privacy (SP), pp. 3–18. IEEE (2017)
33. Song, C., Raghunathan, A.: Information leakage in embedding models. In: Proceedings of the 2020 ACM SIGSAC Conference on Computer and Communications Security, pp. 377–390 (2020)
34. Thakkar, O.D., Ramaswamy, S., Mathews, R., Beaufays, F.: Understanding unintended memorization in language models under federated learning. In: Proceedings of the Third Workshop on Privacy in Natural Language Processing, pp. 1–10 (2021)
35. Vaswani, A., et al.: Attention is all you need. Adv. Neural Inf. Process. Syst. **30**, 1–11 (2017)
36. Wang, B., Komatsuzaki, A.: Gpt-j-6b: A 6 billion parameter autoregressive language model (2021)
37. Wolf, T., et al.: Huggingface's transformers: state-of-the-art natural language processing. arXiv preprint arXiv:1910.03771 (2019)
38. Zhang, C., Ippolito, D., Lee, K., Jagielski, M., Tramèr, F., Carlini, N.: Counterfactual memorization in neural language models. arXiv preprint arXiv:2112.12938 (2021)
39. Zhang, J., Zhao, Y., Saleh, M., Liu, P.: Pegasus: pre-training with extracted gap-sentences for abstractive summarization. In: International Conference on Machine Learning, pp. 11328–11339. PMLR (2020)
40. Zhong, M., Liu, P., Chen, Y., Wang, D., Qiu, X., Huang, X.: Extractive summarization as text matching. arXiv preprint arXiv:2004.08795 (2020)

A Joint Framework to Privacy-Preserving Edge Intelligence in Vehicular Networks

Muhammad Firdaus[1] and Kyung-Hyune Rhee[2]([⊠])

[1] Department of Artificial Intelligence Convergence, Pukyong National University,
Busan 48513, Republic of Korea
mfirdaus@pukyong.ac.kr
[2] Division of Computer Engineering, Pukyong National University,
Busan 48513, Republic of Korea
khrhee@pknu.ac.kr

Abstract. The number of internet-connected devices has been exponentially growing with the massive volume of heterogeneous data generated from various devices, resulting in a highly intertwined cyber-physical system. Currently, the Edge Intelligence System (EIS) concept that leverages the merits of edge computing and Artificial Intelligence (AI) is utilized to provide smart cloud services with powerful computational processing and reduce decision-making delays. Thus, EIS offers a possible solution to realizing future Intelligent Transportation Systems (ITS), especially in a vehicular network framework. However, since the central aggregator server is responsible for supervising the entire system orchestration, the existing EIS framework faces several challenges and is still potentially susceptible to numerous malicious attacks. Hence, to solve the issues mentioned earlier, this paper presents the notion of secure edge intelligence, merging the benefits of Federated Learning (FL), blockchain, and Local Differential Privacy (LDP). The blockchain-assisted FL approach is used to efficiently improve traffic prediction accuracy and enhance user privacy and security by recording transactions in immutable distributed ledger networks as well as providing a decentralized reward mechanism system. Furthermore, LDP is empowered to strengthen the confidentiality of data sharing transactions, especially in protecting the user's private data from various attacks. The proposed framework has been implemented in two scenarios, i.e., blockchain-based FL to efficiently develop the decentralized traffic management for vehicular networks and LDP-based FL to produce the randomized privacy protection using the IBM Library for differential privacy.

This research was supported by the Republic of Korea's MSIT (Ministry of Science and ICT), under the ICT Convergence Industry Innovation Technology Development Project (2022-0-00614) supervised by the IITP and partially supported by the Republic of Korea's MSIT (Ministry of Science and ICT), under the 2022 technology commercialization capability enhancement project (2022-BS-RD-0034) supervised by the INNOPOLIS.

I. You and T.-Y. Youn (Eds.): WISA 2022, LNCS 13720, pp. 156–167, 2023.
https://doi.org/10.1007/978-3-031-25659-2_12

Keywords: Edge intelligence · Blockchain · Federated learning · Local differential privacy · Smart contracts · Incentive mechanism · Vehicular networks

1   Introduction

Recently, the number of internet-connected devices has been exponentially growing with great potential utilization in myriad applications, such as Intelligent Transportation Systems (ITS) [29], smart grids [25], smart healthcare [22], and smart industry [2]. It is followed by the massive volume of heterogeneous data generated from various devices, resulting in a highly intertwined cyber-physical system. In terms of ITS, the concept of edge intelligence [28] system (EIS), which leverages the merits of Mobile Edge Computing (MEC) and artificial intelligence (AI) technology, has been widely deployed to form the next generation of vehicular networks (VNs). MEC offers real-time communications with high bandwidth and low latency by locating the computing and processing infrastructure close to the end-user in the edge network. On the other hand, AI provides smart cloud services with high performance and reduces decision-making delays [5]. Thus, EIS is designed to manage intelligent resource orchestration, enable self-aggregating communication systems, offer powerful computational processing, and reduce decision-making delay by leveraging edge resources on local edge networks [30].

Nevertheless, the traditional AI technique, such as machine learning, suffers from severe privacy leakage risk by centralizing and aggregating the user's training data containing private information on a centralized server. Federated learning (FL) as a decentralized machine learning paradigm has lately developed to address the privacy challenges by allowing mobile devices (e.g., vehicles) to collaboratively perform AI training without giving raw data containing the user's private information to the central aggregator [11]. The FL approach allows the users to perform a local training model that never leaves their own devices. In this sense, the user's raw data is only used to train and update a current global model and send an updated model to the central aggregator in each iteration. Then, the central aggregator generates a new global model by aggregating these updated and trained models gathered from the participated users to be used in the next iteration. This process is repeated in multiple iterations until the global model achieves a particular accuracy [1].

Although FL brings several advantages for edge intelligence systems, the existing FL framework still potentially experiences various adversarial attacks, such as membership inference and poisoning attacks [20]. Here, in the membership inference attack, attackers might perform reverse engineering to gather user's private data by leveraging the updated model training, whereas a poisoning attack aims to affect the global model by sending the malicious updated models during the collaborative training phase. Furthermore, the central aggregator that is responsible for managing the whole system orchestration has trouble addressing crucial challenges associated with a Single Point of Failure (SPoF)

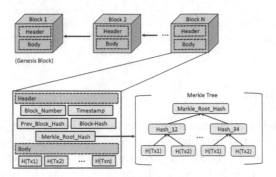

Fig. 1. The illustration of blockchain structure

issue, which may result in the whole FL system failure and lead to the risk of exposing private data. As a result, the users might be hesitant to participate in improving FL-based edge intelligence systems for VNs.

In order to address the above challenges, this paper presents the notion of secure edge intelligence, merging the benefits of Federated Learning (FL), blockchain, and Local Differential Privacy (LDP). The blockchain-assisted FL approach is used to enhance user privacy and security by recording transactions in immutable distributed ledger networks as well as improving an efficient traffic prediction accuracy in a decentralized manner. Moreover, blockchain can be deployed as an incentive mechanism to motivate the users to enhance the global model using their local data collaboratively. We also consider empowering the LDP technique to guarantee the confidentiality of the local training model by shielding the user's data from malicious attackers. Thus, LDP supports heightening the edge intelligence's data sharing transactions protection in VNs.

The structure of this paper is arranged as follows: we explain the background knowledge related to edge intelligence technology components in Sect. 2. Then, Sect. 3 explains the related works. Next, Sect. 4 presents our proposed model, a secure edge intelligence on VNs. We discuss numerical results in Sect. 5. Finally, we conclude this paper in Sect. 6.

2 Background

2.1 Distributed Ledger Technology

Since the introduction of Bitcoin in 2009 by Satoshi Nakamoto [18], blockchain has lately been earning attention from industry researchers and academia to develop decentralized and secure systems for various use cases. Blockchain can be utilized to address the bottleneck of a centralized server. It is an open database that supports anonymous and trustworthy transactions in ensuring data security without requiring any intermediaries. Here, all transactions are marked with a timestamp and recorded into a decentralized ledger where no single authority can endorse events secretly. Blockchain-enabled implementations generally take advantage of the SPoF feature with various consensuses mechanisms that validate and store verified transactions. Figure 1 shows the illustration of blockchain structure, Fig. 1 shows the illustration of blockchain structure. The block is fundamentally composed of two parts, i.e., the block header, which contains information such as block number, previous hash block, Merkle tree root [21], timestamp, etc., and the block body includes the number of user's transactions in the blockchain network.

2.2   Federated Learning

The standard machine learning techniques utilize the training data to train the models by centralizing and aggregating the user's training data containing private information on a centralized server. Nevertheless, these approaches suffer from severe privacy risks, such as the potential of sensitive data leakage, the risk of SPoF, and enormous overhead in collecting and storing the training data. In order to address these issues, Google introduced federated learning as a promising method that permits distributed mobile devices to collaboratively train the models without centralizing the training data and keeps the local data stored on mobile devices. As the user participants, each mobile device downloads the global model from a model provider (i.e., the central server), generates the model update by training the current global model using their local data, and then uploads them to the aggregator server. Then, as an aggregator server, the central server gathers and aggregates all the model updates from the user participants to produces a new global model for the next iteration. Thus, FL significantly enhances mobile device privacy by blocking some attacks for straightforward access to the local training data [30]. Further, in the context of VNs, the federated learning method can be utilized to train prediction models without straightforward access to the private data on the vehicles, which protects the data privacy of vehicles and improves traffic prediction accuracy [14].

Basically, FL aims to facilitate the training model collaboration among participants without conveying their private data; thus, the private or confidential data is kept and never leaves their devices [9]. The FL strives to optimize a global loss function $F(w)$ through an FL optimization objective that can be calculated using the empirical risk minimization approach in Eq. 1,

$$\min_{w} F(w) = \sum_{k=1}^{m} p_k F_k(w) \tag{1}$$

where w, m, p_k, and $F_k(w)$, is notation for model parameters, number of devices, number of data points of device k compared to total number of data points, and loss function of device k, respectively.

2.3 Differential Privacy

Differential privacy (DP) [6] has received much attention as a solution to the privacy-preserving challenges in machine learning [19]. By including random noise, such as Gaussian or Laplacian noise distribution, DP offers a significant standard for data privacy protection. The participants manage the degree of privacy budget (ϵ) that defines the number of noises added. Below is a description of the formal definition of DP [6].

"*A randomized mechanism M provides (ϵ, δ)- differential privacy if for any two neighboring database D_1 and D_2 that differ in only a single entry, $\forall S \subseteq Range(M)$,*

$$Pr(M(D_1) \in S) \leq e^\epsilon Pr(M(D_2) \in S) + \delta \tag{2}$$

if $\delta = 0$, M is said to achieve ϵ-differential privacy.

In order to permit a slight possibility of failure, the term δ is denoted. The less value of ϵ (i.e., more additional noise) yields a better level of privacy, while the increased value of ϵ generates a lower level of privacy, according to Eq. 2.

3 Related Work

An edge computing (EC) network extends the notion of cloud computing concept to perform its capability to the network's edge. The main aims of EC are almost similar to cloudlets or fog computing in other references. Moreover, EC offers data storage, and computational processing is locally performed in the edge infrastructure to be closer to the data provider or user. As a result, edge computing offers real-time services, location-aware, and low-latency communication. Further, it also reduces delay and saves the bandwidth of transferring data for the remote node in the vehicular network system. Moreover, current efforts utilized FL to improve the usability of MEC in reaching edge intelligence systems for wireless networks. In [23], the authors explored an FL model over wireless networks to improve FL's activities utilizing a control algorithm approach by respecting energy consumption as well as communication and computation latency. The authors in [4] focus on improving system performance and solving the FL loss function problem during the training phase by optimizing resource allocation and user selection mechanisms. Further, the authors in [17] deployed FL to form collaborative edge intelligence in mitigation situations of vehicular cyber-physical systems for detecting data leakage and protecting user's privacy information.

Blockchain as a distributed ledger technology is suggested to address the weakness of a traditional data management system in VNs. In the FL-based EIS, blockchain can be used to provide a decentralized incentive mechanism, verify the trustworthiness of the updated model training, and support a fair global model's aggregation. Lately, some research has offered to merge FL and blockchain to strengthen privacy. In [16], the authors suggested a privacy-preserving data sharing mechanism in industrial IoT for a distributed multi-parties scenario. They integrate the consensus mechanism of permissioned blockchain with FL. Meanwhile, the work from [15] designed the framework to refuse dishonest users from the FL system by automatically enforcing smart contracts to defy model or data poisoning attacks. Furthermore, the authors in [27] proposed the DeepChain protocol that employs a blockchain-based incentive mechanism to provide a secure, auditable, fair, and distributed deep learning system. Here, the incentive is utilized to force participants to act rightly and substitute a centralized approach's drawbacks.

In order to guarantee the confidentiality of the local training model from malicious attackers, some study concentrates on employing differential privacy for users' data privacy protection. In [24], the authors proposed a hybrid approach to tackle the problem of inference attacks and provide privacy-preserving federated learning using differential privacy and secure multi-party computation (SMPC). This approach aims to address the FL challenges, such as inference attacks and lack of accuracy, as well as recede the enlargement of noise injection when the number of users rises in diverse use cases and applications. Further, the study in [26] proposed the NbAFL framework to evade data leakage using a differential privacy technique by adding noise before FL model aggregation. This study focuses on solving the information leakage in the distributed stochastic gradient descent (SGD) based FL and develops a theoretical convergence bound for the trained FL model's loss function.

4   Towards Secure Edge Intelligence

As illustrated in Fig. 2, we propose the joint framework by leveraging the advantages of FL, LDP, and blockchain technology to form a secure edge intelligence in VNs. We use the blockchain to enhance the privacy and security of model parameters in the edge resource of federated learning by encrypting the data with a particular cryptography technique. Moreover, blockchain as a distributed ledger technology effectively overcame a centralized server's drawbacks and handled the uploaded parameters of updated models transparently. Furthermore, LDP is empowered to strengthen the confidentiality of transactions, primarily in defending the sensitive or private user's data on the trained local model uploading process.

In this architecture, vehicles and roadside units (RSUs) are the primary nodes, act as the user's participants and aggregator server, respectively. They communicate with each other by forming vehicle-to-vehicle (V2V) and vehicle-to-infrastructure (V2I) communication. These two types of communications refer to dedicated short-range communication (DSRC) standards that facilitate single or multi-hop communication among VNs entities [12]. Here, we consider vehicles as distributed edge users and utilize their local data to train FL models. Also, they are equipped with simple communication and computation capabilities supported by onboard units (OBUs), consisting of various sensing devices. On the

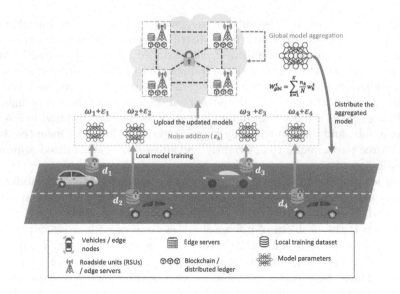

Fig. 2. Design architecture of secure edge intelligence on VNs.

other hand, RSUs are equipped with edge computing servers and designed as the distributed edge servers stationed along the road, providing wireless communications from roadside infrastructure to vehicles. Further, RSUs are considered as intelligent edge servers, providing and aggregating global models from distributed edge users in VNs.

Our proposed design architecture comprises three parts: the local data training executed by vehicles, model parameter validation and protection by empowering LDP-based blockchain, and global aggregation in the distributed edge aggregator server. First, the system is started with the initial learning model process, where initial model parameters of the global model W^0 are uploaded to the blockchain-empowered distributed RSUs. Then, the edge users (i.e., vehicles, donated by k) in iteration t retrieve global parameters W^t from blockchain and execute local training to generate the updated models w_k^t using their local dataset d_k based on Eq. 1. Then, the LDP mechanism is conducted by adding random noise ϵ to the updated models w_k^t to strengthen the privacy during uploading the trained local model and defend against linkability attacks, such as membership inference attacks. In this case, k adds noise ϵ_k to achive ϵ-differential privacy based on Eq. 2 using Gaussian mechanism, which is defined by:

$$f(D) + N(0, S_f^2 \sigma^2) \tag{3}$$

where $N(0, S_f^2 \sigma^2)$ is the normal distribution with mean 0, and standard deviation $S_f \sigma$ [7].

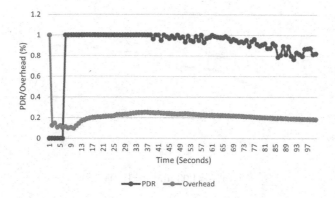

Fig. 3. Packet delivery ratio against MAC/PHY overhead.

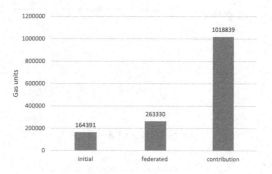

Fig. 4. Initial migration and deploying smart contracts.

After that, k uploads w_k^t with ϵ to the blockchain over distributed RSUs. In short, through this phase, vehicles train their dataset locally and upload the trained model updates collaboratively. Later, a particular consensus mechanism verifies and aggregates w_k^t to obtain a new global model W_{gbl}^t for the next iteration $(t+1)$, where:

$$W_{gbl}^t = \sum_{k=1}^{K} \frac{n_k}{N} w_k^t \qquad (4)$$

where n_k is the number of samples generated by k and N is the total number of data points (samples). Thus, the iteration continues until the model reaches a precise accuracy or the number of iterations exceeding the upper limit. Therefore, in this model, the edge servers (i.e., RSUs) maintain the blockchain and legitimate for performing the global aggregation process to generate a new global model in the VNs.

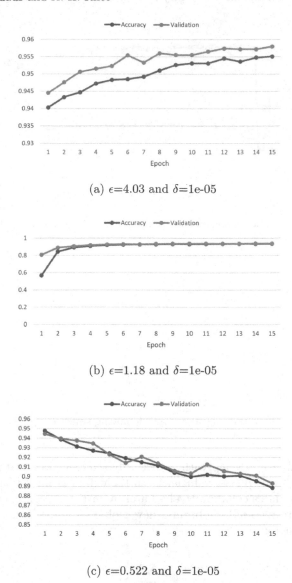

(a) ϵ=4.03 and δ=1e-05

(b) ϵ=1.18 and δ=1e-05

(c) ϵ=0.522 and δ=1e-05

Fig. 5. Privacy budget ϵ against accuracy

5   Numerical Results and Discussion

The proposed framework has been implemented in two scenarios, i.e., blockchain-based FL to efficiently develop the decentralized traffic management for vehicular networks and LDP-based FL to produce the randomized privacy protection using the IBM Library for differential privacy. The vehicular network prototype was designed using a discrete event simulator with an optimized link-state routing protocol to analyze network performance; the detailed prototype can be seen in our previous work [8]. Figure 3 shows the Packet Delivery Ratio (PDR) against MAC/PHY overhead during a simulation time of 100 s. As seen in the figure, after 17s of simulation time, the overhead is practically consistent within the range of 0.2 to 0.25, and it even gradually decreases. The lower the vehicle overhead, the greater the performance of the system, and vice versa. Our proposed protocol is relatively efficient based on the preceding results because it does not incur a significant amount of overhead.

In order to form a decentralized FL system based on blockchain technology, we use the consortium setting [3] that leverages blockchain to realize the decentralized FL transaction, transparently evaluate the participants' contributions to the global model, and develop a decentralized incentive system. In this experiment, MNIST [13] datasets are used as a standard image classification with 10.000 images for the testing examples and 60.000 images for the training examples. Each example is a 28×28 size gray-level image. Figure 4 shows the initial migration and deploying smart contracts using the Ethereum platform. The figure shows that we need 164391 (0.00328782 ETH), 263330 (0.0052666 ETH), and 1018839 (0.02037678 ETH) units of gas for initial migration, federated smart contract, and deploying participants' contribution implementation, respectively. After deploying smart contracts, we can customize the number of participants involved for local model training and calculate their contribution fairly based on blockchain. Then, to implement the FL with DP model, we use a python-based open-source library that IBM developed for the experimentation, simulation, and deployment of differential privacy tools and applications [10]. Figure 5 shows DP-based FL experiment using different privacy budget degrees, i.e., $\epsilon = 4.03$, $\epsilon = 1.18$ and $\epsilon = 0.522$, in 15 epochs. According to simulation results, Fig. 5a with privacy budget $\epsilon = 4.03$ achieves 95.80000024915344 model accuracy. In contrast, Fig. 5b and 5c with privacy budget $\epsilon = 1.18$ and $\epsilon = 0.522$, generates a model accuracy of 93.77999901771545 and 89.31000232696533, respectively. Thus, the smaller value of ϵ (i.e., more noise added) generates higher privacy (i.e., based on the gap between accuracy and validation) but lower accuracy, and vice versa.

6 Conclusion and Future Work

In this paper, we presented the notion of secure edge intelligence for the VNs by leveraging the merits of FL, blockchain, and LDP. We use the blockchain to overcome a centralized server's drawbacks. Moreover, blockchain can be used to form a decentralized incentive system to encourage participants to share their trained model. Furthermore, we use LDP to strengthen the confidentiality of data sharing transactions, especially in protecting the user's private data from various attacks. However, even though the FL approach is a promising method to implement in a decentralized system, there are some significant challenges, especially in user selection issues for the model training process as well as system and statistical heterogeneity. Further, we need to consider the effect of the privacy budget ϵ on the accuracy in future work, where the smaller value of ϵ (i.e., more noise added) generates higher privacy but lower accuracy. Thus, it is essential to consider these challenges for future research direction.

References

1. Anh, T.T., Luong, N.C., Niyato, D., Kim, D.I., Wang, L.C.: Efficient training management for mobile crowd-machine learning: a deep reinforcement learning approach. IEEE Wirel. Commun. Lett. **8**(5), 1345–1348 (2019)
2. Boyes, H., Hallaq, B., Cunningham, J., Watson, T.: The industrial internet of things (iiot): an analysis framework. Comput. Ind. **101**, 1–12 (2018)
3. Cai, H., Rueckert, D., Passerat-Palmbach, J.: 2cp: decentralized protocols to transparently evaluate contributivity in blockchain federated learning environments. arXiv preprint arXiv:2011.07516 (2020)
4. Chen, M., Yang, Z., Saad, W., Yin, C., Poor, H.V., Cui, S.: A joint learning and communications framework for federated learning over wireless networks. IEEE Trans. Wirel. Commun. **20**(1), 269–283 (2020)
5. Yueyue Dai, D.X., Maharjan, S., Qiao, G., Zhang, Y.: Artificial intelligence empowered edge computing and caching for internet of vehicles. IEEE Wirel. Commun. **26**(3), 12–18 (2019)
6. Dwork, C.: Differential privacy: a survey of results. In: Agrawal, M., Du, D., Duan, Z., Li, A. (eds.) TAMC 2008. LNCS, vol. 4978, pp. 1–19. Springer, Heidelberg (2008). https://doi.org/10.1007/978-3-540-79228-4_1
7. Dwork, C., Roth, A., et al.: The algorithmic foundations of differential privacy. Found. Trends Theor. Comput. Sci. **9**(3–4), 211–407 (2014)
8. Firdaus, M., Rhee, K.-H.: On blockchain-enhanced secure data storage and sharing in vehicular edge computing networks. Appl. Sci. **11**(1), 414 (2021)
9. Hard, A., et al.: Federated learning for mobile keyboard prediction. arXiv preprint arXiv:1811.03604 (2018)
10. Holohan, N., Braghin, S., Aonghusa, P.M., Levacher, K.: Diffprivlib: the ibm differential privacy library. arXiv preprint arXiv:1907.02444 (2019)
11. Kang, J., Xiong, Z., Niyato, D., Zou, Y., Zhang, Y., Guizani, M.: Reliable federated learning for mobile networks. IEEE Wirel. Commun. **27**(2), 72–80 (2020)
12. Kenney, J.B.: Dedicated short-range communications (dsrc) standards in the united states. Proc. IEEE **99**(7), 1162–1182 (2011)
13. LeCun, Y., Bottou, L., Bengio, Y., Haffner, P.: Gradient-based learning applied to document recognition. Proc. IEEE **86**(11), 2278–2324 (1998)
14. Le, L., Ye, H., Li, G.Y.: Toward intelligent vehicular networks: a machine learning framework. IEEE Internet Things J. **6**(1), 124–135 (2018)
15. Yi, L., Peng, J., Kang, J., Iliyasu, A.M., Niyato, D., El-Latif, A.A.A.: A secure federated learning framework for 5g networks. IEEE Wirel. Commun. **27**(4), 24–31 (2020)
16. Yunlong, L., Huang, X., Dai, Y., Maharjan, S., Zhang, Y.: Blockchain and federated learning for privacy-preserved data sharing in industrial iot. IEEE Trans. Ind. Inf. **16**(6), 4177–4186 (2019)
17. Yunlong, L., Huang, X., Dai, Y., Maharjan, S., Zhang, Y.: Federated learning for data privacy preservation in vehicular cyber-physical systems. IEEE Netw. **34**(3), 50–56 (2020)

18. Nakamoto, S.: Bitcoin: a peer-to-peer electronic cash system. In: Decentralized Business Review, p. 21260 (2008)
19. Shokri, R., Shmatikov, V.: Privacy-preserving deep learning. In: Proceedings of the 22nd ACM SIGSAC Conference on Computer and Communications Security, pp. 1310–1321 (2015)
20. Shokri, R., Stronati, M., Song, C., Shmatikov, V.: Membership inference attacks against machine learning models. In: 2017 IEEE Symposium on Security and Privacy (SP), pp. 3–18. IEEE (2017)
21. Szydlo, M.: Merkle tree traversal in log space and time. In: Cachin, C., Camenisch, J.L. (eds.) EUROCRYPT 2004. LNCS, vol. 3027, pp. 541–554. Springer, Heidelberg (2004). https://doi.org/10.1007/978-3-540-24676-3_32
22. Tian, S., Yang, W., Grange, J.M.L., Wang, P., Huang, W., Ye, Z.: Smart healthcare: making medical care more intelligent. Glob. Health J. **3**(3), 62–65 (2019)
23. Tran, N.H., Bao, W., Zomaya, A., Nguyen, M.N.H., Hong, C.S.: Federated learning over wireless networks: optimization model design and analysis. In: IEEE INFOCOM 2019-IEEE Conference on Computer Communications, pp. 1387–1395. IEEE (2019)
24. Truex, S., et al.: A hybrid approach to privacy-preserving federated learning. In: Proceedings of the 12th ACM Workshop on Artificial Intelligence and Security, pp. 1–11 (2019)
25. Al-Turjman, F., Abujubbeh, M.: Iot-enabled smart grid via sm: an overview. Future Gener. Comput. Syst. **96**, 579–590 (2019)
26. Wei, K., et al.: Federated learning with differential privacy: algorithms and performance analysis. IEEE Trans. Inf. Forensics Secur. **15**, 3454–3469 (2020)
27. Weng, J., Weng, J., Zhang, J., Li, M., Zhang, Y., Luo, W.: Deepchain: auditable and privacy-preserving deep learning with blockchain-based incentive. IEEE Trans. Depend. Secure Comput. **18**(5), 2438–2455 (2019)
28. Zhi Zhou, X., Chen, E.L., Zeng, L., Luo, K., Zhang, J.: Edge intelligence: paving the last mile of artificial intelligence with edge computing. Proc. IEEE **107**(8), 1738–1762 (2019)
29. Li, Z., Yu, F.R., Wang, Y., Ning, B., Tang, T.: Big data analytics in intelligent transportation systems: a survey. IEEE Trans. Intell. Transp. Syst. **20**(1), 383–398 (2018)
30. Zhu, X., Li, H., Yu, Y.: Blockchain-based privacy preserving deep learning. In: Guo, F., Huang, X., Yung, M. (eds.) Inscrypt 2018. LNCS, vol. 11449, pp. 370–383. Springer, Cham (2019). https://doi.org/10.1007/978-3-030-14234-6_20

Vulnerability Analysis

Recovering Yaw Rate from Signal Injection Attack to Protect RV's Direction

Hyunsu Cho[1], Sunwoo Lee[1], Wonsuk Choi[2], and Dong Hoon Lee[1(✉)]

[1] Korea University, Seoul 02841, Republic of Korea
{hscho20,2015573004,donghlee}@korea.ac.kr
[2] Hansung University, Seoul 02876, Republic of Korea
wonsuk@hansung.ac.kr

Abstract. Angular velocity can be measured by a gyroscope, which provides essential information to determine the heading direction of a vehicle. In particular, the z-axis of a gyroscope represents the vehicle's rotation, information that is used to determine the current location. However, it is known that the current gyroscopes that are designed based on MEMS (Micro-Electromechanical Systems) have a vulnerability by which the gyroscope measurements can be damaged. When an acoustic signal with a resonant frequency of the MEMS gyroscope is injected, the MEMS gyroscope would incorrectly measure yaw rates. For this reason, it is important to protect the yaw rate from an acoustic signal injection attack to maintain the safety of the vehicle system. In this paper, we propose a recovery method for damaged yaw rates based on measurements from an accelerometer. Our method enables a vehicle to maintain its current location even if the signal injection attack attempts to manipulate its yaw rate measurement. In addition, we present the evaluation results showing that our method is able to properly estimate yaw rates based on x-axis and y-axis measurements of an accelerometer.

Keywords: Signal injection attack · Yaw rate · Recovery

1 Introduction

The three axes of a gyroscope each represent roll, pitch, and yaw rates. In particular, yaw rates measured from the z-axis of a gyroscope are used for direction detection or stabilization in automotive systems, such as navigation systems, ESC (Electric Stability Control), ADAS (Advanced Driver Assistance System), and so on. For example, in the ESC system, yaw rates are used to detect a vehicle's turn rate, which is used to stabilize a moving vehicle. Since the gyroscope is the only sensor from which yaw rates are measured in a vehicle, it is difficult to provide any safety-related functions with a vehicle without the gyroscope.

Currently, gyroscopes are generally developed as the MEMS (Micro-Electro mechanical Systems) type that enables low price, small size, and low power consumption. For this reason, the MEMS gyroscopes are widely used in many

© Springer Nature Switzerland AG 2023
I. You and T.-Y. Youn (Eds.): WISA 2022, LNCS 13720, pp. 171–184, 2023.
https://doi.org/10.1007/978-3-031-25659-2_13

applications, such as drones and vehicles. However, it is known that the MEMS gyroscopes are easily affected by signals with audible frequency. Even when the MEMS gyroscope is in stationary, a signal with audible frequency is transmitted around it will cause it to sense a movement [10,13,14]. Accordingly, the MEMS gyroscope is vulnerable to attacks that inject acoustic signals. Hereinafter, we call the MEMS gyroscope simply the gyroscope. There are many studies examining signal injection attacks that cause a malfunction in a gyroscope-equipped system. For example, Son et al. have demonstrated that the drones where a gyroscope is installed can be caused to fall with an acoustic signal injection [23]. Pöllny et al. have shown that a vehicle can be controlled because the ESC system with a gyroscope can incorrectly measure the direction of a vehicle with the injection of an acoustic signal [20]. Accordingly, the acoustic signal injection is able to manipulate yaw rates so that a vehicle would lose its direction.

To address this signal injection attack, defense methods for securing gyroscope measurements have been proposed, which are classified into shielding methods and recovery methods. The shielding methods require additional hardware to physically block injected acoustic signals [12,16,23,25,28]. However, they are not available on current gyroscopes that do not have the additional hardware. To apply these methods, manufacturers would need to consider them at the chip-level design stage. The other type of method centering the concept of recovering correct data from manipulated measurements does not require any additional hardware [11,30]. Unlike the shielding methods, these recovery methods are available on off-the-shelf gyroscopes because these methods can be implemented in software. A deep learning algorithm is employed in these recovery methods, for which a large dataset is required. The difficulty in gathering the sufficient volume of training data is one limitation of deep-learning-based recovery methods.

In this paper, we propose a recovery method for yaw rates that uses a mathematical model for the relation between a gyroscope and an accelerometer. Unlike deep-learning-based recovery methods, our method does not require a large volume of data. In addition, the gyroscope and accelerometer are both mandatory components vehicles, which means that our method can be employed without any additional hardware. We create a linear system model for estimating yaw rates in a robotic vehicle (RV). We evaluate that our method is able to successfully recover manipulated yaw rates with an error of 0.033rad/s on average. As a result, our method enables a RV to maintain its direction even in the event of a signal injection attack for yaw rate manipulation. Our detailed contributions are as follows.

- To show the feasibility of our method, we perform the signal injection attack on a commercial RV.
- We identify a linear system model for the relation between a gyroscope and an accelerometer, by which our method is able to recover manipulated yaw rates.
- Our method does not need any additional sensors to prevent the signal injection attack. In our method, only the default sensors (gyroscope and accelerometer) that are necessarily installed in a vehicle are used.

The remainder of this paper is structured as follows: Sect. 2 describes related works which perform signal injection attacks exploiting the vulnerability of MEMS gyroscope. After that, we introduce detection and recovery methods against signal injection attacks. In Sect. 3, we describe the resonant frequency of the MEMS gyroscope which is caused by its internal structure. Furthermore, we experimentally explain the relation between accelerometer measurements and yaw rates used in our method design. Section 4 proposes an attack model that performs a signal injection attack with a consumer-grade speaker and Sect. 5 explains the detailed design of our recovery method. Finally, in Sect. 6, the evaluations of our recovery method will be described.

2   Related Works

2.1   Attack on Gyroscopes

In early 2000 s, the effects of acoustic signals on MEMS gyroscopes were analyzed. Researchers found that an acoustic signal in resonant frequencies could manipulate the measurements of the gyroscopes [10,13,14]. After that, a simple denial-of-service attack was performed on a drone by injecting an acoustic signal into a drone's gyroscope [23]. This was the first study to attack a real system that equipped gyroscopes using an intentional acoustic signal injection. Wang et al. demonstrated acoustic signal injection attacks on gyroscope-equipped VR devices, drones, and self-balancing vehicles [28]. Tu et al. proposed advanced attack techniques that allow attackers to precisely control yaw rates [26]. The attacks were able to be carried out at a distance of up to 7.8 m with a sound level of 135 dB. Pöllny et al. introduced a study that analyzed the effect of acoustic signals on gyroscopes installed in vehicles' ESC systems [20]. They injected acoustic signals into the gyroscope to manipulate the yaw rate and induced the vehicle's malfunction.

2.2   Signal Injection Detection Methods

As various signal injection attack methods for MEMS gyroscopes were introduced, the methods for detecting them have also been studied. Abbaspour et al. proposed a method for detecting fault data injection in Inertial Measurement Unit (IMU) sensors using an adaptive neural network [6]. Shin et al. introduced a technique to detect errors in IMU sensor data based on DNN [22]. Tarayil et al. published software-based physical-level attack detection methods for IMU sensors [24], which used machine learning and sensor fusion to detect attacks. Methods for detecting sensor attacks based on the physical invariants of the autonomous driving system have also been studied. Quinonez et al. modeled the nonlinear dynamics of RVs and drones and proposed a real-time sensor attack detection method [21]. The proposed method is implemented as a module of RVs, showing the performance of detecting attacks in 0.1 s. These studies introduced only attack detection methods for gyroscopes and did not deal with recovery after the detection.

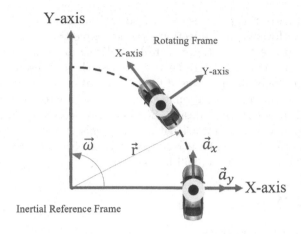

Fig. 1. Accelerations while rotational motion

2.3 Recovery Methods

Researchers have also studied the real-time recovery of manipulated sensor measurements to maintain vehicle safety. Zhang et al. introduced a linear time-varying (LTI) model for attack resilience sensors [30]. This method involves procedures that remove contaminated data from the attack, estimate the current system state, and proceed to the next system target state. Dash et al. proposed an automated attack recovery method to detect and defend against signal injection attacks on gyroscopes [11]. When the attack occurs, the proposed method uses the main controller to recover the RV and allow the mission to be completed successfully.

3 Background

3.1 Resonant Frequencies of MEMS Gyroscopes and Accelerometers

MEMS gyroscopes are designed in a small integrated circuits (IC) package and are low in price, small in size, and have low power consumption. Due to these positive characteristics, MEMS gyroscopes are widely used in cyber-physical systems (CPS), including vehicles and drones. The microstructure inside the MEMS gyroscope consists of a sensing mass and a spring holding it, so the sensing mass vibrates along the operation axis to measure roll, pitch, and yaw rate [14]. The elastic modulus of the spring is adjusted according to the purpose and environment of the gyroscope, and the resonant frequency of the gyroscope is determined by the adjusted elastic modulus. The resonant frequencies of gyroscopes used in vehicles are generally designed to be 14–30 kHz [9,13,29]. Since frequencies below 30 kHz can be output from consumer-grade speakers, attackers can easily attack using acoustic signals to induce resonance, resulting in errors in gyroscope measurements [16].

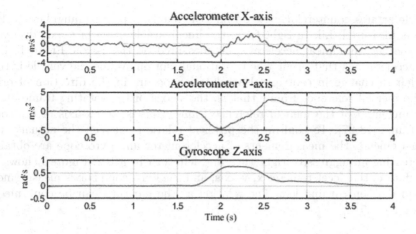

Fig. 2. Raw data of accelerometer and gyroscope in a left turn

The MEMS accelerometers also have resonant frequencies due to their internal microstructure. Similar to the gyroscopes, low-cost MEMS accelerometers resonate within the output frequencies of consumer-grade speakers [25]. However, environments such as a vehicle or a drone are where continuous external vibration is applied to the sensors. In that environment, vibration frequencies are generally between 5–10 kHz, depending on the vehicle or drone's mass and road conditions [7]. Therefore, to minimize the effect of external vibration, accelerometers for vehicles are designed to have resonant frequencies in a much larger band than the frequency of vibration that may occur in the vehicles [8,19]. For this reason, it is difficult to produce the resonant frequency of the accelerometers for vehicles from consumer-grade speakers.

3.2 Relation Between Accelerometer X, Y-Axis and Gyroscope Z-Axis

In this section, we describe the relation between linear acceleration measured by an accelerometer and angular acceleration measured by a gyroscope. In a two-dimensional plane, the sensor measurements associated with the vehicle's motion are the accelerometer x and y-axis and the gyroscope z-axis [15]. Since a vehicle performs a translational or rotational motion (right turn and left turn), these two cases will be described separately. First, in translational motion, the accelerometer x-axis corresponds to the vehicle's traveling direction, so if there is no particular noise and no other movement, the change in acceleration can be measured by the accelerometer x-axis. In this case, no change in angular acceleration in the gyroscope z-axis is observed.

Rotational motion is divided into right and left turns. Since the right turn rotates clockwise around the z-axis, negative angular acceleration is measured on the gyroscope z-axis. At this time, linear acceleration decreases at the accelerometer x-axis (traveling direction), and positive linear acceleration occurs at the accelerometer y-axis (center of the radius of rotation). In a left turn, since the

vehicle rotates counterclockwise around the z-axis, a positive angular acceleration is measured. Like a right turn, the linear acceleration of x-axis decreases,
but the negative linear acceleration is measured on the y-axis. Figure 1 shows
the accelerations that occur when rotational motion. While the vehicle is turning left, a change in centripetal acceleration occurs in the direction of origin
of the inertial reference frame, that is, the y-axis of the rotating frame and in
the tangential of the inertial reference frame, that is, the x-axis of the rotating frame [18, 27]. To confirm the physical relation between the actual sensor
measurements, the measurements of accelerometer and gyroscope are obtained
by creating an aggressive right turn and left turn in a RV. Figure 2 shows the
raw data of the accelerometer x, y-axis, and the gyroscope z-axis measurements
obtained when turning left. The relation at the left-turn can be confirmed at
about 1.7–2.5 s.

4   Attack Model

In this section, we present the attack model on which our method is based. In this
attack model, the attackers' main goal is assumed to be to control a vehicle that
determines its direction based on yaw rates. As such, the attacker may inject an
acoustic signal to make a gyroscope incorrectly measure yaw rates. To manipulate yaw rates through acoustic signal injection, the attacker needs to know
the resonant frequency of a gyroscope. The resonant frequency of a gyroscope
is commonly located between 5 kHz and 30 kHz. We assume that the attacker
is able to obtain the corresponding information about the resonant frequency
by analyzing the same brand of vehicle as the target in advance. However, the
attacker is not able to physically contact the target vehicle; therefore, hardware
modifications cannot take place. According to Tu et al. [26], it is known that the
maximum distance of the acoustic signal injection attack is 7.8m. Even without
physical contact with the target vehicle, the attacker is able to remotely inject
acoustic signals from the vicinity of the target vehicle. Lastly, we assume that
an attacker cannot manipulate the accelerometer measurements by an acoustic
signal injection because the accelerometers used in vehicles usually have much
higher resonant frequencies than audible frequencies [8, 19]. Accordingly, it is
impossible to inject the resonant signals of accelerometers with a consumer-grade
loudspeaker because these cannot generate those high frequencies. Figure 3 shows
an example in the attack model, where the ESC system operates incorrectly due
to the signal injection attack.

5   Our Method

In this section, we describe the system design of the recovery module. To construct our method, we employ a system identification which builds a mathematical system model by optimizing input/output data [17]. A system model is the
best way to find a relation that can identify the approximation of the physical
characteristics of the actual system. We use the MATLAB System Identification
Toolbox [2].

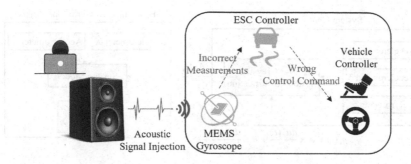

Fig. 3. Attack model

5.1   Dataset Collection

In our method, a system identification is employed to construct the relation between gyroscope and accelerometer measurements. In the system identification, statistical methods are used to build mathematical models of dynamic systems from measured data (i.e., input/output). In our method, input and output data should be defined by x-axis and y-axis measurements from an accelerometer and z-axis measurements from a gyroscope, respectively. Accordingly, the accuracy of the mathematical models depends on the dataset that is used for the system identification. As a result, our method needs to collect the dataset that is measured when a RV performs as many operations as it can. For example, a RV should be accelerated, decelerated, and turn right/left to provide the outperformed dataset.

5.2   Linear System Identification

In this step, the system identification is performed from the collected dataset so that the system model is constructed for the relation between z-axis measurements of the gyroscope and x-axis and y-axis measurement of the accelerometer. In other words, the system model enables us to estimate the z-axis measurements of the gyroscope based on x-axis and y-axis measurements of the accelerometer. We present a linear differential equation that describes the system model as shown on Eq. 1.

$$g_z(t) = A \times \frac{da_x(t)}{dt} + B \times \frac{da_y(t)}{dt} + C \tag{1}$$

where t is time and $g_z(t)$ is z-axis measurement from gyroscope. $a_x(t)$ and $a_y(t)$ are x-axis and y-axis measurement from accelerometer, respectively. With the system identification, coefficients of A and B and a constant of C can be determined as those that minimize estimation errors. Figure 4 shows the overview of system identification procedure based on a linear differential equation.

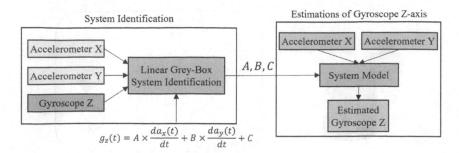

Fig. 4. System identification procedure

5.3   Estimation of Gyroscope Z-Axis

The system model which results from this system identification can be constructed using a linear differential equation with determined A, B, and C. It is used to estimate z-axis measurements of a gyroscope. For these estimations, the x-axis and y-axis measurements of an accelerometer are used as input for the system model. The output of the system model comes from estimations of a gyroscope z-axis, which are the results of the linear differential equation. Validating how well the estimations of a gyroscope are generated from the system model through a comparison with the actual measurements is of utmost importance. To validate the system model, we calculated residuals by comparing estimations and actual measurements. Details of generating estimations of a gyroscope z-axis are described in the evaluation 6.3.

6   Evaluation

In this section, we demonstrate how we evaluate our method by conducting a signal injection attack on a real RV with a gyroscope and an accelerometer installed. In addition, we show how accurately our method estimates yaw rates based on x-axis and y-axis measurements of an accelerometer. Finally, we apply our method to an application for location estimation with gyroscope measurements not using GPS data. We show that our method is able to recover manipulated measurements by a signal injection attack. As a result, the RV is able to maintain its mission even under a signal injection attack.

6.1   Experiment Setup

In the RV we used for the evaluation, ROS2 (Robot Operating System) is installed and a 9-axis IMU module is equipped, which represents the 3-axis measurement of a gyroscope, 3-axis measurement of an accelerometer, and 3-axis measurement of a magnetometer [3–5]. By injecting acoustic signals into the IMU module, we searched for the resonant frequency of one axis representing z-axis of a gyroscope. We injected a frequency ranging from 15 kHz to 30 kHz in

Fig. 5. Experiment setup

a unit of 0.01 kHz and checked if the IMU measurement is affected or not. As a result, we found that 22.5 kHz $\pm$ 0.3 kHz is the resonant frequency. The speaker we used to generate acoustic signals can generate a frequency of up to 40 kHz with 16W output power [1]. We created an audio file including a sine wave of 22.5 kHz frequency at a sampling rate of 96 kHz, encoded by FLAC.

To measure the dataset representing various conditions of the RV, we conducted many operation types of the RV (e.g., acceleration, deceleration, and right/left turn). In addition, we operated the RV on the wide flat ground. For each operation, we aggressively controlled the RV to generate the dataset measures that accurately reflect its movement. The sampling rate of the accelerometer and gyroscope 50 Hz, which is sufficient to reflect the physical movement. Since measurements contain environmental noises, we pre-processed measurements with a noise filter. After that, we used the pre-processed dataset for the system identification to create a system model. Figure 5 shows the experiment setup which is used for the evaluation of our method.

6.2   Impacts of Acoustic Signal Injection

Before evaluating our method, we first checked how much the RV is affected by the signal injection attack. We programmed the RV to move straight forward, placed the speaker on the ground at a distance as close as 50cm from the moving RV. With our focus on z-axis of the gyroscope, we employed the corresponding resonant frequency to make the RV to incorrectly measure its current position. In other words, The goal of this signal injection attack is to manipulate the RV's measurement for its direction by damaging the yaw rate. Figure 6 shows the result in which it can be seen that the RV is not able to move straight forward when the signal injection attack is conducted. The blue and red line are y-axis coordinate of the RV with and without the signal injection attack, respectively.

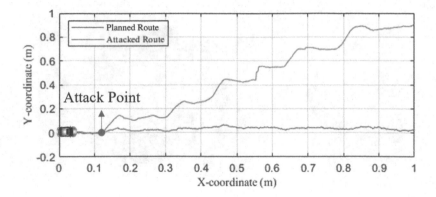

Fig. 6. Planned route and attacked route of RV

6.3 Yaw Rates Estimation

To evaluate our method for estimation accuracy, we measure raw signals for the x-axis and y-axis of the accelerometer and z-axis of the gyroscope. With the measurements for the x-axis and y-axis of the accelerometer, our method is able to estimate the yaw rates. Accordingly, we compare the estimated measurement with the actual measurement for the z-axis of the gyroscope. In addition, the RV is controlled to turn left twice and turn right once during the measurement. Figure 7 shows that the estimated measurement and actual measurement are similar to each other. The correlation between the two measurements is 0.9880 which implies that the two signals are almost the same. The average residual is obtained by 0.030 rad/s and the maximum residual is obtained by 0.0373 rad/s. The experiment results of yaw rate estimation are summarized in Table 1. Among the 10 times experiment, we used different driving datasets which include yaw rates measured while left turn, right turn, and straight run. Therefore, we conclude that our method is able to correctly estimate z-axis of a gyroscope with x-axis and y-axis of an accelerometer.

6.4 Recovery of Odometry System

We also evaluate whether our method is able to recover manipulated yaw rates so that the RV is able to maintain traveling along the planned route. We employ the odometry system that uses sensor data including yaw rate to determine the RV's change in position relative to a known position. In other words, the odometry system is used to measure a driving route of the RV without a GPS sensor. To mount the signal injection attack on this odometry system, we first measure normal sensor data that is used in the odometry system. Subsequently, from the measured normal sensor data, we craft manipulated sensor data by inserting the sensor data for manipulated yaw rate by the signal injection attack. The detection of a manipulated yaw rate is necessary before its recovery. We employ a threshold of 0.3 rad/s. If a residual between actual and estimated yaw rate is

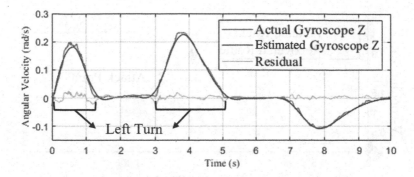

Fig. 7. Comparison between actual and estimated measurement for yaw rates

Table 1. Experiment results of yaw rates estimation

	Operations	Correlation	Maximum residual (rad/s)	Average residual (rad/s)
1	L, R, S	0.9789	0.042	0.039
2	L, R, S	0.9762	0.050	0.041
3	L, R, S	0.9894	0.041	0.033
4	L, R, S	0.9912	0.037	0.024
5	L, R, S	0.9781	0.048	0.037
6	L, R, S	0.9942	0.039	0.033
7	L, R, S	0.9917	0.037	0.034
8	L, R, S	0.9963	0.029	0.023
9	L, R, S	0.9899	0.047	0.037
10	L, R, S	0.9928	0.035	0.029

L: Left Turn, R: Right Turn, S: Straight Run

larger than the threshold, our method would start recovery of the manipulated yaw rate. Figure 8 shows x and y coordinate the odometry system generates. It can be seen that there is no difference between a normal route and the recovered route. This implies that our method is able to perfectly recover a manipulated yaw rate from a signal injection attack; as a result, the odometry system enables the RV's proper change. In addition, our method is able to detect the manipulation with a threshold of 0.3 rad/s. The difference between the normal and recovered routes is measured approximately as 0.2355 m on average; the maximum difference is 0.2447 m and the standard deviation is 0.0105 m.

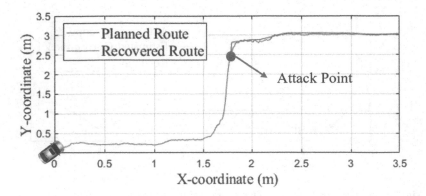

Fig. 8. Comparison of recovered and planned route

7   Conclusion

In this paper, we proposed a recovery method for directional stability under a signal injection attack. The z-axis estimations of a gyroscope were generated through linear system model based on accelerometer measurements. We evaluated the accuracy of our recovery method on a RV. The estimations showed a high correlation with the actual measurements, and the recovery method allowed an RV to drive on the correct route even under a signal injection attack. Since the proposed recovery method uses system identification based on the physical characteristics of the sensor measurements, it has the advantage that it can be extended for uses beyond RVs. We expect that our method will be widely used for maintaining a vehicle's directional stability.

Acknowledgements. This work was supported by the Institute for Information and Communications Technology Promotion (Development of Security Primitives for Unmanned Vehicles) and the National Research Foundation of Korea (NRF) grant funded by the Korea Government (MSIT) under Grant 2020-0-00374 and NRF-2020R1C1C1007446.

References

1. Anker soundcore3 a3117. https://ankerkorea.com/shop_view/?idx=113
2. Matlab r2022a. https://www.mathworks.com/products/matlab.html
3. Mw-ahrs v1. https://github.com/ntrexlab/MW_AHRS_Manual
4. Robot operation system 2. https://docs.ros.org/en/foxy/index.html
5. Stella n1. https://idearobot.gitbook.io/idearobot/
6. Abbaspour, A., Yen, K.K., Noei, S., Sargolzaei, A.: Detection of fault data injection attack on UAV using adaptive neural network. Procedia Comput. Sci. **95**, 193–200 (2016)
7. Ahirrao, N., Bhosle, S., Nehete, D.: Dynamics and vibration measurements in engines. Procedia Manuf. **20**, 434–439 (2018)

8. Aikele, M., et al.: Resonant accelerometer with self-test. Sens. Actuators, A **92**(1–3), 161–167 (2001)
9. Brown, T.G.: Harsh military environments and microelectromechanical (mems) devices. In: SENSORS, 2003 IEEE, vol. 2, pp. 753–760. IEEE (2003)
10. Castro, S., Dean, R., Roth, G., Flowers, G.T., Grantham, B.: Influence of acoustic noise on the dynamic performance of mems gyroscopes. In: ASME International Mechanical Engineering Congress and Exposition, vol. 43033, pp. 1825–1831 (2007)
11. Dash, P., Li, G., Chen, Z., Karimibiuki, M., Pattabiraman, K.: Pid-piper: recovering robotic vehicles from physical attacks. In: 2021 51st Annual IEEE/IFIP International Conference on Dependable Systems and Networks (DSN), pp. 26–38. IEEE (2021)
12. Dean, R., et al.: Vibration isolation of mems sensors for aerospace applications. In: SPIE Proceedings Series, pp. 166–170. Society of Photo-Optical Instrumentation Engineers (2002)
13. Dean, R.N., et al.: On the degradation of mems gyroscope performance in the presence of high power acoustic noise. In: 2007 IEEE International Symposium on Industrial Electronics, pp. 1435–1440. IEEE (2007)
14. Dean, R.N., et al.: A characterization of the performance of a mems gyroscope in acoustically harsh environments. IEEE Trans. Industr. Electron. **58**(7), 2591–2596 (2010)
15. Halliday, D., Resnick, R., Walker, J.: Fundamentals of Physics. John Wiley & Sons, Hoboken (2013)
16. Khazaaleh, S., Korres, G., Eid, M., Rasras, M., Daqaq, M.F.: Vulnerability of mems gyroscopes to targeted acoustic attacks. IEEE Access **7**, 89534–89543 (2019)
17. Lennart, L.: System identification: theory for the user. PTR Prentice Hall, Upper Saddle River, NJ, vol. 28, pp. 540 (1999)
18. Monteiro, M., Cabeza, C., Marti, A.C., Vogt, P., Kuhn, J.: Angular velocity and centripetal acceleration relationship (2014)
19. Ohlckers, P., et al.: An integrated resonant accelerometer microsystem for automotive applications. In: Proceedings of International Solid State Sensors and Actuators Conference (Transducers 1997), vol. 2, pp. 843–846. IEEE (1997)
20. Pöllny, O., Held, A., Kargl, F.: The effect of sound on the gyroscopes in your car. In: 2021 IEEE 93rd Vehicular Technology Conference (VTC2021-Spring), pp. 1–5. IEEE (2021)
21. Quinonez, R., Giraldo, J., Salazar, L., Bauman, E., Cardenas, A., Lin, Z.: {SAVIOR}: securing autonomous vehicles with robust physical invariants. In: 29th USENIX Security Symposium (USENIX Security 20), pp. 895–912 (2020)
22. Shin, J., Baek, Y., Eun, Y., Son, S.H.: Intelligent sensor attack detection and identification for automotive cyber-physical systems. In: 2017 IEEE Symposium Series on Computational Intelligence (SSCI), pp. 1–8. IEEE (2017)
23. Son, Y., et al.: Rocking drones with intentional sound noise on gyroscopic sensors. In: 24th USENIX Security Symposium (USENIX Security 15), pp. 881–896 (2015)
24. Tharayil, K.S., et al.: Sensor defense in-software (SDI): practical software based detection of spoofing attacks on position sensors. Eng. Appl. Artif. Intell. **95**, 103904 (2020)
25. Trippel, T., Weisse, O., Xu, W., Honeyman, P., Fu, K.: Walnut: waging doubt on the integrity of mems accelerometers with acoustic injection attacks. In: 2017 IEEE European Symposium on Security and Privacy (EuroS&P), pp. 3–18. IEEE (2017)

26. Tu, Y., Lin, Z., Lee, I., Hei, X.: Injected and delivered: fabricating implicit control over actuation systems by spoofing inertial sensors. In: 27th USENIX Security Symposium (USENIX Security 18), pp. 1545–1562 (2018)
27. Urone, P.P., Hinrichs, R.: Angular acceleration. College Physics (2012)
28. Wang, Z., Wang, K., Yang, B., Li, S., Pan, A.: Sonic gun to smart devices: your devices lose control under ultrasound/sound. BlackHat USA (2017)
29. Weinberg, M.S., Kourepenis, A.: Error sources in in-plane silicon tuning-fork MEMS gyroscopes. J. Microelectromech. Syst. **15**(3), 479–491 (2006)
30. Zhang, L., Chen, X., Kong, F., Cardenas, A.A.: Real-time attack-recovery for cyber-physical systems using linear approximations. In: 2020 IEEE Real-Time Systems Symposium (RTSS), pp. 205–217. IEEE (2020)

A Survey on Sensor False Data Injection Attacks and Countermeasures in Cyber-Physical and Embedded Systems

Jinhong Choi[✉][iD] and Yeongjin Jang[iD]

Oregon State University, Corvallis, OR 97331, USA
{choij2,yeongjin.jang}@oregonstate.edu

Abstract. Cyber-physical system (CPS) and embedded system (ES) has been growing rapidly, embracing safety-critical systems such as automobiles and airplanes. While such systems are traditionally operated by human, recent technology enables autonomous operation, even making critical control decisions by itself. Since decision-making process highly depends on sensor data, it is crucial for safety that outputs from sensors should remain trustworthy at all times. Sensor false data injection (SFDI) attacks target sensors of CPS and ES, to affect their outputs, ultimately to perturb behavior of the entire system.

In a sensor, raw signal is processed at multiple stages to return the measurement. We group them into three layers where signal changes its form. The simple three-layer view can help analyze existing attacks and defenses systematically: where the root cause of an attack is, how an attack is propagating, which layer a defense can protect.

The goals of the survey are to (1) understand the literature of SFDI attacks and defenses clearly, (2) identify current challenges and potential approaches to make sensors secure.

Keywords: Sensor security · Data injection · Cyber-physical system

1 Introduction

Both CPS and ES are a computer system, where computer-based algorithms are in charge of control. They include emerging products such as Internet-of-Things (IoT) devices and Unmanned Aerial System (UAS), and traditional products adopting more cyber components (e.g. computers) like cellphones and automobiles. The industries related with CPS and ES have been growing rapidly. With increasing popularity, various attacks and vulnerabilities have been discovered.

Early works attacked on the cyber components directly: infiltrating the internal network of an automobile [27], exploiting Wi-Fi network or operating system of UAS [40]. However, these individual vulnerabilities are limited to the specific systems; the adversary must somehow find an entry point to gain access to the internal network [27] or proper implementation of security protocol can eliminate vulnerability [40].

© Springer Nature Switzerland AG 2023
I. You and T.-Y. Youn (Eds.): WISA 2022, LNCS 13720, pp. 185–203, 2023.
https://doi.org/10.1007/978-3-031-25659-2_14

On the other hand, the attack on sensors is an indirect way of attacking the cyber components that control the entire system. Traditional security techniques, merely enhancing the security of the cyber components, can neither detect nor prevent SFDI attacks, which originate in sensors. To effectively defend SFDI attacks, signals must remain intact from raw input to the final measurement.

Objectives. The goal of this survey is to understand 1) the attack surfaces of SFDI attacks of CPS and ES, 2) the proposed defenses to detect and prevent such attacks. First, the survey presents a summary of SFDI attacks against various types of sensors in a broad definition of CPS and ES. We summarize attacks to the following sensors: broadcasted message sensors, inertial measurement unit (IMU), microphone, lidar, radar, etc. Example target systems are including (but not limited to): UAS, autonomous vehicles, IoT devices and even smartphones, all of which are interacting with physical environment (or other systems) via sensors. Second, the survey presents a summary of countermeasures to existing SFDI attacks in to CPS and ES. In this regard, countermeasures are categorized by the layer where the defense is placed to detect or prevent.

Survey Criteria. The survey starts with collecting articles from four major security conferences: IEEE Symposium on Security and Privacy (Oakland), ACM Conference on Computer and Communication Security (CCS), USENIX Security Symposium, and the ISOC Network and Distributed Systems Security (NDSS) Symposium. That is, we include articles from these sources, and then, recursively include articles that are referenced (and relevant to the survey context) from the article. To ease this process, we used a website [3], which offers a graph of relevant articles for given article, based on co-citation, including both backward and forward articles.

2 Background

What is a Sensor? A sensor is a device that detects physical events in environment and returns an appropriate measurement as an output [22,58]. Figure 1 illustrates how a CPS processes sensor inputs in general. Particularly, the process has three layers: receiver, signal processing, and control layer.

Receiver Layer. The receiver layer is at the front-end of the sensing chain. It is the receiver that accepts input—stimulus—from environment. A stimulus is a physical signal carrying information for measurement. Received stimulus is transformed into analog signal by the receiver. If incoming stimulus is already an analog signal such as radio frequency (RF), no transformation is necessary. Active sensors have the emitter to send the stimulus to the environment beforehand and capture responses from the environment. Diverse physical quantities can be stimulus: acoustic pressure, force, RF, electromagnetic (EM) field, etc. Analog signal output from the receiver is conveyed to the signal processing layer.

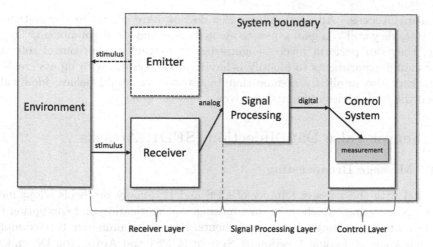

Fig. 1. The three layers processing sensor inputs in CPS. Signals flow from left to right through each layer. A physical stimulus transforms into analog signal, and it is processed to generate digital signal. Finally, it is translated into measurement.

Signal Processing Layer. Signal processing layer receives analog signal as input, then returns digital signal. The primary function of signal processing layer is to transform analog signal into digital signal. In addition, to achieve better conditioning of digital signal, signal amplification, noise reduction and/or other signal processing techniques may occur. Thereby hardware components in signal processing layer may mostly contain electronic components such as power amplifier, filter and analog-to-digital converter (ADC).

Control Layer. Finally, digital outputs from the signal processing layer are translated into a measurement at the control layer, based on underlying physics of sensing and characteristics of the receiver, or protocols that digital signal should comply with. The control layer also includes other logics for the system such as making control decisions.

3 Threat Model

Attack Scope. First, we assume attackers have neither physical nor remote access to the target system including sensors. It is also assumed that adversaries do not have access to digital signals in the signal processing layer and measurements in the control layer. However, attackers can select a medium (e.g., sound, light, RF, etc.), create false signals, and direct them to the target. This does not mean that adversaries can create false *physical* environment (e.g. putting a false road sign) or modify a genuine environment with their own (e.g. covering a genuine road sign).

System Access. Although adversaries do not have access to the system of interest, they still can gain access to an equivalent device or component. Therefore, they can perform reverse engineering to extract model/control software or conduct experiments to identify behavior of the system with inputs created. Attackers also implicitly assume that target system would behave identically when the same series of inputs are given.

4   Sensor False Data Injection (SFDI) Attacks

4.1   Message Broadcasting

To deal with the massive number of CPS and ES, many protocols adopt message broadcasting, which often miss message authentication and encryption for easy-sharing of messages among the clients. Here, we summarize two examples of such systems, Global Positioning System (GPS) and Automatic Dependent Surveillance-Broadcast (ADS-B), for their preliminary information and discovered attacks.

GPS Preliminaries. GPS is one of the global navigation satellite systems, which is owned and operated by the United States of America [5]. In total, thirty-one (31) GPS satellites orbit the Earth as stationary, and they are broadcasting signals continuously. The receivers on the ground capture the signals from a GPS satellite in order to measure the distance to the satellite. In particular, a message broadcasted from a satellite contains ephemeris and time of week to indicate when the signal was generated. Based on the time and satellite location in the message, a GPS receiver can calculate the distance to the satellite by multiplying the time by the signal speed—the speed of light. Combining distances from multiple satellites, preferably having four or more distance measures, a GPS receiver can estimate its location and velocity. The receiver can track the signal from the satellite by analyzing Doppler frequency shift, establishing a *lock*.

Attacks: Spoofing/Jamming. Attackers may spoof a GPS receiver because the message broadcasted from the GPS satellites is neither encrypted nor authenticated. In particular, each GPS satellite transmits a Coarse Acquisition (C/A) code signal for civilian use and a P(Y) code signal for military use. While P(Y) code is encrypted, C/A code is neither encrypted nor authenticated [49]. By exploiting this unencrypted and unauthenticated messages, an attacker may forge and broadcast a GPS C/A code as if they are a legitimate GPS satellite. In case that the forged signal is stronger than legitimate signals from the GPS satellites, the victim GPS receiver can be spoofed [26]. Additionally, attackers may launch a jamming attack, where the spoofing signal is not aligned with legitimate signals at the target receiver. Then it leads to losing the existing locks from the target receiver. This is referred as *hard GPS spoofing* [36] or *overt capture* [26], because the victim may detect the attack based on the status of lock. Although detectable, the hard GPS spoofing can still be effective because a loss of lock can also occur due to the natural causes (e.g., urban buildings, tunnel), which is hard to be distinguished from a spoofing attack [36]. On the other hand, attackers may try *soft GPS spoofing* [36] or *covert capture* [26] in order not to be noticed by the victim. In this case, attackers first transmit a spoofing signal synchronized with a satellite. By increasing strength of the spoofing signal gradually, the signal can takeover the existing lock [52]. GPS spoofing/jamming attacks have been demonstrated against modern GPS application systems such as smartphone, automobiles and UAS [23,30].

ADS-B Preliminaries. ADS-B is a surveillance protocol for air traffic control and also a component of the NextGen national airspace strategy of the United States [56]. Thereby, ADS-B applies only to aircraft—including UAS if it meets the requirement of Federal Regulations 14 CFR 91.225 [1]. According to the protocol, every aircraft should broadcast message including its location periodically. This is unlike with GPS where the signal is from satellites; ADS-B message is generated from aircraft. Therefore, an aircraft can send and receive ADS-B messages through ADS-B *Out* and ADS-B *In* modules. However, it is not a two-way communication since ADS-B *Out* and ADS-B *In* are independent. Here we focus only on how false inputs to ADS-B *In* affect the system.

Attacks: Spoofing/Jamming/Message Injection. Similarly with GPS, the ADS-B messages are neither encrypted nor authenticated by the protocol. ADS-B protocol is thereby vulnerable to eavesdropping [34], jamming, message modification or injection attacks [18,31,32]. A hardware-in-the-loop (HITL) simulation shows that autopilot system for aircraft abruptly changes direction when ghost aircraft is injected close to the existing aircraft [32].

4.2 Inertial Measurement Unit (IMU)

Some CPS and ES include sensors that can capture the movement and mobility of the system. Examples of such sensors are accelerometer, gyroscope, magnetometer, etc., and they are often implemented as Inertial Measurement Unit (IMU). In the following, we describe what is IMU, and then introduce SFDI attacks against sensors included in IMU.

What is IMU? The purpose of IMU is to measure the system's specific force, angular velocity, orientation and heading reference [57]. IMU is typically built as combination of accelerometer, gyroscope and magnetometer. It is attached to the physical body of the system, rendering the inertial behavior of itself as measuring the behavior of the system. Because IMU can measure the movement of the system in physical space, it is a critical sensor component for navigation purposes of aircrafts and land vehicles. Additionally, even mobile devices adopt IMU to measure the human user movements. For example, they can be utilized as fitness trackers to check the orientation of device (e.g., portrait/landscape mode) and track the motion of the user.

MEMS-based IMU. Microelectromechanical systems (MEMS) are widely used in small scale systems where size and weight is restricted [43]. In a MEMS sensor, a sensing mass is designed to move to physical stimulus (e.g., lateral acceleration, rotation rate, etc.). Resulting mechanical movement causes change in the connected electronic circuit (e.g., capacitance voltage).

Attack Surface – Resonant Frequency. An ideal MEMS sensor would only respond to designated physical stimuli. In reality, any external source would affect the output of the sensor if it is strong enough to move the sensing mass. External noise is typically negligible due to the lack of force. However, if it has the same or close to resonant frequency of the MEMS sensor, resulting motion is amplified and governed by resonance. Exploiting this physical phenomenon, researchers have found ways to inject false signals into MEMS sensors.

Denial-of-Service (DoS) Attacks. MEMS-based IMUs are susceptible to denial-of-service attacks. If a signal with resonant frequency arrives at the MEMS-based IMU, the sensing mass would vibrate even if the system is stationary. This phenomenon will cause the sensor output unreliable, possibly resulting in a denial-of-service status.

For example, a small UAS usually includes MEMS-based IMU inside the body. These sensors should respond to motion, rotation and heading reference (measuring the Earth's magnetic field), respectively. However, Son et al. [48] demonstrated that a MEMS gyroscope can be disturbed by sending acoustic noise at the resonant frequency. In particular, the authors found that almost half of 15 different commercially available MEMS gyroscopes have resonant frequencies within or close to audible frequency range. Authors leveraged it and caused false outputs from MEMS gyroscope by placing an audio source (e.g., speaker) close to the gyroscope. Authors also conducted experiments at a system level with a small UAS. As the attack is launched, targeted UAS lost its balance and crashed into the ground. This attack targets the receiver layer and causes an abnormal analog signal. Apparently following layers did neither verify its validity nor filter out-of-band signal.

Spoofing Attack via Signal Modulation. MEMS-based IMUs can suffer from spoofing attacks via signal modulation. In the previous work [48], the attacker cannot control the system behavior using resonant frequency. However, signal modulation techniques enable attackers to inject messages rather than just disturbance, using resonant frequency signal as a carrier. Using a carrier signal with a fixed frequency, amplitude modulation (AM) or phase modulation (PM) are considered, where the desired input signal is modulated in a varying amplitude or phase of carrier signal [53].

Accelerometer. Trippel et al. demonstrated that attacks using resonant frequency can actually spoof MEMS accelerometers [53]. They pointed out how insecure components in the signal processing layer can be exploited: *low-pass filter* and *amplifier*. Although an ideal low-pass filter should cut off signals outside designated frequency range, a typical low-pass filter cannot block those completely. The fluctuation still remains in the filtered signal, which is streamed to the control layer. Likewise, due to limitation of power, an actual amplifier clips high amplitude input signal, introducing a direct current (DC) component in the ouptut signal.

Image Stabilizer. An image stabilizer, equipped in a camera, may suffer from the spoofing attack. To have clear images, incoming light should remain at the same position of the image sensor during exposure—or the image would be blurred. To reduce blurring caused by body motion of the system, both mechanical and digital image stabilization techniques have been developed. Optical image stabilization (OIS) mechanically shifts camera lens or image sensor to the opposite direction of body motion so that projected image can remain still with respect to the image sensor [29]. To measure the body motion, MEMS-based IMU are widely integrated in an OIS hardware.

Ji et al. exploited the resonant frequency to spoof image stabilizers and to affect the image recognition system [24]. They first found that blurred images can result in failures in detecting or misclassifications in the image recognition system inside the control layer, which is typically based on machine learning model. Since the image stabilizer can be spoofed via resonant frequency, crafted malicious signal, combined with adversarial machine learning, can lead to incorrect image recognition in a controllable manner.

Hard Disk. Bolton et al. demonstrated an attack on hard disk drive (HDD) by an acoustic noise, causing false movement from embedded shock sensor [12]. The piezoelectric shock sensor senses vibration of HDD, and prevents read/write head from heading away from the right track or crashing into the surface. However, as the shock sensor work similarly to MEMS-based IMU, resonant frequency can be exploited to spoof the shock sensor to recognize false movements, even if the HDD remains stationary. As a result, false compensation from the shock sensor causes throughput loss of read/write.

4.3 Microphone

Many CPS and ES use one or more microphones. In modern smartphones and IoT devices, human user can speak commands to control the device or connected devices via popular voice assistants such as Apple Siri [7], Amazon Alexa [2], Google Assisant [4]. The processing algorithm works as follows. After acoustic wave is accepted by a microphone and the analog input signal is pre-processed, the feature extraction algorithm extracts voice features. Then the voice recognition system, typically a machine learning based model, generates text predictions. However, systems often fail to check whether the voice is actually originated from a human, is from an authenticated person, is forming a valid speech, or is even an audio signal. Researchers have analyzed the components in different layers if they can inject voice command without the voice from a genuine owner.

Injecting Noise Audio. Early attacks exploited voice recognition algorithm. Authors created voice commands understood by the machine, but they sound like noise to humans [14,54]. They exploit the fact that the output depends on the voice feature extraction algorithm. Specifically, they focused on the Mel-frequency cepstral coefficients (MFCC). After authors reverse engineered the MFCC, they created a tool that can output a mangled voice command when a text is given. Output sounds like noise to human, but still retains sufficient features that MFCC can extract voice features. However, the spoofing signal still has to be loud enough to be captured—unusual noise in the context of environment can be suspicious, and human possibly can distinguish the spoofing signal depending on the content.

Injecting Inaudible Audio, i.e., Ultrasound. To create an attack that is inaudible to human, spoofing signal should be carried in a signal outside audio frequency (AF), generally known as 20–20,000 Hz. A series of work use ultrasound to suffice the condition [42,61,62]. They found nonlinearity in diaphragm and amplifier—receiver and signal processing layer. Considering quadratic terms in their transfer functions, a signal, modulated by the ultrasound via AM, can result in shadow signal within the frequency band of low-pass filter.

Injecting Electromagnetic Signal. Microphones are susceptible to an attack that injects electromagnetic (EM) signal. Specifically, Kune et al. [28] and Kasmi et al. [25] demonstrated spoofing attacks using electromagnetic interference (EMI). In particular, these attacks used the microphone and cable as an antenna to receive EM signal from the attacker instead of microphone picking up acoustic pressure. Due to lack of shielding or proper low-pass filter in the devices that authors tested, high frequency signal, EMI, carrying the spoofing voice signal could arrive at the control layer.

Additionally, a laser can be a medium to inject signals into a microphone. It was found that the diaphragm in MEMS microphones is sensitive to light, while it is supposed to respond only to acoustic waves for the purpose [51]. In fact, this phenomenon is known as photoacoustic effect, found in 1880 [11]. Authors illuminated laser on the diaphragm of MEMS microphones [51]. Voice commands are carried by the laser via AM. Some commercial voice assistant speakers and smartphones, such as Amazon Echo, Google Home, Apple iPhone and Samsung Galaxy, are found vulnerable. Note that light is different medium from what the microphone is supposed to respond—sound. Advantage of this is clear;the attack is inaudible. In addition, by selecting a laser with invisible wavelength, it can also avoid being spotted by human eyes. Because laser has very small beam divergence angle, it can maintain coherence without losing focus to the distant point [6]. As a result, the attack can be launched from a distant location to the target (e.g., outside of house). Authors achieved distances of up to 110 m in their experiments, mentioning that it can be further extended if attackers have more powerful sources and optics. However, small beam divergence also has a disadvantage that the attacker must acquire line-of-sight to the target. In addition, because the laser must directly arrive at the diaphragm of the microphone, the orientation of the target device also highly affects whether the attack can succeed.

4.4 Active Sensors

Active sensors are the sensors that not only receives the signal from the physical environment but also transmits signals to the environment. In the following, we summarize attacks against lidar, radar, and ultrasonic sensors as examples of SFDI attacks.

Lidar. Lidar is an active sensing method to measure the distances to obstacles nearby. Lidar emits light pulses and measures the time it takes to be reflected by a distant surface. These laser pulses are commonly fired by rotating scanner thousands of times per second, creating a sequence of laser pulses. Lidar can provide 360-degree viewing angles and 3-dimensional representation of environment, instead of 2-dimensional images from cameras. Therefore, lidar can be used for Collision Avoid System (CAS) and Adaptive Cruise Control (ACC) [39] in autonomous vehicles [8].

Denial-of-Service Attacks to Lidar. Early attacks attempted to cause the target sensor to lose its functionality. Certain sensors are designed to show linear behavior with respect to strength of inbound physical stimulus as long as it is below the limit of linearity. As input exceeds this region, sensor output is no longer linear, and it cannot reflect the input accurately, which is called saturation. Saturation can be an attack surface against lidars [39,45]. To perform the saturation attack, sufficiently intensive light source, with the same wavelength as one used by the target lidar, should be illuminated at the receiver [39,45].

Spoofing Attacks to Lidar. Petit et al. demonstrated a spoofing attack by relaying the lidar laser pulses to create a fake response [39]. Then a fake echo will be shown in the target lidar further than the location of the spoofer. Moreover, Shin et al. showed that it is possible to induce multiple fake spots with one attack transmitter [45]. They also could create fake spots closer than the actual location of spoofer by analyzing the pulse repetition time (PRT) and rotational speed of lidar scanner. Although attacker can create a few fake spots in different location, blindingly created fake dots do not guarantee that the control layer would recognize those as a certain type of object intended by the attacker. Because the lidar responses including fake signals would be processed through objection detection process, possibly based on machine learning model. Thus attackers that want to create a fake object should spoof the algorithm in the control layer that performs classification of objects.

Cao et al. applied the adversarial machine learning to achieve it [13]. Under the limitation in the number of fake dots that they can create, they formulated an optimization problem and design modeling for input perturbation function, to create fake obstacles near front of the victim vehicle. They could reach around 75% success rate upon simulation (Baidu Apollo), and also demonstrated cases by showing emergency brake attack and freezing attack.

Radar and Ultrasonic Sensors. Radar and ultrasonic sensors are active sensors that use radio waves and ultrasound respectively. Although they use different media, the principle of attack is equivalent to what is shown above for lidars. Chauhan performed spoofing attacks on Frequency-modulated continuous-wave (FMCW) radars, capable of decreasing the distance measured by victim radar [15]. Yan et al. also demonstrated jamming, spoofing attacks on mmWave radars and ultrasonic sensors equipped in the automotive [60]. Xu et al. extended the attack to the distance increasing attack against ultrasonic sensors by cancelling the original response by destructive interference [59].

4.5   Other Sensors

Medical Devices. Medical infusion pump has a drop counter, consisting of an infrared emitter and a receiver continuously monitoring the strength of the signal. If a drop of medicine is falling though the tube, it will instantaneously reduce the intensity and receiver will detect such change. By illuminating infrared light from an external source (e.g., laser), with the same wavelength used by the emitter, the receiver can be saturated and cannot detect actual drops [37]. In addition, by exploiting the algorithm of detecting drops, the attacker also can create fake drops by changing the intensity of external illumination. Furthermore, to maximize attacker's capability, authors also analyzed the control layer. They extracted the firmware and analyzed the anomaly detection algorithm. As a result, the attacker can maintain the attack to a certain extent of duration without being detected. Finally, authors demonstrated the over-infusion (300%) and under-infusion (55%) attacks.

Wheel Speed Sensor. Anti-lock brake systems (ABS) optimally controls brakes of automobiles to prevent wheels from being locked and thus the vehicle from sliding under a sudden stop [9]. ABS became mandatory for passenger cars in many countries including the United States [35]. To decide whether a wheel is locked—the wheel lost its grip to ground—it is necessary to measure the speed of each wheel. A wheel speed sensor captures the difference of magnetic flux as a geared ring (e.g. tone ring) rotates, which is attached to the wheel.

This wheel speed sensor can be disturbed or spoofed if an external magnetic field is applied close to the sensor [46]. To control the sensor output, both a magnetic sensor and a magnetic actuator are needed to measure magnetic flux created from wheel and create a spoofing magnetic signal. The fact that the wheel speed sensor is a part of the feedback loop should be also taken account to spoof the victim vehicle as intended by the attacker. An actual attack scheme would be that an attack module (sensor, actuator and controller) should be placed between the tone ring and sensor—it is probably attached to the wheel speed sensor.

Capacitive Touch Screen. Capacitive touch screen, widely used in modern smartphones, can be targeted to create a false user input [33]. A capacitive touch-screen is formed by grid of two intersecting electrodes, transmitter (TX) electrodes and receiver (RX) electrodes, creating capacitance between them. Because human body can be thought as a capacitor, the capacitance between the TX and RX electrodes will change when the screen is touched. An external electric field can disturb this process. In experiments, electric field is created near the capacitive touchscreen by placing a copper plate below touchscreen. It is connected to an electric circuit that provides a large alternating voltage. The external electric field causes changes in the current in electrodes, and the changes are treated as if a touch event occurs. By combining false touches and malicious near-field communication (NFC) tag, authors present the scenario of a Wi-Fi attack. The attack aims to cause the "CONNECT" button pushed by false touches in the modified pop-up message, altering reading the malicious NFC tag.

5   Countermeasures

5.1   Receiver Layer

Shielding. Shielding, or physical isolation, can provide protection for sensors from unwanted noise or intended disturbance. Especially it is a valid defense if attack signal is carried in out-of-band frequency, since blocking in-band signal can cause degrading the sensing fidelity.

Acoustic Noise. It is found that one of tested gyroscopes that is not affected by acoustic noise is encased by hardware circuit [48]. Authors conducted experiments with four different materials for isolation, and isolation performances were not very different. Although surrounding the sensor with acoustic isolating or dampening materials can offer sufficient shielding, size and cost are sacrificed as a result. Thus, it might not be feasible in most embedded systems where compact size is required and resource is limited.

EMI. Shielding from electromagnetic radiation is well-known and achieved by applying conducting materials around the system [28]. Authors coated the exterior of the webcam with a conducting materials [28]. The achieved attenuation of EMI signal is over 40 dB, even with several holes for microphone and some other components, meaning that attacker should apply 10^4 more powerful EMI signal. However, conducting materials can only eliminate electric field and thus attacks using magnetic near field would be still valid under such protection [44]. Ferrimagnetic materials may be used to provide magnetic shielding, however, such shielding technique is not generally adopted due to weight and cost [44].

Saturation. To protect the saturation of the cameras, a photochromic lens that darkens under brighter light is proposed [39].

Securing Input Channel. A fundamental approach is to apply security principles such as confidentiality, integrity and authenticity into input channels between the system and environment.

Broadcasting Protocols. For digitized messages broadcasted via radio frequency, it is relatively easy to come up with applying security measures by borrowing encryption and/or authentication scheme from digital networks. For example, GPS satellites already support standardized signal encryption, although it is restricted for military use. For ADS-B protocol, encryption and authentication schemes has been proposed [38,50]. Considering the operating environment in the airspace, the security scheme should be lightweight in terms of overhead for encryption/decryption and tolerant of loss or errors in messages. However, applying encryption scheme would hurt usability to a certain extent and require changes in protocol itself, which is under government regulations.

Challenge-Response for Active Sensors. An active sensor emits sensing signal and receive signal from environment, believing the matter of interest will respond or reflect the emitted signal. However, attacker can forge a fake signal and send it as a reply, resulting in a fake response recognized by the victim [13].

PyCRA. The idea that causality of sending and receiving signal can be utilized as a defense scheme was proposed, called as *PyCRA* [47]. If probing signal can be randomly turned off and the attacker does not stop sending their signal, the existence of such attackers can be easily revealed. By randomly stop emitting the signal and expecting no incoming signal during the period, it creates a challenge to the attacker that should respond in a timely manner. Unless the attacker has a novel and fast way of measuring probing signal and turning off attack signal, it can serve as a proper authentication method. This shows that a simple challenge in the physical world can add tremendous effort from the attackers' side to overcome.

Extensions of PyCRA. Backing PyCRA, variations have been proposed in several publications. Xu et al. proposed Physical Shift Authentication (PSA) for ultrasonic sensors [59]. Instead of turning off the emitter randomly, transmitting ultrasonic pulses have randomized waveforms. After the receiver collects response, a correlation between two signals is measured. If the correlation is below a pre-set threshold, the response would be deemed as not legitimate and rejected. Clearly PSA is based on the assumption that the waveform of legitimate response should be correlative to the emitted signal and the attacker that does not have knowledge of the emitted signal will fail to respond correctly. PSA has an advantage over PyCRA because it does not suffer from loss of sensing by skipping the probing signal at times. Similarly, randomizing chirp pattern, changing frequency and/or bandwidth for radar [15] and randomizing pulse period, pulse form, pulse firing sequence in lidar sensors are suggested [39, 45]. Constructing a challenge-response scheme using the probing signal and response can help system detect the spoofing attacks significantly and ignore the output from the sensor under attack. However, it does not apply to passive sensors.

Redundancy. Adding more receivers can be one way to defend against SFDI attacks in the receiver layer. Using two or more sensors that can measure same physical quantity to build robust measurement system is generally called as *sensor-fusion*. In literature, the scope of sensor-fusion is broad, including both the same type receivers (e.g. two gyroscopes) and heterogeneous ones (e.g., gyroscope and GPS). In this section, adding the same sensors is mainly focused. Combining the results from different sensors to detect SFDI attacks will be discussed in Sect. 5.3. Defense by redundancy has an underlying assumption that at least one sensor should remain trusted.

For example, an array of microphones can be embedded in the voice assistant speaker to protect against LightCommands attack [51]. Because of narrow focus of laser, it is more difficult that single laser can attack more than one microphone simulataneously. Although the attacker can use multiple laser sources or widen the focus of laser with optics, possibility of a successful attack still can be very low depending on the positions and orientations of microphones.

Differential comparator introduced by Kune et al. also falls into this category [28]. By using two leads, the difference in potential between two voltages can be measured. If there is an interference affecting both leads, the same pattern of signal can be filtered out. Using the differential comparator is also suggested to protect MEMS gyroscopes from resonant frequency [48]. The second gyroscope with a different structure that responds only to the resonant frequency of the first gyroscope, the system can cancel out the resonance from the first gyroscope.

Multiple Sensor Consistency Check (MSCC) suggested by Xu et al. also utilizes multiple ultrasonic receivers [59]. The MSCC scheme for ultrasonic sensors is based on single-transmitter multiple-receiver structure. When an ultrasonic transducer emits a forged echo, it disperses with a certain angle like flashlight. Thereby outputs from multiple receivers can be combined to check consistency. According to authors, the system can maintain resiliency under their attack (adaptive spoofing) and localize the attacker if three or more receivers are used.

5.2 Signal Processing Layer

Defenses in signal processing layer focuses on filtering malicious signals while legitimate inputs remain intact. Thus, the defenses in signal processing layer can be effective against attacks carried in out-of-band frequency or a specific frequency band.

Band-pass Filters. Different types of filters (low/high/band-pass) can be used to eliminate noise or attack signals in certain frequency band if legitimate signal would never fall into that band [28,53,62].

Randomized Sampling. To create DC offset after being processed by ADC, signal aliasing is exploited by applying high frequency noise whose frequency is multiple of the sampling frequency of ADC [53]. To eliminate such predictability, randomized sampling is proposed [53]. Using varying sampling interval instead of a fixed one can prevent the attacker from stabilizing (DC alias) the fluctuation.

5.3 Control Layer

In this section, defenses that can be deployed in the control layer are explored. If a malicious injection uses in-band signal and the same medium, it will neither be blocked nor filtered from front layers. Researchers had proposed how the system can be robust and resilient even if malicious inputs reach the control layer.

Physical Invariants. Invariants of the system can be defined as properties that should always hold during operation, or a certain period. By monitoring the invariants, the system can detect anomalies. It is actually well-known in software security to detect runtime anomalies by monitoring invariants, which should be met at all times during program execution. For examples, runtime verification in software security can generate monitors automatically from specified properties and integrate them with the existing program [16]. Control Flow Integrity (CFI) examines the violation of call chains [10]. It utilizes the fact that rules for function calls and returns are written, and they must be always met during runtime. However, sensor readings, which represent physical status, cannot be validated by such invariants.

Physical invariants are thus established based on control or physical properties of the system to verify sensor readings [17,21,41]. For instance, governing equations, or state-space representation can be derived, which can describe the system state. Based on the current readings of sensors and control commands, the sensor readings in the next timeframe can be estimated, typically using a Kalman filter [55]. The system continuously monitors the difference between estimated values and measured ones, then determines whether behavior of a sensor is abnormal if the difference is greater than a threshold.

Sensor-Fusion. As discussed in Sect. 5.1, sensor-fusion utilizes the results from two or more sensors to check whether measurements are aligned. To fuse multiple sensors, they should either measure or deduce the same physical quantity. For example, measurement from GPS/IMU/lidar contain information regarding localization. Thus, sensor-fusion can be established upon combining GPS, IMU and lidar [20]. Similarly, because lidar/radar and camera can serve as seeing the environment, combining results can make the system more robust and accurate [24]. By establishing sensor-fusion, it can increase attack overhead in terms of cost and effort to force attackers to target multiple sensors simultaneously.

6   Research Challenges

Attacks. Most SFDI attacks have so far focused on the sensors capturing external environment. However, there are many sensors to check the internal states of the system. Oxygen sensor, for example, measures air-fuel ratio in the automobile's exhaust system, and the controller relies on this information to adjust fuel injection and engine timing. If an adversary can inject false information into the oxygen sensor, the combustion engine will perform poorly, or even fail permanently.

For small UAS, Remote ID has been effective in USA [19], and will be mandated in 2023. Like ADS-B, it is a broadcasting message protocol. Since Remote ID messages will not be secured, similar vulnerabilities found in ADS-B are expected.

Defenses. Although randomizing emitting signal [47] is an effective solution to detect SFDI attacks, it is only applicable to the active sensors. For passive sensors, it is not possible to generate such randomization that can be used for authentication. A potential approach for passive (and active) sensors is to verify a sensor by combining various sensors by machine learning, even if they cannot be combined by traditional sensor-fusion.

7   Conclusion

Recent CPS and ES need to incorporate various sensors to make correct control decisions. Sensor false data injection (SFDI) attacks can affect this process, and in fact various sensors has been found vulnerable. In this survey, we analyze each vulnerability and locate the root cause in the layers of signal chain. We discuss pros and cons of the proposed defenses at each layer. In addition, we conclude with identifying future research challenges and potential approaches regarding SFDI attack and defense.

References

1. 14 CFR 91.225 - Automatic Dependent Surveillance-Broadcast (ADS-B) Out equipment and use. https://www.ecfr.gov/current/title-14/chapter-I/subchapter-F/part-91/subpart-C/section-91.225
2. Amazon Alexa Voice AI. https://developer.amazon.com/en-US/alexa.html
3. Connected Papers. https://www.connectedpapers.com/

4. Google Assistant. https://assistant.google.com/
5. GPS: The Global Positioning System. https://www.gps.gov/
6. Properties of Lasers. https://www.worldoflasers.com/laserproperties.htm
7. Siri. https://www.apple.com/siri/
8. Waymo. https://waymo.com/company/
9. What are Anti-Lock Brakes & ABS. https://www.wagnerbrake.com/technical/parts-matter/automotive-repair-and-maintenance/guide-to-abs-brakes.html
10. Abadi, M., Budiu, M., Erlingsson, Ú., Ligatti, J.: Control-flow integrity. In: Proceedings of the 12th ACM Conference on Computer and Communications Security, pp. 340–353. CCS 2005, Association for Computing Machinery, New York, NY, USA (2005). https://doi.org/10.1145/1102120.1102165
11. Bell, A.G.: On the production and reproduction of sound by light. Am. J. Sci. **s3–20**(118), 305–324 (1880). https://doi.org/10.2475/ajs.s3-20.118.305
12. Bolton, C., Rampazzi, S., Li, C., Kwong, A., Xu, W., Fu, K.: Blue note: how intentional acoustic interference damages availability and integrity in hard disk drives and operating systems. In: 2018 IEEE Symposium on Security and Privacy (SP), pp. 1048–1062. IEEE, San Francisco, CA, May 2018. https://doi.org/10.1109/SP.2018.00050
13. Cao, Y., et al.: Adversarial sensor attack on LiDAR-based perception in autonomous driving. In: Proceedings of the 2019 ACM SIGSAC Conference on Computer and Communications Security - CCS 2019, pp. 2267–2281. ACM Press, London, United Kingdom (2019). https://doi.org/10.1145/3319535.3339815
14. Carlini, N., et al.: Hidden voice commands. In: 25th USENIX Security Symposium (USENIX Security 16), pp. 513–530. USENIX Association, Austin, TX, August 2016
15. Chauhan, R.: A platform for false data injection in frequency modulated continuous wave radar. All Graduate Theses and Dissertations, May 2014. https://doi.org/10.26076/6adb-d066
16. Chen, F., Roşu, G.: Mop: an efficient and generic runtime verification framework. In: Proceedings of the 22nd Annual ACM SIGPLAN Conference on Object-Oriented Programming Systems, Languages and Applications, pp. 569–588. OOPSLA 2007, Association for Computing Machinery, New York, NY, USA (2007). https://doi.org/10.1145/1297027.1297069
17. Choi, H., et al.: Detecting attacks against robotic vehicles: a control invariant approach. In: Proceedings of the 2018 ACM SIGSAC Conference on Computer and Communications Security, pp. 801–816. CCS 2018, Association for Computing Machinery, New York, NY, USA (2018). https://doi.org/10.1145/3243734.3243752
18. Costin, A., Francillon, A.: Ghost in the air(Traffic): on insecurity of ADS-B protocol and practical attacks on ADS-B devices. In: EURECOM (ed.) BLACKHAT 2012, 21–26 July 2012, Las Vegas, NV, USA. Las Vegas (2012)
19. FAA: Remote Identification of Unmanned Aircraft. https://www.federalregister.gov/documents/2021/01/15/2020-28948/remote-identification-of-unmanned-aircraft. Accessed January 2021
20. Gao, Y., Liu, S., Atia, M.M., Noureldin, A.: INS/GPS/LiDAR integrated navigation system for urban and indoor environments using hybrid scan matching algorithm. Sensors **15**(9), 23286–23302 (2015). https://doi.org/10.3390/s150923286
21. Giraldo, J., et al.: A survey of physics-based attack detection in cyber-physical systems. ACM Comput. Surv. **51**(4) (2018). https://doi.org/10.1145/3203245
22. Göpel, W., Hesse, J., Zemel, J.N.: Sensors: a comprehensive survey (1989)
23. Huang, L., Yang, Q.: Low-cost GPS simulator GPS spoofing by SDR. In: DEF CON 23 (2015)

24. Ji, X., et al.: Poltergeist: acoustic adversarial machine learning against cameras and computer vision. In: 2021 IEEE Symposium on Security and Privacy (SP), pp. 160–175. IEEE, San Francisco, CA, USA, May 2021. https://doi.org/10.1109/SP40001.2021.00091

25. Kasmi, C., Lopes Esteves, J.: IEMI threats for information security: remote command injection on modern smartphones. IEEE Trans. Electromagn. Compat. **57**(6), 1752–1755 (2015). https://doi.org/10.1109/TEMC.2015.2463089

26. Kerns, A.J., Shepard, D.P., Bhatti, J.A., Humphreys, T.E.: Unmanned aircraft capture and control via GPS spoofing. J. Field Robot. **31**(4), 617–636 (2014). https://doi.org/10.1002/rob.21513

27. Koscher, K., et al.: Experimental security analysis of a modern automobile. In: 2010 IEEE Symposium on Security and Privacy, pp. 447–462, May 2010. https://doi.org/10.1109/SP.2010.34

28. Kune, D.F., et al.: Ghost talk: mitigating EMI signal injection attacks against analog sensors. In: 2013 IEEE Symposium on Security and Privacy, pp. 145–159, May 2013. https://doi.org/10.1109/SP.2013.20

29. La Rosa, F., Virzì, M.C., Bonaccorso, F., Branciforte, M.: Optical image stabilization (OIS). STMicroelectronics (2015). http://www.st.com/resource/en/white_paper/ois_white_paper.pdf. Accessed 12 Oct 2017

30. Luo, A.: Drones Hijacking - multi-dimensional attack vectors and countermeasures. In: DEF CON 24 (2016)

31. Magazu, D.: Exploiting the Automatic Dependent Surveillance-Broadcast System via False Target Injection. Theses and Dissertations, March 2012

32. Manesh, M.R., Mullins, M., Foerster, K., Kaabouch, N.: A preliminary effort toward investigating the impacts of ADS-B message injection attack. In: 2018 IEEE Aerospace Conference, pp. 1–6, March 2018. https://doi.org/10.1109/AERO.2018.8396610

33. Maruyama, S., Wakabayashi, S., Mori, T.: Tap 'n ghost: a compilation of novel attack techniques against smartphone touchscreens. In: 2019 IEEE Symposium on Security and Privacy (SP), pp. 620–637 (2019). https://doi.org/10.1109/SP.2019.00037

34. McCallie, D., Butts, J., Mills, R.: Security analysis of the ADS-B implementation in the next generation air transportation system. Int. J. Crit. Infrastruct. Prot. **4**(2), 78–87 (2011). https://doi.org/10.1016/j.ijcip.2011.06.001

35. NHTSA: Federal Motor Vehicle Safety Standards; Electronic Stability Control Systems. https://www.nhtsa.gov/fmvss/federal-motor-vehicle-safety-standards-electronic-stability-control-systems-0

36. Noh, J., et al.: Tractor beam: safe-hijacking of consumer drones with adaptive GPS spoofing. ACM Trans. Priv. Secur. **22**(2) (2019). https://doi.org/10.1145/3309735

37. Park, Y., Son, Y., Shin, H., Kim, D., Kim, Y.: This ain't your dose: sensor spoofing attack on medical infusion pump. In: 10th USENIX Workshop on Offensive Technologies (WOOT 16). USENIX Association, Austin, TX, August 2016

38. Perrig, A., Canetti, R., Tygar, J., Song, D.: The TESLA broadcast authentication protocol. RSA CryptoBytes **5** (2002). https://doi.org/10.1007/978-1-4615-0229-6_3

39. Petit, J., Stottelaar, B., Feiri, M., Kargl, F.: Remote attacks on automated vehicles sensors: experiments on camera and LiDAR. In: Black Hat Europe, November 2015

40. Pleban, J.S., Band, R., Creutzburg, R.: Hacking and securing the AR.Drone 2.0 quadcopter: investigations for improving the security of a toy. In: Mobile Devices and Multimedia: Enabling Technologies, Algorithms, and Applications 2014, vol.

9030, p. 90300L. International Society for Optics and Photonics, February 2014. https://doi.org/10.1117/12.2044868

41. Quinonez, R., Giraldo, J., Salazar, L., Bauman, E., Cardenas, A., Lin, Z.: SAVIOR: securing autonomous vehicles with robust physical invariants. In: 29th USENIX Security Symposium (USENIX Security 20), pp. 895–912. USENIX Association, August 2020

42. Roy, N., Hassanieh, H., Roy Choudhury, R.: BackDoor: making microphones hear inaudible sounds. In: Proceedings of the 15th Annual International Conference on Mobile Systems, Applications, and Services, pp. 2–14. MobiSys 2017, Association for Computing Machinery, New York, NY, USA (2017). https://doi.org/10.1145/3081333.3081366

43. Scheiermann, S.: MEMS Sensors Are the Heart of a Drone. https://www.fierceelectronics.com/components/mems-sensors-are-heart-a-drone. Accessed January 2019

44. Selvaraj, J., Dayanıklı, G.Y., Gaunkar, N.P., Ware, D., Gerdes, R.M., Mina, M.: Electromagnetic induction attacks against embedded systems. In: Proceedings of the 2018 on Asia Conference on Computer and Communications Security, pp. 499–510. ASIACCS 2018, Association for Computing Machinery, New York, NY, USA (2018). https://doi.org/10.1145/3196494.3196556

45. Shin, H., Kim, D., Kwon, Y., Kim, Y.: Illusion and dazzle: adversarial optical channel exploits against lidars for automotive applications. In: Fischer, W., Homma, N. (eds.) CHES 2017. LNCS, vol. 10529, pp. 445–467. Springer, Cham (2017). https://doi.org/10.1007/978-3-319-66787-4_22

46. Shoukry, Y., Martin, P., Tabuada, P., Srivastava, M.: Non-invasive spoofing attacks for anti-lock braking systems. In: Bertoni, G., Coron, J.-S. (eds.) CHES 2013. LNCS, vol. 8086, pp. 55–72. Springer, Heidelberg (2013). https://doi.org/10.1007/978-3-642-40349-1_4

47. Shoukry, Y., Martin, P., Yona, Y., Diggavi, S., Srivastava, M.: PyCRA: physical challenge-response authentication for active sensors under spoofing attacks. In: Proceedings of the 22nd ACM SIGSAC Conference on Computer and Communications Security, pp. 1004–1015. CCS 2015, Association for Computing Machinery, New York, NY, USA (2015). https://doi.org/10.1145/2810103.2813679

48. Son, Y., et al.: Rocking drones with intentional sound noise on gyroscopic sensors. In: 24th USENIX Security Symposium (USENIX Security 15), pp. 881–896. USENIX Association, Washington, D.C., August 2015

49. Spilker Jr, J.J., Axelrad, P., Parkinson, B.W., Enge, P.: Global Positioning System: Theory and Applications, vol. I. American Institute of Aeronautics and Astronautics, Reston (1996)

50. Strohmeier, M., Lenders, V., Martinovic, I.: On the security of the automatic dependent surveillance-broadcast protocol. IEEE Commun. Surv. Tutor. **17**(2), 1066–1087 (2015). https://doi.org/10.1109/COMST.2014.2365951

51. Sugawara, T., Cyr, B., Rampazzi, S., Genkin, D., Fu, K.: Light commands: laser-based audio injection attacks on voice-controllable systems. In: 29th USENIX Security Symposium (USENIX Security 20), pp. 2631–2648. USENIX Association, August 2020

52. Tippenhauer, N.O., Pöpper, C., Rasmussen, K.B., Capkun, S.: On the requirements for successful GPS spoofing attacks. In: Proceedings of the 18th ACM Conference on Computer and Communications Security, pp. 75–86. CCS 2011, Association for Computing Machinery, New York, NY, USA (2011). https://doi.org/10.1145/2046707.2046719

53. Trippel, T., Weisse, O., Xu, W., Honeyman, P., Fu, K.: WALNUT: waging doubt on the integrity of MEMS accelerometers with acoustic injection attacks. In: 2017 IEEE European Symposium on Security and Privacy (EuroS&P), pp. 3–18 (2017). https://doi.org/10.1109/EuroSP.2017.42

54. Vaidya, T., Zhang, Y., Sherr, M., Shields, C.: Cocaine noodles: exploiting the gap between human and machine speech recognition. In: 9th USENIX Workshop on Offensive Technologies (WOOT 2015). USENIX Association, Washington, D.C., August 2015

55. Welch, G., Bishop, G., et al.: An introduction to the Kalman filter (1995)

56. Wikipedia contributors: Automatic dependent Surveillance-Broadcast – Wikipedia, the free encyclopedia

57. Wikipedia contributors: Inertial measurement unit–Wikipedia, the free encyclopedia

58. Wikipedia contributors: Sensor – Wikipedia, the free encyclopedia

59. Xu, W., Yan, C., Jia, W., Ji, X., Liu, J.: Analyzing and enhancing the security of ultrasonic sensors for autonomous vehicles. IEEE Internet Things J. 5(6), 5015–5029 (2018). https://doi.org/10.1109/JIOT.2018.2867917

60. Yan, C., Xu, W., Liu, J.: Can you trust autonomous vehicles: contactless attacks against sensors of self-driving vehicle. In: DEF CON 24 (2016)

61. Yan, C., Zhang, G., Ji, X., Zhang, T., Zhang, T., Xu, W.: The feasibility of injecting inaudible voice commands to voice assistants. IEEE Trans. Dependable Secure Comput. 18(3), 1108–1124 (2019). https://doi.org/10.1109/TDSC.2019.2906165

62. Zhang, G., Yan, C., Ji, X., Zhang, T., Zhang, T., Xu, W.: DolphinAttack: inaudible voice commands. In: Proceedings of the 2017 ACM SIGSAC Conference on Computer and Communications Security, pp. 103–117. CCS 2017, Association for Computing Machinery, New York, NY, USA (2017). https://doi.org/10.1145/3133956.3134052

DAZZLE-ATTACK: Anti-Forensic Server-side Attack via Fail-Free Dynamic State Machine

Bora Lee[1], Kyungchan Lim[2], JiHo Lee[1], Chijung Jung[1], Doowon Kim[2], Kyu Hyung Lee[3], Haehyun Cho[4], and Yonghwi Kwon[1(✉)]

[1] University of Virginia, Charlottesville, VA, USA
{boralee,jiholee,cj5kd,yongkwon}@virginia.edu
[2] The University of Tennessee, Tennessee, USA
klim7@vols.utk.edu, doowon@utk.edu
[3] University of Georgia, Georgia, USA
kyuhlee@uga.edu
[4] Soongsil University, Seoul, South Korea
haehyun@ssu.ac.kr

Abstract. Server-side malware is one of the prevalent threats that can affect a large number of clients who visit the compromised server. In this paper, we propose DAZZLE-ATTACK, a new advanced server-side attack that is resilient to forensic analysis such as reverse-engineering. DAZZLE-ATTACK retrieves typical (and non-suspicious) contents from benign and uncompromised websites to avoid detection and mislead the investigation to erroneously associate the attacks with benign websites. DAZZLE-ATTACK leverages a specialized state-machine that accepts any inputs and produces outputs with respect to the inputs, which substantially enlarges the input-output space and makes reverse-engineering effort significantly difficult. We develop a prototype of DAZZLE-ATTACK and conduct empirical evaluation of DAZZLE-ATTACK to show that it imposes significant challenges to forensic analysis.

1 Introduction

Malware analysis is a crucial task in revealing the real intentions and actors behind cyber attacks. Analyzing malware can lead to various forensic evidence, such as what sensitive information the malware wants to leak and to where (e.g., addresses of attacker-controlled servers). In recent years, malware gets more sophisticated in hiding its code using various techniques such as code obfuscation and remote code execution. In response, advanced malware analysis techniques have been proposed: (1) program analysis techniques including symbolic execution and forced execution [21,23,24,28,32,33,35,39,41,44,51,53,59–63,68,78,80] that can uncover hidden malicious logic in malware and (2) deep

---

B. Lee and K. Lim—Co-first authors and listed in alphabetical order.

I. You and T.-Y. Youn (Eds.): WISA 2022, LNCS 13720, pp. 204–221, 2023.
https://doi.org/10.1007/978-3-031-25659-2_15

packet inspection techniques [19,25,46,69] that can see through malicious payloads delivered through network packets. While it is challenging to dissect malware completely, analyzing behaviors of malware often results in critical hints for triaging the attacker (e.g., via network addresses they connect to).

In this paper, we explore the possibility of creating a forensically stealthy malware. Specifically, we present an anti-forensic attack, dubbed DAZZLE-ATTACK[1]. It collects inputs from multiple *benign and uncompromised websites* that are *not associated with cyber attackers* (e.g., www.npr.org). The input content is ordinary (i.e., not influenced by the attacker), avoiding detection from network packet inspection techniques and leaving no forensic evidence in the network trace. DAZZLE-ATTACK does not include executable malicious code itself, making static analysis based forensic analysis (e.g., anti-virus techniques) ineffective.

The inputs are later used to construct a malicious payload through a special state machine proposed by [37,38], which is carefully designed to make the analysis of DAZZLE-ATTACK inconclusive. Specifically, the state-machine can take any inputs and generate varying outputs depending on inputs, making the input-output space extremely large. As such, DAZZLE-ATTACK evades state-of-the-art malware detection techniques, including reverse-engineering and forensic triaging. We design and implement a set of tools that can create DAZZLE-ATTACK from the following two inputs: (1) malicious code snippet to deliver and (2) a set of benign contents. The created DAZZLE-ATTACK will run the specialized state-machine to convert the predetermined benign contents into the malicious code snippet when all the benign contents appear together.

Our contributions are summarized as follows:

- We propose DAZZLE-ATTACK, an anti-forensic technique that transforms ordinary contents from benign websites to malicious payloads.
- We leverage the concept of ambiguous translator [37,38] for translating input words to malicious payloads to impose challenges in reverse-engineering.
- We implement a set of automated tools to create DAZZLE-ATTACK, including a website crawler, statistical analyzer, and the ambiguous translator generator.
- Our evaluation result shows that DAZZLE-ATTACK is effective in delivering malicious payloads without being analyzed and detected.

Threat Model. We assume a forensic/malware analysis scenario. Specifically, we assume that an attacker already compromised a victim server and placed the malware. While the malware might be executed, it did not deliver the malicious payload (i.e., attack) yet. Exploiting servers can be done by leveraging software vulnerabilities [26,64] in Internet-facing server programs. The exploitation of web servers is out of the scope of this paper, but is typical in advanced cyber attack scenarios [12,29,40,48]. We assume that the victim server may log network requests, but may not know when the malware delivered the malicious payload.

---

[1] The name DAZZLE-ATTACK is originated from Dazzle camouflage which is a family of ship camouflage consisted of complex patterns of geometric shapes [67].

2   Motivating Example

We show the effectiveness of the DAZZLE-ATTACK by following a forensic analyst's perspective. Assume that a forensic analyst finds an instance of DAZZLE-ATTACK in a compromised server[2], *before it launches the attack*. Then, he aims to understand (1) the purpose and (2) the actors behind the DAZZLE-ATTACK.

Forensic Analysis of DAZZLE-ATTACK. We present four different analysis attempts on DAZZLE-ATTACK, to demonstrate its resilience to forensic analyses.

1) Analyzing inputs (i.e., network trace): The forensic investigator obtains available network logs including network packet headers and actual payloads *before the attack happens*. Unfortunately, from the domain names, IP addresses, and the content that DAZZLE-ATTACK has interacted with, the investigator cannot understand what it does. A naive way of attributing the attack to the benign websites, as shown in ❶ in Fig. 1, is misleading the analysis.

2) Dynamic analysis: The analyst tries to execute the DAZZLE-ATTACK sample, hoping that it can exercise intended malicious behaviors so that they can be analyzed (❷). However, without knowing the particular input that can trigger the intended attack (which we call *attack triggering input*), the DAZZLE-ATTACK instance does not expose its real intention (e.g., malicious code). Note that DAZZLE-ATTACK will only generate malicious payloads when *the inputs from benign websites are presented as the attacker expected*. If not, it will generate a non-malicious output (i.e., a string that does not look any malicious or another malicious code for obscuring the real objective). For example, in Fig. 1, DAZZLE-ATTACK launches an attack (i.e., translates inputs to a malicious payload) when it receives "...Airlines say..." from *www.cnn.com*, "...Cloudy in..." from *www.weather.com*, and "...Amazon recommends..." from *www.amazon.com* as shown in the second row of Fig. 1(d). However, when the analyst executes the program, it obtains "...President will..." (Ⓑ), "...Cloudy in..." (Ⓐ), and "...Amazon announces..." (Ⓑ), where Ⓐ means that the input is a part of attack delivering input and Ⓑ represents a non-attack delivering the input. As a result, the malicious payload (the third row of Fig. 1(d)) is not generated.

3) Static analysis: The analyst tries to use static analysis techniques including symbolic execution to learn the real intention of the DAZZLE-ATTACK instance. However, they suffer from over-approximation. They may obtain a set of all possible inputs and outputs *without a particular order*, which cannot provide a concrete malicious code snippet. Moreover, among the identified outputs, there are no suspicious outputs (e.g., those look like code such as `unlink()`). This is because the state-machine can generate outputs that are different from the annotated outputs of the state machine. In other words, it can generate a malicious code snippet 'fwrite' without having the exact word 'fwrite' annotated in the state machine (Details are elaborated in Sect. 3.2.1). As a result, even

---

[2] The assumption on the compromised servers in cyber attacks is typical [12,29,48].

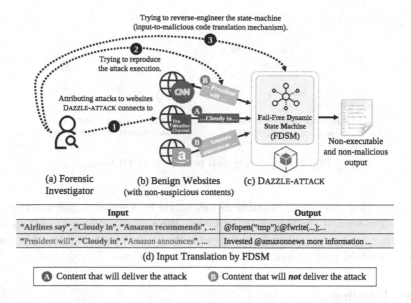

(a) Forensic Investigator

(b) Benign Websites (with non-suspicious contents)

(c) DAZZLE-ATTACK

Input	Output
"Airlines say", "Cloudy in", "Amazon recommends", ...	@fopen("tmp");@fwrite(...);...
"President will", "Cloudy in", "Amazon announces", ...	Invested @amazonnews more information ...

(d) Input Translation by FDSM

Ⓐ Content that will deliver the attack   Ⓑ Content that will *not* deliver the attack

Fig. 1. Forensic analysis on DAZZLE-ATTACK. Malicious output is not generated without the attack triggering input.

after exploring millions of possible paths and inputs via symbolic execution tools [15,28,34,57], the attack delivering inputs were not found (Details are described in Sect. 4).

4) Manual analysis: The analyst manually reads the source code to understand how the input words are translated and what the hidden malicious behaviors are (❸). The analyst collects all possible inputs that can be processed by the state machine and tries to construct inputs hoping it can reveal malicious payloads. However, he observes it is not possible to establish a one-to-one mapping because the same state transition can be triggered by multiple inputs, which implies he may need to test almost every possible word (due to *dynamic output translation* in Sect. 3.2.1).

3 Design

To create DAZZLE-ATTACK, we first profile websites to identify candidate input contents (Sect. 3.1) and then construct the ambiguous translator (Sect. 3.2).

3.1 Identifying Input Words via Profiling

DAZZLE-ATTACK operates on the contents obtained from benign websites that are *not controllable* by attackers (e.g., a headline news title on *www.cnn.com*). This design choice is crucial to deceive forensic investigators (i.e., hide the identity of

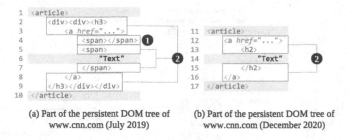

(a) Part of the persistent DOM tree of
www.cnn.com (July 2019)

(b) Part of the persistent DOM tree of
www.cnn.com (December 2020)

Fig. 2. Comparing two persistent DOM trees.

attackers). However, uncontrollable inputs might be unreliable because they may
have changed when the attack is launched. We mitigate this issue by choosing
inputs that are *statistically reliable* via website content profiling. In addition, we
propose a DOM path update resilient parsing technique.

3.1.1   Profiling

The website profiler takes a set of web pages as input and generates multiple
InputVector candidates, consisting of *Input Words* and *Statistics*. Input words are
essentially the chosen inputs that make DAZZLE-ATTACK launch the attack (i.e.,
deliver the malicious payload). It crawls the web pages regularly for a specified
period (e.g., every hour for one month by default) so we have multiple snapshots
for each page.

- **Obtaining a persistent DOM tree.** From the crawled website snapshots,
  we compute a *persistent* DOM tree that only includes elements that appear
  in *all crawled instances* so that unreliable contents will be excluded.
- **DOM parsing resilient to updates.** We leverage a parsing technique that
  is resilient to updates in websites' DOM structures. Specifically, we eliminate
  nodes that do not contain any text. In addition, for an element only contain
  another element (i.e., a holder element), we consider it can be reduced when it
  is compared. For instance, " <h3> Text </h3> "
  and "<div> Text </div>" are considered equivalent in the profiler and
  DAZZLE-ATTACK. In addition, nodes with empty content will also be ignored
  as well (e.g., " "). These two techniques handle cosmetic changes
  in websites. Figure 2 shows an example of two persistent DOM trees obtained
  from www.cnn.com from (a) July 2019 and (b) December 2020. Observe that
  they have different DOM trees. However, after we remove tags that do not
  have any content (❶) and consider placeholders (❷) between the two DOM
  trees are equivalent, we identify the two are semantically identical (as the
  highlighted parts are same). This parsing technique is used by all the components of DAZZLE-ATTACK.
- **Reliability of a persistent DOM tree.** To better understand the reliability of the persistent DOM tree, we obtain 5 persistent DOM trees collected
  from July 2019 (1st to 31st), November 2019 (1st to 30th), March 2020 (1st

to 31st), July 2020 (1st to 31st), and November 2020 (1st to 30th) for 10 websites[3]. Then, we compare the five persistent DOM trees of each website. The result shows that 94.7% of the persistent DOM tree's elements reliably appear during the first 4 months. The percentage of reliable elements becomes smaller as time goes: 85.5% for 8 months, 76.3% for 12 months, and 71.3% for 16 months. This suggests that DAZZLE-ATTACK is quite reliable in its first four months. Moreover, to improve the reliability further, we use multiple DOM elements and use them as alternative elements (i.e., backup options) as explained in Sect. 3.1.2.

- **Extracting input words.** For each DOM element in the persistent DOM tree, we extract all words that are longer than three characters. Shorter words (e.g., "for" and "or") are not good candidates in general because they usually do not have much meaning and are too frequently seen across different pages. The extracted words are annotated with their positions found in the text of the DOM element. For example, a text "*Episode 976: Terms of Service*" is annotated as follows: "Episode" = 1st, "976:" = 2nd, "Terms" = 3rd, and "Service" = 4th. Observe that the word "of" is *not considered* as its length is *not longer than 3*. At runtime, the position will be used to extract input words.

- **Computing input word statistics.** Given the extracted words, the TextRank algorithm [56] is used to identify frequently observed words among them. The top ten (the number of words is configurable) words from the result are chosen. Then, we compute the statistics of the chosen words. Specifically, for each input word, we calculate (1) coverage, (2) regularity, and (3) distribution of the word during the profiling period.

1) Coverage: This represents the percentage of an input word in a DOM element appearing during the profiling. For example, suppose that we crawl every hour for 5 days, resulting in 120 ($=24*5$) data points. If an input word appears 100 out of 120 data points, its coverage is $\frac{100}{120}$. Intuitively, an input word with a higher coverage has a higher probability of being observed in the future.

2) Regularity: The regularity represents how regularly the content will appear. To compute the regularity, for each input word, we measure the variance of time distances between the two adjacent appearances. Specifically, given N data points, the distances between the adjacent two points, n and $n+1$, are calculated, resulting $N-1$ distances: $d_1, d_2, ..., d_{N-1}$. Then, we count the number of unique distances, denoted as $CNT_{unique\_distances}$. If all the distances are equal (i.e., they regularly appear), the value (i.e., regularity) will be 1.0 (i.e., 100%). We compute the regularity as follows: $1.0 - \frac{CNT_{unique\_distances}}{N-1}$. Intuitively, an input word with a higher regularity will appear in a more predictable way than an input word with a lower regularity.

---

[3] www.cnn.com, www.npr.org, www.gnu.org, 19hz.info, techtonic.fm, earthquaketrack.com, news.ycombinator.com, www.kimbellart.org, lite.poandpo.com, chromereleases.googleblog.com.

Algorithm 1: Computing distribution

Input   : D: a set of data including all the profiled data points,
            N: the number of data points. W: input word.
            R: the number of iterations for distribution computation.
Output: DIST: distribution value for the input word W.

1   **procedure** Distribution(D, N, W)
2   $\quad$ $G \leftarrow 24$, DIST $\leftarrow 0$, $r \leftarrow 1$
3   $\quad$ **while** $r \neq R$ **do**
4   $\quad\quad$ $i \leftarrow 0$, $D_c \leftarrow 0$
5   $\quad\quad$ **while** $i \neq G$ **do**
6   $\quad\quad\quad$ $r \leftarrow N/G$
7   $\quad\quad\quad$ $n \leftarrow i + 1$
8   $\quad\quad\quad$ $D_{sub} \leftarrow D_{[i*r, n*r]}$
9   $\quad\quad\quad$ $i \leftarrow i + 1$
10 $\quad\quad\quad$ **if** $W \in D_{sub}$ **then**
11 $\quad\quad\quad\quad$ $D_c \leftarrow D_c + 1$

12 $\quad\quad$ DIST $\leftarrow$ DIST $+ \frac{D_c}{G}$
13 $\quad\quad$ $G \leftarrow G * 2$, $r \leftarrow r + 1$

14 $\quad$ **return** DIST / R

---

3) Distribution: It represents how an input word *appeared evenly* during the profiling period. This is complementary to the regularity because some input words with high regularity may not be evenly distributed. For instance, if a particular input word appears only three times but at the beginning, in the middle, and at the end of the profiling period, it would have a high regularity score. However, it is not well distributed over the period. A higher distribution value means an input word has been observed evenly and frequently during the profiling period. Algorithm 1 shows how we compute the distribution value (DIST). First, given a sequence of N data points (the input D), we divide them into G groups ($G = 24$ in this paper, line 2) so that each group includes N/G data points (line 8 as D_{sub} represents the group). Then, we count whether the content appears in each group (line 10) and divide it by the value of G (lines 11–12). After that, we multiply G by 2 and repeat the above process (line 13). After we repeat this R times ($R = 5$ in this paper), we add the computed value for different Gs and divide by R (line 14). To this end, an input word that appears in more groups will have a higher distribution value.

3.1.2 Handling Unexpected DOM Changes

A website may change its DOM structure. As DAZZLE-ATTACK walks on a DOM tree to locate the input words, changes in the DOM structure can affect the input word collecting process.

To handle this problem, we *chain alternative input words* from multiple DOM elements so that DAZZLE-ATTACK can reliably deliver the payload even with unexpected DOM changes. Specifically, for each selected input word, we identify input words from *other DOM elements that always appear together* with the selected input word. The selected alternative DOM elements should *not share* many DOM elements in their DOM paths (e.g., no more than 20%) so that the alternative input words can work when a significant portion of DOM structure (e.g., 80% of the DOM structure) is changed. If there is no such alternative input word within the same webpage, we use input words from other pages. In practice, a website often has many duplicated contents across multiple sub-webpages. For instance, https://www.npr.org/'s front page [5] and it's National News Section [6] have identical contents because top news in the "National News" section also appear in the front page. Such contents can be potential alternative input words to tolerate unexpected DOM changes. At runtime, if DAZZLE-ATTACK fails to extract an input word from a webpage (e.g., from the front page) because the DOM element containing the input word cannot be located, it tries an alternative input word on another page (e.g., from the National News Section sub-page). If it fails again, it continues trying the next alternative input words until it succeeds. In this paper, we chain *4 alternative DOM elements* for an input word. The number of alternative DOM elements is configurable.

3.2 DAZZLE-ATTACK Creator

Two inputs are required to create DAZZLE-ATTACK: (1) chosen input words from the profiler and (2) payloads to deliver (e.g., source code of existing malware).

3.2.1 Fail-free Dynamic State Machine

The core of DAZZLE-ATTACK is the fail-free dynamic state machine (FDSM). The technique is borrowed from an existing work [37]. It has two distinctive anti-forensic characteristics. First, it is a *fail-free* state machine that *always transits states* regardless of the current state and input, even if the input is *not annotated with the state transitions* (**C1**). In a typical state machine, a state transition only happens when there is a transition that can accept the current input. If not, the state machine will be stuck and fail to make a transition which can be traced by a forensic analyst to infer that the provided input is *not valid*. Second, the output generation rule of FDSM during state transition is *dynamic* (**C2**). This means that the output is changing based on a concrete input at runtime. This significantly enlarges the search space of the possible inputs and outputs.

- **Making transitions on any inputs (C1).** FDSM is designed to make transitions from any state on any inputs. If an input does not match with any possible transitions from the current state, it makes a transition to a state which has a transition condition most similar to the provided input. Specifically, for all next states from the current state, it calculates the distance (by subtracting values from each byte offset) between the current input and the transition conditions. Then, it selects a transition with the smallest distance.
- **Dynamic output translation (C2).** FDSM takes any inputs and generates outputs where each input leads to a *unique output*. When FDSM makes a transition on an input that is not exactly matched with the input of the transition, it changes the output translation rule by applying the differences between the current input and the input annotated on the transition. This makes the output space very large as the output can vary as much as the input varies.

Consider FDSM taking I as input and making a transition T^x where the transition's annotated input and output are denoted as T^x_{IN} and T^x_{OUT} respectively. Now, assume a scenario when an input with no matching transitions from the current state is given. In this case, FDSM makes a transition T^x if the distance (i.e., the sum of the distance between characters) between I and T^x_{IN} is the smallest compare to other transitions' annotated inputs (i.e., T^{others}_{IN}). Moreover, we extend the output space by dynamically changing T^x_{OUT} based on the current input I. Specifically, given I that is different from T^x_{IN}, and assume that the state machine makes T^x transition, instead of generating T^x_{OUT} according to the state machine, we generate an output computed by $T^x_{OUT} - (T^x_{IN} - I)$ on each byte of T^x_{OUT}, T^x_{IN}, and I and '$-$' operator represents subtraction on each byte between the two operands (with the same byte offsets).

3.2.2   Constructing FDSM

First, we create states and transitions for translating the chosen input to the given malicious payload, so that it can generate malicious payload when the predefined attack delivering inputs are provided. We then add dummy states and transitions to connect all states. Note that the dummy states and transitions can also be used to create decoy (i.e., fake) payloads so that it can mislead the forensic analysis. Inputs/outputs of the transitions to the dummy states are chosen in a way that the inputs of all transitions *look similar*, making it challenging to know which transitions are for malicious payload generations. Specifically, for each newly added transition, its input is derived by choosing a similar word (i.e., synonyms/antonyms in dictionaries [2,7]) to its neighboring transition's input.

4   Evaluation

4.1   Reliability of DAZZLE-ATTACK

DAZZLE-ATTACK takes input from webpages that are not under the control of the attacker, meaning that the reliability of DAZZLE-ATTACK's attack is probabilistic. To understand the reliability of DAZZLE-ATTACK in practice, we create a mock attack with real-world websites and show the result.

Experiment with Real-World Websites. To understand how reliably input words will show during an attack, we conduct an experiment from May 2019 to June 2019 (40 days). In particular, we profile 5 websites (Twitter: Houston Rockets, Trinity Church Boston, NASA Image of the Day, eBay, and Oracle Arena)[4] for the first 20 days, and observe the websites for the next 20 days to check whether the input words appear. We select an input word from each of the websites, resulting in 5 input words in total. As shown in Fig. 3(a), during the profiling period, there are about *19 h that all desired input words appear*

---

[4] https://twitter.com/houstonrockets, https://www.trinitychurchboston.org, https://www.nasa.gov/multimedia/imagegallery/iotd.html, https://www.ebay.com, https://www.theoaklandarena.com.

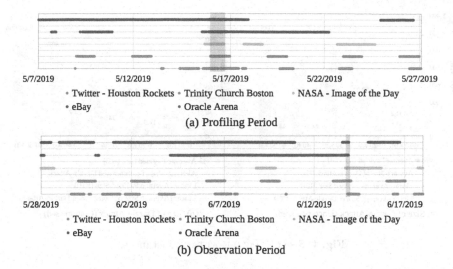

(a) Profiling Period

(b) Observation Period

Fig. 3. Input words appearing during the experiment. X-axis represents the date and Y-axis represent the appearance of input words from websites.

together (highlighted). Figure 3(b) shows the input words that appeared on the websites during the observation period (May 28th, 2019 ∼ June 17th, 2019). There are about 4 h all the input words appeared together. We present two more such experiments on our website [11], showing that creating reliable and stealthy attacks is possible.

4.2 Anti-forensic Capability of DAZZLE-ATTACK

Datasets for Payloads. We collect 573 server-side malware from known malware collection repositories [9,17,18,20,58,66,73,75–77,79]. The samples consist of eight types: webshells, backdoors, bypassers, uploaders, spammers, SQLShells, reverse shells, and flooders. For each category, we collect a similar number of samples (e.g., 61∼79). Details of each type of the samples can be found in Appendix A.1.

Statistics of DAZZLE-ATTACK. We generate DAZZLE-ATTACK instances for all 573 collected malware samples as shown in Fig. 4. We categorize them by the samples' sizes. As shown in Fig. 4(a), the sizes of DAZZLE-ATTACK are significantly larger than the original samples (from to 26 to 67 times roughly). To mitigate this significant size increase, we apply compression, e.g., gzip, to reduce the size of DAZZLE-ATTACK. Figure 4(b) shows the sizes after the compression. Except for the first group, the size of DAZZLE-ATTACK is about 5 times larger than the original sample. DAZZLE-ATTACK in the smallest group is 10 times bigger than the original sample. However, their sizes are less than 30 KB, which is commonly observed in real-world PHP applications.

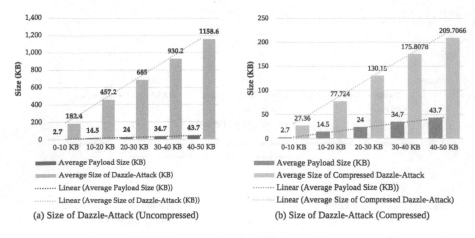

(a) Size of Dazzle-Attack (Uncompressed)   (b) Size of Dazzle-Attack (Compressed)

Fig. 4. Size of DAZZLE-ATTACK instances.

4.3   Comparison with Existing Obfuscators

We compare DAZZLE-ATTACK with state-of-the-art obfuscation techniques. We prepare two sets of samples: benign samples and malicious samples. We apply existing obfuscators to obtain obfuscated versions of samples. We also create DAZZLE-ATTACK of the samples. Then, we run existing malware detectors to see whether the obfuscated samples and DAZZLE-ATTACK instances are detected.

Obfuscator Selection. Four state-of-the-art obfuscators are chosen based on their popularity: PHP Obfuscator [30], YAK Pro [43], Best PHP Obfuscator [1], and Simple Online PHP Obfuscator [47].

Malware Detector Selection. We use three widely used malware detectors (PHP Malware Finder [72], Linux Malware Detector [4], and Shellray [8]) and a recently released PHP malware scanning tool called MalMax [55] that handles multiple layers of obfuscations and exposes all hidden malicious behaviors of malware. We do not use popular anti-virus software [52,71] because they perform worse than the malware detectors we selected as mentioned in [55].

Malicious Sample Selection and Methodology. From the 573 malware we collected, malware samples that are *not detected by existing malware detectors* are excluded from this experiment. Specifically, PHP Malware Finder identifies 413 samples, Linux Malware Detector flags 185 samples as malware, and Shellray detects 524 samples. To this end, we use the different numbers of samples for experiments with each malware detector. Then, each obfuscator is applied to the samples and obtains obfuscated malicious payloads. Finally, the four malware detectors scan all the samples obfuscated by existing obfuscators and DAZZLE-ATTACK instances.

Result for Malicious Samples. Table 1 shows that all existing malware detection tools are unable to detect DAZZLE-ATTACK (0%), while most of the malware

Table 1. Detection results on malicious and benign samples.

Obfuscator	PHP Mal. Finder		Linux Mal. Detect		Shellray		MalMax	
	Mal.	Benign	Mal.	Benign	Mal.	Benign	Mal.	Benign
PHP Obfuscator [30]	399/413	161/573	98/185	0/573	479/524	0/573	573/573	0/573
YAK Pro [43]	264/413	139/573	16/185	0/573	239/524	1/573	573/573	0/573
Best PHP Obfuscator [1]	412/413	573/573	25/185	0/573	505/524	557/573	573/573	0/573
Simple PHP Obfuscator [47]	413/413	573/573	0/185	0/573	524/524	573/573	573/573	0/573
DAZZLE-ATTACK	0/413	0/573	0/185	0/573	0/524	0/573	0/573	0/573

Green cells on 'Mal.' columns indicate that techniques are effective against malware detectors (Detected less than 5%, and lighter green if 5%~50%) while green cells on 'Benign' columns mean that they have no false positives (Lighter green if 5%~50%). Red cells represent the opposite (undesirable) results.

samples obfuscated by the other tools can be detected by at least three detectors: PHP Malware Finder (averagely 89.5%), Shellray (83%), and MalMax (100%). The detection rate of Linux Malware Detector (LMD) is relatively lower than others as LMD is not specifically designed for PHP server-side malware.

Understanding False Alarms. Some malware detectors often consider *any obfuscated programs as malicious*, causing high false positive rates. To understand false positive, 573 benign PHP program files from popular PHP programs' codebases (including WordPress [10], Joomla [3], phpMyAdmin [27], and CakePHP [50]) are collected. Initially, none of the 573 benign files are flagged as malware by the existing detectors. However, once they are obfuscated by PHP Malware Finder and ShellRay, we observe many of them are detected as malware (i.e., high false positive rates) by Best PHP Obfuscator [1] and Simple Online PHP Obfuscator [47]. Linux Malware Detector has no false positives, while it misses many PHP malware samples in general (i.e., low true positive rate).

Result from MalMax. MalMax [55] detects all the malicious code hidden by the four existing obfuscators without flagging any benign obfuscated samples. However, MalMax detects none of the DAZZLE-ATTACK instances. This is because MalMax focuses on executing all statements without precisely identifying attack triggering inputs. Simply executing all statements of a target is sufficient for analyzing the existing obfuscators but not sufficient for DAZZLE-ATTACK.

5   Discussion

Mitigation. To effectively analyze DAZZLE-ATTACK, an automated analysis technique specialized for FDSM is needed. In other words, an analysis engine that can understand and explore a finite state machine may reveal malicious payloads hidden in DAZZLE-ATTACK. However, due to a large number of states and transitions coupled with the fail-free transition and dynamic output translation (Sect. 3.2.1), it still requires significant effort to reverse-engineer DAZZLE-ATTACK even with an analysis specialized to a state machine. A real-time detector and monitoring tool can prevent DAZZLE-ATTACK from damaging the victim's system. However, it is limited to preventing damages. Investigating DAZZLE-ATTACK is still challenging.

Availability of Attack Delivering Inputs for Analysts. We assume that an analyst does not know the attack delivering input, and the goal of the analyst is to identify it by analyzing the malware. If an analyst knows the attack delivering inputs, malicious payload hidden in DAZZLE-ATTACK can be exposed by executing it directly. Note that, in practice, server-side network logs only include HTTP requests (without contents of HTTP responses) because logging contents will increase the log size significantly.

6 Related Work

Advanced Malware Analysis. A group of research [13,14,16,22,28,36,39, 42,45,49,54,65,68,70,74] tries to detect and analyze malware. In particular, a dynamic analysis based forced execution technique [41] aims to handle evasive JavaScript malware. They forcibly drive execution into every branch even if the branch condition is not satisfied. While they are effective in detecting malware that hides malicious code behind sophisticated predicates, it is not effective in exposing malicious payload in DAZZLE-ATTACK because it is encoded as states and transitions of the FDSM. Moreover, there are static, symbolic [31], and fuzzing tools for malware analysis that can reveal malicious behaviors. As discussed in Sect. 4, DAZZLE-ATTACK is resilient to such malware analysis techniques.

Network Traffic based Analysis. There are also forensic analysis and network traffic analysis approaches that analyze the causal relationship between network and system events [14,74]. For such techniques, DAZZLE-ATTACK is difficult to analyze as it gets all inputs from common benign websites where many other applications and systems may access them when DAZZLE-ATTACK is active. As a result, understanding who are the actors behind the attack is particularly challenging. There are approaches that detect common patterns of malware [39, 42]. While they are effective in traditional malware, DAZZLE-ATTACK can evade such techniques as DAZZLE-ATTACK can be implanted into existing programs.

7 Conclusion

In this paper, we present DAZZLE-ATTACK, a new type of attack that secretly delivers malicious payloads while imposing fundamental challenges to post-mortem forensic analysis. We leverage FDSM that effectively thwarts various forensic analysis attempts. Our evaluation shows that DAZZLE-ATTACK is highly effective in preventing forensic analysis.

Acknowledgement. We thank the anonymous referees for their constructive feedback. The authors gratefully acknowledge the support of NSF 1916499, 1908021,

1850392, 2145616, and 2210137. This research was partially supported by Science Alliance's StART program, National Research Foundation of Korea (NRF) grant funded by the Korea government (MSIT) (No. NRF-2021R1A4A102 9650), and gifts from Cisco Systems and Google exploreCSR. Any opinions, findings, and conclusions or recommendations expressed in this material are those of the authors and do not necessarily reflect the views of the sponsor.

A Appendix

A.1 Payload types

A webshell is malware that enables attackers to access a compromised server via a web browser that acts like a command-line interface. Backdoor is used to provide remote access to an infected machine for attackers. Bypassers are used to avoid detections of local or remote security mechanisms (e.g., firewalls). Uploaders are used to remotely inject additional malware into victim machines. Spammers compose and send spoof/spam emails. SQLShells allows remote attackers to access databases of compromised servers, similar to webshells. A reverse shell is a type of shell that communicates back to the attacker's machine from a victim's machine. Flooders are used to launch Denial of Service (DoS) attacks by sending an excessive number of network packets.

References

1. Best PHP Obfuscator (2018). http://www.pipsomania.com/best_php_obfuscator.do
2. A text file containing 479 k English words (2019). https://github.com/dwyl/english-words
3. Joomla: Content Management System (CMS) (2019). https://www.joomla.org/
4. Linux Malware Detect (2019). https://www.rfxn.com/projects/linux-malware-detect/
5. NPR: National Public Radio (2019). https://npr.org/
6. NPR: News and National Top Stories (2019). https://npr.org/sections/national/
7. PHP: Pspell Functions (2019). https://www.php.net/manual/en/ref.pspell.php
8. Shellray: A PHP webshell detector (2019). https://shellray.com/
9. VirusShare (2019). https://virusshare.com/
10. WordPress (2019). https://wordpress.com/
11. Dazzle-Attack: Supplementary Materials (2020). https://sites.google.com/view/dazzle-attack-additional/home
12. Agency, C.I.S.: Russian State-Sponsored Advanced Persistent Threat Actor Compromises U.S. Government Targets (2020). https://us-cert.cisa.gov/ncas/alerts/aa20-296a
13. Anderson, H.S., Kharkar, A., Filar, B., Evans, D., Roth, P.: Learning to evade static PE machine learning Malware models via reinforcement learning. arXiv preprint arXiv:1801.08917 (2018)
14. Aqil, A., et al.: Detection of stealthy TCP-based dos attacks. In: MILCOM 2015–2015 IEEE Military Communications Conference, pp. 348–353. IEEE (2015)

15. van Arnhem, B.: PHPScan: symbolic execution inspired PHP application scanner for code-path discovery (2017). https://github.com/bartvanarnhem/phpscan
16. Balzarotti, D., et al.: Saner: composing static and dynamic analysis to validate sanitization in web applications. In: 2008 IEEE Symposium on Security and Privacy (S&P), pp. 387–401. IEEE (2008)
17. Bart, P.: PHP-backdoors: a collection of PHP backdoors
18. BDLeet: public-shell: Some Public Shell (2016). https://github.com/BDLeet/public-shell
19. Becchi, M., Crowley, P.: A hybrid finite automaton for practical deep packet inspection. In: Proceedings of the 2007 ACM CoNEXT Conference, p. 1. ACM (2007)
20. BlackArch: webshells: Various webshells (2019). https://github.com/BlackArch/webshells
21. Cadar, C., Dunbar, D., Engler, D.R., et al.: Klee: Unassisted and automatic generation of high-coverage tests for complex systems programs. In: OSDI, vol. 8, pp. 209–224 (2008)
22. Christodorescu, M., Jha, S., Seshia, S.A., Song, D., Bryant, R.E.: Semantics-aware malware detection. In: 2005 IEEE Symposium on Security and Privacy (S&P), pp. 32–46. IEEE (2005)
23. Dahse, J., Schwenk, J.: Rips-a static source code analyser for vulnerabilities in PHP scripts (2010). Accessed 28 Feb 2012
24. Designsecurity: progpilot: a static analysis tool for security (2016). https://github.com/designsecurity/progpilot
25. Dharmapurikar, S., Krishnamurthy, P., Sproull, T., Lockwood, J.: Deep packet inspection using parallel bloom filters. In: 11th Symposium on High Performance Interconnects, 2003. Proceedings, pp. 44–51. IEEE (2003)
26. Erdődi, L., Jøsang, A.: Exploitation vs. prevention: the ongoing saga of software vulnerabilities. Acta Polytech. Hung. **17**(7) (2020)
27. Fauth, M.M.: phpMyAdmin: a web interface for MySQL and MariaDB (2019). https://github.com/phpmyadmin/phpmyadmin
28. Filaretti, D., Maffeis, S.: An executable formal semantics of PHP. In: Jones, R. (ed.) ECOOP 2014. LNCS, vol. 8586, pp. 567–592. Springer, Heidelberg (2014). https://doi.org/10.1007/978-3-662-44202-9_23
29. FIREEYE: APT41: Double Dragon, a dual espionage and cyber crime operation (2019). https://content.fireeye.com/apt-41/rpt-apt41
30. Fonk, M.: PHP-obfuscator: a parsing PHP obfuscator (2019). https://github.com/naneau/php-obfuscator
31. Fratantonio, Y., Bianchi, A., Robertson, W., Kirda, E., Kruegel, C., Vigna, G.: TriggerScope: towards detecting logic bombs in android applications. In: 2016 IEEE symposium on security and privacy (SP), pp. 377–396. IEEE (2016)
32. Grimes, H.Y.: Eir–static vulnerability detection in PHP applications (2015)
33. Hauzar, D., Kofroň, J.: WeVerca: web applications verification for PHP. In: Giannakopoulou, D., Salaün, G. (eds.) SEFM 2014. LNCS, vol. 8702, pp. 296–301. Springer, Cham (2014). https://doi.org/10.1007/978-3-319-10431-7_24
34. Jensen, T., Pedersen, H., Olesen, M.C., Hansen, R.R.: THAPS: automated vulnerability scanning of PHP applications. In: Jøsang, A., Carlsson, B. (eds.) NordSec 2012. LNCS, vol. 7617, pp. 31–46. Springer, Heidelberg (2012). https://doi.org/10.1007/978-3-642-34210-3_3
35. Jovanovic, N., Kruegel, C., Kirda, E.: Pixy: a static analysis tool for detecting web application vulnerabilities. In: 2006 IEEE Symposium on Security and Privacy (S&P), p. 6. IEEE (2006)

36. Jovanovic, N., Kruegel, C., Kirda, E.: Static analysis for detecting taint-style vulnerabilities in web applications. J. Comput. Secur. **18**(5), 861–907 (2010)
37. Jung, C., et al.: Hiding critical program components via ambiguous translations. In: 2022 IEEE/ACM 44rd International Conference on Software Engineering (ICSE). IEEE (2022)
38. Jung, C., Kim, D., Wang, W., Zheng, Y., Lee, K.H., Kwon, Y.: Defeating program analysis techniques via ambiguous translation. In: 2021 36th IEEE/ACM International Conference on Automated Software Engineering (ASE), pp. 1382–1387. IEEE (2021)
39. Kapravelos, A., Shoshitaishvili, Y., Cova, M., Kruegel, C., Vigna, G.: Revolver: an automated approach to the detection of evasive web-based malware. In: Presented as part of the 22nd USENIX Security Symposium, pp. 637–652 (2013)
40. Kasturi, R.P., et al.: TARDIS: rolling back the clock on CMS-targeting cyber attacks. In: 2020 IEEE Symposium on Security and Privacy, SP 2020, San Francisco, CA, USA, 18–21 May 2020, pp. 1156–1171. IEEE (2020). https://doi.org/10.1109/SP40000.2020.00116
41. Kim, K., et al.: J-force: forced execution on JavaScript. In: Proceedings of the 26th international conference on World Wide Web, pp. 897–906. International World Wide Web Conferences Steering Committee (2017)
42. Kinder, J., Katzenbeisser, S., Schallhart, C., Veith, H.: Detecting malicious code by model checking. In: Julisch, K., Kruegel, C. (eds.) DIMVA 2005. LNCS, vol. 3548, pp. 174–187. Springer, Heidelberg (2005). https://doi.org/10.1007/11506881_11
43. Kissian, P.: YAK Pro: PHP Obfuscator (2019). https://www.php-obfuscator.com/
44. Kneuss, E., Suter, P., Kuncak, V.: Phantm: PHP analyzer for type mismatch. In: FSE 2010 Proceedings of the Eighteenth ACM SIGSOFT International Symposium on Foundations of Software Engineering, No. CONF (2010)
45. Kolosnjaji, B., et al.: Adversarial malware binaries: evading deep learning for malware detection in executables. In: 2018 26th European Signal Processing Conference (EUSIPCO), pp. 533–537. IEEE (2018)
46. Kumar, S., Dharmapurikar, S., Yu, F., Crowley, P., Turner, J.: Algorithms to accelerate multiple regular expressions matching for deep packet inspection. In: ACM SIGCOMM Computer Communication Review, vol. 36, pp. 339–350. ACM (2006)
47. Lie, R.: Simple online PHP obfuscator: encodes PHP code into random letters, numbers and/or characters (2019). https://www.mobilefish.com/services/php_obfuscator/php_obfuscator.php
48. Magazine, C.: New Report Reveals Chinese APT Groups May Have Been Entrenched in Some Servers for Nearly a Decade Using Little-Known Linux Exploits, CPO Magazine (2020). https://www.cpomagazine.com/cyber-security/new-report-reveals-chinese-apt-groups-may-have-been-entrenched-in-some-servers-for-nearly-a-decade-using-little-known-linux-exploits/
49. Mao, J., et al.: Detecting malicious behaviors in JavaScript applications. IEEE Access **6**, 12284–12294 (2018)
50. Masters, L.: CakePHP: The Rapid Development Framework for PHP (2019). https://cakephp.org/
51. Medeiros, I., Neves, N.F., Correia, M.: Automatic detection and correction of web application vulnerabilities using data mining to predict false positives. In: Proceedings of the 23rd International Conference on World Wide Web, pp. 63–74. ACM (2014)

52. Microsoft: Microsoft Defender Advanced Threat Protection (2019). https://docs. microsoft.com/en-us/windows/security/threat-protection/microsoft-defender-atp/microsoft-defender-advanced-threat-protection
53. Mirtes, O.: PHPStan: PHP Static Analysis Tool (2019). https://github.com/ phpstan/phpstan
54. Moser, A., Kruegel, C., Kirda, E.: Exploring multiple execution paths for malware analysis. In: 2007 IEEE Symposium on Security and Privacy, pp. 231–245. IEEE (2007)
55. Naderi-Afooshteh, A., Kwon, Y., Nguyen-Tuong, A., Razmjoo-Qalaei, A., Zamiri-Gourabi, M.R., Davidson, J.W.: MalMax: multi-aspect execution for automated dynamic web server malware analysis. In: Proceedings of the 2019 ACM SIGSAC Conference on Computer and Communications Security, pp. 1849–1866 (2019)
56. Nathan, P.: Pytextrank, a python implementation of textrank for text document nlp parsing and summarization (2016). https://github.com/ceteri/pytextrank/
57. Nguyen, H.V., Nguyen, H.A., Nguyen, T.T., Nguyen, T.N.: Auto-locating and fix-propagating for html validation errors to PHP server-side code. In: Proceedings of the 2011 26th IEEE/ACM International Conference on Automated Software Engineering, pp. 13–22. IEEE Computer Society (2011)
58. nixawk: fuzzdb: Web Fuzzing Discovery and Attack Pattern Database (2018). https://github.com/nixawk/fuzzdb
59. Nunes, P.J.C., Fonseca, J., Vieira, M.: phpSAFE: a security analysis tool for OOP web application plugins. In: 2015 45th Annual IEEE/IFIP International Conference on Dependable Systems and Networks (2015)
60. Olivo, O.: TaintPHP: Static Taint Analysis for PHP web applications (2016). https://github.com/olivo/TaintPHP
61. OneSourceCat: phpvulhunter: A tool that can scan php vulnerabilities automatically using static analysis methods (2015). https://github.com/OneSourceCat/ phpvulhunter
62. Papagiannis, I., Migliavacca, M., Pietzuch, P.: PHP Aspis: using partial taint tracking to protect against injection attacks. In: 2nd USENIX Conference on Web Application Development, vol. 13 (2011)
63. Peng, F., Deng, Z., Zhang, X., Xu, D., Lin, Z., Su, Z.: X-force: force-executing binary programs for security applications. In: 23rd USENIX Security Symposium, pp. 829–844 (2014)
64. Piantadosi, V., Scalabrino, S., Oliveto, R.: Fixing of security vulnerabilities in open source projects: a case study of apache http server and apache tomcat. In: 2019 12th IEEE Conference on Software Testing, Validation and Verification (ICST), pp. 68–78. IEEE (2019)
65. Preda, M.D., Christodorescu, M., Jha, S., Debray, S.: A semantics-based approach to malware detection. ACM SIGPLAN Not. **42**(1), 377–388 (2007)
66. Ridter: Pentest (2019). https://github.com/Ridter/Pentest
67. Ruslan Budnik: The Fantastic Idea of Dazzle Camouflage (2019). https://www. warhistoryonline.com/instant-articles/dazzle-camouflage.html
68. Saxena, P., Akhawe, D., Hanna, S., Mao, F., McCamant, S., Song, D.: A symbolic execution framework for JavaScript. In: 2010 IEEE Symposium on Security and Privacy, pp. 513–528. IEEE (2010)
69. Sherry, J., Lan, C., Popa, R.A., Ratnasamy, S.: BlindBox: deep packet inspection over encrypted traffic. ACM SIGCOMM Comput. Commun. Rev. **45**(4), 213–226 (2015)

70. Shu, X., Yao, D., Ramakrishnan, N.: Unearthing stealthy program attacks buried in extremely long execution paths. In: Proceedings of the 22nd ACM SIGSAC Conference on Computer and Communications Security, pp. 401–413. ACM (2015)
71. Symantec: Norton^{TM}–Antivirus & Anti-Malware Software (2019). https://us.norton.com/
72. Systems, N.: GitHub - nbs-system/php-malware-finder: Detect potentially malicious PHP files (2019). https://github.com/nbs-system/php-malware-finder/
73. tanjiti: webshellSample: Webshell sample for WebShell Log Analysis (2018). https://github.com/tanjiti/webshellSample
74. Taylor, T., et al.: Detecting malicious exploit kits using tree-based similarity searches. In: Proceedings of the Sixth ACM Conference on Data and Application Security and Privacy, pp. 255–266. ACM (2016)
75. tennc: webshell: A webshell open source project (2019). https://github.com/tennc/webshell
76. Troon, J.: PHP-webshells: Common PHP webshells (2016). https://github.com/JohnTroony/php-webshells
77. tutorial0: WebShell: WebShell Collect (2016). https://github.com/tdifg/WebShell
78. vimeo: psalm: A static analysis tool for finding errors in PHP applications (2019). https://github.com/vimeo/psalm
79. xl7dev: WebShell: Webshell & Backdoor Collection (2017). https://github.com/xl7dev/WebShell
80. Yang, Q.: Taint-em-All: a taint analysis tool for the PHP language (2019). https://github.com/quanyang/Taint-em-All

vkTracer: Vulnerable Kernel Code Tracing to Generate Profile of Kernel Vulnerability

Hiroki Kuzuno[1](✉)🆔 and Toshihiro Yamauchi[2](✉)🆔

[1] Graduate School of Engineering, Kobe University, Kobe, Japan
kuzuno@port.kobe-u.ac.jp
[2] Faculty of Natural Science and Technology, Okayama University, Okayama, Japan
yamauchi@okayama-u.ac.jp

Abstract. Vulnerable kernel codes are a threat to an operating system kernel. An adversary's user process can forcefully invoke a vulnerable kernel code to cause privilege escalation or denial of service (DoS). Although service providers or security operators have to determine the effect of kernel vulnerabilities on their environment to decide the kernel updating, the list of vulnerable kernel codes are not provided from the common vulnerabilities and exposures (CVE) report. It is difficult to identify the vulnerable kernel codes from the exploitation result of the kernel which indicates the account information or the kernel suspension. To identify the details of kernel vulnerabilities, this study proposes a vulnerable kernel code tracer (vkTracer), which employs an alternative viewpoint using proof-of-concept (PoC) code to create a profile of kernel vulnerability. vkTracer traces the user process of the PoC code and the running kernel to hook the invocation of the vulnerable kernel codes. Moreover, vkTracer extracts the whole kernel component's information using the running and static kernel image and debug section. The evaluation results indicated that vkTracer could trace PoC code executions (e.g., privilege escalation and DoS), identify vulnerable kernel codes, and generate kernel vulnerability profiles. Furthermore, the implementation of vkTracer revealed that the identification overhead ranged from 5.2683 s to 5.2728 s on the PoC codes and the acceptable system call latency was 3.7197 μs.

Keywords: Kernel vulnerability · Dynamic analysis · System security

1 Introduction

An operating system (OS) kernel has the threat of vulnerable kernel codes, which can lead to memory corruption or denial of service (DoS), among other problems [1]. The identification of vulnerable kernel code in a running kernel is challenging. Although the common vulnerabilities and exposures (CVE) summarizes the overviews of kernel vulnerability, the CVE report does not contain the details of vulnerable kernel codes [2]. As modern kernels are complex and lengthy, it

© Springer Nature Switzerland AG 2023
I. You and T.-Y. Youn (Eds.): WISA 2022, LNCS 13720, pp. 222–234, 2023.
https://doi.org/10.1007/978-3-031-25659-2_16

is hard for service providers or security operators without kernel development knowledge to identify which kernel codes relate to which kernel vulnerabilities.

This leads to the following research problem that addresses how to easily identify vulnerable kernel code and provide that information as an indication of kernel vulnerability. Service providers or security operators require the detailed information of vulnerable kernel codes (e.g., function names and virtual addresses) are contained in the kernel on their environment to decide the kernel updating. Because they have to prevent the security incident through the vulnerable kernel codes that could lead to kernel exploitation.

This paper describes a novel security approach known as the vulnerable kernel code tracer (vkTracer). It has a tracking mechanism that identifies the information of vulnerable kernel codes that contains virtual address ranges and kernel function names to create a kernel code list, which serves as the profile of kernel vulnerabilities. It focuses on the behavior of proof-of-concept (PoC) code of known kernel vulnerabilities (e.g., CVE) that subvert the running kernel.

The implementation of vkTracer reserves the attaching placement of kernel code invocation using the kernel tracing features (i.e., `kprobe` and `tractpoints`) while executing PoC code. Moreover, vkTracer prepares the kernel component information for profile generation. It can relate the virtual address range and function name of kernel codes to invocated kernel codes using running and static kernel images containing debug with an attributed record format (DWARF) and symbol information. It ensures that vkTracer identifies the invoked kernel code, and then creates a profile of kernel vulnerability that relates to memory corruption or DoS. The contributions of this study are as follows:

1. The proposed vkTracer method is a novel approach for tracking the vulnerable kernel code for an adversary's user process at the kernel layer. The key functionality of vkTracer is to identify vulnerable kernel code information (e.g., virtual address ranges and function names) on the modern OS kernel. This paper presents the tracing model, security features, limitations, and portability of vkTracer, as well as any future research directions envisioned.
2. The effectiveness of the vkTracer implementation is based on how well it identifies the invocation of vulnerable kernel codes through proven kernel vulnerabilities using the PoC code. The measurement of the implementations of vkTracer reveals that the tracing overhead is between 5.2683 s and 5.2728 s for user applications, the maximum overhead for system call is 3.7197 μs.

2   Background

2.1   Kernel Vulnerability and PoC Code

Kernel Vulnerability: The incorrect implementation of kernel results in kernel vulnerabilities, which can eventually lead to kernel attacks [1]. The running kernel can be damaged in a variety of ways through a kernel attack. The typical attacks include privilege escalation through memory corruption, which can lead to administrator privileges (e.g., root account) and DoS through unusual kernel data modification, defeating the stability of the kernel [1].

Table 1. Available PoC code for Linux kernel vulnerability list. DoS: denial-of-service, Mem. Corr.: Memory Corruption

CVE ID	Types	Description
CVE-2016-4997 [5]	DoS, Mem. Corr.	Boundary check error
CVE-2016-9793 [6]	DoS, Mem. Corr.	Boundary check error
CVE-2017-6074 [3]	DoS	Use after free
CVE-2017-7533 [7]	DoS, Mem. Corr.	Race condition
CVE-2017-16995 [4]	DoS, Mem. Corr.	Boundary check error
CVE-2017-1000112 [8]	Mem. Corr.	Race condition

PoC Codes: Several kernel vulnerabilities have been reported for Linux kernels [2]. PoC codes are small programs that directly invoke vulnerable kernel codes to exploit a known vulnerability. Table 1 summarizes some of the available PoC codes. These include the execution techniques to invoke vulnerable kernel code in a specific version of the Linux kernel. In this study, the following kernel vulnerabilities [3,4] are applied for the evaluation of vkTracer:

- **Privilege escalation**: This overwrites credential information through the corruption of stack or heap areas and exploits kernel vulnerability to achieve privilege escalation.
- **DoS**: This leads to unstable behavior that forcibly terminates the running kernel. A system becomes vulnerable to DoS attacks because a variable is accessed or freed after its memory has already been freed (known as a use-after-free (UAF) vulnerability), deadlock of mutual exclusion, or finite loops when the flag control fails.

3   Precondition of Environment and Scenario

Environment: The assumed environment of vkTracer for an eventual deployment to kernel attack verification. vkTracer involves a user that attempts to access vulnerable kernel codes using a PoC code as follows.

- **User**: A user uses a normal user account and PoC codes that exploit kernel vulnerabilities.
- **Kernel**: A kernel contains kernel vulnerabilities, which are directly used by PoC codes. A kernel (e.g., Linux) provides internal tracing features (e.g., `kprobes` and `tracepoints`) for kernel code invocation, static kernel image, and debug information.
- **Kernel vulnerability**: A kernel vulnerability that has already been discovered or demonstrated. Vulnerable kernel codes are identified as a known piece of kernel vulnerability.

Scenario: In the assumed scenario, vkTracer attaches to the PoC code of a user process, which accesses and executes the invocation of the vulnerable kernel

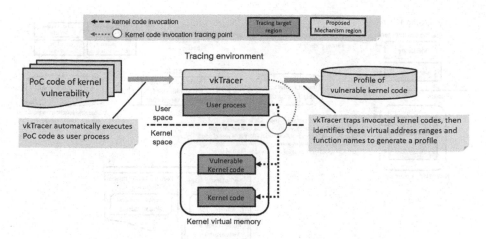

Fig. 1. Overview of the vulnerable kernel code tracer (vkTracer)

code. If successful, the user process can subsequently cause damages, including privilege escalation via memory corruption, DoS via UAF or critical section on the running kernel. vkTracer forcibly hooks on to the vulnerable kernel code during the kernel attack process. Thereafter, it gathers the entire vulnerable kernel code invocation list from the tracing environment. Finally, vkTracer generates the profile of vulnerable kernel code information (e.g., kernel function names and virtual address ranges).

4   Design

4.1   Concept

The purpose of this study was to design and develop vkTracer to fulfill the following requirements for tracking the invocation of vulnerable kernel code.

- **Requirement 1**: Trace the invocation of a vulnerable kernel code that leads to memory corruption or DoS. The tracing feature must trap the behavior of the user process and kernel while the vulnerable kernel codes are invoked on the running kernel.
- **Requirement 2**: Identify the vulnerable kernel code. The profile of the kernel vulnerability must contain the list of function names and virtual address ranges. These are identified from the invoked vulnerable kernel codes.

These requirements are enough for the raising the question of how to provide necessary information for the constructing of the profile of kernel vulnerability for the decision of the kernel updating on the user's environment.

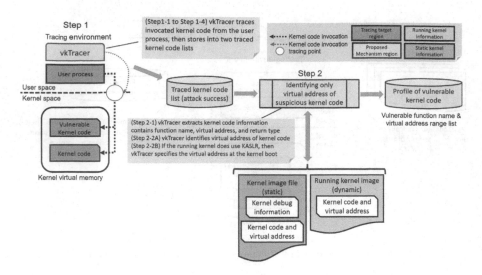

Fig. 2. Overview of the steps of profile generation

4.2 Approach

vkTracer addresses the aforementioned requirements by enhancing the capabilities of the kernel. Figure 1 outlines how vkTracer generates a profile by tracing the invocation of a vulnerable kernel code from the PoC code. vkTracer executes the PoC code as a user process in the tracing environment. Thereafter vkTracer traps the invocation of vulnerable kernel codes that is requested when the user process attempts to exploit a kernel vulnerability. vkTracer identifies the vulnerable kernel code and generates a profile of kernel vulnerability. The following approach provisions for tracing and restriction must be fulfilled:

– **Vulnerable kernel code dynamic tracing and analysis**
  vkTracer provides a mechanism for dynamic kernel tracing and for the analysis of a user process (e.g., execution of PoC codes) in the running kernel. vkTracer traps the invocation of vulnerable kernel codes that is requested when the user process attempts to exploit a kernel vulnerability. Furthermore, this mechanism utilizes the symbol and debugging information of the static kernel image during tracing. This mechanism ensures that vulnerable kernel code information (e.g., function name and virtual address range) is used to generate a profile of a specific kernel vulnerability.

4.3 Profile of Vulnerable Kernel Codes

vkTracer traps all invocations of the kernel codes. The generated profile of kernel vulnerability is defined as follows:

- **Profile**: This profile consists of a list of the kernel code invocations, virtual address ranges, and function names. vkTracer automatically collects the invocations of the kernel code instigated by the user process and then identifies the virtual address range and function name of the vulnerable kernel code.

5   Implementation

5.1   Profile Generation

vkTracer is implemented on Linux for the x86_64 CPU architecture. vkTracer automatically generates a profile of the kernel vulnerability. Figure 2 illustrates the steps of profile generation, which employs the trapping of the invocation of the kernel code and the identification of the virtual address ranges of the running kernel. This is achieved through the following steps:

- **Step 1-1:** The user executes the PoC code as a user process. vkTracer attaches to the user process and then registers the tracing target pid for trapping.
- **Step 1-2:** The user process starts the kernel attack, which invokes the vulnerable kernel code by exploiting the kernel vulnerability.
- **Step 1-3:** vkTracer determines whether the user process id is the tracing target pid, and then collects information on the kernel code that is invoked by the user process during each system call invocation.
- **Step 1-4:** vkTracer terminates the trapping of the user process when the kernel is compromised through kernel vulnerability.
- **Step 2-1:** vkTracer extracts the necessary kernel information (e.g., invocation of kernel codes) from static and dynamic kernel images to generate a profile of the kernel vulnerability.
- **Step 2-2A:** If the running kernel does not use KASLR, then vkTracer creates a relationship among the kernel code, function name, and virtual address ranges using the debug information of the kernel for the profile.
- **Step 2-2B:** If the running kernel does use KASLR, then vkTracer specifies whether the kernel image contains the kernel code as part of the profile. The complement of the virtual address ranges is identified for the profile at the kernel boot.

5.2   Kernel Code Tracing and Virtual Address Range Identification

Kernel Code Tracing: vkTracer uses the kernel tracing capabilities (c.g., bpftrace and tracepoints) to associate the running kernel with the user process behavior.

- **tracepoints**: This is a static embedded placement of a kernel that calls the tracing mechanism to record kernel processing.
- **kprobes**: This is a dynamically registered placement of a kernel that uses the symbol information of a function name for the kernel tracing capability.

Table 2. DWARF information for profile (✓ is adopted).

Item	Description	Profile
DW_AT_name	Function name	✓
DW_AT_low_pc	Lower virtual address of function	✓
DW_AT_high_pc	Higher virtual address of function	✓

The implementation of vkTracer employs the entire suite of kernel symbols and hooks the invocations of kernel code through kprobes and tracepoints. The implementation of vkTracer registers both tracing capabilities as a user-defined enhanced Berkeley Packet Filter (eBPF) program. Therefore, vkTracer gathers the actual kernel code invocation history (e.g., function name list) from the target user process for the generation of the profile.

Virtual Address Range Identification: vkTracer analyzes the static and dynamic kernel images to identify the virtual address ranges for each kernel code for profile generation.

- **Static analysis of the kernel**: vkTracer employs several sections of the Linux kernel. These are DWARF and symbol information, and include .debug_info and .text, which contain the kernel code and virtual address information.
- **Dynamic analysis of the kernel**: vkTracer dynamically identifies the virtual address range of the kernel code using the function name from kprobes and tracepoints of the eBPF program. Thereafter, vkTracer prepares the Linux kernel module (LKM) that requires the modified Linux kernel to employ EXPORT_SYMBOL for almost all kernel functions. It allows the LKM of vkTracer to directly access the virtual address of the specified kernel function.

For the purpose of generating profiles, vkTracer parses the entire set of records, and creates a relationship among the traced kernel code, virtual address range, and function name. Table 2 lists the DWARF information for the static analysis of the kernel. However, if the kernel uses KASLR, randomizes the virtual address range of the kernel code at each kernel boot, then vkTracer depends on a dynamic analysis of the kernel image to avoid infection by KASLR.

5.3 Termination Condition

vkTracer outputs the history of the kernel code's invocation while the execution of user process. Additionally, vkTracer implements the following conditions for tracing completion:

- **Privilege escalation**: The user process forcibly modifies its credential information (e.g., UID is 0) from normal privilege to administrator privilege.
- **DoS**: The user process forcibly suspends the running kernel after exploiting the kernel vulnerability. vkTracer writes the history of the vulnerable kernel code's invocation to the disk or sends these data to a remote server.

6   Evaluation

6.1   Evaluation Environment

Equipment: The security evaluation environment was implemented on virtual machines containing one traced environment server and a log collection server. The environment for the PoC code and kernel for measuring the performance cost was implemented on a physical machine equipped with an Intel (R) Core (TM) i7-7700HQ (2.80 GHz, x86_64) processor with 16 GB memory.

Implementation: To evaluate the tracing capability, two known kernel vulnerabilities [3,4] were introduced into Linux kernel 5.0.0. One kernel vulnerability leads to privilege escalation via memory corruption, and the other leads to DoS on the running kernel:

- **Privilege escalation:** PoC code 01 exploits vulnerable kernel code 1 that refers to CVE-2017-6074 [3] to achieve privilege escalation. It is implemented as system call `sys_kvuln01`, `support_sys_kvuln01_01`, and `support_sys_kvuln01_02`.
- **DoS:** PoC code 02 exploits vulnerable kernel code 2 that refers to CVE-2017-16995 [4] to force a DoS on the running kernel. It is implemented as system call `sys_kvuln02` and `support_sys_kvuln02_01`.

In addition, to evaluate the performance cost, vkTracer calculated the execution times of the PoC codes. vkTracer required 712 lines for the application. The proven kernel vulnerabilities required 192 lines for four files, whereas the PoC code for the Linux kernel 5.0.0 required 143 lines.

6.2   Tracing and Identification Consideration

The ability of vkTracer to identify vulnerable kernel code information, when a user process attempts to exploit a proven kernel vulnerability in invoking a system call, was evaluated.

Case of Privilege Escalation: Fig. 3 shows that the user process attempted to invoke the `support_kvuln01_01` and `support_kvuln01_02` functions during the `sys_kvuln1` system call in lines 6 to 8. vkTracer was able to trace and identify the invocation of vulnerable kernel codes. The user process upgraded from a normal user account (e.g., user id is 1000) to obtain the administrator account privilege, as shown by the user process id (e.g., user id is 0) at line 10. Then, vkTracer determined the function names and virtual address ranges of the vulnerable kernel codes in lines 18 to 20. This tracing result was correct, as evidenced by the symbol information in lines 28 to 30. Finally, vkTracer generated the profile of `sys_kvlun1` and other functions in line 31 to 33.

Case of DoS: Fig. 4 shows that the user process attempted to invoke the `support_kvuln02` and `support_kvuln02_01` functions in lines 4 to 7, after which

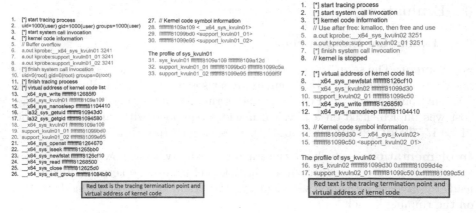

Fig. 3. Attack tracing cases of proven privilege escalation kernel vulnerability

Fig. 4. Attack tracing cases of proven DoS kernel vulnerability

the running kernel was terminated. Subsequently, in lines 9 to 10, vkTracer determined the function names and virtual address ranges of the vulnerable kernel codes at the remote server. This tracing result was correct, as evidenced by the symbol information in lines 14 to 15. Finally, vkTracer generated the profile of `sys_kvlun2` and `support_kvuln02_01` in lines 16 and 17.

Therefore, vkTracer identified the vulnerable kernel codes and extracted the kernel code information as a profile containing the function name and virtual address range.

6.3   Performance Measurement

The performance evaluations were performed to measure the overhead cost of a kernel with vkTracer.

Measurement of Vulnerable Kernel Code Identification: To evaluate the tracing overhead, the processing costs of a vanilla kernel and a kernel with vkTracer were compared. The tracing overhead is a measure of the processing time of PoC codes that exploit proven kernel vulnerabilities. The kernel compilations were run five times to determine the average processing time of two different PoC codes as the user process. Table 3 lists the performance scores. vkTracer required 5.2728 s and 5.2683 s for the two PoC codes.

Measurement of The Kernel Overhead: To measure the kernel performance overhead, LMbench was executed five times to determine the average system call overhead between a vanilla kernel and a kernel with vkTracer.

LMbench invokes two system call counts for open/close and the other system calls count is one. Table 4 shows that the open/close system calls have the highest overhead of 7.4394 µs (3.7197 µs for each once), whereas the fstat system call has the lowest overhead of 3.2292 µs.

Table 3. Tracing overhead of vkTracer (s)

Application	Vanilla kernel	w/vkTracer	Overhead
PoC code 01	0.2047	5.4775	5.2728
PoC code 02	0.1034	5.3717	5.2683

Table 4. One time system call invocation overhead of vkTracer (μs)

System call	Vanilla kernel	w/vkTracer	Overhead
open/close	1.6049	9.0443	7.4394
read	0.3545	4.0560	3.7015
write	0.2997	3.5443	3.2446
stat	0.5831	3.9714	3.3883
fstat	0.4068	3.6360	3.2292

7 Discussion

7.1 Evaluation Result Consideration

Tracing and Identification Consideration: vkTracer identifies the invocation of a vulnerable kernel code under the execution of a PoC code without any infection. It also generates a profile that contains the necessary data, including a virtual address range and function name, from the kernel image and kernel debug information. In addition, it does not have any effect on the behavior of the user process.

vkTracer requires only the PoC code, one of the PoC codes demonstrated in this paper had 143 lines, whereas the vulnerable kernel code had 192 lines. It is possible to identify the execution of the vulnerable kernel code from the source code file. To evaluate the tracing and identification capability, vkTracer needs to measure the accuracy of vulnerable kernel code identification using the latest CVE database.

Performance Consideration: The implementation of vkTracer requires additional overhead for the kernel. The identification cost for the vulnerable kernel code requires the analysis of the kernel image and debug information. It takes a few seconds after the PoC code is executed. It depends on the size of the kernel components despite the necessary cost of vkTracer for the accuracy of the kernel vulnerability's profile.

The tracing cost of vkTracer requires the registration time and additional callback processing costs of `tracepoints` and `kprobes` for the running kernel. Both tracing features increase the performance cost due to the additional kernel processing time required. To measure this, LMbench was used to calculate the cost of the overhead that occurs with the actual latency in the kernel layer.

7.2 Limitation

Design Limitation: vkTracer focuses on the behavior of a specific PoC code to identify an already known kernel vulnerability (e.g., privilege escalation and DoS). Although it invokes the vulnerable kernel code and reports it to the CVE database and developer communities (e.g., Linux kernel mailing list) [2,9], vkTracer's capability would be enhanced if it also provided support for identifying other types of vulnerabilities in kernel code for kernel attacks. Additionally,

Table 5. Portability of vkTracer for OSs (✓ is supported; • is available on x86_64).

OS	Kernel tracing	vkTracer
Linux	✓	✓
FreeBSD	✓	•
XNU kernel	✓	•
Windows	✓	•

Table 6. Comparison of tracing approaches for kernel code invocation

Design	kRazor [17]	KASR [18]	vkTracer
Target	AP	AP and kernel	PoC code
Tracing	Kernel tracing	VMM tracing	Kernel tracing
Limitation	AP and kernel update		Kernel update

vkTracer needs to investigate the kernel code used by the actual application, then provide the CVE information for the security analyst.

Implementation Limitation: The implementation of vkTracer relies on the Linux `kprobes`, which supports available symbol information for the kernel and Linux `tracepoints`, which supports static placement in the kernel code. To cover the entire kernel behavior, the dynamic tracing of kernel data (i.e., variable read and write) is necessary for additional security capability. Moreover, to focus on the detail of kernel vulnerability, reducing the tracing log and the identification mechanism of the root cause of vulnerability are required from the location of kernel corruption.

7.3 Portability

The Linux implementation of vkTracer serves as a reference for the kernel layer. Table 5 outlines the portability of vkTracer for different OSs. The implementation of vkTracer in other OS kernels depends on the tracing of the OS kernel. For example, `ktrace` and `dtrace` functionalities are available for kernel tracing in the FreeBSD and XNU kernels [10,11]. Meanwhile, Windows supports kernel loggers and tracing mechanisms [12,13]. These features can extract kernel code invocations while the execution of the user process. Therefore, the tracing of kernel behavior is available and supports the implementation of vkTracer on modern OS kernels.

8   Related Work

Kernel Tracing for Fault Tolerance: Stable kernel behavior requires the kernel to be protected from identified malicious or buggy device drivers. iKernel adopts a virtual machine monitor that traces and separates buggy devices on virtual machines [14]. SIDE traces each driver, then provides a dedicated page table for the interaction mechanisms between the kernel and drivers [15].

Kernel Tracing for Attack Surface Reduction: PerspicuOS demonstrates privilege minimization by manually tracing the kernel mechanism for hardware management [16]. kRazor and KASR require the tracing of application, related kernel code, and kernel data to statically create the available kernel code list or kernel image [17,18]. Multik customizes the kernel image to create a profile that contains the necessary kernel code for each traced application [19].

8.1 Comparison

Regarding tracing capabilities, Table 6 presents a comparison of the gap in the tracing techniques between vkTracer and previous mechanisms [17,18]. Although kRazor and KASR collect a minimum set of executable kernel functions from the benign application and whole of kernel behavior [17,18], vkTracer needs only the PoC code and the vulnerable kernel code. To complement the remaining tracing capabilities of the kernel components, vkTracer and previous mechanisms had to correspond to the latest kernel code updating the collection behavior of the running kernel with the tracing target user process.

9 Conclusion

Vulnerable kernel codes can open a system to attacks via kernel memory corruption and DoS. Although CVE provides information about kernel vulnerability, service providers or security operators cannot identify the details of vulnerable kernel codes. vkTracer, however, presents a novel approach for the tracing and identification of vulnerable codes. It involves the collection of an invoked vulnerable kernel code with a virtual address and function name using PoC code to provide a profile of vulnerable kernel codes. The evaluation results show that the proposed method supports several types of kernel vulnerabilities in identifying vulnerable kernel codes. The performance cost of PoC code tracing ranges from 5.2683 s to 5.2728 s for each kernel vulnerability. Moreover, the performance overhead of the maximum system call invocations was 3.7197 μs.

Acknowledgment. This work was partially supported by the Japan Society for the Promotion of Science (JSPS) KAKENHI Grant Number JP19H04109, JP22H03592, ROIS NII Open Collaborative Research 2022 (22S0302), and JST, PRESTO Grant Number JPMJPR22PB, Japan.

References

1. Chen, H., Mao, Y., Wang, X., Zhow, D., Zeldovich, N., Kaashoek, M.F.: Linux kernel vulnerabilities - state-of-the-art defenses and open problems. In: Proceedings of the Second Asia-Pacific Workshop on Systems, pp. 1–5. ACM (2011). https://doi.org/10.1145/2103799.2103805
2. Linux Vulnerability Statistics. https://www.cvedetails.com/vendor/33/Linux.html. Accessed 5 July 2019
3. CVE-2017-6074. https://nvd.nist.gov/vuln/detail/CVE-2017-6074. Accessed 16 Sep 2021
4. CVE-2017-16995. https://nvd.nist.gov/vuln/detail/CVE-2017-16995. Accessed 16 Sep 2021
5. CVE-2016-4997. https://nvd.nist.gov/vuln/detail/CVE-2016-4997. Accessed 16 Sep 2021
6. CVE-2016-9793. https://nvd.nist.gov/vuln/detail/CVE-2016-9793. Accessed 16 Sep 2021

7. CVE-2017-7533. https://nvd.nist.gov/vuln/detail/CVE-2017-7533. Accessed 16 Sep 2021
8. CVE-2017-1000112. https://nvd.nist.gov/vuln/detail/CVE-2017-1000112. Accessed 16 Sep 2021
9. VGER.KERNEL.ORG.: Linux kernel mailing list. http://vger.kernel.org/vger-lists.html#linux-kernel. Accessed 16 Sep 2021
10. ktrace. https://www.freebsd.org/cgi/man.cgi?ktrace. Accessed 16 Sep 2021
11. dtrace. https://www.freebsd.org/cgi/man.cgi?dtrace. Accessed 16 Sep 2021
12. NT Kernel Logger Trace Session. https://docs.microsoft.com/en-us/windows-hardware/drivers/devtest/nt-kernel-logger-trace-session. Accessed 16 Sep 2021
13. Event Tracing for Windows. https://docs.microsoft.com/en-us/windows/win32/etw/event-tracing-portal Accessed 16 Sep 2021
14. Tan, L., et al.: iKernel: isolating buggy and malicious device drivers using hardware virtualization support. In: Proceedings of the third IEEE International Symposium on Dependable, Autonomic and Secure Computing. IEEE (2007). https://doi.org/10.1109/DASC.2007.16
15. Sun, S., Chiueh, T.: SIDE: isolated and efficient execution of unmodified device drivers. In: Proceedings of the 43rd Annual IEEE/IFIP International Conference on Dependable Systems and Networks. IEEE/IFIP (2013). https://doi.org/10.1109/DSN.2013.6575348
16. Dautenhahn, N., Kasampalis, T., Dietz, W., Criswell, J., Adve, V.: Nested Kernel: an operating system architecture for intra-kernel privilege separation. In: Proceedings of the 20th International Conference on Architectural Support for Programming Languages and Operating Systems, pp. 191–206. ACM (2015). https://doi.org/10.1145/2694344.2694386
17. Kurmus, A., Dechand, S., Kapitza, R.: Quantifiable run-time kernel attack surface reduction. In: Dietrich, S. (ed.) DIMVA 2014. LNCS, vol. 8550, pp. 212–234. Springer, Cham (2014). https://doi.org/10.1007/978-3-319-08509-8_12
18. Zhang, Z., Cheng, Y., Nepal, S., Liu, D., Shen, Q., Rabhi, F.: KASR: a reliable and practical approach to attack surface reduction of commodity OS kernels. In: Bailey, M., Holz, T., Stamatogiannakis, M., Ioannidis, S. (eds.) RAID 2018. LNCS, vol. 11050, pp. 691–710. Springer, Cham (2018). https://doi.org/10.1007/978-3-030-00470-5_32
19. Kuo, H.C., et al.: MultiK: a framework for orchestrating multiple specialized kernels. https://arxiv.org/abs/1903.06889v1. Accessed 16 May 2019

Security Engineering

ARMing-Sword: Scabbard on ARM

Hyeokdong Kwon[1], Hyunjun Kim[1], Minjoo Sim[1], Siwoo Eum[1],
Minwoo Lee[1], Wai-Kong Lee[2], and Hwajeong Seo[1]

[1] IT Department, Hansung University, Seoul 02876, South Korea
hwajeong84@gmail.com
[2] Department of Computer Engineering, Gachon University,
Seongnam, Incheon 13120, South Korea
waikonglee@gachon.ac.kr

Abstract. Scabbard, one of the Post-quantum Key Encapsulation
Mechanisms (KEM), is a improved version of Saber that Lattice-based
Key Encapsulation Mechanism. Scabbard has three schemes, called Florete, Espada, and Sable. Florete is a Ring-LWR-based KEM that effectively reuses the hardware architecture module used in Saber. Espada is
a Module-LWR-based KEM that can be parallelized, requires very little memory, and is advantageous for operating in a resource-constrained
environment. Finally, Sable adjusted the parameters to reduce the standard deviation of errors occurring in the Saber. In this paper, we propose
ARMing-sword that optimized implementation of Scabbard on ARM
processor. For the efficient implementation, a parallel operation technique using vector registers and vector instructions of the ARM processor
is used. We focused on optimizing the multiplier, which takes majority
execution time for Scabbard computation, and propose a Direct Mapping and Sliding Window methods for accumulating computation results.
ARMing-sword has a performance difference of up-to 6.34× in the multiplier and a performance difference of up-to 2.17× in the encryption
algorithm to which the optimization technique is applied.

Keywords: Post-quantum cryptography · Saber · Scabbard · Software
implementation · 64-bit ARMv8 processors

1 Introduction

Quantum computers can compute huge data at once through qubit that based
on the quantum mechanics principles [1]. Therefore, the computation power of

This work was partly supported by Institute for Information & communications Technology Promotion(IITP) grant funded by the Korea government(MSIT) (No.2018-0-
00264, Research on Blockchain Security Technology for IoT Services, 50%) and this
work was partly supported by the National Research Foundation of Korea(NRF) grant
funded by the Korea government(MSIT) (No. NRF-2020R1F1A1048478, 50%) and this
work was partly supported by Institute of Information & communications Technology
Planning & Evaluation (IITP) grant funded by the Korea government(MSIT) (No.2022-
0-00627, Development of Lightweight BIoT technology for Highly Constrained Devices,
25%).

© Springer Nature Switzerland AG 2023
I. You and T.-Y. Youn (Eds.): WISA 2022, LNCS 13720, pp. 237–250, 2023.
https://doi.org/10.1007/978-3-031-25659-2_17

quantum computers is stronger than classical computers. With quantum computers, Shor and Grover algorithms utilized this characteristic [2]. These algorithms help solve the NP-hard problem. NP-hard problems are generally difficult to solve and become a stumbling block in many situations [3]. However, in cryptography, the NP-hard problem is the basis for securely using ciphers. So the advent of quantum computers, public key cryptographic systems and symmetric key cryptographic algorithms are threatened [4].

Therefore, the National Institute of Standards and Technology (NIST) held a post-quantum cryptography standardization competition to create a safety online environment under the quantum computer era [5]. This competition, which started in 2016, reached Round 3 in 2020, and in the Public-Key Encryption (PKE) category, Classic McEliece [6], CRYSTALS-Kyber [7], NTRU [8], and Saber [9] were selected as final algorithms [10].

Among them, Saber is a lattice-based cipher based on the Module ring learning with rounding (Module-LWR) problem. It has advantages that short key length and fast computation. Due to these advantages, Saber guarantees even under a resource-constrained environment. Afterwards, the Scabbard, which improved the internal structure of Saber, was proposed. Scabbard utilizes parallel operators provided on a specific platform and is designed to operate appropriately in a resource-constrained environment like Saber. In this paper, we propose ARMing-sword that optimized implementation of Scabbard on ARMv8 processor. The main contributions of this paper is as follows.

1.1 Contributions

- **Step-by-step optimization of multiplier.** In this paper, we focused on high-speed implementation of multiplier, which is heavily used in Scabbard operations. Multiplier of the Scabbard consists of three steps (i.e. Evaluation, Multiplication, and Interpolation). In the proposed method, evaluation and multiplication are implemented efficiently by using parallel operators. In the implementation, we reduce the number of iterative operations by utilizing vector registers and vector instructions of ARM processor. Finally we reduce the computational load. The target processor is Apple M1 processor (@3.2GHz). As a unit, we use the average of the clock cycles where we run each algorithm a million (for multiplier) or ten thousand (for cipher) times. In the case of Evaluation it took up to 137.6 (Single), 329.6 (3-way), and 92.8 (4-way) clock cycles, respectively. In total, the multiplier takes 8,736 (Espada) and 425.6 (Florete, Sable) clock cycles, respectively. Performance improvements of multiplier are 3.35× and 1.17× then Scabbard multiplier. When we applied proposed multiplier to ARMing-sword algorithm, the result of measuring the operation time of Keygen+Encap+Decap, ARMing-sword Florete takes 203.8 clock cycles, Espada shows 720.4 clock cycles, and Sable needs 247.5 clock cycles. The case with the best performance improvement is Espada Decapsulation, which shows a performance improvement by 2.17×.
- **Optimized implementation for each scheme.** Scabbard has three schemes, including Florete, Espada, and Sable. Each has a different inter-

nal structure. Florete and Sable have similar structures, but Espada has a completely different form. Therefore, different approaches are applied to each algorithm.

- **First implementation of Scabbard on ARMv8 processors.** Saber, the previous implementation of Scabbard, has an optimized implementation on ARMv8, and the implementation is optimized by implementing the Toom-cook multiplication algorithm used inside in parallel. Scabbard is an improved algorithm of Saber. However, the same implementation techniques cannot be applied due to the different internal structure. In this paper, we propose ARMing-sword, which is the optimized implementation of Scabbard, and focused on the optimized implementation of all schemes of Scabbard.

1.2   Organization of the Paper

The organization of the paper is as follows. Section 2 shows the backgrounds of Scabbard algorithm and target processor ARMv8. In Sect. 3, we introduce ARMing-sword that optimized implementation of Scabbard on ARMv8. Detailed optimization techniques and implementation methods are described. In Sect. 4, we present performance evaluation of the previous Scabbard and the proposed ARMing-sword. Finally, Sect. 5 concludes this paper.

2   Backgrounds

2.1   Scabbard: A Suite of Post-quantum Key-Encapsulation Mechanisms

Scabbard was proposed in 2021 as an improved key-encapsulation mechanism (KEM) of Saber. Scabbard is a lattice-based cryptography that uses ring learning with rounding the same as the original cipher, Saber. Scabbard has three schemes, and they are called Florete, Espada, and Sable, respectively [11].

Florete. Scabbard Florete focused on reusing the hardware architecture and software modules developed for Saber to ensure efficient KEM. In lattice-based cryptography, such as Scabbard, the part that generates the largest computational load is polynomial multiplication, which is necessary because of the binomial distribution of lattice-based cryptography. In Florete, polynomial multiplication based on an asymptotically faster Number Theoretic Transform (NTT) cannot be used because the moduli have already been selected. In order to apply NTT technique to implementation, it should use a larger NTT friendly prime. Instead, Florete used a generic Toom-Cook polynomial multiplication [12].

To efficiently implement Scabbard Florete, quotient ring $\mathbb{R}_q^n$ was changed to $\mathbb{Z}_q[x]/(x^{768} - x^{384} + 1)$. Before multiplying the two polynomials a and $b \in \mathbb{R}_q^n$, Toom-Cook 3-way evaluation and b is applied. Through this, the polynomials of length 256 are divided into 5 polynomials. After that, polynomial multiplication of 256×256 is performed, and then $c = a \times b \in R_q^n$ is calculated through Toom-Cook 3-way interpolation. Since the computational load of Toom-Cook 3-way evaluation and interpolation is small, the time to perform multiplication of five 256×256 polynomials is similar to the time to calculate one 768×768 polynomial multiplication. Table 1 shows that Florete has fewer multiplications than Saber and works effectively in pseudo-random number generation.

Table 1. Size of pseudo random number and number of 256×256 polynomial multiplications in Saber and Scabbard-Florete.

Name	Pseudo-random number (Bytes)	256×256 multiplications		
		KeyGen	Encap	Decap
Florete	1152	5	10	15
Saber	4512	9	12	15

However, polynomial coefficients need to be within 16-bit for efficient multiplication operation on FPGA or IoT devices. Therefore, while applying Toom-Cook interpolation, it is sometimes necessary to divide field elements by $r = 2d \times m$ with $gcd(m, 2) = 1$. Last, Florete targets NIST security level 3 and does not support level 5, but can be provided as 7 polynomial partitions of length 256 using Toom-Cook 4-way.

Espada. Scabbard Espada aimed to have a system that has a small memory footprint and can be parallelized in a resource-constraint environment. In this way, Espada maintains the performance of other platforms within a lightweight environment and aims to achieve 128-bit or higher post-quantum security.

Espada further reduced the length of the polynomial (n). Parallel operations can be performed, effectively. In particular, as n decreases, the faster operation is possible and requires a smaller area. In this way, multiple instances of $n \times n$ polynomial multipliers can be executed in batches. Therefore, using this method is similar to applying Toom-Cook evaluation to decompose larger multiplications and then using small polynomial multipliers in parallel. Considering this point, Espada uses n as an optimal value of 64.

Sable. Scabbard Sable is a lattice-based KEM manufactured in another form of Saber. Previous Saber used rounding error with continuous uniform distribution rather than discrete uniform distribution. At this time, the parameters are adjusted in order to prevent a decrease in security due to different standard deviations of the error. First, Sable sample the secret value from the Centered Binomial Distribution (CBD) where $\eta = 1$. In this case, the secret coefficient is -1, 0, or 1. When $\eta = 1$, we can store the secret value using only 2 bits per coefficient, reducing the memory requirements for the Sable.

In Saber, polynomial multiplication is performed in the form of $a \times s$, where a is randomly determined from R_q^n or R_p^n, and s is sampled according to the distribution β_η. Saber uses η as 3, 4, and 5 according to each scheme. Sable keeps η because it is advantageous to keep η and change p and q. It is easy to use this distribution for efficient implementation because secret values have a specific distribution.

2.2 Target Processor: Apple M1 Processor

The Apple M1 processor is a processor belonging to the ARMv8 family and was first shown in 2020. Same as ARMv8 processor, it has 64-bit general purpose register and 128-bit vector register capable of parallel operation. One vector register can store up to 128-bit. However, according to the arrangement specifier, the data inside the register is treated as the size specified by the specifier. If $16B$ specifier is used, the vector register treats the internal value as 16 bytes. The overall arrangement specifier can be found in Table 2 [13]. However, it is specified in the instruction, not in the arrangement specifier register. This allows the value in the register to be treated as a different unit each time an instruction is executed.

Table 2. List of arrangement specifiers specifying register packing of vector registers.

Data type	Unit	Specifier	Number of data
Byte	8-bit	8 B	8
		16 B	16
Half-word	16-bit	4 H	4
		8 H	8
Single-word	32-bit	2 S	2
		4 S	4
Double-word	64-bit	1 D	1
		2 D	2

2.3 Optimized Implementations of Post-Quantum Cryptography on ARM Processors

Kwon et al. [13] implemented FrodoKEM on Apple A10X Fusion processor, one of ARMv8 processors. The proposed method parallelizes matrix multiplication. The multiplication is performed at a high speed, and the AES module used for random number generation is operated at a high speed using an AES accelerator. As a result of performance comparison, it was shown that it operates up to 10.22× faster than the reference FrodoKEM-640.

Song et al. [14] implemented Saber, the predecessor of Scabbard, on ARM Cortex-A72, an ARMv8 processor. The proposed method operates the multiplication algorithm Toom-Cook at high speed using vector instructions and registers. The proposed method improves the operation speed of the multiplier up-to $5\times$ faster than the existing multiplier of Saber.

Kim et al. [15] implemented Falcon, an NTRU based cryptography. The implementation targets the Jetson Xavier CPU, which is widely used in autonomous driving environments. Jetson Xavier CPU is ARMv8.2 and uses the same instruction set as ARMv8, but it has added functions such as half-precision floating-point processing. The proposed method implements FFT-based multiplication and NTT-based multiplication, separately, and utilizes the NEON engine. As a result of performance comparison, the proposed method showed a performance improvement of up-to 65.4% in the verification process compared to the existing Falcon-512.

Kwon et al. [16] optimally implemented the rainbow signature algorithm, a multivariate based cryptography, on Apple M1 processor. The main optimization technique is to change polynomial multiplication to multiplication based on look-up table. In addition, by using vector instructions and registers, the table look-up is executed in parallel. The multiplication is completed quickly. The multiplication performance of the proposed method was improved by a maximum of $167.2\times$ compared to the existing method. When the multiplier was applied to the Rainbow signature, there was a performance improvement of up-to $51.6\times$.

3   Proposed Techniques

The goal of code optimization is to speed up the program or reduce the resources it consumes [17]. In this paper, we focus on speeding up the algorithm. The multiplier used in Scabbard consists of three stages (Evaluation, Multiplication, and Interpolation). The proposed method is to improve the performance by applying the optimal implementation to each step.

3.1   Instruction Set

ARMv8 processor provides various instructions, and these instructions divided into general instructions and vector instructions. In this paper, vector instructions are mainly used together with some general instructions. Table 3 lists instructions used to implement the ARMing-sword, and it can easily check the usage and effect of each instruction.

3.2   Evaluation: Direct Mapping

In the Evaluation stage, the variable is set to a 256-bit length and a set number of values is secured. At this time, the composition of evaluation is different for each scheme. Espada divides the initial input value for each section and creates it, and Florete and Sable create a value by performing a specific operation on the initial input value.

Table 3. List of ARMv8 instructions used for proposed implementation in alphabetical order [18]; Xd, Vd: destination register (general, vector), Xn, Xm, Vn, Vm: source register (general, general, vector, vector), Xt, Vt: transferred register (general, vector), T: Arrangement specifier, i: Index.

Vector instructions			
asm	Operands	Description	Operation
ADD	Vd.T, Vn.T, Vm.T	Add vector	Vd ← Vn + Vm
LD1	Vt.T, [Xn]	Load multiple single-element structures	Vt ← [Xn]
LD1R	Vt.T, [Xn]	Load one single-element structures and Replicate	Vt ← [Xn][i]
SHL	Vd.T, Vn.T #shift	Shift Left	Vd ← Vn << #shift
ST1	Vt.T, [Xn]	Store multiple single-element structures	[Xn] ← Vt
SUB	Vd.T, Vn.T, Vm.T	Subtract vector	Vd ← Vn - Vm
General instructions			
asm	Operands	Description	Operation
ADD	Xd, Xn, Xm	Add a register values	Xd ← Xn + Xm
CBNZ	Xt, (Label)	Compare and Branch on Nonzero	Go to Label
MOV	Xd, #imm	Move immediate maximum 64-bit	Xd ← #imm

In the Evaluation process, all the values of each array are traversed and stored in different variables. It takes a lot of time. In the case of Espada, Evaluation is performed twice in succession, and this requires more time than Florete and Sable. Vector registers and instructions are used to optimally implement Evaluation step. Since Scabbard operates in 16-bit units, a maximum of 8 variables are stored using $8h$ arrangement specifier in single vector register. This can reduce the number of loops by 8 times.

For the efficient operation, the structure of Evaluation is changed and it performed once instead of twice. Evaluation stage of the Scabbard Espada can be confirmed in the form of pseudo code of Algorithm 1. It shows the for loop is run twice. As such, Evaluation of Espada has a larger computational load compared to Florete and Sable. Visualizing this one shown in Fig. 1(a). Figure 1(b) shows only an example for $AW0$, but $AW1$ and $AW2$ go through the same process.

The proposed method is the **Direct Mapping** that directly stores the initial input value in the output value. To implement Direct Mapping, we first figure out saving rules of each array value. Values stored in $AW00$ and $AW02$ in Algorithm 1 are as Eq. 1.

$$AW00[0] \leftarrow AW0[0 + M] = A1[0 + L + M]$$
$$AW02[0] \leftarrow AW0[0] = A1[0 + L]$$
$$AW00[1] \leftarrow AW0[1 + M] = A1[1 + L + M]$$
$$AW02[1] \leftarrow AW0[1] = A1[1 + L]...$$
$$AW00[j] \leftarrow AW0[j + M] = A1[j + L + M]$$
$$AW02[j] \leftarrow AW0[j] = A1[j + L]$$

$$(1)$$

Algorithm 1. Pseudo-code of Scabbard Espada Evaluation step.

Input: N length of 16-bit array $A1$, middle length $M = N/2$, output length $L = N/4$.

Output: L length of 16-bit array $AW00$, $AW01$, $AW02$, $AW10$, $AW11$, $AW12$, $AW20$, $AW21$, $AW22$.

1: $i \leftarrow 0$
2: **for** i to M **do**
3:     $AW0[i] \leftarrow A1[i + L]$
4:     $AW2[i] \leftarrow A1[i]$
5:     $AW1[i] \leftarrow A1[i] + A1[i + L]$
6:     $i \leftarrow i + 1$
7: **end for**
8: $j \leftarrow 0$
9: **for** j to L **do**
10:     $AW00[j] \leftarrow AW0[j + M]$
11:     $AW01[j] \leftarrow AW0[j] + AW0[j+M]$
12:     $AW02[j] \leftarrow AW0[j]$
13:     $AW10[j] \leftarrow AW1[j + M]$
14:     $AW11[j] \leftarrow AW1[j] + AW1[j+M]$
15:     $AW12[j] \leftarrow AW1[j]$
16:     $AW20[j] \leftarrow AW2[j + M]$
17:     $AW21[j] \leftarrow AW2[j] + AW2[j+M]$
18:     $AW22[j] \leftarrow AW2[j]$
19:     $j \leftarrow j + 1$
20: **end for**
21: **return** $AW00$, $AW01$, $AW02$, $AW10$, $AW11$, $AW12$, $AW20$, $AW21$, $AW22$

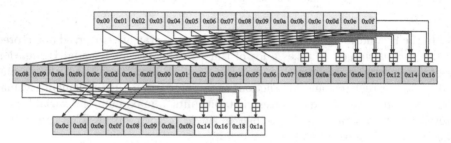

(a) $AW0$ is passed to generate $AW00 \sim 02$. All values are moved one at a time and iterates through the array until it is traversed.

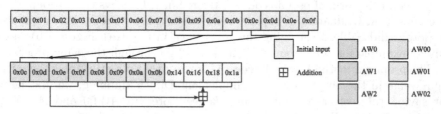

(b) Direct Mapping technique of ARMing-sword. $AW00 \sim 02$ are created directly without intermediate values. $AW01$ is created by the sum of $AW00$ and $AW02$. The number of iterations is reduced by shifting multiple values at once.

Fig. 1. Evaluation step of scabbard.

It can be seen that $AW02$ gets the value from the middle value of $A1$, which is the initial input value, and $AW00$ gets the value from the 3/4 point of $A1$. In the case of $AW01$, it can be calculated by adding the values of $AW00$ and

$AW02$. Similarly, in the case of $AW20$ and $AW22$, it is similar to $AW00 \sim 02$, except that the starting value of $A1$ is imported. Therefore, the overall form is the same as $AW00 \sim 02$. Finally, the following Eq. 2 rules can be found for the values of $AW10$ and $AW12$.

$$
\begin{aligned}
AW10[0] &\leftarrow AW1[0+M] = A1[0+M] + A1[0+M+L] \\
AW12[0] &\leftarrow AW1[0] = A1[0] + A1[0+L] \\
AW10[1] &\leftarrow AW1[1+M] = A1[1+M] + A1[1+M+L] \\
AW12[1] &\leftarrow AW1[1] = A1[1] + A1[1+L]... \\
AW10[j] &\leftarrow AW1[j+M] = A1[j+M] + A1[j+M+L] \\
AW12[j] &\leftarrow AW1[j] = A1[j] + A1[j+L]
\end{aligned}
\tag{2}
$$

$AW10$ is derived from the sum of the intermediate values of the initial input value $A1$, and $AW12$ consists of the sum of the starting values of $A1$. Therefore, it can be seen that all values from $AW00$ to $AW22$ can be calculated directly from $A1$ without going through $AW0$, $AW1$, and $AW2$. However, the values of $A1$ requested by $AW10$, $AW11$, and $AW12$ have already been stored by calculating $AW00 \sim 02$, $AW20 \sim 22$. Therefore, $AW01 \sim 12$ can be calculated by adding $AW00 \sim 02$ and $AW20 \sim 22$. The Direct Mapping technique calculates the final value directly without going through an intermediate step like this. The Evaluation step of ARMing-sword to which Direct Mapping is applied can be expressed as Algorithm 2. If it is expressed visually, it can be expressed as Fig. 1(b), and it shows how the values of $A1$ correspond from $AW00$ to $AW02$ at once. Figure 1(b) In Fig. 1(b), only $AW00 \sim 02$ case is expressed, but the rest of the values are calculated in the same way.

Algorithm 2. Pseudo-code of Direct Mapping technique for ARMing-sword.

Input: N length of 16-bit array $A1$, middle length $M = N/2$, output length $L = N/4$.

Output: L length of 16-bit array $AW00$, $AW01$, $AW02$, $AW10$, $AW11$, $AW12$, $AW20$, $AW21$, $AW22$.

```
1:  i ← 0
2:  for i to L do
3:      AW00[i] ← A1[i + L + M]
4:      AW02[i] ← A1[i + L]
5:      AW01[i] ← AW00[i] + AW02[i]
6:      AW20[i] ← A1[i + M]
7:      AW22[i] ← A1[i]
8:      AW21[i] ← AW20[i] + AW21[i]
9:      AW10[i] ← AW00[i] + AW20[i]
10:     AW12[i] ← AW01[i] + AW21[i]
11:     AW11[i] ← AW02[i] + AW22[i]
12:     i ← i + 1
13: end for
14: return   AW00, AW01, AW02,
            AW10, AW11, AW12, AW20, AW21,
            AW22
```

Direct Mapping changes the order of operations to minimize memory access. In particular, in the case of $AW10 \sim 12$, it can be calculated by adding $AW00 \sim 02$ and $AW20 \sim 22$, respectively. This can shorten the time to access the memory to get a value from $A1$, and it is an effective operation because the number of addition instructions can be reduced only for $AW11$. Algorithm 3 describe the Direct Mapping in source codes. In line 1–4, $A1$ values are loaded from address of $A1$ to vector registers. At that time, the value is loaded into the vector registers corresponding to the output address. In line 5–6, $AW01$ values are calculated and line 7–8, $AW21$ values are calculated. In line 9–14, $AW10$, $AW12$, and $AW11$ values are calculated. In line 15–19, each value is stored to output address. From Algorithm 3, $AW00$, $AW02$, $AW20$, and $AW22$ don't seem to have any operations. Since these values only need to get the specific value of $A1$, the calculation is actually completed as soon as values from lines 1–4 are loaded.

Algorithm 3. Source codes for Direct Mapping technique.

Input: $A1$ address = x0, AW
    address = x1
Output: $AW00$, $AW01$,
    $AW02$, $AW10$, $AW11$,
    $AW12$, $AW20$, $AW21$,
    $AW22$ values
1: LD1.8h {v16, v17}, [x0],
    #32
2: LD1.8h {v12, v13}, [x0],
    #32
3: LD1.8h {v4, v5}, [x0], #32

4: LD1.8h {v0, v1}, [x0], #32
5: ADD.8h v2, v0, v4
6: ADD.8h v3, v1, v5
7: ADD.8h v14, v12, v16
8: ADD.8h v15, v13, v17
9: ADD.8h v6, v0, v12
10: ADD.8h v7, v1, v13
11: ADD.8h v10, v4, v16
12: ADD.8h v11, v5, v17
13: ADD.8h v8, v2, v14
14: ADD.8h v9, v3, v15

15: ST1.8h {v0, v1, v2, v3},
    [x1], #64
16: ST1.8h {v4, v5, v6, v7},
    [x1], #64
17: ST1.8h {v8, v9, v10, v11},
    [x1], #64
18: ST1.8h {v12, v13, v14,
    v15}, [x1], #64
19: ST1.8h {v16, v17}, [x1],
    #32

In the case of Florete and Sable, it is implemented according to Toom-Cook 3-way or 4-way. Unlike Evaluation of Espada, Evaluation of Florete and Sable includes a number of processing of input values. Therefore, we focus on minimizing the number of iterations using vector instructions and registers. In some parts, Direct Mapping can be applied. Algorithm 4 is a part of the source code implementing Toom-Cook 3-way Evaluation. Toom-Cook 4-way can be implemented by increasing the scale of 3-way version. In line 1–3, initial input values are loaded from address of $A[0]$, $A[256]$, and $A[512]$. In line 4–5, $p0$ and $p4$ are calculated using the Direct Mapping technique. In line 6–14, 15–19, and 20–32, $p1$, $p2$, and $p3$ values are calculated, respectively. Since Algorithm 4 is part of the whole operation process, it completes all values through iteration.

3.3 Multiplication: Sliding Window

After Evaluation, the multiplication is carried out. The multiplication of Espada is implemented as a nested loop like Algorithm 5 and has a structure in which the calculation result value is accumulated.

However, vector instructions cannot be implemented because the address pointer moves in 32-byte or 64-byte units. For this, the **Sliding Window** technique is utilized. The Sliding Window technique is a technique that processes operations based on the current pointer position. This requires manual adjustment of the pointer. In ARM assembly, address pointers are stored in general

Algorithm 4. Source codes for Toom-Cook 3-way Evaluation.

Input: $A[0]$ address $=$ x0,
$p0 - 4$ address $=$ x1-
5, $A[256]$ address $=$ x6,
$A[512]$ address $=$ x7.
Output: $p0, p1, p2, p3, p4$ values.
1: LD1.8h {v0, v1, v2, v3}, [x0], #64
2: LD1.8h {v4, v5, v6, v7}, [x6], #64
3: LD1.8h {v8, v9, v10, v11}, [x7], #64
4: **ST1.8h {v0, v1, v2, v3},** **[x1], #64**
5: **ST1.8h {v8, v9, v10,** **v11}, [x5], #64**
6: ADD.8h v12, v0, v8
7: ADD.8h v13, v1, v9
8: ADD.8h v14, v2, v10
9: ADD.8h v15, v3, v11
10: ADD.8h v16, v12, v4
11: ADD.8h v17, v13, v5
12: ADD.8h v18, v14, v6
13: ADD.8h v19, v15, v7
14: ST1.8h {v16, v17, v18, v19}, [x2], #64
15: SUB.8h v16, v12, v4
16: SUB.8h v17, v13, v5
17: SUB.8h v18, v14, v6
18: SUB.8h v19, v15, v7
19: ST1.8h {v16, v17, v18, v19}, [x3], #64
20: ADD.8h v16, v16, v8
21: ADD.8h v17, v17, v9
22: ADD.8h v18, v18, v10
23: ADD.8h v19, v19, v11
24: SHL.8h v16, v16, #1
25: SHL.8h v17, v17, #1
26: SHL.8h v18, v18, #1
27: SHL.8h v19, v19, #1
28: SUB.8h v16, v16, v0
29: SUB.8h v17, v17, v1
30: SUB.8h v18, v18, v2
31: SUB.8h v19, v19, v3
32: ST1.8h {v16, v17, v18, v19}, [x4], #64

Algorithm 5. Pseudo-code of Scabbard Espada Multiplication stage.

Input: Evaluation result array A, input array B.
Output: output result C.
1: $i \leftarrow 0$
2: $j \leftarrow 0$
3: **for** i to 32 **do**
4:    **for** j to 63 **do**
5:       $C[0][0][i] \leftarrow A[i] * B[0][0][j]$
6:       $C[0][1][i] \leftarrow A[i] * B[0][1][j]$
7:       $C[0][2][i] \leftarrow A[i] * B[0][2][j]$
8:       $C[1][0][i] \leftarrow A[i] * B[1][0][j]$
9:       $C[1][1][i] \leftarrow A[i] * B[1][1][j]$
10:     $C[1][2][i] \leftarrow A[i] * B[1][2][j]$
11:     $C[2][0][i] \leftarrow A[i] * B[2][0][j]$
12:     $C[2][1][i] \leftarrow A[i] * B[2][1][j]$
13:     $C[2][2][i] \leftarrow A[i] * B[2][2][j]$
14:     $j \leftarrow j + 1$
15:    **end for**
16:    $i \leftarrow i + 1$
17: **end for** C

---

registers. They can be adjusted through general instructions. Algorithm 6 is the source code used for Sliding Window implementation. In line 1–2, B and A values are loaded. In line 3–4, multiplication between A and B is performed. In line 5–7, the multiplication result is accumulated and stored to C. There is no register to store the address of C in the source code. This is because it shares an address with A. In line 8, the address pointer is moved to next value. The operation can be completed by repeating this until the last value of A and B. Florete and Sable exist in five different forms of multiplication. Therefore, 5 different types of multipliers to which Sliding Window is applied are implemented.

Algorithm 6. Source codes of Sliding Window technique for ARMing-sword.

Input: B address $=$ x1, A address $=$ x2.
Output: multiplication result C.
1: LD1.8h {v18, v19}, [x1], #32
2: LD1.8h {v21, v22}, [x2]
3: MUL v23.8h, v18.8h, v0.h[0]
4: MUL v24.8h, v19.8h, v0.h[0]
5: ADD.8h v21, v21, v23
6: ADD.8h v22, v22, v24
7: ST1.8h {v21, v22}, [x2]
8: ADD x2, x2, #2

Table 4. Performance comparison results of multiplier (Unit: clock cycles)

Algorithm	[11]	This work
Evaluation single	272	**137.6**
Evaluation 3-way	1,740.8	**329.6**
Evaluation 4-way	588.8	**92.8**
Multiplier Espada	29,286.4	**8,736**
Multiplier Florete/Sable	496	**425.6**

4   Evaluation

This Section shows evaluation result of proposed ARMing-sword and previous Scabbard implementation[1]. The target processor is Apple M1 processor (@3.2GHz) which used for Apple product line (e.g. MacBook and iPad). The implementation is carried out through the Xcode IDE, and compiled with compile option -O3 (i.e. fastest). The performance is measured through the average time of 1,000,000 iterations (i.e. 10,000 times for multiplier and ARMing-sword algorithm in average timing). The unit is clock cycles.

First, performance of the multiplier is compared. Table 4 shows performance comparison results. Evaluation single is only for Espada, and Evaluation single of Scabbard takes 272 clock cycles. Our proposed ARMing-sword Evaluation single needs 137.6 clock cycles. It has 1.97× better performance than Scabbard. Evaluation 3-way and 4-way is used for Florete and Sable, Scabbard show 1,740.8 and 588.8 clock cycles, respectively. On the other hand, ARMing-sword Evaluation 3-way and 4-way take 329.6 and 92.8 clock cycles respectively. It is 5.28× and 6.34 × better performance than Scabbard. Finally, as a result of operating multiplier, Multiplier of Scabbard-Espada takes 29,286.4 clock cycles. However, ARMing-sword-Espada multipliers only takes 8,736 clock cycles, and it 3.35 × performance improvement. However, multipliers of Florete and Sable have almost the same performance. This is because optimized implementation of Evaluation is well done, but the structure of Multiplication Florete/Sable is not friendly to ARM processor compared to Espada.

Second, we compare the performance of the previous work and the proposed method. The overall performance comparison results are shown in Table 5. The proposed method has better performance than the previous work. In particular, the performance improvement in Espada is outstanding. Among them, decapsulation shows the best performance improvement with 2.17×.

---

[1]   https://github.com/josebmera/scabbard.

Table 5. Performance comparison results of previous implementation and proposed implementation (Unit: $\times 10^4$ clock cycles).

Scheme	Algorithm	[11]	This work
Sable	KeyGen	80.8	**75.7**
	Encapsulation	89.8	**84.1**
	Decapsulation	93.4	**88.4**
	All	263.2	**247.5**
Espada	KeyGen	475.6	**230.7**
	Encapsulation	505.4	**239.7**
	Decapsulation	521.2	**241.7**
	All	11497.4	**720.4**
Florete	KeyGen	53.2	**50.8**
	Encapsulation	72.5	**72.6**
	Decapsulation	86.0	**78.9**
	All	222.1	**203.8**

5 Conclusion

In this paper, we propose ARMing-sword that optimized version of Scabbard algorithm. ARMing-sword uses Direct Mapping and Sliding Window techniques for multiplication algorithms. As a result of the performance comparison, multiplier shows performance improvement by 6.34× in Evaluation 4-way. In the case of ARMing-sword implementation by applying a multiplier to Scabbard, decapsulation shows most performance improvement that 2.17× than previous works.

References

1. Deutsch, D.: Quantum theory, the church-turing principle and the universal quantum computer. Proc. R. Soc. Lond. A Math. Phys. Sci. **400**(1818), 97–117 (1985)
2. Leuenberger, M.N., Loss, D.: Quantum computing in molecular magnets. Nature **410**(6830), 789–793 (2001)
3. Boualem, A., De Runz, C., Ayaida, M.: Partial paving strategy: application to optimize the area coverage problem in mobile wireless sensor networks. J. Wireless Mobile Netw. Ubiquitous Comput. Dependable Appl. **13**(2), 1–22 (2022)
4. Kirsch, Z., Chow, M.: Quantum computing: the risk to existing encryption methods (2015). https://wwwcs.tufts.edu/comp/116/archive/fall2015/zkirsch.pdf
5. Moody, D., et al.: Status report on the second round of the NIST post-quantum cryptography standardization process (2020)
6. Bernstein, D.J., et al.: Classic McEliece: conservative code-based cryptography (2017)
7. Avanzi, R., et al.: CRYSTALS-Kyber algorithm specifications and supporting documentation. NIST PQC Round **2**(4), 1–43 (2019)

8. Chen, C., et al.: NTRU algorithm specifications and supporting documentation. In: Second PQC Standardization Conference (2019)
9. D'Anvers, J.-P., Karmakar, A., Sinha Roy, S., Vercauteren, F.: Saber: module-LWR based key exchange, CPA-secure encryption and CCA-secure KEM. In: Joux, A., Nitaj, A., Rachidi, T. (eds.) AFRICACRYPT 2018. LNCS, vol. 10831, pp. 282–305. Springer, Cham (2018). https://doi.org/10.1007/978-3-319-89339-6_16
10. Auten, D., Gamage, T.: Impact of resource-constrained networks on the performance of NIST round-3 PQC candidates. In: 2021 IEEE 45th Annual Computers, Software, and Applications Conference (COMPSAC), pp. 768–773. IEEE (2021)
11. Mera, J.M.B., Karmakar, A., Kundu, S., Verbauwhede, I.: Scabbard: a suite of efficient learning with rounding key-encapsulation mechanisms. IACR Trans. Cryptographic Hardware Embed. Syst. **2021**, 474–509 (2021)
12. Knuth, D.E.: Art of Computer Programming, Volume 2: Seminumerical Algorithms. Addison-Wesley Professional, Boston (2014)
13. Kwon, H., et al.: ARMed Frodo. In: Kim, H. (ed.) WISA 2021. LNCS, vol. 13009, pp. 206–217. Springer, Cham (2021). https://doi.org/10.1007/978-3-030-89432-0_17
14. Song, J., Kim, Y., Seo, S.: Optimization study of Toom-Cook algorithm in NIST PQC SABER utilizing ARM/NEON processor. J. Korea Inst. Inf. Secur. Cryptol. **31**(3), 463–471 (2021)
15. Kim, Y., Song, J., Seo, S.C.: Accelerating falcon on ARMv8. IEEE Access (2022)
16. Kwon, H., Kim, H., Sim, M., Lee, W.-K., Seo, H.: Look-up the rainbow: efficient table-based parallel implementation of rainbow signature on 64-bit ARMv8 processors. Cryptology ePrint Archive (2021)
17. You, G., Kim, G., Cho, S.-J., Han, H.: A comparative study on optimization, obfuscation, and deobfuscation tools in android. J. Internet Serv. Inf. Secur. **11**(1), 2–15 (2021)
18. ARMv8-A instruction set architecture. https://documentation-service.arm.com/static/613a2c38674a052ae36ca307. Accessed 26 June 2019

Optimized Implementation of Quantum Binary Field Multiplication with Toffoli Depth One

Kyungbae Jang, Wonwoong Kim, Sejin Lim, Yeajun Kang, Yujin Yang, and Hwajeong Seo

IT Department, Hansung University, Seoul, South Korea
hwajeong84@gmail.com

Abstract. Shor's algorithm models discrete logarithms on binary elliptic curves and provides polynomial-time solutions. One of major overheads in applying Shor's algorithm is implementing binary elliptic curve arithmetic in quantum circuits. Among operations of elliptic curves over binary fields, the multiplication is essential and cost-critical even in the quantum field.

In this paper, we aim to optimize quantum binary field multiplication. Previous works on quantum multiplication focused on minimizing the number of Toffoli gates or qubits. In contrast, our work presents strategies for optimizing Toffoli depth and full depth, which are key factors in the Noisy Intermediate-Scale Quantum (NISQ) era. To achieve our goal, Karatsuba multiplication using divide-and-conquer approach is adopted. In a nutshell, we present an optimized quantum multiplication with Toffoli depth one. Furthermore, under the influence of the optimized Toffoli depth, the full depth is naturally reduced.

In order to show the effectiveness of proposed method, the performance is evaluated by various metrics, such as, qubits, quantum gates, depth, and qubits-depth product. To the best of our knowledge, this is the first study on quantum multiplication that optimizes Toffoli depth and full depth.

Keywords: Shor's algorithm · Binary elliptic curves · Quantum multiplication · Toffoli depth

1 Introduction

The large-scale quantum computers that will emerge in the near future are considered to be a major threat to the cryptography community. Quantum com-

This work was partly supported by Institute for Information & communications Technology Promotion(IITP) grant funded by the Korea government(MSIT) (No. 2018-0-00264, Research on Blockchain Security Technology for IoT Services, 50%) and this work was partly supported by Institute for Information & communications Technology Planning & Evaluation (IITP) grant funded by the Korea government(MSIT) (<Q|Crypton>, No. 2019-0-00033, Study on Quantum Security Evaluation of Cryptography based on Computational Quantum Complexity, 50%).

ⓒ Springer Nature Switzerland AG 2023
I. You and T.-Y. Youn (Eds.): WISA 2022, LNCS 13720, pp. 251–264, 2023.
https://doi.org/10.1007/978-3-031-25659-2_18

puters with quantum algorithms can model and solve problems for which cryptographic algorithms are based on their security. Quantum computers capable of running the Shor algorithm [1] can solve factorization and discrete logarithm problems, which are the challenges of Rivest-Shamir-Adleman (RSA) and Elliptic Curve Cryptography (ECC). As such, it is well known that the Shor's algorithm violates the security of public key cryptography. In this current situation, the analysis of potential quantum computer attacks on public key cryptography should be considered for a robust security system [2,3].

In [4], Häner et al. presented that $2n + 2$ qubits are required to apply the Shor algorithm to RSA with an n-bit key. As another quantum analysis of RSA, Gideny presented that RSA with an n-bit key requries $2n + 1$ qubits when applying the Shor algorithm [5].

In Asiacrypt'17 [6], Roetteler et al. estimated the quantum resources required to solve the elliptic curve discrete logarithms, and showed that ECC is more vulnerable to quantum computers than RSA. In PQCrypto'20 [7], Häner et al. reduced the number of qubits and circuit depth by improving the results of [6]. In [6,7], prime curves are targeted, and when solving discrete logarithm problems, optimizing scalar multiplication on elliptic curves, which is the most expensive, is key in determining the cost.

In CHES'20, Banegas et al. estimated the cost of solving discrete logarithm problems on binary curves and showed that it is possible to attack with fewer qubits and depth than prime curves. In the work of Banegas et al., Van Hoof's work [8] was used to implement quantum multiplication of binary fields. Van Hoof's quantum multiplication is based on the Karatsuba algorithm and features a space-efficient implementation that reduces the number of qubits, while reducing the number of Toffoli gates.

As it can be seen from previous works, optimizing binary field multiplication on a quantum computer is an essential building block for high-performance quantum cryptanalysis. Most recent works about quantum multiplication focus on reducing the number of qubits or Toffoli gates, but do not give much consideration to the depth of the circuit [8–12]. A few years ago, the number of available qubits in a quantum computer was small. But today's quantum computers are no longer considered small. Also, the upcoming quantum computers are obviously not small, as seen in IBM's quantum computer development roadmap[1]. Toffoli depth is an important metric for quantum computing where errors should be controlled [13], and full depth determines the circuit's operating time [14]. Regarding the importance of full depth, in the quantum security requirements[2] of the National Institute of Standards and Technology (NIST), the complexity of quantum attacks is calculated as the product of the number of gates and the full depth (the number of qubits is not included) [15].

The main target of this paper is to optimize binary field multiplication on a quantum computer. We focus on Toffoli depth and full depth, and propose a

---

[1] https://research.ibm.com/blog/ibm-quantum-roadmap.

[2] https://csrc.nist.gov/CSRC/media/Projects/Post-Quantum-Cryptography/documents/call-for-proposals-final-dec-2016.pdf.

quantum binary filed multiplication that is optimized with Toffoli depth one and has the lowest full depth. The proposed multiplication requires additional qubits, and the number of qubits is still an important factor in quantum computers. In this trade-off, the proposed work is evaluated by various metrics, including the number of qubits, number of quantum gates, depth, product of Toffoli depth, and number of qubits.

In most quantum-related studies, quantum circuits are simulated on a classical computer using quantum programming tools, such as ProjectQ [16], Qiskit [17], and Q# [18] (i.e. logical level with no errors). This is because it is difficult to access real quantum computers and errors that occur must be considered (i.e. physical level with errors). In this work, the quantum programming tool ProjectQ is used to implement quantum circuits and estimate detailed quantum resources.

1.1 Our Contribution

The contribution of this paper is summarized as follows:

1. **Optimized quantum binary field multiplication using the Karatsuba algorithm.** (Sects. 3.1 and 3.2). We present the optimized quantum binary field multiplication with Toffoli depth one. Since all Toffoli gates operate in parallel, all products are generated, simultaneously. The full depth of quantum multiplication is mostly derived from Toffoli gates. The full depth of proposed quantum multiplication is naturally reduced.
2. **Efficient quantum circuit implementation techniques**. Additionally, efficient implementation techniques are presented together. How to offset the overhead of increasing qubits in our quantum multiplication (Sect. 3.3), quantum multiplication of T-depth one (Sect. 3.4), and optimal modular reduction (Sect. 3.5) are discussed.
3. **Optimized primitives for quantum cryptanalysis of ECC.** Our work can be used to optimize quantum cryptanalysis of elliptic curves over binary fields. Quantum binary field multiplication is essential for the Shor algorithm to solve discrete logarithm problems on binary elliptic curves. Our work shows the best trade-off between Toffoli depth and number of qubits.

2 Background

2.1 Binary Field Multiplication

Multiplication of $\mathbb{F}_{2^n}$ performs n-bit polynomial multiplication and modular reduction by irreducible polynomial N. The multiplication of f and g of $\mathbb{F}_{2^n}$ is as follows.

$$h = f \cdot g \bmod N \tag{1}$$

For the generated product of f and g, the modular reduction is performed over n bits in length. As a result, h, the product of f and g, becomes an element of $\mathbb{F}_{2^n}$.

2.2   Karatsuba Multiplication

It is well known that the Karatsuba algorithm [19] can reduce the complexity of multiplication by using addition operations. For the multiplication of polynomials f and g of size n (i.e. $h = f \cdot g$), the Karatsuba algorithm divides the two input polynomials f and g into the size of $s = n/2$ as follows:

$$f = f_1 x^s + f_0$$
$$g = g_1 x^s + g_0 \tag{2}$$

After two input polynomials (f and g) are divided as above, the Karatsuba multiplication is done as:

$$f_0 \cdot g_0 + \{(f_0 + f_1) \cdot (g_0 + g_1) + f_0 \cdot g_0 + f_1 \cdot g_1\}x^s + f_1 \cdot g_1 x^{2s} \tag{3}$$

Using the Karatsuba algorithm, the multiplication complexity of $O(n^2)$ is reduced to $O(n^{\log_2 3})$ by performing addition operations.

2.3   Quantum Gates

This Section briefly describes the CNOT and Toffoli gates for implementing binary field multiplication consisting of XOR and AND operations.

Figure 1(a) is a quantum CNOT gate that can replace the classical XOR operation. In the CNOT gate, one control qubit is used to determine the value of the target qubit ($\mathrm{CNOT}(x, y) = (x, x \oplus y)$).

Figure 1(b) is a quantum Toffoli gate that can replace the classical AND operation. In the Toffoli gate, two control qubits are used to determine the value of the target qubit ($\mathrm{Toffoli}(x, y, z) = (x, y, z \oplus (x \cdot y))$). In practice, the Toffoli gate in Fig. 1(b) has a high cost as it is implemented as a combination of quantum gates [20].

Quantum gates in reversible quantum computing can compute a unique input from a given output. In quantum circuits, the reverse operation means returning from the output to the input by reversing the previous quantum gates. When the reverse operation is performed on the output of the quantum gates in Fig. 1, it returns to the input.

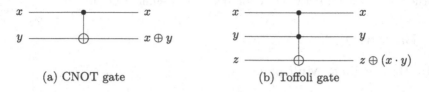

(a) CNOT gate   (b) Toffoli gate

Fig. 1. Reversible quantum gates.

In this section, quantum multiplication using the Karatsuba algorithm with Toffoli depth one for any field size is described first. Then, quantum multiplication of T-depth one is presented by applying the Toffoli gate of T-depth one introduced in [21].

We apply the Karatsuba algorithm recursively, making all multiplication operations independent. With this technique, we present a quantum multiplication of Toffoli depth one that performs all multiplication operations simultaneously. The proposed quantum multiplication also reduces the full depth, since the Toffoli depth in multiplication has an impact on counting the full depth. NCT

3 Optimized Implementation of Quantum Binary Field Multiplication

In quantum multiplication, the majority of the cost is spent on Toffoli gates to compute the products (i.e. performing AND operations). Karatsuba algorithm, which reduces the number of multiplication operations, is obviously an efficient technique in quantum computers.

We propose a special quantum Karatsuba multiplication that reduces the number of Toffoli gates, Toffoli depth, and circuit depth. With this technique, we present a quantum binary field multiplication of Toffoli depth one that performs all multiplication operations, simultaneously. The proposed quantum multiplication reduces the full depth, since the Toffoli depth in multiplication has an impact on counting the full depth.

3.1 Parallel Quantum Multiplication with the Karatsuba Algorithm

Let h be the product of two polynomials f and g of size n (i.e. $h = f \cdot g$). As illustrated in Fig. 2, $f \cdot g$ with Schoolbook multiplication (which is general) requires n^2 Toffoli gates.

In the proposed method, we apply the Karatsuba algorithm once to reduce the size of the multiplication, which is called Level-1. In Level-1, it is divided into three multiplications $f_0 \cdot g_0$, $f_1 \cdot g_1$, and $(f_0 + f_1) \cdot (g_0 + g_1)$. The size of each multiplication is reduced to $(n/2)$ and $3 \cdot (n/2)^2$ Toffoli gates are required. This result reduces the use of Toffoli gates from n^2 to $3 \cdot (n/2)^2$, but may not be completely parallel, which means the three multiplications are not performed, simultaneously. In the Level-1 layer of Fig. 2, multiplications $f_0 \cdot g_0$ (low part) and $f_1 \cdot g_1$ (high part) are performed, simultaneously, but $(f_0 + f_1) \cdot (g_0 + g_1)$ in the rectangle (middle part) is performed sequentially after the previous multiplications are finished. Operands of the multiplication of the middle part $(f_0 + f_1, g_0 + g_1)$ are overwritten in f_0, g_0 or f_1, g_1 (i.e. $f_0 = f_0 + f_1$, $g_0 = g_0 + g_1$), and it is possible only after the multiplication of the high part and the low part is finished, as in [8,10,11].

Before multiplications, we allocate clean qubits (rectangle of Level-1 layer in Fig. 2) and independently prepare the middle part operands $(f_0 + f_1)$ and $(g_0 + g_1)$ using CNOT gates. Preparing this middle part requires n clean qubits and $2n$ CNOT gates. (i.e. $2/n$ clean qubits $= f_0 + f_1$ and $2/n$ clean qubits $= g_0 + g_1$) Three multiplications of low, middle, and high become independent of each other and can be performed, simultaneously. As a result, in Level-1, quantum multiplication of reduced Toffoli depth is presented. If the Karatsuba

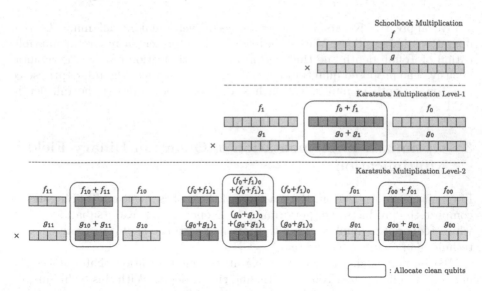

Fig. 2. Overview of the proposed method.

multiplication is terminated, additions between the generated products $f_0 \cdot g_0$, $f_1 \cdot g_1$, and $(f_0 + f_1) \cdot (g_0 + g_1)$ are performed using CNOT gates to complete the multiplication. Furthermore, we apply the Karatsuba algorithm recursively to optimize the Toffoli depth and full depth.

The quantum resources of multiplication according to the Karatsuba Level is shown in Table 1. In practice, the Toffoli gate is implemented as a combination of several quantum gates. In this work, we decompose the Toffoli gate into 7 T gates + 8 Clifford gates, T-depth 4, and full depth 8 following the frequently adopted method [20]. However, for a bird's eye view of comparison, in Table 1, without decomposing the Toffoli gate, only the full depth is assumed to be 8. In subsequent resource estimates, we completely decompose the Toffoli gates.

Modular reduction is not included in Table 1 and will be described in Sect. 3.5, because the complexity slightly different depending on the irreducible polynomial of the field and does not significantly affect the overall cost.

Table 1. Quantum resources required for each Karatsuba level of multiplication.

Field size 2^n	#CNOT	#Toffoli	Toffoli depth	#Qubits	Full depth
Schoolbook	·	n^2	$3n-2$	$4n-1$	$8 \cdot (3n-2)$
Karatsuba Level-1	$5n-4$	$3 \cdot (n/2)^2$	$3n/2-2$	$3 \cdot (2n-1)$	$8 \cdot (3n/2-2)+5$
Karatsuba Level-2	$(5n-4)+$ $3 \cdot (5n/2-4)$	$3^2 \cdot (n/2^2)^2$	$3n/2^2-2$	$3^2 \cdot (n-1)$	$8 \cdot (3n/2^2-2)+10$
Karatsuba Level-3	$(5n-4)+3 \cdot (5n/2-4)$ $+9 \cdot (5n/4-4)$	$3^3 \cdot (n/2^3)^2$	$3n/2^3.-2$	$3^3 \cdot (n/2-1)$	$8 \cdot (3n/2^3-2)+15$

3.2 Toffoli Depth Optimization with Recursive Karatsuba Algorithm

In Level-2, the Karatsuba algorithm is applied to each of the three multiplications divided by Level-1. Similar to Level-1, in Level-2 there is a dependency on multiplications for middle parts. Thus, we allocate 3× clean qubits and prepare the 3× middle parts using CNOT gates again (rectangles of Level-2 layer in Fig. 2). Preparing these middle parts requires $3 \cdot (n/2)$ clean qubits and $3n$ CNOT gates. As a result, nine multiplications become completely independent of each other and are performed, simultaneously. In Level-2, Toffoli gates and Toffoli depth that were reduced in Level-1 are reduced once more to $3^2 \cdot (n/2^2)^2$ for Toffoli gates and $(3n/2^2 - 2)$ for Toffoli depth.

In this way, the Karatsuba algorithm is applied recursively until it is divided into multiplications of size one, and the dependencies of all multiplications are released. Then, we can perform quantum multiplication of Toffoli depth one by generating all products in parallel. Finally, the proposed quantum multiplication circuit achieves the best performance of Toffoli depth one, providing high performance even for full depth.

According to field size 2^n, the required Karatsuba Level for multiplication of Toffoli depth one is different. This is calculated as Level-$\log_2 n$ according to field size 2^n. For example, Level-2 for field size $n = 4$ and Level-3 for field size $n = 8$. In Table 2, we compare quantum resources required for multiplication of Toffoli depth one by field size. As the Karatsuba level increases, there is a trade-off between Toffoli gates, depth, and number of qubits (See Table 1). Proposed quantum multiplication provides the best performance at the highest Karatsuba Level, but implementation designer can flexibly set the Karatsuba Level by considering this trade-off.

Table 2. Quantum resources required for multiplication of Toffoli depth one.

Field size 2^n	Karatsuba Level	#CNOT	#1qCliff	#T	T-depth*	#Qubits	Full depth
$n = 4$	2	88	18	63	4	27	17
$n = 8$	3	300	54	189	4	81	23
$n = 16$	4	976	162	567	4	243	28

※: Toffoli depth one has a T-depth of four.

3.3 Recycling Qubits with Reverse Operation

In our quantum multiplication, new qubits for the middle parts are allocated each time the Karatsuba algorithm is applied, which is obviously an overhead. However, these qubits can be initialized by the reverse operation of the CNOT gates used previously in the middle parts.

The initialization of the qubits is performed after the operation of the Toffoli gates that generate the products. If all products are generated at once in the lowest layer, we initialize (cleaning) the qubits from the lower layer to the upper layer by performing the reverse of the operations that prepared the middle parts. As a result, the qubits allocated for the middle parts are initialized to zero (i.e. clean state).

This initialization, which cleans the qubits, can be used if the multiplication is merged with other operations (i.e. not stand-alone multiplication). This means that in subsequent multiplications, the previously initialized qubits can be reused without allocating new qubits for middle parts. Besides multiplication, these initialized qubits can be reused for other operations that require new clean qubits. Since the multiplication is primitive in cryptography, the qubit initialization is effective. Also, we found that this reverse operation for initialization does not increase the circuit depth, as it can be done while the multiplication is being performed (when combining products or modular reduction). With this technique, we can effectively offset the overhead of qubits in our quantum multiplication. When qubits are reused in subsequent multiplications, $17, 43$, and 113 qubits are required for $n = 4, 8$, and 16, respectively (reduced from $27, 81$, and 243 qubits).

3.4 Optimized Implementation of Quantum Multiplication of T-Depth One

For T-depth optimization, we apply the quantum AND gate of T-depth one introduced in [21] instead of the Toffoli gate. The AND gate illustrated in Fig. 3(a) uses one ancilla qubit and has a T-depth of one. In the AND gate, an ancilla qubit is initialized to zero. It can be reused in the next AND gate. However, without reuse, we allocate a new ancilla qubit for each AND gate to operate all AND gates, simultaneously.

Since all Toffoli gates operate in parallel (i.e. Toffoli depth is one) in the proposed quantum multiplication, we allocate the same number of ancilla qubits as the number of Toffoli gates required. As a result, all AND gates are successfully operated in parallel, and a quantum multiplication of T-depth one is implemented. AND gates require additional qubits, but these qubits are initialized at the end. They can be reused in subsequent multiplications or other operations that require clean qubits (Similar to Sect. 3.3). Table 3 shows the quantum resources required for quantum multiplication of T-depth one when the AND gate is adopted.

3.5 Quantum Modular Reduction

In quantum multiplication, the modular reduction can be customized according to the irreducible polynomial of the field. In this Section, we customize modular reduction for $\mathbb{F}_{2^8}/(x^8 + x^4 + x^3 + x + 1)$ (used in AES) and analyze the required quantum resources.

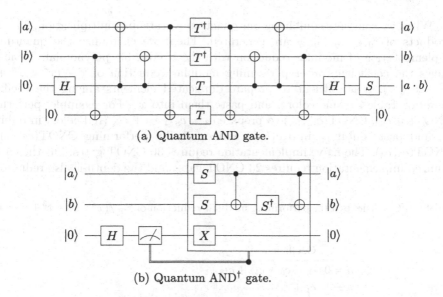

(a) Quantum AND gate.

(b) Quantum AND† gate.

Fig. 3. Quantum AND gate of T-depth one.

Table 3. Quantum resources required for multiplication of T-depth one using AND gate.

Field size 2^n	Karatsuba Level	#CNOT	#1qCliff	#T	T-depth	#Qubits	Full depth
$n = 4$	2	106	27	36	1	36	16
$n = 8$	3	354	81	108	1	108	22
$n = 16$	4	1138	243	324	1	324	27

In [10], after generating products, the authors omit the combining step and compute according to linear combinations of products after modular reduction. That is, combining and modular reduction are considered as one step without separate, and the coefficients are computed. For $\mathbb{F}_{2^8}/(x^8 + x^4 + x^3 + x + 1)$ with this approach, if we consider combining and modular reduction as one step and compute linear combinations of products, then 70 CNOT gates are used and the full depth is 27 for this. However, unlike in [10], if the coefficients are computed by separating the combining step and modular reduction, 85 CNOT gates are used and the full depth is 17.

In our implementation, we separate the combining step and modular reduction (which is kind of general) because it is more valuable to reduce the depth instead of using more CNOT gates. Firstly, we perform optimal CNOT operations on linear combinations of combining (62 CNOT gates) and then complete quantum multiplication by performing optimal CNOT operations on linear combinations of modular reduction (23 CNOT gates).

When we complete combining our quantum Karatsuba multiplication, $2n-1$ products of $c_0, c_1, ..., c_{2n-2}$ are generated. Then, we customize the quantum implementation of modular reduction with the irreducible polynomial. Table 4 shows the coefficients after performing modular reduction of $\mathbb{F}_{2^8}/(x^8 + x^4 + x^3 + x + 1)$. It is efficient to prepare duplicated elements among the coefficients in Table 4 (same colors) and paste them into x^n. For example, perform $\text{CNOT}(c_9, c_8)$, $\text{CNOT}(c_{14}, c_8)$ to prepare $c_8 = c_8 + c_9 + c_{14}$ (red color) in qubit c_8, and paste qubit c_8 into $c_1(x^1)$ and $c_4(x^4)$ by performing $\text{CNOT}(c_8, c_1)$, $\text{CNOT}(c_8, c_4)$. The naïve implementation requires 30 CNOT gates, but the customized implementation requires 23 CNOT gates and the depth is also reduced.

Table 4. Coefficients after performing modular reduction of $\mathbb{F}_{2^8}/(x^8 + x^4 + x^3 + x + 1)$.

x^n	Coefficient
$n = 0$	$c_0 + c_8 + c_{12} + c_{13}$
$n = 1$	$c_1 + c_8 + c_9 + c_{12} + c_{14}$
$n = 2$	$c_2 + c_9 + c_{10} + c_{13}$
$n = 3$	$c_3 + c_8 + c_{10} + c_{11} + c_{12} + c_{12} + c_{13} + c_{14}$
$n = 4$	$c_4 + c_8 + c_9 + c_{11} + c_{14}$
$n = 5$	$c_5 + c_9 + c_{10} + c_{12}$
$n = 6$	$c_6 + c_{10} + c_{11} + c_{13}$
$n = 7$	$c_7 + c_{11} + c_{12} + c_{14}$

Quantum resources required for multiplication of $\mathbb{F}_{2^8}/(x^8 + x^4 + x^3 + x + 1)$ including modular reduction are shown in Table 5 (Tables 1, 2, and 3 only include up-to the combining step).

Table 5. Quantum resources required for multiplication of $\mathbb{F}_{2^8}/(x^8 + x^4 + x^3 + x + 1)$.

Field size 2^n	Karatsuba Level	#CNOT	#1qCliff	#T	T-depth	#Qubits	Full depth
$n = 8^\star$	3	323	54	189	4	81	32
$n = 8^\diamond$	3	377	81	108	1	108	31

$\star$: Using the Toffoli gate decomposition in [20].
$\diamond$: Using AND gate.

4   Performance

In this Section, we review previous works on quantum multiplication and discuss the effectiveness of proposed work.

In [9], Banegas et al. introduced quantum binary field multiplication to solve discrete logarithm problems for binary elliptic curves. Authors implemented schoolbook multiplication. n^2 Toffoli gates are used for the multiplication of $\mathbb{F}_{2^n}$. They prioritize the upper products $c^n, c^{n+1}, \ldots, c^{2n-2}$ (where modular reduction occurs) for $h = f \cdot g$ to optimize the number of qubits. Then, the result of modular reduction of the upper products is stored in n-qubit h. Through this, quantum multiplication is implemented using $3n$ qubits for f, g, and h. Their works use a small number of qubits. Since it is based on a general schoolbook multiplication, many Toffoli gates are used and the Toffoli depth is also high. The quantum resources required for the multiplication of $\mathbb{F}_{2^8}/(x^8 + x^4 + x^3 + x + 1)$ using their schoolbook multiplication are shown in Table 6 (Source [9]).

In [10], Kepley et al. presented quantum multiplication using the Karatsuba algorithm, which classically reduces the complexity of multiplication. Since the Karatsuba algorithm using the divide-and-conquer approach reduces the number of multiplication operations, quantum multiplication with a reduced number of Toffoli gates is presented in [10]. The quantum resources required for the multiplication of $\mathbb{F}_{2^8}/(x^8 + x^4 + x^3 + x + 1)$ using their Karatsuba multiplication are shown in Table 6 (Source [10]).

In [8], Van Hoof presented another quantum multiplication using the Karatsuba algorithm. The work in [8] reduced the number of qubits used in [10]. In [10], additional qubits are used to store the Karatsuba products, but the author of [8] uses the LUP decomposition. $3n$ qubits equal to schoolbook multiplication are used. In [8], the number of gates and qubits used in their implementation is reported, but not the full depth. The full depth estimated by decomposing Toffoli gates is not reported. Only the depth estimated at the NCT (NOT, CNOT, and Toffoli) level is reported. Multiplication in [8] uses fewer qubits than that of [10], but we assume the full depth is higher in [8]. This is because the operation of gates in a reduced space (reduced number of qubits) becomes a bottleneck for parallelism and increases the depth. The depth estimated in [8] for $\mathbb{F}_{2^8}/(x^8 + x^4 + x^3 + x + 1)$ is 139 (NCT level), and it increases when the full depth is estimated.

Table 6 compares the quantum resources required for the multiplication of $\mathbb{F}_{2^8}/(x^8 + x^4 + x^3 + x + 1)$. Although no specific full depth is reported in [8], it is confirmed that the NCT depth of [8] is higher than the full depth of [10].

Table 6. Comparison of quantum resources required for multiplication of $\mathbb{F}_{2^8}/(x^8 + x^4 + x^3 + x + 1)$.

Field size 2^n	Source	#CNOT	#1qClff	#1	Toffoli depth	#Qubits	Full depth	$TD \cdot M$
$n = 8$	This work (Sect. 3.5)	323	54	189	1	81	32	81
	[9]	405	30	448	28	24	216	672
	[10]	270	54	189	8	43	88	344
	[8]	382	54	189	N/A	24	N/A	N/A

TD = Toffoli depth, M = number of qubits.

Our quantum multiplication is optimized with Toffoli depth one for any field size. In quantum multiplication, Toffoli depth has a huge impact on counting full depth. Thus, under the influence of the optimized Toffoli depth, our work achieves the lowest full depth.

Quantum computers in the upcoming NISQ era are no longer small, but they still need quantum error correction. In error correction, the metric of Toffoli depth is probably the most important. However, since the number of qubits is still important, it is important to consider the trade-off between qubits and depth. Our quantum multiplication requires relatively more qubits, but achieves the best trade-off of $TD \cdot M$ (TD is Toffoli depth, M is the number of qubits). This metric ($TD \cdot M$) represents the trade-off for quantum circuits and is adopted in [13].

As mentioned in Sect. 3.3, if it is not stand-alone multiplication, the overhead of using more qubits can be offset. One representative example is an inversion based on the Itoh-Tsujii algorithm [22] that requires multiple multiplications (squaring operations are also required, but they are implemented simply with fewer quantum resources compared to multiplication). In this case, multiplications after the first multiplication are implemented more efficiently because previously allocated qubits can be reused.

5   Conclusion

In response to the upcoming post-quantum era, optimizing quantum cryptanalysis is of great interest to the cryptographic community.

In this paper, we present an optimized quantum binary field multiplication, which is essential for quantum cryptanalysis of ECC. Our main contribution is quantum multiplication that is optimized with Toffoli depth one for any field size. Further, we describe the reverse operation to offset the overhead of qubits, optimization with T-depth one, and an efficient implementation of modular reduction. This is the first implementation of quantum multiplication to optimize Toffoli depth and full depth. We show the impact of our work by comparing it to other implementations in various metrics.

Future work is to find another optimization for quantum cryptanalysis building blocks of ECC. We note the direction of optimization that should be pursued in quantum implementations. We will also explore an optimized quantum cryptanalysis of ECC consisting of efficient quantum arithmetic operations.

References

1. Shor, P.W.: Polynomial-time algorithms for prime factorization and discrete logarithms on a quantum computer. SIAM Rev. **41**(2), 303–332 (1999)
2. Desnitsky, V., Levshun, D., Chechulin, A., Kotenko, I.V.: Design technique for secure embedded devices: application for creation of integrated cyber-physical security system. J. Wirel. Mob. Netw. Ubiquitous Comput. Dependable Appl. **7**(2), 60–80 (2016)

3. Yan, Z., Geng, G., Nakazato, H., Park, Y.-J.: Secure and scalable deployment of resource public key infrastructure (RPKI). J. Internet Serv. Inf. Secur. **8**(1), 31–45 (2018)
4. Häner, T., Roetteler, M., Svore, K.M.: Factoring using $2n + 2$ qubits with Toffoli based modular multiplication. arXiv preprint. arXiv:1611.07995 (2016)
5. Gidney, C.: Factoring with $n+2$ clean qubits and $n-1$ dirty qubits. arXiv preprint. arXiv:1706.07884 (2017)
6. Roetteler, M., Naehrig, M., Svore, K.M., Lauter, K.: Quantum resource estimates for computing elliptic curve discrete logarithms. In: Takagi, T., Peyrin, T. (eds.) ASIACRYPT 2017. LNCS, vol. 10625, pp. 241–270. Springer, Cham (2017). https://doi.org/10.1007/978-3-319-70697-9_9
7. Häner, T., Jaques, S., Naehrig, M., Roetteler, M., Soeken, M.: Improved quantum circuits for elliptic curve discrete logarithms. In: Ding, J., Tillich, J.-P. (eds.) PQCrypto 2020. LNCS, vol. 12100, pp. 425–444. Springer, Cham (2020). https://doi.org/10.1007/978-3-030-44223-1_23
8. Van Hoof, I.: Space-efficient quantum multiplication of polynomials for binary finite fields with sub-quadratic Toffoli gate count. arXiv preprint. arXiv:1910.02849 (2019)
9. Cheung, D., Maslov, D., Mathew, J., Pradhan, D.K.: On the design and optimization of a quantum polynomial-time attack on elliptic curve cryptography. In: Kawano, Y., Mosca, M. (eds.) TQC 2008. LNCS, vol. 5106, pp. 96–104. Springer, Heidelberg (2008). https://doi.org/10.1007/978-3-540-89304-2_9
10. Kepley, S., Steinwandt, R.: Quantum circuits for $\mathbb{F}_{2^n}$-multiplication with sub-quadratic gate count. Quantum Inf. Process. **14**(7), 2373–2386 (2015). https://doi.org/10.1007/s11128-015-0993-1
11. Jang, K., Choi, S.J., Kwon, H., Hu, Z., Seo, H.: Impact of optimized operations $A \cdot B$, $A \cdot C$ for binary field inversion on quantum computers. In: You, I. (ed.) WISA 2020. LNCS, vol. 12583, pp. 154–166. Springer, Cham (2020). https://doi.org/10.1007/978-3-030-65299-9_12
12. Jang, K., et al.: Binary field montgomery multiplication on quantum computers. Cryptology ePrint Archive (2021)
13. Zou, J., Wei, Z., Sun, S., Liu, X., Wu, W.: Quantum circuit implementations of AES with fewer qubits. In: Moriai, S., Wang, H. (eds.) ASIACRYPT 2020. LNCS, vol. 12492, pp. 697–726. Springer, Cham (2020). https://doi.org/10.1007/978-3-030-64834-3_24
14. Bhattacharjee, D., Chattopadhyay, A.: Depth-optimal quantum circuit placement for arbitrary topologies. arXiv preprint. arXiv:1703.08540 (2017)
15. NIST. Submission requirements and evaluation criteria for the post-quantum cryptography standardization process (2016). https://csrc.nist.gov/CSRC/media/Projects/Post-Quantum-Cryptography/documents/call-for-proposals-final-dec-2016.pdf
16. Steiger, D.S., Häner, T., Troyer, M.: ProjectQ: an open source software framework for quantum computing. Quantum **2**, 49 (2018)
17. Cross, A.: The IBM Q experience and Qiskit open-source quantum computing software. In: APS March Meeting Abstracts, vol. 2018, pp. L58–003 (2018)
18. Svore, K., et al.: Q# enabling scalable quantum computing and development with a high-level dsl. In: Proceedings of the Real World Domain Specific Languages Workshop, vol. 2018, pp. 1–10 (2018)
19. Karatsuba, A.: Multiplication of multidigit numbers on automata. Sov. Phys. Doklady **7**, 595–596 (1963)

20. Amy, M., Maslov, D., Mosca, M., Roetteler, M., Roetteler, M.: A meet-in-the-middle algorithm for fast synthesis of depth-optimal quantum circuits. IEEE Trans. Comput. Aided Des. Integr. Circuits Syst. **32**, 818–830 (2013)
21. Jaques, S., Naehrig, M., Roetteler, M., Virdia, F.: Implementing grover oracles for quantum key search on AES and LowMC. In: Canteaut, A., Ishai, Y. (eds.) EURO-CRYPT 2020. LNCS, vol. 12106, pp. 280–310. Springer, Cham (2020). https://doi.org/10.1007/978-3-030-45724-2_10
22. Itoh, T., Tsujii, S.: A fast algorithm for computing multiplicative inverses in $GF(2^m)$ using normal basis. Inf. Comput. **78**, 171–177 (1988)

Time-Optimal Design of Finite Field Arithmetic for SIKE on Cortex-M4

Mila Anastasova[1(✉)], Reza Azarderakhsh[1(✉)], and Mehran Mozaffari Kermani[2]

[1] Computer and Electrical Engineering and Computer Science Department and I-SENSE at Florida Atlantic University, Boca Raton, FL, USA
{manastasova2017,razarderakhsh}@fau.edu
[2] Computer Engineering and Science Department at University of South Florida, Tampa, FL, USA
mehran2@usf.edu

Abstract. The advances in quantum technologies and the fast move toward quantum computing are threatening classical cryptography and urge the deployment of post-quantum (PQ) schemes. The only isogeny-based candidate forming part of the third round of the standardization, the Supersingular Isogeny Key Encapsulation (SIKE) mechanism, is a subject of constant latency optimizations given its attractive compact key size lengths and, thus, its limited bandwidth and memory requirements. In this work, we present a new speed record of the SIKE protocol by implementing novel low-level finite field arithmetics targeting ARMv7-M architecture. We develop a handcrafted assembly code for the modular multiplication and squaring functions where we obtain 8.71% and 5.38% of speedup, respectively, compared to the last best-reported assembly implementations for p434. After deploying the finite field optimized architecture to the SIKE protocol, we observe 5.63%, 3.93%, 3.48%, and 1.61% of latency reduction for SIKE p434, p503, p610, and p751, respectively, targeting the NIST recommended STM32F407VG discovery board for our experiments.

Keywords: Supersingular Isogeny Key Encapsulation (SIKE) · Post-Quantum cryptography (PQC) · ARM Cortex-M4

1 Introduction

Public key cryptography is essential for the security and integrity of data conveyed across an unsecured channel. The classical cryptographic protocols, however, such as RSA and ECC, relying on the difficulty of factoring large prime numbers and the Elliptic Curve Discrete Logarithm Problem (ECDLP), are vulnerable to quantum attacks. Thus, a transition to post-quantum robust protocols is required to offer secure data transmission in the era of large-scale quantum computers. Forming part of the alternate group of PQ candidates, the Supersingular Isogeny Key Encapsulation (SIKE) [1] mechanism is the candidate with the smallest public key and ciphertext sizes, thus it is suitable for deploying it in scenarios with limited bandwidth and memory resources.

© Springer Nature Switzerland AG 2023
I. You and T.-Y. Youn (Eds.): WISA 2022, LNCS 13720, pp. 265–276, 2023.
https://doi.org/10.1007/978-3-031-25659-2_19

In this work, we focus on the NIST-recommended platform for performance evaluation on embedded devices - the ARMv7-M Cortex-M4-based STM32F407VG microcontroller.

Contribution. In this paper, the time-optimal architecture for finite field arithmetic operations, base of SIKE, is proposed for the resource-constrained ARM Cortex-M4 processor. The breakdown of our contributions is as follows:

- We present the first multi-precision multiplication, squaring, and reduction architecture based on a hybrid method that integrates both product- and operand-scanning approaches in the inner multiplication loop design.
- We observe 8.71%, 5.99%, 4.46%, and 2.04% of latency reduction for the execution of modular multiplication based on prime lengths of 434, 503, 610, and 751 bits, respectively. We achieve 5.38%, 6.43%, 14.64%, and 6.42% of speedup compared to the counterparts in [2] for the modular squaring routine.
- We integrate the suggested multi-precision multiplication, squaring and reduction routines in the SIKE implementation and we obtain more than 5.6% of speedup for SIKEp434. We report 3.93%, 3.48%, and 1.61% of latency reduction for SIKEp503, SIKEp610, and SIKEp751, respectively.

2   Related Work

SIKE is the PQ primitive requiring the smallest communication latency, allowing for rapid data transmission even when bandwidth is constrained.

The pyramidal structure of the isogeny-based protocol permits optimization of its many levels. High-level isogeny optimizations of the SIKE protocol proposing an optimal solution for the calculation of the heavy isogeny maps are presented in [3–6]. The execution latency, however, of SIKE, remains relatively high and a target-specific implementation of the low-level computations is required. The authors in [7] base their work on the x86 AVX-512 extended Advanced Vector Extensions SIMD instruction set. Another line of research demonstrates ongoing efforts to optimize SIKE on ARMv8 architecture deploying the NEON advanced Single Instruction Multiple Data (SIMD) architecture extension for the A-profile and R-profile processors technology [8–12].

In addition to the several high-end target-specific implementations, the focus has remained on low-end devices due to the difficulty of fitting such a computationally intensive protocol into devices with limited resources. The authors in [2,13,14] provide implementation solutions for the low-level finite field arithmetic of SIKE and compressed SIKE and achieve a record speedup on the target platform, running the SIKE protocol in 139MCCs for security Level I. The nature of the SIKE protocol, based on supersingular elliptic curves defined over a quadratic extension of a finite field, benefits from the previous work on low-level arithmetic for classical protocols such as RSA and ECC. Thus, implementation strategies proposed for ECC optimizations [15–20] are applicable to the isogeny-based PQ protocol if not targeting a specific finite field size. Nonetheless, despite the low computational cost and extremely small key sizes, this classical crypto scheme

Key Generation	Encapsulation	Decapsulation
Input: -	*Input:* pk_A	*Input:* s, sk_B, pk_B, c
Output: s, sk_A, pk_A	*Output:* c, ss	*Output:* ss
1. $sk_A \in_R \mathbb{Z}/2^{e_A}\mathbb{Z}$	1. $m \in_R \{0,1\}^t$	1. $\phi_A' : E_B \to E_{BA}$ with
2. $\phi_A : E_0 \to E_A$ with	2. $r = H(m\|pk_A)mod3^{e_B}$	$ker(\phi_A') =$
$ker(\phi_A) = \langle P_A + [sk_A]Q_A \rangle$	3. $\phi_B : E_0 \to E_B$ with	$\langle \phi_B(P_A) + [sk_A]\phi_B(Q_A) \rangle$
3. $pk_A =$	$ker(\phi_B) = \langle P_B + [r]Q_B \rangle$	2. $m' = c_1 \oplus K(j(E_{BA}))$
$(E_A, \phi_A(P_B), \phi_A(Q_B))$	4. $pk_B =$	3. $r' = H(m'\|pk_A)mod3^{e_B}$
4. $s \in_R \{0,1\}^t$	$\{E_B, \phi_B(P_A), \phi_B(Q_A)\}$	4. $\phi_A'' : E_0 \to E_{B'}$ with
	5. $\phi_B' : E_A \to E_{AB}$ with	$ker(\phi_A'') = \langle P_B + [r']Q_B \rangle$
	$ker(\phi_B') =$	5.
	$\langle \phi_A(P_B) + [r]\phi_A(Q_B) \rangle$	$pk_B' = \{E_{B'}, \phi_A''(P_A), \phi_A''(Q_A)\}$
	6. $c = (pk_B\|K(j(E_{AB})) \oplus m$	6. IF $pk_B' = pk_B$
	7. $ss = (J(m\|c))$	$ss = (J(m'\|c))$
		ELSE $ss = (J(s\|c))$

Fig. 1. SIKE algorithm [1]. H, K and J denote hash functions. $p = 2^{e_A}3^{e_B} - 1$, $E_0/\mathbb{F}_{p^2}$, $\{P_A, Q_A\}$ and $\{P_B, Q_B\}$ are public parameters.

will not ensure secure data transmission in the case of large quantum computers, necessitating the NIST post-quantum standardization effort and a substantial effort on implementing hybrid systems providing both classical and quantum security [21–24].

3   Preliminaries

In the next part, we provide an overview of the SIKE protocol and the Cortex-M4 platform. We refer the readers to [1] and [25] for further details.

3.1   SIKE

The Supersingular Isogeny Key Encapsulation process provides post-quantum resilience since it relies on difficult mathematical issues that are thought to be resistant to large-scale quantum computers. The SIKE protocol, which is based on pseudorandom walks on isomorphic graphs, assures that both communication parties reach a shared secret based on a curve j-invariant.

An elliptic curve is defined as $E_{a,b}/\mathbb{F}_{p^2} : ay^2 = x^3 + bx^2 + x$. SIKE elliptic curve elements are defined by two coordinated x, y defined over the quadratic extension of a finite field such that $x, y = ai + b$ with $a, b \in \mathbb{F}_p$. The value of the prime p has the shape of $p = 2^{e_A}3^{e_B} \pm 1$ where the values of e_A and e_B vary depending on the security level of the deployed protocol.

Two elliptic curves E and E' are said to be isogenous if they are of the same order, thus $\#(E) = \#(E')$. An isogeny map φ is defined as $\varphi : E_0 \to E_0/\langle G \rangle$ with G the kernel of the isogeny. The isomorphism is a mapping function, which ensures that the original and projection curve feature the same j-invariant. After executing SIKE, both communication parties reach the same isomorphic class, thus, deducing the same value for a j-invariant Fig. 1.

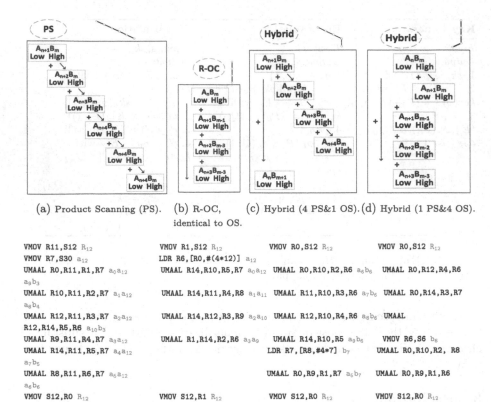

(a) Product Scanning (PS).   (b) R-OC,   (c) Hybrid (4 PS&1 OS). (d) Hybrid (1 PS&4 OS).
identical to OS.

VMOV R11,S12 R_{12} VMOV R1,S12 R_{12} VMOV R0,S12 R_{12} VMOV R0,S12 R_{12}
VMOV R7,S30 a_{12} LDR R6,[R0,#(4*12)] a_{12}
UMAAL R0,R11,R1,R7 a_0a_{12} UMAAL R14,R10,R5,R7 a_0a_{12} UMAAL R0,R10,R2,R6 a_6b_6 UMAAL R0,R12,R4,R6
a_9b_3
UMAAL R10,R11,R2,R7 a_1a_{12} UMAAL R14,R11,R4,R8 a_1a_{11} UMAAL R11,R10,R3,R6 a_7b_6 UMAAL R0,R14,R3,R7
a_8b_4
UMAAL R12,R11,R3,R7 a_2a_{12} UMAAL R14,R12,R3,R9 a_2a_{10} UMAAL R12,R10,R4,R6 a_8b_6 UMAAL
R12,R14,R5,R6 $a_{10}b_3$
UMAAL R9,R11,R4,R7 a_3a_{12} UMAAL R1,R14,R2,R6 a_3a_9 UMAAL R14,R10,R5 a_9b_6 VMOV R6,S6 b_6
UMAAL R14,R11,R5,R7 a_4a_{12} LDR R7,[R8,#4*7] b_7 UMAAL R0,R10,R2, R8
a_7b_5
UMAAL R8,R11,R6,R7 a_5a_{12} UMAAL R0,R9,R1,R7 a_6b_7 UMAAL R0,R9,R1,R6
a_6b_6
VMOV S12,R0 R_{12} VMOV S12,R1 R_{12} VMOV S12,R0 R_{12} VMOV S12,R0 R_{12}

Fig. 2. Deployed list of inner multi-precision loop execution flows along with the associated assembly instruction set.

3.2   ARMv7-M Architecture

The fast expansion of the Internet of Things necessitates low-cost devices that can be integrated into real-time embedded systems. For resource-constrained devices, NIST has designated the STM32F407VG as the target microcontroller. The PQM4 library [26] was created as a consequence of the standardization effort low-end recommended target. The STM32F407VG microcontroller features 1 MB of flash memory and 192 KB of RAM.

The ARMv7-M Cortex-M4 platform has 16 32-bit GPRs and 32 32-bit Floating-Point Registers (FPRs). Two GPRs are designated for the Stack Pointer and the Program Counter. The whole of FPR is available to the user, and data transmission between GPRs and FPRs is instantaneous via VMOV instruction, unlike data accessing instructions like LDR and STR which might cause stall cycles if not correctly planned.

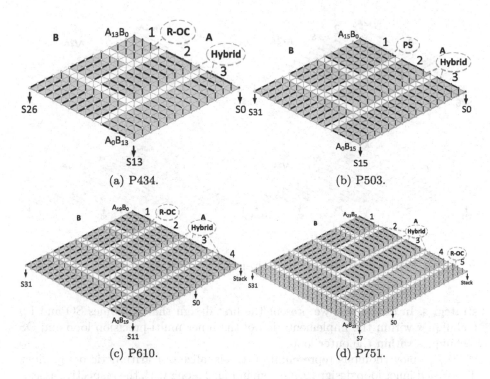

Fig. 3. Proposed architecture for multi-precision multiplication for all SIKE primes.

The powerful Multiply ACcumulate (MAC) instructions allow the execution of up to three operations in a single clock cycle; hence, we integrate the use of UMULL and UMAAL in our work.

4   Proposed Design for SIKE Field Arithmetic

In this section, we present the proposed multi-precision multiplication, squaring, and reduction techniques, and analyze their performance compared to the counterparts.

4.1   Notation

In this paper, a novel implementation technique for multi-precision multiplication, square, and reduction is proposed and deployed into the SIKE PQ protocol. To our knowledge, our multi-precision architecture is the first to integrate hybrid Operand Scanning (OS) and Product Scanning (PS) techniques in the inner multiplication loop. The authors of [13] present a hybrid multi-precision arithmetic approach in which the outer and inner multi-precision loops, respectively, implement non-hybrid OS and PS techniques. The work presented by [2] presents improved design based on the same independent PS inner and OS outer loop

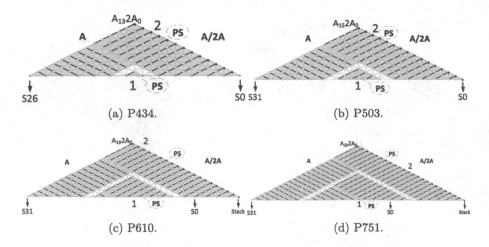

Fig. 4. Proposed architecture for multi-precision squaring for all SIKE primes.

strategies. In this paper, we present the first design that combines SO and PS techniques within the implementation of the inner multi-precision loop and OS techniques within the outer loop.

We employ rhombus representation to visualize our arithmetic design flow. The varied inner loop designs are shown in Fig. 2 along with the respective assembly code design. While the PS and Refined-Operand Caching (R-OC) strategies are not novel, we combine them to create a more optimum and time-efficient hybrid inner loop execution phase.

The PS Fig. 2a requires larger number of memory accesses for accessing the previously calculated partial results, however, allow computing a larger set of partial values per iteration. It facilitates the register set usage by loading a single word from one operand and a large set of words from the second operand; hence, it allows increasing the size of the inner loop iteration. The R-OC Fig. 2b uses an Operand Scanning technique in the inner multiplication loop, which allows reusing the values of the operands when modifying the increasing and decreasing indices of operand words (i.e., when changing the direction of the flow).

In this work, we benefit from both techniques and propose a hybrid design Fig. 2c and Fig. 2d where we increase the size of the loop iteration and still keep the partial results values in the register set without the need of moving them into the memory. In Fig. 2c, four partial results are generated based on PS and one based on OS. In Fig. 2d, four R-OC and one PS steps are used. The former hybrid design uses requires a single register for storing the second operand, minimizing the register use. The latter hybrid design reserved three registers for the second operand, which benefits the R-OC principal at the mid-point of each row.

Table 1. Instruction count and clock cycles for memory access and register move operations.

Memory accesses												
Design	SIKEp434			SIKEp503			SIKEp610			SIKEp751		
	Memory	VMOV	CC	Memory	VMOV	CC	Memory	VMOV	CC	Memory	VMOV	CC
Seo et al. [27]	170	–	340	220	–	440	335	–	670	474	–	948
Anastasova et al. [2]	70	100	240	100	140	310	139	190	468	230	240	700
This work	58	88	**204**	68+2×(16+1)	112	**214**	118	168	**404**	148	212	**508**

4.2 Multi-precision Multiplication

Optimizing multi-precision multiplication is critical for cryptographic protocols, especially when costly calculations like isogeny maps among supersingular elliptic curves are required.

We propose efficient multi-precision multiplication for all four SIKE security levels, based on prime lengths of 434, 503, 610, and 751 bits. We used a novel hybrid method in the inner multiplication loop to improve row size and hence reduce memory accesses for partial values. Depending on the prime number, we apply a combination of the three inner iteration designs. The purpose of this effort is to increase row size, hence the number of operand words and the maximum applicable row size determines which iteration strategy is applied.

In Fig. 3 we show the four prime multiplication processes in a rhombus, with the row sizes highlighted in grey. For the execution of SIKEp434 multiplication routine Fig. 3a we combine the new hybrid iteration design and R-OC. By deploying the hybrid iteration we increase the row sizes and thus decrease the number of rows by one compared to the counterparts [2]. SIKEp503 multiplication design featured optimized row sizes already, proposed in [2], however, basing our work on the hybrid iteration step Fig. 3b, we avoid multiple word reloads, thus, obtaining better results. We also implement the PS strategy for the first row of the implementation, which additionally allows saving operand memory accesses. SIKEp610 is the only prime with a number of words divisible by the size of the hybrid row design, thus, it features hybrid rows only Fig. 3c. Similarly, SIKEp751 Fig. 3d, uses a hybrid design for all rows except the last one. This paper provides optimum multi-precision multiplication techniques for all four SIKE prime numbers, based on the new hybrid inner iteration pattern. Table 1 presents the reduced number of instructions and clock cycles for all primes multi-precision multiplication routines compared to our counterparts.

4.3 Multi-precision Squaring

The multi-precision squaring procedure was earlier improved in [2] by proposing new row architecture. Using their approach, we reduce the number of rows while increasing their size using a PS-only inner loop iteration pattern.

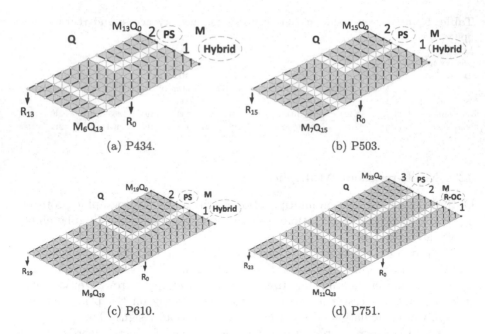

Fig. 5. Proposed architecture for multi-precision reduction for all SIKE primes.

The use of PS allows reserving one and six registers for the operands and reaching the maximum row size on the target platform. Although we do not benefit from the R-OC operand caching when the increasing index is changed (i.e., in the mid-point of each row), this adds simply five additional operand accesses per row, which when kept in the FP set, is insignificant. However, it reduces the partial results kept in the stack.

Figure 4 shows all SIKE primes multi-precision squaring procedures. Our design uses the double operand technique, where we double the operand when the indexes are different (e.g., $A_i \cdot A_j$ with $i \neq j$) and use the original value when the indexes are the same (e.g., $A_i \cdot A_j$ with $i = j$).

The design for SIKEp434, SIKEp503, SIKEp610, and SIKEp751 are shown in Fig. 5a, Fig. 5b, Fig. 5c, and Fig. 5d, respectively. The use of PS iteration minimizes memory access for all primes since it reduces the size of the first row and hence the number of partial values stored in memory for subsequent accumulation. Additionally, the new squaring design reduces the number of rows for p610 and p751 by one in comparison to the results in [2]. By using the PS approach for squaring, we reduce partial results and consequently memory accesses.

Table 2. SIKE finite field arithmetic latency targeting STM32F407VG

Implementation	Latency [CC]							
	$\mathbb{F}_p$mul	$\mathbb{F}_p$sqr	$\mathbb{F}_p$mul	$\mathbb{F}_p$sqr	$\mathbb{F}_p$mul	$\mathbb{F}_p$sqr	$\mathbb{F}_p$mul	$\mathbb{F}_p$sqr
	SIKEp434		SIKEp503		SIKEp610		SIKEp751	
SIDH v3.3 [28]	17,964	17,964	23,364	23,364	35,047	35,047	49,722	49,722
Seo et al. [27]	1,110	981	1,333	1,139	–	–	2,744	2,242
Seo et al. [27]	1,011	889	1,221	1,024	1,869	1,535	2,577	2,066
Anastasova et al. [2]	769	594	952	734	1,506	1,171	2,103	1,543
This work	**702**	**563**	**895**	**684**	**1,435**	**997**	**2,062**	**1,444**

4.4 Multi-precision Reduction

A new row pattern (i.e., outer loop execution flow) has been proposed in [2], ensuring a minimal number of rows. In this study, we use our hybrid inner loop architecture to maximize row sizes and therefore delay.

In Fig. 5 we present the optimized multi-precision reduction routine. We have deployed the hybrid inner loop pattern to the SIKEp434 Fig. 5a, SIKEp503 Fig. 5b, and SIKEp610 Fig. 5c architecture. Their designs include one hybrid and one PS row, with the latter allowing for p610 row expansion to six. Thus, we reduce the number of rows by one compared to the counterparts. Due to the 2-piece row shape, the hybrid inner loop does not require extra cycles for reloading the operand, so the R-OC and PS have the same cost. As for the implementation of p751 Fig. 5d, we employ two R-OC rows and one PS, the former ensuring lowest cost row 1, owing to reuse cached operand values, and the latter to ensure row size of five with an extra free register saved for address destination. Based on the modulus length, multiple inner loop iteration patterns were used to enhance the multi-precision reduction.

4.5 Performance Evaluation

The latency of the finite field arithmetic operations developed in this work is reported in CCs in Table 2. Since our approach is constant-time, we are protected from side-channel attacks such as Simple and Differential Power Analysis (SPA & DPA). Our results are based on the STM32F407 Discovery Board @24MHz for exact latency.

We report 702, 895, 1435, and 2062 CC for the execution of modular multiplication for p434, p503, p610, and p751, respectively. We achieve optimized latency by 8.7%, 0.0%, 4.5%, and 2.0% for the aforementioned prime sizes, compared to the best-known findings in [2] where the improvement is based on the previous effort of assembly implementation of low-level arithmetic. We obtain modular squaring latency of between 5% and 14% better timing for all the primes, with particularly outstanding results for p610 due to the reduced row count.

Table 3. Report of SIKE timing results in terms of clock cycles and speedup percentage on STM32F407 running @24MHz

Implementation	Timing [cc×10^6]							
	KeyGen	Encaps	Decaps	Total	KeyGen	Encaps	Decaps	Total
	SIKEp434				SIKEp503			
SIDH v3.3 [28]	650	1,065	1,136	2,202	985	1,623	1,726	3,350
Seo et al. [27]	74	122	130	252	104	172	183	355
Seo et al. [27]	54	87	94	181	74	121	129	250
Anastasova et al. [2]	41	67	72	139	58	96	102	197
This work	**39.0**	**63.6**	**68.0**	131.6	**55.9**	**91.8**	**97.7**	189.5
	SIKEp610				SIKEp751			
SIDH v3.3 [28]	1,819	3,348	3,368	6,716	3,296	5,347	5,742	11,089
Seo et al. [27]	-	-	-	-	282	455	491	946
Seo et al. [27]	131	241	243	484	225	365	392	757
Anastasova et al. [2]	106	195	196	391	182	295	317	613
This work	**102.5**	**188.1**	**189.3**	377.4	**179.4**	**290.5**	**312.1**	602.7

5 SIKE Performance Speedup

We present broad findings for every Cortex-M4-based platform, which may vary depending on the target microcontroller's specifications.

We report the results in MCCs in Table 3. We note that we achieve Key Generation, Encapsulation, and Decapsulation in 39.0, 63.6, and 68.0 MCCs for SIKEp434, respectively. The total execution timing of SIKEp434 becomes 131.6 MCC which is around 5% better than the previous best-reported results. We report 189.5, 377.4, and 602.7 MCC for SIKE security Levels II, III, and V, achieving a speedup of up to 3.9%.

In Table 3, we describe the timing of the quantum-safe isogeny-based primitive. We highlight our final results in green color. This result is reached after two complete NIST standardized optimization rounds and three handmade assembly code SIKE protocol optimizations on Cortex-M4. Thus, our results show a considerable reduction in protocol execution speed and a unique multi-precision strategy that may be applied to other cryptographic protocols.

6 Conclusions

In this work, we presented the first hybrid architecture for the inner loop of the long-integer multi-precision multiplication, squaring, and reduction routines. We provide a handcrafted assembly implementation of the finite field routines for all SIKE security levels, reaching a new speed record, while keeping our design constant-time, thus, the architecture remains robust against side-channel attacks such as SPA and DPA. We report 5.63%, 3.93%, 3.48%, and 1.61% improved execution time for SIKE p434, p503, p610, and p751, respectively.

Acknowledgment. This work has been supported in parts by an award from NSF CNS-2101085.

References

1. Jao, D., et al.: Supersingular isogeny key encapsulation. Submission to the NIST Post-Quantum Standardization Project (2017). https://sike.org/
2. Anastasova, M., Azarderakhsh, R., Kermani, M.M.: Fast strategies for the implementation of SIKE round 3 on ARM Cortex-M4. IEEE Trans. Circuits Syst. I Regul. Pap. **68**(10), 4129–4141 (2021)
3. Costello, C., Longa, P., Naehrig, M.: Efficient Algorithms for supersingular isogeny Diffie-Hellman. In: Robshaw, M., Katz, J. (eds.) CRYPTO 2016. LNCS, vol. 9814, pp. 572–601. Springer, Heidelberg (2016). https://doi.org/10.1007/978-3-662-53018-4_21
4. Costello, C., Hisil, H.: A simple and compact algorithm for SIDH with arbitrary degree isogenies. In: Takagi, T., Peyrin, T. (eds.) ASIACRYPT 2017. LNCS, vol. 10625, pp. 303–329. Springer, Cham (2017). https://doi.org/10.1007/978-3-319-70697-9_11
5. Costello, C., Longa, P., Naehrig, M., Renes, J., Virdia, F.: Improved classical cryptanalysis of the computational supersingular isogeny problem. Cryptology ePrint Archive, Report 2019/298. https://eprint.iacr.org/2019/298
6. Tian, J., Wang, P., Liu, Z., Lin, J., Wang, Z., Groszschaedl, J.: Efficient software implementation of the SIKE protocol using new data representation. IEEE Trans. Comput. **71**, 670–683 (2021)
7. Cheng, H., Fotiadis, G., Groszschädl, J., Ryan, P. Y.: Highly vectorized SIKE for AVX-512. IACR Trans. Cryptographic Hardware Embed. Syst. **2022**, 41–68 2022
8. Koziel, B., Jalali, A., Azarderakhsh, R., Jao, D., Mozaffari-Kermani, M.: NEON-SIDH: efficient implementation of supersingular isogeny Diffie-Hellman key exchange protocol on ARM. In: Foresti, S., Persiano, G. (eds.) CANS 2016. LNCS, vol. 10052, pp. 88–103. Springer, Cham (2016). https://doi.org/10.1007/978-3-319-48965-0_6
9. Jalali, A., Azarderakhsh, R., Kermani, M.M.: NEON SIKE: supersingular isogeny key encapsulation on ARMv7. In: Chattopadhyay, A., Rebeiro, C., Yarom, Y. (eds.) SPACE 2018. LNCS, vol. 11348, pp. 37–51. Springer, Cham (2018). https://doi.org/10.1007/978-3-030-05072-6_3
10. Seo, H., Liu, Z., Longa, P., Hu, Z.: SIDH on ARM: faster modular multiplications for faster post-quantum supersingular isogeny key exchange. IACR Trans. Cryptograph. Hardware Embed. Syst. **2018**, 1–20 (2018)
11. Jalali, A., Azarderakhsh, R., Kermani, M.M., Campagna, M., Jao, D.: ARMv8 SIKE: optimized supersingular isogeny key encapsulation on ARMv8 processors. IEEE Trans. Circuits Syst. I Regul. Pap. **66**(11), 4209–4218 (2019)
12. Seo, H., Sanal, P., Jalali, A., Azarderakhsh, R.: Optimized implementation of SIKE round 2 on 64-bit ARM Cortex-A processors. IEEE Trans. Circuits Syst. I Regul. Pap. **67**(8), 2659–2671 (2020)
13. Seo, H., Anastasova, M., Jalali, A., Azarderakhsh, R.: Supersingular isogeny key encapsulation (SIKE) round 2 on ARM Cortex-M4. IEEE Trans. Comput. **70**(10), 1705–1718 (2020)
14. Anastasova, M., Bisheh-Niasar, M., Azarderakhsh, R., Kermani, M.M.: Compressed SIKE round 3 on ARM Cortex-M4. In: Garcia-Alfaro, J., Li, S., Poovendran, R., Debar, H., Yung, M. (eds.) SecureComm 2021. LNICST, vol. 399, pp. 441–457. Springer, Cham (2021). https://doi.org/10.1007/978-3-030-90022-9_24
15. Hutter, M., Wenger, E.: Fast multi-precision multiplication for public-key cryptography on embedded microprocessors. In: Preneel, B., Takagi, T. (eds.) CHES

2011. LNCS, vol. 6917, pp. 459–474. Springer, Heidelberg (2011). https://doi.org/10.1007/978-3-642-23951-9_30

16. Seo, H., Liu, Z., Choi, J., Kim, H.: Multi-precision squaring for public-key cryptography on embedded microprocessors. In: Paul, G., Vaudenay, S. (eds.) INDOCRYPT 2013. LNCS, vol. 8250, pp. 227–243. Springer, Cham (2013). https://doi.org/10.1007/978-3-319-03515-4_15

17. Seo, H., Kim, H.: Consecutive operand-caching method for multiprecision multiplication. J. Inf. Commun. Convergence Eng. 13(1), 27–35 (2015)

18. Hutter, M., Schwabe, P.: Multiprecision multiplication on AVR revisited. J. Cryptogr. Eng. 5(3), 201–214 (2015). https://doi.org/10.1007/s13389-015-0093-2

19. Fujii, H., Aranha, D.F.: Curve25519 for the Cortex-M4 and beyond. In: Lange, T., Dunkelman, O. (eds.) LATINCRYPT 2017. LNCS, vol. 11368, pp. 109–127. Springer, Cham (2019). https://doi.org/10.1007/978-3-030-25283-0_6

20. Anastasova, M., Bisheh-Niasar, M., Seo, H., Azarderakhsh, R., Kermani, M.M.: Efficient and side-channel resistant design of high-security ed448 on arm cortex-m4. In: 2022 IEEE International Symposium on Hardware Oriented Security and Trust (HOST), pp. 93–96, IEEE (2022)

21. Crockett, E., Paquin, C., Stebila, D.: Prototyping post-quantum and hybrid key exchange and authentication in TLS and SSH. Cryptology ePrint Archive (2019)

22. Campagna, M., Crockett, E.:Hybrid post-quantum key encapsulation methods (PQ KEM) for transport layer security 1.2 (TLS). Internet Eng. Task Force, Internet-Draft draft-campagna-tls-bike-sike-hybrid, 1 (2019)

23. Paquin, C., Stebila, D., Tamvada, G.: Benchmarking post-quantum cryptography in TLS. In: Ding, J., Tillich, J.-P. (eds.) PQCrypto 2020. LNCS, vol. 12100, pp. 72–91. Springer, Cham (2020). https://doi.org/10.1007/978-3-030-44223-1_5

24. Anastasova, M., Kampanakis, P., Massimo, J.: PQ-HPKE: Post-Quantum Hybrid Public Key Encryption. Cryptology ePrint Archive (2022)

25. ARM, "Cortex-M4 ISA". https://developer.arm.com/documentation/100166/0001

26. Kannwischer, M.J., Rijneveld, J., Schwabe, P., Stoffelen, K.: pqm4: testing and benchmarking NIST PQC on ARM Cortex-M4 (2019)

27. Seo, H., Jalali, A., Azarderakhsh, R.: SIKE round 2 speed record on ARM cortex-M4. In: Mu, Y., Deng, R.H., Huang, X. (eds.) CANS 2019. LNCS, vol. 11829, pp. 39–60. Springer, Cham (2019). https://doi.org/10.1007/978-3-030-31578-8_3

28. Microsoft Team, "Sidh library". https://github.com/Microsoft/PQCrypto-SIDH

Analysis of Radioactive Decay Based Entropy Generator in the IoT Environments

Taewan Kim[1], Seyoon Lee[1], Seunghwan Yun[1], Jongbum Kim[2], and Okyeon Yi[1(✉)]

[1] Department of Financial Information Security, Kookmin University, Seoul, Korea
{ktw0308,custmor,schneeleopard,oyyi}@kookmin.ac.kr
[2] Radioisotope Research Division, Korea Atomic Energy Research Institute, Daejeon, Korea
jong@kaeri.re.kr

Abstract. In cryptography, random numbers are the most important element for security. Random numbers are generated through RNG (Random Number Generator), and collecting sufficient entropy sources is essential to generate random numbers. However, it is difficult to collect sufficient entropy sources due to limited resources in the IoT environment. In this paper, we have α- and β-based radioactive decay noise sources to solve this problem, and generated entropy using proper entropy generation methods respectively. The result is as follows: β-based noise sources can generate entropy about 32 times faster than α-based noise sources.

Keywords: QRNG · Entropy · IoT

1 Introduction

Random numbers are elements used in cryptographic systems such as secret keys, nonce, and initialization vectors. Based on the security of random numbers, cryptographic algorithms can provide confidentiality, integrity, authentication, and non-repudiation. When using cryptographic algorithms, random numbers underlying cryptographic algorithm's security can be predicted, or if they are vulnerable to attacks, the cryptographic algorithm's security can be less secure. Therefore, for the use of secure cryptographic algorithms, random numbers must be generated using secure RNG(Random Number Generator). However, the cryptographically secure RNG is determined by the initial value seed and the seed consists of entropy sources generated through the noise source. A noise source can be collected from a software or hardware operating environment, but in general, process clock, mouse, keyboard, disk information, interrupt request, etc.,

This research was financially supported by the Institute of Civil Military Technology Cooperation funded by the Defense Acquisition Program Administration and Ministry of Trade, Industry and Energy of Korean government under grant No. 21-CM-AU-09.

I. You and T.-Y. Youn (Eds.): WISA 2022, LNCS 13720, pp. 277–288, 2023.
https://doi.org/10.1007/978-3-031-25659-2_20

can be used in a software environment such as an operating system. In hardware environments, radioactive decay, photoelectronic effects, etc. may be used. When generating entropy, a noise source that can provide entropy must be selected and used in consideration of the operating environment, the purpose of using random numbers, etc. [11]. For example, when generating random numbers using /dev/random in a Linux with insufficient entropy pool, it may become blocked. Therefore, in this case, entropy must therefore be collected quickly.

Unlike operating systems that can collect a variety of noise sources, it is difficult to collect noise sources to generate entropy sources in environments with limited resources such as IoT environments. To solve this problem, noise sources are collected using sensors equipped with IoT device, typically using accelerometers, gyroscopes, geomagnetic sensors, cameras, microphones, etc. [3]. However, these noises are only available in certain environments that are operating or require external input. Therefore, noise sources that rely on a specific environment are difficult to solve the problem of noise sources in IoT devices. Another method for collecting noise sources is to collect noise sources using entropy chips. A typical example is the collection of noise sources utilizing the natural radioactive decay, a physical phenomenon [8,9]. This method can collect sufficient random numbers without physical constraints [2]. In this paper, the contributions are as follows:

- Derive entropy generation method using radioactive decay noise source in IoT device.
- Demonstrate the availability of entropy generation using Quantum Entropy Source in IoT environment.

2   Background

2.1   Random Number Generator

Cryptographically secure random numbers must be generated from cryptographically secure RNG and used in cryptographic systems. A cryptographically secure RNG is defined as a structure in which a TRNG and a PRNG are combined, as shown in Fig. 1. A cryptographic RNG is configured to output a cryptographically secure random number by using seed, an output value of TRNG, as an input of PRNG. The international standard for RNG, ISO/IEC 18031 [5] and SP 800-90 [1], which deals with cryptographic random number constructions, the output value of TRNG is non-deterministic bits, so TRNG is expressed as a NRBG(Non-deterministic Random Bit Generator), the output value of PRNG is deterministic bits, so PRNG is expressed as a DRBG(Deterministic Random Bit Generator) [7].

The NRBG collects noise sources with unpredictable characteristics and generates seed through digitization and post-processing. Noise sources are divided into physical noise sources and non-physical noise sources, and physical noise

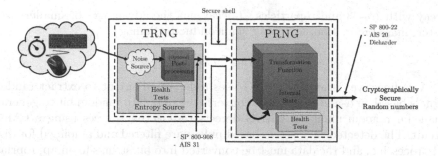

Fig. 1. Cryptography secure pseudo random number generator

sources include mouse, keyboards, quantum effects, etc. As the non-physical noise source,/dev/(u)random or the like of Linux exists. A DRBG generates a pseudo-random number sequence using the seed generated by the NRBG as an input of a deterministic algorithm. If the same value is used to the algorithm according to the deterministic characteristics of the DRBG, the random number being the output value of the DRBG becomes the same. Therefore, it is important to generate unpredictable seed when configuring DRBG.

2.2 Quantum Random Number Generator

QRNG(Quantum Random Number Generator) is a type of physical TRNG that uses the value generated by quantum phenomena as seed. Quantum phenomena include optical method, radioactive decay method, quantum state overlap, Heisenberg uncertainty, quantum turning, etc. [6]. QRNG using quantum phenomena provides faster generation speed and reliable randomness than conventional physical noise source generation [4]. Among them, RNG using the radioactive decay method is not affected by external factors such as temperature and power conditions, and thus the most ideal random number can be generated. Using this, IoT devices can generate entropy independently of the operating environment. According to a recent study, the radiation used to generate random numbers is divided into α and β [8,9].

A method for radioactive decay using α-rays uses α-particles emitted during the decay of a radioisotope(AM-241). In α-decay, the nucleus of a radioisotope emits α-particles, reducing the mass number by 4 and the atomic number by 2. AM-241 undergoes α-decay with NP-237 and α-particles. The generated α-particles have a large detection signal, so it can be detected with a simple CMOS circuit. Therefore, it was first commercialized.

$$_{95}^{241}AM \rightarrow _{93}^{237}NP + _{2}^{4}He(=\alpha) \tag{1}$$

A method for radioactive decay using β-rays uses β-particles emitted during the decay of a radioisotope(Ni-63). β-decay causes the nucleus of a radioisotope to change from a neutron to a proton and release electrons. Ni-63 undergoes β-

decay with Cu-63 and β-particles. β-decay has the advantages of smaller sizes, faster, mass production, and lower semiconductor damage [9].

$$^{63}Ni \rightarrow^{63} Cu + \beta^-$$ (2)

A radioactive decay based RNG uses a detection circuit to extract random signals based on α-and β-rays, and converts the data into random bit to generate quantum random numbers. QRNG detects radioactive sources using a CMOS circuit. The detected radioactive-based pulses are filtered and amplified for digital processing, and the data must be converted into bit strings in an appropriate method to make the collected data random. There are various methods for converting radioactive pulses into random bits, typically using digital counters to convert radiation pulses into random bits [4,10]. In this paper, we describe several bit conversion methods that can generate one bit per pulse, and experiment with entropy characteristics according to quantum entropy generator types. Also, since QRNG is a kind of physical TRNG, it is necessary to estimation Quantum Entropy Source(QES) generated from QRNG. Therefore, in this paper, a radioactive decay based entropy source is used with IoT device, and entropy for collected data is estimated using NIST SP 800-90B. Finally, when entropy is generated using QRNG in IoT device, analyze the results respectively.

3   Materials and Method

3.1   Digital Data Harvesting

Configuring entropy as shown in Fig. 2 consists of an entropy source collection and a post-processing process. When collecting entropy source, a noise source that can provide entropy should be selected considering the amount, type, speed of the noise sources that make up the entropy. After the entropy is collected, the post-processing process is selectively performed according to the characteristics of the entropy. Due to the properties of IoT device with resource and buffer constraints, there is a limit to processing a lot of data quickly. Therefore, in order to generate entropy with IoT device, it must be composed of noise sources that are appropriate to collect from the device. This is because if the amount of information from the noise source is large or the collection speed is fast, data leakage or loss can occur. Accordingly, no matter how good a noise source is, if

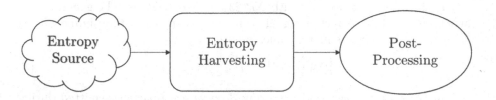

Fig. 2. Random number generation process

the noise source cannot be collected correctly by IoT device, the entropy characteristics possessed by the noise can be deteriorated. Therefore, when generating entropy sources in IoT environments, noise sources that can provide entropy should be selected considering the amount, type, speed, etc. of noise sources. In this paper, radiation pulses are collected by using a Raspberry Pi 4 in a simulated IoT environment, and entropy is constituted by utilizing a corresponding noise source.

3.2   Analysis of Pulse Collector for IoT Devices

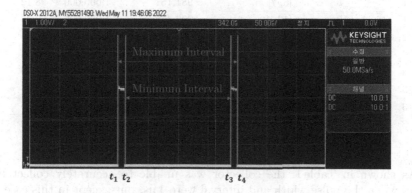

Fig. 3. Measurement of pulse interval

RNGs using radioactive decay are α- and β-ray based [8,9]. If IoT device can accurately collect entropy sources generated from α- and β-rays, then entropy can be generated using the data. However, IoT environments where entropy is difficult to collect can have problems processing large amounts of data precisely because of low computing power. Accordingly, even if a RNG capable of generating a good entropy can be used, the entropy of the RNG can be generated worse than the original if the IoT device cannot accurately process the noise source of the RNG. Therefore, in order to apply random number generator to IoT devices, the ability of IoT devices to process according to pulse generation time must be confirmed and a corresponding noise source must be supplied.

In this paper, we analyze the collection accuracy according to the pulse generation time in Raspberry Pi 4. When various intervals of pulses occurred using the Wiring Pi library with the GPIO pin of Raspberry Pi, the accuracy of the collector was analyzed by comparing the time of the pulse collected by Raspberry Pi with the original pulse generation time. As shown in Fig. 3, the maximum value of the pulse generation interval occurs when the pulse is generated (t_1) and when the next pulse ends (t_4), and the minimum value can occur when the pulse ends (t_2) and when the next pulse starts (t_3). That is, the error range of the pulse generation interval is a value obtained by adding the width w of the two pulses from the interval d of the generated pulse. Therefore, the accuracy of pulse collection can be calculated as follows:

$$Accuracy = \frac{\# \, of \, pulses \, collected \, within \, the \, margin \, of \, error \, (Pulse \, counting)}{Actual \, number \, of \, pulses \, generated \, (Total \, pulse)}$$

(3)

Table 1. Accuracy of pulse collector

No	Width(us)	Delay(us)	Range($[d, d+2w]$)	Pulse counting	Total pulse	Accuracy(%)
1	1	1	[1, 3]	146,569	1,000,000	**14.66**
2	1	5	[5, 7]	981,151	1,000,000	98.12
3	1	10	[10, 12]	993,468	1,000,000	99.35
4	2	1	[1, 5]	959,385	1,000,000	95.94
5	2	5	[5, 9]	995,384	1,000,000	99.54
6	2	10	[10, 14]	993,854	1,000,000	99.39
7	3	1	[1, 7]	996,666	1,000,000	99.67
8	3	5	[5, 11]	995,520	1,000,000	99.55
9	3	10	[10, 16]	994,243	1,000,000	99.42

As shown in Table 1, the collector was unable to accurately collect most pulses when the pulse width and interval were 1 us, but except in this case, the pulse interval was measured with high accuracy. In other words, when generating entropy using Raspberry Pi, a noise source should be selected in consideration of the collection speed, and an appropriate post-processing process should be applied to the collected noise source.

3.3   Methods to Extract Random Bits from Short Pulses

QRNG detects radioactive sources using a CMOS circuit. The detected radioactive pulses are filtered and amplified for digital processing, and the data must be converted into bit strings in an appropriate method to make the collected data random. There are various methods for converting radioactive pulses into random bits, and in general, a digital counter is used to convert radioactive pulses into random bits [8,9]. In this paper, we describe several bit conversion methods that can generate one bit per pulse, and experiment with entropy characteristics according to quantum entropy generator types.

Method 1, called the Fast Clock method, constructs entropy using intervals for the collected process time as shown in the Fig. 4 [4]. i.e., the entropy is constructed by calculating the difference between the $i+1$-th pulse generation time and the i-th pulse generation time. If the interval between the first pulse and the second pulse is odd, then 1, and if it is even, it becomes zero, and the eight of these pulses are collected to produce a 1-byte random number. Method 1 may generate a 1-byte random number per pulse by extracting the least signification

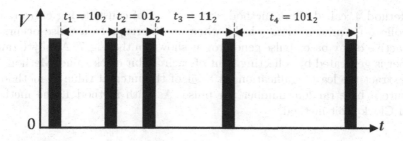

Fig. 4. Fast Clock method (Method 1)

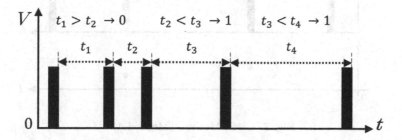

Fig. 5. Time difference Method (Method 2)

bit 8-bit of the interval value. In this paper, the method is called fast clock 8-bit method.

Method 2, called the Time Difference method, using the entropy configuration method of method 1 as shown in the Fig. 5. We first obtain an interval for pulse generation and compare the sizes of i-th and $i + 1$-th intervals to construct entropy. If the interval of the i-th is greater than the interval of the $i + 1$-th, configure it as 1, else 0 [10]. Method 2 also collects these eight intervals as shown in method 1 to generate a 1-byte random number.

Method 3, called the Slow Clock method, configures entropy by counting the number of pulses generated within a specific time as shown in the Fig. 6. The entropy bit is 1 when the count is odd and 0 when even. In this paper, it is based on the average interval of pulses collected at a specific time [10].

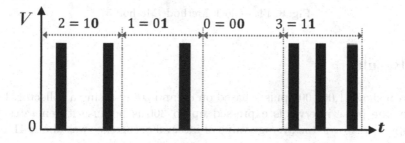

Fig. 6. Slow Clock Method (Method 3)

Method 4, called Clock method, is a method of constructing entropy using the collector's process time (clock) when an interrupt to a pulse occurs in a radioactive decay based pulse generator as shown in the Fig. 7. A 1-byte random number is generated by collecting 1 bit of each 32-bit clock value. Method 4 can also extract the least signification bit 8-bit of the interval value as method 1 to generate a byte random number per pulse. As with method 1, the method is called Clock 8-bit method.

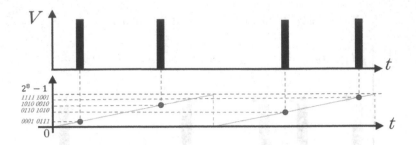

Fig. 7. Clock Method (Method 4)

Finally, the entropy configuration method 5, called Flag Clock method, compares the size of the interval between a specific value($flag$) and the generated pulse to construct the entropy as shown in the Fig. 8. In this paper, we calculate the flag as the average interval of the collected pulses. If the pulse interval is greater than the flag, configure it as 1 and else 0.

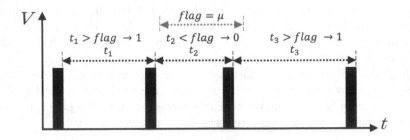

Fig. 8. Flag Clock Method (Method 5)

4   Result

Figure 9 shows 1,000,000 pulses based on α- and β-rays using a collector. In the figure, the pulse interval is expressed up to 300 us because it generates 8-bit entropy. For α-rays, the average value of interval occurrence was about 41,416 us

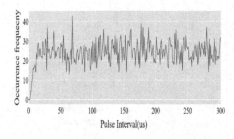 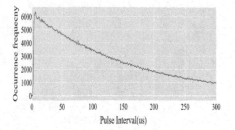

Fig. 9. Pulse interval according to α (left) and β (right)

and about 24 pulses per second. For β-rays, the average value of interval occurrence was about 161 us and 6,211 pulses per second. As shown in Fig. 9, the frequency of occurrence for various interval values is relatively uniform, but for β, as the interval increases starting with the interval of 5 μs, the frequency decreases significantly, and thus the frequency is not uniform relatively. This confirms that when radioactive based RNGs are used in IoT devices, entropy must be generated by applying different methods depending on the noise source used.

Figure 10 is the result of the entropy value generated using the Fast Clock 1-bit method. The Fast Clock 1-bit method produced similar results for both α- and β-rays. All possible 8-bit entropy values occurred uniformly, and the distribution of entropy values was also uniform. Figure 11 is the result of the entropy value generated using the Time Difference method. Time Difference also produced similar results for both α- and β- rays. Unlike the Fast Clock 1-bit method, all possible 8-bit entropy values were not uniform, and the distribution of entropy values was also visually dense. Therefore, even if entropy is generated using the same noise source, the characteristics of the entropy generated may be affected by which post-processing method is used.

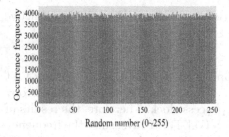 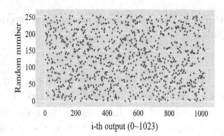

Fig. 10. Fast clock 1-bit method occurrence (left) and output (right) for α- and β-radioactive pulses.

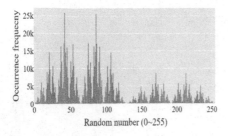

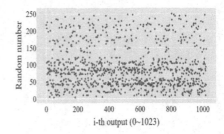

Fig. 11. Time difference method occurrence (left) and output (right) for α and β-radioactive pulses.

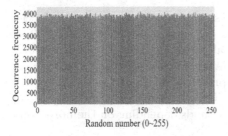

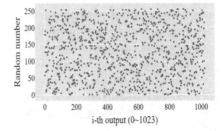

Fig. 12. Fast clock 8-bit method occurrence (left) and output (right) for α-radioactive pulses.

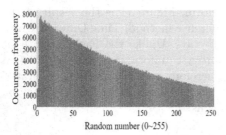

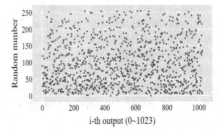

Fig. 13. Fast clock 8-bit method occurrence (left) and output (right) for β-radioactive pulses.

Figures 12, 13 are the results when applied to each α- and β-ray using Fast Clock 8-bit. Fast Clock 8-bit is a post-processing method that generates entropy using 8-bit of the interval of the collected process clock. Therefore, the results of post-processing are affected by the pulse interval. For α-rays, since the frequency of the collected pulse intervals is relatively uniform, the output value is also uniform after post-processing. However, for β-rays, the frequency of collected pulse intervals is not uniform, so the output value is biased to one side. Therefore, when generating entropy, it should be generated by considering both the type of noise source and the post-processing method.

Table 2. Min-entropy of entropy outputs

	Fast Clock (8-bit)	Fast Clock (1-bit)	Time Difference	Slow Clock	Clock (8-bit)	Clock (1-bit)	Flag Clock
α-entropy	7.88	7.88	5.25	**Fail**	7.87	7.89	**Fail**
β-entropy	**Fail**	7.89	5.24	6.59	**Fail**	7.89	5.37

Table 2 is the entropy value after post-processing in Chap. 3 between the collected α- and β-ray based pulses. Fast Clock 8-bit and Clock 8-bit, which generate an entropy of 1-byte per pulse using the interval of pulse generation, are affected by the noise source collection time. That is, it is difficult to generate a good entropy if collection time is inaccurate. As shown in Fig. 13, β-ray based noise sources that emit large amounts of noise per second are difficult to measure the exact collection time in the collector by 8-bit, resulting in an entropy evaluation failure. On the other hand, the α-ray based noise source passes the entropy test because the interval between pulses is measurable. The method of generating 1-byte of entropy with eight pulses(Fast Clock 1-bit, Time Difference, etc.) in both α and β passes all entropy tests. However, if entropy is generated by selecting a specific flag, the characteristics of the entropy are determined by how the flag is selected. Flag in this paper defined as the average of pulse generation intervals, and for β, the entropy test is passed when the flag is set as the average value because the deviation is small, but for an α, the test is failed when the flag is set as the average value.

For the results, α-ray based noise sources can be collected 24 pulses per second and use them to generate entropy, the Fast clock 8-bit and Clock 8-bit methods of post-processing are the fastest and highest entropy. Thus, the entropy generation rate is 192 bps. In addition, β-ray based noise sources can be collected 6,211 pulses per second, and the Fast Clock 1-bit and Clock 1-bit methods are the best methods to use them. In this case, the entropy generation rate is 6,211 bps. That is, when entropy is generated using each of the best methods, β-rays may generate entropy about 32 times faster than α-rays. If seed is generated considering the 128-bit security strength, it will take about 666 ms for α and about 20 ms for β. Therefore, it is effective to use β-entropy for IoT equipment used in environments where random number generation time is critical.

5   Conclusion

In this paper, radioactive decay based noise sources were collected with IoT device and entropy characteristics by noise source types were analyzed by applying various post-processing methods. For α-ray based noise sources, device can properly collect noise sources, but entropy generation is relatively slow. On the other hand, for β-ray based noise sources, the pulse generation rate is significantly faster than α, so the noise source generation rate is fast, but appropriate post-processing methods are needed when using the noise source with IoT device. Therefore, in order to use QRNG in an IoT environment, the performance of the device and the characteristics of the noise source should be considered. If QRNG can be used to IoT device, random number generation problems can be solved with various IoT device currently in use. It will also help secure IoT information security and future quantum computing security.

References

1. Barker, E.B., Kelsey, J.M.: Recommendation for random bit generator (RBG) constructions. US Department of Commerce, National Institute of Standards and Technology (2012)
2. Bera, M.N., Acín, A., Kuś, M., Mitchell, M.W., Lewenstein, M.: Randomness in quantum mechanics: philosophy, physics and technology. Rep. Prog. Phys. **80**(12), 124001 (2017)
3. Cho, S.M., Hong, E., Seo, S.H.: Random number generator using sensors for drone. IEEE Access **8**, 30343–30354 (2020)
4. Herrero-Collantes, M., Garcia-Escartin, J.C.: Quantum random number generators. Rev. Mod. Phys. **89**(1), 015004 (2017)
5. ISO/IEC18031: Information technology - security techniques- random bit generation. International Organization for Standardization and International Electrotechnical Commission (2011)
6. ITU: Quantum noise random number generator architecture. ITU-T Rec X.1702 (2019)
7. Park, H.: A study on the security evaluation for cryptographically secure random number generators. Kookmin University, pp. 1–162 (2021)
8. Park, J., Cho, S., Lim, T., Tehranipoor, M.: QEC: a quantum entropy chip and its applications. IEEE Trans. Very Large Scale Integr. (VLSI) Systems **28**(6), 1471–1484 (2020)
9. Park, K., et al.: A lightweight true random number generator using beta radiation for IoT applications. ETRI J. **42**(6), 951–964 (2020)
10. Rohe, M., et al.: Randy-a true-random generator based on radioactive decay. Saarland University, pp. 1–36 (2003)
11. TTA: Guideline for the collection and application of noise sources on operating systems. TTAK.KO-12.0235/R2 (2020)

Security Management

A Novel Metric for Password Security Risk Against Dictionary Attacks

Binh Le Thanh Thai$^{(\boxtimes)}$ and Hidema Tanaka

National Defense Academy of Japan, 1-10-20 Hashirimizu, Yokosuka,
Kanagawa 239-8686, Japan
binhbe603501@gmail.com, hidema@nda.ac.jp

Abstract. Passwords are still the most used method of user authentication in the usage of information systems, and they have an important role in practical security. Despite the fact that researchers have discovered various vulnerabilities in the usage of passwords, this authentication method is still frequently used. The main issue with passwords is their quality or strength, i.e., how hard they can be guessed by an attacker, and there are various password strength metrics have been proposed so far. In this paper, we propose a new metric for password strength that takes into account the risk of dictionary attacks. We create datasets from leaked password lists and regard them as Markov information sources. Then we calculate the password self-information and compare it to the threshold value we specified to determine the password strength. With this numerical value, we can know how risky a password has against dictionary attacks, and can easily compare the strength of several passwords. Through experimental results, we show that our method is very effective, does not require huge computational resources, and can effectively help users create stronger passwords.

Keywords: Password strength · Security risk · Dictionary attack · Self-information

1 Introduction

1.1 Background and Motivation

In the field of information security, passwords are still a predominating approach for user authentication because of their convenient simplicity and sound implementation. Although researchers recently showed several vulnerabilities in the use of passwords, this authentication method is still given attention.. Meanwhile, when the Internet became a necessity for society from business activities to the everyday life, the number of opportunities to use passwords has also increased rapidly. Therefore, it is very important to choose strong passwords to fulfill the user authentication role. This fact leads to the password strength, i.e., how hard it can be guessed by an attacker, has become the main issue and many password strength metrics (PSMs) have been proposed so far [3,8,11]. When generating a

© Springer Nature Switzerland AG 2023
I. You and T.-Y. Youn (Eds.): WISA 2022, LNCS 13720, pp. 291–302, 2023.
https://doi.org/10.1007/978-3-031-25659-2_21

Table 1. Example of password strength score of `password$1`

Service	Strength	Score
Apple	Moderate	2/3
Dropbox	Very weak	1/5
eBay	Medium	4/5
Google	Fair	3/5
Microsoft (v3)	Medium	2/4
Skype	Poor	1/3
Twitter	Perfect	6/6
Yahoo!	Very strong	4/4

password, convenience and security conflict [21]. Simple passwords such as patterns that combine dictionary words and consecutive numbers, e.g., `hello123`, are convenient to use because they are easy to remember but are not secure. On the contrary, complex passwords that include uppercase and lowercase letters, digits, and special characters are strong but are inconvenient. Current studies [2,6,23] show that users intend to choose weak passwords, which are usually easy-to-remember but vulnerable to being guessed. Furthermore, passwords are often reused, which is also a security risk [7].

Motivated to prevent users from generating weak passwords, we propose a new PSM based on the risk of dictionary attacks. Paper [5] shows that a password that is evaluated as strong by some PSMs also maybe not really strong if it has already leaked. Based on this consideration, we collect the leaked passwords to create datasets to evaluate the password strength. We regard these datasets as Markov sources to calculate the value of self-information of the target passwords and use this value to show the risk of dictionary attacks. Through experiments, we confirm that the proposed method can more effectively show the risk against dictionary attacks than previous PSMs. This is our first contribution.

On the other hand, even if the same password is used, the password strength differs greatly depending on the PSMs. Table 1 shows the example for the strength of the password `password$1` evaluated by some service vendors [4]. From Table 1, we can find that Dropbox and Skype gave the password `password$1` the minimum score, whereas it has the maximum score in Twitter and Yahoo!. This fact may make users confused whether their passwords are really strong. Here, the users face the problem that they do not know what PSMs have been used by these service vendors. Furthermore, the PSMs shown in Sect. 2.1 empirically evaluate passwords and do not clarify how to determine the indicators or points. Meanwhile, the proposed method evaluates passwords from statistical results, so users can check the strength of their passwords and can ignore the score of these service vendors. This is our second contribution.

In the followings, we use the common notations in Table 2 and the standard charsets in Table 3.

Table 2. Notation

Variable	Definition
pw	The password
l	The length of the password
n	The number of charsets in pw
L	Lowercase characters
U	Uppercase characters
D	Digits
S	Special characters
N	The size of the charset
$\mathbf{C} = \mathbf{L} \cup \mathbf{U} \cup \mathbf{D} \cup \mathbf{S}$	All printable characters

Table 3. Standard charsets

Charset	size N
$\mathbf{L} = \{a, b, \cdots, z\}$	26
$\mathbf{U} = \{A, B, \cdots, Z\}$	26
$\mathbf{D} = \{0, 1, \cdots, 9\}$	10
$\mathbf{S} = \{\sim \text{'}!@\#\$\%\hat{}\& * ()\text{-}\{\} - []+ = | : \text{"} <>?;', ./\backslash\}$	32

1.2   Targeted Password Cracking Method

There are many well-known password cracking methods such as the brute-force attack, the rainbow table attack, and the dictionary attack. Among them, the brute-force attack greatly relies on the computing power; thus, it is only effective in the case of cracking short passwords. The success or failure of this attack method is determined only by the length of the password, so it is not the target of our study. On the other hand, the rainbow table attack [17] targets the hash values of the passwords; thus, it is affected by only the length of hash value. Hence, it is also not the target of our study. With the dictionary attack [16], this method is more effective than the brute-force attack and is greatly affected by the word or character choices. Therefore, it should be considered when evaluating the password strength. In this study, we contribute to the security analysis of passwords against the dictionary attack.

2   Previous Works

2.1   Entropy

National Institute of Standards and Technology (NIST) proposes a metric to calculate password strength using entropy in *Electronic Authentication Guidelines* [3]. The entropy is defined as follows.

$$H(pw) = \log_2 N^l \tag{1}$$

The high value of entropy means that password has higher uncertainty. That is, the password is harder to guess by an attacker, so the password is evaluated as strong. However, this method is too naive because it is obvious that long passwords from large charsets will have high entropy values. Therefore, NIST proposes another method for estimating password entropy H with consideration of password length, use of multiple charsets, and the possibility of a dictionary attack. The entropy H is estimated as follows.

$$H = \begin{cases} +4 & \text{first character} \\ +2 & \text{for each of the 2nd to 8th characters} \\ +1.5 & \text{for each of the 9th to 20th characters} \\ +1 & \text{for each of the 21st and above characters} \\ +6 & \text{use uppercase and non-alphabetic characters} \\ +6 & \text{not in dictionaries} \end{cases} \tag{2}$$

The basic idea is to use well-known Shannon's estimate of the entropy in ordinary English text as the starting point to estimate the entropy of user-selected passwords [19]. Shannon conducted experiments where he gave people strings of English text and asked them to guess the next character in the string. From this result, he estimated the entropy of each successive character. In this case, he only used 26 English lowercase letters and the space. On the other hand, NIST assumes that passwords are selected from the normal keyboard of 94 printable characters shown in Table 3. Furthermore, NIST also considers some rules of forcing to include uppercase letters, non-alphabetic characters, and the existence of passwords in dictionaries. With these considerations, the above entropy H is derived.

2.2   Password Quality Indicator [11]

Most users know the risk of dictionary attacks and avoid using passwords listed in dictionaries. However, users want to choose easy-to-remember passwords like a word with small changes, e.g., use number 0 instead of character O, use special character $ instead of character S, etc. On the other hand, methods of dictionary attack also adopted various word-mangling rules to match a password with words in dictionaries. Therefore, password strength should be evaluated by how hard to correct it to match some words in the dictionaries. Based on this consideration, a method using a linguistic distance between a dictionary word with the password, that is called the "*Levenshtein distance*" [9], is proposed to measure it. This metric calculates the distance between two strings by counting the minimum number of single-character manipulations required (deletion, modification, and insertion) to make the two strings the same. Table 4 shows examples.

The password quality indicator (PQI) of a password pw is defined as $\lambda = (D, L)$, where D is the Levenshtein distance of the password to the base dictionary words, and L is the effective password length as follows.

$$L = l \log_{10} N \tag{3}$$

Table 4. Example of Levenshtein distance

String 1	String 2	Levenshtein distance
amazon	amazon	0
amazon	amaz0n	1
amazon	amazone	1
amazon	4m4z0n	3
amazon	@D$5	6

With $\lambda = (D, L)$, the password is at least D characters different from the base dictionary words and there are at least 10^L possible password candidates to be tried to crack. A password that has $D \geq 3$ and $L \geq 14$ is evaluated as strong.

2.3 Password Complexity Metric [8]

Most service vendors, e.g., Microsoft, Skype, Apple, etc., use a PSM based on the "LUDS requirements", and some use the metric based on the "patterns in passwords". The LUDS requirements is that passwords must consist of characters from **L**, **U**, **D** and **S** (see Table 3). Meanwhile, the patterns in passwords is how common a password is according to several sources, such as common passwords in leaked password sets, general names from census data, and general words in Wikipedia. Although the users are aware of using different charsets to compose passwords, they are likely to put characters from the same charset together rather than mixing them up. For example, the password amazon123 is usually used more than the password ama12zo3n. With this consideration, Gongzhu Hu proposes a metric called the "password complexity metric" (PCM) that is based both on LUDS requirements and patterns in passwords.

PCM searches for substrings in a password that are from the same charset and counts the number of such substrings. Using the above example, the number of substrings in amazon12345 is 2 (amazon and 12345), whereas it is 5 in ama12zo3n (ama, 12, zo, 3, and n). Gongzhu Hu also cared about the position of special characters and applied a penalty to this pattern if the password uses only 2 charsets (including the special charset). The complexity of a password is calculated as follows.

$$C(pw) = \begin{cases} 0 & , \ l < 4 \\ n + (k/l) + s - p - (d/l) \,, & l \geq 4 \end{cases}$$

$$s = \begin{cases} 0.5, & pw \text{ contains special characters} \\ 0, & \text{otherwise} \end{cases} \tag{4}$$

$$p = \begin{cases} 0.5, & \begin{array}{l} n \leq 2 \text{ and a special character is at the} \\ \text{beginning or the end} \end{array} \\ 0, & \text{otherwise} \end{cases}$$

where k denotes the number of same-charset-substrings, and d is the length of substring that is listed in dictionaries.

3   Proposed Method

3.1   Basic Idea

As is shown above, many PSMs have been proposed so far. However, they only estimate password strength based on an empirical choice of what condition has a great influence on the password strength and the evaluation results are not stable. Furthermore, the evaluation values calculated in these methods assume that the password is generated from a memoryless source, the use of the alphabet for the password is not considered based on the linguistic personality. On the other hand, a huge number of passwords have been leaked as a result of intensifying cyber-attacks [15,20,22]. It is obvious that a dictionary attack with these leaked passwords is very effective. Therefore, a password is not strong, even if it is evaluated as strong by the methods shown in Sect.2, if it has already been leaked. Due to these facts, we should consider a new method to evaluate the risk of dictionary attacks based on the leaked passwords. That is, our method shows the risk of passwords by quantitative comparison with the leaked password lists.

From previous works, we discovered the following facts and tendencies.

- There is a large bias in the combination of **LUDS**, e.g., the probability that uppercase is chosen for the first character is high.
- A weak password usually has the Levenshtein distance less than 3. That is, such a password is easy to be predicted from the viewpoint of patterns in passwords.
- A weak password usually has less than 3 such sub-strings used in the PCM.

To quantitatively evaluate such tendencies from the leaked password lists, it is appropriate to focus on the connection of the characters in the passwords. In other words, we re-execute the entropy of Shannon's experiment [19] based on the leaked passwords by computer experiments. From the viewpoint of such entropy, the large value means that the password is unlikely to be used, so such a password is hard to be guessed by dictionary attacks with the leaked password datasets. Adding these above characteristic is the advantage of the proposed method over the previous works.

3.2   Self-information-Based Metric

In information theory, self-information is a basic quantity derived from the probability of a particular event occurring from a random variable and also can be interpreted as quantifying the level of "surprise" of a particular outcome. Our basic idea is to calculate the self-information of a password with Markov information sources and use this value to evaluate its strength. The leaked password lists have duplicates of popular weak passwords, e.g., `123456`, `Qwerty`, `Password`, etc. We use the frequency of such duplicate as a weight of passwords.

Firstly, we calculate conditional probabilities with weight for the leaked password lists in the order of appearance of characters. Next, considering the connection of the characters in the passwords, we split the target password into two-character pieces, e.g., the result of password `amazon123` is [am, ma, az, zo, on, n1, 12, 23], and calculate the self-information I [bit] as follows.

$$I = \sum_{i=1}^{l-1} \log_2 \frac{1}{P(x_{i+1}|x_i)} \tag{5}$$

where x_i denotes the i-th character of pw and $P(\cdot|\cdot)$ denotes the conditional probability.

The value of self-information I indicates how ambiguous the target password is concerning the leaked password. From the viewpoint of the leaked passwords, if the frequency of the input password's characters is low, the system will "surprise" and the value of self-information will become larger. Therefore, the high self-information value means that the password is further from the leaked password. That is, the password with a large self-information can be evaluated as "strong" against a dictionary attack. We call our method the "*self-information-based metric*" (SBM).

3.3   Update of Dataset

In the proposed method, we use leaked password lists to create datasets for password evaluations. While evaluating passwords by SBM, we constantly need to update the dataset by adding the target evaluation password into them because of the following reasons.

- $P(x_{i+1}|x_i)$ does not exist in some cases
- The frequency of appearance of characters always changes.

The dominant calculation cost is processing the dataset of leaked password lists. This process only needs to be executed at the beginning of the whole process. The necessary calculation cost for evaluation of passwords including the update of the dataset is negligible. The specific calculation cost is shown in the experiments in Sect.4.

3.4   Threshold Value Based on 3σ Rule

In statistics, the 3σ rule [18], also known as the 68-95-99.7 rule, shows the percentage of values that lie within an interval estimate in a normal distribution. That is, 68%, 95%, and 99.7%, respectively, of the values lie within 1, 2, and 3 standard deviations of the mean.

$$Pr(\mu - 3\sigma \leq X \leq \mu + 3\sigma) \approx 99.7\% \tag{6}$$

where $Pr(\cdot)$ denotes the probability function, X denotes an observation from a normally distributed random variable, μ denotes the mean of the distribution, and σ denotes the standard deviation. A weak 3σ rule derived from Chebyshev's inequality shows that at least 88.8% of cases fall within properly calculated 3σ

Table 5. Self-information threshold for each password length

	l							
	6	7	8	9	10	11	12	13
Dataset-1	70.19	82.82	101.89	109.13	140.18	132.01	150.25	189.27
Dataset-2	66.95	78.43	99.64	103.60	123.30	133.72	148.64	164.46

intervals even for non-normally distributed values. Based on this rule, we consider that passwords with self-information more than the mean and 3 standard deviations are away from at least 88.8% of leaked passwords, so such passwords can be evaluated as strong. We call the value of the mean and three standard deviations as the "threshold value" and evaluate the password pw as follows.

$$\begin{cases} I_{pw} < \mu + 3\sigma & \text{Weak} \\ I_{pw} \geq \mu + 3\sigma & \text{Strong} \end{cases} \tag{7}$$

Note that the values of μ and σ are derived from the values I_{pw} of all passwords in the datasets.

4 Experimental Results

4.1 Preliminary

In our experiments, we use the leaked password lists from GitHub [12–14] and BlueLeaks [1] to create 2 types of datasets for password evaluations. Notably, the data of [12] contains 5 kinds of small datasets. With the data from GitHub, we only use passwords with $l \leq 49$ because we found that passwords with $l \geq 50$ are obviously processing errors. This dataset contains 6,988,152 passwords in total, and we refer to it as the "Dataset-1". On the other hand, since the data from BlueLeaks is very huge, we only use a part of this data to create the "Dataset-2". This dataset contains 23,665,875 passwords in total. From these datasets, we calculate the value of self-formation threshold for each password length and show the results in Table 5.

We use Apple Mac mini 2018 (CPU 3 GHz 6-Core Intel Core i5, Memory 8 GB 2667 MHz MHz DDR4) and Python 3.9.8 in our experiments. With this computer environment, the time for processing the Dataset-1 and the Dataset-2 are about 8 s and 26 s, respectively, and the time for evaluating a password is less than 1 s. The calculation cost for the values shown in Table 5 is about 50 s. Table 6 shows the results of various methods for some passwords. The password c6V#ihGyUJ is generated by a random password generation site [10] with the condition that $l = 10$ (the same length as password\$1, see the example shown in Sect. 1) and $n = 4$, and the other ones are generated by us.

Table 6. Examples of comparison

| Password | SBM (our proposal) | | NIST | PQI | PCM |
	Dataset-1	Dataset-2	Entropy	$\lambda = (D, L)$	
c6V#ihGyUJ	143.34/Strong	160.00/Strong	33	$(10, 19.73)$/Strong	5.3
password$1	132.97/Weak	104.12/Weak	27	$(2, 18.33)$/Weak	3.7
#111$apple	104.70/Weak	113.52/Weak	27	$(5, 18.33)$/Strong	3.8
1111111111	68.51/Weak	64.62/Weak	27	$(10, 1)$/Weak	1.1
111#apple	89.93/Weak	97.10/Weak	26.5	$(4, 16.49)$/Strong	3.72
111APPLE	85.18/Weak	89.83/Weak	24	$(3, 12.45)$/Weak	2.125
111apple	64.58/Weak	63.95/Weak	24	$(3, 12.45)$/Weak	2.125

4.2 Comparison with the Previous Methods

The password c6V#ihGyUJ is evaluated as strong by the PQI and also has high scores by other methods. With our method, it also has the self-information value larger than threshold and is evaluated as strong. Next, let us consider the results of 2 passwords password$1 and #111$apple. With consideration of the results of the NIST entropy, the PQI, and the PCM, #111$apple is stronger than password$1; notably, the PQI tells that #111$apple is strong, whereas password$1 is weak. Meanwhile, from the viewpoint of leaked passwords, SBM shows that both self-information values of #111$apple and password$1 are less than the threshold value and are evaluated as weak. This result shows that the proposed method effectively shows the risk of dictionary attacks based on the statistic of the leaked passwords.

The password 111#apple is evaluated as strong by the PQI and also has quite high scores by the NIST entropy and the PCM. However, this password is evaluated as weak by the SBM in both cases using the Dataset-1 and the Dataset-2. Especially, in the case using the Dataset-1, this password has the self-information value that is about 30 [bit] less than the threshold (see Table 5). That is, if an attacker uses the Dataset-1 to try to crack this password, he/she can easily succeed. From these results, we can conclude that the proposed method can effectively show the security risk of passwords against dictionary attacks.

4.3 Analysis of the Differences in the Datasets Used

From the analysis of 2 datasets, we confirm that users usually create passwords that have $(l, n) = (8, 2)$. With this consideration, we created two passwords 111APPLE and 111apple. Let us analyze the evaluation results of these passwords. Both of these are weak passwords and they also have the same strength evaluated by the NIST entropy, the PQI, and the PCM. Meanwhile, the proposed method shows that 111APPLE is stronger than 111apple. In general, people have more opportunities to use lowercase letters than uppercase letters, e.g., when writing a sentence, only the beginning is uppercase. It is regarded that people also have this tendency when generating a password. For this reason, when entering a password, the systems usually warn us when CAPSLOCK is on. Therefore, 111apple should be weaker than 111APPLE when considering a dictionary attack. That is, the proposed method has a more rational result. Furthermore, the NIST entropy tells that 1111111111 is stronger than 111APPLE. This result is derived only by that 1111111111 has $l = 10$, whereas 111APPLE has $l = 8$. However, this result is not rational because 1111111111 uses only one character, whereas 111APPLE uses a mix of two charsets. Therefore, we can also conclude that it is not appropriate to use the NIST entropy when considering the risk of dictionary attacks.

Another point worth mentioning the evaluation results of password$1 and #111$apple. Intuitively, #111$apple is regarded as stronger than password$1. The PQI and the PCM also tell that #111$apple is stronger than password$1; notably, there is a large difference in the value D of these two passwords in the PQI. However, in the proposed method, even both are evaluated as weak, password$1 is evaluated to be about 28 [bit] stronger in the small size Dataset-1. On the other hand, in the sufficiently large size Dataset-2, it is evaluated to be about 9 [bit] weaker, and the result follows the intuition and the evaluation of the PQI and the PCM. From this result, we can confirm that the larger size of the dataset, the more detailed and effective evaluation is executed.

5 Discussion

In this study, we use 2 datasets built from leaked passwords from GitHub and BlueLeaks. The size of Dataset-1 is around 1/3 that of Dataset-2, as indicated above. As a result, there is a discrepancy in the frequency distribution of self-information. The frequency distributions of self-information of passwords with $l = 10$ of two datasets, for example, are shown in Fig. 1. The horizontal axis represents self-information, whereas the vertical axis represents frequency. We may deduce from the findings in Fig. 1 that the larger the dataset, the closer the self-information frequency distribution approaches the normal distribution. That is, the 3σ rule becomes more exact, allowing for a more precise determination of password strength. Therefore, the proposed method can conduct a more effective assessment if we can generate a larger dataset. Including the obfuscated passwords in the dataset is one approach to increase its size. Leetspeak is considered an effective method for such a purpose. Indeed, leetspeak passwords are a well-known countermeasure against dictionary attacks, and we found a large number of them in our datasets. We expect that converting current datasets to leetspeak will allow us to create larger datasets for more accurate evaluation. This is our future work.

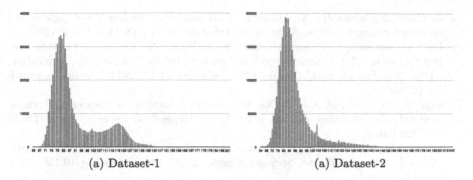

(a) Dataset-1   (a) Dataset-2

Fig. 1. Frequency distributions of self-information of passwords with $l = 10$

6 Conclusion

The "self- information-based metric" is a novel method for evaluating password strength that we propose in this paper. We create datasets from the leaked passwords and compare the evaluation results to the findings of previous methods to confirm the effectiveness of the proposed method. The proposed method has the following two advantages.

- The proposed method analyzes the tendencies of character connections from the leaked passwords and evaluates the password strength against dictionary attacks quantitatively using self-information value.
- The proposed method uses statistics to determine if a password is strong or weak, whereas previous studies used experimental or empirical methods.

However, for more accurate evaluation, a big dataset is necessary, and future work should include obfuscation. To use the proposed method, all that is necessary is the acquisition of a dataset, and the computational cost required to execute is very low. Furthermore, since the strength of passwords can be numerically compared, we can conclude that our method is very effective for generating stronger passwords. In our forthcoming paper, we will aim to verify the threshold value in detail and propose a more practical password evaluation system.

References

1. Blueleaks. https://ddosecrets.com/wiki/BlueLeaks
2. Bishop, M., Klein, D.V.: Improving system security via proactive password checking. Comput. Secur. 14(3), 233–249 (1995)
3. Burr, W., Dodson, D.F., Newton, E., Perlner, R., Polk, W., Gupta, S., Nabbus, E.: NIST special publication 800–63-2 electronic authentication guideline. Comput. Secur. Div. Inf. Technol. Lab. Nat. Inst. Stan. Technol. (2013)
4. de Carné de Carnavalet, X., Mannan, M.: From very weak to very strong: analyzing password-strength meters. In: 21st Annual Network and Distributed System Security Symposium, NDSS 2014, San Diego, California, USA, February 23–26 2014. The Internet Society (2014)

5. de Carné de Carnavalet, X., Mannan, M.: A large-scale evaluation of high-impact password strength meters. ACM Trans. Inf. Syst. Secur. **18**(1), 1:1–1:32 (2015)
6. Das, A., Bonneau, J., Caesar, M., Borisov, N., Wang, X.: The tangled web of password reuse. In: 21st Annual Network and Distributed System Security Symposium, NDSS 2014, San Diego, California, USA, February 23–26, 2014. The Internet Society (2014)
7. Han, W., Li, Z., Ni, M., Gu, G., Xu, W.: Shadow attacks based on password reuses: a quantitative empirical analysis. IEEE Trans. Dependable Secur. Comput. **15**(2), 309–320 (2018)
8. Hu, G.: On password strength: a survey and analysis. In: Lee, R. (ed.) SNPD 2017. SCI, vol. 721, pp. 165–186. Springer, Cham (2018). https://doi.org/10.1007/978-3-319-62048-0_12
9. Levenshtein, V.I., et al.: Binary codes capable of correcting deletions, insertions, and reversals. In: Soviet Physics Doklady, vol. 10, pp. 707–710. Soviet Union (1966)
10. LUFTTOOLS: Random password generation site. https://www.luft.co.jp/cgi/en/
11. Ma, W., Campbell, J., Tran, D., Kleeman, D.: A conceptual framework for assessing password quality. Int. J. Comput. Sci. Netw. Secur. **7**(1), 179–185 (2007)
12. Miessler, D.: Leaked passwords - 1. https://github.com/danielmiessler/SecLists/tree/master/Passwords/Leaked-Databases
13. Miessler, D.: Leaked passwords - 2. https://github.com/danielmiessler/SecLists/blob/master/Passwords/dutch_passwordlist.txt
14. Miessler, D.: Leaked passwords - 3. https://github.com/danielmiessler/SecLists/tree/master/Passwords/Common-Credentials
15. Mikalauskas, E.: Rockyou 2021: largest password compilation of all time leaked online with 8.4 billion entries. https://cybernews.com/security/rockyou2021-alltime-largest-password-compilation-leaked/
16. Nam, J., Paik, J., Kang, H., Kim, U., Won, D.: An off-line dictionary attack on a simple three-party key exchange protocol. IEEE Commun. Lett. **13**(3), 205–207 (2009)
17. Oechslin, P.: Making a faster cryptanalytic time-memory trade-off. In: Boneh, D. (ed.) CRYPTO 2003. LNCS, vol. 2729, pp. 617–630. Springer, Heidelberg (2003). https://doi.org/10.1007/978-3-540-45146-4_36
18. Pukelsheim, F.: The three sigma rule. Am. Stat. **48**(2), 88–91 (1994)
19. Shannon, C.E.: A mathematical theory of communication. Bell Syst. Tech. J. **27**(3), 379–423 (1948)
20. Whitney, L.: Billions of passwords leaked online from past data breaches. https://www.techrepublic.com/article/billions-of-passwords-leaked-online-from-past-data-breaches/
21. Woods, N., Siponen, M.T.: Improving password memorability, while not inconveniencing the user. Int. J. Hum Comput Stud. **128**, 61–71 (2019)
22. Woollacott, E.: Cybersecurity incident at ubisoft disrupts operations, forces company-wide password reset. http://portswigger.net/daily-swig/cybersecurity-incident-at-ubisoft-disrupts-operations-forces-company-wide-password-reset
23. Yan, J.J., Blackwell, A.F., Anderson, R.J., Grant, A.: Password memorability and security: empirical results. IEEE Secur. Priv. **2**(5), 25–31 (2004)

Towards Evaluating the Security of Human Computable Passwords Using Neural Networks

Issei Murata[✉], Pengju He, Yujie Gu, and Kouichi Sakurai

Graduate School of Information Science and Electrical Engineering, Kyushu University, Fukuoka, Japan
murata.issei.662@s.kyushu-u.ac.jp, {gu,sakurai}@inf.kyushu-u.ac.jp

Abstract. Passwords are playing a major role for authentication in our daily life. However contemporary passwords are typically either difficult to remember or vulnerable to various attacks. In 2017, Blocki, Blum, Datta and Vempala introduced the concept of human computable passwords as a promising authentication method. The fundamental concerns for designing human computable passwords are their usability and security. So far, the security evaluation on human computable passwords authentication schemes is mainly based on complexity-theoretic analysis. In this paper, we initially investigate the security of human computable passwords against neural network-based adversarial attacks. Specifically, we employ the typical multilayer perceptron (MLP) model to attempt to attack the human computable passwords authentication scheme proposed by Blocki-Blum-Datta-Vempala. We present implementation results and the corresponding analysis as well. Our results imply that it is possible for an MLP to learn a simple function, but is difficult for an MLP to learn piecewise functions well.

Keywords: Human computable password · Neural network · Multilayer perceptron

1 Introduction

With the development of Internets and infrastructure of networks, people worldwide get their accounts on various websites which could offer services for them. Nowadays, passwords are the mainstream authentication technology for accessing the accounts and playing a major role in our daily life. Since each website usually requires one account, it is quite challenging for users to manage all of their accounts. For instance, to avoid resetting passwords frequently, users often adopt insecure passwords or adopt same passwords on different accounts [1–5,11,12].

To develop more promising authentication schemes, Blocki, Blum, Datta and Vempala proposed the concept of human computable passwords, which aims to explore a trade-off between the usability regarding human efforts and the security against various attacks [2]. They proposed a model for human-computable password based on images which is briefly described as follows. First, the user

© Springer Nature Switzerland AG 2023
I. You and T.-Y. Youn (Eds.): WISA 2022, LNCS 13720, pp. 303–312, 2023.
https://doi.org/10.1007/978-3-031-25659-2_22

memorizes a secret mapping $\sigma : Imgs \rightarrow [d]$ from a set $Imgs$ of n images to numbers $[d] := \{0, 1, \ldots, d-1\}$ and sets a human computable (hash) function $f : [d]^k \rightarrow [d]$ in advance. When the user attempts to access, the system will generate a series of challenges, where each challenge consists of k randomly selected images $I_1, \ldots, I_k$ from $Imgs$, to the user, and the user needs to calculate a response $(f \circ \sigma)(I_1, \ldots, I_k)$ using the mapping σ and the function f for complete the authorization. A detailed description is referred to Sect. 3.

The two main concerns for human computable passwords are usability and security, which are both closely related to the setting of n, k, d, σ and f in the Blocki-Blum-Datta-Vempala model [2]. The usability has been investigated in the literature, see [2,6–8,11] for example. In this paper, we mainly focus on the security viewpoint.

To evaluate the security of Blocki-Blum-Datta-Vempala human computable passwords, the existing research has attempted to recover the secret mapping σ based on a collection of sample pairs of (challenge, response). In [2], Blocki, Blum, Datta and Vempala exploited CSP solver to decipher (i.e. exactly recover) the secret mapping σ, see also [3,6]. Accordingly, the security evaluation on human computable passwords mainly relies on the complexity theory so far.

In this paper, we initially consider the security evaluation for human computable passwords based on neural networks. It is worth noting that in contrast with the security regarding the *exact recovery* of secret mapping σ in the previous work, we consider the security regarding the *approximation* of the secret mapping σ here. It is quite meaningful in the practical application since once the password could be correctly guessed with high probability, the authentication system is not secure any more. Concretely, we consider the adversarial attacks for human computable passwords based on the typical multilayer perceptron (MLP) [8]. In principle, the MLP is employed to learn the composition of the secret mapping σ and the human computable function f (in the black-box setting). We provide the Python implementation results and a corresponding analysis. Notably, our results imply that using simple MLP model, it is possible to learn a simple (non-smooth) function, while is difficult to learn a (sophisticated) piecewise function.

The remainder of this paper is organized as follows. Section 2 describes the Bloki-Blum-Datta-Vempala model and reviews the security evaluation of human computable password with CSP solver. Section 3 presents our attack model based on neural networks. Section 4 shows the implementation results. Section 5 presents an analysis according to the simulation results. Finally, Sect. 6 presents the conclusion of the paper and future work.

2   Bloki-Blum-Datta-Vempala Model

2.1   General Setting

In [2], Blocki, Blum, Datta, and Vempala proposed a generic model for human computable password management schemes. In this setting, users construct their (dynamic) passwords by computing responses with respect to challenges. In particular, the *human computable* item refers to simple modular arithmetic operations (e.g. addition modulo 10) based on user-stored secrets. Generally speaking, in the Bloki-Blum-Datta-Vempala model, users only need to memorize a *secret* mapping $\sigma : Imgs \to \mathbb{Z}_d$, where $Imgs$ is a collection of n images, and a human computable (hash) function $f : \mathbb{Z}_d^k \to \mathbb{Z}_d$.

The user authenticates by responding to a series of single-digit challenges, where each challenge consists of k images and is responded by a single digit. Let C denote a challenge and $(f \circ \sigma)(C) = f(\sigma(C))$ denote the corresponding response to C. In an authentication scheme, the user needs to respond to λ single-digit challenges $C_1, C_2, \ldots, C_\lambda$, where λ is a positive integer. Accordingly, the user obtains a λ-digit password $f(\sigma(C_1)), f(\sigma(C_2)), \ldots, f(\sigma(C_\lambda))$.

2.2 Candidate Functions

In this section, we present the specific mapping σ and the candidate function f as in [2]. Let $d = 10$ (notice that $d > 10$ would be difficult for humans to compute and remember) in the secret mapping $\sigma : Imgs \to \mathbb{Z}_d$. Accordingly, for the image I_i we have

$$\sigma(I_i) = x_i \text{ for some } x_i \in [10].$$

For simplicity, the image I_i is also written as image i. The total number of images in $Imgs$ is n, and the user needs to memorize a number for each image accordingly. Figure 1 illustrates an example of such mapping σ.

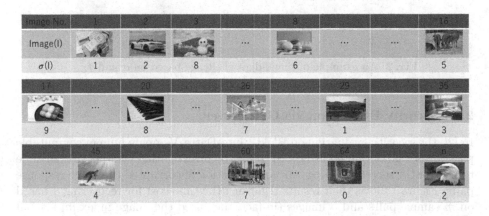

Fig. 1. An example of mapping σ

Next we show a specific candidate function f as in [2]. For given integers $k_1 > 0$ and $k_2 > 0$, define the function $f_{k_1,k_2} : \mathbb{Z}_{10}^{10+k_1+k_2} \to \mathbb{Z}_{10}$ as follows.

$$f_{k_1,k_2}(x_0,\ldots,x_{9+k_1+k_2}) = x_j + \sum_{i=10+k_1}^{9+k_1+k_2} x_i \mod 10 \tag{1}$$

where

$$j = \sum_{i=10}^{9+k_1} x_i \mod 10. \tag{2}$$

Now we introduce the single-digit challenge by considering the case when $k_1 = k_2 = 2$ (our experiments are also conducted under this setting). In this case, each single-digit challenge consists of $10 + k_1 + k_2 = 14$ images $I'_0,\ldots,I'_{13}$. The user computes a single-digit by using the secret mapping σ and the human computable function $f_{2,2}$, i.e. $f_{2,2}(\sigma(I'_0,\ldots,I'_{13}))$, as a response to the challenge.

A concrete example is shown in Fig. 2.

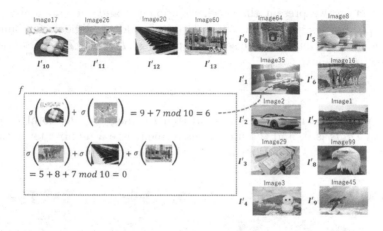

Fig. 2. An example of single-digit challenge based on σ and $f_{2,2}$

2.3   Security Evaluation via CSP Solver

In [2], the security evaluation on Bloki-Blum-Datta-Vempala human computable passwords was conducted using CSP solver by investigating whether it is possible to recover the secret mapping σ from a collection of corrupted challenge-response pairs. Figure 3 shows their results regarding the time cost for recovering σ based on m sample pairs and n images (in fact, they used the image index $[n]$ instead of the real images). If the solver fails to recover the mapping σ within 2.5 days, (n, m) is marked as HARD, and for the case that the solver has not attempted yet, it is indicated as UNSOLVED.

	$m = 50$	$m = 100$	$m = 300$	$m = 500$	$m = 1000$	$m = 10000$
$n = 26$	23.5h	40min	4.5h	29min	10min	2min
$n = 30$	HARD	UNSOLVED	2.33h	35.5min	10min	20s
$n = 50$	HARD	HARD	HARD	HARD	UNSOLVED	7h
$n = 100$	HARD	HARD	HARD	HARD	HARD	UNSOLVED

Fig. 3. Evaluation by CSP solver [2]

3   Security Evaluation via Neural Networks

In this section, we propose the security evaluation on human computable passwords against neural network-based attacks. In contrast to the existing security evaluation regarding the *exact recovery* of secret mapping σ, we focus on the *approximation* of secret mapping σ (more precisely, the composition of secret mapping σ and human computable function f, in the black-box setting).

3.1   Learning Functions by Neural Networks

Neural networks could deal with predictive modeling and have numerous applications in artificial intelligence. It is also known that neural networks could approximate continuous functions well, see [8–10] for example. The *universal approximation theorem* states that a neural network with three layers can represent any continuous function (with negligible error) if the number of parameters per layer is sufficiently large. Also, the *approximation error rate* examines the effect of the number of parameters of the neural network. When the function to be represented is smooth, the mathematical results suggest that at most three layers of a neural network are sufficient. When the function is non-smooth, the approximation error rate of a neural network with five or more layers theoretically achieves the optimal value, while a neural network with a small number of layers or conventional methods before deep learning cannot achieve that rate. In other words, it can be expressed by increasing the number of layers to five or more.

Notice that the mappings considered in this paper are not continuous (i.e. non-smooth). Based on the above theoretical results, we know that the functions in this paper could be cracked (theoretically) by using neural networks with five or more layers, i.e., with at least three middle layers. Therefore, it would be interesting to find out the explicit (practical) neural networks which could achieve this goal.

3.2   Experimental Settings

In our experiment, the multilayer perceptron (MLP), a typical class of feedforward artificial neural network, will be exploited. Informally, a multilayer perceptron is a neural network that consists of multiple (simple) perceptrons connected together to form a multiple structure, where a simple perceptron has only one input layer and one output layer.

This paper aims to evaluate the security level of human computable passwords by exploring the question: *Is it possible to use MLPs to predict the challenge-response relationship?* In principle, it is equivalent to the approximation of the composite function $f \circ \sigma$.

The experimental settings are as follows.

(1) *Dataset*

The number of images is denoted by n. The dataset consists of a collection of (challenge, response) sample pairs, where each challenge is composed of 14 images indices from $[n]$ (i.e. "X0 to X13" in Table 1) and the corresponding response is an integer between $0 \sim 9$ (i.e. "Z" in Table 1). As shown in Table 1, each row is a (challenge, response) sample pair.

Table 1. The (challenge, response) sample pairs

single-digit challenge: 14 images indices														Ans
X0	X1	X2	X3	X4	X5	X6	X7	X8	X9	X10	11	X12	X13	Z
19	16	25	3	9	47	90	62	48	51	69	4	77	46	4
1	45	28	99	63	46	24	33	70	75	65	54	58	13	6

(2) *Model setting*

The dataset is divided into training and test data, and the training data is used to train the MLP. The input data in the MLP is the image indices (i.e. challenge), and the output data is the answer/response to the challenge. The number of input nodes is equal to the number of images in each challenge (here is 14 input nodes). The number of output nodes is 10, where each node represents a class (see Fig. 4 for example).

4   Experimental Results

In this section, we present the experimental results in terms of three different scenarios.

4.1   To Learn Function $f \circ \sigma$

The experiments are performed with $n = 26, 30, 50$, and 100. The results are shown in Table 2.

It can be seen that the prediction accuracy is around 10% regardless of the value of n, the middle functional layer, or the number of nodes.

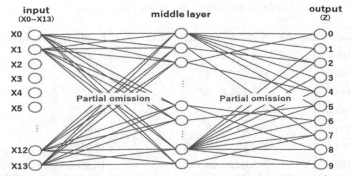

※ The number of middle layers is set to one here, but there can be more than one.

Fig. 4. An example of MLP model

Table 2. Prediction accuracy on function $f \circ \sigma$

Size of dataset	Number of middle layer node	Prediction accuracy n=26	Prediction accuracy n=30	Prediction accuracy n=50	Prediction accuracy n=100
1000	128,64,32	8.00%	9.75%	10.33%	8.00%
1000	128,64,32,16	9.00%	8.50%	11.33%	9.50%
1000	256,128,64,32	10.67%	8.50%	10.33%	8.00%
10000	128,64,32	10.17%	10.50%	9.80%	10.60%
10000	128,64,32,16	9.87%	8.60%	8.90%	9.05%
10000	256,128,64,32,16	9.80%	9.15%	10.17%	10.10%
100000	128,64,32,16	11.74%	10.13%	10.12%	9.91%
100000	256,128,64,32,16	10.45%	10.41%	9.96%	9.76%
100000	512,256,128,64,32,16	10.22%	10.32%	9.90%	10.07%

4.2 To Learn Function f

Based on Sect. 4.1, we would like to explore the reason why $f \circ \sigma$ is difficult to learn. Therefore we conduct experiments to see whether the function f could be learned by MLP or not. The dataset in this case is constructed by removing the effect of σ. The experimental results are shown in Table 3.

As for the function f in Table 3, the MLP had a prediction accuracy of around 10% as well. We notice that the function f defined in (1) varies with different inputs and j from (2), which might be a factor of the difficulty of predicting f by MLPs. To be sure with it, we continue to conduct another experiment in Sect. 4.3.

4.3 To Learn Function g

In this case, we would like to conduct experiment on a function whose formula does not change with respect to inputs. To that end, a new function g is defined as follows.

Table 3. Prediction accuracy on function f

Size of dataset	Number of middle layer node	Prediction accuracy
1000	128,64,32	9.00%
1000	128,64,32,16	11.00%
1000	256,128,64,32	8.50%
10000	128,64,32	9.65%
10000	128,64,32,16	9.05%
10000	256,128,64,32,16	10.70%
100000	128,64,32,16	10.26%
100000	256,128,64,32,16	10.23%
100000	512,256,128,64,32,16	12.97%

$$g(x_0, x_1, \ldots, x_{13}) = x_i + x_{12} + x_{13} \quad \text{mod } 10 \tag{3}$$

where i is a fixed index (see Table 4 as well). Here, function g is a simplified version of function f and is a human computable function. The reason for evaluating the function g is to measure the security level of simple human computable functions with respect to MLP based attacks.

Table 4. Prediction accuracy on function g

Size of dataset	Number of middle layer node	Prediction accuracy $g = x_2 + x_{12} + x_{13}$	Prediction accuracy $g = x_5 + x_{12} + x_{13}$
1000	128,64,32	10.00%	10.50%
1000	128,64,32,16	8.00%	10.50%
1000	256,128,64,32	11.50%	11.50%
10000	128,64,32	78.96%	86.30%
10000	128,64,32,16	74.20%	61.55%
10000	256,128,64,32,16	54.00%	49.25%
100000	128,64,32,16	99.97%	99.38%
100000	256,128,64,32,16	99.97%	99.99%

The experimental results are shown in Table 4. In this case, when the number of data is 10000, the prediction accuracy is around 80%, which is almost 70% higher than the prediction accuracy of function f. It was also found to be 99% predictable when the number of data is 100000.

5   Analysis

In this section we perform an analysis according to the experiments in Sect. 4. Notice that f in (1) is in fact a piecewise function as below.

$$F_{f,k_1,k_2}(x_0,\ldots,x_{9+k_1+k_2}) = \left\{ x_j + \sum_{i=10+k_1}^{9+k_1+k_2} x_i \mod 10 \mid j \in [10] \right\}.$$

In particular, when $k_1 = k_2 = 2$,

$$F_{f,2,2}(x_0,\ldots,x_{13}) = \begin{cases} x_0 + x_{12} + x_{13} \,(\text{mod}\,10), & \text{if } x_{10} + x_{11} \equiv 0 \,(\text{mod}\,10) \\ x_1 + x_{12} + x_{13} \,(\text{mod}\,10), & \text{if } x_{10} + x_{11} \equiv 1 \,(\text{mod}\,10) \\ \vdots & \\ x_9 + x_{12} + x_{13} \,(\text{mod}\,10), & \text{if } x_{10} + x_{11} \equiv 9 \,(\text{mod}\,10) \end{cases}$$

$$(4)$$

The experimental results show that it is possible (see Sect. 4.3) for MLPs to learn a (one-level) piecewise/non-smooth function $g(\cdot)$ in (3), while it seems difficult (see Sects. 4.1 and 4.2) for a simple MLP to learn a (two-level) piecewise function $F(\cdot)$ in (4) well.

6   Conclusion and Future Work

In this paper we investigated the security of human computable passwords against neural network-based adversarial attacks. The experimental results imply that the non-smooth functions $f \circ \sigma$ and f are difficult to learn using a simple MLP, while simple piecewise functions such as function g can be learned well by MLPs. In other words, human computable passwords would be insecure when a simple (non-smooth) function is used.

As a future work, it is of interest to explore more on using MLPs and other neural network models to attack the human computable passwords authentication schemes in order to evaluate its security against neural network-based attacks and to build more secure passwords systems for practical applications. In addition, it is also interesting to investigate the case when the training dataset is small, since the number of leaked samples is usually assumed to be not too large in the practical setting.

Acknowledgement. The last author, Kouichi Sakurai, is grateful to Support Center for Advanced Telecommunications Technology Research (SCAT) for their academic support on this research.

References

1. Guan, Y., Zhang, Y., Chen, L., Bian, K.: A neural attack model for cracking passwords in adversarial environments. In: IEEE/CIC International Conference on Communications in China (ICCC), pp. 183–188 (2019)

2. Blocki, J., Blum, M., Datta, A., Vempala, S.: Towards human computable passwords. In: Innovations in Theoretical Computer Science (ITCS), pp. 10:1–10:47 (2017)
3. Blum, M., Vempala, S.: The complexity of human computation via a concrete model with an application to passwords. In: Proceedings of the National Academy of Sciences of the USA (PNAS), vol. 117, pp. 9208–9215 (2020)
4. Rosenfeld, E., Vempala, S., Blum, M.: Human-usable password schemas: Beyond information-theoretic security. arXiv:1906.00029 (2019)
5. Samadi, S., Vempala, S., Kalai, A.: Usability of humanly computable passwords. In: 6th AAAI Conference on Human Computation and Crowdsourcing (HCOMP), pp. 174–183 (2018)
6. Blum, M., Vempala, S.: Publishable humanly usable secure password creation schemas. In: 3rd AAAI Conference on Human Computation and Crowdsourcing (HCOMP), pp. 32–41 (2015)
7. Blocki, J., Komanduri, S., Cranor, L., Datta, A.: Spaced repetition and mnemonics enable recall of multiple strong passwords. In: 22nd Annual Network and Distributed System Security Symposium (NDSS), San Diego, California, USA (2015)
8. Taud, H., Mas, J.F.: Multilayer perceptron (MLP). In: Camacho Olmedo, M.T., Paegelow, M., Mas, J.-F., Escobar, F. (eds.) Geomatic Approaches for Modeling Land Change Scenarios. LNGC, pp. 451–455. Springer, Cham (2018). https://doi.org/10.1007/978-3-319-60801-3_27
9. Belkin, M., Hsu, D., Ma, S., Mandal, S.: Reconciling modern machine learning practice and the classical bias-variance trade-off. In: Proceedings of the National Academy of Sciences (PNAS), **166**, 15849–15854 (2019)
10. Rotskoff, G., Vanden-Eijnden, E.: Neural networks as interacting particle systems: asymptotic convexity of the loss landscape and universal scaling of the approximation error. arXiv: 1805.00915 (2018)
11. Blocki, J., Blum, M., Datta, A.: Naturally rehearsing passwords. In: Sako, K., Sarkar, P. (eds.) ASIACRYPT 2013. LNCS, vol. 8270, pp. 361–380. Springer, Heidelberg (2013). https://doi.org/10.1007/978-3-642-42045-0_19
12. Yampolskiy, R.: Unexplainability and incomprehensibility of artificial intelligence. J. Artif. Intell. Conscious. **7**, 277–291 (2020)

Markov Decision Process for Automatic Cyber Defense

Xiaofan Zhou[1], Simon Yusuf Enoch[2,3]([envelope]) [iD], and Dong Seong Kim[1] [iD]

[1] The University of Queensland, St Lucia, QLD 4072, Australia
dan.kim@uq.edu.au
[2] Federal University, Kashere, Gombe State, Nigeria
simonpuks@gmail.com
[3] Pen Resource University, Gombe, Gombe State, Nigeria
simon.enoch@pru.edu.ng

Abstract. It is challenging for a security analyst to detect or defend against cyber-attacks. Moreover, traditional defense deployment methods require the security analyst to manually enforce the defenses in the presence of uncertainties about the defense to deploy. As a result, it is essential to develop an automated and resilient defense deployment mechanism to thwart the new generation of attacks. In this paper, we propose a framework based on Markov Decision Process (MDP) and Q-learning to automatically generate optimal defense solutions for networked system states. The framework consists of four phases namely; the model initialization phase, model generation phase, Q-learning phase, and the conclusion phase. The proposed model collects real network information as inputs and then builds them into structural data. We implement a Q-learning process in the model to learn the quality of a defense action in a particular state. To investigate the feasibility of the proposed model, we perform simulation experiments and the result reveals that the model can reduce the risk of network systems from cyber attacks. Furthermore, the experiment shows that the model has shown a certain level of flexibility when different parameters are used for Q-learning.

Keywords: Automation · Cyber-attacks · Defense · Deep learning · Reinforcement learning · Machine learning · Q-learning

1 Introduction

Cyber-attacks have grown over the past few years to become more effective. In particular, cyber-criminals are now incorporating artificial intelligence (AI) to power cyber-attacks (e.g., deep locker [13]) and to outsmart conventional defense mechanisms using various approaches [1,8,11]. For instance, a group of researchers at McAfee [9] in their 2020 threat prediction report have predicted the potential raise of less-skilled attackers to become more powerful to create and weaponize deepfake content. In addition, they have predicted that cyber-criminals will use AI to produce convincing real data capable of bypassing many user authentication mechanisms. Besides, the current state-of-the-art

© Springer Nature Switzerland AG 2023
I. You and T.-Y. Youn (Eds.): WISA 2022, LNCS 13720, pp. 313–329, 2023.
https://doi.org/10.1007/978-3-031-25659-2_23

defense enforcement methods require the security expert to manually deploy cyber-defenses, thus faced with uncertainties about the best countermeasures to enforce in order to achieve optimal security.

To address these challenges, we propose a novel approach to automatically select and deploy cyber defense by formulating Markov Decision Process (MDP) that reflects both attack and defense scenarios. Specifically, we propose an automatic MDP modeling-based approach to automate defense deployment and selection using a Q-learning model (A Q-learning is a reinforcement learning policy that finds the next best action, given a current state). Here, we use the Q-learning model with the MDP framework to learn the quality of a defense action in the states. The proposed framework is divided into four phases; model initialization, model generation phase, Q-learning phase, and the conclusion phase. The model initialization phase takes a real network situation as the input and converts it into structured data; the model generation phase generates all the possible states for the MDP model using a breadth-first search algorithm; the Q-learning phase implements a Q-learning iteration which trains the model to learn the space and update the quality for each state-action pair, and the conclusion phase searches for the optimal solutions using the Q-table trained after the previous phase. The focus of this paper is to use an AI technique to automate cyber defense and thwart attacks. The main contributions of this paper are as follows:

- To design and implement an automation framework based on MDP and a deep learning algorithm for the automatic cyber defense of networked systems.
- To collect real network data and generate an MDP structure model based on the real data.
- To develop a Q-learning model which can train itself and generate an optimal defense solution.
- To build a testbed and to demonstrate the usability and applicability of the proposed framework based on our framework.

The rest of the paper is organized as follows. Section 2 provides the related work on defense automation based on different approaches. Our proposed MDP-based framework model is presented in Sect. 3. In Sect. 4, we provide the experimental setup and analysis of the obtained results. We conclude the paper in Sect. 5.

2   Related Work

In this section, we briefly survey related work on defense automation for both the traditional defense and AI-based approaches.

Ray et al. [12] proposed a framework based on UML-based use cases, statechart diagrams, and XML to show attacker, attack actions, and the possible defense method. This work is still theoretical. Applebaum et al. [2] developed a practical framework based on MITRE Adversarial Tactics, Techniques, and Common Knowledge (ATT&CK) to test for weaknesses and train defenders. In their work, they used classical planning, Markov decision processes, and Monte

Carlo simulations to plan attack scenarios and to proactively move through the entire target networked systems searching for weakness and training the defenders on possible defenses to deploy.

The authors in [7] presented a framework for automating threat response based on a machine learning approach. Also, Noor *et al.* [10] presented a framework for data breaches based on semantic analysis of attacker's attack patterns from a collection of threats. The focus of these papers is different from our work, as they have focused on automating threat responses from a given repository, while our proposed automation framework is based on simulation of real networks.

Zheng and Namin [14] presented a defense strategy against Distributed Denial-of-Service (DDoS) in a Software-Defined Networking (SDN) using Markov Decision Process. The authors used three parameters to model the finite set states of the MDP model, including Flow Entry Size (F), Flow Queue Size (Q), and Transmitted Packets Count (T). The rewards function is related to these three parameters F, Q, and T. Each of them has been applied with different weight factors because they have different impacts on the network. Their results show that the model can keep the flow traffic optimized and detect potential DDoS attacks at an early stage. This work also showed that the model can control how the system makes a transition by adjusting the rewards weight factor. Also, Booker and Musman [3] presented a theoretical model-based automated cyber response system, where they frame a cyber response problem as a Partially Observable Markov Decision Problem (POMDP). In another work, the authors extended their work where the POMDP is used to frame automated reasoning for defensive cyber-response that searches for a policy that maps to system states, and probabilistic beliefs.

The authors in [15] proposed a Markov Decision Process to model Moving Target Defense with the interaction between the defend and attack sides. the paper uses four states (Normal, Targeted, Exploited, Breached) with three possible defense strategies (wait, defend, reset) to describe the model. It also uses the Bellman equation and value iteration method to find out the optimal policy for each state. Their result demonstrated how much impact the cost will have on the optimal policy and how that will help the defender to make better defense strategies. Other authors such as [4,5] developed a blue team framework that can perform cyber defense generation, defense enforcement, and security evaluation using a defined workflow. However, the work did not use any AI technique to enhance system attack learning or to thwart cyber attacks.

3   The Proposed Approach

In this section, we describe the proposed framework for automatic cyber defense based on MDP. The workflow of the framework comprises of four phases; Initialization Phase, Generation Phase, Q-learning Phase, and Conclusion Phase. We explain them in detail as follows.

3.1 Model Initialization Phase

The first phase is the initialization phase. During this phase, the program takes some real network situations as the inputs. These inputs need to be recognized and transformed into programmed data and later implemented into the MDP model. Here, the more detailed the description of the network situation is, the more complex the model will become.

3.2 Model Generation Phase

The second phase is the model generation phase. During this phase, the program will generate all the possible states for the MDP using the input data collection from the previous phase. To guarantee all the states will be visited in a well-designed order, it is necessary to have a traversal method (and the Breadth-First Search (BFS) algorithm will be used in this phase). Algorithm 1 and Algorithm 2 are used for the model generation, including the generation of the next state and the defense states.

Algorithm 1: Initialize States

```
queue.add(initialState);
while queue not empty do
    currentState ← queue.pop();
    states.add(currentState);
    GenerateNextState(currentState);
end
```

Algorithm 2: Generate Next State

```
/* Generate Attack States                                            */
if attackPath is None then
    for host ← adjacentHost do
        if !host.compromised & host.hasVulnerabilities then
            state ← AttackAction(host);
            queue.add(state);
        end
    end
end
else
    host ← GetNextHostOnPath();
    if !host.compromised & host.hasVulnerabilities then
        state ← AttackAction(host);
        queue.add(state);
    end
end
/* Generate Defense States                                           */
for action ← defenseActionsList do
    state ← DefenseAction(action);
    queue.add(state);
end
```

There are two major assumptions during the model generation phase. Firstly, the attacker can only attack the host which is next to a compromised host or public internet. For example, if the attacker attempted to compromise one host in the network, this is only possible to happen when there is at least one neighbor host compromised, or the host is directly connected to the public internet. Secondly, there is no value to patch vulnerabilities on a host that has already been compromised. Once a host is marked as compromised in the model, it is assumed that the data on the host has already been fully breached or the host has already been controlled.

After all the states have been generated, a transition table will be constructed. The table has size s by s where s is the number of all states. Each cell contains transition information between the row state and the column state, or none represents no transition available between two states. The transition information includes data such as action, success rate, reward after success transition, and reward after the fail transition.

3.3   Q-Learning Phase

The third phase is the Q-learning phase. During this phase, the model will keep learning the space until the iteration is over. Before starting the learning process, a Q-value table will need to be initialized with rows and possible actions, and columns as all generated states. Here, each q-value represents the "quality" of a state and action pair. During this learning phase, the Q-table will keep updating until it has reached the maximum iteration.

Four parameters are needed for the Q-learning; learning rate, epsilon, epochs, and gamma (γ) or discounted factor which is ranging from 0 to 1. The γ parameter decides how important the future rewards will be. It is also used to approximate the noise in future rewards. The Q-learning phase is described by Algorithm 3. In this phase, if gamma is close to one, it means the agent mostly considers the future rewards while being willing to delay the immediate rewards. If gamma is close to zero, it means the agent will mostly only consider the immediate rewards.

Algorithm 3: QLearningTrain

Input: gamma, lrnRate, epsilon, maxEpochs;
for *i in range(maxEpochs)* **do**
  currS ← 0;
  while *True* **do**
    /* Decide to explor or exploit   */
    if *random.uniform(0, 1) < epsilon* **then**
      action ← GetRandomNextAction(currS);
    else
      action ← GetMaxAction(currS);
    nextS = GetStateFromAction(action);
    /* Finish if no following state   */
    if *nextS is None* **then**
      break;
    /* Whether the action is successful or fail   */
    if *random.uniform(0, 1) < trans[currS][nextS].rate* **then**
      reward ← rewards[currS][nextS].success;
    else
      reward ← rewards[currS][nextS].fail;
      nextS ← currentS;
    nextA ← GetMaxNextAction(nextS);
    futureQ ← QTable[nextS][nextA];
    /* Update Q Table   */
    QTable[currS][action] ← QValueCalculation();
    currS ← nextS;

Equation (1) shows the detail calculation for the function *QValueCalculation()*.

$$Q(s,a) = ((1 - \alpha) * Q(s,a)) + (\alpha * (reward + (\gamma * Q(s',a')))) \tag{1}$$

Here, the Q-learning needs to make sure every q-value has been updated with sufficient times to reflect the actual quality. The agent can increase the number of iterations (epochs) to increase the overall updated times. The agent can also adjust the epsilon to balance between exploration and exploitation.

3.4   Conclusion Phase

After the Q-learning process has been completed and the Q-table has finished its updates, the process will enter the conclusion phase. The main task in this phase is to find the optimal solution(s) for the current network state.

4   Experimental Setup

In this section, we use a real network to illustrate the framework used for the attack and defense scenarios.

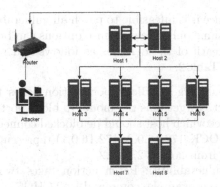

Fig. 1. Real network structure

The Network and Attack Model: The network structure is shown in Fig. 1. The network consists of 8 hosts, named host 1 - host 8. The network has a router that controls access between the networked hosts. Hosts in the network have vulnerabilities that may or may not be patchable. Table 1 shows the vulnerabilities of each host. In the Table, we use V_i to denote vulnerability ID, CVSS Score for Common Vulnerability and Scoring System Base Score, and Patch cost for the cost of patching vulnerabilities. The CVSS score is based on the severity scores provided by National Vulnerability Database [6], and we assume the patch cost value. We assume an attacker is located outside the network. The attacker is trying to compromise the host in the internal network. The attacker can directly connect to host 1 and host 2.

In our model, we represent the connections between hosts with links. For example, the hosts (h_i) information is going to be recorded as a list such as $[h_1, h_2, ...,h_n]$, and links will be represented as $[(h_1, h_2), (h_2, h_1), (h_1, h_3) ...]$. In a real situation, the network connections between two hosts are not always bi-directional. It is possible for a host to stop receiving packages from another host while it is still able to send packages to that host. Therefore, all the links recorded in the program are uni-directional.

Table 1. Hosts and vulnerabilities information

Host address	Vulnerability ID	CVSS score	Patch cost
172.16.0.1	V_1	4.3	8.0
172.16.0.2	V_2	2.1	5.0
172.16.0.3	V_3	10.0	6.5
172.16.0.4	V_4	4.3	3.5
172.16.0.5	V_5	7.5	4.5
172.16.0.6	V_6	8.8	5.0
172.16.0.7	V_7	8.8	6.0
172.16.0.8	V_8	6.1	7.0

Defense Model: Since it is infeasible to patch all vulnerabilities in real network environments, we assume only a few defense options can be selected for possible defense. We explain each of the defenses as follows and we show the available defense strategies in Table 2.

- BLOCK(target, sub-target): Block port action takes two parameters, target, and sub-target. Target tells the model to block port on which host, while sub-target indicates which host should be blocked connection from. For example, command BLOCK(172.16.0.2, 172.16.0.1) represents the host 172.16.0.1 should block port from host 172.16.0.2.
- PATCH(target, vulnerability): Patch action takes two parameters, target, and vulnerability. For example, command PATCH(172.16.0.3, V3) represents patching vulnerability V3 on host 172.16.0.3.

Table 2. Available defenses options

Defenses ID	Defense detail
D1	Block port to Router on 172.16.0.1
D2	Patch V7 on 172.16.0.7
D3	Block port to Router on 172.16.0.2
D4	Block port to 172.16.0.7 on 172.16.0.3
D5	Patch V4 on 172.16.0.4
D6	Patch V6 on 172.16.0.6

4.1 Results and Analysis

In this section, we use the network scenario described to illustrate the phases of the framework with their results.

Initialization Phase. One of the features and an MDP-based model assumes that the environment is fully observable and known by the agent. In this phase, the hosts and vulnerabilities are collected and provided as input to the model, it is presumed that the data collected have covered all the hosts and vulnerabilities in the space. For this experiment, the following network data were collected:

- Host Address: The IP address for the host. This data is treated as the identifier for each host in the model.
- CVSS Score: This value is collected from NVD. The number has a range from 0 to 10. The higher the number, the more severe the vulnerability is when it is compromised by attackers. This number will be used as a negative offset in the model's rewards calculation for state transition, particularly for an "attack" transition.
- Vulnerability ID: is an identifier for each vulnerability. Hosts can have more than one vulnerability.
- Patch Cost: is a number that represents the total cost of patching the vulnerability on the host. The number has a range from 0 to 10. For example, the cost of patching V_1 is 8.0 and the cost of patching V_3 is 6.5. The number will be used as a negative offset in the model's rewards calculation for state transition, particularly for a "patch" transition.

Attack Path is an optional input for the model, it decides whether the model is trying to solve a more particular problem or a wide-ranged problem. If the attack path is given, the attacker will only attack the host which is on the path. If the attack path is not specified in the model, the model will assume the attacker will attack any feasible host for the attacker to attack. The attack patch is an important element during the model generation phase. For this experiment, the following attack path (Fig. 2) is used:

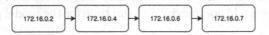

Fig. 2. The attack path

Model Generation Phase. Figure 3 shows how the BFS algorithm starts exploring the space from its root node, which corresponds to the initial state in the model. It explores the next level of states using all possible attack and defense actions. There are four possible actions to perform in the initial state in the figure, and thus it expands its branches to those four states. The algorithm will finish exploring all of the neighbor states at the same level before moving to the next depth level.

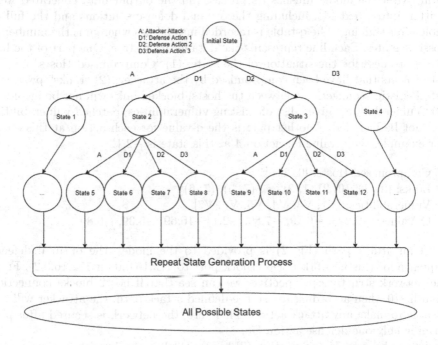

Fig. 3. State generation diagram

Each node in the BFS exploration tree will be visited only once, however it is still possible for two nodes to have the same state. This is because doing different actions in a different sequence is possible to result in the same state. Therefore, it is necessary to check duplications before adding the node to the state set in the MDP model.

Here, the attack path is an important element during the exploration of the BFS algorithm. If the attack path is not specified, the algorithm assumes the attacker will attack any feasible host (i.e., the host being attacked is adjacent to a compromised host and the host has at least one vulnerability.) Not specifying the attack path will add complexity and run time for the model generation phase.

Q-Learning Phase. In this phase, the Q-Value Table shown in Fig. 4 is initialized. Initially, the Q values in the cells are all zero. Each Q-value represents the "quality" of a state and action pair.

The parameters for Q-learning iteration is listed as follows:

- γ (Discount Factor) : 0.9
- α (Learning Rate) : 0.1
- ϵ : 0.7
- epochs : 5000

For this simulation experiment, 1492 possible states have been generated in total. After the model finishes its process, all the output data generated were written into a text file, including the optimal defense solutions and the full q-table after training. The q-table is recorded into n lines where n is the number of possible states. Each line represents the data for each state. One part of the line is used to describe the situation of the state, (1) "Compromised Hosts" gives a list of hosts that have been compromised by the attacker; (2) "Links" provide a list of existing connections between the hosts, blocked links will not be included; (3) "Vulnerabilities" give a list of existing vulnerabilities, patched vulnerabilities will not be included. Another part is the q-value for each action at this state. For example, the q-value for action 4 at this state is -2.1.

Compromised Hosts: [0, 2, 6]
Links: [(0, 1), (0, 2),(1, 2), ..., (7, 5), (7, 6)]
Vulnerabilities: [V1, V3, V4, V5, V6, V7]
Q-Values: $-9.298, -6.19, -7.89, -2.1, -10.69, -5.39, -6.89$

If an attack path (Fig. 2) is provided to the model, the optimal defense sequence for this network is D3 (Block port to 172.16.0.0 on 172.16.0.2). From the network structure perspective, we can see that if host2 blocks connection from host0, then according to the pre-defined attack path, the attacker will not be able to make any attack action. Therefore, the network is secured after performing only one defense action-D3.

From the q-table perspective (Table 3), D3 has the largest q-value at the State0 (Initial State), so D3 is added to the output sequence. For State5 (the state after performing D3 at State0), the q-value for attack action is 0 which is larger than any other defense action. Therefore, the model concludes that there is no need to perform any defense actions, and the search ends.

Table 3. Q-Table for real network example with attack path (Partial)

State	Attack Action	D1	D2	D3	D4	D5	D6
State0 (Initial State)	−9.298	−6.19	−7.89	−2.1	−10.69	−5.39	−6.89
State5 (T(State0, D3) = State4)	0.0		−4.3	−6.0	0.0	−8.8	−3.5	−5.0

If the attack path is not provided to the model, the optimal defense sequence for this network is D3-D1. From the network structure perspective, if host1 and host2 both block connection from host0, then the rest of the network is fully protected because host1 and host2 are the only passes where the attack can proceed its attack. From the q-table perspective (Table 4), D3 has the largest q-value at the State0 (Initial State), so D3 is added to the output sequence. D1 has the largest q-value at State5 (Initial State), so D1 is then added to the output sequence. For State29 (the state after performing D1 at State5), the q-value for attack action is 0 which is larger than any other defense action.

Table 4. Q-Table for real network example without attack path (Partial)

State	Attack action	D1	D2	D3	D4	D5	D6
State0 (Initial State)	−9.298	−6.19	−9.296	−5.97	−12.363	−7.283	−8.274
State4 (T(State0, D3) = State5)	−5.33	−4.3	−9.411	None	−12.415	−7.203	−8.667
State29 (T(State5, D1) = State29)	0.0	0.0	−5.948	0.0	−8.622	−3.478	−4.946

The output result may significantly depend on the network situation, such as the cost of patching a vulnerability, the cost of blocking ports on a host, or the damage to a host after being attacked. For some network systems, blocking ports on host1 (D1) may result in further damage to the organization's service, because it not only blocks the attacker but also blocks all other normal users from accessing. In that case, the cost of D1 will be raised significantly, and as a result, the optimal defense sequence may not include D1. The model may choose other alternative defense strategies, such as patching vulnerabilities on host4 (D5), to minimize the damage.

Conclusion Phase. In this phase, all the q-values in the table are negative since the implementation of cyberdefense is a costly task. Either patching a vulnerability or host compromised puts a negative effect on the whole system. It is impossible to profit and earn positive rewards.

Finding the optimal strategy for one certain state can be achieved by looking at the corresponding q-value in the q-table. The larger the q-value is, the less damage the action will result. For example in Fig. 4, Action1 has the largest q-value in the State1 column, which means Action1 theoretically is the best action to take at State1. On the contrary, Action 4 is the worst action to take.

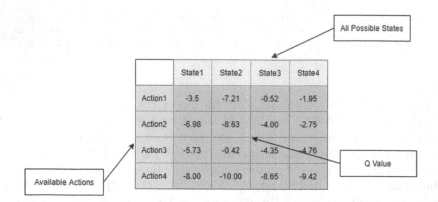

Fig. 4. Q-Value table

Finally, the model will look for a sequence of actions from the initial state. The model will keep searching through the q-table by using the following steps:

1. Find the best action in the initial state, add the action to the sequence;
2. Go to the consequence state with the action. For example, performing Action1 in State1 will result in State2.
3. Find the best action at that state and add the action to the sequence. Keep iterating step 2 & 3 until there is no following states, or the q-value shows there is no need to do any defense actions. (When the q-value of action attack is larger than any other defense actions, it means that performing any defense actions will be redundant and cause more damage to the system. That is when there is no need to do any defense actions).

After performing the above steps, the model will output a sequence of actions such as Action1-Action3-Action2. This action sequence is the solution that optimized the rewards, therefore minimizing the overall cost and damage to the network system. The initial state can be replaced by any state for this searching mechanism, which allows the agent to find an optimal solution in any situation in the network.

4.2   Effect of Q-Learning Parameters on Optimal Reward

Different parameters' values may have a significant effect on the output result of the model. In this section, Q-learning parameters such as discount factor, epsilon, and iterations are investigated. This section will assess their performance with different data, and a suitable combination of parameters should be concluded to maximize the overall performance of the model.

Fig. 5. Impact of discount factor on optimal reward

Discount Factor (γ) in Q-learning, $\gamma \in (0, 1)$, indicates the importance of the future rewards compared to the immediate rewards. If γ is larger, it means the agent considers the future rewards more and is willing to delay the immediate rewards. As the figures show, the optimal solution reward grows almost linearly as the discount factor increase. As the model digs deeper into space, the more certain it realizes that the optimal solution has a better effect on defending the network system. This explains why the damage becomes less when the discount factor increases.

Secondly, epsilon (ϵ) is a factor that balances exploration and exploitation. If ϵ is larger, the agent will have more possibility to explore the space (i.e. to choose action randomly). If ϵ is lesser, the agent will be more likely to choose the action with the highest q-value. Changing ϵ has a minor effect on the overall optimal rewards value, therefore in this experiment, the percentage improvement of the optimal solution's reward, compared to the rewards of not defending, is used as an index to test the performance of the model. The percentage is calculated by Eq. (2) (where OSR is Optimal Solution Reward, NDRs is No Defend Rewards).

$$Improvement\ Percentage = -\frac{OSR - NDRs}{NDRs} \qquad (2)$$

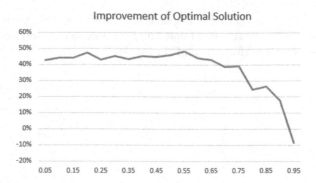

Fig. 6. Improvement of optimal solution with different epsilon

Since the rewards are all negative, so the result needs to be negated. Figure 6 shows the improvement almost stays at 40% to 50% level when ϵ is less than 0.75. However, after the ϵ gets larger than 0.75, the improvement drops substantially and even decreases below 0% (the optimal reward is less than the attack reward) at 0.95. This shows when ϵ gets larger than a certain point, the agent tends to explore more paths. As a result, the agent did not give much weight to the optimal solution, therefore, reducing the difference between every action.

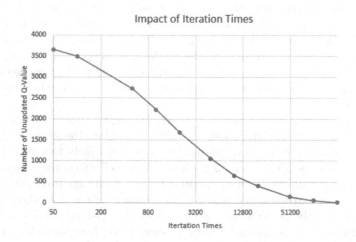

Fig. 7. Improvement of iteration times on the number of un-updated Q-value

Lastly, iteration times (epochs) represent the maximum number of iterations the Q-learning will iterate. As the iteration times increase, the overall quality and completeness of the output result are also increased. However, larger iteration times can also increase the run time for the model. Therefore, it is necessary to find a suitable number of iteration times that allows both a decent run time and an acceptable quality of the output results.

As Fig. 7 shows that the iteration times increase, the number of un-updated q-value decreases (Note that the x-axis is in log-scale). The un-updated q-value means the q-value in the q-table that has not been updated once. Since the q-table for the experiment has a size of 13594 q-values, likely, some of them are not updated during the process. The pattern of the graph is similar to a logarithm equation. When epochs are relatively small, the un-updated q-values decrease substantially. When epochs are relatively large, the un-updated q-values only decrease a small amount. That is because when there is more and more q-value being updated, the probability for the agent to reach an un-updated q-value becomes less.

Although the parameters for Q-learning can vary between different tasks, an appropriate range of those parameters has been concluded for a network defense problem.

- Discount Factor (γ): The experiment reveals that the larger the γ is, the more rewards will be received from the optimal solution. However, it is also not proper to weigh too much on the future rewards, since the immediate rewards still need to be considered in some cases. In summary, the experiment suggests a range of 0.8 to 0.9 for the discount factor.
- Epsilon (ϵ): The experiment shows that if ϵ increases over 0.75, the overall difference between the optimal solutions and other solutions will be reduced. Therefore, it will become hard to distinguish between a "good" and "bad" action. While if ϵ gets too small, the agent will be less likely to find alternative strategies that can further reduce the overall damage to the network system. As a result, the experiment suggests a range of 0.5 to 0.7 for the ϵ.
- Iteration Times (epochs): The experiments prove that as epochs increase, the overall quality and completeness of the output result is also increased. However, the efficiency of improving the result decreases, and the run time raises when epochs increase to a larger number. Therefore, the experiments suggest a range of 5000 to 10000 for the epochs.

4.3   Model Efficiency Experiments

In the area of cyber defense, algorithm efficiency is also a key element to determine whether the system can successfully defend against the attacker. If the attacker's efficiency is better than the defense side, the optimal solution output from the model may be no longer applicable to the environment.

The experiment uses a network with different numbers of hosts to test the efficiency of the model. Normally, if there are more hosts in the network, the model will become more complex and there will be more possible states to generate. As the state number increases, the complexity of training the model also increased.

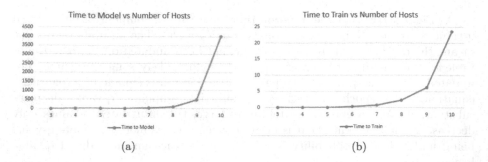

Fig. 8. Time efficiency for model generation

Figure 8 shows when the number of hosts is less than 8, the time to generate and the time to train the model does not increase much as the number of hosts increases. The time for model generation stays under 1 min and the time for training stays under 5 s. However, when the number of hosts is greater than 8, the time spent starts to grow exponentially. On the other hand, the time to train the model is relatively faster than the time to generate the model.

5   Conclusion and Future Work

In this paper, we have presented an MDP-based optimal solution model for cyber defense. The model is composed of four sequential phases. The model initialization phase takes some real network situation as the input and converts it into structured data; the model generation phase generates all the possible states for the MDP model using a breadth-first search algorithm; the Q-learning phase implements a Q-learning iteration which trains the model to learn the space and update the quality for each state-action pair; the conclusion phase searches for the optimal solutions using the q-table trained after the previous phase. Real network simulation experiments have been done to test the usability and functions of the model. The result demonstrates the model can reduce the attack impact on the network system from a cyber-attack, in either network structure perspective or q-table perspective. In the future, we plan to add more defense actions to the model. Another potential development for the model is to make it a POMDP (Partially observable Markov decision process). Besides, We plan to collect more usable and real data from a bigger network.

References

1. Alavizadeh, H., et al.: A survey on cyber situation awareness systems: framework, techniques, and insights. ACM Comput. Surv. (CSUR) **55**(5), 1–37 (2022)
2. Applebaum, A., Miller, D., Strom, B., Korban, C., Wolf, R.: Intelligent, Automated Red Team Emulation. In: Proceedings of the 32nd Annual Conference on Computer Security Applications, pp. 363–373 (2016)

3. Booker, L.B., Musman, S.A.: A model-based, decision-theoretic perspective on automated cyber response. arXiv preprint. arXiv:2002.08957 (2020)
4. Enoch, S.Y., Mendonça, J., Hong, J.B., Ge, M., Kim, D.S.: An integrated security hardening optimization for dynamic networks using security and availability modeling with multi-objective algorithm. Comput. Netw. **208**, 108864 (2022)
5. Enoch, S.Y., Moon, C.Y., Lee, D., Ahn, M.K., Kim, D.S.: A practical framework for cyber defense generation, enforcement and evaluation. Comput. Netw. **208**, 108878 (2022)
6. FIRST: CVSS v3.1: Specification Document. Forum of Incident Response and Security Teams (2019). https://www.first.org/cvss/v3.1/specification-document
7. Iqbal, Z., Anwar, Z.: SCERM-a novel framework for automated management of cyber threat response activities. Future Gener. Comput. Syst. **108**, 687–708 (2020)
8. Kaloudi, N., Li, J.: The AI-based cyber threat landscape: a survey. ACM Comput. Surv. (CSUR) **53**(1), 1–34 (2020)
9. McAfee: Mcafee labs 2020 threats predictions report (2019). https://www.mcafee.com/blogs/other-blogs/mcafee-labs/mcafee-labs-2020-threats-predictions-report/
10. Noor, U., Anwar, Z., Malik, A.W., Khan, S., Saleem, S.: A machine learning framework for investigating data breaches based on semantic analysis of adversary's attack patterns in threat intelligence repositories. Futur. Gener. Comput. Syst. **95**, 467–487 (2019)
11. Park, M., Seo, J., Han, J., Oh, H., Lee, K.: Situational awareness framework for threat intelligence measurement of android malware. JoWUA **9**(3), 25–38 (2018)
12. Ray, H.T., Vemuri, R., Kantubhukta, H.R.: Toward an automated attack model for red teams. IEEE Secur. Priv. **3**(4), 18–25 (2005)
13. Stoecklin, M.P.: Deeplocker: how AI can power a stealthy new breed of malware. Security Intell. (2018)
14. Zheng, J., Namin, A.S.: Defending sdn-based iot networks against ddos attacks using markov decision process. In: 2018 IEEE International Conference on Big Data (Big Data). IEEE (2018)
15. Zheng, J., Namin, A.S.: Markov decision process to enforce moving target defence policies. arXiv preprint. arXiv:1905.09222 (2019)

Influence Through Cyber Capacity Building: Network Analysis of Assistance, Cooperation, and Agreements Among ASEAN Plus Three Countries

Yu-kyung Kim⬤, Myong-hyun Go⬤, and Kyungho Lee(✉)⬤

Korea University, Seoul, Republic of Korea
{rladb1125,mhgo,kevinlee}@korea.ac.kr

Abstract. ASEAN is fast emerging as a key strategic region amidst the intensifying geopolitical competition between the United States and China. Important global actors, including China, Japan, and South Korea, have each formulated regional policies with strong ASEAN saliency. The ASEAN Plus Three are global ICT powerhouses that have developed strong economic and political ties with the region, and the Plus Three countries have leveraged their significant cyber capability to extend their influence in the region. This study evaluates the relative performances of the Plus Three countries' cyber outreach efforts to the region by visualizing the complex web of actors and cyber cooperation and assistance activities with network analysis tools and open source databases. The study finds that the Plus Three countries, despite the outward similarity in their respective regional strategies, are a study of contrasts, with one of them emerging as an influential yet silent power in the regional cyber diplomacy domain.

Keywords: Cybersecurity · ASEAN · ASEAN Plus Three · Cyber capacity building · Cyber cooperation

1 Introduction

The Association of Southeast Asian States (ASEAN) is emerging as a critical strategic bloc that stands at the confluence of China's expansive Digital Silk Road [29], its territorial ambitions in the South China Sea [28], as well as the United States' Indo-Pacific strategy that is set to counter both. The wide-ranging Asia-Pacific community is recognized as a neutral organization, with ASEAN playing an important role in international cybersecurity cooperation in the context of United States-China strategic competition [7]. ASEAN member states are important parts of the global ICT supply chain and partake in fast-growing export of ICT services [27]. Besides its strategic importance, ASEAN stands on its own merit. The combined ASEAN population is about 659 million and its

Supported by a grant-in-aid of HANWHA SYSTEMS.

I. You and T.-Y. Youn (Eds.): WISA 2022, LNCS 13720, pp. 330–343, 2023.
https://doi.org/10.1007/978-3-031-25659-2_24

Gross Domestic Product (GDP) is expected to exceed US$ 4 trillion by 2022, making it the world's seventh-largest market. ASEAN's digital economy has the potential to add US$ 1 trillion more to GDP over the next decade [10].

The three Northeast Asian powerhouses of South Korea, Japan, and China are deepening cooperation with ASEAN, including in the field of cyber diplomacy and security cooperation. Each of these three countries have formulated dedicated national strategies with strong ASEAN salience: South Korea with the "New Southern Policy", Japan with "Free and Open Indo-Pacific strategy", and China with the "Digital Silk Road strategy". South Korea has been pursuing improved cooperation with ASEAN through the New Southern Policy (NSP). The NSP was promulgated by President Moon in 2017 and has since strengthened relations with ASEAN in various fields, including people-to-people exchanges, economic exchanges, and diplomatic cooperation [14]. NSP can be considered as South Korea's effort to strengthen its influence with Southeast Asia at a time when the strategic competition between the US and China is intensifying in the wider Indo-Pacific region. Japan's ASEAN strategy is taking place within the framework of the Quadrilateral Security Dialogue, of the "Quad", composed of Australia, India and the United States. The former Prime Minister Shinzo Abe has been strengthening relations with ASEAN starting with bilateral policy dialogues with ASEAN in February 2009. Japan is perhaps the most consistent player when it comes to cybersecurity among the three Northeast Asian countries that compose the "Plus Three" in ASEAN Plus Three. It enacted the Basic Cybersecurity Act in 2014 and is consistently pursuing international cooperation policies with ASEAN, the European Union (EU), and the United States. China diverges from its Northeast Asian neighbors in that it aims to replace existing cyber norms with a new China-centric order. The "Digital Silk Road", part of the grander infrastructure building program, the Belt and Road Initiative, is China's main conduit to Southeast Asia. China is also making active use of international forums and organizations dedicated to forming international standards for cybersecurity such as the Shanghai Cooperation Organization (SCO), ASEAN Regional Forum (ARF), and traditional international organizations like the UN GGE and ITU.

Cybersecurity in particular has been an emerging and critical area for cooperation and assistance in the field of ASEAN member states, except for the members with advanced economies, lag significantly behind in terms of cyber capacity and readiness. ASEAN member states rank low in the cybersecurity rankings of the ITU's Global Cybersecurity Index and Estonia's National Cyber Security Index. Another challenge is the uneven cyber development within the regional bloc: according to the Global Cybersecurity Index 2018, Singapore, Malaysia, Brunei, Indonesia, Philippines, Thailand, and Vietnam have scores above 0.8, while Cambodia, Laos, and Myanmar score below 0.2 [8]. National Cyber Security Index shows similar intra-group inequality, with Singapore and Malaysia scoring more than 70 points while the average for the rest is estimated at around 28 points [1]. This capacity divide in the backdrop of rapidly rising demand for ICT technologies driven by economic development, population growth, and cross-border ICT connectivity susceptible to cyber threats [7], increase ASEAN member states' vulnerabilities in the cybersecurity area.

Thus, assistance for cyber capacity building is a critical dimension for improving ASEAN's cyber capacity, and it also creates opportunities for cooperation between ASEAN and major global and regional actors. These connections not only help the ASEAN member states, but also allow major global and regional actors to promote trade opportunities and expand influence in the region. There is certain competitive element among major actors jockeying for regional influence in Southeast Asia, which in turn can lead to the rapid expansion of assistance and cooperation.

In this study, we focus on three major actors: South Korea, Japan, and China. Unlike other major global actors operating in the region, these three East Asian countries are formally connected to ASEAN through the regional expansion mechanism called the ASEAN Plus Three [22,24]. The Plus Three countries have parlayed their competitive advantages in ICT industries to advance foreign policy goals. The confluence of foreign policy and cybersecurity deepens the complexity and facets of cooperation and assistance programs. It is in the cyberspace that the geopolitical characteristics based on technological power best manifest themselves in complex security and foreign policy strategies. It is through the intertwined links of cooperation and assistance that the performance of the regional strategies of respective powers can be evaluated. This study uses the network analysis techniques to first visualize and then quantify the relative influences of the three Northeast Asian actors among the ASEAN member countries.

2   Literature Review

Securing cyberspace is a fundamental prerequisite for ASEAN security and digital economies, which can be addressed by reviewing members' cybersecurity strategies and laws [23]. Southeast Asian countries' willingness to address cyber policy issues depends largely on their cyber maturity [25], on which cybersecurity strategies should be planned and implemented. The complex foreign policy relations and diplomatic cooperation among ASEAN member states echo the current competition for supremacy in cyberspace [15]. To understand how ASEAN member states are cooperating in cyberspace, we need to analyze cyberspace cooperation in ASEAN in depth. The existing literature has several shortcomings. Research in this field is limited as publicly available information on ASEAN cyber policies is scarce. In addition, it is difficult to easily analyze the cyber policy direction of independent ASEAN member states, because these nations do not openly discuss their policies. Fortunately, a few studies have compared and analyzed cyber policy strategies within regional organizations such as ASEAN as well as various cyber-agreements consultative bodies. Based on these studies, one can elucidate the state of affairs in ASEAN's cyber cooperation and agreements.

2.1   Assessing National Cybersecurity Capabilities

Evaluation of national cybersecurity capabilities is a precondition for cooperation in cyberspace. Unfortunately, the indices that measure cybersecurity capabilities are diverse and not integrated. Common evaluation metrics have never been formally discussed to assess the capabilities of cybersecurity. Indicators for cybersecurity assessment are developed by international organizations or think tanks and evaluated through policies, organizations, national strategies, and cooperation. Some indicators are compared through measurements between countries, while others provide exponential scores based on the indicators. We present three indicators that evaluate global cybersecurity capabilities that are considered in this study.

The Global Cybersecurity Index (GCI) compiles information on cybersecurity efforts by 193 ITU member states. GCI is evaluated according to five factors, legal, technical, organizational, capacity development, and cooperation, and summarized into 25 indicators. GCI evaluation methods consist of surveys, with questions about each of the five factors that are weighted as determined by a group of experts [8]. According to the 2018 GCI, the United Kingdom topped the global rankings with a score of 0.931, while Singapore ranked sixth with a score of 0.898. Besides Singapore, the global rankings of the ASEAN Plus Three countries in descending order were Malaysia (0.893, 8th), Japan (0.88, 14th), South Korea (0.873, 15th), China (0.828, 27th), Thailand (0.796, 35th), Indonesia (0.776, 41st), Vietnam (0.693, 50th), Philippines (0.643, 58th), Brunei (0.624, 64th), Laos (0.195, 120th), Myanmar (0.172, 128th), and Cambodia (0.161, 131st). Singapore's high ranking was due to its strong cybersecurity capabilities as ASEAN's cybersecurity hub and Malaysia scored high thanks to its focus on strategic publications and legal frameworks. In addition to GCI, this study uses data from Global Forum on Cyber Expertise (GFCE) and UNIDIR Cyber Policy Portal. Comprised of 115 members, the Global Forum on Cyber Expertise (GFCE) aims to strengthen the cyber capacity building ecosystem and international collaboration. The initiative participants consist of governments, international organizations, non-governmental organizations, private firms, and academia [16]. The GFCE combines various organizations to help coordinate efforts to build the prerequisites to norms adoption, implementation, and accountability. The outcome from the 2015 GFCE meeting in the Hague initiated a platform for policymakers, practitioners, and experts [18].

The UNIDIR Cyber Policy Portal is an interactive map of the global cyber policy environment and is published by the United Nations Institute for Disarmament Research (UNIDIR). In addition to various intergovernmental organizational and multilateral frameworks, UNIDIR provides cyber policy profiles of 193 UN member states [26]. Data from the UNIDIR Cyber Policy Portal is collected and linked to publicly available online sources. The advantage of the portals is high reliability of the information offered, since they consist of official documents distributed by national or intergovernmental organizations. As a result, salient studies on cyber governance make use of data in the UNIDIR Cyber Policy Portal: Solar et al. (2020) [20] examined military agencies dedicated to cybersecurity in emerging democracies, such as Argentina, Brazil, Indonesia, Philippines, and Mexico. Gramaglia et al. (2013) [6] studied the organization and structure responsible for cyber defense in NATO member states based on UNDIR data. The study analyzed cyber commands, military CERT, and special cyber units through the national profile of UNIDIR in 28 NATO member states.

3   Analysis of Cyber Cooperation and Assistance Activities Framework

ASEAN Plus Three countries have long emphasized cooperative relations in cybersecurity. But given the loose, non-binding nature of ASEAN agreements and policies, there is much leeway with which ASEAN member states enter into bilateral and multilateral cyber agreement and assistance programs. For instance, the Philippines accepted U.S. assistance to combat cyber terrorism in ASEAN [5], but Malaysia did not on the ground that it infringed upon its national sovereignty. Indonesia also refused U.S. assistance because other ASEAN member states pressured them to decline the aid. In other words, ASEAN's cybersecurity efforts show high degree of heterogeneity in terms of cooperation, agreement, and reaction to external influence. In contrast to the United States, China takes an approach that is more sensitive to the issue of sovereignty: it works with ASEAN on non-traditional security cooperation with focus on national sovereignty, which flexibly leads to various formal agreements [2]. This perspective embodies an approach to security that reflects the norms of authoritarian developmentalism.

ASEAN is characterized by a wide range of levels of economic development, which is fully reflected in the region's heterogeneity in terms of development of the ICT sector [25]. In other words, ASEAN member's efforts on cyber policy issues is hampered by differing levels of cyber maturity. Countries with high cyber development, such as Singapore, tend to push for developments in norms adoption, capacity-building measures, and other cyber-policy aspects. In contrast, countries such as Myanmar is more focused on establishing protective measures for its national infrastructure [25]. As a result, the direction of each member state's cybersecurity policy is associated with the maturity and complexity of the ICT sector as well as national strategies of each ASEAN member state. In turn, the level of maturity is associated with the degree of cybersecurity cooperation of each member state. By visualizing cyber assistance and agreements through the social network analysis, one can infer the effectiveness of the Plus Three countries' ASEAN strategies in the cyber domain. This paper will identify the relationship of cybersecurity assistance, cooperation, and agreements to find the characteristics of relationships of ASEAN member states with the Plus Three countries.

4   Method

This study is descriptive in nature and provides an intuitive understanding of the state of affairs in the ASEAN cyberspace through the use of network analysis visualization aids. To that end, the study employs data from the Global Forum on Cyber Expertise (GFCE) and UNIDIR. The data source is comprised of various aspects of the cyber cooperation on the topics of policies, strategies, cyber crime, and infrastructure protection. We extracted 43 entries from the GFCE dataset in which the recipient is one of the ASEAN Plus Three countries in the period between 2015 and 2021. We have also added information on international cybersecurity cooperation from the latest UNIDIR data, which provides profiles of the cyber policies of all 193 UN member states. This study compared and analyzed international and domestic cyber activities, framing the analysis based on these countries' latest cybersecurity strategy documents.

The collected datasets are classified into bilateral and multilateral assistance, cooperation, and agreements. There are differences among the three indicators of cybersecurity cooperation. Assistance and cooperation can encompass both governmental and non-governmental activities, whereas agreements in this study are limited to official state-to-state understandings. Assistance are dialogues and exercises that are related to cyber policy matters at the state level [26]. Agreements include treaties, conventions, and memoranda of understanding. Cybersecurity assistance relationships have to have at least one funding country ("Funder") and one recipient country "Receiver"), as well as information on financial assistance to be classified as such. Others that do not meet the definition of assistance are considered as cooperation relationships. Cooperation is defined as legally binding and non-legally binding dialogues, exercises, related to cyber policy matters that a state has entered into with another state. Cybersecurity agreement is defined as international treaties relating to cyber policy matters.

Based on the data compiled from information in GFCE and UNIDIR, we have visualized cybersecurity assistance, cooperation, and agreement relationships using social networks analysis techniques. Social network analysis is a powerful technique to model social structure [17]. In particular, the concept of structure as a relational construct presented by social network analysis helps us understand the structure of international relations in cyberspace. The analyses and graphs in this study were made using Polinode [13] social network analysis software. We used representative social network metrics such as "In Degree" and "Out Degree" for quantifying assistance and cooperation relations, and "Total Degree" for agreements of cybersecurity. "In Degree" represents relations where the country ("node" in network parlance) is the recipient of assistance or cooperation initiative. "Out Degree" is its opposite. Following the same logic, agreements are best measured by the "Total Degree" statistic given its reciprocal nature.

But the most salient metric in this study concerns the centrality of a country in the complex web of cyber policy relations. Literally, the level of influence will directly correspond to how central a country is in the relations network of assistance, cooperation, and agreements. The most straightforward of such network centrality is degree centrality, and is computed as the (raw or normalized) sum of connections that the node possesses. Nodes are state actors or in some instances international organizations, the sizes of which indicates the prominence of a particular node in the network. In addition to degree centrality, This study also uses relative centrality. Unlike degree centrality, relative centrality of a given node takes into consideration how central its neighboring nodes are [28], and are denoted by the relative size of the node. Thus, node sizes can be a more precise indicator of influence in a network than degree centrality. The width of the links between nodes indicated the frequency of cybersecurity-related agreement or assistance activities taking place between any given two countries. The "In Degree" and "Out Degree" are defined as in Eqs. (1) and (2).

$$indegree_{ik} = \sum_{i=1}^{N} Z_{ijk} = Z_{jk} \tag{1}$$

$$outdegree_{ik} = \sum_{i=1}^{N} Z_{ijk} = Z_{jk} \tag{2}$$

Equation (1) is the number of relationships from actor i to all other actors j. "indegree" is the number of relationships an actor i receives from all other actors j in the k network. Equation (2) is the number of relationships that actor i receives from all other actors j. "outdegree" is the number of relationships from actor i to all other actors j in the k network.

5   Findings

5.1   Assistance Relationship of Cybersecurity

The "in degree" and "out degree" metrics were used to quantify the Assistance Relationship of Cybersecurity through the collected dataset. Figure 1 illustrates Funder-Receiver assistance relations among the ASEAN Plus Three countries, which include South Korea, Japan, and China. Japan has the most significant influence in cybersecurity assistance (Node Size = 83.7, Total Degree = 195), followed by Singapore and South Korea. Indonesia, Myanmar, and Malaysia receive more assistance for cybersecurity than any other ASEAN member states, although the differences among the ASEAN recipient states are minimal (Indonesia Node Size = 20.7, Myanmar Node Size = 20.7, Malaysia Node Size = 20.3, Indonesia Total Degree = 38, Myanmar Total Degree = 38, Malaysia Total Degree = 37). Among ASEAN member states, Singapore and Thailand are the ones that contribute most in terms of assistance. Singapore has significant influence as a funder state (Node Size = 52, Total Degree = 116).

However, the conclusion that Japan is the most central player in providing assistance and thus gaining influence over ASEAN member states should be qualified by the fact that China has umbrella bilateral discussions with ASEAN member states, which are not limited to non-monetary cooperation. Often China's assistance agreements are operationalized through military agreements that include cybersecurity sub-section. When it comes to norm building, China prefers multilateral cybersecurity discussions at regional cooperation organizations such as the Shanghai Cooperation Organization (SCO) and ASEAN

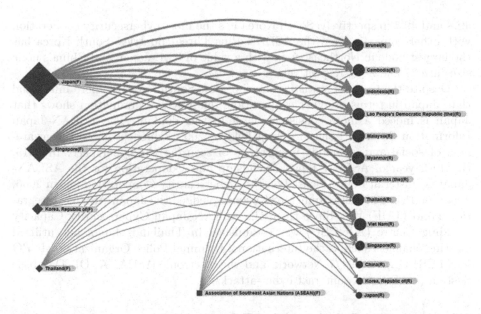

Fig. 1. Assistance relationship of cybersecurity. This figure illustrates a social network analysis of cybersecurity assistance relationships based on the GFCE data. The left column lists the Funder countries, and the right side consists of Receiver countries.

Regional Forum (ARF), in addition to working within the framework of international organizations such as the United Nations GGE and ITU [12]. China's influence in the region is prominent but difficult to quantify. Thus, the result in the assistance analysis should be considered in the light of the limitation inherent in the dataset used in the study.

5.2 Cybersecurity Cooperation Relationships

This section analyzes the cybersecurity cooperative relations among the ASEAN Plus Three countries in Fig. 2. This figure illustrates cybersecurity cooperation among the ASEAN Plus Three countries. Figure 2 shows South Korea, Japan, and China are actively engaged in cybersecurity exchanges and cooperation on bilateral or multilateral relations almost indiscriminately, which are manifested in the high degrees of connection observed: South Korea's total degree is 43, Japan's 42, and China's 41. Singapore is again the central player in cybersecurity cooperation within ASEAN, with the total degree of 81 if relations with the Plus Three countries are excluded from the sample. Despite this, a cluster composed of Vietnam, Myanmar, Cambodia, and Laos emerges from the cornucopia of cooperation relations. This likely reflects the more active cooperation formalized through the informal country grouping of Cambodia-Laos-Myanmar-Vietnam or CLMV group [3]. If all connections are considered, the most central ASEAN cyber cooperation players are Singapore and Thailand, which have node sizes of

49.8 and 49.7, respectively. South Korea has the most cybersecurity cooperation with other countries from the ASEAN Plus Three countries. South Korea has the largest node in Northeast Asia with a value of 39.1. Japan and China's node sizes are 37 and 34.6, respectively.

Despite the network statistics showing that South Korea is more influential than Japan in terms of cyber cooperation, qualitative examination shows that Japan is indeed a more consistent actor in this domain. The ASEAN-Japan Information Security Policy meeting held in 2009 helped promote the awareness of social and economic importance of securing the cyberspace. In 2013, the 40th year of ASEAN-Japan Friendship and Cooperation for the ASEAN-Japan Ministerial Policy focused on the Cybersecurity Cooperation [4]. In 2006, Japanese Prime Minister Junichiro Koizumi pledged the Japan-ASEAN Integration Fund (JAIF) [11]. Since then, the ASEAN-Japan Cybersecurity Capacity Building Centre (AJCCBC) was established in Thailand. Japan has utilized existing channels such as the International Criminal Police Organization (ICPO - INTERPOL), G8 24/7 Network, and the electronic ASEANAPOL Database System (e-ADS) to counteract cyber-attacks.

5.3   Agreement Relationship of Cybersecurity

Cybersecurity agreement strongly reflects the reality of cyberspace rather than aid or cooperation. Many national governments have cooperated informally by sharing cyber threat intelligence, investigating attacks or crimes, preventing or stopping harmful conduct, providing evidence, and arranging for the rendition of individuals to a requesting state [19]. But cybersecurity agreements are indicative of long term cooperation and partnership and provide useful foundation for continued cooperation in the future.

In this section we examined the cybersecurity agreements of the ASEAN countries. The cybersecurity agreements describe specific commitments that apply to the signatory state. Cybersecurity agreements have a stated goal to improve cybersecurity capability. Furthermore, Cybersecurity agreements can be multilateral. Figure 3 illustrates the relationship among ASEAN member states and the Plus Three countries denoted by cybersecurity agreements. Figure 3 shows the strong centrality that South Korea, Japan, and China have in the network. Compared to other ASEAN member states, South Korea is the most significant player with node size of 97.4 and total degree of 23. The result shows that the Plus Three countries formulate their cybersecurity strategies differently. South Korea not only has the most number of connections, i.e., agreements with other ASEAN and Plus Three countries, but the width of edges depicted show that South Korea has often multiple cyber agreements with the same country. Compared to Japan and China, South Korea shows strong relations with Indonesia, Malaysia, Philippines, Singapore, and Thailand, whereas Japan is more focused on Vietnam. Among the Plus Three countries, China differs from its other Northeast Asian peers in that it is more selective in its agreements, shown by China's focus on Indonesia and to a lesser extent, Vietnam. As in the assistance network, China exerts influence on certain ASEAN member states

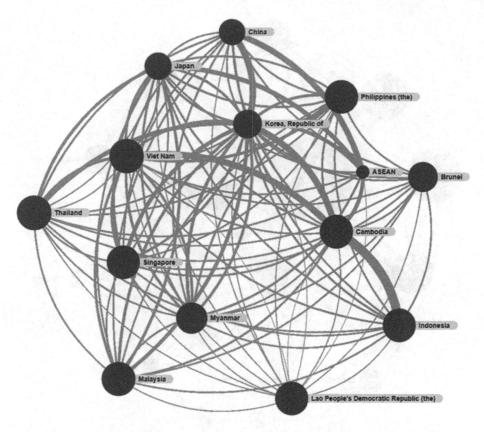

Fig. 2. Cybersecurity cooperation relationships. This figure results from a social network analysis of cybersecurity cooperation relationships based on GFCE data, UNIDIR, and open sources of each country.

with comprehensive agreements that incorporate cyber cooperation, but gauging their true impact is difficult. Singapore can be regarded as the hub in ASEAN member states, given its evenly distributed connection with ASEAN member states as well as the Plus Three countries.

5.4 Discussion

Our analysis shows that Singapore is the leader in terms of ASEAN's cybersecurity cooperation. Singapore is also active in cybersecurity assistance, although Thailand is also a significant player alongside Singapore within the regional group. While Singapore and Malaysia are active on the cybersecurity agreement front, other ASEAN member states like Thailand, have shown relatively low level of interest in engaging the Plus Three countries diplomatically. Singapore as a country with high cybersecurity capability, by definition promotes many activities such as declarations, conferences, and policy discussions. The preponderance of Singapore in the cooperative and diplomatic activities with ASEAN

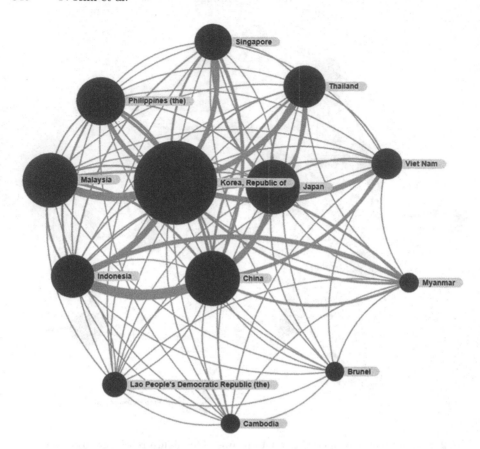

Fig. 3. Agreement relationship of cybersecurity. This figure results from a social network analysis of cybersecurity agreement relationships based on GFCE data, UNIDIR, and open sources of each country.

member states and Plus Three countries means that unless other members dispute its leading role, the directions of the cybersecurity strategies of ASEAN will be quietly but effectively shaped by Singapore's guiding hand.

We also rely on ITU's GCI 2018 and 2020 reports to identify potential relationships between cyber cooperation and cybersecurity capabilities. GCI calculates cybersecurity capability score based on the number of cybersecurity projects and policy documents. It denotes competence and preparedness, but not necessarily technological prowess. But our study shows that high competence in cybersecurity is correlated with high level of international cooperation. According to ITU's GCI 2020 [9], South Korea and Singapore ranked 4th with 98.52. Malaysia ranked 5th with 98.1, Japan 7th with 97.9, Indonesia 24th with 94.9, Vietnam 25th with 94.6, China 33rd with 92.5, and Thailand 44th with 86.5. These are all countries that are active in cyber cooperation according to the analysis. Given the descriptive scope of the current study, we are not able to

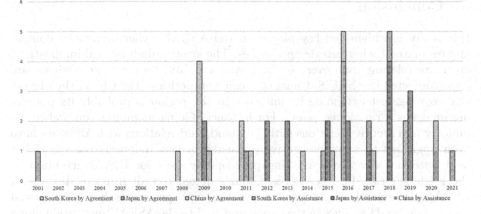

Fig. 4. Assistance and agreement relationship of cybersecurity by Northeast Asia. This figure results from graphs of cybersecurity assistance and agreement relationships based on GFCE data, UNIDIR, and open sources of each country.

establish a clear causal relation between capability and cooperation, i.e., whether capability leads to cooperation or vice-versa. This question will be addressed in follow up studies.

Although South Korea, Japan, and China seem to be equally influential by looking at the relationship graphs, a deeper look reveals that three countries have had differing degrees of effectiveness with their approaches. In particular, Japan shines for its policy consistency. Figure 4 shows the instances of cyber assistance and agreements signed over the last two decades, revealing that in contrast to South Korea, which mostly focused on signing agreements, Japan consistently extended cybersecurity assistance to ASEAN countries. Even though South Korea was seemingly more active on reaching headline grabbing state-to-state agreements, South Korea-ASEAN agreements tend to cluster around specific time points, which suggests that the agreements were driven by internal political factors rather than long term strategic considerations. China has become more active in cyber agreements and assistance only recently, suggesting new priorities associated with the Digital Silk Road are behind the recent uptick in cooperative activities with ASEAN. Although a rather low level of Chinese activities in cyber domain could be due to China's preference for umbrella agreements with ASEAN rather than dealing directly with the member states, one cannot discount the possibility that the low influence level is due to the polarized views of China held by ASEAN member states [8] due, but not limited to, the ongoing spat over maritime borders in South China Sea [21]. Japan's leadership in lending assistance is further backed by grander cooperative schemes. In December 2005 the ASEAN-Japan Cooperation Fund announced that Japan would provide about US$ 70.1 billion in financial support to support ASEAN integration. Japan's other cyber assistance commitments to ASEAN are ASEAN Cyber Capacity Development Projects and ASEAN Joint Operations Against Cybercrime.

6   Conclusion

Our study has identified key players in the ASEAN cyber diplomacy domain and evaluated their strategic approaches. The study's findings and implications are more relevant than ever, as Southeast Asia and its maritime environs are deeply affected by the U.S.-China strategic competition. For China, the biggest challenge against extending its influence in the region is probably its polarizing image as a revisionist power. For instance, China maintains comprehensive military and security relations with Thailand, and relations with Malaysia have been upgraded to a comprehensive partnership. But Indonesia regards China as a potential adversary and Singapore openly calls for U.S. intervention to check China's rise. In other words, China's mixed records in its relations with ASEAN also extends to the cyber cooperation and agreements. South Korea and Japan, two key U.S. allies in the region and tied to the ASEAN institution along with China through the Plus Three mechanism, have a pivotal role in shaping regional dynamics through diplomatic outreach in which cyber cooperation and assistance figure prominently.

While seemingly similar in strategic outlooks, our studies find that South Korea and Japan are a study of contrasts: South Korea is highly active in state-to-state agreements but it will have to inject more substance into its diplomatic endeavors, for instance by providing beefier financial assistance to ASEAN member states. This study finds that Japan is the most successful player that can exert a considerable influence on ASEAN member states through its extensive and consistent cyber assistance and cooperation policies. In combination with its long track record of investments and involvement in the region, it can be said Japan is the silent power that is the most influential state actor in ASEAN 's cyber domain. But it remains to be seen whether Japan's active stance on cyber assistance and cooperation with ASEAN can bear more tangible fruits for Japan's Free and Open Indo-Pacific strategy, which calls for a more active deterrence posture against China that many ASEAN countries, despite their shared misgivings about the rising hegemon, may not agree with.

References

1. National Cyber Security Agency: Malaysia cyber security strategy 2020–2024 (2017). https://www.nacsa.gov.my/
2. Arase, D., Ooi, K.B., Das, S.B., Chong, T.: Non-traditional security in China-ASEAN cooperation: the institutionalization of regional security cooperation and the evolution of east Asian regionalism, pp. 378–383. ISEAS Publishing (2015)
3. ASEAN: Joint media statement of the tenth clmv economic ministers' meeting (2018). https://asean.org/joint-media-statement-tenth-clmv-economic-ministers-meeting/
4. ASEAN-Japan: joint ministerial statement of the ASEAN-Japan ministerial policy meeting on cybersecurity cooperation (2013). https://asean.org/joint-ministerial-statement-of-the-asean-japan-ministerial-policy-meeting-on-cybersecurity-cooperation/

5. Chow, J.T.: ASEAN counterterrorism cooperation since 9/11. Asian Surv. **45**(2), 302–321 (2005)
6. Gramaglia, M., Tuohy, E., Pernik, P.: Military cyber defense structures of NATO members: an overview. Background Paper. International Centre for Defense and Security (RKK/ICDS), Tallinn, Estonia (2013)
7. Heinl, C.H.: Regional cybersecurity: moving toward a resilient ASEAN cybersecurity regime. Asia Policy **18**, 131–160 (2014)
8. Index, G.: Global cybersecurity index 2018 (2018)
9. Index, G.: Global cybersecurity index 2020 (2020)
10. INTERPOL: Interpol report highlights key cyberthreats in Southeast Asia (2020). https://www.interpol.int/News-and-Events/News/2020/INTERPOL-report-highlights-key-cyberthreats-in-Southeast-Asia
11. JAIF: Overview purposes of JAIF. https://jaif.asean.org/overview/
12. Kim, S.: Cybersecurity strategies of major powers in world politics: from the comparative perspective of national strategies. J. Int. Area Stud. **26**(3), 67–108 (2017)
13. Ltd., P.P.: Polinode - powerful network analysis in the cloud. https://www.polinode.com/
14. Oh, Y.A.: Korea's new southern policy: progress, problems, and prospects (2020)
15. Park, S.R.: Cybersecurity international cooperation status in ASEAN. KISA Report **9**, 15–21 (2019)
16. Păunescu, M.: EU cyberspace strategic documents. In: Strategic Changes in Security and International Relations, p. 195 (2020)
17. Scott, J.: Social network analysis. Sociology **22**(1), 109–127 (1988)
18. Slack, C.: Wired yet disconnected: the governance of international cyber relations. Global Pol. **7**(1), 69–78 (2016)
19. Sofaer, A., Clark, D., Diffie, W.: Cyber security and international agreements. In: National Research Council, Proceedings of a Workshop on Deterring Cyberattacks (2009)
20. Solar, C.: Cybersecurity and cyber defence in the emerging democracies. J. Cyber Policy **5**(3), 392–412 (2020)
21. Storey, I.: ASEAN's failing grade in the south China sea. In: Rozman, G., Liow, J.C. (eds.) International Relations and Asia's Southern Tier. AMS, pp. 111–124. Springer, Singapore (2018). https://doi.org/10.1007/978-981-10-3171-7_8
22. Stubbs, R.: ASEAN plus three: emerging East Asian regionalism? Asian Surv. **42**(3), 440–455 (2002)
23. Sunkpho, J., Ramjan, S., Ottamakorn, C.: Cybersecurity policy in ASEAN countries. In: 17th Annual Security Conference, pp. 1–7
24. Three, A.P.: History. https://aseanplusthree.asean.org/about-apt/history/
25. Tran Dai, C., Gomez, M.A.: Challenges and opportunities for cyber norms in ASEAN. J. Cyber Policy **3**(2), 217–235 (2018)
26. UNIDIR: UNIDIR cyber policy portal. https://unidir.org/cpp/en
27. Vu, K.M.: ICT diffusion and production in ASEAN countries: patterns, performance, and policy directions. Telecommun. Policy **41**(10), 962–977 (2017)
28. Wasserman, S., Faust, K.: Social network analysis: methods and applications (1994)
29. Zhou, L.: 'Let's build a digital silk road': Xi Jinping looks to cement China's ties with ASEAN (2020). https://www.scmp.com/news/china/diplomacy/article/3111612/lets-build-digital-silk-road-president-xi-promises-ways-china

Chameleon DNN Watermarking: Dynamically Public Model Ownership Verification

Wei Li[1], Xiaoyu Zhang[1(✉)], Shen Lin[1], Xinbo Ban[2], and Xiaofeng Chen[1]

[1] State Key Laboratory of Integrated Service Networks (ISN), Xidian University, Xi'an 710071, People's Republic of China
{liw,linshen}@stu.xidian.edu.cn, {xiaoyuzhang,xfchen}@xidian.edu.cn
[2] Swinburne University of Technology, Melbourne, VIC 3122, Australia
xban@swin.edu.au

Abstract. Deep neural network (DNN) has made unprecedented leaps in functionality and usefulness in the past few years, revolutionizing various promising fields such as image recognition and machine translation. The trainer's high-performance DNNs are often considered intellectual property (IP) due to their expensive training costs. However, one pre-trained model may face various infringement problems when hacked by a malicious user, such as illegal copying or secondary selling. Digital watermarking is one of the effective methods currently used for model ownership verification. Nonetheless, limited by the ex-ante nature of the watermark embedding phase and the ex-post nature of the verification phase, previous research has only supported private verification or one-time public verification, failing to achieve multiple public verifications. In this paper, we introduce the definition of chameleon DNN watermarking and propose the first DNN watermarking scheme based on chameleon commitment, which allows multiple public verifications to declare the owner's model ownership without exposing the core watermark information. We give a comprehensive security analysis of the verification scheme of chameleon DNN watermarking and prove by experiments that chameleon DNN watermarking can maintain the high-performance and robustness of the model.

Keywords: Deep neural networks · DNN watermarking · Chameleon commitment

1 Introduction

Deep learning has been enormously successful in a variety of machine learning tasks, including image recognition [1,2], medical image processing [3], speech recognition [4], and natural language processing [5]. In practice, training a highly accurate DNN is frequently an expensive process [6], due to (1) the need to collect a large number of high-quality training datasets and process them appropriately for the desired applications and (2) the need to consume expensive computational resources to tune the network architecture and (hyper)parameters of this model.

© Springer Nature Switzerland AG 2023
I. You and T.-Y. Youn (Eds.): WISA 2022, LNCS 13720, pp. 344–356, 2023.
https://doi.org/10.1007/978-3-031-25659-2_25

Therefore, considering the expensive training process, these pre-trained deep models have a high commercial value and are frequently regarded as the model owners' intellectual property (IP), and may even constitute core technologies for some companies or organizations that urgently need to be protected. In light of the diverse and unpredictable properties of model theft, the owners may wish to have sufficient evidence to prove their ownership whenever an illegal act occurs.

Digital watermarking is a significant method to validate intellectual property. So far, researchers have proposed several methods to embed watermarks in DNN models to protect IP [7–9]. As a growing number of pre-trained DNNs are available in open source on the Internet or involved in commercial selling chains, a comprehensive IP protection technology of DNNs should provide both of the following capabilities: (Q1) *proof the ownership of the DNN:* the model owner should always be capable of proving its model's ownership after being published; (Q2) *support for multiple public verifications:* the watermarking scheme should be extended from limited private and single public verifications to multiple public verifications to enhance its IP credibility. Unfortunately, however, all the existing watermarking approaches only satisfy the first requirements (Q1 *proof the ownership of the DNN*) and ignore the second requirement (Q2 *support for multiple public verifications*). For the first time, we ask the following problem: **How to perform multiple public verifications for published models?**

It is challenging to develop such a DNN watermarking scheme that supports multiple public verifications, however, because of: (C1) *after-sales immutability:* models that have been published cannot go back for watermark embedding and modifications; (C2) *exposure of watermarks for public verification* [7]: watermarks embedded into models tend to expose their key watermark information after undergoing one public verification, leading to unreliability of subsequent verification. When the same model needs to be verified multiple times, the act of always adding a new watermark as a proof of identity is not practical under the restriction. In addition, the general watermarking scheme [8–10] leads to the watermark information fully exposed after verification, making the focus (C2 *exposure of watermarks for public verification*) necessary. This paper investigates how to address these challenges and propose the chameleon DNN watermarking scheme as the first promising solution for multiple public verifications. The technical contributions of this paper are summarized as follows:

- We propose the chameleon DNN watermarking scheme to implement multiple public verification requirements for DNNs. In order to deal with the problem that the model cannot be changed after releasing, our solution for the first time expands from single-verification of a single-embedding to multiple-public-verification of a single-embedding, with the ability to perfectly hide the initial watermark information, thus achieving a creative leap forward in model watermarking work.
- We investigate the performance of chameleon DNN watermarking in combination with the scheme in [7]. We have conducted security proofs and comparative experiments to demonstrate the effectiveness, the security, and the robustness in resisting removal attack and overwriting attack of the chameleon DNN watermarking scheme.

2   Background and Definitions

2.1   DNN Watermarking

Inspired by traditional IPR (Intellectual Property Rights) techniques in the media, the first proposal to add bit messages as watermarks for neural network models using regularization techniques was made in [8], which was proposed to protect the IP of AI models such as machine learning and deep learning. From the perspective of watermark verification [11], the watermarking techniques currently proposed can be broadly classified into two main categories: white-box verification [8] and black-box verification [7,9,10]. Since the verification phase does not require querying the model's internal parameters, black-box verification is suitable for a broader range of practical application scenarios. Methods based on backdoor triggering mainly belong to black-box watermarking, where the verification of the watermark usually only requires access to the model API or even satisfies remote verification. There is also the attempt to combine cryptographic schemes with privacy protection for machine learning [12]. Following this idea, subsequent works such as [9,10] suggested the use of adversarial samples or watermarked images as triggers, etc.

The existing model watermarking techniques involve the following two steps: (1) embedding the watermark [8,9,13]: during the model training phase, the digital watermark is embedded into the model by adopting a specific strategy; (2) verifying the watermark [7–10]: extract the watermark information from the model and compare with the embedded watermark to determine whether it is infringing [14]. However, all of the above DNN watermarks only consider the single verification needs, without realizing the multiple verification needs scenarios in the sales and purchase phases as DNN models and machine learning are commercialized. In this paper, we address this limitation of current DNN digital watermarking research and propose a DNN watermarking scheme that supports dynamic multiple verification, thus providing a more complete solution for model intellectual property protection.

2.2   Definitions of Chameleon DNN Watermarking

Commitment is one of the important cryptographic primitives, which consists of two phases: (1) in the commit phase, A inputs the message m and the random value r, computes the commitment value c; (2) in the open phase, B uses A's m and r to verify that c is a commitment to the message m. In particular, the chameleon commitment have critically important applications in modern cryptography due to its trapdoor property. [15] firstly defined the chameleon hash scheme and chameleon signature scheme without key exposure systematically, and [16] went a step further to solve the security problem of chameleon hashing. Based on the above, we first try to combine chameleon commitment with DNN watermarking, and propose the chameleon DNN watermarking scheme.

In our scheme, the model owner generates an initial watermark and the unique key pairs, embeds them in the model training phase, and publishes the version number ID and the commitment value in advance. Whenever facing a public verification requirement, the owner opens the commitment by providing a shadow message pair to verify its ownership while hiding the initial watermark.

Definition 1. *We formalize the definition of chameleon DNN watermarking =* $(\mathcal{CWG}, \mathcal{CWC}, \mathcal{CWE}, \mathcal{CWV}, \mathcal{CWU})$, *which consists of five algorithms.*

- $\mathcal{CWG}$ $(g, q, \{t_t^{(i)}, t_l^{(i)}\}_{i \in [1,n]})$ $\rightarrow$ $(CP, \{sk_t^{(i)}, sk_l^{(i)}, pk_t^{(i)}, pk_l^{(i)}\}_{i \in [1,n]})$: It is implemented by the model owner O. It takes the security parameters (g, q) and the target triggers $\{t_t^{(i)}, t_l^{(i)}\}_{i \in [1,n]}$ as input and takes the system parameters CP, the private-secret key pairs $\{sk_t^{(i)}, sk_l^{(i)}\}_{i \in [1,n]}$ and the public-secret key pairs $\{pk_t^{(i)}, pk_l^{(i)}\}_{i \in [1,n]}$ as outputs.

- $\mathcal{CWC}$ $(m_t, m_l, \text{ID}, \{t_t^{(i)}, t_l^{(i)}, sk_t^{(i)}, sk_l^{(i)}, pk_t^{(i)}, pk_l^{(i)}\}_{i \in [1,n]})$ $\rightarrow$ (mk, vk): The algorithm is conducted by O. On input the current version number ID, initial embedding messages (m_t, m_l), trigger tuples $\{t_t^{(i)}, t_l^{(i)}\}_{i \in [1,n]}$ and keys pairs $\{sk_t^{(i)}, sk_l^{(i)}, pk_t^{(i)}, pk_l^{(i)}\}_{i \in [1,n]}$, it outputs (mk, vk).

- $\mathcal{CWE}$ $(w_i, \text{Dataset}, \{t_t^{(i)}, t_l^{(i)}\}_{i \in [1,n]}) \rightarrow M$: It takes the current model parameters w_i, the training dataset Dataset and the trigger tuples $\{t_t^{(i)}, t_l^{(i)}\}_{i \in [1,n]}$ as input and the embeded model M as output.

- $\mathcal{CWV}$ $(M, \{t_t^{(i)}, t_l^{(i)}\}_{i \in [1,n]}, (m_t^{(j)}, m_l^{(j)})_{j \in [1,k]}, vk) \rightarrow 0/1$: O provides mutiple shadow message pairs $(m_t^{(j)}, m_l^{(j)})_{j \in [1,k]}$ for the public verification, if it outputs 1, the verification is successful, otherwise the verification fails.

- $\mathcal{CWU}$ $(\text{ID}_N, \text{ID}, (mk, vk))$ $\rightarrow$ $(\text{ID}_N', \text{ID}', (mk', vk'))$: It is done by O, with dynamically updating of the sequence number ID_N, the current version number ID and (mk, vk).

2.3 Security Requirements

A secure chameleon watermarking scheme should satisfy the following properties:

- **Resistant to forgery:** Without the knowledge of private-secret key pairs, there is no efficient algorithm that allows arbitrary third parties to forge any correct shadow messages pairs.
- **Global semantic security:** Given the initial messages pairs and any shadow messages pairs, the probability distributions of the commitment values of both are computational indistinguishability.
- **Non-exposure of the watermark information:** As long as the Computation Diffie-Hellman Problem (CDHP) in the cyclic multiplicative group G is intractable, the initial watermark information embed in the model will always have the non-exposed property.

3 Chameleon DNN Watermarking

3.1 Overview

Figure 1 demonstrates the global pipeline of the chameleon DNN watermarking scheme. Chameleon DNN watermarking consists of such two principal phases:

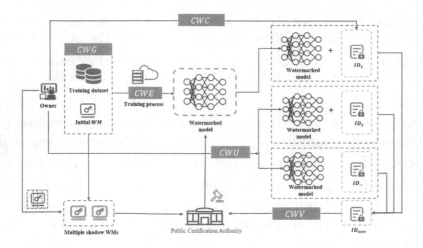

Fig. 1. Workflow of chameleon DNN watermarking.

chameleon watermark embedding and verification. Chameleon watermark verification is further divided into a double verification of triggered watermark verification, and chameleon commitment verification, where critical information hiding relies on the chameleon temporary watermarking algorithm and the implementation of dynamic watermark public verification is based on the chameleon update algorithm.

3.2   Algorithm Details

This section shows the details of the algorithm of chameleon DNN watermarking based on the chameleon commitment without key exposure [15]. In summary, the chameleon DNN watermarking scheme is described as follows:

- $\mathcal{CWG}\ (g, q, \{t_t^{(i)}, t_l^{(i)}\}_{i \in [1,n]}) \to (CP, \{sk_t^{(i)}, sk_l^{(i)}, pk_t^{(i)}, pk_l^{(i)}\}_{i \in [1,n]})$:
    - Select target triggers $T_t = \{t_t^{(1)}, t_t^{(2)}, ...t_t^{(n)}\}$ and mark them with specific target labels set $T_l = \{t_l^{(1)}, t_l^{(2)}, ...t_l^{(n)}\}$.
    - Selecting an element g and a large prime q, a Gap Diffie-Hellman group G is generated by g, where the order is q. Denote a secure cryptographic hash function by $H : \{0,1\}^* \to G^*$. Define the system parameters as $CP = \{G, q, g, H\}$.
    - For each $t_t^{(i)} \in T_t, t_l^{(i)} \in T_l$, define a hash function $\{h(t_t^{(i)}) = sk_t^{(i)}, h(t_l^{(i)}) = sk_l^{(i)}\}_{sk_t, sk_l \in Z_q^*}$. Get the secret keys by triggers $SKT = \{sk_t^{(1)}, sk_t^{(2)}, ..., sk_t^{(n)}\}$ and secret keys by labels $SKL = \{sk_l^{(1)}, sk_l^{(2)}, ..., sk_l^{(n)}\}$.
    - Given $\{sk_t^{(i)}, sk_l^{(i)}\}_{i \in [n]}$, calculate the chameleon public keys $\{pk_t^{(i)}, pk_l^{(i)} = g^{sk_t^{(i)}}, g^{sk_l^{(i)}}\}_{i \in [n]}$. Get the public keys by triggers $PKT = \{pk_t^{(1)},$

$pk_t^{(2)}, ..., pk_t^{(n)}\}$ and the public keys by labels $PKL = \{pk_l^{(1)}, pk_l^{(2)}, ..., pk_l^{(n)}\}$. O publishes $\{PKT, PKL\}$.

- $\mathcal{CWC}$ $(m_t, m_l, \text{ID}, \{t_t^{(i)}, t_l^{(i)}, sk_t^{(i)}, sk_l^{(i)}, pk_t^{(i)}, pk_l^{(i)}\}_{i \in [1,n]}) \rightarrow (mk, vk)$:
  - Following "Customized Identities" in [17], define $\text{ID} = H(\text{ID}_O \| \text{ID}_M \| \text{ID}_N)$, where $\text{ID}_O, \text{ID}_M,$ and ID_N denote the identity of O, M, and the current sequence number N.
  - O selects a pair of initial embedding messages (m_t, m_l), and randomly chooses a pair of integers $(r_t, r_l) \in Z_q^*$.
  - Sample n trigger groups $\{t_t^{(i)}, t_l^{(i)}\}_{i \in [n]}$, and generate $2n$ commitment values $\{c_t^{(i)}, c_l^{(i)}\}_{i \in [n]}$:

$$c_t^{(i)} \rightarrow \text{Com}(t_t^{(i)}, sk_t^{(i)}, pk_t^{(i)}, g, m_t, r_t, \text{ID}) = (g * \text{ID})^{m_t} pk_t^{(i)^{r_t}},$$
$$c_l^{(i)} \rightarrow \text{Com}(t_l^{(i)}, sk_l^{(i)}, pk_l^{(i)}, g, m_l, r_l, \text{ID}) = (g * \text{ID})^{m_l} pk_l^{(i)^{r_l}}; \qquad (1)$$

   where $\text{Com}(\cdot)$ is a chameleon committing operation.
  - Set $mk \leftarrow \{\{t_t^{(i)}, t_l^{(i)}, sk_t^{(i)}, sk_l^{(i)}\}_{i \in [n]}, r_t, r_l, m_t, m_l, \text{ID}\}$, $vk \rightarrow \{c_t^{(i)}, c_l^{(i)}\}_{i \in [n]}$ and return (mk, vk).

- $\mathcal{CWE}$ $(w_i, \text{Dataset}, \{t_t^{(i)}, t_l^{(i)}\}_{i \in [1,n]}) \rightarrow M$:
  - We embedded trigger tuples to model M:

$$M \leftarrow \text{Training}(\{t_t^{(i)}, t_l^{(i)}\}_{i \in [n]}, \text{Dataset}, w_i). \qquad (2)$$

  - Public M and $vk \rightarrow \{c_t^{(i)}, c_l^{(i)}\}_{i \in [n]}$.

- $\mathcal{CWV}$ $(M, \{t_t^{(i)}, t_l^{(i)}\}_{i \in [1,n]}, (m_t^{(j)}, m_l^{(j)})_{j \in [1,k]}, vk) \rightarrow 0/1$: Whenever a property dispute occurs and ownership verification is required, O needs to make a public verification.
  - O releases k couples of random messages:

$$m_v = \{(m_t^{(1)}, m_l^{(1)}), (m_t^{(2)}, m_l^{(2)}), \ldots, (m_t^{(k)}, m_l^{(k)})\}. \qquad (3)$$

  - For each $(m_t^{(j)}, m_l^{(j)})_{j \in [k]}$: given (mk, vk), for each $(sk_t^{(i)}, sk_l^{(i)})$, compute a hash collision:

$$\mathcal{F}(sk_t^{(i)}, c_t, m_t, g^{r_t}, pk_t^{(i)^{r_t}}, m_t^{(j)}, \text{ID}) = (g^{r_t^{(j)}}, pk_t^{r_t^{(j)}}),$$
$$\mathcal{F}(sk_l^{(i)}, c_l, m_l, g^{r_l}, pk_l^{(i)^{r_l}}, m_l^{(j)}, \text{ID}) = (g^{r_l^{(j)}}, pk_l^{r_l^{(j)}}); \qquad (4)$$

   where $g^{r_t^{(j)}} = g^{r_t}(g * \text{ID})^{(sk_l^{(i)})^{-1}(m_l - m_t^{(j)})}, g^{r_l^{(j)}} = g^{r_l}(g * \text{ID})^{(sk_l^{(i)})^{-1}(m_l - m_l^{(j)})}$
   and $pk_t^{r_t^{(j)}} = pk_t^{(i)^{r_t}}(g * \text{ID})^{m_t - m_t^{(j)}}$, $pk_l^{r_l^{(j)}} = pk_l^{(i)^{r_l}}(g * \text{ID})^{m_l - m_l^{(j)}}$.

   Such a shadow message pairs $\{(g^{r_t^{(j)}}, pk_t^{r_t^{(j)}}), (g^{r_l^{(j)}}, pk_l^{r_l^{(j)}})\}$ satisfies:

$$\text{Com}(t_t^{(i)}, sk_t^{(i)}, pk_t^{(i)}, g, m_t^{(j)}, r_t^{(j)}, \text{ID}) = \text{Com}(t_t^{(i)}, sk_t^{(i)}, pk_t^{(i)}, g, m_t, r_t, \text{ID}),$$
$$\text{Com}(l_l^{(i)}, sk_l^{(i)}, pk_l^{(i)}, g, m_l^{(j)}, r_l^{(j)}, \text{ID}) = \text{Com}(t_l^{(i)}, sk_l^{(i)}, pk_l^{(i)}, g, m_l, r_l, \text{ID}).$$

- O should generate multiple $\{(g^{r_t^{(j)}}, pk_t^{r_t^{(j)}}), (g^{r_l^{(j)}}, pk_l^{r_l^{(j)}})\}_{j \in [k]}$ for each $(m_t^{(j)}, m_l^{(j)})_{j \in [k]}$ and release them.
- **Verification based on the chameleon commitment:**
  For all $i \in [n], j \in [k]$, checking to ensure if:

$$\text{Open}(c_t^{(i)}, \text{ID}, m_t^{(j)}, g^{r_t^{(j)}}, pk_t^{r_t^{(j)}}) = 1,$$
$$\text{Open}(c_l^{(i)}, \text{ID}, m_l^{(j)}, g^{r_l^{(j)}}, pk_t^{r_t^{(j)}}) = 1, \tag{5}$$

  where $\text{Open}(\cdot)$ is a chameleon opening operation. Otherwise output 0.
- **Verification based on the triggered black-box:**
  For all $i \in [n]$ test that $\text{Classify}(t_t^{(i)}, M) = t_l^{(i)}$. If this is true for all but $\varepsilon|T_t|$ elements from T_t then output 1, else output 0.

- $\mathcal{CWU}$ $(\text{ID}_N, \text{ID}, (mk, vk)) \rightarrow (\text{ID}_N', \text{ID}', (mk', vk'))$: Once a public verification is finished, the ID is exposed, that's why O needs to dynamically update the (mk, vk).

  - Update the current sequence number $\text{ID}_N \rightarrow \text{ID}_N'$.
  - Calculate $\text{ID}' = H(\text{ID}_O||\text{ID}_M||\text{ID}_N')$.
  - Update (mk', vk') from the new ID':

$$mk' \leftarrow \{\{t_t^{(i)}, t_l^{(i)}, sk_t^{(i)}, sk_l^{(i)},\}_{i \in [n]}, r_t, r_l, m_t, m_l, \text{ID}'\}_{i \in [1,n]},$$
$$vk' \leftarrow \{c_t^{(i)'}, c_l^{(i)'}\}_{i \in [1,n]}. \tag{6}$$

  - Subsequent validations will always be with the recently updated (mk', vk').

4   Security Analysis

Theorem 1. *The chameleon DNN watermarking scheme is resistant to forgery, i.e., without private-secret key pairs $\{sk_t^{(i)}, sk_l^{(i)}\}_{i \in [1,n]}$, any E cannot forge thus shadow messages pairs $(m_t^{(j)}, g^{r_t^{(j)}}, pk_t^{r_t^{(j)}})$ or $(m_l^{(j)}, g^{r_l^{(j)}}, pk_l^{r_l^{(j)}})$, which satisfies $\{m_t^{(j)} \neq m_t, m_l^{(j)} \neq m_l\}$ but $\text{Open}(c_t^{(i)}, \text{ID}, m_t^{(j)}, g^{r_t^{(j)}}, and pk_t^{r_t^{(j)}}) = 1$, $\text{Open}(c_l^{(i)}, \text{ID}, m_l^{(j)}, g^{r_l^{(j)}}, pk_l^{r_l^{(j)}}) = 1$.*

Proof. There is no PPT algorithm $\mathcal{A}$, without sk_t, obtains two pairs (m_t^1, r_t^1), $(m_t^2, r_t^2) \in R$, which satisfies $m_t^1 \neq m_t^2$ and $c_t sk_t(m_t^1, r_t^1) = c_t sk_t(m_t^2, r_t^2)$ with non-negligible probability. The probability is both related to sk_t and the random coins thrown by the algorithm $\mathcal{A}$. □

Theorem 2. *The chameleon initial messages have the semantic security, i.e., neither the chameleon commitment value c_t nor the shadow message pairs $(g^{r_t^{(j)}}, pk_t^{r_t^{(j)}})$ expose the information about m_t.*

Proof. Semantic security is in two parts: semantic security in the commit phase and in the open phase. The semantic security of the commit phase is to guarantee that the chameleon commitment value c_t of the message m_t does not disclose any information about m_t in the commit phase. The semantic security of the open phase can be as the correctness of the commitment, i.e., the verification can be accurately achieved.

- **Semantic security proofs for the commit phase:** Given the chameleon commitment value c_t of the initial message m_t, the conditional entropy $H[m_t \mid c_t]$ of m_t is equal to the entropy $H[m_t]$ of m_t.
- **Semantic security proofs for the open phase:** The proof is similar to [15]. Given a commitment value c_t, and each message $m_t^{(j)}$, and the current version number ID, there exists exactly one pair $(g^{r_t^{(j)}}, pk_t^{r_t^{(j)}})$ such that $c_t = \mathrm{Com}(t_t^{(j)}, sk_t, pk_t, g, m_t^{(j)}, r_t^{(j)}, \mathrm{ID})$.
- **Semantic security proofs of the commitment values:** The commitment values are perfectly hidden. Since $pk_t^{r_t}$ hides $(g * \mathrm{ID})^{m_t}$ in an information-theoretic sense, the commitment values are random number unrelated to the initial message, so even if E has infinite computational power, he cannot distinguish between the different commitment values.
- **Semantic security proofs of the initial message:** The conditional entropy $H[(m_t, r_t) \mid c_t]$ of the initial messages (m_t, r_t) is not reduced by the collision $(m_t^{(j)}, r_t^{(j)})$. That is:

$$H[(m_t, r_t) \mid c_t, (m_t^{(j)}, r_t^{(j)})] = H[(m_t, r_t) \mid c_t]. \tag{7}$$

That is, O can publicly disclose any multiple pairs of shadow messages $(m_t^{(j)}, r_t^{(j)})$, while E cannot reverse the initial messages (m_t, r_t). $\qquad\square$

Theorem 3. *As long as the CDHP in a cyclic multiplicative group G is intractable, then the open phase would only expose the ID, but not the private-secret key pairs $\{sk_t^{(i)}, sk_l^{(i)}\}_{i \in [1,n]}$.*

Proof. – We have $c_t = \mathrm{Com}(t_t, sk_t, pk_t, g, m_t, r_t, \mathrm{ID}) = (g * \mathrm{ID})^{m_t} pk_t^{r_t}$.
- Given collisions $(m_t, g^{r_t}, pk_t^{r_t})$ and $(m_t^{(j)}, g^{r_t^{(j)}}, pk_t^{r_t^{(j)}})$, which could satisfy $c_t = \mathrm{Com}(t_t, sk_t, pk_t, g, m_t^{(j)}, r_t^{(j)}, \mathrm{ID}) = \mathrm{Com}(t_t, sk_t, pk_t, g, m_t, r_t, \mathrm{ID})$, i.e., $(g * \mathrm{ID})^{m_t^{(j)}} pk_t^{r_t^{(j)}} = (g * \mathrm{ID})^{m_t} pk_t^{r_t}$.
- So we could deduce $(g * \mathrm{ID})^{sk_i^{-1}} = (g^{r_t}/g^{r_t^{(j)}})^{(m_t^{(j)} - m_t)^{-1}}$.
- Each version number ID will cause E to recover the information $(g * \mathrm{ID})^{sk_t^{-1}}$.
- But once the sequence number is updated, the attacker will not be able to use it to calculate the information $(g * \mathrm{ID}')^{sk_t^{-1}}$ for $\mathrm{ID}' \neq \mathrm{ID}$, which is equivalent to solve CDHP in G. $\qquad\square$

In summary, the forgery resistance of the shadow messages pairs ensures the binding of the owner O to the model M; the hidden property of the initial messages enables one-time embedding without changing the embedded (m_t, r_t);

the non-exposing property of the private keys $\{sk_t^{(i)}, sk_l^{(i)}\}_{i \in [1,n]}$ allows O to achieve dynamic verification by dynamically updating the version number ID.

5   Experimental Evaluation

In this section, we perform an experimental analysis of the watermarking scheme described in Sect. 3. We demonstrate that it is possible to embed watermarks with our approach without affecting the performance of the host network, and the generated watermarks have good maintenance of functionality, with the robust to removal attack and overwriting attack.

5.1   Evaluation Settings

To demonstrate the maintenance of functionality and robust of our scheme, we apply the proposed watermark embedding method to the image classification of two representative datasets, CIFAR-10 and CIFAR-100. We follow the classical settings in image classification and use the well-known 18-layer ResNet-18 model as a training model. As for the trigger settings, we use similar settings as mentioned in [7], with selecting 100 images as the set of triggers for all tasks. To embed watermarks, we optimize the model using both the training set and the trigger set. Note that, unlike [7], we only study the FROMSCRATCH method that trains the model and the trigger set from scratch and discard the PRE-TRAINED method, cause the model's creator will be the one embedding the watermark. During the training period, for each batch, we follow the trigger set image sampling setting of $k = 2$ in [7]. Unlike [7] where batch-size $= 100$, our experiments set batch-size to 128 (a multiple of 8) for both CIFAR-10 and CIFAR-100 to improve the efficiency of parallel computation inside the GPU and to do normalized experiments at the same time.

5.2   Maintenance of Functionality

To maintain the model's functionality, in the case of the classification task, we require that the watermarked model shall have the same accuracy on the clean dataset that the clean model performs. Also, it should be clear that unlike [7], the purpose of our scheme is positioned as the trainer of the model to embed the watermark in order to declare its ownership, so the embedding of the watermark is only considered to be trained FROMSCRATCH with the trigger-set.

Table 1 summarizes the classification accuracy of the test and trigger sets of our chameleon DNN watermarking model and the scheme in [7] on CIFAR-10 and CIFAR-100; (I) model without watermark (NO-WM); (II) model trained from scratch with trigger set (FROMSCRATCH). It can be seen that the NO-WM model and the WM model have the nearly identical test-set accuracy for the clean CIFAR-10 and CIFAR-100 datasets. As for the dataset containing triggers, the WM model is performing as expected, with 100% trigger-set accuracy for both datasets.

It is clear from the experimental data that the prediction accuracy of the chameleon DNN watermarking scheme and the scheme in [7] is very similar for the test set. Even the chameleon DNN watermarking scheme results are superior to the initial watermarking, which we attribute to the adjustment of batch-size, which proves that our batch-size setting is more reasonable for the training and optimizing of the model.

Table 1. Comparison of our proposed scheme and the scheme in [7] for classification accuracy of the CIFAR-10 and CIFAR-100 datasets on the test and trigger-sets.

Dataset	Scheme	Model	Test-set acc.	Trigger-set acc.
CIFAR-10	Our scheme	NO-WM	93.42%	–
		WM	93.81%	100%
	Scheme in [7]	NO-WM	92.58%	–
		WM	92.69%	100%
CIFAR-100	Our scheme	NO-WM	74.01%	–
		WM	73.67%	100%
	Scheme in [7]	NO-WM	72.12%	–
		WM	72.27%	100%

5.3   Robust to Removal Attack

This section investigates the robustness of the chameleon DNN watermarking model to model-changing operations that remove the watermark while keeping the model functionality unchanged. We focus on fine-tuning the experiments. In many practical and realistic scenarios, users need to fine-tune their downloaded models by using their private datasets. Therefore, for models with chameleon watermarks, the watermarks should not be corrupted by such fine-tuning operations. We perform the experiments with the strong assumption that the adversary has the capability to fine-tune the model with the same number of training examples and batches that were used for the initial training phase.

We used four different fine-tuning processes: **Fine-Tune Last Layer(FTLL)**: freeze the parameters of all except for the output layer, but only the parameters of the last layer are updated, which can also be considered as we only fine-tune the output layer. **Fine-Tune All Layers(FTAL)**: update the parameters of all layers of the model. **Re-Train Last Layers(RTLL)**: freezing the parameters of all layers except for the output layer, initializes the parameters of the output layers with random weights, and updates them only. **Re-Train All Layers(RTAL)**: initializes the output layer parameters using some random weights and updates all layers of the network.

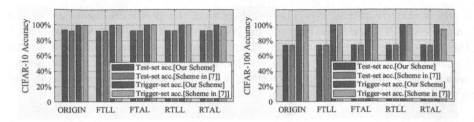

Fig. 2. Classification accuracy of the test and trigger sets of CIFAR-10 and CIFAR-100 using four different fine-tuning techniques.

Figure 2 shows the results of the watermarking models generated by our scheme and the scheme in [7] on the test and trigger-sets for the datasets CIFAR-10 and CIFAR-100, and demonstrat the application of four different fine-tuning techniques. *Test-set acc.* references to the accuracy of the test set with our chameleon DNN watermarking scheme and the scheme in [7]; *Trigger-set acc.* is the accuracy of the trigger set in two scheme. It can be observed that the robustness of our chameleon DNN watermarking scheme compared to the scheme in [7] against the fine-tuning operation is essentially the same, i.e., our chameleon DNN watermarking does not negatively affect the watermark itself.

5.4   Robust to Overwriting Attack

In the setting of experiments on watermark overwriting, we will explore the scenario where an adversary wants to illegally claim the ownership of a model by overwriting the original watermark and applying a new one. For this purpose, we collect a new set of triggers containing 100 different images, labeled PICSNEW, and embed them in the model with PICSORIG embedded (the adversary will use this new set of triggers to claim ownership of the model). To fairly compare the robustness of the fine-tuned set of triggers, we used the same number of attached graphs as the original set of triggers to embed the new set of triggers.

Concretely, the adversary tries to fraudulently claim ownership of the model in the ownership verification step by providing its own new trigger PICSNEW as training data to the model by embedding new watermarks. As a defensive measure, we wish to remove the adversary's watermark while preserving the initial watermark through some powerful fine-tuning methods. Observing the experimental data, we believe that if the model can identify PICSORIG with high probability and PICSNEW with low probability after fine-tuning, then it indicates that our scheme is robust to watermark coverage when ensuring ownership. Through our experimental evaluations, we found that FTAL and RTAL are the more effective fine-tuning methods, which is also similar to the findings in [7]. In addition, our comparative experimental data show that the chameleon DNN watermarking scheme performs similarly to the scheme in [7] in resisting overwriting attacks, proving that the chameleon DNN watermarking does not degrade the performance of the original watermark.

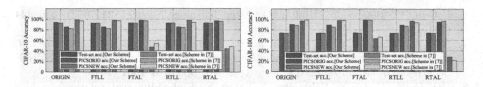

Fig. 3. Classification accuracy after overwriting attacks on CIFAR-10 (left) and CIFAR-100 (right) datasets.

6 Conclusion

With the increasing commercialization of deep learning, it will be an urgent and realistic problem to systematically protect the intellectual property rights of pre-trained models and verify them publicly multiple times. Inspired by the trapdoor feature of the chameleon commitment in cryptography, this paper proposes the first chameleon DNN watermarking scheme that supports single embedding as well as multiple public validations. We provide an exhaustive security analysis of the scheme from a cryptographic perspective and demonstrate that our scheme has a high detection rate and a low false alarm rate in model ownership verification. Furthermore, The experimental results show that our scheme can embed watermarks without affecting the performance of deep neural networks, and the embedded watermarks do not disappear even after model modification attacks such as fine-tuning or overwriting. Although our scheme achieves good results, there are still many challenges in resisting attacks such as model extraction, which leaves to our future work.

Acknowledgment. This work is supported by the National Nature Science Foundation of China (No. 62102300).

References

1. He, K., Zhang, X., Ren, S., Sun, J.: Deep residual learning for image recognition. In: Proceedings of the IEEE Conference on Computer Vision and Pattern Recognition, pp. 770–778 (2016)
2. Krizhevsky, A., Sutskever, I., Hinton, G.E.: ImageNet classification with deep convolutional neural networks. Commun. ACM **60**(6), 84–90 (2017)
3. Zhang, J., Chen, Y., Hong, S., Li, H.: REBUILD: graph embedding based method for user social role identity on mobile communication network. In: Tan, Y., Takagi, H., Shi, Y. (eds) Data Mining and Big Data. DMBD 2017. LNCS, vol. 10387, pp. 326–333. Springer, Cham (2017). https://doi.org/10.1007/978-3-319-61845-6_33
4. Graves, A., Mohamed, A.R., Hinton, G.: Speech recognition with deep recurrent neural networks. In: 2013 IEEE International Conference on Acoustics, Speech and Signal Processing, pp. 6645–6649 (2013)
5. Vaswani, A., et al.: Attention is all you need. Adv. Neural. Inf. Process. Syst. **30**, 5998–6008 (2017)

6. LeCun, Y., Bengio, Y., Hinton, G.: Deep learning. Nature **521**(7553), 436–444 (2015)
7. Adi, Y., Baum, C., Cisse, M., Pinkas, B., Keshet, J.: Turning your weakness into a strength: watermarking deep neural networks by backdooring. In: 27th USENIX Security Symposium (USENIX Security 2018), pp. 1615–1631 (2018)
8. Uchida, Y., Nagai, Y., Sakazawa, S., Satoh, S.: Embedding watermarks into deep neural networks. In: Proceedings of the 2017 ACM on International Conference on Multimedia Retrieval, pp. 269–277 (2017)
9. Zhang, J., et al.: Protecting intellectual property of deep neural networks with watermarking. In: Proceedings of the 2018 on Asia Conference on Computer and Communications Security, pp. 159–172 (2018)
10. Le Merrer, E., Perez, P., Trédan, G.: Adversarial frontier stitching for remote neural network watermarking. Neural Comput. Appl. **32**(13), 9233–9244 (2020)
11. Zhang, X., Chen, C., Xie, Y., Chen, X., Zhang, J., Xiang, Y.: Privacy inference attacks and defenses in cloud-based deep neural network: a survey. arXiv preprint arXiv:2105.06300 (2021)
12. Zhang, X., Chen, X., Liu, J.K., Xiang, Y.: DeepPAR and DeepDPA: privacy preserving and asynchronous deep learning for industrial IoT. IEEE Trans. Industr. Inf. **16**(3), 2081–2090 (2019)
13. Zhang, J., et al.: Model watermarking for image processing networks. In: Proceedings of the AAAI Conference on Artificial Intelligence, vol. 34, pp. 12805–12812 (2020)
14. Zhang, X., Chen, X., Yan, H., Xiang, Y.: Privacy-preserving and verifiable online crowdsourcing with worker updates. Inf. Sci. **548**, 212–232 (2021)
15. Chen, X., Zhang, F., Kim, K.: Chameleon hashing without key exposure. In: Zhang, K., Zheng, Y. (eds.) ISC 2004. LNCS, vol. 3225, pp. 87–98. Springer, Heidelberg (2004). https://doi.org/10.1007/978-3-540-30144-8_8
16. Chen, X., Zhang, F., Susilo, W., Tian, H., Jin, L., Kim, K.: Identity-based chameleon hashing and signatures without key exposure. Inf. Sci. **265**, 198–210 (2014)
17. Ateniese, G., de Medeiros, B.: Identity-based chameleon hash and applications. In: Juels, A. (ed.) FC 2004. LNCS, vol. 3110, pp. 164–180. Springer, Heidelberg (2004). https://doi.org/10.1007/978-3-540-27809-2_19

Author Index

Printed in the United States
by Baker & Taylor Publisher Services